LOU HARRISON

LOU HARRISON

American Musical Maverick

BILL ALVES *and* **BRETT CAMPBELL**

Indiana University Press

This book is a publication of

Indiana University Press
Office of Scholarly Publishing
Herman B Wells Library 350
1320 East 10th Street
Bloomington, Indiana 47405 USA

iupress.indiana.edu

The paper used in this publication meets the minimum requirements of the
American National Standard for Information Sciences—Permanence of
Paper for Printed Library Materials, ANSI Z39.48-1992.

Manufactured in the United States of America

Library of Congress Cataloging-in-Publication Data

Names: Alves, Bill, author. | Campbell, Brett, [date] author.
Title: Lou Harrison : American musical maverick / Bill Alves and Brett
    Campbell.
Description: Bloomington ; Indianapolis : Indiana University Press, 2017. |
    Includes bibliographical references and index.
Identifiers: LCCN 2016056931| ISBN 9780253025616 (cl : alk. paper) | ISBN
    9780253026156 (pb : alk. paper) | ISBN 9780253026439 (eb)
Subjects: LCSH: Harrison, Lou, 1917-2003. | Composers—United
    States—Biography.
Classification: LCC ML410.H2066 A7 2017 | DDC 780.92 [B]—dc23
    LC record available at https://lccn.loc.gov/2016056931

1 2 3 4 5 22 21 20 19 18 17

This whole round living world of music—the Human Music—rouses and delights me, it stirs me to a "transethnic," a planetary music.

—Lou Harrison

CONTENTS

Part 4: Full Circle

Part 5: Pacifica

Part 6: The Great Melody

FOREWORD: HAIL, LOU!

Mark Morris

This book is a marvel. From knowing Mr. Harrison, from reading and through conversation with many others who knew him better than I did, I thought I'd heard it all. I'm happy to say that I was way off. His story and the story of his music are very satisfyingly presented here. So many fascinating details are revealed that I felt renewed respect, awe, and love for the subject: the Divine Lou Harrison. Harrison's music—or musics, considering the many diverse styles and modes and methods he employed in his compositions—promoted pleasure and peace. His devotion to beauty and consonance resulted in a deep trust relationship with his audience: hearing an engaging tune makes you feel better, and everyone wants to feel better. He was unafraid of the emotional resonance of a ravishing melody and, like his beloved Henry Cowell, was long denied respect by the Music Police. The deep, theoretical, personal immersion in music of the Rest of the World paid off by allowing him to produce an astounding variety of sonorities and compositional practices and structures, resulting in the amazing, huge embrace that his aesthetic presents to a willing listener.

You either love Lou's music or you haven't heard it yet. It sings and it dances. I first heard his call in the early 1980s from an out-of-print LP of *Four Strict Songs*. That recording led me to hunt for more and then more. I can't imagine how I'd been ignorant of the music for so long. Since my early teenhood I'd been drawn to the work of Satie, Cowell, Thomson, Nancarrow, Hovhaness, Cage, Ives, and particularly Harry Partch. My first good dance was set to Partch's *Barstow*. I'd been to Indonesia and was smitten with all things gamelan. I'd been to Korea and Japan and Thailand. I already loved the music of Asia and Polynesia. I adored Peking Opera. I'd sung madrigals and Croatian music and Appalachian and shape-note hymns and the Carter Family. I sang (enthusiastically if not beautifully) baroque music and rounds and catches and lute songs with similarly interested friends. I loved American Sign Language and hula and Esperanto and popular songs of the 20s and 30s. I was a flamenco dancer, a folk dancer, a modern dancer, a ballet dancer. I was already an active, confident choreographer at fifteen. I'd even read most of Partch's *Genesis of a Music*, at least the parts I could comprehend.

Lou's music hit me in the same way that my first trip to India hit me: it felt like Home. It was strange and satisfying and just right. In the way that Lou claimed he wished he'd written "Take Me Out to the Ball Game," I felt that I myself could somehow have come up with what I heard in his music. What I heard was magic, trust, power, Eros, kindness, fear, an overwhelming mystery, and vast inclusion. I try to perpetuate those qualities in my own work as a choreographer. I've learned through conversation with friends who knew Lou (Merce Cunningham, Dennis Russell Davies, Willie Winant, Eva Soltes, John Luther Adams, Michael Tilson Thomas, Jody Diamond, Remy Charlip . . .) that we all knew him best and loved him most. He was impossibly kind. He was generous and bossy. He was grand and shy. Superstrong and super-gay. I found his music irresistible and inescapable. Over the years, I've choreographed many of his pieces and presented many more in my curation of concerts, and I plan to set even more dances to his music as time goes on.

I visited Lou and Bill Colvig numerous times at their home in Aptos. They were wonderful, fascinating old friends. Yes, there was the perpetual soup pot on the stove, the Tchaikovsky and Ives rooms, the carpets, the garden with its plants from antiquity. They attended my dance company's performances in Berkeley and in New York, even if the program didn't include music that Lou had written. Lou came to my mother's birthday party in Seattle wearing galoshes instead of shoes. The two of them, so fond and funny with each other, were mildly lascivious with me and my male friends. Bill would dart past, naked, out of Lou's view. They smelled of the Forest and the Temple. In our very satisfying collaboration on the piece that became *Rhymes With Silver*, I was lucky to be caught up in the thrilling compositional process of a fully realized choreomusical presentation. Lou consulted Yo-Yo Ma on bowing and fingering, adjusted phrasings and lengths to suit dancing's needs, revised and improved the already gorgeous music both new and repurposed; he throughcomposed most of the sections but also generously dumped several "kits" in my lap to cope with in my own way. He always served me and paid for lunch at the Mexican café near his house.

In 2003 I was at work choreographing a solo for myself to *Serenade for Guitar*. In the dance, I played finger cymbals during one part (the "Usul") and thought I should also play castanets for the last part (which sounded to me like Scarlatti). I was getting ready to call Lou for official permission to add that little bit of percussion to his music. Before I got around to making that call (don't put it off!), I learned that Lou, darling Lou, had died. I guess it was time. I took his silence as tacit approval. I strapped on my castanets and danced to his memory and to his unequaled influence on the Great Big World of Music. Hail Lou!

PREFACE: LOU'S WORLD

The bus dropped me off at a stop on the side of the road, just off a major highway near Santa Cruz, California. I looked around. This appeared to be the right place, but there was no building nearby, just forested hillsides on both sides of the road. It was June 1995, and I was supposed to be meeting composer Lou Harrison at his house for the first time in half an hour, for our first formal interview in the biography I had just begun with Bill Alves. I had assumed I would take a taxi to his front door, but in our phone conversation, Harrison pointed out that it would be a lot cheaper and "more fun" to ride the bus from the home I was house-sitting in Walnut Creek and then hike "up the hill" from the back. "You'll see the trail" that Harrison's life partner, Bill Colvig, had blazed himself many years before, Harrison assured me.

I looked around and finally spotted what might—or might not—have been the path. Toting my tape recorder and laptop, I plunged into the forest and followed the path uphill.

Bill Alves and I decided to write the book when I was looking for a final project in my literary nonfiction master's program at the University of Oregon. In the mid-1980s, when Bill was a music composition graduate student at the University of California, his interests in just intonation and gamelan had led him to Lou's music, at a time when recordings of Lou's gamelan music had recently become available. After having helped arrange for a residency for Lou at USC, Bill was surprised when two white-bearded, flannel-shirted men pulled up in a ramshackle old camper. Lou and Bill hit it off right away, with Lou even conceding his admiration for Bill's computer music, a medium that Lou normally disdained, and they corresponded thereafter.

Meanwhile, I had been entranced by a public radio broadcast of Lou's *Pacifika Rondo* and asked Bill to introduce us. We met up with Lou and Bill Colvig after a talk Lou was giving at a local college, in which he used the history of the Western piano to demonstrate that there is no such thing as a pure musical tradition. At dinner afterward, we proposed our biography project, and they agreed to participate. "What composer doesn't like to talk about himself?" chuckled Lou.

Thus I trudged my way up that coastal hillside, at the fringe of the Forest of Nisene Marks State Park, marveling at how after only a couple of minutes of walking through the quiet shade of pine, redwood, and eucalyptus trees—so cooling after the hour-long ride in Santa Cruz's un-air conditioned bus—I felt worlds away from the area's suburban sprawl and noxious highways. I spied a couple of deer darting away, tuned into a chorus of birdcalls, inhaled the arboreal fragrance.

A few minutes later, I spied a fence and a clearing. Opening the gate, I emerged into a lovely garden, with purple agapanthus and other lilies and more in full summer bloom. There at the picnic table sat Lou (wearing a batik shirt) and Bill (wearing a lumberjack-style shirt and hiking shorts), enjoying a snack. I felt as though I'd entered some kind of magic garden. They invited me inside.

To enter Harrison's house was to immerse yourself in a realm resplendent in modern art (some by famous painters Lou had known, like Ben Shahn), artifacts (wall hangings, statues, tiles from Iran, and more), shelves upon shelves of books (with even more scattered about everywhere), strange percussion instruments, even food from all over the planet. And of course music—LPs and cassettes of traditional music and Lou's own recordings and scores. After a couple of hours of interviewing, Lou walked me to the back fence, and I plunged into the forest and descended back to the real world.

I repeated that journey (an hour each way by bus) a few times a week for the next month or so, trying hard not to overburden Lou, who was nearly seventy, and already starting to feel the pressures—increasingly incessant phone calls and faxes, mail, invitations, and other importunings that chipped away at his composing time. But he was almost always voluble, funny, brilliant (he had inherited Henry Cowell's habit of prefacing some relatively arcane knowledge of history, science, or art with "As you know …"), and, as many older people are, amazingly detailed in his memories of his childhood, teenage years, and twenties. I'd learned interview techniques to elicit just such memories, but I also learned that Lou was at the time engaged in similar reminiscences with his therapist, which probably helped. By the end of that summer, I knew I had one of the great stories of twentieth-century art.

For the next eight years, Bill Alves and I would return several times a year to Aptos whenever Lou's increasingly hectic schedule, and ours, permitted. He encouraged Bill to root around in his piles of manuscripts, then just being put into order by Lou's doughty archivist, Charles Hanson, and to use his home copier and stacks of kenaf paper. In formal sit-down interviews, over lunches at Manuel's, and during other encounters in Eugene, Portland, Los Angeles, and San Francisco, Lou would share his memories and ideas, musical and otherwise.

Then one February day in 2003, we received the devastating news that Lou had died, en route to an extensive four-day music festival in his honor at the Ohio State University. I was due to meet him there the next day, to cover the festival for the *Wall Street Journal*, and when I arrived in Columbus, I found everyone stunned, still reeling from the sudden departure of the artist whose music, whose world, had so long enchanted us.

After Lou's death, boxes of scores, recordings, notebooks, and memorabilia passed into storage at UC Santa Cruz, which hired Charles Hanson to catalog it. Thanks to his work and that of others at UCSC, these archives became an invaluable resource for us. While interviewing Lou's friends (such as Terry Riley, John Luther Adams, Mark Morris, Burt Bacharach, David Harrington, and David Lang) for unrelated stories, I would ask them about Lou, and their faces would light up, eager, like so many others, to share their memories.

Everyone smiles when they talk about Lou. His contagious sense of wonder and discovery—about history, science, art, music, politics, and more—rekindles that same spark in all of us. As we excavated further his full life, we discovered more about his troubled past and terrible temper, and one of the only regrets Lou ever expressed to us was about the terrible way he had sometimes treated people. Yet those who knew him during his youth—Remy Charlip, John Dobson, Judith Malina, Ned Rorem—remembered first his charm, his laughter, his infectious excitement. Remembering Lou made you feel, as he did, that the world was a bounteous trove of wonder.

I can still recall the moment—every biographer has one—when we found a document that, combined with evidence from interviews, for the first time really illuminated a searing turning point in his life. And whenever I encountered fellow citizens of Planet Lou, in the course of research or other journalistic assignments or visits, we would share more memories of the musician who touched so many through both his music and his ebullient attitude toward life.

Throughout his eventful career, Harrison would pursue the magic he first experienced amid the Asian art treasures gracing his childhood home in Portland's Silver Court apartments. He'd find it in mysterious shops in San Francisco's Chinatown, in Korean temples and Indonesian percussion orchestras, Medieval musical modes, ancient Greek tunings, in new instruments contrived from junkyard detritus. From those unlikely ingredients, he would fashion beguiling new sounds far removed from the conventional music of his time and place. Like his mother, he would embrace beautiful strangeness—and make it feel like home.

Just as Lou re-created, in his home and his music, the exotic world of the Silver Court of his childhood, or the colorful Chinatown and the rest of San Francisco of his adolescence, we have tried to conjure up Lou's world, the one I and so many others glimpsed when we entered that rambling house bordering the woods, or when they heard his increasingly popular and influential music.

After Lou died, new owners demolished the house I'd climbed up to that summer, the property now having become too pricy to harbor the quirky compound of music and memories we and his other visitors knew. I never could bring myself to go back to that spot on the hill. Eva Soltes preserved some of the contents, and she manages Harrison House, the desert retreat Lou designed at the end of his life, probably the best place to encounter a tangible environment that preserves his spirit. In a way, more and more of us, especially on the West Coast, are living in the world Lou helped create, a world in which music and art and culture from all over the world converge as part of our everyday lives.

And of course this spirit lives in Harrison's wondrous music, so much of which embraces, in an organic rather than a contrived fashion, the sounds of so many other cultures. It's there that he really re-created the sense of worldly wonder he felt as a boy at the Silver Court. We hope that this book also captures the feeling of that world, the one Lou glimpsed as a child in Portland and re-created in the house and garden at the edge of the woods—and the continent—in Aptos. As I emerged from the woods into a magical garden, I found myself in a portal to the vast and rich world of history, art, nature, music, and delight that Lou Harrison created during his eighty-five years on this planet, and that resounds in the music he made.

—Brett Campbell

ACKNOWLEDGMENTS

We are indebted to a great many people for the creation of this book, most espe-cially many of Lou's close friends, who generously and gleefully shared detailed memories of their time with Lou, always, always with a wistful smile and a chuckle, including Remy Charlip, Bill Colvig, Richard Dee, Jody Diamond, Charles Han-son, Robert Hughes, Daniel Schmidt, and Eva Soltes. Now good friends of ours as well, they helped in many ways, from providing key documents and photographs to tracking down acquaintances and other valuable information. We're grateful to Eva Soltes for allowing us access to her research for her 2012 documentary *Lou Harrison: A World of Music*. Lou's friend Charles Shere, who began an insightful Lou Harrison biography of his own but went on to other projects, graciously allowed us access to his manuscript. The memories of Judith Malina and Ned Rorem helped open up a crucial but underappreciated part of Lou's story in New York, in part because his own memories, damaged by his breakdown there, were so sketchy.

Like all researchers, we are also grateful to the librarians and archivists who helped us search through the monumental collection of scores, recordings, docu-ments, and other artifacts of Lou's life: those at the University of California, Santa Cruz, Special Collections—including Rita Bottoms, Christine Bunting, Luisa Had-dad, and Charles Hanson—and Janice Braun at Mills College. We're sure there is much more information in these archives, and there are more stories worth telling. We hope future researchers will find these collections as fascinating.

We are also very grateful to Jeff Abell, John Luther Adams, Susan Alexan-der, Anahid Ajemian, Debbie Alves, Charles Amirkhanian, Burt Bacharach, Erik Bauersfeld, Jack Body, Robert Brown, Mark Bulwinkle, Todd Burlingame, Linda Burman-Hall, the Cabrillo Music Festival, Bonnie Callantine, Hal Callantine, Peter Cavagnaro, John Chalmers, Duncan Charters, John Dobson, David Doty, Frank Eng, Margaret Fisher, Frank Foreman, Holly Gardinier, Peter Garland, Don Gillespie, Kraig Grady, David Harrington, David Harsany, Susan Heinlein, Mark Hoffman, Joseph Horowitz, James Irwin, Daniel Kelley, Lorle Kennedy, David Lang, Kerry Lewis, Frederic Lieberman, Larry London, Eric Marin, Vincent McDermott, Don-ald McKayle, Jim McKee, Midiyanto, Leta Miller, Danlee Mitchell, Mark Morris,

Trish Neilsen, Matthew Paris, Peter Poole, Jarrad Powell, Terry Riley, John Rockwell, Joel Sachs, John Schneider, Chloe Scott, Jon Siddall, William Slye, Jennifer Shennan Thomas, Andrew Timar, Larry Warren, Jeffrey Wash, Raymond Weisling, I Nyoman Wenten, William Winant, Daniel Wolf, Randall Wong, Wu Man, George Zelenz, and Michael Zwiebach.

Our thanks go to the editorial staff and others at Indiana University Press, who were so helpful and supportive of this large and challenging project, including Raina Polivka, Janice Frisch, and Gary Dunham. We also gratefully acknowledge support from Harvey Mudd College. We are especially thankful to our teachers, other supportive friends and colleagues, and, of course, our beloved family members—parents, partners, children, and felines.

PART 1

Oregon Trails

By the time he turned eighty in May 1997, Lou Harrison had reached a pinnacle few American musicians ever attain. San Francisco mayor Willie Brown declared June 14, 1996, Lou Harrison Day.[1] Across the street from City Hall, at a concert at Davies Symphony Hall, San Francisco Symphony music director Michael Tilson Thomas read Brown's proclamation to the audience at the orchestra's American Mavericks Festival, which honored Harrison and his friends and fellow music pioneers Henry Cowell and John Cage. There, just steps from the War Memorial Opera House where, fifty-seven years before, Harrison had received his first orchestral performance, Thomas conducted several Harrison compositions, including *Canticle #3*, a now classic composition for percussion ensemble that San Franciscans had first heard a mile and a half away at the Fairmont Hotel's auditorium in 1941, played by Harrison, Cage, and a group of amateur percussionist friends.

In New York, where Harrison lived for a decade, Lincoln Center presented an eightieth birthday exhibition of Harrison memorabilia, a solo recital by pianist Michael Boriskin, and the premiere of Harrison's *Concerto for Pipa and String Orchestra*. A concert at the 92nd Street Y presented Harrison's music for the "American Gamelan," a set of percussion instruments Harrison had designed and built with his life partner, Bill Colvig. At the Brooklyn Academy of Music, the country's most innovative dance group, led by Mark Morris, performed three evenings' worth of dances set to Harrison's music, including *Rhymes with Silver,* featuring superstar cellist Yo-Yo Ma, which had debuted earlier that year in Berkeley.

In between the start of his artistic life, living on the edge of poverty, and his celebration as one of America's leading composers, Harrison helped bring American music from the generation of fearsome modernist iconoclasts to the generation of world music and minimalism. In 1930s San Francisco, he helped to pioneer music for percussion ensemble as well as a DIY mentality that extended to forming his own band and even making his own instruments long before classical composers did such things. His early explorations in noise, global music cultures, early music, and unusual musical tunings also anticipated the larger world by decades, as did his countercultural convictions of pacifism and open homosexuality. An unrepentant eclectic in a time that celebrated singular artistic visions, he composed propulsive dance scores and unabashedly modal melodies alongside his experiments in atonality. Also unlike many modernists, Harrison never thought of his many innovations as revolutionary musical statements, just the next potentially rewarding creative avenue to explore, often inspired by mentors and books that opened his imagination to new possibilities.

Like other ambitious radical artists, he headed for the headwaters of American new music, New York City, but despite his formative connections and experiences there, he found a musical and personal dead end. He returned to California, leaving the musical mainstream both geographically and musically for the quiet solace of nature and a perspective looking out over the Pacific. His trajectory between these extremes was unlike that of any of his contemporaries—to outsiders, he seemed to have suddenly abandoned a seemingly promising career to pursue, in near isolation, eccentric interests in Asian music and tuning. At a time when the musical avant-garde exploded with futurist electronics, wild experimentation, and inscrutable complexity, Lou Harrison vacated "the overcrowded city space of modern music," said *New Yorker* critic Alex Ross, "to camp out in a desert landscape of long drones and mesmeric patterns."[2] A troubled life and a long wait for acceptance never shook Harrison from his stalwart faith in transcendent melody, a resolutely westward view (away from Europe and toward Asia), and an ideal of harmonic purity in music as well as society.

Through his isolation, he came to value the joys of making music with friends over a career in search of conventional markers of success. By the gentle gravitational attraction of his ebullient personality, Harrison drew a steadily widening circle of sympathetic fellow travelers to his side in his journey, often creating a supportive community to perform and listen to the new sounds he was conceiving. His contagious enthusiasm for ideas, artistic and beyond, inspired devotion and support from key figures who helped him throughout his life, because he made so many of those around him imagine that they could do what he did: continuously embrace the joy of exploring new horizons, and continuously reinvent himself throughout his long and fruitful life.

By the 1980s, Harrison's recordings were winning legions of listeners beyond the hermetic Western avant-garde aficionados, and his multiculturalism was moving beyond the esoteric to the mainstream. At the San Francisco Symphony's 1996 American Mavericks Festival, conductor Michael Tilson Thomas placed Harrison's music squarely in the lineage of American music, alongside his mentors and musicians he influenced, from Charles Ives to John Cage, and even with Bay Area rock legends the Grateful Dead.

Throughout his long and meandering creative journey, Harrison never stopped learning and exploring, and the acclaim of the Davies Symphony Hall audience, Deadheads and all, showed that this path had found a surprisingly wide range of listeners. And that path's direction was set nearly eighty years before, several hundred miles up the Pacific Coast, where his mother surrounded him with the elegance of Asian art and his father read James Joyce out loud to the family.

THE SILVER COURT (1917–1934)

Whenever Lou Harrison came home, it was like stepping into another world. From as early in childhood as he could remember, wherever he looked in his family's apartment in Portland, Oregon's Silver Court Apartments, young Lou saw colorful paintings from various Asian cultures mounted on walls covered by Japanese grass wallpaper. Chinese carved teak furniture perched on Persian rugs, colorful Japanese lanterns dangled from the ceiling, cloisonné objects filled the mantel, and the rooms boasted other artifacts from Asia and the Middle East. Compared to the prosaic furnishings and fixtures of the rest of the young Harrison's post-World War I Pacific Northwest life, his home was an almost magical place.

The exotic decor sprang from the ambitions of his mother. Born in Seattle in 1890, Calline Silver grew up in the Alaskan frontier with her sister, Lounette. Despite these rough circumstances, their father saw to it that both girls had music lessons, at a time when music was an important marker of good breeding and refinement for young women. After her father died and Cal raised herself from this rustic beginning to a middle-class ideal, she became a woman of strong will and determination, qualities that her son would inherit. She married affable, fair-skinned Clarence Harrison, a first-generation American born in 1882, whose Norwegian father had, like many immigrants, changed his surname from exotic (de Nësja) to blend-in conventional: Harrison.

Like many upwardly mobile West Coasters, Cal Harrison was attracted to the allure of Asia and regarded exotic artifacts as exemplars of refined taste. Such decorations were common in Portland homes since the 1905 Lewis and Clark Centennial and American Pacific Exposition and Oriental Fair. Japan alone spent a million dollars on its exhibit, which featured exotic (to American eyes) arts and crafts, sparking a local infatuation with Asian art and culture. Many middle- and upper-class houses boasted "Oriental Rooms" festooned with Asian and Middle Eastern furniture and art, "Turkish corners," and other symbols of what many Americans still regarded as the mysterious East. That Pacific exoticism also manifested in music. When Lou was born on May 14, 1917, Hawaiian music was the most popular genre in America. Radio broadcasts of Hawaiian slide guitars and the clacks of his mother's mah-jongg tiles supplied the soundtrack to some of his earliest memories—and inspired his final great composition eight decades later.[1]

The Silver Court's surrounding Irvington neighborhood in northeast Portland had been developed as an exclusive enclave only twenty years before Lou was born. Connected to downtown Portland's cultural riches by trolley, the "streetcar park" originally catered to the toffs (including lumber barons). During Lou's childhood, however, the changing neighborhood's new Queen Anne revival, Craftsman, and Prairie School-style homes welcomed more middle-class people like the Harrisons. They had built the handsome Silver Court Apartments (which still stands at 22nd and Hancock streets) shortly after Lou's birth, when Calline received a substantial inheritance from her family in Ohio, who owned a manufacturing business; her grandfather's widow's death in 1910 led to a partition of the estate, and the Harrisons used their share to build the three-story, thirty-unit apartment building. The money allowed them to hire a family to take care of the apartments, including their own.

They also bought the tire business where Lou's father worked, inculcating a lasting family tension: Cal never let Clarence forget that it was her money that put him in business. "It was mother's belief that the man should wear the skirts," Lou wrote in his journal many years later.[2] After all, the apartment building they lived in and managed was called Silver Court, not Harrison House—and it later seemed to Lou that his father was always on trial.

Clarence and Calline did share a love of cars—she was reputedly the first woman to drive across Portland's Steel Bridge—and the family enjoyed then-common Sunday drives and picnics in the country. They appreciated the scenic beauty—waterfalls, the spectacular Columbia River Gorge, Mt. Hood (which dominated the eastern skyline), and nearby Mt. Tabor—and gave Harrison and his brother, Bill (born three years later), a lasting love of the outdoors.

Calline had intended to name the baby for her sister Lounette, but "when they discovered I was a male, they cut off the 'nette.' I became Lou, so I'm not Lou-vig, or Louis, or any of that, just plain Lou."[3] Like their apartment building, Lou was also named for his mother's maiden name, giving his name a uniqueness that was later commemorated in the title of his ballet *Rhymes with Silver*. In childhood, though, Lou Silver Harrison was mostly called by his nickname, Buster. Harrison never met his grandparents and had little contact with extended family during childhood, so his parents exerted the greatest family influence on their eldest son. Their two most persistent legacies were his lifelong loves: arts and reading. Aunt Lounette played violin, often accompanied by Calline on the piano, and little Buster would dance.

He took the stage early. Calline worked in a Portland beauty shop, and one of her regular customers, Verna Felton, ran a small theater company that in 1920 was producing Jean Webster's 1912 play *Daddy-Long-Legs*.[4] They needed a young boy for a silent walk-on role as a little orphan, and Calline volunteered two-year-old Buster, who, encouraged by candy, improvised his lines—for the irrepressible little Lou, it turned out not to be a silent role after all—and won the audience's heart, getting his picture in the daily *Oregonian* newspaper and an invitation to reprise the role on a Northwest tour and in another production in Washington.[5] The experience gave

Harrison both a taste for performance and a deep set of separation anxieties that never left him.[6]

> Aged three
> I was on stage
> & touring with the troupe—
> the child's still me in my rounds and duties
>
> The stage
> was large, the scene
> was dim, the actress was,
> I knew, woman my mother
> much loved.
> > frightened
> > by commotion
> > in the hall—applause
> > laughter?—loud, so many grown-ups
> > clapping!
> So large
> the stage! the plot
> unknown, the lines unsure,
> & the scenes done as reverse glass
> paintings.
> > So much
> > for all the pain—
> > costumes and glitter keep
> > our solemn frivolity
> > alive.[7]

LOST TREASURES

Along with the Asian art in her home and the European art in the Silver Court lobby, Calline imparted artistic culture to her children. Just two and a half miles away and over the Broadway or Steel bridges across the Willamette River that separated the Irvington neighborhood from downtown's theaters and studios, the city's relatively rich classical music, dance, and theater scenes provided an outlet for Calline's ambitions for her family's artistic enlightenment.

Oregonians liked to say that when the pioneers moved west over the Lewis and Clark Trail, the settlers who wanted gold turned left and headed for California, while those who wanted to set up a culture turned right and brought their schools, pianos, and other cultural trappings to Oregon. Portland fancied itself as more cultured than other West Coast boomtowns, and its 1920s music scene reflected that cultivated sensibility, including recitals by famous musicians like Maurice Ravel, Igor Stravinsky, Sergei Rachmaninoff, Béla Bartók, Jascha Heifetz, and Fritz Kreisler. Lou remembered seeing movies like the 1925 epic *The Lost World* at the Hollywood Theater.

As Buster grew older, he'd join the rest of the family in singing popular music, old tunes like "Bicycle Built for Two," "Blue Lagoon," and "By the Bend of the

River"—the last a pentatonic melody that, he later recalled, "haunted" his music for years, "just as Virgil Thomson was haunted by 'Jingle Bells.'"[8] The family owned a phonograph that Lou once modified by putting a bigger horn on it.[9] Cal signed the boys up for music and ballroom dance lessons. "I remember learning the schottische when I could barely toddle," said Harrison.[10] Although his brother, Bill, was not very interested in music, Lou was happy to stay home and play violin, harmonium, and the family piano on Portland's rainy winter and spring days.

Lou also inherited what he called his mother's tendency toward "hysteria" to get what she wanted. His later friend Remy Charlip said that Lou told him how, at the age of five, he would get his way: He stood in the middle of the room and screamed. "Lou remained," said Charlip, "a diva throughout his life."[11] Even his faintly formal and slightly archaic manner of speaking and writing seemed to originate in his mother's upwardly mobile ambitions.

If Harrison associated his mercurial mother with the beautiful things in life, his father, known as Pop, symbolized "industrial grease iron" and masculine detachment.[12] Once, when Lou rushed up to embrace his father after an absence, Pop's response was, "Men don't do that." Only years later would Harrison come to appreciate what a gentle and kind person Pop Harrison really was.[13]

Despite his childhood close connection with his mother, Lou received one crucial legacy from his father: a love of reading. When Pop came home each night from his job at a Portland tire company, he enjoyed a cocktail and hours of reading books and magazines, even reading James Joyce's *Ulysses* aloud to the family.[14] Little Buster often read from an encyclopedia set for young readers called *Our Wonder World* with a section titled "Queer Peoples of the World."[15] Lou inherited his dad's bibliomania (and his taste for alcohol) and was immersed in at least one book practically every day of his life.

However, Harrison's Portland idyll—as he remembered it—of arts and books and nature ended when he was eight. In the mid-1920s, boosters in what was then Oregon's second-largest city, Astoria, were advocating for the construction of a new bridge across the Columbia River. Anticipating an impending North Coast economic boom that ultimately never arrived, the Harrisons swapped the Silver Court for a resort hotel in the declining coastal city. The failure of this investment prompted them to leave the state entirely. Clarence's rich brother Harry (known as "H. O.") was an automobile distributor in San Francisco and agreed to set up Clarence in his business.[16]

Harrison's Oregon upbringing left lasting impressions on the budding young musician: an inclination toward the outdoors and nature's beauty, an affection for high-culture art and music, and a performer's sense of the stage and the audience. But leaving the only home he'd ever known is tough on any child, and now, as the family drove south along Highway 101, following the conquistadors' old Road of Kings, El Camino Real, the alluring, Asian-tinged world that had nurtured nine-year-old Buster Harrison was receding. The loss of that world would be compounded by the economic upheavals roiling not just his family's prospects but also the nation's. Much later, toward the end of one of the richest lives ever lived in American arts, the then-octogenarian Harrison came to realize that in pursuing, studying, and ultimately creating original music deeply informed by the traditional sounds of Asia, he was "trying to recapture the lost treasures of my youth."[17]

"I was surrounded by a household of very fine Asian art," he said, "and as I grew up, I wanted to reproduce that. My problem and my drama has been, could I recover the lost treasures of childhood? Well, I discovered that if I couldn't make enough money to buy them, at least I could make some."[18]

Yet mere imitation of music of other times or cultures, however elegant and graceful, would not fulfill Harrison's quest. He would soon discover a thrilling world of modern American composition blazing paths into previously unheard worlds of sounds. This creative tension between recapturing ancient beauty and finding new excitement in revolutionary sounds would fuel Harrison's lifelong musical journey.

CALIFORNIA MISSIONS

> the great valley's heat & birds & blooms,
> my beautiful brother bicycling with me
> on the banks of rivers,
> the melons that my father loved
> & that in summer crawl laden
> out upon the roads,
> reedy rivers, blackbirds, & the perilous canals.
>
> —Lou Harrison[19]

"When Dad announced that we were going to move to California," Harrison recalled, "I had this image of a sombreroed rider on a burro, and cactus. It turned out not to be true—we moved to Woodland. And there were the missions."[20]

A brown, rural landscape replaced the regal security of the Silver Court, little resembling Astoria's chilly coastal seascape or Portland's verdant neighborhoods. Flat, small (three thousand people), and broiling in summer, Woodland was a farm town outside Sacramento in California's fertile agricultural breadbasket, where Lou and Bill would play among orchards and irrigation canals. Lou's uncle H. O. hired his brother Clarence to set up regional car dealerships around the area. As a result, the family became itinerant, changing cities every year or two as Clarence received new assignments: in Sacramento itself after Woodland, next in marshy Stockton.

Young Buster was just beginning a peripatetic stretch in which he would live at twenty-eight different addresses by the time he graduated from high school.[21] Although thanks to the advanced Oregon schools, Lou did fine in his studies, even jumping ahead a grade when he got to California, "I learned early on that you shouldn't form really close relationships, because you were going to move," Harrison remembered.[22] He was already starting to feel different from the other boys, and every time he entered a new and unfamiliar school, he kept to himself and out of sight of bullies. A series of childhood illnesses also served to isolate both brothers. Lou retreated to his books, art, and music, and he later wondered whether his interest in music "did not come from the weariness of having to relocate all the time."[23] Family life was often dominated by a tempestuous mother who lashed out at his father, whom she blamed for the family's misfortune.

For solace, Lou kept a trunk of precious possessions—photos, scores, books, mementos—that became his portable world of imagination, an island of beauty and stability amid the shifting currents of the family's turbulent peregrinations. The trunk's greatest treasure—a self-created, portable replacement for the Silver Court's lost glories—was what it embodied for Harrison: his response to the challenges of adolescence. In this period of discovery over the next few years, through junior high and high school, he would surmount those challenges by vastly expanding his knowledge of music, arts, the world, and himself. Throughout his life Harrison would continue to pursue his vision of beauty from his lost happy childhood and the Silver Court.

His music lessons continued, and when he heard of the death of a family friend whose farm they had frequently visited in rural Oregon during their Portland years, Lou wrote his first composition, an "Elegie," contributing his own watercolor image and hand calligraphy to the score cover and signing it "Lou Silver Harrison, 10 years old." The elegy is really a waltz, which Lou had learned in ballroom dance lessons, a charming little piece full of block major and minor chords, often misspelled in a crude but earnest hand. This juvenilium already reveals a longing for rural surroundings that would recur in his life and music; the dead friend represented the country pleasures that the citified Portlanders enjoyed on visits.[24]

The family's next move took them from rural to suburban California, as they relocated to Berkeley, where Lou started junior high school and even joined the football team with his brother (Lou played center). His mother found him a new piano teacher in nearby Oakland, one who could also teach him jazz. Harrison was never particularly a jazz enthusiast, but it was a broadening experience for the young musician, who had to learn to navigate harmonies through all twelve keys and quickly find various chords. However, 1929 was the heyday of the stride piano style, in which the pianist's left hand must speedily leap from bass notes to chords, and twelve-year-old Lou simply did not have hands the size of James P. Johnson's or Fats Waller's. Frustrated, he abandoned this jazz experiment when they next moved, but its influence would later resurface. "I was never successful as a jazz pianist because . . . I never could do the oompahs right. So I flunked out as a performing artist there, but I gained a lot theoretically."[25]

The more cosmopolitan college town also offered another opportunity for diversifying Buster and Bill's educational background. Although the family wasn't especially religious, Cal wanted her kids to be exposed to as many religions as possible so they could make up their own minds about their spiritual direction. Lou later credited his exposure to a multitude of Protestant churches and Sunday schools for his many explorations into traditions farther afield, from mystical Christianity to Buddhism. "I never regretted this run-around," he explained, "because it gives you a comparative sense of things and also it just went right on into world religions too and general philosophies."[26]

But any sense of stability was again short-lived. Uncle Harry, like so many others in *Grapes of Wrath*-era California, went bankrupt, and Pop started taking on extra jobs, including managing apartment houses and office work. After a brief stay in Los Gatos, the family moved to the bayside town of Redwood City, from which Pop would commute twenty-five miles north to San Francisco.

At Sequoia Union High School, Lou soon found opportunities to become much more serious about music. At thirteen, he was still featured as a boy soprano soloist and for a while could sing both soprano and bass. "I did a lot of singing those days," he remembered, from madrigals to popular songs to Gilbert and Sullivan tunes. "I think that my attitude towards music, that it's basically a song and a dance, comes from both things: first I was a singer, then I was a dancer."[27]

Lou also learned the rudiments of conducting and could passably play French horn and clarinet. The school choir director, also a composer who played organ in a downtown church, invited Harrison to dinner with his family and eventually gave Lou the key to the church organ loft so that he could play the pipe organ there whenever he could find time not already committed to his newspaper route and school.[28] Soon Harrison had composed a rather romantic organ sonata (marked "Andante Religioso").

His new piano teacher also encouraged Lou and even took him to concerts in the area, and piano compositions soon followed.[29] Despite its reliance on Clementi models (Alberti basses and big block chords), an ambitious four-movement sonatina (dated, with a hint of pride and his later prolificacy, "begun Nov. 10, 1931, completed Nov. 11, 1931") shows a clear grasp of conventional forms, including sonata form and a minuet and trio. For all of their puerile romanticism, his early piano works display an increasing confidence, facile musical handwriting, and a willingness to experiment with unusual chord progressions and key changes.

Harrison's creativity found other outlets, including writing poetry and taking an art class in school. He did well academically, especially in science classes, beginning a lifelong interest in science. He read library books by science writer Arthur Eddington and all the science fiction he could find.[30] He even invented his own shorthand alphabet to facilitate note-taking in school. However, unlike his brother, Lou detested gym class, where he felt awkward (except in wrestling) and was taunted for being a "sissy" and thrown into the swimming pool.[31]

The bullies sensed what Harrison himself had already suspected. He had already felt unsatisfied urges directed toward older men and realized he was different. The following year, at a high school party, the action moved to the rumble seats of the parked cars, and he discovered that he had no sexual interest whatsoever in the girls there. "I knew I was different—that's when it struck me," he recalled. "It made me very sad, very melancholy."[32]

He found solace at the Redwood City public library, where he would eagerly devour books on art, literature, and science fiction. And he realized that he could pursue his particular interests as deeply as he wanted, by checking out the books cited in footnotes and repeating the process with those books in turn. He remembered reading a couple of books each evening—a practice he never abandoned. "My afternoons after school . . . largely consisted of studying and reading and . . . long sessions at the piano trying to work out scores," he remembered. "And also, being gay kept me away from parties. All the straights were having a lot of parties, whereas I didn't have that, so I had a lot of reading time and practice time, making instruments time too."[33]

But he was not entirely alone. Lou began to play music with Ivan Harris, a violinist from school, and then their duets became even closer. "He was very sensuous and a very nice guy," Harrison remembered, fondly recalling writing poetry together and romantic trysts in a tent in summer. "We were friends for many, many years. He was very nice, very intense, very pleasurable. He taught me a lot and shared concepts and ideas. It was romantic and soft and warm and sexy."[34] Harrison now knew that his attraction to men was real and serious, and that it could even be fun.

The older Ivan introduced Lou to a new musical world. One day over at Ivan's house, Ivan played records from his collection for Harrison. Out of the tinny speaker came music of flabbergasting intensity and dissonance. It was Stravinsky's ballet score *The Rite of Spring*. Next was the strangely austere counterpoint of the same composer's *Octet* and *Piano Concerto*, pieces then less than ten years old. But for a lesson on how ancient and modern could intermingle, Harrison preferred Manuel de Falla's *El Retablo del Maese Pedro* (*Master Peter's Puppet Show*), a short, delightful chamber opera that would later inspire one of Harrison's landmark compositions. Instead of following Stravinsky's detached, almost mechanistic reinterpretation of baroque idioms, the Spanish composer's recent (1923) setting of this episode from *Don Quixote* was melodically opulent and sparkled with the then-novel timbre of the harpsichord. Harrison also heard in Falla's melodies and (more surprisingly) Stravinsky's rhythms a Latin character that connected with his romance of colonial period California.

One day when they visited a pianist friend of Ivan's, Lou noticed some curious sheet music with a distinctive art deco cover, called simply *New Music*. It contained music, written by mostly American composers, that appeared to have little in common with Stravinsky's neoclassicism. Although Harrison wouldn't delve into these mysterious scores until he rediscovered them in the San Francisco Library after high school, leafing through them gave him a brief glimpse of a world of contemporary music. Harrison's own portal to that world would be the very editor of *New Music*, America's "ultramodernist" composer Henry Cowell.

BAROQUE AND BRAHMAN

A bit of incense
Rising from a tiny pot
But now—see the fern!

—Poem in the form of a Japanese haiku by fifteen-year-old Harrison published in a local paper[35]

Just as Harrison was settling into Redwood City, though, the family moved again, to Burlingame, just up the peninsula, where Clarence was running a car wash. And it was there that Lou's intellectual and artistic lives really blossomed. In his high school English class and during subsequent library trips, Harrison developed intense literary obsessions, especially for the works of William Blake and William Butler Yeats (both of whom would influence subsequent work), and he recognized the homosexual overtones in works he admired by Walt Whitman, igniting what became a lifelong passion for poetry with "congested and intense quality of sound" and "lots of tone language."[36] He helped edit the school poetry journal and also contributed original linoleum block print illustrations.

A friend active in the theater department, Bob Metcalf, introduced Harrison to the works of Gertrude Stein, and the boys even traveled up to Stanford for a rare opportunity to hear Stein herself read. Impressed, Harrison wrote Stein a fan letter and received a polite response from her partner, Alice Toklas. Harrison then submitted a Stein-influenced piece to the senior-year issue of his school's poetry journal. Metcalf would continue to be a good friend after graduation, as they both became active in the Bay Area arts community.[37]

Harrison's intellectual explorations often transcended his school lessons. A conscientious teacher spotted something in an essay he wrote and pointed him toward the Vedanta Society, devoted to the study of the centuries-old Hindu Brahman philosophy. Harrison admired the philosophy's emphasis on the pursuit of knowledge and the compelling talks delivered by the current temple leader, Swami Ashokananda. "When I was there, I had the sensation that I was being looked right through, that I was absorbing what he absorbed in some way," Harrison recalled. "I guess it was good music, intelligent preachment [that] seemed more like philosophical discussion, and appealed to me emotionally as well as [to my] intellectual interests. There was no intermediary between God and you. An adolescent hunting inside himself is apt to regard that, I suppose, as a kind of aid too."[38]

Pop Harrison patiently indulged his older son's interests, even if he didn't understand them. When the boy wanted to learn about medieval music, he drove him up to San Francisco's historic Mission Dolores for Gregorian chant choir—an hour driving, a two-hour wait during Lou's rehearsal, and another drive home. There Lou learned about the so-called church modes, scales beyond the major and minor he knew from piano lessons, and recitation tones, the extended pitches on which many syllables of prose or irregular verse could be repetitively chanted and framed by melodic motives called *initium* and *terminatio*. He even saved up to buy a copy of the *Liber Usualis*, the Catholic Church's thick standard compilation of chant, and, helped by his high school Latin classes, learned to read the thirteenth-century-based notation.

When Lou wanted more formal training in music theory, Pop paid for lessons with Howard Couper, a graduate student of Domenico Brescia, the elderly Italian composer who headed the music theory department at Mills College in Oakland. For about a year, Harrison received a firm grounding in traditional counterpoint and theory from Couper via copious exercises in such forms as fugues and variations. Harrison welcomed the lessons in baroque counterpoint, as he loved music from this period, particularly that of George Frideric Handel. "The divine Mr. Handel has been with me since I can't remember. It's so old, my love for Handel," he reminisced. "And there was a period in my life when I would get up, go to the phonograph, and put on something by Handel as my first act of the morning."[39]

To Harrison, the baroque aesthetic was no mere textbook abstraction. He recognized it in the architecture of the Dolores Mission and other survivals of California's colonial past. During those years, "everybody's living room had a least one picture of the [Spanish] Alhambra [Palace]," he said.[40] Harrison pursued the Spanish connection in local public libraries, where he found the monumental collections of Spanish Renaissance and baroque music edited by Spanish nationalist Felipe Pedrell, who also collected folk and popular songs. Harrison spent hours playing through volumes of seventeenth-century Spanish keyboard music, a pursuit that led directly to his first composition that he kept on his list of acknowledged works.

Harrison called this creation a "sonata," not after the well-known classical form, but instead in the earlier sense of a piece "to be sounded" as used by the Italian-Spanish baroque composer Domenico Scarlatti. Like those models, this sonata is in binary form (two repeated halves) and written not for piano but rather the baroque harpsichord. Although Harrison lacked access to a harpsichord, he decorated the melody with appropriate ornaments. Unlike his earlier compositions, the spare, clean textures sometimes resemble the inventions of Bach. Over the next few years, Harrison gradually added more sonatas to form a collection representing what Harrison called his "Mission period" and reflecting, he said, the "romance and geometry of impassioned Spain."[41]

Harrison frequently brought to Couper these "voluntary" pieces (that is, pieces written apart from his assignments), many of which show his preoccupation with early music, including a set of folk song variations for a whole Renaissance ensemble.[42] Upon receiving one of these unorthodox experiments, the astonished Couper told Harrison, "You're either going to amount to a lot or you'll collapse."[43] In the end, Harrison would do both.

Harrison graduated from Burlingame High in December 1934, performing with a student flutist his new composition *Blue Glass* at the ceremony.[44] In those critical years, he had confronted initial challenges—his dislocation from his family's comfortable, Asian-accented Portland life; his outsider status resulting from his frequent moves and being gay—and found his identity through the study of ideas, through art and literature, and in creating art. "When you're adolescent, that's when everything opens up—the whole world," he said later. "It's not only your pelvic girdle, it's also your mind, and they sort of bloom at once."[45]

Harrison's blossoming would continue in San Francisco, where his family was moving and where he planned to enroll at San Francisco State College. The city was home to some of his high school friends, such as Bob Metcalf, who helped Harrison navigate an intoxicating artistic atmosphere.

PART 2

The Vast Acreage

Although Harrison's family had lived in the environs of San Francisco since he was twelve years old, their move into the city itself in January 1935 revealed to Harrison a vibrant cultural world. The next seven years—the period that shaped his career—would also introduce him to the other major elements he would combine in fruitful fusion for the rest of his life: dance, percussion, European and American avant-garde music, early music, Asian music. Harrison often said that he laid out his toys on a vast acreage early on and spent much of the rest of his life picking them up, examining them, using and combining them as he pleased.[1] In his old age, he called San Francisco "the city where I attained my maturity—I can't say I grew up here, because I haven't yet."[2]

At the time, though, Harrison didn't know he wanted to be a composer. In fact, to the end of his life, he claimed that he never did make that decision. Then as later, Harrison's guileless charm proved attractive to others who shared his many enthusiasms, and they, in turn, opened many of San Francisco's doors of discovery to him.

To the voluble, energetic young Harrison, San Francisco was "a lavish, very social city with friendship and pleasure above all."[3] In the quarter century since it had been leveled by an earthquake and fire, the city had developed into a busy metropolis of art deco skyscrapers and cable cars, jazz clubs and Victorian row houses. Traditional musicians played along the fragrant alleyways of Chinatown, and sizable communities of immigrants from Japan, the Philippines, and India contributed their flavors to the port city's rich cultural stew. Until the completion of the San Francisco–Oakland Bay Bridge in 1936 and the Golden Gate Bridge in 1937, ferries crisscrossed the bay, with small musical ensembles often furnishing entertainment for the passengers.

The Depression hit San Francisco's longshoremen and others at the bottom of the economic ladder especially hard. Much of their plight was invisible to the city's social elite, who had already established San Francisco as the leading arts center on the West Coast, founding the San Francisco Symphony in 1911 and the city opera in 1923. In 1936, the socialites who controlled the symphony board scored an artistic coup when they enticed the famous French conductor Pierre Monteux, who had conducted the notorious premiere of Stravinsky's *The Rite of Spring*, to come to San

Francisco. Monteux would establish the orchestra as one of the nation's finest. Critic Alfred Frankenstein devoted most of his weekly column in the *Chronicle* to the symphony, just as the society pages faithfully chronicled the goings-on of Monteux and his family.

But rarely did newspapers touch on the other San Francisco—the teeming mix of bohemian artists, leftist radicals, and religious visionaries, of iconoclasts and misfits that the seventeen-year-old Harrison discovered shortly after his arrival. Harrison's encounter with this other San Francisco began when he enrolled at San Francisco State College's old downtown campus, just walking distance from his family's new house on Buena Vista Hill.[4] Just on the other side of the tunnel lived Jim Cleghorn, another aspiring composer who sang in the college madrigal singers and chamber choir with Harrison. Harrison and his new friend became "close artistically and intellectually," and soon Cleghorn was introducing Harrison to communities of artists, dancers, and musicians, where his real education began.[5]

After an inward-looking existence necessitated by his family's frequent moves and his failure to fit into adolescent cliques, Harrison found a welcoming artistic milieu waiting for him in the city. "I just entered the network that already existed," he remembered. "It was a place where you could go and attend a party and within a week know practically everybody. I'd go whenever I was invited and wasn't working—at least once a week. We'd smoke cigarettes and drink and recite poetry, play instruments, tell jokes, and enjoy the latest in gossip."[6]

A man he met at a theater party introduced Harrison to the city's gay underground. Homosexuality was so accepted within Harrison's social circles that he never hid his orientation from most friends and acquaintances. The first gay bars sprung up after Prohibition was repealed, and in the 1930s and 1940s, the city's gay and lesbian communities frequented the same bars, including the "quasi-dangerous" Mona's ("where we encountered many a fistfight").[7]

Harrison soon became friends not just with musicians and dancers, but also with the artists and poets who created San Francisco's thriving underground arts community in downtown lofts and high school auditoriums. Much of their work was made possible by the Works Progress Administration (WPA), which in 1935 established federal projects for the arts. Unlike today's National Endowment for the Arts, "the projects" directly employed artists as craftspeople to do what they did best—paint, compose, write, stage plays, play music. The Bay Area's several WPA orchestras employed scores of musicians and, in keeping with the program's philosophy, tended to play new American music—a rarity on most other symphony programs.

"We all went to WPA concerts and ballets because there was minimal admission," Harrison recalled. "It was a wonderful period for American arts. They had the notion that an artist was also a workman and craftsman and deserved to be paid just like any working craftsman. For a young person growing up in that atmosphere and with friends who were working with WPA and giving concerts and exhibitions and decorating public buildings, it was really quite an insight into what the arts can be, and I've never forgotten it. Art was part of our daily lives."[8]

It all added up to a creative environment as rich as any in American history. An article in the 1937 *Dance Observer*, for example, lists the number of events San Francisco critics had attended between October and May: forty-nine operas, twenty-six orchestral concerts, twenty-eight dance programs, twenty-two piano recitals, sixteen singers, eight violinists, seventeen chamber music ensembles, nine choral programs, and ten miscellaneous.[9] Two-thirds of the dancers were locals, but they could benefit from exposure to visiting national figures such as Martha Graham.

The WPA also brought the visual arts closer to Harrison, who attended exhibitions at the old Museum of Modern Art and at Coit Tower by artist friends, and who saw plenty of Japanese and Chinese paintings, which reminded him of the lost luxury of his family's Portland home. Harrison often visited San Francisco's Palace of Fine Arts with his high school friend Bob Metcalf, who lived with his mother nearby. He and friends frequented galleries, admiring the works of Klee and Dali.[10] Harrison took classes at the Art Institute from the Japanese painter Chiura Obata, as well as watercolor classes from another well-known California artist, Helen Frank, and he learned to work in egg tempera from an artist who was paid by the WPA to produce three panels in that medium every month.

Harrison's companion on many of his early San Francisco adventures, John Dobson, gained even greater early exposure to Asia: he was born in what Americans then called Peking, where his father had taught before taking a teaching position at San Francisco's Lowell High School, where James Cleghorn's father also taught.

Cleghorn had introduced Harrison to the long-haired Dobson—bright, talkative, excited about ideas, and, to Harrison, very beautiful—who quickly became the most important person in Harrison's life. When Harrison visited the Dobson family house, which stood just on the other side of Buena Vista Hill, he found it, like his own, teeming with Asian art. At dinner, the family conversation would occasionally lapse into Mandarin. Dobson's father decided that his three sons should review Chinese history and language, and John's new friend Lou was soon included in the lessons. (He found it useless in San Francisco's Chinatown—whose inhabitants mostly spoke Cantonese.) Harrison frequently picked up his friend for a night in Chinatown, where, during the height of the Depression, for a quarter each, they could eat till they were full, and then head for the opera.[11]

2

A WONDERFUL WHIRLIGIG (1935–1936)

As Lou Harrison and his young friend entered the theater, they saw a turquoise silk stage curtain with embroidered dragon and phoenix on both sides—and the word "Bromoseltzer" in giant silver letters. The curtain—and its advertisement—was the Chinatown theater's main concession to Western culture. Instead of the quiet reverence that accompanies European opera, Chinese opera competed with children lining up by the stage, friends gossiping—but no one applauded. Huddled together in the unheated building, most of the Chinese patrons knew the ritualized stories of the opera and were there to experience the atmosphere of the performance or perhaps the solo of the top-billed singer.

Clamorous, colorful, the music seemed a world away from refined Western string quartets or piano recitals. Harrison, whose Asian interest had ignited early at his childhood home in Portland's Silver Court, and who had already had read something about Chinese music in the library, loved it. His attitude was rare among non-Asian San Franciscans, many of whom viewed what they regarded as cacophony with distaste. A 1936 essay parodied the typical white citizen's reaction: "San Francisco has had concerts featuring the music of Schoenberg, which makes it hopeful that some day Occidental music will overtake its Oriental rival in the matter of discord."[1] Before he ever saw a European opera, Harrison had seen dozens of productions of Chinese opera. Harrison and his friends would come to these thrilling performances at least once a week, at a time when European opera was expensive, infrequent, and, in Harrison's opinion, "pretty stuffy."[2]

Other than the occasional tourists, Harrison and his friends usually found themselves the only non-Chinese patrons in the theater, but later at night, a quarter bought you a table with snacks of candied coconut and sugarcane, pumpkin seeds and dried plums. This night in 1935, Harrison enjoyed a bowl of delicious ginger ice cream.

As the curtain rose, giant pantomime paper dragons danced on stage, flames (made of yellow and red silk) gushing from their nostrils. Lights flashed, smoke poured out. Actors tumbled acrobatically across the stage; others suddenly began dancing or breaking into song, accompanied by supple falsetto voices singing and narrating (in Cantonese, of course) the highly stylized dramatic form. A half dozen or more players played instruments like the lute-like *yueqin* or the *jinghu*, a two-string fiddle. Clattering cymbals and gongs punctuated the actors' movements. By the end, long after midnight, the heroes won, adorned with peacock feathers on their crests.

As the gaudy Bromoseltzer curtain descended, Harrison and Dobson headed home. But they would be back. And they'd be seeing each other even sooner.

OUT IN THE OPEN

There is a friend beside me whose soul when he wishes is as light as a bird's body and can twist our air into beauty as swiftly and joyfully as any bird's wing.

—Lou Harrison, 1935[3]

Later that summer in 1935, Harrison got up early one morning, grabbed his bedroll and a pot and pan, and packed some dry rice, raisins, and powdered Klim ("milk" spelled backward). When clear mountain water was added—in less than the recommended amounts—the tasty malted milk flavor was irresistible. He and his new friend, John Dobson, had an appointment in the mountains. At the streetcar stop, Harrison met Dobson, clad in his usual blue jeans and blue work shirt; he had dropped out of the University of California as a sophomore, and it was the custom for sophs to wear jeans before graduating to corduroys the next year. As the streetcar clacked its way to the ferry, they talked nonstop—about politics, society, philosophy, music, and practically anything else.

When Harrison met him, Dobson had just left Berkeley after a year and a half studying physics. "I didn't belong in the halls of academia," he recalled. "I felt like a bird out of a cage."[4] Dobson's rebellious streak started early. When his frequent hikes caused him to miss not only classes but also haircut appointments, he enjoyed the provocation his long hair caused and decided to keep it long—a radical notion for that time and place. If people could get so upset over "this dead stuff on our heads," he reasoned, then all of society's attitudes—toward church, education, religion—were open to question.[5] "People tell me I'm the original hippie," Dobson laughed. "In the mid-'30s, I lived on Ashbury above Haight Street and had long hair and a beard."[6]

When the streetcar arrived at the ferry, the two teenagers hoisted their bedrolls and knapsacks, found a seat, and resumed their conversation as the ferry steamed across the bay to what were then undeveloped, pastoral landscapes—Marin County, Inverness, Point Reyes, even as far as Tomales Bay.

Old oak trees puttered about
The hills like thick tangles of string.
Underfoot
The hills' vertebrae poked.
A needless moon wintered the east and a
Stifled sun punctuated seven oclock against
Another range.
You and I will unravel ourselves in the white fatting of a flower field,

in the wonderful seclusion of an open hill, walking, and at times
  forgetting ourselves so much as to fly.
    We shall avoid, for a day, all the unseemly order of the streets and walk
from cabbage and cabbage to the sea, where telephone poles will cease.[7]

On the trail, Harrison hurried to keep up with the athletic Dobson's quick pace. Sometimes Dobson would teach him some Mandarin words, or Harrison would teach him to sing canons or clap cross-rhythms out in the open air. Dobson inherited his musical inclinations from his mother, a piano teacher who kept a harp in the parlor.

Dobson, as intellectually ravenous as Harrison, proved as welcome a companion in conversations about ideas as he did on hikes. When conversation in their group of friends turned to music, Harrison always held forth about new techniques and the music of other cultures. He would play them recordings on his Victrola, including works by Stravinsky and Schoenberg, whose unusual music Harrison found more intriguing than Dobson did. Harrison enjoyed leading their friends in an exercise: they would all listen to a piece of music and then write down their individual emotional associations with and responses to it. Then they would compare notes, and Dobson was shocked at how the same piece of music could affect various people so differently. "Our reactions were never the same," he said.[8]

They spotted a stream and stopped for their lunch of raisins, rice, and Klim, along with some fruit Dobson had brought. As they looked back down the hills, Harrison marveled at the beauty of the Bay—the air and water, crystal clear then, the wide-open spaces quiet and uninhabited. After lunch, they resumed their hike, with Dobson, whose father was a zoologist, pointing out natural features, identifying plants and animals. Once, returning home from a hike, they caught a rattlesnake and took it home and cooked it. After another malty meal, the two campers unrolled their bedrolls and lay side by side upon them, Dobson pointing out constellations in the clear night sky. As the moon climbed over the hills, Harrison reached over to his friend. By now, as their friendship grew into love, their excursions had become a way to explore their sexuality far from judgmental eyes.

In the brilliant nite
Your perfect body in my arms
Immobile
And your hair lying about
Like bellstrings between us
All this,
That is unbelievable
Save at the moment
Everything at all
Immured in five convenient minutes
When you will grant the semblance of your reality
And when your lips are given in a quiet immolation.[9]

Harrison awoke with a start. The moon was high, lighting up the clearing where they had pitched their camp. He heard a rustling in the stillness and gently turned in its direction. About three feet away stood a cougar. Harrison froze, gazing raptly at the beautiful creature. It looked at him, then sniffed around their campsite, then strode majestically away.

SOCIAL CIRCLES

By end of 1935, the eighteen-year-old Harrison decided that he was ready to live with Dobson. He had never told his parents directly about his romantic feelings for other men, and he didn't want to now, so the break was somewhat awkward. "Mother particularly complained that I left, but I think she knew why," Harrison recalled. "Dad didn't say much about it. My brother was already flying away; he already had a group of friends and girlfriends. I guess I decided I wanted to be with my peer group."

There was another reason for the move. "At this time, the family was not too well integrated," Harrison remembered. "It was split down the middle, my mother and me, and Bill and Dad. It got to the point where we'd sit this way: me across from Mom and Bill across from Father. I remember once [Dad] said, 'Would you tell your mother . . .' when she was sitting right there. It was pretty rough."

Harrison recalled the basis of the split being his mother's resentment of his father's business troubles; she had sold the Portland apartment house for money that he invested. Much later, after his father died, Harrison asked his mother if he had made back the money she had given him, and she said he had. "So it was mainly a power thing," Harrison speculated. "Mother was a hysteric in many ways. But it was at that time an unhappy marriage and definitely an unhappy home—another reason to move out."[10] His parents separated shortly after that but would later reunite.

In December 1935, Harrison, Dobson, Cleghorn and his wife Fern, and another San Francisco State student moved into a big, three-story Victorian house at 1423 Willard Street, just up from the streetcar track, nestled against a hill abutting Sutro Forest, where Dobson and Harrison spent hours exploring the woods; sylvan imagery would appear in Harrison's music throughout his career. Many of the trees had a fungus that gave them a golden hue that Cleghorn wrote of in a paean to the city. Dobson recalled his verse nearly seven decades later:

> In the heart of the city, there is a golden forest singing its soft music over the brown breasts of hills and waves of blue flame.[11]

The house had one other boarder, another new friend of Lou's. Dorothy James (later Russell) had lived with her family in Java in 1932–1933 and brought back early recordings of gamelan music, which Harrison eagerly listened to, along with her tales of Java. James brought a number of people into their circle. "She was a born salon hostess in many ways," Harrison remembered. "She used to give Sunday breakfasts and make wonderful dishes—finnan haddie, say—and have music and poetry. She was a singer and loved music."[12]

The house had a piano in the parlor, on which Harrison composed many of his works during his San Francisco period. Despite the Depression, it was an idyllic existence in many ways. Dobson would buy large bags of wheat or oatmeal and cook cereal for breakfast every morning, and then they would head off to school.

The college offered no music major, so Harrison took courses in anything that interested him—astronomy, classics, he failed a journalism course—but gravitated toward the music department, taking lessons in horn and clarinet and singing in campus choral groups, including music by Renaissance composers such as Palestrina as well as nineteenth- and twentieth-century composers, hymns, folk songs, spirituals, Christmas carols, and more.

But the college's biggest contribution to his career came from the school's "ancient music" ensemble. Still beguiled by the baroque, Harrison was lucky to find one of America's few early music groups, whose instruments and historically informed approach were then real rarities. Each musician typically played a variety of instruments, giving Harrison the opportunity to learn harpsichord and recorders, in addition to his usual singing (bass). They performed music by Elizabethan composers (John Dowland, William Byrd, Orlando Gibbons), and by baroque masters including J. S. Bach and Handel. Harrison arranged and occasionally even composed works for the group, which he played with even after he left college. Ensemble director Eileen McCall's historically correct meantone temperament showed Harrison that equal temperament was not music's only option and that tuning could greatly affect the sound of a composition.

Harrison scoured the San Francisco Public Library for more information about early music, especially Elizabethan virginal composers. Those discoveries led to an intense study of the entire Tudor collection of madrigals and church music and English viol consorts of the seventeenth century, including the works of John Jenkins and William Lawes and culminating in the fantasias of Henry Purcell. This uncompromisingly concentrated polyphony would greatly influence his own compositions.

McCall nurtured not only Harrison's love of pre-classical music but his composing as well. The forms of pre-classical music—saraband, fugue, concerto grosso, passacaglia—marked Harrison's compositions from the 1930s, continuing his "mission style." His sketchbooks from the period include a "Pavan" for two recorders and bass viol and a later *Suite for Recorder and Lute* that included an "Alman," a "Pavan," and a "Bourée." He played one of his *Cembalo Sonatas* as part of a college noon concert by the group. But rather than adopting the ironic, self-conscious neoclassicism so common among European composers at that time, Harrison drew upon the styles and forms of these composers as naturally and unpretentiously as another composer might write a sonata or as Harrison himself later would draw upon Asian music.

At the library and bookstores near campus, Harrison also pursued other wide-ranging intellectual interests: Jehovah's Witnesses religious tracts (following the smorgasbord of religious interests his parents had early on encouraged him to explore) and then "as an antidote," he said, "the little blue books"—radical or progressive monographs by writers such as Sinclair Lewis that introduced Harrison to the liberal and socialist ideals that would stay with him and inform some of his work from the 1930s on.[13] Dobson wore a button for Socialist candidate Upton Sinclair, and they boycotted a restaurant because it refused to serve black people. Harrison was always carrying books and scores home from the library. Harrison remained a bookaholic and a library supporter ever after.

Dobson was also intensely interested in philosophy, and in 1937, Harrison took the opportunity to introduce him to the Vedanta society he had first explored in high school. Vedanta's mysticism interested Harrison but soon obsessed Dobson. They attended a lecture by Swami Ashokananda at the Century Club that proved to be a fateful turn in Dobson's life, as he devoted more and more of his time to its study.

Yet despite his intellectual and artistic pursuits, Harrison also enjoyed a thriving social life, much of it in private house parties where gay people and others from the theater, dance, and art scenes congregated over wine and cheese, music and poetry, and lots of heavy smoking, all of which Harrison indulged in. "Everybody was having a good time all the time," he remembered. "Sometimes parties were where you met your next lover!"[14] He said, "I met dancers, set designers, artists, other musicians, writers. This was fairly common. You'd get one idea after another—constant ideas and learning, learning all the time. For example, that's where I found out about Hart Crane. Someone at a party said he was gay, and I looked him up for that reason."[15] Although many of his friends were gay, "all of us were part of the straight world," he explained. "Our oddity was acceptable coin. We were musicians, poets, artists, and so on, and there was no problem about our boyfriends or girlfriends."[16]

Even though these artists were creating a vibrant modernism, neither Harrison nor his friends adopted the kind of self-consciously avant-garde identity common among inhabitants of other bohemias. "It was no big deal. We were just having fun," Harrison said. "We were occupied doing what we were doing. And we had friends who liked doing it too, and that constituted a party. Absolutely, it was a big community thing. . . . If you don't feel you can play some things with your friends, what's the point?"[17]

Harrison's friend Sidney Robertson, who spent those years in San Francisco before marrying Harrison's teacher Henry Cowell, later reminisced that in the San Francisco of that period, everyone respected you more for doing something that nobody else had done before. Artists were expected to blaze their own trails.[18] Harrison would do just that.

By the end of his second year in San Francisco, immersed in an astonishingly dynamic new world of fascinating art and ideas and people, Harrison had rekindled his passion for Asian arts, acquired his first real lover and identity as a gay man, joined a vibrant and varied circle of young artists and other intellectually and artistically voracious bohemians, and developed a deep affection for nature. From the lonely, friendless adolescent who had sequestered himself with music and mementos had emerged a breathlessly energetic, charming young artist now surrounded by convivial and sympathetic friends.

"I was giddy at that time—being interested in almost everything," he remembered. "I spent many a night and day just burrowed in books and thinking and writing. But I was also out and about all the time. It was a grand time then, no doubt of that. And I realized it then. It was a wonderful whirligig."[19]

Most wondrous of all was the new music he was discovering. At one concert in Chinatown, a slight, balding man approached the grand piano, but instead of sitting down at the keys, he reached under the lid. By plucking, strumming, and striking the strings of the piano directly with one hand while the other formed chords on the keyboard, he was able to coax unearthly sounds from this most familiar of instruments. Dobson and Harrison were astonished—neither had ever heard anything like it. The man who took a bow was none other than the composer Harrison had read about who was at the nexus of the American avant-garde music scene, and who was to become Harrison's mentor and most important teacher: Henry Cowell.

3

THE ULTRAMODERNIST (1935–1936)

> *Remembering Henry I realize*
> *His central kindness & the gentle smile.*
> *I remember his certain eagerness*
> *To like & to be liked, & that he brought*
> *A hundred kindred composers to know*
> *Each other out of that same amity.*
> *The wide life of his mind, I remember,*
> *Was serene & free, as he was also*
> *Perfectly fearless in his melody*
>
> —Lou Harrison[1]

Settling into his seat in June 1935 after paying the 25¢ admission, Lou Harrison saw a stage that was bare except for only a giant box, whose contents were hidden from the audience. His high school friend Bob Metcalf, the Palo Alto Community Theater lighting designer, had told him about its strange new play called *Fanati*, written by Stanford University professor Ralph Emerson Welles, another of San Francisco's seemingly inexhaustible community of mystics, socialists, and free-thinking artists.[2] Even more exciting: the music was composed by Welles's friend Henry Cowell.

As the lights went down, the hypnotic sound of exotic, repeating percussion patterns emerged from the box. "If you go far enough from here, you will come to the channel and Channel Island and the Lighthouse," a narrator intoned, and the action, such as it was, commenced.

Welles's play was a highly stylized pacifist allegory with spare white sets and Metcalf's mysterious lighting suggesting a shadowy Greek classicism. The fantasy recounted the conflict between working people and the Fanati—corrupt tycoons, politicians, religionists, and journalists who ruled the dystopia called Unitasia. The characters declaimed the poetic text in a deliberate, chant-like fashion similar to traditional Noh drama of Japan, with the poetic speaking rhythm matching that of the percussion ensemble. Cowell used his knowledge of the similarly styled Japanese forms to write the incidental music. Just as he had borrowed the concept of hidden chambers for the musicians from Kabuki theater, Cowell employed the Noh technique of layering percussion lines to conjure a haunting sonic fabric throughout each scene.

The plot in Noh dramas often matters less than their mood of floating timelessness, and the spare sounds supplied by the musicians in the box—five percussionists, with occasional flourishes of trumpet and piano—matched the play's mood. Along with a few songs sung onstage and some piano pieces from his repertoire, Cowell deployed a large battery of exotic percussion: Chinese drums, Javanese temple bells, a Japanese cymbal-gong, Korean wood blocks, and a *jaltarang* (Indian ceramic bowls played with chopsticks). Harrison instantly understood how percussion instruments could be used not only as loud noisemakers as in Chinese opera, but instead as subtle mood inducers, capable of generating expressive nuances in intricate patterns. It wasn't all bang and clang.

The mysterious, suspended atmosphere hovered till the play's end—at which point, it was unveiled to the audience that the box on stage contained a piano surrounded by an array of percussion instruments. At the center stood the composer— the man whose music, philosophy, and teaching perhaps influenced Harrison's life and music more than anyone else's.

NEW MUSICAL RESOURCES

One day in 1935, Lou Harrison rode the Powell streetcar to meet with the author and musician whose writings he'd been obsessively absorbing for the last few months. His friend Jim Cleghorn, knowing Harrison's enthusiasm for Henry Cowell's writings, had told him that Cowell was returning to his native West Coast to teach a class. Harrison was nervous because he couldn't afford the tuition. Yet he had to take that class.

Henry Cowell was born in Menlo Park, California, in 1897, to parents whose anarchic ideas about religion, government, and education inspired Cowell's open-minded and ecumenical approach to music. Cowell grew up in the San Francisco Bay region familiar with British folk music, music from Chinatown, and Beethoven in roughly equal measure. In one of his first piano recitals, the sixteen-year-old Cowell entertained the San Francisco Music Club by smashing his palm or fist over entire regions of keys in his composition *Adventures in Harmony*.[3] Harrison would later borrow this famous "tone cluster" technique. At the University of California, the pioneering musicologist Charles Seeger encouraged Cowell to systematize such enthusiastic experiments, an effort resulting in Cowell's celebrated book *New Musical Resources*.[4]

Propelled by Seeger's inclusionary but rigorous philosophy that encompassed medieval chant to folk songs to European avant-garde, Cowell was soon applying these attention-grabbing, unprecedented gestures to notorious piano recitals across the United States and Europe, spending as much time reaching inside the piano, coaxing all manner of exotic sounds from the instrument, as at the keyboard. Journalists called him America's "ultramodernist," and he became new music's envoy, connecting with composer organizations in New York and Europe.

In 1925, he brought their models back to the West Coast, where he established the New Music Society experimental concert series and a quarterly, *New Music*, which (unlike other American publications) issued only scores of contemporary, mostly

American music—including the startlingly unorthodox music of a retired insurance executive named Charles Ives. Remembering that copy of *New Music* he had seen on a piano in high school, Harrison quickly scoured all the issues at the public library after moving to San Francisco, also finding *American Composers on American Music*, an invaluable series of essays that Cowell had edited.

But when Harrison brought home *New Musical Resources*, it transformed his understanding of music. Rather than cataloguing what composers did in the past, as other music texts did, Cowell's *New Musical Resources* shows what composers could do in the future—and to do that, Cowell wrote, they had to go back to fundamentals. The book explained that every pitch is really a composite of many waves in a naturally occurring pattern of frequencies called the harmonic (or "overtone") series. Although the entire European harmonic system is based on the lowest few in the series (the first three harmonics in the Middle Ages, then up to the fifth harmonic by the Renaissance), Cowell proposed that, over the centuries, listeners accepted intervals higher and higher up the harmonic series as consonances. In the twentieth century, music from jazz to Debussy admitted the second (represented by the ninth harmonic) as an acceptable consonance. A few composers, such as Charles Ives, went even further, dividing the octave into quartertones, whose finer gradations allowed musicians to climb even further up the unexplored territory of the harmonic series.[5]

Fascinated by these insights into the nature of sound, the teenaged Harrison in early 1935 worked out the quartertone approximations of the harmonic series and the "undertone series" (its inversion), as given in Cowell's tables, using square note heads to indicate quartertones. Realizing that fretless instruments of the violin family could play these pitches that lie "in the cracks" between the piano keys, he began a new composition for nine strings in quartertones and optional organ. His first of many experiments inspired by Cowell's book, *The Geography of Heaven* was also Harrison's first excursion into alternate tunings. The three movements have William Blake-like titles: "Saints," "Angels in a Summer Landscape," and "Soul Soaring Aflame." It is music of adolescent mysticism, its angular quasi-tonality quite different from either Harrison's cembalo sonata or earlier experiments, more reminiscent of scores by American composer Carl Ruggles that had appeared in *New Music*.

Along with his adventures in tuning, Cowell offered Harrison a new perspective of music, in which Cowell saw no reason to segregate his appreciation of Chinatown's music from that of European classical music. Determined to discover other musical treasures, Cowell in 1931 had studied Asian and African music with the pioneering ethnomusicologist Erich von Hornbostel in Berlin, and with others. Those studies and his copies of many of von Hornbostel's archival recordings informed his course at New York's New School for Social Research called "Music Systems of the World," at a time when his academic treatment of non-European music was as rare as von Hornbostel's recordings. In 1935, he brought the course, retitled "Music of the Peoples of the World," to the University of California's extension program, which offered nontraditional public courses off campus.

At their first meeting, the nervous Harrison told Cowell about his predicament: He deeply desired to take the class, but he couldn't afford the tuition. His enthusiasm was so genuine that Cowell made Harrison the "course monitor," which involved taking roll and acting as Cowell's assistant—allowing him to take the class for free.

A WHOLE WORLD OF MUSIC

Cowell's course, probably unique in the United States at the time, focused on the classical music traditions of Japan, China, Java, Persia, India, and more. Cowell added his own perspective as a composer, and Harrison remembered the class as one in which all music was treated on an equal footing as sound—a perspective that extended his compositional horizons far beyond those of a typical music conservatory student. Unlike the early colonialist researchers who labeled it the study of "primitive music," Cowell taught that these musical traditions were not less "advanced" than the European tradition, and that in fact in areas such as melodic invention and rhythm, they might actually be far more sophisticated.

Harrison began attending Cowell's New Music Society (NMS) events, including an April 1935 concert that featured a *shakuhachi*, the ancient and expressive bamboo flute of Japan, a shamisen (plucked long-neck lute), a koto (plucked zither), and a vocalist. "Since the music, although ancient, is new to most Occidentals," Cowell wrote in the program, "the New Music Society feels it to be within its province to sponsor this presentation."[6] Harrison loved it, he told Cowell, who immediately put him in touch with a Japanese merchant who would import records for him.

A more ambitious NMS program presented music of Arnold Schoenberg, conducted by the composer himself, whose atonal scores and twelve-tone method had already made him notorious as the leading musical radical of the time. Although Schoenberg's *Pierrot Lunaire* proved so difficult that the group Cowell put together for the concert was able to perform only one-third of the song cycle (and even then not up to the exacting Austrian's standards), the concert exhilarated Harrison, for whom Schoenberg's music would soon become a singular passion, and Cowell introduced the young student to the Viennese master.[7]

Harrison was so taken with his new teacher that he invited Cowell to dinner at his parents' house—without asking them first. While Harrison's surprised mother, Calline, scrambled to set the family table with the good linens and china, Lou worried about his car-dealer father's reaction to their surprise guest. The elder Harrison had little interest in or knowledge of music; what would they talk about?

"Very quickly," Harrison recalled, "in not too many sentences, Henry found out what Dad's interests were, and he regaled us for the whole evening with the fact that he had just crossed the continent in a newly converted diesel motorcar, and Dad was enthralled because automobiles were his thing."[8] Displaying the engaging personality that helped make him American music's great connector, Cowell charmed the whole family that night.

September 11, 1935.

Dear Mr. Harrison,

If you can come to visit me on the evening of Sept. 13th (this Friday) at about 8:15 at 171 San Marcos Ave. (Forest Hill district, San Francisco) I shall be very happy. Perhaps you can bring along anything you would like me to see. . . .

Sincerely,

H. Cowell[9]

Lou Harrison never earned a college degree. Instead, he learned about music, dance, and art the old-fashioned way: through voracious curiosity, assiduous study, and wise mentors like Cowell. When Harrison asked Cowell if he would look at some of his own scores, Cowell invited him to the house of his stepmother, Olive Cowell, where he was staying in the city. When Harrison arrived at the striking modernist structure cascading down the nearly vertical hillside, Cowell was gracious and encouraging to the unknown eighteen-year-old, whose scores showed a good grounding in conventional counterpoint and enthusiastic experiments in many directions. As Cowell had before him, Harrison needed rigor while retaining his eagerness to innovate.

Harrison's catch-as-catch-can lessons with the ever-busy Cowell were as likely to happen in a car as in a classroom. Rather than assign emulations of past styles (as had Harrison's earlier teacher, Howard Couper), Cowell broke down music to its essential qualities—melody, rhythm, counterpoint—and systematically assessed the possibilities they provided composers.

Dear Mr. Cowell,

I didn't know whether you would be interested in seeing what I did while you were away. . . . The piano piece (by the way, it's the only piano piece I have written since the suite) was finished a week or so ago, and the other is still a draft. I sent the second because I think it shows harmonic development.

I want to thank you very much for your kindness in helping me to take your most valuable courses; I would have been unable to take them any other way.

Lou Harrison

P.S. As much as I heard of that court music is absolutely haunting me![10]

Harrison's formal instruction with Cowell lasted less than a year, but as their relationship changed from teacher and student to mentor and protégé, Harrison gleaned immense knowledge of musical styles from what Cowell called "the whole world of music." Harrison admired Cowell's cheerfully anti-establishment attitude as well as his Irish raconteur ability to frame lessons of music history as stories. Cowell showed Harrison how the scores he had seen in *New Music* were actually put together—how Ives, whose scores especially fascinated Harrison, wove complex polytonal webs of sound from repetitions of relatively simple elements, how Schoenberg manipulated melodic cells and developed his as yet unpublished twelve-tone method.

"Henry Cowell's view of teaching composition was that it couldn't be taught, but that an exchange of ideas with a more experienced colleague might be a stimulant to someone who already knew where he was going," Cowell's wife, Sidney, remembered. "So if one of his few private pupils, such as John Cage and later Lou Harrison, picked up something from the lively consultations and ran with it, Henry was delighted."[11]

Cowell's method emerges in the way Harrison experimented with two techniques in 1935 and 1936: polyrhythm (two or more distinct simultaneous meters) and polytonality (two or more distinct simultaneous tonal centers, or keys). Composers such as Stravinsky and Darius Milhaud exploited these techniques extensively, but none did so earlier than—or more persuasively as—Charles Ives. Ives loved to recount the times in his Danbury, Connecticut childhood when multiple bands played simultaneously, creating a wonderful cacophony. In his *The Fourth of July*, published in *New Music Quarterly* in 1932, Ives represents the spirit of America through the stalwart individualism of this kind of musical "democracy": the orchestra divided into different distinct layers of rhythm and tonality, each representing a different band or viewpoint speaking at once and yet resulting in an organic whole. Without this "freeing of melodic lines from any formal prearrangement as to the kind of chords their several junctures should make," wrote Harrison, "the daring venture of what [Ives] called a 'prose' style could not have existed."[12]

Cowell employed polyrhythm and polytonality in several pieces that explored how different layers can be unified on a deeper level, including a piano work he showed Harrison titled *Fabrics*. At first Harrison struggled with its polyrhythms—far more complicated than those of the Renaissance madrigals he sang in high school and college. To hear what some of the patterns really should sound like, Harrison made radial scratches at regular angles in the lead-out groove of a record. The resulting pops would repeat whatever rhythmic pattern Harrison had worked out. To take a simple example, if he wanted to hear two against three, he would scratch at 0 degrees and 180 degrees; he would hear two beats for every rotation. Then, to hear three overlaid, he would also scratch at 0 degrees, 120 degrees, and 240 degrees. He would end up with four different scratches (since they both line up at 0 degrees). The result was a single rhythm made up of two overlaid rhythms—polyrhythm.

In his First Piano Sonata (dated March 1936), Harrison experimented with notating each polyrhythmic layer on a separate staff with its own time signature (as he had seen in a modern edition of a polyrhythmic madrigal): the lowest voice (which plays an ostinato of five dissonant chords) notated in five, the next highest voice (played by the right hand) in four, and the highest (also played by the right hand) in three. Unfortunately, its mostly even flow of quarter notes makes it difficult for the listener to delineate the separate meters. The second movement, "Discussion," recalls Ives's use of polyrhythm in his second string quartet (whose first movement is titled "Discussions") to emulate an airing of different points of view—each with its own rhythm. Harrison's discussion is a double fugue, the left hand having two voices in a meter of seven and the right hand two voices in a meter of five. The final movement, "Jubilation," experiments with "counterchords," an idea Cowell proposed in *New Musical Resources*: chord-against-chord polyphony rather than traditional counterpoint's note-against-note polyphony.[13] The counterchords thicken the texture until the piece ends in thunderous clusters. Harrison called this early experiment a "sort of a bicycle trip through modern music" and played it at a reception at the Cowells' house.[14]

Two months later, Harrison took greater rhythmic and polytonal liberties in *Project #2* for piano. Apparently, a few measures into the piece, bar lines became superfluous for Harrison, as he crossed out the first few and did not use them again for the duration of the piece. He said later that liberating his rhythms from these metrical prison bars was the next logical step after using different bar lines in each part.[15] He had studied similarly bar line-less preludes of French baroque composers and the "Emerson" movement of Ives's *Concord* sonata, which his friend Douglas Thompson had performed at the same recital as Harrison's sonata and which Harrison himself played at San Francisco State the same month. Cowell had pointed out that when Satie dispensed with bar lines, it was in reaction to the "metrical monotony" of conventional music.[16] Harrison would return to this kind of flowing, chant-like free meter in works throughout his career, from his *Prelude for Grandpiano* of 1937 to *Incidental Music for Corneille's Cinna* of 1956 and *Music for Bill and Me* of 1967. Even late in his career, Harrison often waited to add bar lines to a melody until after it was composed, or he compromised by placing the lines between staves rather than through them (as modern editors of Renaissance works often do).

COUNTERPOINT

Besides polyrhythms and polytonality, Cowell bestowed on Harrison facility with different kinds of counterpoint—the art of combining melodies. Even if some composers had recently accepted the interval of the second, Cowell regarded the practice of counterpoint as essentially unchanged since the time of Bach. To take counterpoint further, Cowell reasoned, a composer must use dissonant (to 1930s ears) rather than consonant chords as resting points.

Cowell's teacher Charles Seeger had arrived at the same conclusion as early as 1914.[17] In order to create something really new, Seeger suggested that composers try a kind of inversion of traditional counterpoint: instead of seconds resolving to thirds, thirds should "resolve" to seconds. In this system, bare consonances must function entirely as non-harmonic tones, "outside" the harmony primarily made up of seconds, sevenths, or other traditional dissonances. Seeger called this procedure "dissonant counterpoint," a term Cowell adopted in his book. Cowell used the technique as far back as 1916, soon followed by Carl Ruggles, Ruth Crawford, and others.

Cowell assigned Harrison to develop a theme using both traditional (third-based, or tertial) counterpoint and dissonant (second-based, or secundal) counterpoint. Dissonant counterpoint permeates Harrison's *Saraband* for piano of 1937.[18] When texture consisted of only two lines, Harrison controlled the consonances just as carefully as he would dissonances in traditional counterpoint. When the texture thickened to three or more lines, he formed stacks of seconds ("secundal" harmony) instead of thirds ("tertial" harmony). Harrison continued to experiment with balancing harmonic interest with contrapuntal integrity in a dissonant context, eventually finding models in Schoenberg and Ruggles.

EXAMPLE 3.1. These two measures from Harrison's *Saraband* (top two staves) are collapsed into a single octave and rhythm below to show the dissonant counterpoint. The circled pitches are the non-harmonic tones, which must "resolve" to seconds. Courtesy of Special Collections, University Library, University of California Santa Cruz, Lou Harrison papers.

He found yet another approach during his constant scouring of the San Francisco Public Library. Like Cowell, music theorist Joseph Yasser in his innovative *A Theory of Evolving Tonality* viewed the history of harmony and counterpoint as evolving up the harmonic series, starting with the fifth-based pentatonic systems of China and medieval Europe, extending to third-based diatonic music of later Europe, and finally to a proposal for a nineteen-tone microtonal system. Yasser argued that, just as tertial counterpoint was appropriate for diatonic music, a counterpoint based on fifths ("quintal") was natural for pentatonic scale systems—supplying Harrison another type of counterpoint to augment Cowell's examples of secundal and tertial. Quintal counterpoint allows only perfect fourths, fifths, and octaves as consonances and treats all other intervals, including thirds and sixths, as dissonances.[19] With his eye on Yasser's quintal "harmonizations" of Chinese, Celtic, and even Tchaikovsky melodies, Harrison experimented with the technique using pentatonic Appalachian folk tunes, and when Cowell would assign him a counterpoint exercise to be completed in tertial and secundal style, Harrison would sometimes add a third in quintal. Next to the astringent sound of Cowell's dissonant counterpoint or the sweetness of tertial counterpoint, quintal counterpoint sounded austere and stark, and it reminded Harrison of the deserts of the American West and California's Mission Period.[20]

As their titles suggest, Harrison's first surviving works based on quintal counterpoint, the *Double Fugue* and *Ground* in E minor, both from September 1936, follow neoclassical forms. The *Ground* was inspired by the music of English baroque composer Henry Purcell, who often used this form featuring variations over a repeating bass line. Unlike the quintal counterpoint demonstrated by Yasser, based on pentatonic scales, these pieces "decoupled" mode and counterpoint type to allow the pieces to retain their spicy chromaticism in the surprising context of bare-sounding fifths and fourths.[21]

Harrison had already absorbed an immense variety of musical and other influences, but nothing played a greater role in his artistic development than his study

Moderato

EXAMPLE 3.2. In this excerpt from Harrison's *Ground*, the boxed intervals are the non-harmonic tones, which must resolve to perfect fourths, fifths, or octaves in this example of quintal counterpoint. Courtesy of Special Collections, University Library, University of California Santa Cruz, Lou Harrison papers.

with his first and most important mentor. "Henry was the central information booth for two or three generations of American composers," Harrison said. "You asked Henry a question, and if he didn't know the answer, as he often did, he knew who did and had the phone number."[22]

The great connector Cowell would shortly provide Harrison with another tremendously important contact. Harrison's willingness to share his own great breadth of interests and to devote himself to music reminded him, Cowell told Harrison one day, of another student of his in New York, who had just moved back to his native Los Angeles. You have a lot in common, Cowell mused. Someday, you must meet him.

EMANCIPATION OF NOISE

[Percussion music] arose from necessity on the West Coast. We had percussion orchestras made up of dancers who were studying the modern dance, to dance to percussion music. . . . They developed percussion orchestras that had to be played by amateur percussers, but they were very interested in the possibilities of orchestration.

—Henry Cowell[23]

Harrison's studies with Cowell and his experience at Cowell's *Fanati* helped propel him toward one of his most important legacies to music: percussion. Modernist composers such as Stravinsky, William Walton, and George Antheil had already elevated percussion from occasional orchestral add-ons to a new fountain of timbral possibilities. In 1933, following a notorious Hollywood Bowl performance of Edgard Varèse's all-percussion *Ionisation*, Cowell published the piece in *New Music*, and the next year, his New Music Society brought it and its composer to San Francisco, with choreography. At the reception at the Cowell house, Cowell introduced Harrison to Varèse and invited him to play something for him. Harrison chose his recent *ricercare* on Bach's name in dissonant counterpoint. Although the French composer was quite polite, his intense, mad-scientist gaze "scared the wits" out of the lanky young Californian.[24]

The percussion works of Varèse, Johanna Beyer, John Becker, and William Russell led an emancipation of noise analogous to Schoenberg's famous "emancipation of the dissonance." Cowell received submissions of fifteen percussion ensemble pieces for *New Music* in 1933 alone, and in 1936, his quarterly published an entire issue devoted to percussion music.[25] Along with the avant-garde fascination with new sounds, composers were also drawn to percussion by an interest in folk or non-Western traditions. The first all-percussion works in the Western classical tradition, two 1930 compositions by Cuban composer Amadeo Roldán, were inspired by then-popular Latin American nationalism and his country's Afro-Hispanic heritage.

Both approaches appealed to Henry Cowell, whose 1934 *Ostinato Pianissimo* for percussion ensemble, which includes a *jaltarang* and a tambourine without jingles that resembles an Arabic frame drum (*daff*), reflected his recent ethnomusicological studies in Berlin.[26] Few of the instruments in *Ostinato Pianissimo* demand any special techniques; most can be played by non-percussionists.

The German dancer Mary Wigman, whose disciple Henrietta Greenwood had choreographed the dance scenes in *Fanati*, had introduced the use of percussion instruments for dance in the early 1930s. Inspired by Wigman, American choreographer Lester Horton had amassed a collection of percussion instruments for his company. Modern dancers appreciated the fact that while using a piano and most other instruments requires hiring a specialist, many percussion instruments can be played by non-specialists or even dancers themselves.

By the mid-1930s, percussion instruments were nearly as common as the piano in modern dance schools, and the most prominent American advocate of their use in dance was Henry Cowell, who in the summer of 1935 taught classes for dancers at Mills and Stanford in rhythm and percussion accompaniment. "Percussion instruments are essential as aids in defining rhythmic change," he wrote. "All dance is of course dependent on a well-defined beat; when the beat shifts constantly, as in much of modern dancing, it is vitalizing to have the changes sharply indicated on percussion instruments."[27]

Harrison's interest in percussion thus emerged from several sources—the world music introduced to him by Cowell, the sound-liberating possibilities that also inspired Varèse, and its value in dance accompaniment demonstrated in *Fanati*. But percussion also appealed to his lifelong sense of practicality. Some percussion instruments could be improvised out of everyday objects: old Folgers coffee cans became a metallophone when mounted in a frame, and the distinctive boing of alarm clock coils became an eerie sound source when attached to a discarded guitar resonator. Harrison's openness to foraged or modified instruments would stay with him throughout his life.

Harrison didn't have to wait long to put to use his inspiration from Cowell's *Fanati*. Already his friend James Cleghorn had introduced him to Lenore Peters Job, director of the Peters-Wright Dance School, where many in the San Francisco dance community congregated, including Sally Rand. A composer friend recommended Harrison to one of the teachers at the Peters-Wright Dance School, a Martha Graham student named Carol Beals.

After leaving Graham's company in New York, Beals had arrived in San Francisco at about the same time as the Harrisons and judged the dance scene to be "in the dregs."[28] She and her husband, Mervin Leeds, founded the Dance Council of Northern California as a way to establish cooperation among the many Bay Area groups. Beals soon came to know Cleghorn and Cowell, who spoke at least one of the Dance Council events, and then Harrison, who for the first time earned a paycheck for music, by accompanying her classes. "Carol was as sweet as they come," he recalled. "She improvised beautifully. After class, I'd ask her to improvise while I played."[29]

But to revitalize the dance scene, Beals thought, artists needed to make their work relevant to peoples' lives, especially in these desperate times. She had a subject for a new ballet that was both politically controversial and highly relevant for the time and place: the great San Francisco waterfront strike of 1934.

ON THE WATERFRONT

One day in early 1936, burly longshoremen streamed into San Francisco's massive Ferry Building, trudged up the stairs to the second floor, found seats, and gazed upon the boxing ring. But instead of pugilists, the workers saw a dozen or so willowy dancers. A teenaged musician crouched nervously below the ring, surrounded by a passel of percussion instruments. Those were heady times for the proponents of class consciousness. The strange juxtaposition of dockworkers and dancers took place at a benefit for the Longshoreman's Union. And providing the music, in his first major performance event, was the eighteen-year-old Lou Harrison.

A year and a half earlier, on a steamy day in July 1934, as his father drove Lou into the city, they came to a police barricade. A policeman asked the elder Harrison to explain why he was coming to the city. A father taking his son to sing Gregorian chant evidently proved an acceptable reason, and their car was waved on. The Harrisons had run into one of the tensest moments of the Depression. The conservative state government and business leaders' attempt to forcibly open the docks closed by striking longshoremen led to violence on July 5, since known as "Bloody Thursday," during which police killed two strikers. A three-day general strike followed, and the situation was defused only when the Roosevelt administration compelled negotiations that ultimately settled the dispute.

For many Californians, the strike and police violence became a radicalizing or at least consciousness-raising episode. To them, the Depression illustrated the excesses of unbridled capitalism and greed and inspired social activism and even leftist radicalism among many modern artists. In the "revolutionary" journal *New Theatre* in 1934, dancer Jane Dudley called for "the mass dance"—revolutionary dances on socially relevant topics, with "such instruments as drums, cymbals, piano, gongs, even voice, chants, songs . . . in order to provide rhythm, and so keep the unity of movement, and to help build intensity."[30] As an example, she suggested the San Francisco waterfront strike and outlined a possible scenario.

Both Dudley and Carol Beals had been involved in the politically radical New Dance League and New Dance Group in the early thirties. Beals and her husband, Mervin Leeds, were politically active and friends with the leader of the strike, Harry Bridges, so a dance commemorating the strike was a natural production for her company. Harrison was already reading radical pamphlets he found at the corner bookstore near his dad's Market Street shop.

When Harrison commenced work on *Waterfront, 1934* in late 1935, he remembered Cowell's *Fanati* and decided to write for solo percussion—appropriate for a piece whose second movement was called "Strike!"—and play it himself.[31] The surviving part of the *Waterfront* score includes parts for three different drums, a large and a small cymbal, Chinese woodblocks, and a gong. The first movement, "Speed Up," reflected the corporate demand for faster and faster handling of the cargo, a precipitating incident in the strike. "Strike!" portrayed the gathering solidarity of working people rising up to defend themselves against capitalist exploitation. The third movement, "Bloody Thursday," depicted the violent response of the reactionary government and business alliance.

The longshoremen in the audience were bemused to see the fey young composer sitting just outside the ring, surrounded by odd percussion instruments, as the tiny Beals and her dancers cavorted in the ring, their limbs occasionally swinging out over him.[32] Though the stevedores looked askance at the long-haired Dobson, playing a working man who was shot by police, and "dying" in that affected way dancers do, they were mollified when he doffed his shirt, revealing his wiry, muscular physique. "They really clapped," Dobson recalled. The dance ended with the waterfront union workers and friends joining in a solemn funeral march, a reminder that the martyred protester hadn't died in vain.[33]

But the afterglow of Harrison's first major success as a composer soon succumbed to chilling, shocking news. Just a week after a performance with Beals's group at the Veteran's Auditorium concert in May 1936, Harrison headed over to Cowell's Menlo Park house and accompanied his mentor to Stanford University, where Cowell had been commissioned for a swimming ballet. He played Harrison some of that music, as well as some of Harrison's favorites among his older works, on the piano. The next morning, Harrison was stunned to learn that Cowell had been arrested. He was in the Redwood City jail.

4

THE GRAND MANNER (1936–1937)

Occasionally during 1936, Lou Harrison would make his way across the bay to California's San Quentin prison. He presented his pass at the gate, was led inside, and was searched for contraband. The wary guard rifled through Harrison's bag and found a sheaf of papers covered with lines and dots and other mysterious markings. Was he exchanging code with the notorious felon? Harrison nervously explained he was there for composition lessons. Finally, he was escorted to see his teacher, the great composer Henry Cowell. He was hardly the only visitor—such luminaries as conductor Leopold Stokowski, choreographer Martha Graham, and composer Carlos Chávez (after conducting the San Francisco Symphony) came to visit. Once, Harrison was joined by his friend John Dobson, who then composed a small piece with Cowell-esque tone clusters.

Cowell's arrest had shocked Harrison and the circle of musicians and artists drawn into the great connector's attractive orbit. Cowell had been letting groups of teenage boys use a swimming hole on his Menlo Park property and even borrow his ramshackle car. According to Cowell's own naively frank account, the boys "played on his own homosexual inclinations" and Cowell had "joined in" some sexual acts already in progress among the boys.[1] A couple of older boys from outside the neighborhood then tried to blackmail Cowell into giving them his car. When he ignored them, one of them reported Cowell to the police, who arrested him early in the morning of May 22, 1936.[2]

Cowell was charged with one count of having oral sex with another man (then a felony in California), not with having sex with a minor, since the person in question was legally an adult. Nevertheless, wildly lurid newspaper accounts portrayed him as a sex-crazed pedophile. (The most scurrilous stories apparently resulted from Cowell's failure to pay blackmail money to a San Francisco street rag.[3]) "The San Francisco papers tried to make an Oscar Wilde trial out of it," recalled Harrison, who read about the arrest in the following morning's newspaper.[4] Indeed, the *San Francisco Examiner*'s front-page photo of the composer behind bars was captioned "California Oscar Wilde Jailed!"[5]

The case quickly became politicized, and some of Cowell's friends—including Carl Ruggles and Charles Ives—broke off contact.[6] Others rushed to his defense, including prominent musicians such as Nicolas Slonimsky, Percy Grainger, and Charles Seeger. "I have never known a more honest, truthful, or guileless individual," said Lewis Terman, a Stanford psychologist who first knew Cowell as a subject in his study of child geniuses. This guilelessness (even naivety), a fear that a court trial could result in even more serious charges, and a long-held distrust of lawyers, all led Cowell to confess to the charge, even without the representation of a defense counsel.[7] By the time his family did find him a lawyer, it was too late.

Cowell's confession set off a series of legal consequences that ended in the dark cells of San Quentin. The Board of Prison Terms and Paroles consisted of political appointees who had no incentive to hand out anything but the maximum sentence to a by-then notorious sex criminal.[8] Slonimsky suspected that Cowell's well-known leftist connections, including his visit to the Soviet Union, might have played a role in the board's stiff sentence of fifteen years—staggering even by the standards of the day.[9] Harrison wrote to Olive Cowell:

> The day before I left I read of Henry's sentence, and I want to tell you how it agonizes me. This seems not such an unjust world as totally justiceless.... I cannot say how this whole thing has affected me, the strength of ignorance and prejudice and the prevailing lack of balanced perception in the great mass was never so wholly apparent to me before. It seems that all one can do to be good in this world is to follow one's own precepts.... And the tragedy of it all is that the good, productive, penetrative, and holiest life seems by this arrangement to be unhappy at best, almost inevitably.[10]

The Cowell affair sent shivers through Harrison and his friends, many of whom were gay. (Harrison later admitted that he "flirted like mad" with his teacher, receiving only a knowing smile in return.)[11] His own hardships did not prevent Cowell from composing in prison almost as prolifically as he had when he was free. When Harrison came to him relaying a proposal that he compose a score for Mills choreographer Marian Van Tuyl, Cowell began to think about how he could convincingly write accompaniment to a dance that he was unable to see. How could he collaborate while incarcerated?

Cowell found his answer in his own 1935 *Mosaic* string quartet, where he had experimented with allowing modules of precomposed music to be rearranged into different possible configurations for each performance, prefiguring by many years similar experiments by John Cage and the 1950s avant-garde.[12] So in response to Van Tuyl's invitation, Cowell wrote a series of fragments: melodies, drones, percussion ostinatos, and so on. He gave these to Harrison and entrusted him to combine them in ways that would fit the dance, performed as *Ritual of Wonder* in 1937.[13]

Harrison came to call this set of recombinant materials a "kit" and adopted the technique a few years later for his theater work *Jephthah's Daughter*. The Old Testament story, which Harrison sets as rhythmic speech, describes a woman, danced by Carol Beals, given by her father to God. A percussionist would freely draw upon a set of both composed segments and shorter ostinatos to accompany the action as required.[14]

Cowell's arrest made their lessons difficult, but his mentor's example and contacts continued to influence the young composer's career. Just before Christmas 1936, a life-changing legacy of his mentorship arrived at the communal house Harrison shared with Dobson and the others. The name above the return address on the large crate read "Charles Ives."

FREE AND FANTASTIC

> Dear Mr. Ives:
> I am a student at State College in San Francisco. It seems that there are favorable opportunities to perform your works on what we have as student recitals and in theory and history classes.[15]

Since his teenage encounter with Charles Ives's work in *New Music* and with Cowell's essay about him in *American Composers on American Music*, Harrison had been fascinated by the works of the visionary New Englander. He performed the "Emerson" movement of Ives's difficult, ruminative *Concord* piano sonata at a San Francisco State noon concert in the spring of 1936. Around the same time, he had the rare opportunity to hear orchestral Ives when Bernard Herrmann conducted the multilayered fugue from Ives's Symphony #4 on a CBS radio program. Frustrated that so few Ives works were available, he groused to Cowell, who knew that Ives was always generous to those genuinely interested in his music. Why don't you write him a letter asking for more? Cowell suggested. In March 1936, two months before Cowell's arrest, Harrison took his advice.

Harrison's work on the "Emerson" movement inspired him to ask for copies of Ives's two other piano sonatas. Instead, Harrison received a photostatic copy of the then-unknown Third Symphony and a "curious edition" of the *Concord* sonata with some intriguing changes to the "Emerson" movement.[16] Emboldened, he sent off another letter suggesting that members of the local Youth Congress would be able to program Ives's chamber works. After some months passed with no response, Ives's nephew Chester wrote to Harrison telling him to expect "some chamber music pieces" to arrive in the mail.

> Dear Mr. Harrison:
> Mr. Ives says that he hopes you will not feel in any way obligated to have any of his music played just because so much is being sent, or if it bothers the players too much, which is often the case. But he greatly appreciates your interest and generosity in taking the time and trouble about it.[17]

"Some chamber music pieces" turned out to be a crate that included the piano sonatas, eleven volumes of chamber music, and 117 songs—all the more remarkable because the copies had been made by an early photostatic process, which, at the height of the Depression, could cost a dollar a page. Ivesian angular harmonies and atonality began to show up in Harrison's works, such as his "quite free and fantastic" *Variations* for violin and piano, probably written in 1936.[18]

Variations opens with the pianist smashing both forearms down on the piano as loudly as possible, in increasingly wide tone clusters. Although this distinctive technique is associated with Cowell, Ives had anticipated it in the "Hawthorne" movement of the *Concord* sonata. The violin's angular melody rides a series of dissonant, atonal chords that form the harmonic basis for the following variations, which bristle with inversions and swapped roles between the instruments and hands, build up to a climax, and tumble back down, like Ives's thickly dissonant "Emerson" movement.

But more than specific techniques, the Ives crate gave Harrison an expansive compositional attitude that he also relished in the music of his beloved Handel. "I could sense the grand manner in the sonatas, and that led to my being able in a sense to write symphonies," he recalled. "Ives was a great help in learning how to write big pieces, because he had the sense of the grand manner."[19]

Ives's music liberated Harrison's. "The first thing I learned was if Mr. Ives could permit himself this, then I could permit myself other things too," Harrison recalled. "It was a freedom that was gained."[20] Ives also provided a model for Harrison's eclecticism, which (in contrast to the single-mindedness of Cage or Schoenberg) would become a hallmark of his career: "I got the idea intellectually from Mr. Ives of inclusivity—that you don't do exclusively one kind of thing. I really like what Henry Brant calls the 'grand universal circus,' and I think that Charles Ives was the great creator musically of this, just as Whitman was poetically.... [T]he Ives achievement is total. It's complete, it's grand, it's world-scale, and it's there forever."[21] Harrison wrote to Ives in February 1937, saying, "The world will see as time goes on that there are no 'mistakes of mind or heart' in your symphony, it's too accurately realized a vision to swerve far from the truth that was in your heart when you did it."[22] In less than ten years, Harrison would introduce that symphony to the world, establishing a milestone in Ives's career.

BUILDING MELODIES

When the fall semester of 1936 rolled around at San Francisco State, Harrison saw little reason to enroll again. He was already busy earning his way as a dance accompanist, and between his self-guided library research and his guided study with Cowell, Harrison was effectively putting together an independent study course in music.

Cowell had often assigned his protégé to craft different kinds of melodies out of the transformations of short cells of three or four notes, which Harrison began calling "melodicles." Harrison distinguished melodicles from conventional motives first in their lack of a specific rhythm—rhythmic permutations ("rhythmicles") can be used simultaneously but independently. More important, repetitions and variations of a motive in Beethoven's music, for example, serve as one unifying force within the overall phrase structure of a theme. Harrison's melodicles, though, may be strung together into a kind of linear mosaic. Cowell showed him that, through variation, a single cell contained enormous possibilities. When the notes are played in inversion, retrograde, or some other transformation, listeners might not recognize the original tune, but the characteristic intervals remain, serving as a kind of aural glue that can hold a piece together for listeners.[23]

Harrison discovered similar techniques throughout the world and music history—for example, in the Middle Ages, when composers sometimes pieced together chants by a similar process. Harrison also discerned in Ives's music "a polyphony in which phrase and section cumulate from motive-germinated melodies alone,"[24] and he analyzed the intricate motivic transformations in Schoenberg's works, such as the *Kleine Klavierstücke* of opus 19.[25] Through Cowell's class and recordings, he found that melodicles are also central to much non-Western music, including that of India and (most significantly for Harrison's later development) Java. Harrison later called the use of melodicles "the oldest known method of musical composition, probably deriving from Mesopotamia and Egypt."[26]

Composing melodically in this way played to Harrison's gift for melody and enabled him to build tunes by joining units of melody together—rather than by plotting a rigid hierarchy of harmonic structures. A single melodicle announced by the first violin forms the basis of the first section of Harrison's *France 1917–Spain 1937* (dated June 16, 1937) for string quartet and two percussionists. The same melodicle (in retrograde variations) underlies a contrasting section, and its pitch set defines the piece's harmony.[27] Harrison's introduction for a Mills College production of *The Eumenides* consists nearly entirely of transpositions and inversions of a melodicle of a major third leap followed by a semitone in the opposite direction.[28]

While these early works use melodicles to define their direction, in *First Concerto for Flute and Percussion* (1939), Harrison used melodicles throughout as a fundamental structural element. The jaunty opening movement consists almost entirely of two basic melodicles in transposed, inverted, and retrograde variations. Harrison also assigned each melodicle a characteristic rhythmicle—the rhythmic counterpart of the melodicle—and varied the rhythms independently of the melodicles by switching the characteristic rhythm of the two halves of the measure. The many different transpositions spice this movement with chromatic variety, but at the same time, Harrison maintained its unity by sticking to the same intervals, linking most of the melodicles to the preceding one by the interval of a minor third (the main interval of the first melodicle) or a major second (the main interval of the second melodicle).

As with many of Harrison's methods, this independent variation of rhythm and melodicles has a precedent in early music in a technique known as isorhythm, in which (in Harrison's terms) a melodicle repeats along with a rhythmicle but often non-coincidentally. The *First Concerto*'s percussion ostinato, for example, is three measures long, while each of the flute phrases is two measures in length.[29] Although this cubist approach to constructing melodies may leave listeners without a hummable tune, the result is nevertheless irresistibly tuneful, especially the sinuous, slow second movement.

The *First Concerto for Flute and Percussion* kicked off a whole series of works for solo instrument plus percussion, sometimes labeled "concerto" but in the term's original sense of two opposing forces playing against each other. Although it may not have sounded much like the music that still dominated contemporary composition,

EXAMPLE 4.1. The opening melody of Harrison's *First Concerto for Flute and Percussion* is nearly entirely made up of two melodicles ("a" and "b") and their transformations, including transposition (starting at a different pitch), inversion (upside down), retrograde (backward), and retrograde inversion. Copyright © 1964 by C. F. Peters Corporation. Used by permission. All rights reserved.

Harrison's studies showed him that the texture of a melodic instrument accompanied by percussion and optional drone was both ancient and common, "of course, world-wide," he wrote later. "This is the standard usage in India, in Islam, in Sinitic folk (if not in the cultivated) music, in Africa—and where not else?"[30]

These seemingly wildly diverse musical approaches—early music, Asian music, dissonant counterpoint, dance, percussion—shared a common primary element: an emphasis on melody. Harrison's lifelong inclination toward melodic composition would distinguish him from most of the other classical composers of his generation, even though Harrison also heard a focus on the linear dimension of music in the music of the most prominent prophet of the musical avant-garde.

EXPANDING TONES, RESTRICTING INTERVALS

There have been times when I seemed incapable of listening to music other than Schoenberg's. His music allured me more intensely that that of any European composer but Handel.

—Lou Harrison[31]

In the age before instantly available publications, Harrison enjoyed greater access to the newest developments in music than did most young American composers of the era, through Cowell, *New Music*, and the San Francisco Public Library. And beginning in May 1936, he found another resource—and a job. At the Cowell house, he met the proprietor of Herbert Wilson's Record Rental Library, who hired Harrison as a clerk. The new position—a lucky break during the Depression—presented the nineteen-year-old composer with an independent income and a feast of new music, which he eagerly devoured, spending most of his salary renting and buying records from his employer. The store boasted glass listening booths and a distinguished clientele. Harrison enjoyed the proprietor's custom of taking a 4:00 PM brandy break every day. In the two years he worked there, Harrison explored music ranging from Javanese gamelan to Dmitri Shostakovich to the microtonalist Julián Carrillo. Echoes of the orchestral factory depicted in the Russian futurist Alexander Mossolov's *The Iron Foundry* found their way into some of Harrison's percussion music.[32]

But ever since the New Music Society concert when he met the man, Harrison recalled, "I developed a passion for Schoenberg's music."[33] Though critics delighted in blaming Schoenberg for alienating audiences with unremitting dissonance, Harrison heard an uncompromising compositional integrity. "During [that period] I would barely study any music besides Schoenberg's," he remembered. "What I liked about the music was its intense self-contained musicality. For it seemed to me that those small mobile melodies, so swiftly and adroitly developed, imitated, inverted, retrograded, collapsed into chords, augmented, ornamented, contracted or otherwise treated, did create a closed garden of purely musical interest, purely musical existence."[34]

After having been liberated by Ives's "anything is permitted" example, and by Cowell's all-embracing musical omnivoracity, Harrison's enormous palette needed discipline. "In addition to the expressive powers in Mr. Ives and the sense of freedom, there is the need for method," he said. "The friction of the polarity between the free and the controlled . . . is very stimulating. You have to have both. . . . And it was this sense of order that I needed from Schoenberg. I love systems and methods."[35]

The most famous answer to the twentieth-century composer's quest for structure was Schoenberg's twelve-tone method, but in 1936, little had been written in English about the twelve-tone method. Cowell, one of the few people in the country then conversant with the twelve-tone technique, was happy to show it to Harrison.[36] Inspired, Harrison analyzed the Schoenberg works found in the San Francisco Public Library and realized that twelve-tone music wasn't that far from what he had been doing himself—it was essentially composition with a single melodicle. Like any melodicle, the row of a dozen pitches is transposed, inverted, or played backward, creating the fabric of the piece.[37]

Harrison took his first tentative steps composing with the twelve-tone method in a sketch titled *Slow (Symphony for Organ)* dated February 10, 1937, and in an unnumbered piano sonata, but these experiments remained in his stack of notebooks, unperformed.

Then he heard on the radio a revolutionary composition that proved to him that a reconciliation of tonality and the twelve-tone method was possible: Alban Berg's fervid 1935 *Violin Concerto*. "It really walloped me," he recalled.[38] The Wilson Record Library soon received the inaugural recording with the commissioning violinist, Louis Krasner. In a 1947 article in *Listen* magazine, Harrison called Berg's work "among the highest musical achievements of the century."[39] Berg's example showed Harrison (and many other composers of the day) that a consistent chromaticism was possible within a tonal context, and this combination would later become a distinctive part of Harrison's stylistic repertoire.

BALANCING FREEDOM AND UNITY

Yet however powerful and cogent the twelve-tone method can be, Harrison came to view Schoenberg's method as often limiting, restricting the choice of pitches at any given point too greatly. Paradoxically, what initially seemed to represent liberation from the strictures of tonal harmony soon proved confining. Once a form of the row has been chosen for a point in a piece, in Schoenberg's authoritarian system, the composer is obligated to follow through all twelve pitches. Harrison soon found that a twelve-tone composer has to live with this sense of no turning back, even when another pitch might sound better at some point. "If you're using all twelve tones in a serial form," Cowell told him, "those damn last tenth, eleventh, twelfth, you don't want [them]—really, why should you [use them]?"[40]

The search for a way to balance choice and structural integrity (or unity) led Harrison to invent another technique. Like Cowell's teacher Charles Seeger, Harrison found an inconsistency in the use of intervals in different dimensions of traditional music: while harmony is based on thirds, melodies move most often by seconds and bass lines by fourths or fifths. Seeger had suggested that taking dissonant counterpoint to its logical ends meant using dissonant intervals at all levels, but when Harrison tried it, the result grew too complex to keep track of, so he tried limiting all the melodic intervals to just a few of his own choosing.[41]

In this method, which Harrison called "interval controls," the composer permits only a limited number of melodic intervals. (Inversions or octave displacements of these intervals may or may not be allowed, depending on how strictly the composer defines the method.) In the twelve-tone method, once the composer starts using a form of the row, he has only one choice for the next note. But with interval controls with, for example, two allowable intervals, a composer at any point has at least four choices for the next pitch: interval 1 up or down or interval 2 up or down (more if inversions are allowed). As with Schoenberg's method, much of the power of the interval technique lies in its simplicity. If the intervals are chosen and applied with care, the resulting chromatic melody will still retain a great deal of unity.

Harrison's consistent use of a few melodicles naturally led to interval controls. Because the three-note melodicle of his First Piano Sonata, from March 1936, is so pervasive, the resulting melody moves only by fifths and seconds. Another 1936 composition, *Project #2* for piano, contains a section in which all harmonic intervals are constrained to the sequence third, seventh, and fifth (forward or in retrograde).

Harrison's first major pieces that consistently use interval controls, the *Saraband* and *Prelude for Grandpiano* ("For Henry Cowell"), dated May and September 1937 respectively, were also his first published pieces, appearing in the July 1938 *New Music Quarterly*, along with his friend James Cleghorn's *How Do You Like This? Three Ironies for Piano*.[42] The resulting national attention proved a mixed blessing. "None too original pieces in that old radical tradition," declared Aaron Copland in his review of the issue published in *Modern Music*.[43] Copland's dismissive sentence reflected the current rivalry between the traditionalist and experimentalist camps of American composers, and Copland—then entering the phase that would produce populist works like *Billy the Kid*—was probably reacting to Harrison's early works' uncompromising chromaticism and dissonance.

Beyond those surface characteristics of the "radical" school, however, these experiments in interval controls and dissonant counterpoint today seem more original than Copland's first impression. The darkly potent *Prelude's* lack of bar lines and the rapid sweeps of a single melody played in octaves evoke the rhapsodic expressiveness of its model, Bach's *Chromatic Fantasy and Fugue*.[44] The *Prelude* retains the flash and drama of the Bach as well as baroque-style unity, while the surface of its "radical tradition" is very different from the tonal, contrapuntal neoclassicism that Walter Piston, for example, was then writing. (Harrison remembered getting indignant when Cowell once compared his music to Piston's.)[45] Befitting a piece dedicated to Cowell, it also includes polytonal chords, secundal harmonies, and plucking and strumming inside the piano. Harrison's technique of interval controls unifies the bold atonality of both the *Prelude* and the *Saraband*, but he left the countermelody of the floating, less cohesive *Saraband* unconstrained so that he could maintain dissonant counterpoint.[46] Harrison intended the *Saraband* to convey "the grandeur and cruelty of the Spanish Baroque," he said later, comparing it to Goya's painting *The Dream of Reason*.[47]

Harrison's 1938 Third Piano Sonata features a much stricter use of interval controls throughout its three movements, banishing inversions. The dissonant intervals imbue the first movement with an ominous, "turbulent lyricism";[48] the second (marked "Fast & rugged") brutally hammers away like Cowell's early piano assaults in pieces such as *Dynamic Motion*. Nevertheless, the sonata fades away with a hauntingly serene (though still dark), even singing melody, which, like the *Prelude*, is mostly in octaves and which finally "settle[s] down with a certain nobility towards the end chords."[49]

The most important composition to emerge from this experimentation with interval controls was Harrison's 1940 *Concerto for Violin with Percussion Orchestra*, which would remain unperformed until 1959. As he had in the *Prelude, Saraband*, and Third Piano Sonata, Harrison chose the minor second and major third together with a larger interval, in this case the major sixth. He called this combination of the minor second and major third "very affecting and very useful," and it would become a signature combination even in works half a century later.[50] After a muscular and sharply angular opening statement by the violin, punctuated by metal pipes and brake drums over a rolled bass drum and tam-tam, a brisk contrapuntal section follows (as in a baroque overture), the "counterpoint" provided by layers of interlocking pipes, brake drums, and coffee cans. As in his other percussion pieces, Harrison divides the non-violin parts between sustained (that is, rolled) and dry timbres, achieving contrast in the movement's middle section with long, sustained violin tones with the annotation (in the 1959 version) "the violin chants." The bittersweet melodies of the second movement especially recall one of its inspirations: Berg's Violin Concerto. The sparse and more transparent percussion accompaniment provides a gently dreamlike context with soft wind chimes, triangles, sistra (metal rattles), and other novel timbres.

Limiting the number of available intervals can unify harmonic as well as melodic language, and Harrison liked combinations such as semitones and perfect fifths, which didn't limit him to the language of either secundal or quintal harmonies—in effect they are conflated, offering elements of each when needed. The Third Sonata's harmonies consist mostly of perfect fifths and major seconds—intervals lacking in the melody and thus providing a welcome foil.[51]

EXAMPLE 4.2. Harrison used his technique of interval controls for the violin melody of his *Concerto for Violin with Percussion Orchestra*, restricting the melody to the intervals of a minor second (m2), major third (M3), and major sixth (M6). Copyright © 1964 by C. F. Peters Corporation. Used by permission. All rights reserved.

Harrison also used a wide vocabulary of both semitones and fifths in his "private meditation" *Largo Ostinato* (dated January 1937 and dedicated to "John L. D[obson]"), amid polytonal interlocking F major and Db major triads.[52] Harrison later credited the influence of Edwardian Romantic Edward Elgar for its expressively searching melody and Charles Ives's "In the Night" for its haunting atmosphere.[53]

These works show Harrison leavening the possibilities offered by Schoenberg, Ives, Cowell, and others with his own distinctive techniques. He would fill notebooks with these experiments, and the sketches would proliferate when an important performance was approaching. "For pieces done on commission or on spec, I could fuss around and erase a lot more, try the different routes the piece could take," he explained.[54]

In fact, Harrison's most important source of commissioned work was now the stage. Shortly after he began collaborating with Carol Beals, and just before Cowell's arrest, Harrison went to dinner one night at the Cowell house. One of the other guests was a tiny, moon-faced woman with long limbs and large hands named Tina Flade, a dancer who had come directly from Wigman's company in Germany. She was the new dance instructor at Mills College in Oakland, and she needed an accompanist for her class. She approached Cowell, who had also taught a class at Mills, but Cowell recommended his promising young protégé. Harrison would now have a regular salary from composing music for dance.

5

CHANGING WORLD (1937–1938)

Just two years out of high school, a couple of weeks short of his twentieth birthday, Lou Harrison looked out on the cavernous Curran Theater in downtown San Francisco, where his latest ballet, *Changing World: Illusions of a Better Life*, was about to be premiered. The performance was the climax of the Dance Council of Northern California's conference, and in the large audience were choreographers from all over the region, the critic for the *Chronicle*, Alfred Frankenstein, and Harrison's parents (who rarely attended his performances). Harrison's growing collection of percussion instruments sprawled around the Curran's grand piano and his fellow musicians: his neighbor Douglas Thompson (a WPA artist and gifted pianist) and his best friend and lover, John Dobson. More accustomed to performing on stage, Dobson was pressed into his percussionist role after experiencing a sharp pain and a sound like a rifle shot during rehearsal. He had snapped a tendon, and his dancing days were over.

The performance began as Harrison's woodblocks, gongs, and drums resounded in the hall. At one point his friend and housemate Dorothy James, whom he had enlisted to sing the vocalise he had written for her, glimpsed the audience, blanched, and succumbed to stage fright, unable to utter a sound. Harrison just smiled encouragement up from the pit, and they continued without her. For the third scene, his double percussion fugue in the hands of Thompson and Dobson, Harrison ran up onto the stage to dance his own choreography.

In the short journey from a union hall boxing ring to San Francisco's most prestigious theater, Harrison had become a prolific and expert composer for dance, even as he worked at the record store, studied Ives and library scores, and composed his own experimental music—what he called his "voluntary" works. Before the invention of the tape recorder, modern dancers who wanted an up-to-date sound to accompany their modern choreography had to hire musicians and pay them to compose new pieces for them, creating for Harrison what was even then a rare opportunity: a paid composing gig. After *Waterfront*'s 1936 premiere, Beals introduced him to Veronika Pataky, a Wigman school choreographer who shared Mary Wigman's enthusiasm for percussion. Harrison's first performance with the company took place in February 1936, and he later went on tour with them.

Accompanying Beals's and Pataky's companies forced Harrison to quickly learn to improvise and compose for piano, percussion, and whatever melodic instruments were available, and to learn the ins and outs of modern dance so that he could write music appropriate to the dance style. Beals showed Harrison Martha Graham's tense angularity and poetry of the body, while Pataky taught him Wigman's German expressionist style, fueled by dramatic use of space and emotional gesture. For Beals and Pataky, Harrison mostly composed and performed solo piano or percussion scores, occasionally recruiting dancers to play in his ensemble if they could read music.

Beals and Pataky also introduced Harrison to social and artistic concerns preoccupying American choreographers and other artists of the times. Beals's husband, Mervin Leeds, exposed him to nineteenth-century socialist writers such as William Morris. After *Waterfront*, Beals reorganized her company as a "dance collective"—a social and artistic experiment that favored egalitarian collaboration over the traditional totalitarian model. In May 1937 the Dance Council of Northern California invited the collective to present a major new work at a conference of dancers from eleven western states.

That's how Harrison wound up both onstage and in the music pit at downtown San Francisco's Curran Theatre. A collaboration between twelve different choreographers (including Harrison) in eight scenes, *Changing World* covered themes of country life (gleaners and field workers), city life (intellectuals and night-lifers), women's struggle for independence, the rise of democracy, and (in that third episode Harrison had choreographed and danced in) religious tolerance; its title, "All Religions Are One," from William Blake, must have appealed to Harrison's ecumenical upbringing.

Harrison's first major print reviews were mixed, as the critics predictably found the choreographic grab bag uneven. Alexander Fried in the *Examiner* complained that Harrison used "a tiresome lot of percussion," though Marjory Fisher in *Musical America* judged the score "excellent" and "an attempt to compromise the exigencies of musical with dance form."[1] Harrison's parents were somewhat bewildered by the whole spectacle. Once Harrison made the mistake of asking his father how he liked a percussion piece. "It was okay," the elder Harrison replied, "but I'd rather have the music added."[2]

This perspective notwithstanding, Harrison's melodicism emerges even from his battery of drums, Chinese woodblocks, gongs, clay "bells," steel bells, rattles, and a "witch's stick," often because he arranged them in sets of "relatively tuned" (arranged in low-pitched to high-pitched order) instruments.[3] Harrison then structured these melodies of relative though indistinct pitches through neoclassical forms: sonata-allegros, a march, a passacaglia, and a double fugue (perhaps inspired by William Russell's percussion fugue that had appeared in *New Music*). Like other composers of the period, Harrison usually worked by writing down the metrics of the dance as it developed in the studio and then composing works that would fit the resulting mold.

For Harrison and the other fiery young members of Beals's collective, the production's relevance transcended artistic beauty. On the day *Changing World* premiered, Harrison found time to write in his journal:

May 2 1937
In our guilt years

A world too taken over
Too in our hands
Too planned
Claps off the plain roar of war
And what will happen to us,
What will happen?[4]

The war was the Spanish Civil War, a rallying point for American leftists. Beals's company staged a concert for the Spanish Relief Fund to benefit the anti-fascist forces; Harrison himself danced to one of his favorite pieces, Manuel de Falla's *Harpsichord Concerto*. The summer after the *Changing World* premiere, he expressed his outrage at fascist aggression in a chamber work titled *France 1917–Spain 1937*.

Later that year, Beals's group performed in a dance festival benefiting the Young Communist League, also at the Curran. This time, the do-it-yourself ethic of the percussionists worked against them, as they learned just before curtain that union rules prohibited any performance at the Curran without the theater's pit musicians being paid for it—even if they didn't play. They held the curtain for half an hour until Harrison could hurry to the bank, withdraw $300, and pay the musicians to sit quietly in the pit while the dancers pounded out percussion patterns in their tribute to the working class.

MUSIC AT MILLS

While continuing to compose for Pataky's and Beals's companies in the fall of 1937, Harrison regularly took the ferry across the Bay to Oakland for Flade's classes at Mills College.[5] In addition to accompanying dance classes at the private women's college, Harrison composed for theater productions, including the annual fall Shakespeare play and spring ancient Greek play at the outdoor Greek Theater. That fall he pulled together a student ensemble of string quartet, flute, trumpet, and percussion for a score to *The Winter's Tale*. "Mills is one of those places where you sort of played around doing what you wanted," Harrison explained, "and if you found a sympathetic soul who was doing something, you went along with it."[6] Among these many sympathetic souls were student composer and fellow dance accompanist Esther Williamson, later to be his colleague in New York, and the music librarian, Evelyn Hinrichsen, later to be his publisher.

In the Mills dance studio, Harrison sat at the piano and the percussion instruments, accompanying Flade's classes. He usually began by improvising as the dances took shape. Sometimes these sessions would provide him practice at techniques such as melodicle variation—once devoting an entire session to variations of the four-note theme of Eddie Cantor's radio show.[7] "When you accompany dancers . . . for hour after hour in the studio, . . . you get a certain facility at getting around the keyboard," he remembered. "You have to, because they won't put up with just single-finger stuff for very long!"[8]

Uninterested in improvisation for its own sake, Harrison preferred to write out a complete score for the public performance, carefully setting the rhythms to fit the metrics of the dance. Even when time demands prohibited completing a written-out score, Harrison permitted only what he called "controlled improvisation," as had Cowell in *Fanati*. Because of the Wigman school's emphasis on improvisation, Tina Flade might change counts depending on the feel of the moment, throwing Harrison's precisely prepared score into disarray. To prevent her from perpetrating these disruptive changes, Harrison asked Pataky to teach him Labanotation (a method of notating dance invented by Wigman's teacher, Rudolf von Laban) so he could remind her how she had choreographed a passage at the preceding session.[9]

Learning Labanotation, which borrows from music such concepts as a staff with its metaphorical division of space, "scales" of movement, and the idea of notation itself, demonstrated to Harrison that human movement could be a kind of melody. Ideally, his music should form a counterpoint with it, in the same ways that his musical lines were interwoven. Accordingly, his dance music never tries to either overpower or merely accompany the choreography but rather works in tandem with it. As the great choreographer Bella Lewitzky (who danced to Harrison's work when she was with Lester Horton's Los Angeles-based company) noted, his scores also left space for the dancers to shine through.[10]

Soon Harrison was well known throughout the Bay Area dance community. Evidently retaining the kinetic knowledge gained in those preschool dance lessons, he danced in other productions after his stint in *Changing World*; sometimes, he would stop accompanying and join the class. He picked up some of Graham's technique, some classic ballet, and other styles, such as Lester Horton's. "At one point," he said, "I could fall to the ground and get up in four or five different ways—Horton, Graham, Wigman, you name it."[11]

By then Harrison was one of the more active male dancers in San Francisco—which, he would point out, wasn't necessarily saying much, as male dancers were always in demand. Still, he received good notices. "I danced my own choreography to my own music, and I must say, I never understood why, but people liked it," he said. "Dancers seem to like to use my music, but when I did choreography and danced to it myself, I had a *terrible* time."[12] At one point a solo modern dancer asked Harrison to choreograph for him, but Harrison couldn't get far, and he gave up. He even tried forming a dance group of his own, though they never got to the point of renting a hall and staging a performance. Nevertheless, the lessons he learned from the inside during this intensive period of composing and choreographing for dance, working with dancers, and even dancing himself would inform most of Harrison's music for the rest of his career.

INVITATION TO THE DANCE

After the final curtain at San Francisco's Community Playhouse on a Sunday afternoon in April 1938, Lou Harrison escaped his seat and slipped backstage. He had witnessed a riveting dance version of Oscar Wilde's notorious *Salome*, created by the celebrated Los Angeles choreographer Lester Horton. Frankenstein in the *Chronicle* noted that the "brutal" and "gripping" treatment was accompanied by "the innumerable percussive effects beloved of modern dancers . . . woven together in a large symphonic form."[13] Backstage, Harrison marveled at Horton's collection of exotic percussion, including Native American instruments and a *bonang* (a rack of tuned bronze gongs), the first Javanese gamelan instrument Harrison had seen.

He was equally impressed with the charming choreographer and leader of the company—dapper in his trademark loose sweater with an open collar. They began to chat. In a few weeks, Horton, his instruments, and his lead dancer, Bella Lewitzky (electrifying in the title role of *Salome*), would be joining Harrison at the Mills College summer session.

Harrison's own world began to change after the 1937 production of *Changing World*. His paid composing assignment from Tina Flade's dance class afforded him the financial independence to join the rest of his friends in moving to another house, on Telegraph Hill. One day, Dobson came down to breakfast and found Cleghorn staring fixedly at his plate. He looked up at Dobson. "What I do is getting farther and farther from what I think," Cleghorn announced. "You've got to take me to the booby hatch."[14] Dobson and Cleghorn's wife escorted him to the hospital. He and Harrison lost touch until years later, when Cleghorn became the principal arts and music librarian for the San Francisco Public Library and invited Harrison to give a lecture there.

Not long after the incident with Cleghorn, Dobson was sitting on the living room floor with Dorothy James, rubbing her foot. He decided to tickle her with a key—but she didn't feel it at all. This loss of sensation was one of a series of symptoms of what turned out to be Hansen's disease (leprosy), contracted during her family's stay in the Pacific. Another of Harrison's best friends was gone: She abruptly moved to Seattle to stay with family members and to get treatment for the still-stigmatized disease, without telling the others (except for Dobson) the reason.

Dobson himself soon left the house to return to college, in part to avoid what many assumed would be a return of the draft. He and Harrison had already begun to drift apart, as Dobson plunged deeper and deeper into the study of meditation that he had first encountered when Harrison took him to Ashokananda's lecture sponsored by the Vedanta Society, and in 1944, Dobson joined the swami's ashram and became a Vedanta monk. "Lou more or less lost me to Swami," he said.[15]

But Dobson continued his interest in the sky he had displayed during those long hikes with Harrison, ultimately founding the Sidewalk Astronomers of San Francisco, which spread around the world and made Dobson one of the most celebrated—if iconoclastic—astronomers and popularizers of science in America. "I think he was looking for God within and couldn't find him," Harrison said, "so he looked up to the universe." Dobson wouldn't see Harrison again until the 1960s.[16]

Changes were afoot at Mills, too. At the beginning of the spring 1938 semester, a new dance instructor came to Mills. Another Martha Graham protégée, Marian Van Tuyl's adoption of that style disappointed Harrison, who preferred the more narrative Wigman approach. "My impulse musically is *toward* things, left to right," he explained. "That's like fall and recovery. Not like Graham, which is contract and release."[17] The collaboration was also a mixed success for Van Tuyl. "I liked our investigations together of stress and duration and permutation," remembered Van Tuyl.

"But he was difficult to have as an accompanist! . . . With our intellectual delight and aesthetic delight in musical experimentation, in teaching a class I had to face Lou instead of the class to keep him on target for any technique because he wanted to go on to ramifications which the class couldn't do and which they didn't have the strength to hold up against."[18]

Despite their differences, Harrison produced his first score for Van Tuyl, *Tribunal*, that spring—one of a prodigious number of productions he was involved in. On March 24, he played recorder with Eileen McCall's early music group at Burk Auditorium. A month later, he danced in the world premiere of Harvey Raab's opera *Ming Yi* at the Opera House. A month after that, the day after his twenty-first birthday, he played a percussion interlude he had composed between two movements of Falla's *Harpsichord Concerto* at a lecture/demonstration by Beals at the San Francisco Art Museum. And a month after that, his original music accompanied the Mills outdoor production of Euripedes's *Electra*, which Flade choreographed. Just three years after moving to San Francisco, Harrison had become one of San Francisco's busiest and most creative young performing artists.

But it was a performance he *wasn't* involved in that spring—that powerful, percussion-propelled April 1938 show by the Horton Dance Group—that would change the course of Harrison's career, ultimately enticing him from the wonderful whirligig he'd managed to ride to such artistic accomplishment.

Lester Horton had made his entry into the world of modern dance through the unlikely venue of the then-popular "Indian pageant," huge outdoor productions of white actors and dancers portraying Native American legends. Convinced he was part Indian himself, Horton became something of an amateur authority on indigenous cultures and had even taken time out from his rising dance career to collect and study Indian artifacts, including musical instruments. Inspired by Wigman, Horton and his partner, Bill Bowne, improvised music with those instruments to add dramatic backgrounds and exclamation points to the dancers' fluid movements.[19]

"The dances were wonderful," Harrison recalled. "The technical virtuosity was astounding. [Horton] always managed to set an intense mood or feeling. He was an expressionist. He had theatrical presence, and so did his dancers," including the brilliant Lewitzky, who later gained acclaim for her own troupe's work.[20] Harrison also admired Horton's political inclinations. In the mid-1930s, Horton made the transition from storytelling pageants to more lyrical—and political— dances dealing with the social problems (colonialism, the Ku Klux Klan, unemployment) of the time and thereby earning attacks from Los Angeles's right-wing press.[21] Harrison judged Horton to be an "epicurean" like himself, enthusiastic about new possibilities and multicultural influences in all forms of art. Uncharacteristically for the time, Horton reveled in the sounds, foods, and art of Asian and Latin American cultures; he was as entranced as Harrison was upon first encountering California's Mexican imagery.

And Harrison would soon be working with him. Both Harrison and Horton had been invited to participate in Mills's 1938 summer session. The Mills College summer dance program was well known throughout the dance world, and the small West Coast women's college managed to consistently bring out some of the leaders of the field to teach and run workshops during the six-week session. Also in residence that year was Bonnie Bird, a prominent choreographer from Seattle's Cornish School, who, like Horton, would become an important creative collaborator for Harrison.

Just as the summer arrived, so did another, even more important soon-to-be partner. One day in May 1938, Harrison was at the piano in the parlor of the communal house when he heard a knock at the door. He opened it to find a clean-cut, freckle-faced young man he had never met.

"My name is John Cage," the visitor announced, "and Henry Cowell has sent me."[22]

6

DOUBLE MUSIC (1938–1939)

Cage and Harrison had a lot in common. Born in Los Angeles in 1912, Cage was five years older than Harrison, but both had been inspired by the same mentor. A year before Harrison enrolled in Cowell's Music of the Peoples of the World class in San Francisco, Cage took the course from Cowell at New York's New School for Social Research.[1] After studying with Cowell and Adolph Weiss in New York, Cage wrote *Two Pieces for Piano*, using the twelve-tone method in an utterly unorthodox way by breaking up the tone row into what he called "cells," in which the note patterns are freely rearranged and transformed.

In 1935, back in Los Angeles, Cage studied with another of Harrison's influences: Arnold Schoenberg.[2] The consistency and coherence of Schoenberg's twelve-tone method impressed Cage, who sought rigorous mathematical systems to structure his works, realizing that "a composer must create a system of obstacles (strictly adhered-to pre-compositional rules) in order to free the composer to be truly creative."[3] Although few if any of Cage's works resemble Schoenberg's, Cage said he "worshipped" the stony Austrian composer.[4] When he met Harrison, Cage was carrying the score of another quasi-serial piece, the *Sonata for Two Voices*, and he showed Harrison the *Three Pieces* for two flutes he had written while studying with Schoenberg.

Cage also embraced Cowell's ardor for percussion music. After hearing the controversial performance of Edgard Varèse's landmark percussion work *Ionisation* at the Hollywood Bowl, Cage began writing percussion ensemble music with his revolutionary 1935 *Quartet*.[5] At junkyards or around the house, Cage found interesting objects to bang on, and he began organizing impromptu concerts with his new wife, Xenia, and others in Los Angeles. When invited to one of these concerts, Schoenberg replied that he would not be free that night ... nor any other night.[6] Cage composed music for dance at UCLA, as Harrison did at Mills College, and, inspired by the "string piano"—Cowell's name for his trademark plucking, strumming, and scraping the strings of the piano—even experimented with tying objects to the piano strings.[7]

After the end of the spring semester in 1938, Cage headed up to San Francisco to study further with Cowell, perhaps hoping to work for the summer dance and theater program at Mills. That's when, at Cowell's urging, he knocked on Harrison's door, commencing a lifelong creative partnership that deeply affected both composers and American music. "We were like brothers," Harrison said.[8]

Over conversations in restaurants and coffee shops, during walks around San Francisco, the two intellectually voracious musicians shared the fruits of their study. Cage was especially interested in Harrison's knowledge of Asia. Despite the parallels between the two composers, their differences were just as pronounced—and vital to their collaboration. In contrast to the ebullient, mercurial Harrison, "a tall, brown-eyed Californian with a subtle mind for metaphysics and a smile that suggests Buddha as a schoolboy,"[9] Cage projected a cool, wry persona, winking at the world from which he always seemed to stand a bit aloof. Yet he was as driven and energetic as Harrison, always eager to promote their work and push to get it produced. Harrison called Cage "the president of the company" and himself "the research and development department."[10]

But while Cage looked relentlessly forward, Harrison felt as much enthusiasm when mining the distant past for new techniques. Although Cage thought of music abstractly, "not as self-expression, but as Expression,"[11] many of Harrison's works were intensely personal and emotional. Although Harrison freely used a wide variety of techniques, he never used them as a way to remove his own voice from the resulting notes; Cage's experiments were abstract and impersonal. Harrison cared more about having fun and creating beauty than about Cage's self-conscious avant-gardism. Despite these differences, for the next few years, the two young composers' related interests would converge to fuel one of the most exciting developments in American music.

But when he knocked on Harrison's door in the late spring of 1938, Cage wasn't seeking a creative partner or new insights into the future of music. He was looking for a job. Cowell had recommended seeking out Harrison because of Lou's extensive network of contacts in the modern dance world.

One of those new contacts, Bonnie Bird, was looking for a new accompanist in Seattle and offered Harrison the job. Harrison said he was quite happy where he was, but (just as Cowell had passed the Mills job opening on to him) he had another musician to recommend. Within days of their first meeting, Harrison introduced Cage to Bird at San Francisco's Modern Art Museum, and she offered him the job. It was one of several job offers Cage received via Harrison, and—enticed by promises of a closet full of percussion instruments on campus—he agreed to join Bird in the fall.

Harrison also arranged a summer teaching job for Cage at Mills and made sure Cage was invited to the Mills summer music festivals that summer and the next. As part of the summer dance program, Harrison offered beginning and advanced courses on percussion music for dancers, with the resulting music used in Horton's evening workshops. Harrison and Flade also offered a dance composition class, with Harrison teaching baroque dance forms.[12]

At Bird's workshop that summer, Harrison noted the mutual flirtation going on between Cage and Bird's assistant, Mercier Cunningham, whom Cage recruited to play in the percussion ensemble. Harrison teased the married Cage that he was being greedy.[13] The following summer, Cunningham's virtuosic, athletic performance caught the eye of Martha Graham at the Mills program. If you come to New York, she told Cunningham, you can join my company. He did, and he would become a crucial presence in the lives of Cage and Harrison there.

That summer, the two composers and their exotic instruments would become a common sight around the Mills campus. The composer Arthur Berger recalled the two of them stopping his car to greet him when he first drove to Mills, recognizing him from photographs. "The California sky was crystal clear but Harrison said, in a dark monotone that suggested some Eastern guru before they were the rage, 'It's going to rain.' I asked, how did he know, it certainly didn't look it. In the same monotone, and in words that were really guru-like, he said, 'The drums never lie.'"[14]

CONQUEST

> The ancient Mexicans moved gracefully in a ceremonial, pastoral dance, displaying their gratitude to the white-feathered serpent god Quetzalcoatl, who gave the arts to humanity. Then two sorcerers arrived, bearing what seemed to be a great gift: a potion that relaxed the mind and soothed the spirit. As the Mexicans drank more of this new elixir, however, their mood quickly darkened, culminating in a drunken, staggering bacchanal dance. Quetzalcoatl, angry at his people for allowing alcoholic brews to poison their paradise, stormed away, flying east, leaving behind his mask to be reclaimed upon his return.

So began *Conquest*, the ballet Lester Horton created as a finale to the 1938 Mills summer dance session. For music for his ambitious new work, a four-part dance recounting the Spanish subjugation of the Aztecs, Horton turned to the twenty-one-year-old summer session accompanist and percussion instructor, Lou Harrison. Harrison remembered Horton as an electric personality who, during rehearsals, chomped on a cigar, hand on hip, while lost in profound contemplation. The dancers had to take a break when his cigar smoke drifted down to the level of their heads.[15]

> Centuries later, the Mexicans gathered to welcome the pale, strangely clad visitors who'd sailed over the waves from the east, believing them to be descendants of Quetzalcoatl, returning as he'd promised long ago. But the Spanish conquistadores took advantage of the Mexicans' confusion to ravage and enslave the people and destroy the mask.[16]

The program noted that it "depicts imperialism in its most wicked form," and the subject of pre-Columbian America dovetailed with Harrison's own fascination with the history of California. "It was Lester who 'full-scale' alerted me to the glories of Mexico as 'folk culture' and 'classical ancient culture,'" Harrison wrote.[17]

Harrison used the controlled improvisations he taught in his afternoon percussion music courses (which the students would then try out for Horton's evening work-shop) to seed his score for piano, flowerpots, thundersheet (a sheet of metal shaken to imitate thunder), and, to represent the spirit of indigenous Mexico, a conch shell and an ocarina. Although he used Cowell's kit method and improvisation for the sake of flexibility and expediency, Harrison carefully worked out all metrics to match the choreography. While he was teaching three classes and accompanying others every day during the intensive session, Harrison somehow found time to design the Indian-flavored decor with Horton.

Premiering at Mills on August 5, 1938, the show was choreographed by Horton and his prize dancer, Bella Lewitzky, who played the tortured Indian and also the prophet who returned at the end to reclaim the Spirit of the People from centuries of European oppression. Merce Cunningham performed too.

> A native prophet emerged from the chaos ... inspiring the people, who danced close to the floor—the land—using rhythmic footwork. In contrast, the Spanish conquerors moved airily, elegantly in almost courtly dances. Gradually, the Mexican music and movements overcame the European styles, and then the woman embodying the Spirit of the People descended, ... celebrating independence and freedom, the victory of the people over their oppressors.

Before Horton returned to Los Angeles, he invited Harrison to accompany his dancers on a tour of Southern California, where they performed several of Harrison's pieces written for the production, including "Dance of the Pulque" and "Tierra y Libertad" (the famed motto of the Mexican revolution—Land and Liberty).[18] "Maybe due to his own driving intensity, I have never lost my pleasure in doing all sorts of things other than the music for which I am known," Harrison later wrote. "Lester's type—the type of the full artist—should 'create all over the place'— have a ball—PLAY! When we are children we go about our play very seriously and absorbedly indeed. We do this because, of course, it isn't play unless it is serious and absorbing. When we are 'grown up' we do the same thing—we play—& we then call it Civilization. Lester never forgot that for a moment!"[19] Neither did Harrison.

Horton and Cage weren't Harrison's only new partners. In late 1938, at one of those smoke-filled parties (Harrison, like all his friends, began smoking heavily around this time) of people from the dance, music, and art worlds that Harrison frequented, he met Sherman "Sherry" Slayback. With Dobson having left to pursue spiritual enlightenment, Harrison and Slayback moved in together in a "railroad flat" (an apartment with a long central hallway and rooms to the sides) on Telegraph Hill. Later, Bob Metcalf and his partner rented the apartment next door, and Harrison sublet the front room to a deaf friend from the ballet who taught Harrison some basic sign language. Later, they moved to an apartment over a dance studio where Harrison held his percussion rehearsals.[20]

Nine years older than Harrison, the gregarious Slayback moved easily in intellectual social circles and introduced Harrison to various University of California professors, writers, and artists. At a party given by a lesbian poet and her companion, Slayback introduced Harrison to the writer Elsa Gidlow, whose 1923 *On a Gray Thread* was the first explicitly lesbian poetry published in the United States. She became an occasional visitor to Harrison's studio, even attending some percussion rehearsals, and they remained lifelong friends. In 1941, he set to music one of her poems, "May Rain," and that year also dedicated his *Simfony #13* to her.[21]

Harrison's intense but sometimes tempestuous relationship with Slayback mirrored that of Harrison's parents in many ways, with Lou assuming his mother's occasional hysteric persona. But unlike his parents, who preferred to stay home so much that they seldom even saw Lou's shows, Harrison and Slayback fully indulged in San Francisco social life—so much so that they finally decided that, to get any work done, they would spend Friday nights at home and invite all their friends over for wine and cheese, in return for which their friends promised not to bother them the rest of the week.[22]

The wine was usually cheap, the bread a day old. This was the Depression, and many mornings, Slayback would grab a gunnysack and walk down the hill, where trucks heading for the markets would often spill fruit and other food—which often became their breakfast or lunch. Slayback was only occasionally employed as a nurse and a jukebox repairman, and the two lived off Harrison's salary from the Wilson record store and Mills College.

His new romantic partner had to share space in Harrison's world with his new creative partners, Horton and John Cage. As 1939 dawned, Harrison began working on the music they would make that coming summer.

JUNKYARD SIMFONIES

For a fledgling American composer of the time, European study and a good deal of luck might catch the attention of a conductor or classical ensemble, but Harrison and Cage were financially and aesthetically disinclined to follow such a path. Harrison was grateful for the opportunities in dance and theater, but he yearned for an outlet for their concert music. "John and I weren't about to go through a conservatory, get a degree, present our large symphonies to the local conductor and get them refused," Harrison said. "This was nonsense and we knew it. But in the irrepressible good spirits of youth and having fun—we would invent our music, so we did, and we got very good musician friends who were interested in having the fun of giving concerts and we literally, with Henry Cowell's stimulus, invented the percussion orchestra."[23]

Before meeting Cage, Harrison had relied on percussion as an important ingredient in his dance scores. Now he was inspired to try all-percussion forms for the concert stage. For Harrison, the percussion ensemble represented something more personal and emotional: Composed of dancers and musicians he'd been working with in dance shows, it was the kind of community of simpatico friends he'd been seeking since those lonely preadolescent days when he'd been ripped from his comfortable Portland surroundings and exiled for nearly a decade with little more than books and music for comfort. In forming his percussion ensemble, Harrison commenced a lifelong pattern of forming creative communities to make music with. Unlike many composers who labored in isolation and watched their music being performed onstage from a prime seat in the audience, Harrison would always be happiest when playing the music he wrote—and playing with friends.

What to Harrison was good-spirited fun and community was something bigger to Cage. "Percussion music," he wrote, "is revolution."[24]

THE PRESENT METHODS OF WRITING MUSIC, PRINCIPALLY THOSE WHICH EMPLOY HARMONY AND ITS REFERENCE TO PARTICULAR STEPS IN THE FIELD OF SOUND, WILL BE INADEQUATE FOR THE COMPOSER, WHO WILL BE FACED WITH THE ENTIRE FIELD OF SOUND. . . . Percussion music is a contemporary transition from keyboard-influenced music to the all-sound music of the future. Any sound is acceptable to the composer of percussion music; he explores the academically forbidden "non-musical" field of sound.[25]

Cage would lead this revolution from the Cornish School in Seattle.[26] He corresponded with Harrison about organizing a percussion ensemble for a spring 1939 concert in Seattle, followed by a concert at the next Mills summer session. The two of them invited contributions from other composers in Cowell's circle, including William Russell, Gerald Strang, Virgil Thomson, and Johanna Beyer, the reclusive New York composer whom Cowell had hired as his "secretary" to help run the New Music Society in his absence.[27]

Cage was less interested in controls of pitch and harmony than of duration, because rhythm, he pointed out, determines all other musical parameters (including silence). As Cowell taught, durational controls could also be applied to large-scale structures as well as small, so Cage experimented with processes of composing rhythm and structure that were just as strict as Schoenberg's twelve-tone method.[28] One of Cage's solutions Harrison named the "square-root form."[29] "His principal contribution," Harrison said, "was the concept of making a phrase, and then within it, breaking a phrase, so that there were maybe at least two sections, and then using that structure, both in every phrase, and in the entire piece. It was a microscopic/macroscopic form. That was the basic thing that he did. I've used it, and others have used it, too. It's a fascinating way of making the piece." Harrison found this structure very useful and said, "The result suggests a Mandala—balanced and temporally symmetric."[30]

In Harrison's *Fifth Simfony* (the intentionally wayward spelling distinguished it from the traditional orchestral form), Harrison built up his own "mandala" out of one-measure rhythmicles that he could manipulate just as he did melodicles. The transformations in the *Fifth Simfony* are entirely retrogrades—that is, the one-measure rhythmicles are played forward and backward. Harrison reflected this transformation on the large scale by playing whole sections of the piece in retrograde. Each large section of the first and third movements consists of two halves of exactly thirty-two measures, the second half being the retrograde of the first, like a series of mirror images. The second movement is a two-part form, each of the two sections in mirror halves (this time sixteen measures each). Like Cage's structures, "it was quite Cubistic," Harrison said.[31]

Harrison likened composing in such a strict durational form to composing with a lost-wax process—the form is there from the beginning, and the artist simply pours the molten metal (or notes) into it to form the piece.[32] When trying to systematically determine how many different rhythms were possible, given a certain number of pulses, Harrison enlisted the help of a mathematics professor at Mills. The mathematician showed Harrison that for any given pulse, the choices are exactly two: a sound or silence. Therefore, two pulses gives four possible combinations, three pulses eight, and so on. Harrison worked out many of these possibilities during his San Francisco to Oakland commute.[33]

Harrison's other contribution to their project, *Counterdance in Spring*, varied rhythmicles in yet other ways, through augmentation (lengthening) and diminution (shortening), to create fascinating variations of a single rhythmicle, which then combine polyrhythmically.[34] The work represented the daylight half of Persephone's curse to live half the year above ground and half in the Underworld. He intended to pair it with a movement evoking the River Styx boatman's arrival in Hell, including the most terrifying sound imaginable—shrilling alarm clocks—but apparently he could not find satisfactory ones in time, so Cage's group performed only the *Counterdance*.[35]

Another piece from that spring did not make it onto the program: Harrison's brief *Bomba*, inspired by the percussion music of Cuban composers Amadeo Roldán and José Ardévol that had appeared in *New Music*. It has *Counterdance*'s propulsive polyrhythms but not its consistent rhythmicles.[36] Instead, Harrison created yet another new technique to build up intensity: "*ictus* controls."[37] *Ictus* means "attack" or the beginning of a note, and Harrison would control how many appeared in a measure, though he would freely choose their distribution within the measure and among the different instruments. Thus the beginning of *Bomba* has two *icti* per measure, then three, later four, and finally five, creating a gradual buildup in intensity.

During that same busy spring, Harrison also composed the *First Concerto for Flute and Percussion*, wrote a score for a Lenore Peters Job production of *The Trojan Women*, and performed with Marian Van Tuyl's dance group at Mills and at San Francisco's Federal Theater, including a new solo dance, *Uneasy Rapture*.[38] "It was the first time I had heard a Chinese gong dipped in a tub of water," Van Tuyl remembered. This technique, which produces an otherworldly swooping sound, was an innovation of Cage's, though perhaps originating with Cowell.[39] The title of Harrison's ballet *Usonian Set* appropriates Frank Lloyd Wright's term of populist idealism, and its movements, "Reel," "Rangesong," and "Jig," suggest a Cowell-like evocation of Anglo pioneer spirit.

While Cage was blazing trails in Seattle, Harrison continued working at Mills, and the following summer he and Cage were together again, teaching and accompanying classes.[40] For the 1939 Mills summer dance program, Mills brought out the entire dance department of Bennington College, the country's leading academic center for dance, including choreographers Martha Graham, Doris Humphrey, Louis Horst, and Hanya Holm; José Limón was an assistant.

Cage brought with him the core performers of his Seattle ensemble, including his wife, Xenia, pianist Margaret Jansen, and dance instructor Doris Dennison, and he and Harrison continued accumulating instruments. As Henry Cowell had long espoused what Harrison called the "wickedly subversive" notion of using "found" percussion—anything that could make a good noise was fair game, if the composer used it appropriately—the young musicians scoured junkyards, thrift shops, anywhere they could find cheap "instruments."[41] "[Cowell] was very stimulating on the subject of new instruments or things you could find, junk art, like putting a Kurt Schwitters together," Harrison explained, referring to the German Dada collagist. "You could do a work of art collage system with junk sounds, so to speak."[42]

A store on Market Street yielded a *quijada*, the jawbone of an ass, used in South American music.[43] Chinatown shops held all manner of gongs, tuned wooden temple blocks, various drums, porcelain bowls, and other colorful noisemakers. Cage raised money from an art collector to buy some temple gongs,[44] and Cage's bargaining skill came in handy when a merchant invited them into back rooms for tea and polite negotiations. Harrison and Cage each wound up with a $45 tam-tam (a large, unpitched metal gong)—quite a sum in those days[45]—and Harrison kept it till the end of his life. "Our senses were very much alive and if we found ourselves able to buy beautiful, deep sounding tam-tams, why of course, it would thrill the pants off you."[46]

To young composers living at the poverty line during the Depression, junkyards provided treasures like car brake drums, which at the time were made of spun steel and, when struck, released a bright, bell-like sound.[47] Their scores omitted typical orchestral percussion instruments, like timpani, which were expensive to rent and required advanced techniques to play.[48]

Harrison polemicized about this necessity in the journal *The Dance Observer*, once again appropriating Frank Lloyd Wright's term "usonian":

> The only music which may be considered creative and therefore important today is being pursued by a small group of inadequately supported amateurs.... The result of this is that there are two mediums most safe (as far as the line of probable actualization goes) for the composer: the forever present human voice or the field of percussion. In the last named field the amateur still reigns with his clear and vigorous head on his shoulders and his anxious hands on a drum or whatever. Here the course of musical sound tends by force of art—history, love and economics.... [T]o anyone who feels for the importance of usonian culture these things will seem of import.... Shall we extol and neglect? We would rather get a "kick" out of usonian art and keep it out in the air! Let's to work![49]

The musicians and dancers all invited their friends, and the audience (more than fifty the first time, more at subsequent concerts) was large enough to cover the costs and a bit more. The audience also held an august personage: the *San Francisco Chronicle's* Alfred Frankenstein, one of the country's most influential music critics. "We are still very far from the subtlety and rhythmic speech the Arabs and Indians get out of their little hand drums or the symphonic grandeur of the Balinese percussion orchestras," he wrote, "but such experiments as that of last night point toward interesting developments."[50]

Frankenstein made a point to announce each subsequent percussion concert in the newspaper, and the audiences for the musical mayhem grew. "We didn't have electronics in those days and when we wanted to blow down the house, we played loud!" Harrison recalled. "In fact, John once said he thought the ideal end of the concert would be for a great pile-driver to crash into the auditorium."[51]

By the end of that first percussion concert, it was clear that the two young composers had created a successful new kind of music and found a way to bring it to the public without going through the elitist art music institutions that excluded so many listeners as well as composers. Not that its historical significance mattered much to Harrison at the time. "We were having fun," he said.[52] What mattered was that in the past year, he'd found exciting new creative and artistic partners, he had a new vehicle—the percussion ensemble—for exploring and expressing his music, and he was having the time of his life.

Somehow, amid his first percussion concert and summer session dance program, Harrison found time to attend other events that stoked his interest in Asian music. Although Harrison was not part of the Mills music department, he took advantage of the cultural opportunities there. In October 1939 he encountered Pauline Benton's Red Gate Players, an American version of traditional Chinese shadow puppetry that would become an inspirational model for Harrison. He found the mesmerizing polychrome projections of her puppets on the screen "beautiful beyond belief, and with the bright sounds of Chinese music."[53] Benton's musical director, William Russell, was the same percussion music composer whose scores Harrison had studied in Cowell's *New Music*. His works would appear alongside Harrison's in concerts later that year. Russell, an authority on jazz long before it attracted scholarly interest, gave Harrison a crash course in jazz, showing up at his San Francisco apartment with stacks of records and educating if not converting his younger colleague.[54]

Harrison also explored the 1939 Golden Gate International Exposition, then sprawling across Treasure Island in San Francisco Bay. There he wandered through the gardens of the Japan pavilion and the Chinese Village, but one in particular struck him as he wandered over to the Dutch East India Company's exhibit.

A strange and beautiful sound emerged from the pavilion overlooking a lake, surrounded by an enraptured audience. As he drew closer, Harrison realized that he was hearing, for the very first time live, gamelan music from Bali. He was acquainted with the music through Cowell's course and the writings of Cowell's friend Colin McPhee, the pioneering Canadian ethnomusicologist who would become the West's first authority on Balinese gamelan.[55] But Harrison had never heard this magical music live before, and he was entranced at this other kind of percussion music that was as melodic as anything in a Western orchestra.

Not long after, at San Francisco's Geary Theatre, he heard a recording of the more languorous Javanese style of gamelan and was beguiled by the Javanese dancer onstage, moving so slowly, gracefully, the nuanced movements of her limbs, fingers, and facial expressions all part of the dance, its subtlety so different from the flashy extremes then in vogue in Western dance styles. That summer of 1939, he returned again and again to the Treasure Island pavilion and its beautiful interwoven melodies. That sound never left him, and decades later, Harrison would call upon it again to make perhaps his most famous contribution to music.

7

DRUMS ALONG THE PACIFIC (1939–1941)

Time's endless flowering of tone & tune here streams across to each embodied matrix song, heart's gift of ancestry & dreams. Behind the singer's song stands quietly (or dancing) the strange remembered body of the mode. Or is it fashioned piecewise (that body) from the rhymes & purlings of the tune? Sure, scales are not. These sit, immotive, on systemic right. Perhaps modes meld from melodies themselves.

—Lou Harrison[1]

As Lou Harrison waited for his cable car at Market and Stockton streets on September 2, 1939, a glance at the newspaper headlines shocked him. Harrison regarded the German invasion of Poland as the next phase of the fascism he had already condemned in such works as *France 1917–Spain 1937*. As he sat numb on the Powell Street cable car, he pulled out his pocket music notebook and began writing. Soon, he found himself in a sort of "transported state," composing a melody for a mass.

"I wrote the vocal part in the modes for the entire *Mass* before I did anything else," he recalled. "Very simple vocal melodies. The entire *Mass* is tied to the vocal part, which in turn is tied to the words."[2]

Since he had moved to California from Oregon, Harrison had been fascinated by the region's history of Native American and Spanish cultures. The music he chose for his *Mass* reveals just how much Harrison's interest in Native American culture (reignited a year earlier by Horton's *Conquest*) was influencing his artistic vision. He had just read a book that revealed one of the crafty methods of converting the heathen to Christianity: California's Franciscan missionaries would "invite the Indians into the Mission with their own instruments—rattles, drums, scratches, whatever they had—then gradually teach them a kind of rhythmitized Gregorian Chant, still with their own instruments," eventually taking away the instruments and leaving them with only their voices and the Lord. "Well, the intermediate stage as described in the book . . . struck me as too marvelous. This I had to do."[3]

Harrison's choice of a mass to respond to the horror of war reflected his ecumenical spirituality as well as his interest in California's period of Spanish Catholicism.

Like many other modern composers, he used the mass form as an artistic structure rather than as liturgy. Harrison, already a devoted pacifist, surely felt some of the same sentiments shared by millions at the time—profound disillusionment at an apparent recurrence of the bloody carnage the world hoped it had left behind a generation earlier in the Great War.

Rather than set his *Mass* for traditional polyphonic choir, Harrison composed just a single melody of limited range for unison choir, like Gregorian chant, although alternations between men and women and other contrasts provide variety. Like his earlier percussion music with single melody instruments, this one would be a solo "rhythmitized chant" with the kind of percussion accompaniment he had been employing for the past few years in his dance works. As with Gregorian chant, the foundation for Harrison's melodies came not from his chromatic experiments but instead from what he would come to recognize as the most ancient of melodic structures: modes.

Harrison's enchantment with modes grew out of his love of melody. Like many composers of the early part of the century, most famously Claude Debussy, Harrison experimented with scales other than the traditional major and minor, particularly the other diatonic modes prevalent in the European Middle Ages—known by their supposed Greek names such as Lydian, Phrygian, Dorian, and Mixolydian. "Modality" or "neo-modality" in the early twentieth century came to refer to the self-consciously archaic use of these modes, sometimes called "church modes" because of their textbook association with Gregorian chant. But Cowell explained that in some other cultures, the concept of mode may include (along with the simple scale) characteristic motives, melodic ranges, particular ornamentation, associations of mood or character—the whole melodic basis of composition.[4] Harrison (as in his ode to modes above) saw in them potential for new melodic structures, freed from the conventional harmonic architecture to which melody had been chained in the classical European tradition.

While studying with Cowell, Harrison concentrated on contrapuntal techniques—dissonant counterpoint, quintal counterpoint, polytonality. But soon other primarily melodic devices—melodicles, interval controls, isorhythm—began to take a much more prominent place. Although he applied these techniques with ecumenical openness to both tonal and atonal scores, echoing the split compositional personality of his teacher,[5] his exploration of modes and his enthusiasm for melody soon predominated, as it would for most of his life. His often spare, hastily written dance scores sometimes focus on the melody to the point of having only a single melodic line. While other neoclassical composers mined the baroque period for its contrapuntal complexity, Harrison drew upon the single-melody-line toccata for his *Prelude for Grandpiano*. Even when he used counterpoint, two voices were often enough. Many of his Mills works and the *First Concerto for Flute and Percussion* consist of single melodies accompanied by percussion—a texture he would continue to use throughout his career.

Harrison's recent study and work equipped him well for his journey into modal writing. His composition with melodicles already had many similarities to some of the Asian music Cowell had introduced in his class. And Harrison was already using diatonicism—the white-key scales from which the "church modes" are constructed—to provide dramatic contrast in his music of this period, as a foil to sections of dissonant chromaticism. Dramatic works such as *Electra* or *Ecstatic Moment* start with a dissonant introduction, followed by a largely diatonic dance, or even alternating phrases of chromatic and modal material.

Harrison dedicated one of his first modal pieces to Cowell—a reel, an Irish dance that nods to both his then-imprisoned mentor's Irish heritage and his interest in folk music.[6] Like Cowell's Irish dance music, Harrison's 1939 piano work *Reel, Homage to Henry Cowell* is entirely in a pentatonic mode.[7] The deceptively simple tune echoes the repeating form of the reel, though the ten-measure B section raffishly undermines the dance's traditional foursquare patterns. Even with just five tones, Harrison created a highly unified melody with a satisfying rise and fall, retaining enough surprises to hold a listener's interest. What keeps the piece "modern," though, are the palm and forearm clusters that thicken the melody when repeated, as well as the accompanying ostinatos (repeating melodicles) that use different pentatonic sets (five-note combinations) than the right hand—a kind of pentatonic polytonality.[8]

Modality permeates another piece from the same year, one that turned into a milestone in Harrison's career. In the overture he wrote for a production of *The Trojan Women* at Mills, a slow and solemn melody in the Phrygian mode evokes ancient Greece with the same simple dignity as Erik Satie's earlier *Socrate*, whose timelessness and disarming simplicity entranced Harrison when he discovered it at the San Francisco Public Library.[9] A slow repeating phrase accompanies this melody in *The Trojan Women*, and the counterpoint between them reflects the starkness of late medieval motets, with their stratified levels of speed and contrapuntal freedom. As in the *Reel*, Harrison thickens one of the melodies through the use of clusters, a technique he called "crossing Appalachian Mountain modality with Henry Cowell."[10] Harrison also used clusters to thicken a modal melody in his 1941 song *King David's Lament for Jonathan*, a simple but moving expression of grief for one fallen in war, which, like the *Trojan Women* overture, evokes a solemn procession.[11]

In late 1939, Harrison's current obsessions—modes, percussion music, and Native America—all found their way into the *Mass* sketched in the wake of Hitler's invasion. Its somber first movement, Kyrie, pleads for mercy from God while the percussion part raps out a chilling military march. The movement is in Phrygian, the "darkest" of the medieval modes, and emphasizes the falling semitone, the baroque period's musical symbol of grief.[12]

The next movement, Gloria, erupts in bright, exuberant celebration, accompanied in the percussion by every type of bell Harrison could think of, like the tolling of dozens of church bells. "John Cage and I agreed that a superfluous number of bells is just about right," he recalled.[13] Except when the mode changes briefly in a contrasting middle section to reintroduce the tragic falling semitone motive from the first movement on the text and "takes away the sins of the world," the jubilant movement sharply contrasts with the first, heightened by the B♭ tonality, the pitch furthest in the cycle of fifths away from the opening E key center.

The consoling third movement's key of G lies exactly in between the previous two, drawing them together with "the comforting feeling of someone telling his beads over and over," Harrison explained, "because it's a little melody that rotates around in a comforting way." The Sanctus next returns to an E key center, but now in the Dorian mode, with the opening Benedictus (the *Mass*'s only chromatic section) section in a "hushed, mystical vein."[14] The second Hosanna section of the Sanctus swells joyously but, like the rest of the *Mass*, is shadowed by clouds that never entirely disappear. The ending Agnus Dei movement provides solace through one of Harrison's most captivating melodies. Despite its attempts at consolation, the *Mass*'s ultimate feeling is, as befits a work written at the outset of war, melancholy. Unfortunately, Harrison's *Mass*, which would turn out to be one of his most moving creations, would languish, unfinished, in his notebook for more than a decade.[15]

THE SONG OF QUETZALCOATL

With no choir at his disposal for a performance of his *Mass*, Harrison aimed his next hybrid of Native American and European spirituality at a singer whose voice was powerful enough to constitute "a sort of a chorus" by itself.[16] A friend of Cowell's, Radiana Pazmor, packed a dramatic contralto voice (every bit as memorable and beautiful as her name) that transfixed Harrison when he heard her sing Ives's "General William Booth Enters into Heaven" on New Music Quarterly Recordings. At a post-concert reception, he met the singer, "a majestic woman, very tall . . . quite beautiful, in a grand and glamorous way," and he proposed a new song for her voice and piano.[17]

Harrison's *Sanctus* again sets the "Sanctus" and "Hosanna" sections of the mass and in the same six-tone mode that ended his earlier *Mass*, now with aggressive ostinatos and cross-rhythms in the piano inspired by Stravinsky's *Les Noces*.[18] The contrasting "Pleni sunt coeli" and Benedictus sections, though, inhabit a mysterious non-diatonic mode of the Kwakiutl Indians of the Pacific Northwest that Harrison discovered in a book.[19] When Pazmor sang it at a November 1940 recital that also included songs by Cowell and Ives, the *San Francisco Examiner* critic Alexander Fried thought Harrison's percussiveness "unfittingly barbarous and noisy."[20] But *Chronicle* critic Alfred Frankenstein wrote, "[Harrison's] work seems to say we might learn something by investigating the non-European musical systems that serve the great majority of the human race, and so his enormously dramatic and forceful *Sanctus* uses primitive scales treated in highly unprimitive fashion."[21]

In late 1939, Harrison pursued his growing fascination with Native American and Spanish culture by making a pilgrimage. He and Slayback hiked overnight to a remote rancho near Big Sur to learn about Native American culture from a man Sherry Slayback had introduced him to a few months earlier.[22] The French-born linguist and writer Jaime de Angulo had set out to study the languages of indigenous Californians but ended up living so closely with many that he became the most important ethnographer of the region's Indians of the time. Though not a musician, de Angulo recognized the importance of music to the cultures he studied and made an effort to learn their songs. His friend Henry Cowell helped de Angulo transcribe the songs, which, Harrison found, show a variety of diatonic and pentatonic modes and their subsets.[23]

Harrison also found insight into Latin American music from yet another Cowell friend, the great Mexican composer Carlos Chávez. Chávez saw native influences as a way to demonstrate a distinctly Mexican national voice, distant from Iberian influence, during this period of Latin American nationalism, and in Chávez's book *Towards a New Music*, Harrison read, "Civilized Occidentals generally call [American Indian] music savage. It seems to me, however, to be among the most refined music I know. Its sincerity can only with difficulty be matched in the occidental music."[24] When Chávez came to San Francisco to conduct his symphony, Harrison made his way backstage to enlist his help in freeing the recently arrested Cowell.

These Native American influences soon began springing up in the second and fourth *Cembalo Sonatas*, which use, respectively, a mostly diatonic mode and an entirely pentatonic mode—the two scale types shown in de Angulo's collection. The second sonata is a propulsive Indian dance with repeated notes on the harpsichord taking the place of drumbeats, and the fourth sonata's florid ornaments, though characteristic of European harpsichord music, here also suggest American Indian flute music.[25] The other movements directly reference Spanish influences, particularly the Falla-influenced fifth sonata.[26] By 1943, Harrison had completed six sonatas, the traditional baroque number in a set, and they were published in *New Music Quarterly*. The whole set was part of his "Mission Period," his personal version of the 1930s American regionalist art movement, and was "directly stimulated by my studies about and feelings for the land, peoples and history of California."[27]

As in the *Mass*, Harrison's interest in indigenous American music soon found its way into the other percussion music he was writing. Inspired by the Aztec myth of Quetzalcoatl (depicted in *Conquest* two years earlier) and an experimental film in which a camera slowly panned over a painting, Harrison thought he might write a soundtrack to such a film depicting the art of the ancient Aztec codices. Alas, he lacked access to film equipment, but a cinematic atmosphere would pervade *The Song of Quetzalcoatl*, one of Harrison's major percussion works of the period and the culmination of Harrison's fertile "Mission Period."

During the fall and winter of 1939 and beginning of 1940, along with these sacred, modal, and Native American-influenced works, Harrison continued composing for choreographers. Van Tuyl's work for the spring 1940 dance concert at Mills, *Goin' to Be a Party in the Sky*, featured another kind of spiritual influence: "revival hymn music by Lou Harrison" that he called *Skyparty*.[28] And just after Van Tuyl choreographed the score Harrison had assembled from Cowell's "kit" *Ritual of Wonder*,[29] Harrison learned that, after four years of concerted efforts by friends from around the world, Henry Cowell would finally be released. The composer Percy Grainger had agreed to employ him as his secretary in New York—the prospect of secure employment and a home was crucial to the proposal—and in anticipation of a meeting by the parole board, his friends and family amassed a stack of supportive testimonials. Then Olive

Cowell told Harrison the good news: the board had voted to parole Henry. On June 9, 1940, just before his release, Harrison and Olive attended Cowell's last appearance as conductor of the San Quentin Band.[30]

The morning after Henry Cowell was released, Olive invited Harrison to breakfast with his mentor, herself, and Sidney Robertson. Robertson, whom Cowell would soon marry, had worked tirelessly with lawyers and friends to help secure Cowell's release. As Olive served breakfast, a tense silence hung over the table, and Harrison worried about the transformation that prison had exacted on his previously voluble mentor. Then, after gentle prodding by Olive, Cowell suddenly apologized.

"I forgot!" he exclaimed. "I wasn't allowed to talk during meals in prison!" And then, Harrison recalled, "off he went," chattering on like old times. The experience did mark him for life, however, as Harrison would discover when he met up with Cowell again in New York a few years later.[31]

Although Cowell was leaving San Francisco, Harrison's other musical compadre was returning. Cage's Seattle sojourn had proved immensely fruitful, for the composer and for American music. In March, Bird's student Syvilla Fort needed music for a piece she called *Bacchanale*, but the venue was large enough only for a piano, an instrument Cage had little interest in and one that would never work for the "barbaric" choreography. Inspired by happy accident and Cowell's example, Cage inserted objects like bolts and erasers between and on top of the piano strings, generating strange harmonics and weird, percussive timbres. Eventually he discovered that the right-sized common threaded bolt could be wound down into the strings and would stay put—leading Harrison to call Cage's technique "screwing the piano."[32] Other modifications followed, each altering the sound—muting it, making it tinny or thudding, producing a gamelan-like wide range of sonorities—and Cage realized that the piano itself could become a one-player percussion ensemble: the prepared piano.[33] "Oh, dammit," Harrison said upon first hearing the idea. "I wish I'd thought of that!"[34]

But Cage's Seattle interlude was ending. As the summer of 1940 approached, Harrison received a message from Cage in Seattle: In the wake of turmoil in the dance department, he and Bird had decided to leave Cornish after the 1939–1940 academic year. With the school year ending, he was returning to San Francisco—just in time to prepare for the summer 1940 Mills dance program and a new percussion concert.

PERCUSSORS

During the last two years an extraordinary interest in percussion music has developed on the Pacific coast. In Seattle, San Francisco, Oakland, Los Angeles, orchestras have been formed to play music for percussion instruments alone. They are directed chiefly by two young Western composers, John Cage and Lou Harrison, who have concocted innumerable creations for these instruments. . . . This year, Seattle came down and joined San Francisco. . . . Seventeen "percussors" made up the orchestra.

—Henry Cowell[35]

As members of the audience filed into Mills College's Lisser Hall on July 18, 1940, they saw a spectacle every bit as intriguing as the strange music to be performed. The summer dance program included students from Bennington College as well as the Bauhaus arts school in Chicago, who had transformed the stage into a multilevel set, above which floated a striking mobile designed by Xenia Cage. Projected geometric shapes glowed from the walls. Ropes swept down from the ceiling, with percussion mallets dangling from the ends; shortly, percussionists would wield them upon the enormous battery of strange and exotic percussion instruments. The five players took their positions around the stage, and the show began.

Harrison's *Canticle #1* opened the concert with the delicate rattling of sistrum and gourd, then took listeners on an expedition through combinations of wood rattles, bells (metal, glass, clay), woodblocks, drums, thundersheet, and muted gongs— thirty-eight instruments in all. As they played, moving lights added a visually kinetic dimension to the performance.[36] The next piece, Cage's *Second Construction*, began with an insistent pattern from dancing metal gongs and deep bass fragments from a piano muted by the player reaching inside. The novel sounds, including the spacey, swooping pitch of a gong dipped in water, created a otherworldly atmosphere that contrasted with the melodic focus and dramatic development of Harrison's piece.[37]

Harrison's group had been rehearsing two or three nights a week and three or four hours a night for at least six months.[38] They called in artist friends who made posters; another friend who worked at a radio station made sure it was announced over the air; they bought ads in the newspaper. The preparation paid off, as they looked out on a full house that included a critic from the national magazine *Time*.

"Percussion orchestras mean little in the life of the man in the street," the critic observed. "For Maestro John Cage they are the medium of a rich and exciting fine art, shot through with potentialities."[39] Yet strange as the music must have seemed in those days when Glenn Miller's dance music ruled the airwaves, listeners who paid attention began to enjoy it. "A savage sort of rhythm poured off the stage that had the audience squirming in its seats. At first, because of the serious mien of the performers and the fearful novelty of the percussion orchestra, nobody smiled," wrote a Chicago critic attending Cage's performance of Harrison's *Canticle #1* a few weeks later. "Finally, the audience began to enjoy itself, applauding enthusiastically, to be rewarded with a pleased-as-pie grin from Mr. Cage. 'It's better than Benny Goodman,' said one man in the audience, who had previously announced that 'Bach bores me.'"[40]

Between the review in *Time* and Henry Cowell's article in *Modern Music*, the two young Californians and their irrepressible appetite for new sounds had found national attention. One of the Harrison works that Cowell praised in the Mills College concert originated out of practical necessity. In a single afternoon just before the Van Tuyl company left for its summer 1940 tour of Southern California, Harrison cooked up an instrumental interlude for the percussion ensemble to play during set and costume changes. Harrison deceptively called it "a simple waltz,"[41] but the many syncopated layers cleverly obscured the lilting sense of the dance while retaining its unifying underpinnings. Like Harrison's other percussion works, *Canticle #1* maintains a clear balance of "dry" sounds versus "wet" (sustaining or rolled) sounds in each register (low, middle, and high). In this case, dry A and B sections contrast with the C section's intense buildup of rolls on a spectrum of different instruments. The coda features dry sounds accompanied by a roll on the tam-tam, just as baroque codas would often have an extended pedal point.

The result avoids the cacophony that skeptics expected. The title (a canticle is a biblical song made from prose) suggests how surprisingly melodic Harrison's percussion music could be. "Above all the conductor should see that the players make the most expressive effect with their instruments," Harrison insisted in the score's performance notes, "in order to avoid that regrettable bang bang so often associated with the word percussion!"[42]

SOMETHING TO PLEASE

In addition to the percussion concert, Harrison and Cage continued composing for Mills's 1940 summer dance program, which that summer again included Lester Horton along with choreographers Louise Kloepper and José Limón. Horton's work that summer, *Something to Please Everybody*, was a revue of short scenes in a kaleidoscope of styles (romance, murder mystery, tragedy, surrealism). Harrison's score matches both the eclecticism and "high camp" of Horton's creation, summoning styles of blues (for the movement "Inebria," marked "a la hangover blues"), impressionism (for the movement "Aesthetic Ecstacy"), a horror film soundtrack (for the movement "Occult"), some chinoiserie (for the movement "Orientale"), and even a boogie-woogie.[43] Harrison set Lewitzky's humorous "Striptease for the Tired Businessman" to appropriately sexy music. "At Mills—Strip Tease!" blared the headline of the *Chronicle* review the next day.[44] Like *Something to Please Everybody*, Horton's *Sixteen to Twenty-Four* was a series of "documentary"-style vignettes scored by Harrison, dealing with the troubles suffered by city dwellers facing the Depression and impending war.

Meanwhile, Harrison and Cage taught beginning and advanced percussion music together and also again excitedly exchanged ideas, including Cage's historic innovation. Harrison immediately tried out the prepared piano, first in his score for *Something to Please Everybody* and then in a short song titled "May Rain." The song used simple preparations of a few strings to create a delicate "drizzle" of harmonics to quietly evoke the text by his friend Elsa Gidlow.[45] The unusual eight-tone mode of the "May Rain" melody contributes to its melancholy yet unearthly atmosphere, appropriate for Gidlow's nostalgic poem.

Harrison used another new (to him) instrument in an odd way in his score for a dance by Kloepper titled *Omnipotent Chair*—a double bass beaten on as a percussion instrument—along with a solo violin leaping around pentatonic pitches over a percussion accompaniment that also includes flowerpots, brake drums, and elephant bells. Kloepper's company performed it at the end of the summer, along with Harrison's *Skyparty*.

Cage had tried and ultimately failed to raise money for an experimental music center at Cornish, and so he and Xenia stayed in San Francisco, sharing the percussion studio near Harrison and Slayback's apartment.[46] While Harrison taught a percussion course at Mills in the spring of 1941, Cage did the same through the Berkeley extension. However, the daily cross-Bay commute and playing for classes left little time for Harrison's ambitions. "Working awfully hard to accomplish the bigger things I have had ideas for," Harrison wrote Cowell, "and didn't have time nor energy to do when tied up at Mills."[47] The preceding summer, he told Cage that he wasn't getting along with Van Tuyl, needed a larger salary for the amount of work he was doing there, and really wanted to spend his time working with Horton.[48] Harrison finally quit his regular job at Mills and took a job as a flower arranger in San Francisco's Palace Hotel to replace the income.

Cage's friends from Seattle—pianists Margaret Jansen and Brabezon Lindsey and eurhythmics instructor Doris Dennison—joined Cage, Xenia, and Harrison for rehearsals in the downstairs studio that spring. Now that they had built an audience and were quickly producing a strong repertoire of percussion works, their next concert would feature only their own compositions, in alternation. And this time, it wouldn't happen in a college in Oakland—but instead in downtown San Francisco.

CANTICLES AND CONSTRUCTIONS

On Lou Harrison's twenty-fourth birthday, May 14, 1941, he and Cage and their friends took the stage at the California Club in downtown San Francisco. Once again, Xenia Cage designed a special decor for the concert. Cage's and Harrison's new works already showed an unmatched mature and sophisticated facility with the materials of percussion, along with a major advance in color and complexity over their earlier percussion music.

Harrison's quartet *Song of Quetzalcoatl* opened with a dramatic bang, then silence, the pulsating suspended brake drums and glasses polyrhythmically pulsating in repeating rhythmicles, suggesting a musical analogy to the angular patterns of early Aztec art that Harrison saw in those codices. Although not using silence like his composing partner, sparse and quiet notes on glass wind chimes, tam-tam, and gongs surround the dramatic explosions of the main theme.

After Cage's wild, cyclical *Third Construction*, they played Harrison's other new work, *Simfony #13*, which, like his earlier *Simfony #5*, is pieced together from cells and polyrhythmic interplay. But while the earlier *Simfony* depends on grouping rhythmicles into ostinatos and steadily denser textures, in *Simfony #13* Harrison created extended but engaging melodies, each receiving a spotlight with textures so clear that music writer Peter Yates later wrote of them, "The melodies, rhythm, counterpoint of this *Thirteenth Symphony* are as lucid as a work of Mozart, though the sound producing means allow only the simplest non-tonal melodies, which must be given enlargement by very complex rhythm."[49]

Since the plan was to alternate Cage and Harrison pieces for the concert, Cage suggested that it would be fitting for the last piece in the program to be collaborative, a "festive" end to the evening. That collaboration became *Double Music*, which would turn out to be their most enduring work of the period. They first agreed on a set number of parts (four), measures (Cage suggested two hundred), meter and tempo, and instruments—Harrison suggested mostly metal, because he admired those sounds in Cage's *First Construction*. They assigned instruments to the parts roughly in a high-to-low pitch configuration, like the soprano, alto, tenor, and bass division of a choir. Then Cage went off to write instrument parts one and three, while Harrison took two and four.

Although they discussed the types of motives they would use, they separately wrote the rest, not hearing the result until the parts were complete. Cage, not surprisingly, chose a square root form of fourteen times fourteen measures (with a short coda to make up the remaining four measures at the end), though he did not reflect the macro-structure in the micro-structure as strictly as in his *Constructions*. Harrison chose a form of twenty-one sections each lasting nine and a half measures (plus an extra half measure at the end). By this time, they knew each other's methods and habits so well that, even working apart, they distributed their motives into these molds in less than a day, brought them together the next rehearsal, and never changed a note.[50]

Harrison noted that they used "melodic sets" (i.e., patterns of relative pitch) and rhythmicles: "We could use those in any enchainment. It was a mosaic system, you could put them together in any way and in any amount of repetitions and rests of the same duration, or multiples thereof."[51] Of course, the isolated dual composition process precluded the dramatic unison sections or sudden and clear changes in texture that spice up many of Harrison's other percussion ensembles, but the engaging asymmetrical motives maintain an exciting, dynamic propulsion. As a result, *Double Music* resembles Cage's earlier works in which the music marches through a series of mathematical structures. Nevertheless, Harrison liked *Double Music*, and, when the occasion warranted, he proved as willing as Cage to explore the game-like intellectual puzzles of such forms.

They made enough money from the sold-out California Hall performance to pay for a recording of one piece from the show. In the spirit of democracy, Cage and Harrison asked the audience to vote. The winner, Harrison's *Simfony #13*, was recorded in the Sherman Clay Music building studio the following fall—Harrison's first recording. They paid for a limited number of disc copies for $1 each and gave them out to friends. "There is nothing freakish or strange about the work," Frankenstein wrote in his *Chronicle* review. "It is, rather, an exhilarating lyrical study and quite appealing. It is almost impressionistic compared to the annihilating roar and rage of the only other recorded piece of this type, the notorious *Ionization* of Edgar Varese."[52] Actually, judging by the term they used on the record label—Varèse's "organized sound" rather than the prosaic "music"—the composers evidently did feel indebted to the older composer; but when they sent him a copy, the elder composer telegrammed back, insisting that they not use "his" term.[53]

Shortly afterward, Harrison lost his first great creative partner. Cage and Xenia left San Francisco for Chicago, where Cage accepted a job offer to teach an experimental music class at the famous Chicago School of Design.[54] Harrison would have to carry on by himself.

8

INTO THE LABYRINTH (1941–1942)

From his seat in the empty audience area of San Francisco's vast War Opera House, Lou Harrison gazed up as the august Pierre Monteux asked the members of the San Francisco Symphony to take out their copies of the young composer's *The Trojan Women*. Feeling obliged to support local music, Monteux had selected it from a pile of submissions to be performed in a national broadcast on the Standard Oil Hour. The musicians squinted at his laboriously copied parts, and the hand of the harpist went up. Harrison had written five-tone diatonic clusters to thicken the processional melody and had originally performed it that way on piano at the Mills College performance for Job's company. Now he was called up on stage and informed that, because harpists do not use their little fingers, he would have to choose four out of the five notated pitches for each hand to play. He did so, vowing in future to seek the advice of performing musicians as he wrote his scores.[1]

Despite his brief embarrassment, Harrison received his first national exposure when his hometown symphony broadcast his *Trojan Women* overture on June 13, 1941. It was the first time Harrison had ever heard a piece of his played by an orchestra, much less on national radio; to celebrate, his friends took him out for ice cream that night. That spring, Frankenstein again noted Harrison's non-European influences in his review of the San Francisco music scene for the national magazine *Modern Music*.[2] Just twenty-three years old, Lou Harrison was becoming one of the West Coast's most promising young composers.

Harrison and Cage had now established their summer percussion concert as one of the West Coast's signal annual new music events. In the fall of 1941, as he sat down to plan for the next edition for the summer of 1942, Harrison didn't want to repeat himself. Even with his erstwhile partner Cage in Chicago, Harrison hatched ambitious plans for next summer's percussion extravaganza. He envisioned an ensemble so large that it had to be called a "percussion orchestra" and wrote to Johanna Beyer asking for such a work from her. She replied with a piece he called "the maddest music I'd ever heard, pure space music, . . . [but] so clean and geometric."[3] Inspired, Harrison set about writing such a prodigious piece himself. He called it *Labyrinth #3* "because it was a burrowing into the mysteries of my relation to the

Earth and ancestry," he said. "'Labyrinths' were more subjective [than canticles] and intended to convey psychological and mythical ideas."[4] Those ideas emerge in the movement titles—"Ode," "Passage through Dreams," "Seed," and "Image in the Soil"—reflecting his lifelong concern for the Earth and the connection to nature he found in his many hikes with John Dobson and others.

The enormous battery required for this percussion orchestra reflects the intensity of Harrison's search for new sounds: from the standard orchestra (various triangles, cymbals, drums, cowbells, the eerily swooping flexatone), from Latin America (bongos, claves, maracas, *teponatzli*—an Aztec wooden slit drum), from Chinatown shops (a Javanese gong, tam-tam, cupbells, elephant bells, temple bell, Japanese glass wind chimes, Chinese dance drums, dragonmouths—a set of Asian wooden blocks also called temple blocks), from junkyards and hardware stores (brake drums, saw, thundersheet), and from the household (porcelain bowls, flowerpots, glasses), plus Cowell and Cage's "water gong" and (as in *Omnipotent Chair* and his *Concerto for Violin and Percussion*) a string bass with strings tuned to specified pitches and played like a percussion instrument. The first movement, which features mostly dry instruments, contrasts with the second, which features mostly wet ones (literally, in the case of the water gong).

Harrison constructed his *Labyrinth*'s four movements from the same kinds of one- and two-measure rhythmicles as his other percussion works. With so many more sets of like instruments (bells, drums, woodblocks, etc.), Harrison could emphasize "relative melodies," in which the score indicates indeterminate pitches in relative low-to-high pitch order. And he devised several comparably large-scale forms to contain them. The fourth movement follows a form Harrison called *terza rima*, after the poetic rhyme scheme made famous by Dante's *Divine Comedy*: ABA BCB CDC, and so on. To Dante, these interlocking sets of three symbolized the Christian trinity, but this movement dedicated to the Earth and nature suggests another kind of interconnectedness.[5]

As it turned out, *Labyrinth #3* proved too ambitious. The four completed movements (out of a planned suite of nine) last about twenty minutes and employ eleven percussionists playing a vast arsenal of ninety-four instruments. Unable to secure enough players to realize his vision of a percussion orchestra concert, he was forced to shelve the four completed movements, and the piece, now a landmark in percussion literature, did not receive its first performance until 1961.[6]

Instead, Harrison set to work on another dramatic piece. Carol Beals had secured a slot for her company at the annual Midsummer Musical presented by the Ballet Group of San Francisco at the city's Sigmund Stern Grove in August 1941. In between Ravel's *Noble and Sentimental Waltzes* and the folksy "Arkansas Traveler" (in which Harrison also danced), the company performed Harrison's *Green Mansions*.[7] Harrison based the ballet on William Henry Hudson's 1904 "romance of the tropical forest," whose pacifist themes, South American setting, and Native American respect for nature appealed to Harrison. Hudson's novel was a gift to Harrison from a well-known architect and friend of the Cowells, Irving Morrow—who also happened to be the famed designer of the Golden Gate Bridge and, incidentally, Olive Cowell's distinctively modernist residence and Wilson's Record Library, where Harrison worked. Harrison admired Morrow's appreciation for design and music, and the older man's love of nature reawakened Harrison's own; they took hikes together in Marin County. When Harrison mentioned his love of Falla, Morrow pulled a score of the Spanish composer's puppet opera off his shelf and showed it to Harrison.[8]

In *Green Mansions*, the brooding melodies and ostinatos for piano four hands, recorder, and percussion set up a mysterious forest scene where (in a reversal for the time) hunters are the savages and the indigenous Rima, a child of all races, the representative of nature and beauty, is reflected in Harrison's charmingly light and transparent textures. Harrison both danced and played music for this piece, rushing back and forth in costume.

Cage wasn't the only of Harrison's friends to depart in 1941, as his exhilarating whirligig of a young life in San Francisco began to wind down. His relationship with Sherman Slayback became increasingly tense that fall, and Sherry moved in with another man. Harrison was at once angry, sad, and guilty over the way he had treated Sherry.[9] A friend spotted Harrison one night at the ballet and tried to console him over the loss. "But then you have your music," to sustain you, his friend said. "I just slaughtered [him]," Harrison remembered bitterly. "I thought of that often: 'But then you have your music!'"[10] As he would be reminded often in coming years, music alone wasn't enough.

By winter, Harrison had a new lover, Bill Brown, the singer and dancer with Beals's group for whom Harrison composed *May Rain*. Carol Beals and her husband offered the couple a room in their house. As they crossed the Bay Bridge with a car full of Bill's belongings to move in, on the radio they heard the news that the Japanese had attacked Hawaii.

FUGUE AND SUITE

San Francisco in the days after Pearl Harbor was a city of anxiety and uncertainty. Fears of a possible attack, even an invasion, prompted nightly blackouts and patrols. Harrison worried about some of his friends in the armed forces but also about his Japanese friends: Chiura Obata, the WPA artist that had taught him Japanese ink painting; Kitaro Tamada, the *shakuhachi* (bamboo flute) player and Cowell's teacher; a Japanese merchant who brought him recordings of traditional music; and others. Despite the efforts of some of Harrison's friends to hide them, virtually all ended up in California's internment camps. As the United States entered the war and the newspapers reported the increasing body counts, Harrison felt numb with horror. Although he opposed the aggression of the Nazis and the Japanese forces, at age twenty-four, Harrison was already a committed pacifist and soon to face the draft.

But in early 1942, Harrison continued writing while working at the Palace Hotel. He received letters from Cage, who, after failing to establish an experimental music center in Chicago, had moved with Xenia to New York with only the change in their pockets and their contacts in the art world. Harrison sent his new percussion scores to Cage, who would soon introduce his and Harrison's percussion works to the city at the center of American music.

These works marked the next phase in Harrison's percussion writing, as he explored ways to make his works ever more melodic, subtle, and complex. As he was exploring the nuances of percussion sonorities and melody, Harrison was also fascinated with the mathematics of rhythm. One idea came from an idea Cowell had advanced in his *New Musical Resources*: applying concepts normally used for melodies to rhythm. For example, two pitches a perfect fifth apart are related in frequency by the ratio three to two. So Cowell suggested that in rhythm, those two melodies could be related by the same ratio—three notes in the higher melody to every two in the other.[11]

Harrison decided to apply Cowell's principle to the form of a fugue, in which the same melody enters at staggered points in time but in different keys, traditionally related in fixed ways. One day in 1941, in a pie shop at San Francisco's old Playland at the Beach, between bites of apple pie, he explained his concept to Cage, who helped him work out all the relevant mathematics. In Harrison's *Fugue* for percussion, the second player repeats the melody that the first player introduced, but at a ratio of 3:2; that is, one-third slower—the ratio of frequencies when two pitches are a perfect fifth apart, as in the beginning of a traditional fugue.[12] When completing the piece the following year, Harrison also extended some other characteristics of a traditional fugue to the percussion medium, including sequences (same melody repeated at progressively higher or lower pitch levels) and a pedal point (extended bass note, here played on the flexatone). Much of the material develops in retrograde, including a mirror of the opening exposition that becomes the coda, as in the *Fifth Simfony*.[13] The *Fugue*'s dizzying layers includes rhythms so complex that Harrison did not expect it to be performed at one of their concerts—or, indeed, in his lifetime; to that extent, it more resembled his "voluntary" notebook experiments than his earlier percussion works, all intended for performance.[14]

If the *Fugue* constitutes a kind of culmination of Harrison's exploration of formal rhythmic experiments in his percussion music, the *Suite for Percussion*, also from 1942, represents a peak of his expressive and dramatic use of the medium. Harrison created what he called its "hyper" intensity through a seismic buildup of polyrhythms, answered with dramatic unison sections. An extended "aria" (as Harrison termed it) for dragon's mouths (Chinese tuned woodblocks) of the second movement is answered in the third movement by a "recitative" solo for (of all instruments) the bass drum. These solos percolate with complex rhythms, carefully written to give a *parlando* (free, speech-like rhythm) effect that, even though played on percussion instruments, still sounds lyrical. The *Suite* closes with a canon for brake drums and a series of rhythmic groupings that push to a vibrant climax.

The complexities of these recent works prompted even supporters like critic Alfred Frankenstein to complain that their "delicate, lacy" textures were wearing thin: "Such effects were at one time heavily stressed, perhaps even over-stressed," he wrote, "in an obvious effort to forestall the criticism that percussion music must of necessity be noisy."[15]

The pinnacle of this sort of subtle lyricism, even approaching mannerism, came in *Canticle #5*, composed during Harrison's last days in San Francisco. He asked for a technique also used in the performance of gamelan music: "All instruments are to be stopped immediately with the playing of the next note in the part, thus providing a genuine singing continuity in the line," Harrison wrote in a note in the score. "This makes it essential that the players scrupulously observe rests and dynamic shadings." Like *Labyrinth, Fugue,* and *Suite,* it proved too complex to be performed at the last San Francisco percussion concert.

SEEDS OF CHANGE

The final concert of Cage and Harrison's groundbreaking series took place on May 7, 1942, this time in the Holloway Playhouse of San Francisco's Fairmont Hotel. In Cage's absence, Harrison produced the concert himself. The small venue was packed—in part because some of the players had sold more than their share of tickets—and the compositions much more ambitious than before, including Cage's *Fourth Construction, Two Movements* by Johanna Beyer, and two new Harrison works.

Harrison's cherished pre-Columbian influences return in *Canticle #3,* in which the heated climaxes of traditional Native American instruments and other percussion are cooled by a haunting ocarina (as in his earlier *Conquest,* representing an Aztec instrument) floating over a bubbling bed of percussion. "My *Third Canticle* is composed on a very few rhythmicles and melodicles and makes streaming lines of melody," Harrison recalled. "What I was doing was pushing at the size of it. It was like a young man beginning to conceive of bigger forms and using his elbows to get that way."[16]

His other work, his last of the period, also featured a wind melody instrument: a haunting wooden flute. Another collaboration with choreographer Carol Beals, who also designed the costumes, *Johnny Appleseed* was perhaps the first ballet in which Harrison chose the subject and the shape himself, rather than relying on a choreographer's existing scenario. Harrison himself built a ten-foot "junk mobile" of wood and colored glass, "intended to convey the concept of sparkling deity and the mysticism of Johnny Appleseed."[17] To Harrison, it was an American tale of environmental consciousness, depicting the battle between love of the planet and greed.[18]

To the accompaniment of a bass drum march, Johnny plunges into the unexplored Western territories, haunted by a vision (evoked by the wooden flute, suggesting an itinerant's instrument perhaps itself carved from a tree) of planting apple trees; rattles represent the scattering of seeds. A drum eruption marks his deification by the Native Americans, and ominous ostinatos accompany his battle with "super big forest-killing mythic braggart Paul Bunyan."[19] His work and spirit having ripened into full bloom, the vision (with flute and rattles) then reappears, beckoning him to meet the Ancient of Days in heaven. An ecstatic percussion chorus then erupts in joy as the descendants of the pioneers unite to praise Johnny.

Harrison, Doris Dennison, and Margaret Jansen (percussion concert veterans now calling themselves the San Francisco Percussion Orchestra) performed. Beals played an angel, and Harrison's lover Bill Brown performed the title role. It was Brown who would shortly provide the impetus for Harrison to leave San Francisco, scene of so many musical and other adventures, at summer's end; but even without

Brown, Harrison had fewer and fewer reasons, artistic or social, to remain in San Francisco. His innovative percussion writing had become so refined and complex that it approached a creative dead end. "Sometimes the lack of melodic interest gets on your nerves," the usually sympathetic Alfred Frankenstein wrote in his review.[20]

The twenty-four-year-old Harrison's musical inclinations were turning elsewhere. He was excited to hear, he wrote Cowell, that Monteux had accepted his three-movement orchestral work *Canticle #6* for the San Francisco Symphony's next season, although apparently it was never performed. "I am tired of tossing off too many damned many works . . . which after their first performance collect dust in a trunk," his letter to Cowell continued. "I [am] ready to make a bid for professional musical attention divorced from dance or any other consideration." As for his other musical outlets, realizing how few performance opportunities they offered, "I am determined not to write another score for The Trunk, [and] am determined not to write exclusively for percussion."[21]

Even if he had wanted to continue writing for percussion, with Cage gone, Harrison lacked a creative partner to pursue his passion; percussion ensembles and composer-led ensembles wouldn't become prominent in the United States until the 1960s. Nor was there an outlet for Harrison's nascent interests in non-Western music. As much as San Francisco had given Harrison, at this point in history, it offered little else to satisfy his creative impulses.

Meanwhile, Cage was already making a reputation in the cultural center of the United States, New York, and sent back regular letters with accounts of the vibrant arts scene. Lester Horton had established his dance company in Los Angeles and offered Bill Brown a job there. The larger city to the south offered new artistic opportunities to Brown and Harrison. Most significantly for Harrison, Arnold Schoenberg was now living there and teaching at UCLA. Harrison hoped for a job with Horton but had many other connections through the dance world.

"My parents worried I wouldn't be able to support myself," he remembered. "But they never once raised the problem of how I might support a family. They were just worried about me. If you've got a life that's just filled with all the arts, which is what I was doing, what would you care about plotting a graph for the future? If you're utterly fascinated with what you're up to, why worry? And if you can support yourself so you're not actually starving or lying in the streets, why bother?"[22] They began packing.

Harrison stored most of his percussion instruments with his parents and said good-bye to the medium for the time being. Although a love for percussion and an appreciation for its special qualities would never leave him, Harrison wouldn't write another piece for percussion ensemble for well over a decade. But in the space of four years, he had helped create a new kind of music. Their creations echo today, from college percussion orchestras to electronic music to the junkyard sounds in the dances of *Stomp!*

At an August 9 percussion and dance performance at the Stern Grove Theater in San Francisco, Brown's and Harrison's belongings were already packed into Brown's car, and shortly after the curtain fell, they were on the road to Los Angeles.

9

WESTERN DANCE (1942–1943)

As Bill Brown's car rumbled down the Coast State Highway, emerged from the orange groves of the San Fernando Valley, and crested the Hollywood Hills, Lou Harrison marveled at the twinkling lights below. The warm August breeze that swept through the open windows carried the sweet fragrance of orange blossoms and gardenias. "The air was clear. Everything was in bloom," Harrison said. "It was absolutely beautiful."[1]

Harrison had visited Los Angeles before, once as a child and then in 1938 when he had taken his first airplane flight to accompany the Horton Dance Group's Southern California tour. On a trip to the beach, Harrison, accustomed to San Francisco's frigid bay, was pleasantly surprised to find that he could comfortably swim in the ocean.[2] Now, in the summer of 1942, Harrison was ready to trade San Francisco's sometimes-chilly summers for the welcome sunshine that beckoned a day's drive to the south.

In 1942, Los Angeles was already a city of one and a half million, nearly three times the population of San Francisco, though sprawled out over a bewilderingly immense area. As Brown and Harrison settled into an apartment in Hollywood, the difference in scale between the two cities became apparent. The trip on the city's famous "red car" trolleys down Sunset Boulevard to the University of California Los Angeles in Westwood took well over an hour, and the wartime gasoline shortage made buses and streetcars increasingly crowded. Naturally, the intellectually voracious Harrison quickly located the downtown Los Angeles Public Library, but getting there involved another long ride in the opposite direction. Harrison's neighborhood errands took him past the famous wrought-iron gates to Paramount Studios; he was nearly run over by Bob Hope one day.

Compensating for its initially jarring expanse and bustle, Los Angeles offered a different kind of cultural diversity than Harrison had experienced in San Francisco. He was fascinated by the remnants of colonial Spanish culture, and on a bus shortly after his arrival, he heard Spanish spoken for the first time. "I thought, 'That sounds like a percussion,'" he remembered. "It didn't sound at all mellifluous."[3] At Olvera

Street, the center of Los Angeles's downtown historic Spanish district, Harrison enjoyed a puppet theater, a blind harpist, and "exotic" Mexican food.

The music scene Harrison hoped to enter was as diffuse and sprawling as the population. Henry Cowell had founded his New Music Society in Los Angeles in 1925 but soon moved the operation north. In 1933, Cowell's friend, the conductor Nicolas Slonimsky, was summarily fired after daring to introduce "ultramodern" music to patrons of the Hollywood Bowl, one of whom, the young John Cage, had been inspired by Slonimsky's performance of Edgard Varése's *Ionisation* there. Such conflicts fragmented what might have been a rich cultural landscape, filled with such European émigrés as Sergei Rachmaninoff, Theodor Adorno, Thomas Mann, and Max Reinhardt. The two most famous composers of the century, Arnold Schoenberg and Igor Stravinsky, both lived in west Los Angeles just eight miles apart—yet they rarely spoke, even when attending the same events. Schoenberg and Stravinsky had become standard-bearers for opposing schools of modern composition: The Schoenbergian atonalists disdained Stravinsky's turn toward what they regarded as a regressive neoclassicism.

Brown and Harrison arrived that August in time to see Lester Horton's company perform in downtown Los Angeles. Earlier that spring and summer, the company had performed its revue *Something to Please Everybody* with Harrison's score several times, and now it was performing before feature films at the Orpheum Theater.[4] Perhaps in hopes of taking part in Horton's new season, and conscious of Aaron Copland's recent success with his ballet *Billy the Kid*, Harrison sketched out a scenario for a dance with a Western theme, *The Hangout*. However, within weeks of Harrison's arrival, Horton put his concert works on hold when he received what would be the first of a series of much-needed jobs for the movie industry. Choreographing his company as native dancers in "exotic" B-pics for Universal Studios such as *White Savage* and *Rhythm of the Islands* would preoccupy Horton for the rest of Harrison's stay in Los Angeles.

With prospects of a job as composer or even accompanist for Horton's company fading, Harrison found his first job near his apartment, accompanying dance classes at Hollywood High School. Through his contacts in the dance world, he called Martha Hill, director of the dance program at UCLA, and he soon had another job playing for dance classes there. Later he began teaching courses for UCLA dancers in Labanotation and classical musical form, as he had for the Mills summer sessions. One of the choreographers, Melissa Blake, taught him about various dance styles and history, and she encouraged his musical experiments. With her husband serving in the war, the two of them became a frequent couple at dinners and performances all over town.

Soon after settling in at his Hollywood apartment, Harrison received a letter familiar to millions at the time—his armed forces induction notice. Harrison showed up at the induction center and endured a physical examination. Then it was his turn for the psychiatric evaluation. Let's talk about your sex life, the officer began. "I like men," Harrison replied—and that was the end of the interview. Classified 4F, unfit for service, Harrison was never bothered again.

One day at Melissa Blake's dance class, she introduced Harrison to a friend named Peter Yates and his wife, Frances Mullen, a pianist. Blake had been describing to them this unusual young composer who improvised accompaniments and fugues for her classes, all while reading books propped up on the piano.[5] An amateur poet and musician, Peter Yates shared a love of modern art with his wife and worked to promote her career as a pianist of modern music at a time when such a specialty was a rarity, especially in California. To build her repertoire of little-known and unpublished scores, he began corresponding with several composers, including Henry Cowell and Charles Ives. Like Harrison, who had written Ives around the same time, he received a gracious response but found little interest among California concert programmers.

So the Yateses decided to start a series of their own, outside the city's closed network of conservative concert programs. Unable to regularly rent a hall, they bought an old bungalow and, with the help of the famous modernist architect Rudolf Schindler, built a cozy recital hall on the roof. Under different names and presenters, the Evenings on the Roof concert series served as a foundation of new music in Los Angeles for more than seventy years, and as a venue for skilled performers to play the latest Bartók, Cowell, Schoenberg, or Stravinsky.

Harrison had actually heard Mullen perform before, in 1937 when she had performed the six highly concentrated piano pieces of Schoenberg's opus 19 at Mills College. When they met in Los Angeles, Harrison told her of his long desire to hear a performance of Schoenberg's *Suite for Piano* op. 25. To his delight, she sat down and began playing it then and there.[6] Impressed by the young composer, Frances Mullen requested a piece from Harrison for one of their rooftop concerts. Instead of immediately leaping at the generous offer, Harrison characteristically countered that he would write the work only if Mullen would program Schoenberg's op. 25 as well. She agreed, and Harrison set to work on his first major work for piano, which, like Schoenberg's, was a suite.

The Yateses became Harrison's intellectual and musical companions in Los Angeles and lifelong supporters of Harrison's career. Baroque keyboards and their tunings fascinated Peter, and he introduced Harrison to a friend who built harpsichords and tuned them in baroque meantone temperaments. Knowing Harrison's interest in Ezra Pound's imagistic poetry, Yates introduced Harrison to the work of Wallace Stevens and William Carlos Williams, and they also shared other literary enthusiasms: Rilke, Cummings, Robert Lowell, Millay, Poe, Greek lyric poets, and Chinese poetry.[7] One of Harrison's finds was a curious book of Chinese wisdom known as the *I Ching*, which he would later take to New York and show to John Cage.

Harrison became good friends with another member of the Yates's circle who was a sometime performer on the Evenings on the Roof. The composer Ingolf Dahl, whose style reflected his close connection to his friend and fellow European expatriate Stravinsky, scraped by in Los Angeles as a conductor, pianist, and teacher.[8] Although married, Dahl was gay; nearly a quarter century later, it would be through him that Harrison would meet the love of his life.

Lou Harrison was a little nervous as he waited in line for the teller at the bank just down the street from his house. In an hour, he had an appointment to meet the most influential American composer of the time. Like many young composers of the time, Harrison had been dazzled by a record of Aaron Copland's notorious, groundbreaking 1930 *Piano Variations*; he admired its "steely grandeur," played it often, and studied the score, trying to figure out how Copland had made so much out of the central motive of just three notes.[9] Harrison had also read a number of Copland's articles in *Modern Music* and elsewhere and regarded him as one of America's finest modern composers and its most important promoter of contemporary music. Like the regionalist paintings of Thomas Hart Benton or the prose of John Steinbeck, Copland's homespun sound comforted and inspired an isolationist nation beleaguered by economic depression and war. His uniquely lyrical diatonicism—which seemed to simultaneously evoke the expanse of the prairies, the simplicity of Protestant hymn-tunes, and the snappy rhythms of American urban bustle—converged with the efforts of like-minded composers, notably Roy Harris and Virgil Thomson, and often dominated the concerts of the New York-based League of Composers, whose direction Copland largely determined.

Though Harrison was associated with Cowell's rival circle of "radical" composers, who initially frowned at the League's Americana conservatism, he occasionally adopted elements of Copland's diatonic regionalism, including in the first piece he wrote in Los Angeles: incidental music to a UCLA production of William Saroyan's *The Beautiful People* in November 1942. Reminiscent of Copland's scores for films in the same regionalist genre as Saroyan's play, *Of Mice and Men* (1939) and *Our Town* (1940), Harrison's relatively conventional score for piano and trumpet uses Cowell's "autoharp" technique in which the pianist silently depresses the keys while strumming the strings.

Now Harrison had discovered that Copland was working on a new film just a few blocks from Harrison's apartment, at Samuel Goldwyn Studios on Santa Monica Boulevard. The forty-one-year-old leader of American music, whose previous acquaintance with Harrison's work came only from the publication of *Prelude* and *Saraband* in *New Music* (which Copland had negatively reviewed), graciously made an appointment to meet with the young composer, but first Harrison had to stop at the grocery store and then the bank just down the street from his house. Harrison—wearing an open-neck shirt—was eager to get home to dress up a bit for his first meeting with the great man.

Finally, he reached the teller, withdrew some cash from his new account, and turned to leave—and there stood an angular, bespectacled man that Harrison immediately recognized from dozens of photos he had seen in magazines.

"Mr. Copland," he stammered, "I'm Lou Harrison, and I have an appointment with you in an hour, but first I must go home and get my jacket!"[10]

As they shook hands, Copland's ever-ready laugh reassured him. "I'll see you at my studio in a little while, then," he replied.

The neatly dressed young composer arrived early, bearing some of his music. The film company had provided Copland his own studio with a piano and a couch. Harrison played a bit of his music, including his neoclassical *Gigue and Musette*.

The inspiration for this charming piece came from the UCLA class Harrison was accompanying. When Melissa Blake asked him to provide a minuet for the class, he instead composed this "delightful miniature," just before the class.[11] Like a minuet, it is in binary form with a contrasting trio section. However, instead of the graceful minuet, Harrison chose the rollicking gigue (jig) dance, with a trio section in the form of a musette (a baroque dance imitating a bagpipe). The parallel thirds that sometimes thicken the lines of baroque dances here become parallel fifths of quintal counterpoint, giving the piece a surprisingly austere taste while retaining the lyrical, neo-baroque lilt of the dances.[12]

When Harrison finished playing, Copland smiled, declaring, "I want to become an authority on your music!"[13] They chatted some more, and the older man showed Harrison some of his own music in progress. Harrison felt a mutual attraction, which would later develop into a platonic familiarity when they later frequented the same circles in New York. Then Copland escorted Harrison on a tour of the sets for the film *North Star*.

The meeting with Copland didn't immediately inspire new insights or bring new opportunities for Harrison, although Copland promised to provide introductions for Harrison should he ever make it to New York. But the great man's approbation did give a provincial young composer a needed boost of confidence. At the same time, Harrison, who in just a few months had quickly found his way into Los Angeles new music and dance circles, had found in his new city another mentor, whose music seemed worlds away from Copland's. Somehow, he would find a way to stretch his own artistic vision wide enough to embrace them both.

SCHOENBERGIANA

Only a short walk from the dance studios where Lou Harrison worked, he looked up at the office of the composer whose music had become nearly an obsession for him in San Francisco: Arnold Schoenberg. In seeking employment at UCLA, Harrison harbored an ulterior motive, hoping his position on the staff might provide an entrée to Schoenberg's weekly composition class. Schoenberg's assistant looked over the young man who held a handful of his scores, then led him to the sixty-eight-year-old composer's office.

At his desk, the "birdlike" composer looked up, startled and twitching.[14] Fired from his teaching post in Berlin in 1934 because of his Jewish heritage, Schoenberg, like so many other European intellectuals, immigrated to the United States. Because of his poor health, including dizzy spells and asthma, Schoenberg decided to move with his wife and daughter to the balmy climate of Southern California, settling in Brentwood, where he played tennis with the Marx Brothers and socialized with celebrities such as Charlie Chaplin and George Gershwin. Harrison was impressed by his vigor and curiosity, which Schoenberg applied to his teaching, composing, and his hobby of woodworking.[15] Hesitantly Harrison introduced himself, handing over some recent scores. "We met in San Francisco, when Henry Cowell brought you up for performances of your music," he reminded Schoenberg.

As one of the century's most revered and reviled composers flipped through the pages, he asked the would-be student, "Why do you want to study with me?"

For years Harrison had dreamed of studying with the modernist master. His enthusiasm for Schoenberg's music was "just a total absorption. . . . The very rich texture sonically, plus the intensity of the emotional power [was] unlike anything else for me."[16] Although the rigor of his twelve-tone method had given Schoenberg a reputation as a fearsomely intellectual composer of incomprehensibly cerebral sounds—Harrison remembered him remarking in class one day that many accused him of being a mathematician—Harrison understood that the truth was nearly the opposite, that Schoenberg's language was a distillation of late Romantic expressionism. As Virgil Thomson memorably put it, his music "positively drips with emotivity."[17]

However, Schoenberg recognized that such expressivity was only possible through discipline—discipline of the ear and of the mind. His search for order in atonality (a term he disliked) had ultimately led him to his well-known system, and he was convinced that students should recapitulate the patient and rigorous study of harmonic tradition that led him there.[18] Schoenberg's American students often disappointed him with their lack of knowledge of basic repertory, and though Harrison had diligently studied baroque composers and *New Music Quarterly*, he himself was largely ignorant of much of the Romantic repertory. Cage had already warned Harrison with harrowing tales of Schoenberg's harshness and even cruelty to students who did not measure up to his rigorous standards.[19]

Schoenberg looked up from Harrison's scores. "You can join the class," he said, and he returned to the papers on his desk.

To Harrison at least, Schoenberg proved not to be the fierce pedagogue his reputation suggested. Despite his nervous manner and sometimes halting English, the class's compact size allowed for extensive personal feedback from the teacher, who invited students to bring their works to class. Even in Los Angeles, the horror of his adopted country at war with his homeland, as well as the Nazi persecution of Jews, was never far away. Schoenberg would duck down in mid-sentence when the buzz of passing aircraft came through the windows. Or he might shush the class to listen to a birdsong.[20]

One day, Harrison offered his *Prelude for Grandpiano* and *Saraband*, but with some trepidation, knowing their use of baroque forms would inevitably label them as neoclassical and thus part of the school that, at least in the popular imagination, stood in polar opposition to Schoenberg. Harrison passed the score to his teacher. But Schoenberg instantly plunged in and evaluated Harrison's piece on its own terms. "This is music I understand," he announced to the class, to Harrison's embarrassment. "Why do you not bring me such music?" he frowned, looking around at the other students.[21]

"My admiration for him just skyrocketed because he had no interest in what style it was," Harrison recalled. "It was the musicality and how it was done that interested him. And if you thought he was interested in just one kind of music, he wasn't. He was a very richly learned man."[22]

Besides examining the students' scores, Schoenberg would also bring in classic scores for them to analyze, especially Beethoven symphonies. However, Schoenberg never offered one of his own works, until one day when the class prevailed upon him to bring in his second string quartet and explain its technique. This was a risky request. When John Cage asked him about his own work, Schoenberg replied testily, "That's none of your business."[23] For whatever reason, though, Schoenberg told Harrison's class, "Oh yes, I'll show you. It's very easy."[24] As Schoenberg carefully broke down the score's components, suddenly the forbidding piece seemed comprehensible. The chance to study such scores was rare at that time, and it proved invaluable to Harrison's own music for the next few years.[25]

The first of Harrison's compositions to show a clear debt to Schoenberg's in-class example was a piano work inspired by Ezra Pound's spare, evocative paraphrase of the eighth-century Chinese poem "The River Merchant's Wife" by Li Po.[26] Instead of setting Pound's text as a song, Harrison used floating atonal melodicles and spare Schoenbergian textures to evoke the poem's aching loneliness of a young wife in the absence of her husband. Rather than applying the twelve-tone method, Harrison chose to emulate Schoenberg's earlier reliance on small motives and their transformations to cohere his atonal language. Schoenberg's teaching and Copland's own example of atonal motivic transformation, the *Piano Variations*, reaffirmed the value of Harrison's melodicles. Using such brief melodic cells to shape musical structure became a lasting insignia of Harrison's style.

Harrison's interest in Pound's work led him to other Chinese poetry and books such as Robert van Gulik's *The Lore of the Chinese Lute*. Harrison loved its romantic stories and ink paintings of the famous players of the ancient Chinese zither, the *guqin*. "Chinese poetry gave me a sense of the everyday world as a real and notable thing," Harrison said. "There was a stream of that in my poetry, but it was reemphasized by the little knowledge of Chinese verse."[27] The UCLA dance department choreographed and performed Harrison's *The River Merchant's Wife* that fall, one of his few performances while he lived in Los Angeles.

ONLY THE ESSENTIALS

Lou Harrison was stuck. As he labored to create Frances Mullen's suite using Schoenberg's method, he couldn't figure out how to make this process-propelled piece work. He'd taken a break, heading deep into the stacks of the UCLA library, filling his head with the articles and syllogisms of Thomas Aquinas's monumental *Summa Theologica*. Harrison's study of early music had led to a fascination with the medieval mind's capacity for infinite rationalization, for creating marvelously self-consistent worlds from symbolism, scripture, number, and Thomist logic, in both philosophy and music. Around the same time that St. Thomas was debating the nature of angels at the University of Paris, the Cathedral of Notre Dame had echoed with some of the Western world's earliest polyphony. To Harrison, the internal consistency of a modern process like Schoenberg's twelve-tone system wasn't all that different.[28]

Medieval polyphony at Notre Dame often took the form of a conductus, in which harmonizing voices accreted on top of the long tones of a preexisting chant melody called the cantus firmus. What would happen, Harrison wondered, if he used the modern device of a twelve-tone row as a cantus firmus? It was just another melody, after all. For the third movement of the piano suite he was writing for Mullen, Harrison devised a cantus firmus from the twelve-tone row—repeated twelve times with medievalist (or Cageian) consistency. He'd learned a long time ago that, as Stravinsky had said, freedom comes from the constraints an artist imposes.[29] He began with the first row in prime form (F♯, G, C, A♭ . . .). For the second variation, he started the row on the second pitch—G—of the original row. The third variation began on C. It was just like many of his earlier percussion works—a grand scheme reducible to a musical game of solitaire. He built rapid staccato exchanges of chords between the pianist's hands to contrast with a singing melodic line.

Then he began to bog down. The twelve repetitions of twelve whole notes that underlaid the structure soon became tedious, precluding shaping of a larger structure. He resorted to making the variations around the cantus firmus increasingly complex, but he wasn't very far down this path when he realized that he had reached a nearly impenetrable density—and with a long way yet to go in his structure. He had composed himself into a corner and didn't know how to get out.

Despite some 1937 experiments in Schoenberg's method and some brief instruction in it from Cowell, Harrison was still a twelve-tone novice. In order to create a larger-scale work, Harrison chose the loose structure of a suite, which he could tackle in smaller parts, as Schoenberg had done. Following the recommendations of a thin instruction book on the technique written by Schoenberg's follower Ernst Krenek, Harrison's row contains every possible interval from one note to the next but also emphasizes the perfect fourth, thus enabling Harrison's familiar quintal chords. [30] Harrison also unified the *Suite* by limiting row transpositions to only the perfect fourth (already prominent in the row), reducing the number of row transformations from the possible forty-eight to just four.[31]

But at first, he couldn't figure out how to reconcile his short melodicles with the predetermined sequence of pitches demanded by Schoenberg's method. Harrison soon saw the wisdom in Schoenberg's and Krenek's reliance on rhythmic motives to provide some unity, as in Harrison's second movement, "Aria." Harrison also rendered the technique more tractable by ignoring Krenek's suggestions of ways to combine row forms and instead used the row almost entirely linearly—one tone after the next in all the parts (except for his cantus firmus experiment). Although fascinated by the intellectual calisthenics of composers such as Krenek and Schoenberg, who worked out ways to combine row forms while avoiding overlapping tones, Harrison, ever the melodist, built all melodies and chords from a single linear series weaving its way through all the parts.

But now he was stumped. The obvious solution was to ask his teacher's advice for the troublesome third movement, but Schoenberg's assistant had bluntly warned Harrison that Schoenberg absolutely refused to look at anything twelve-tone. No composer should try that method, he declared, until he had mastered conventional tonal styles. Most of his American students could not come close to meeting his high expectations; rumor among the students had it that Schoenberg on occasion had thrown out the entire class in exasperation. Fortunately, Harrison had set up another meeting with Aaron Copland—maybe he could help. But while he offered encouragement about Harrison's ambitious plan, Copland could not suggest any specific solution. Harrison fretted for hours. Finally, he decided that he had no choice. He would have to approach Schoenberg. After all, the old man had been exceptionally kind to Harrison so far.

The next day, Harrison sat down at the piano in front of his classmates and nervously played his new Prelude. As the last note faded, none of the students dared speak. Schoenberg frowned. "Is it twelve-tone?"

Harrison swallowed. "Yes," was all he could manage.

The founder of the Second Viennese School, avatar of atonality, stood up, strode over to the piano bench, and reached for the page. Harrison held his breath.

"It is good!" Schoenberg exclaimed. "It is good!"

Harrison let out his breath as he realized he was not to be thrown out of class after all.

"Continue!"

Harrison played his second movement.

"It is good! It is good!" Schoenberg was fascinated by the wide, soft spacing in the opening measures. The mood lightened considerably—but the scariest passage lay just ahead.

Harrison played as much of the third movement as he'd completed, halting at the impasse he'd reached in the preceding days. He started to apologize, but Schoenberg was already thoroughly engaged in the piece. The veteran composer immediately perceived the structure that Harrison had established—and just where he'd gone wrong. By increasing the work's complexity, his teacher explained, Harrison was digging himself deeper into the hole he'd created by his strict rules.[32]

"Thin out!" Schoenberg shouted, not angrily but encouragingly. "Less!" he admonished. "Thin! Thinner!"[33] Schoenberg showed that the cantus firmus had to impart some structure so that the long string of whole notes did not become pointlessly plodding. He suggested adding variety by making the middle six repetitions into half notes, giving the movement an underlying ABA structure. Freed from the one-way cul-de-sac implied by an unchanging cantus firmus, Harrison suddenly saw new opportunities for variation and internal structure that would make the movement work. Ultimately the *Suite* would become one of the finest of his early period. Schoenberg's advice, Harrison later recalled, "permanently disposed of for me not only that particular difficulty but also any of the kind that I might ever encounter."[34]

The encounter's value to Harrison extended beyond that single piece. "Simplify" became Schoenberg's own cantus firmus to Harrison's career, steering the young composer away from elaboration and complexity and toward the clarity and transparency of Mozart. For all his reputation as an ultramodernist revolutionary, Schoenberg the teacher remained very much a traditionalist. "He was very open and he took you seriously," Harrison recalled. "Schoenberg constantly moved me, and all his students, in the direction of simplicity—bring out only the salient."[35] Schoenberg admired Harrison's gift for melodic clarity and craved it in his own music: "Everything I touch turns to lead," he once despaired.[36]

Fulfilling Harrison's request, Frances Mullen performed Schoenberg's op. 25 *Suite* during the 1943 Evenings on the Roof season (the fifth in the series), along with Charles Ives's formidable *Concord* Sonata. And, after Schoenberg had showed Harrison how to finish his own *Suite for Piano*, Mullen performed it, the *Gigue and Musette*, and Harrison's *Cembalo Sonatas* the following year.[37]

But Harrison wasn't there to hear them. Less than a year after Bill Brown had come to Los Angeles for a job with Horton's company, the choreographer had decided to move his company to New York City, the capital of dance in America. A combination of the draft and the temptations of the movie industry had reduced his company from thirty-two members down to just eight, and Horton was eager to find a new venue for concert works.[38] A wealthy donor had offered them a venue at his new nightclub, the Folies Bergere. Some of the dancers were skeptical—a nightclub?—but it was a chance to be paid go to New York and perhaps hold the company together. For Horton, whose company was already regarded as perhaps the most important American dance ensemble outside New York, the move represented the last frontier.

Bill Brown—who by then had changed his professional name to William Weaver—went with them in the spring of 1943, and again there was an implication that Harrison could have the job as accompanist for the company. Harrison pondered the decision. Back in San Francisco, someone had told him that if he was going to make it big as a composer, he had to go to Paris, presumably to study with the great teacher Nadia Boulanger, as Copland and so many other American composers had (and would). At that moment, ever the contrarian, he resolved never to go to Paris.[39]

New York, though, was different. He already had a network there: Cage and Cowell were already there, his new friend Copland had moved back after his work on his film score, his idol Charles Ives had a brownstone in Manhattan, and Brown and Horton and Lewitzky—his circle of friends in LA—would all be there for him. Moreover, New York was the center of America's musical universe, hosting major orchestras, dance companies, festivals, publishers, and, crucially, performers and conductors who could perform the music.

At his last lesson with Schoenberg, Harrison told his mentor that he was moving to New York.

"Why are you going?" the old man asked.

"Well, I don't really know," the twenty-six-year-old Harrison replied.

"I know you're going for fame and fortune," Schoenberg said. "And good luck."

Harrison thanked him and rose to leave.

"Don't study with anybody; you don't need to study with anybody," his teacher told him. "Study only Mozart."[40]

Harrison realized then that he had "graduated" from studying Bach's polyphony in Schoenberg's class, because his teacher kept only Bach's and Mozart's music on his desk. Harrison immediately obtained scores of Mozart piano sonatas, which taught him crucial lessons about balance, proportion, and the salient. Two years later Schoenberg would name Harrison as one of America's most promising composers.[41]

On his last day in California, as he headed for the train station with Melissa Blake, Harrison expressed some anxiety about the cross-country trip. Blake stopped to buy him a St. Christopher medallion, so that the patron saint of travelers could keep him safe. Unfortunately, the store did not have St. Christopher, so she bought a St. Anthony medal instead. Why shouldn't St. Anthony help just as well, Harrison asked. "I'm sure that heaven is not a department store."[42] The saint would see him safely across the country, and later he would name the mass he had begun in San Francisco for the last-minute alternative saint.

Harrison may not have had much music to show for his year in Los Angeles, but it was a crucial part of an apprenticeship important not so much for his mastery of the particulars of the twelve-tone method as for the continued construction of a unique melodic voice. As the train rolled out of the station, Harrison could comfort himself with the thought that two of the century's greatest composers had told him that he was ready for the big time. And in a few days, he'd be there.

PART 3

A Hell of a Town

As his train pulled into Manhattan's Penn Station, Lou Harrison gazed at the metropolis's crowded streets and thought of Ishi, the last of the Yahi Indians. Ishi, who had lived in San Francisco from 1911 to 1916, said that what most impressed him were not the tall buildings and other great monuments of white civilization but rather the multitudes of people. As he disembarked, Harrison and his single suitcase were engulfed by hundreds of soldiers, black porters, and white businessmen invariably dressed in gray trilby hats. When he arrived in the summer of 1943, Harrison thought this colossal train station, with its grand art nouveau sculptures and war bond posters, was magnificent. "In those days," he recalled, "you entered New York like a king."[1]

Despite Henry Cowell's best efforts to establish a modern music scene on the West Coast, no one doubted New York's status as the hub of American artistic vitality. This was the city of the League of Composers and their journal, *Modern Music*; the Pan American Association of Composers; of Copland (except when working on films), Virgil Thomson, Edgard Varése, and many, many other composers. The center of the publishing industry, where aspiring novelists seemed as plentiful as yellow cabs, New York also boasted not only the new Museum of Modern Art (when such a focus was a rarity) but also a brand-new, competing Museum of Non-Objective Painting, to become better known under the name of its founder, Peggy Guggenheim. As in Los Angeles, the city harbored a sizable community of refugee artists, from French surrealists to German abstractionists.

Somewhere amid the bustle of Penn Station, Harrison found Bill Brown, who had come to pick him up. After the flooding sunlight of Los Angeles, the streets of Manhattan seemed like cool canyons between the cliffs of skyscrapers (or "scrapers" in the current New York slang). "Ah, New York," wrote Jean Cocteau in *Marriage at the Eiffel Tower*, a play for which Harrison would soon write music, "city of lovers and midday twilights!"[2] Crowded into these buildings were people from almost every conceivable ethnic group, often segregated into cramped neighborhoods that seemed claustrophobic after the expanse of Los Angeles. "It was a squalid place, with too much noise," Harrison concluded, "particularly for a Westerner who's used to being able to walk ten feet without interruption."[3]

Not long after Harrison arrived in New York City, one of his soon-to-be friends, Leonard Bernstein, wrote a musical whose most famous number begins, "New York, New York, a helluva town." While *On The Town* captured the vibrancy of mid-century America's most vibrant city, it also contained songs called "Lonely Town" and "I Wish I Was Dead."[4] As much of Harrison's upbeat San Francisco music reflects the excitement of new friends, discoveries, and experiences, the brooding and introspective works of his early New York years often wove dark thickets of dissonant counterpoint. However, conclusions about causal connections (either way) between Harrison's turbulent life and his moody music at best oversimplify his complex inner state and eclectic inspirations. What is clear is that much of his music from about 1944 to 1947 exudes a tense melancholy, a sorrowful yearning that seems to mirror his emotions of the time—a shadowy soundtrack to disturbing feelings and brushes with madness.

10

THE LONESOME ISLE (1943–1945)

From early on, Harrison walked everywhere around Manhattan island, imbibing its urban wonders. Naturally, one of the first things he acquired was a library card, but he found that almost every book he wanted was missing or checked out. So he acquired the habit—never broken—of buying books at Gotham's many little bookstores. He immediately continued his study of pre-classical music, from medieval religious dramas to Handel, and explored the city's museums and cultural sites.

But the excitement of being in New York quickly faded. Brown had found a tiny apartment on the Upper East Side, which was much noisier than any place Harrison had experienced in California. It had a bed but only a shared bathroom, no kitchen, and, worse, no piano.

One of Harrison's first visits was to the equally diminutive Greenwich Village home of John and Xenia Cage, an apartment so minuscule that guests sometimes had to sit under the piano keyboard during parties. Xenia's small inheritance had quickly been consumed, and Cage was reduced to washing walls at a Brooklyn YWCA.[1] But the Cages were as rich in connections as they were poor in funds, and for Harrison, their compact surroundings were merely a portal to an expansive world of vanguard art.

Upon arriving in New York a year before Harrison, the Cages had stayed with the painter Max Ernst, who had met Cage in Chicago, and the arts philanthropist Peggy Guggenheim. Through such contacts, they (and later, through them, Harrison) met a parade of famous artists: Andre Bréton, Piet Mondrian, Joseph Cornell, and the great Japanese American sculptor Isamu Noguchi, whose Village studio Harrison and Cage visited often. "I was just flabbergasted by the whole situation," Cage recalled later. "Somebody famous was dropping in every two minutes, it seemed."[2]

As soon as he had hit the ground in Manhattan, the ever-enterprising Cage began parlaying these new contacts into musical prospects. His reputation as an ultramodern percussion composer and the support of esteemed critic and composer Virgil Thomson led to a League of Composers-sponsored concert at the Museum of Modern Art.[3] The February 1943 concert, which featured not only Cage's works but also two of Harrison's pieces, received a favorable review by Cage's friend and Thomson protégé Paul Bowles in the *New York Herald Tribune*. The fact that the other reviews were dismissive, if not downright mocking, was less important than the attention and notoriety that resulted.[4] The March issue of *Life* magazine featured a two-page spread with photographs, making Cage overnight one of the most visible composers in New York.

But Peggy Guggenheim's hospitality evaporated when the famously jealous patron discovered that Cage, innocent of New York artistic squabbles, was also performing at MOMA, her archrival. Cage lost not only a benefactor but also his apartment.

A new friend, choreographer Jean Erdman, came to the rescue, offering her Greenwich Village apartment while she and her husband were teaching for the summer in Vermont. Erdman's husband, the dashing, forty-year-old Sarah Lawrence College professor Joseph Campbell, had already electrified the academic world with his pioneering studies of the cultural significance of ancient myths, soon to reach popular audiences in his 1948 book *The Hero with a Thousand Faces*.[5] Campbell analyzed myths through the psychologist Carl Jung's concept of the collective unconscious, elucidating the shared themes that pervade human mythology and religions.

Cage recruited Erdman and Campbell—both of whom would become two of Harrison's most important colleagues in New York—to play in his percussion ensemble. In lieu of paying rent, Cage agreed to compose new pieces for Erdman to choreograph with his friend Merce Cunningham for the Martha Graham company's summer workshop at Bennington College. Graham had invited Cunningham to join her New York company in 1939, and he had become its star, happily reuniting with Cage when he had arrived.

A few months later, after Cage encouraged her to give a concert with Cunningham, Erdman left Graham's company to embark on a solo career. At a February 1943 concert in Chicago, Erdman choreographed an important work she called *Creature on a Journey* to Harrison's *Counterdance in Spring*, after Cage suggested that the music (which he had performed in Chicago the previous February) would suit Erdman's Balinese-inspired choreography. Harrison's colorful polyrhythms complemented Erdman's red-yellow-and-blue-costumed, skittering, birdlike dance.[6]

After creating the role of the Preacher and choreographing his own solo in Copland's landmark *Appalachian Spring* in October 1944, Cunningham also left Graham's company, and Cage would soon write several compelling scores for him and Erdman. So Cage had, in a few short months, become well placed enough to introduce his old friend Lou to a major segment of the progressive New York artistic community.

Also in his first week in New York, Harrison had eagerly reestablished contact and conversation with his other best friend—his old mentor Henry Cowell, now working for the Office of War Information and living with his wife Sidney in an apartment in Greenwich Village. Cowell and his social circle embraced Harrison, providing some of the happiest moments in his otherwise bleak New York years.

Harrison soon found that he needed his old California friends to survive. He had moved to the city counting on getting regular work as a composer for Lester Horton's company, but Horton's troupe already detested the nightclub venue. Horton began rehearsals for revivals of *Tierra y Libertad!* and *Something to Please Everybody*,[7] but the show's backer was an industrialist whose fortune was tied to trade with the Soviet

Union, which had just been attacked by Nazi Germany. The production collapsed, and Horton's company dissolved.[8]

Suddenly jobless only weeks after arriving, Harrison found that his dance world connections didn't count for much in this new city. In December 1943, he found a gig playing percussion for dancer Anna Sokolow, but money woes quickly grew so acute that he took a job as an elevator operator at Radio City Music Hall, where he escorted Shirley Temple and Paul Whiteman to performances.[9]

Just as Harrison had secured job offers for Cage when they first met, Cage now introduced him to Minna Lederman, cofounder of the League of Composers and editor of their journal, *Modern Music,* which Virgil Thomson called "a Bible and a news organ, a forum, a source of world information, and the defender of their faith."[10] With contributors such as Copland, Cowell, Paul Bowles, Edwin Denby, and many other distinguished composers and writers, Lederman "developed a stable of writing composers who wrote with wit and clarity, who were invariably interesting and, in a surprising number of cases, wonderful stylists. Surely no such gathering of superb composer-writers has existed before, nor is it likely to again in the foreseeable future."[11]

And now it would include Lou Harrison. At the interview in her Manhattan office, Lederman immediately assigned him to review new music commissioned for summer band concerts in Central Park and worked with him on his draft until it was publishable. This first writing assignment brought no pay but introduced him to "everyone of importance" in modern music circles.[12] Lederman, a rigorous editor, taught Harrison the basics of arts journalism, a skill that would lead to other opportunities. Harrison also did some editorial work for *New Music,* Henry Cowell's magazine. By 1945, Cowell had named Harrison the magazine's assistant editor. Unfortunately, the editors weren't paid; Cowell, in fact, was subsidizing the magazine.

In *Modern Music,* Harrison proved a thoughtful, balanced, and thoroughly insightful critic, able to incorporate his technical knowledge of composition and music theory while still making reviews accessible to general readers. He was abetted by his native wit and the example of *Herald Tribune* critic Virgil Thomson, who never let caution inhibit his own bons mots: "It was supposed to be built as a Gothic arch and sounded like a prairie," Harrison wrote of a piece by American composer Roy Harris.[13] He judged that Samuel Barber "seems fascinated in turn by each of the famous masks and mantles. If he ever catches up with himself he certainly will be a composer of power and interest."[14]

Harrison had his favorites—Schoenberg, Ives, Wallingford Riegger—but usually managed to help his readers understand the flaws as well as the delights of all of his subjects. "Ives no longer purposes to speak for the rest of us at the gates of heaven; rather, in the best gentleman-scholar fashion . . . he assembles the data of his observed surroundings and tells the tale, not without tenderness, of what he and his friends were like and where they lived. His aim is amazingly close to that of the best Chinese poetry (wherein observed fact is more expressive than referred likeness)."[15]

Harrison also found much to praise in the music of friends such as Cage, Cowell, Paul Bowles, and Thomson, who shared many of his artistic inclinations. But with lesser music, Harrison's pen could be sharp: "Mrs. Rapoport's piece labored over a number of inexplicable silences and curious phrase confusions, while Franco's work cracked up in an unplanned morass of textural ineptitudes."[16]

Like Thomson, Harrison used his reviewer's pulpit to make larger points about the state of music. "One gets quite a shock on hearing the Berg Sonata now to realize how callously the movies live on what they borrow," he wrote. "If ever a Hollywood star made love or sighed on a solitary cliff this music is the unwilling grand-papa of her accompaniment. Commercial musicians ought to be assessed for every idea they take from a creative artist's works, since they tax the capacity of such composers to keep them supplied with ideas to imitate, exploit, and one might add, cheapen."[17]

While he was reacquainting himself with old friends and making new ones, losing one job and gaining others, Harrison's personal life was deteriorating. As fall 1943 turned to winter, Harrison's relationship with Brown soured, and finally Brown left for another man. Unable to afford a place on his own, Harrison temporarily moved in with a dancer friend in Manhattan's then-notorious Hell's Kitchen. Around the same time, he received a letter bearing devastating news: His ex-lover Sherman Slayback had drowned in an accident at the New Jersey coast in September 1943, trying to save a friend. Harrison felt guilty about driving Sherman away, and news of his death plunged him even deeper into depression.

His tenuous emotional state was exacerbated by the phenomenon that would haunt his entire decade in New York: the city's unremitting noise. Sirens, car horns, buses, and foghorns from the waterfront kept him awake and wondering how he would ever be able to compose in such an environment. The lack of air conditioning meant that most apartments had open windows facing into common alleyways, courtyards, or streets. Harrison and Cage frequented sidewalk kosher delis so they could sit outside during the summer heat. But the noise barely abated as the weather cooled.

Harrison was desperate; that winter he wrote Peter Yates, saying that he was planning to move back to California. That February, Yates wrote a glowing profile of the young composer for *Arts and Architecture* magazine, predicting that Harrison would be the most outstanding new American composer since Roy Harris.[18] But the city, unimpressed with Yates's opinion, offered Harrison few opportunities to have his music heard.

Having lost his old lover, his current partner, and his main source of income within a few months of his arrival, and living in dismal, clamorous surroundings with no outlet for his music, in late 1943 Harrison wrote to his brother Bill, who had just gotten married, and said that he was already lovelorn and disillusioned by New York: "The more you see of life and people, the more you will know what a miracle [love] is. . . . You can look about you and see men either made or broken by it. . . . But whether you are made or broken by it, never let it die. Treasure it. It means the difference between real life as it was meant to be or the life of the one who died inside years before."[19]

One frigid day that winter, Harrison trudged home, regarded the depressing squalor of his friend's tiny, grubby flat, turned on the gas—and didn't light the jet.

The streets ran off at odd angles in all directions. She saw storefronts with awnings shading cluttered sidewalks, kids chasing one another in front of a grocery, delivery trucks stopping and starting their way up the street. Walking north on 7th Avenue, she saw the skyscrapers of midtown in the distance and when she turned around, the cluster of tall buildings in the financial district in the south. But in this spot most buildings were two or three stories, and a few higher than five or six. . . . Everywhere she looked she saw people—people talking to one another, it seemed, every few feet, casually dressed women window-shopping, old men with hands clasped on canes sitting on the benches in a triangular park. . . . This was home.[20]

This was the Greenwich Village that Jane Jacobs, soon to become America's fore-most urbanist, saw when she moved there around the same time that Lou Harrison found a "big, mirthless" walkup apartment above an Italian bakery on Bleecker Street in spring 1944.[21] Not long after Harrison had given up his halfhearted suicide attempt after an hour or so (the Hell's Kitchen studio simply took too long to fill up with gas), he learned of a vacancy near his friends Cowell and Cage, in the part of New York that suited him perfectly; he would make his home for the rest of his sojourn there.

Greenwich Village's sense of community spawned a bohemian enclave of poets, philosophers, and political activists. An influx of European refugees added to the neighborhood's intellectual mix; several taught at the iconoclastic New School for Social Research on Twelfth Street, as did Cowell and Copland. The predecessor of the Whitney Art Museum showed modern works on Eighth Street, and painters peri-odically exhibited their works on the streets by Washington Square and gathered at dimly lit jazz clubs and bars such as the Cedar Tavern, the celebrated watering hole of the nascent New York School abstract expressionists.

The Village also teemed with modern musicians. John and Xenia Cage lived near Harrison's new apartment, and just down the street were Henry and Sidney Cowell. Paul Bowles and Peggy Glanville-Hicks lived on nearby Tenth Street, Ben Weber on Eleventh, and Elliott Carter was up on Twelfth. The Cherry Lane Theater and Theater de Lys harbored venues for their music and modern dance.

Along with its artistic richness, Greenwich Village suited Harrison and many of his colleagues because of its hospitality to homosexuality. Allen Ginsberg went to the Village in 1943 because that was where "all the fairies were," and he hung out with William Burroughs, Jack Kerouac, Gregory Corso, and Living Theater found-ers Julian Beck and Judith Malina (soon to become close friends of Harrison's) at Bleecker Street's San Remo bar.[22]

Harrison put up a beautiful purple curtain in his new place and exposed the walls to show the red bricks.[23] Beams projected through the floor, up to a high ceiling. But in winter it was chilly, and lugging kerosene canisters up four flights of stairs soon tempered any romance of living in Greenwich Village, as did a nearby church whose choir preferred cloyingly sweet arrangements. "I swore off parallel thirds after that," he said.[24] Nevertheless, the proximity that his flat provided to nearby sympathetic friends and artists—a hallmark of the Village's creative fertility—provided Harrison a stable launch pad for a series of ever-widening orbits through New York's vibrant cultural landscape. Within days of settling in, he began widening his social circles.

THE STATE OF MUSIC

Lou Harrison sat on the sofa and looked around the ninth-floor apartment he was visiting in New York's famed Hotel Chelsea, temporary home of bohemian celebrity artists from Mark Twain to Dylan Thomas. The spacious, rosewood-paneled front parlor, which smelled of cinnamon and citronella, boasted a bay window that looked down over Greenwich Village. Next to it, near the fireplace, stood a grand piano. Paintings, many by modern European masters (including a portrait of the apartment's tenant and a Duchamp drawing), covered the walls, or at least that part of them unadorned by bookshelves. A closet had been converted into a kitchen, with a long table defining the dining area between parlor and bedroom.[25] For decades this suite constituted the home of the composer and critic who, according to the *New York Times*'s John Rockwell, "had given us as profound a vision of American culture as anyone has yet achieved."[26] And Harrison was about to meet him.

After a brief sojourn in New York, the Kansas City-born Virgil Thomson had spent many years amid post-World War I Paris's American expatriates, where he combined his background as a Baptist organist and Harvard intellectual with a new enthusiasm for the music of Erik Satie to forge a style of calculated naivety, spicing Midwestern simplicity with Gallic wit. Thomson's collaboration with another expatriate, Gertrude Stein, on the landmark opera *Four Saints in Three Acts* became the longest-running opera in Broadway history, brought modernism into the mainstream, and made Thomson a star (though not an income) in New York music circles after its 1934 debut there.[27]

A similarly sharp facility with language earned Thomson a job as an arts correspondent for American publications, leading to the publication of a book that impressed Harrison: the feisty 1939 broadside *The State of Music*, which, contrary to the romantic image, revealed how composers were inextricably bound to and influenced by their patronage and the whole business of music. Driven back to the United States in August 1940 by the impending Nazi invasion of Paris, Thomson became chief music critic for New York's "other" major paper, the *Herald Tribune*, and used that position to advance his agenda of promoting American music while also maintaining his own composing career. Perhaps the finest writer (literally—he never learned to type) in the history of American music criticism, Thomson's usually witty reviews were always trenchantly opinionated, well informed, and often brilliant. "The function of criticism," he wrote, "is to aid the public in digesting musical works. Not for nothing does it so often resemble bile."[28]

While in Los Angeles, Harrison had read and cherished Thomson's tome, not only for its "basic good sense" about music (including denunciations of Wagner and other shibboleths of the musical establishment), but also for its fresh wit and humor, qualities rare in music punditry.[29] Its wry commentary on America's lack of social support for artists may have led Harrison to prankishly write the mayor of New York, asking if his office could arrange a piano for the newcomer.[30]

Harrison resolved to meet Thomson as soon as possible, and he asked Cage to facilitate a meeting. "He had a combination of St. Louis and Paris," Harrison said of the author, who, clad in his usual orange pajamas, came out to greet him.[31] The two quick-witted composers hit it off immediately, and Thomson became one of the most important in the series of vital mentors Harrison found throughout his life. "We're round, pink-faced intellectuals, you and me," Thomson told him, "and we therefore share a certain point of view."[32] They shared more than that: Thomson was also gay, but he kept his sexuality closeted. Thomson could be prickly and catty to many of his friends, but he always regarded Harrison and his music with an affection that Harrison reciprocated.

After a brief interview, Thomson hired Harrison as his copyist (as he had composers Ned Rorem, Paul Bowles, and Ben Weber), and Harrison visited the Chelsea apartment often to copy parts and pass time in conversation about subjects like orchestration, Europe, music history, and American composition. Thomson soon offered Harrison another plum opportunity: writing freelance music reviews for the *Herald Tribune*. Beginning in November 1944, Harrison joined Thomson's stable of composer/critics, which would include Cage, Rorem, Bowles, Carter, Peggy Glanville-Hicks, Arthur Berger, and others.

For many of his New York nights over the next few years, Harrison would attend a concert and then rush over to the *Tribune*'s smoky, stuffy, city-block-sized newsroom to pound out a review on one of its antique typewriters, after which he might repair to the *Trib* staff's Fortieth Street hangout, the Artists and Writers Café (informally known as Bleeck's, after its proprietor), as the paper went to press,[33] "walking past shooting galleries and X-rated movie arcades and novelty shops, past papaya juice stands and Nick's and Bickford's, past strip clubs and jazz clubs and cheap hotels, past Jack Dempsey's and the Latin Quarter and the Paramount, where legions of bobby-soxers lined up on the sidewalk for a chance to swoon over Frank Sinatra," in the words of the paper's movie critic, William Zinsser.[34] Sometimes Harrison would accompany Thomson to concerts, where his job included nudging the *Herald Tribune*'s chief critic when he dozed off during a boring performance.[35]

When one of Harrison's more than three hundred reviews evaluated the music of his friends, he would become more descriptive and less judgmental. "This music is so sensually attractive by reason of the delicacy and color of the sounds its author arranges by muting the piano strings with different materials that it requires much listening for the average ear to find beneath the surface the enormous play of intellect and imagination that is there," Harrison opined about one of Cage's 1946 prepared-piano concerts.[36] Even in other reviews, Thomson required his critics to focus on the event itself, emphasizing that "what you're doing is reporting on an event, like a fire in the Bronx or something," as Bowles recalled. "You go, he says, tell what you see, you don't say 'I didn't like the color of the fire. I don't like the smell of the burning rubber.' Don't tell what you like or don't like because no one cares.... [A] recital at Town Hall or Carnegie Hall was an event. He always stressed that: What happened?"[37]

Like the other *Tribune* critics, Harrison studied the scores as well as attending the concerts and talked about them with the composers, once discussing a score with the great Brazilian composer Heitor Villa-Lobos over melting ice cream as he was preparing a January 1945 essay on the composer's *Chôros* for *Modern Music*.[38] Since Thomson liked to assign his freelancers concerts that matched their interests and knowledge, Harrison often wound up covering concerts involving non-Western music, experimentalists, young composers, and authentic early music performance practice.

His experience at *Modern Music* and the *Tribune* later led to publications in other magazines, including *Listen* and the avant-garde arts magazine *View*. Besides providing him desperately needed income, the *Tribune* job helped flesh out Harrison's musical education. "During my period of sitting in concert halls in New York, I gradually learned the European repertoire which everybody is expected to know," he recalled, "but I heard them live and I heard different interpretations."[39]

PARTY PIECES

Henry Cowell is like a modern music genius, born forth from the shell of a grand piano. His sonorities surge out like smokes and the salt sprays of associations wet your face.

—Lou Harrison, 1946[40]

Henry Cowell sat on the sofa in Lou Harrison's Greenwich Village apartment, scribbling notes on a piece of paper. He folded it and passed it over to John Cage, who did the same, writing a measure of music, folding the paper so that only the last notes of the measure were visible, and passing it over to Harrison, who, after adding his contribution, handed it over to Virgil Thomson. Each composer started with a blank sheet of paper, meaning several sheets were rotating throughout the room in what Harrison described as a "sort of surrealist assembly line."[41] After enough passes around, one of them would play the usually amusing result on the piano.

Throughout his life, Harrison enjoyed making music with friends, from percussion ensembles to gamelans. This particular game was a variation on the French surrealist "exquisite corpse" game—a round-robin drawing in which the paper is folded so that each participant can see only the edge of the previous contribution, with musical notation substituting for the drawings that the surrealist artists used to pass around.[42]

Cowell's apartment also provided Harrison with a social circle. Now safely ensconced in sympathetic if not comfortable surroundings, he began building the network that would sustain him throughout his New York years. "If you were close to Henry, everyone was around all the time," Harrison remembered, including the composers Vladimir Ussachevsky and Otto Luening, both at Columbia University, and Wallingford Riegger.[43] Elliott Carter, with whom Harrison shared a love for the music of Charles Ives, would often stop by. Frank Wigglesworth, a "stout, pink, and jolly" New Englander who had studied with Cowell and with Luening, shared Harrison's interest in medieval music and careful counterpoint.[44] The charming Ben

Weber (like Wigglesworth, nearly the same age as Harrison) possessed a wit as biting as his twelve-tone dissonances. A gourmet cook, he sometimes invited Harrison, Cage, Thomson, and others over for dinner at his apartment.

Cowell also introduced Harrison to composer Merton Brown, whose "doleful blue eyes, fair wavy hair, a small blond moustache, a meager rickety frame, and a dry New England voice"[45] soon became a frequent presence at Harrison's Village apartment, where he often sought musical advice.[46] Brown in turn introduced Harrison to his handsome, sandy-haired partner, John Heliker, a painter whose canvasses were frequently as bright and likable as he was. Heliker and Brown had met in 1942 at the Vermont farmhouse of their mutual friend, the composer (and painter) Carl Ruggles, and often joined Harrison's other friends at his apartment, where Schaefer beer was consumed in liberal amounts.[47]

These get-togethers provided Harrison some of his happiest moments in an otherwise gray and alienating city. The Cowells enjoyed a tradition of musical gatherings, with Henry often contributing small pieces for himself and his wife or for visiting friends. He liked to hand out recorders to the guests, and they would read through a new piece he'd written for the occasion.[48] In 1943 Harrison contributed his own *Serenade*, an affable miniature for three recorders.

Harrison also embraced a charming tonality in "Polka" and "Jarabe," two ultimately unused pieces he composed for the choreographer José Limón, and in the first of three piano waltzes—"Waltz in A" (1944), "Waltz in C" (1945), and "Hesitation Waltz" (1951)—he would later collect as his *New York Waltzes*. The spirit of old-time New York reminded him of such favorites as "Take Me Out to the Ball Game" and "Bicycle Built for Two."[49] Each a delightful miniature in unabashed triadic harmonies, despite the occasional spice of chromaticism and dissonance, their brief simplicity echoes the Francophilic "portraits" Virgil Thomson was writing at the time. That's no surprise, because not only would Thomson become one of the key figures in Harrison's career, but he would also lead him into the most important of New York's artistic circles.

LITTLE FRIENDS

"The trouble with the New York musical world," groused the ever-crusty Edgard Varése, "is that it's dominated by homosexuals."[50] Besides being accomplished composers, most of Virgil Thomson's colleagues, whom he called "the little friends," shared another striking similarity: Practically all of them were gay or bisexual.[51] The perfumed Paul Bowles maintained what Thomson called "a queer marriage" with his lesbian wife, Jane, in their all-white apartment (including piano) that, according to Ned Rorem, reeked of patchouli and ambergris.[52] Leonard Bernstein, also married, vacillated among sexual preferences throughout his life. After his release from prison, Cowell seems to have played it straight, but despite the cowboy associations of his Americana music, Copland was gay.

The association of homosexuality with creativity has occasioned much speculation, but perhaps what is just as important is that the composers, Bernstein excepted, lacked the responsibilities of family life and were able to live a vibrant downtown life of constant artistic and intellectual stimulation. On the other hand, Harrison found that New York's gay life was, in those pre-Stonewall days, much more closeted than he'd experienced in San Francisco. "The first time I encountered that feeling of tightness and constraint, or uptightness," he remembered, "was in New York."[53]

In reviewing a new edition of Tchaikovsky's diaries in 1946, Harrison was struck by poignant scenes of terrible loneliness that led the great homosexual Russian composer to leave his hotel in a strange city to "carouse."[54] The traumatic example of Cowell's imprisonment still haunted musical circles, and in March 1942, Thomson himself had been arrested in a raid of a well-known gay bordello run out of a private home. Although the *Tribune* used its influence to free Thomson and keep his involvement secret, the owner of the house was sentenced to twenty years in prison for sodomy.[55]

It was therefore a shock when a magnetic young poet that Harrison met, Robert Duncan, published an article titled "The Homosexual in Society" in the leftist journal *Politics* in 1944. Duncan's poetry brought together a wild anarchism and an encyclopedic reference to myth and medieval literature that especially appealed to Harrison. Duncan gave a few poetry lessons to Harrison and Cage, assigning them exercises like creating a poem with five or six given words. As the rigorous Thomson left his mark on Harrison's prose, Duncan's influence on Harrison's poetry would last throughout his life, as their friendship continued later in California. Duncan's open advocacy for gay rights likewise remained an inspiration.[56]

As Varèse's homophobic comment above reveals, the "little friends" still faced bigotry in 1940s New York. While publicly supportive of Cage's music, Varèse in private railed against Thomson and his entourage, including Cage and Harrison (who nevertheless innocently continued to admire Varèse, adopting the habit of bowing whenever he passed the composer's apartment).[57] Harrison's friend Ben Weber, who was on friendly terms with Varèse, reported later that the elder composer "never failed to demolish people that he had antipathies toward like John Cage, Lou Harrison and Virgil."[58] Even politically progressive artists worried about the supposedly baleful, feminizing influence of a midcentury "homintern" (a takeoff on the Comintern, or the Communist International).[59]

This repressive atmosphere must have pushed Harrison's composer acquaintances closer together. Harrison's New York life benefited enormously from the instant social circle of "little friends" surrounding Virgil Thomson, including rising young composers David Diamond, Bernstein, Rorem, Bowles, Cage, and many more established composers, such as Samuel Barber and Gian Carlo Menotti.[60] Frequently they converged at Thomson's Chelsea apartment. Thomson was a celebrated host with a fine cook and a penchant for party games. Harrison remembered one such party when Bernstein, who'd just performed that night, was called away to take a phone call and returned to tell the gathering, "A lady just called to tell me I'm a genius."

"Leonard," Thomson replied, "everyone in this room is a genius."[61]

Including its central figure. "Thomson was a genius at social manipulation," his friend, New York City Ballet founder Lincoln Kirstein, said. In lining up support for his own musical projects such as *Four Saints*, Thomson brilliantly sussed out Manhattan salons and other elite New York and other cities' social circles but was also familiar with Harlem. He provided Harrison with a glimpse into, if not patronage from, the elite world of the New York arts establishment.[62]

Harrison soon realized that, even among the tonalists in the League of Composers, two camps had emerged—those aligned with Thomson and those associated with Copland. Harrison learned that this split came to a head over Cage's notorious MOMA percussion concert, which Thomson engineered behind the scenes, outmaneuvering Copland, who firmly opposed the League sponsoring such experimental music.[63]

Thomson privately grumbled that the League had become Copland's private fiefdom and that Copland used his influence to promote his own protégés (as if such an accusation could never be made against Thomson). While the two shared reverence for American folk music forms and were outwardly cordial and mutually supportive, the discreet Copland was never comfortable with Thomson's more flamboyant mannerisms and his use of his newspaper position for self-advancement as a composer.[64] It seemed strange that Thomson should invite the West Coast radicals Cage and Harrison into his clique of tonal composers, but to Thomson, keen intellect and fresh ideas outranked aesthetic differences. In his autobiography, Thomson wrote, "With all his rigors, Cage has a wit and breadth of thought that make him a priceless companion. For hours, days, and months with him one would probe music's philosophy. And after Lou Harrison, with his larger reading and more demanding ear, had arrived from the West, the three of us provided for one another, with Europe and the Orient cut off by war, a musical academy of theory and practice."[65]

After its turbulent false start, by the end of Harrison's second year in New York, he found himself at the center of the city's—and the country's—vibrant contemporary music scene, learning the latest musical developments and making new friends. But of all the friends that Harrison spent time with in New York, two were paramount. One was his erstwhile San Francisco percussion partner and best friend. The other would be his first great love.

11

NEW YORK WALTZES (1945–1946)

Oh you whom I often and silently come where you are, that I may be with you,
As I walk by your side, or sit near, or remain in the same room with you,
Little you know the subtle electric fire that for your sake is playing within me.
—Walt Whitman[1]

Since high school, Harrison had felt a special connection to the sensitive portrayal of a homosexual romance in Walt Whitman's "Calamus" poems. Now immersed in a new love relationship, Harrison set these lines in 1946 in "Fragment from Calamus," a brief, through-composed song for baritone that evokes love's "subtle electric fire," transcending everyday experience in the same way that the piece's dissonant counterpoint lifts the listener from the earthly gravity of tonality. When Ben Weber teased that Harrison had written another "Ich liebe dich," Harrison responded, "Why not? Love songs are the most popular forms of songs, and I'd never done one before."[2]

Since Bill Brown had left him, Lou Harrison had felt adrift. Despite finding old and new friends through Cage, Cowell, and Thomson, Harrison's first year in New York City had been troubled and depressing. While most nights he went out to dinner or perhaps a movie with John Cage,[3] he also took to cruising New York's gay pickup spots—bars and other places where the city's repressive laws forced homosexual men to seek companions. He frequented urinals at Harlem subway stops.[4] Much later, Harrison estimated that he'd had fifteen hundred lovers over his lifetime—most of them, including a half dozen women, during his difficult New York nights.[5] One night in the fall of 1944, at a New York theater on Forty-Second Street, he picked up a tall, very dark, handsome man named Edward McGowan. Unlike many other such brief encounters, this one blossomed immediately.

McGowan, a minister in a Bronx-based African American Methodist Episcopal church, was deeply involved in the nascent civil rights movement, working to change discriminatory practices then prevalent in New York.[6] Besides their liberal political beliefs, McGowan and Harrison shared a warm personality and a gift for conversation that made them easy companions. They attended concerts and theater productions together, including Orson Welles's famous production of *Othello* at Broadway's

Shubert Theater, starring McGowan's friend Paul Robeson and Uta Hagen, who shared a groundbreaking interracial kiss onstage.[7]

With his preacher's charm and amiable humor, McGowan often persuaded artists, actors, and activists to attend his church services in the Bronx. Harrison admired McGowan's sermon-style storytelling, including biblical tales, and McGowan would sometimes come over to Harrison's apartment on Saturdays for help working out a sermon for the next day. Harrison arranged a "fairly rollicking" version of "Onward, Christian Soldiers" for trumpet and organ and heard it performed at McGowan's church.[8]

McGowan introduced Harrison to a whole new world of African American artists and activists, a social circle that revolved around the dancer and painter Frank Neal and his wife, Dorcas. Actor Brock Peters, singer Harry Belafonte, and the jazz composer Billy Strayhorn were among the artists who gathered often for late-night chats and eats in their second floor walkup on Twenty-Eighth Street between Broadway and Fifth Avenue. Cage and Harrison were two of the few white members of what came to be called the "Neal Salon." They also frequented an inexpensive Caribbean restaurant in the Village near Harrison's house known to them as Connie's Calypso, after the owner, where they sometimes chatted with the young waiter and aspiring novelist James Baldwin.[9] In the two-plus years their relationship lasted, McGowan provided a central stabilizing pillar in Harrison's otherwise unsettled life in New York.

THE PERILOUS NIGHT

As Harrison's life finally found some order, Cage's was in turmoil. His relationship with Merce Cunningham led Cage to question his sexual identity, and Cage's friends urged him to seek psychoanalysis. Now, Xenia having expelled him from their apartment, Cage found, in a decaying tenement on Monroe Street, a spacious seventh-floor loft with no kitchen, no bathroom, and no view. He cut windows in the walls, revealing a dramatic river view, created a bathroom and a kitchenette, and painted all the walls white. Eschewing decorations and even furniture, save for a beige studio couch, a drafting table with fluorescent lamp, Lippold mobiles, straw matting for guests to sit on, and a piano (filled with bolts, erasers, and other implements), Cage said this new home "turns its back to the city and looks to the water and the sky" and thus invited quiet contemplation and discussions about aesthetics with Harrison and Merton Brown.[10] And it was probably there that Cage and Harrison had their single, drunken sexual encounter, while both were in a state of flux over their relationships and sexual identity.[11]

Although hardly an autobiographical composer, Cage wrote works in this period whose titles at least echo the upheaval in his life. Joseph Campbell's collection of Irish myths inspired Cage's haunting prepared-piano work *The Perilous Night*, which Harrison's review called "a set of whispers about some unknown plot in some otherworldly bedchamber."[12]

One day Harrison showed up at Merce Cunningham's studio and showed Cunningham and Cage a fascinating book he had discovered in Los Angeles, the *I Ching*.

Perhaps struck by the resemblance between its series of randomly built-up figures called hexagrams and Labanotation, he thought it could be useful for choreography. At the time Cage could not see a use for it, but later he would famously apply its methods to chance composition, an idea that never occurred to Harrison, who was thus unwittingly involved in one of the twentieth century's most important aesthetic developments—one he himself came to deplore.[13]

Both Harrison and Cage were still desperately poor, and each helped the other whenever circumstances allowed—lending each other a few dollars when possible. "John and I instituted a 'floating five,'" Harrison recalled. "In the long run, we never could figure out whose original five it was. 'But, John, I need the five today,' Or, he would say, 'I need the five today,' or something. But that would get us through the day."[14]

CHANGING MOMENT

By proposing a group of musicians playing together, then, made up of melodies which are to one another of right rhythm, considerate direction, and choice interval, it shows between its several voices, in what we differ from one another, in what we resemble one another, but in the whole reflects the affectionate unity of all persons. In this it is pleasing to God. . . . The presence of a formal interval is like the presence of the divine spirit. Anyone who has known what it is to sing or play among a group of others a voice modestly contrived to accord with the others will know of the pleasure and friendliness he feels in that accordance. . . . Formal counterpoint is thus a suitable music for a proud and friendly people, for all among the voices are needed and each goes out to meet a proud and friendly equal. The various voices meet above in the air and are joined together. A good work of formal counterpoint is a listening exercise in the love of friends.

—Lou Harrison[15]

By 1945, as World War II's end approached, the Village artists' spirits seemed to lift accordingly. Lou Harrison's life likewise seemed more stable than it had since he had moved to New York. He was in love, and he was firmly embedded in several vital social and artistic networks. Those feelings of cooperative interaction among highly diverse and fascinating individuals seemed to permeate his music of the moment as well. In the music he wrote during his first New York years, surprisingly varied influences contended for a place in his musical palette. A cheery little dance (like the *Waltz in A* dedicated to McGowan) might be followed a few weeks later by a thorny atonal experiment. A composition might share the most modern experimental techniques—and musical forms from the seventeenth century.

This bifurcation was nothing new to Harrison, whose San Francisco notebooks reveal adventurous "voluntary" experiments quite distinct from the dance pieces he was then writing to order. But with no performance opportunities yet apparent in New York, he was free to try all manner of styles and explore books and theories that would lead his music in new directions. Harrison continued to work with Schoenberg's twelve-tone method, first in an engaging little piano piece offered to Cowell,

A 12-Tone Morning After to Amuse Henry, but more significantly in a large string quartet whose use of Schoenberg's models for creating harmonies from fragments of the row, canons, and other alternatives shows much more confidence in the idiom than his earlier *Suite for Piano*'s strictly linear use of the row.

More startling was his new use of octaves, Schoenberg's verboten interval. Conventional twelve-tone composers thought the emphasis that octave doublings gave to particular pitches betrayed the method's goal of equality of tones, but that very emphasis allowed Harrison's natural instinct for clear melodies to emerge from the thorny thicket of a texture. Excited about this innovation, he boasted to John Cage that in his new string quartet, he had "discovered" the octave. After listening to Harrison play the piece on the piano, Cage laughed, "You discovered the octave? Why Lou, listen to them now!" He did and discovered that the octaves provided only a superficial masking of "various concatenations of discords" decorating a pointless circularity. In his zeal to work out the intellectual puzzle, "I had been lost to sound and sense," he concluded. Harrison abandoned the quartet and would only later discover the reason for his failure to reconcile octaves and atonality when he began his studies of just intonation.[16]

A more successful experiment originated in Harrison's studies of the scores of Edgard Varèse. In *Changing Moment,* a piano work Harrison composed for a Jean Erdman dance in 1946, he applied Varèse's characteristically disjunct motives and pitch sets of adjacent semitones (rather like Cowell's clusters, spread out). The raindrops of staccato notes fall around atmospheric sustained chords, replacing Varèse's hard-edged aggression with clarity and counterpoint.

Although Harrison's tonal works, atonal works, and studies with Cowell and Schoenberg seem so diverse as to come from different composers, they converged in one major respect: counterpoint. Within so-called formal or "strict" counterpoint, he distinguished the different types he had discerned during his study with Cowell: tertial (that is, based on thirds, which is the conventional sort taught in theory textbooks), secundal (based on seconds, Cowell's dissonant counterpoint), quintal or quartal (based on fourths or fifths), and finally, for completeness's sake, octaval (based on the octave). Harrison called the intervals that formed the basis for each style—secundal, tertial, quintal, octaval—the "formal interval" or "choice interval."[17]

But as he came to idealize harmony in both music and his lonely life, counterpoint meant much more than an abstract musical technique. As the quotation above reveals, for Harrison, counterpoint served as a metaphor about how to live one's life. It provided the framework in which melodies, while retaining their individuality, cooperate toward a greater whole, or what he called "our best spirit." In this sense, the music he was making in New York reflected his social circumstances amid Thomson's, McGowan's, Cage's, and Cowell's social networks.

Harrison's equation of music with friendship is a lifelong trope, from his early days in the percussion ensemble through his joy in participating in gamelan ensembles. He was happiest not in making small talk at parties, nor in hermit-like conditions (though composing often required them), but instead in making music together with friends, an activity he now sorely missed.

Quintal counterpoint had given a distinctive sound to such works as the *Gigue and Musette* he wrote in Los Angeles, but it is rather harmonically limiting, especially to a young composer steeped in the complex sonorities of Schoenberg and Ruggles. In his search to reconcile complex harmonies with strict quintal counterpoint, Harrison found one solution through the theories of one of New York's war refugees, a Jewish Viennese composer named Hugo Kauder, who taught counterpoint and violin at a small New York music school. Harrison probably heard some of his gently dissonant, modal compositions in new music concerts around town.[18]

Kauder's application of the principles of counterpoint to non-diatonic scales opened new compositional possibilities for Harrison. Like Joseph Yasser, whose book had first given Harrison his idea for quintal counterpoint, Kauder argued that such counterpoint is most appropriate for pentatonic scales, as found in much Asian music. Kauder, however, extrapolated this idea to more complex sonorities, stacking fourths and fifths, which Henry Cowell had also suggested in his *New Musical Resources*.[19] Harrison saw in Kauder's works the possibility for a solution that yielded yet another variant of his contrapuntal methods: a combination of quintal and dissonant counterpoint that treated perfect fourths as well as minor sevenths (i.e., two stacked fourths) as consonant, along with their inversions, perfect fifths and major seconds. Unlike the bare harmonic resources of strict quintal counterpoint, this quintal/secundal method provides a variety of stable sonorities based on these gently dissonant combinations, comparable to the different sorts of triads in traditional counterpoint.

These theoretical explorations led to new developments in Harrison's music, beginning with a 1940s sketch that later became his *Easter Cantata* when he completed it in 1966. Like a baroque celebratory cantata, it opens with an instrumental Sinfonia that contrasts a slow majestic opening (in quintal counterpoint) with a fast fugue (in quintal/secundal counterpoint). Instead of using conventional recitatives, Harrison sets the biblical prose with *parlando* (speech-like) chorales in the same counterpoint. These "studies in diatonicism," as Harrison called them,[20] extended into movements of his two suites for strings of 1947–1948 that all self-consciously share the careful, intensely introspective counterpoint of the Jacobean viol composers Harrison so admired.[21] Harrison modeled the first movement of his first *Suite for Strings* so closely on these forms that he noted that it almost could have been written by the seventeenth-century composer John Jenkins.[22]

Like his continuing meticulous explorations in chromatic atonality, these experiments would for the most part languish in his notebooks, in some cases for decades, as Harrison struggled to establish himself in his new, unforgiving environment. In contrast, the occasional pieces in his third style of charming tertial tonality radiate an optimism, perhaps inspired by the stability he'd found in his friendships old (Cage, Cowell) and new (Thomson, McGowan, Brown) in 1944–1945, as well as the intellectual stimulation he discovered in Kauder. After so much turmoil, Harrison had briefly achieved the kind of balanced stimulation in music and life he admired in creative musical counterpoint. Then an unexpected new music appeared in his life.

EXAMPLE 11.1. The chorale from Harrison's *Easter Cantata* uses a form of counterpoint based on stacks of perfect fifths and fourths, resulting in major seconds and minor sevenths as harmonic intervals. Courtesy of Special Collections, University Library, University of California Santa Cruz, Lou Harrison papers.

THE COMING OF LIGHT

John Cage and Lou Harrison settled into their seats at New York's Town Hall in June 1945, each in the midst of a new relationship, Harrison with McGowan and Cage with Cunningham. The concert hall was full; it seemed that all the prominent New York composers had turned out to hear the New York debut of this unknown composer from Boston. Two of the soloists, the piano-violin duo Anahid and Maro Ajemian, then just twenty and twenty-three years old and recent Juilliard students, would soon enter Harrison's swelling circle of friends. But nothing he encountered in his New York years would affect his music more than what he was about to hear.

As the concert opened, thoughts about anything but the portentous music emanating from the lowest range of a cello vanished. Harrison was startled, but, too often burned by new music by unknown composers that opened with a striking gesture only to fall back into cliché, he whispered to Cage, "It's going to go oompah any minute."[23] But it didn't. The beautiful, unearthly cello melody was joined by a jittery piano figure, and then the rest of the orchestra joined in with yet another ravishing melody, this one on the violin soaring over the rest. The glorious melodies seemed to spin on and on, traversing ancient modes from Asia rather than plodding the well-tamped path of conventional Western tonality.

Harrison was astonished. He had heard a lot of music but never anything like this single-movement piano concerto, *Lousadzak*, whose Armenian title translates to "The Coming of Light." "This can't go on this way," he said to Cage as the uncertain applause wafted over them. "The next one will be awful."

But the next piece, a violin concerto by the same composer titled *Tzaikerk* ("Evening Song") proved to be one of the most unexpectedly ravishing musical moments Harrison had experienced since first hearing a recording of Alban Berg's violin concerto in San Francisco. Here was a composer who had ingeniously sidestepped the polarized aesthetic positions that New York composers had staked out, by using non-Western modes, gracefully ornamented melodies, and foundations established by drones and ostinatos (short, repeating figures).

"The intermission that followed," Harrison remembered, "was the closest I've ever been to one of those renowned artistic riots. In the lobby, the chromaticists and the Americanists were carrying on at high decibels. What had touched it off, of course, was the fact that here came a man from Boston whose obviously beautiful and fine music had nothing to do with either camp and was in fact its own very wonderful thing to begin with. I dashed off to the *Herald Tribune* and wrote a rave review while John went back to the green room to meet Alan."[24] At the *Tribune* office, Harrison typed, "In these pieces a rigid and hypnotic permanence of the scale and mode ('of Armenian' origin) is the structural basis on which is erected a clean, decorative set of melodic lines, frequently of a highly ornamented nature. There is almost nothing occurring most of the time but unison melodies and very lengthy drone basses, which is all very Armenian. It is also very modern indeed in its elegant simplicity and adamant modal integrity, being, in effect, as tight and strong in its way as a twelve-tone work of the Austrian type."[25]

The tall, mysterious composer, Alan Hovhaness (born Alan Vaness Chakmakjian in 1911 in Somerville, Massachusetts), was the son of an Armenian father and a mother of Scottish descent. Rejecting the growing harmonic complexity and density that characterized so much of contemporary Western classical music, he instead explored the modes of his Armenian ancestors and Asian cultures. The Town Hall concert ignited a career that was to make him at once one of America's most performed composers and one of its most vilified, even by major figures such as Leonard Bernstein and Aaron Copland.[26]

But where critics disdained Hovhaness's "simplistic" aesthetic, Harrison discerned "melody, clarity, discipline, beauty"—qualities conspicuously missing from much modern orchestral music.[27] Its simple clarity and "Eastern" flavor especially intrigued him and Cage, both of whom were beginning to explore Asian music and philosophy. Cage arranged for Hovhaness's work to be published in *New Music*, and Martha Graham commissioned a ballet from him.

Yet although he recognized the value of Hovhaness's breakthrough, Harrison, preoccupied with working out his systems of atonal music at the moment, wasn't immediately ready to apply it to his own compositions. Soon, when he reached a musical and emotional crisis, Harrison would remember Hovhaness's arresting approach and find in it clues to a path to his own artistic salvation. For Harrison, Hovhaness's music would help illuminate the path out of the dark forest of dissonant counterpoint.

GUARDIAN ANGELS

Row, row, row your boat, gently down the stream.

On a late summer day in 1945, a small group of artists and musicians sang on the white, windswept cliffs overlooking Penobscot Bay. They had noticed that the sound of their voices—including Lou Harrison's spirited baritone—bounced back from the cliffs across the bay with enough of a delay to allow them to sing rounds with the echoes of their own voices. The bay breezes quickly swept the small sound away, but they didn't mind. The man who'd invited the band of friends to the Maine coast, Jack Heliker, set up a canvas on a small portable easel and began to paint one of the bright, Cézanne-inspired evocations of New England coastal landscapes that would soon bring him acclaim.

Later, after they returned to the erstwhile lighthouse that Heliker and his partner, Merton Brown, frequented, Harrison, McGowan, and a few other friends passed around a small, high-pitched recorder. Ignoring the instrument's instruction booklet on how to play tunes like "Home, Sweet Home," they instead improvised between snatches of conversation and gaiety. The tiny instrument rang clearly in the wooden and stone rooms, unimpeded by city clamor.

The friends reveled in the vacation from New York's summer noise and heat, but soon they had to return to urban clamor. The New England getaway ignited Harrison's longing for pastoral living, a craving that would go unrequited for years. Missing the quiet nights of the New England coast, Harrison turned an account of their trip for *View* magazine into a plea for portable and modest instruments that "would make possible a revival of genuine music in our lives." He lamented the fact that quiet instruments designed for intimate performances—lutes, viols, and clavichords—were no longer available to the modern composer. Instead, noisy cities, with their "symphony monopolies and managerial rackets," demanded instruments that could play anywhere and all sound the same. He argued that soft instruments would now have a niche among city dwellers who wished to play late at night. "At least three-hundred nights out of the year," he wrote, "I sit in disconsolate anxiety after the dead-line hour gazing at the keyboard of a piano whose voice would wake the entire neighborhood."[28]

The following summer, Harrison followed his own advice and built a clavichord from wood scraps and other spare parts. The baroque period clavichord, considered by Harrison "the most exciting keyboard instrument Europe's ever produced," is the softest of keyboard instruments, clearly audible only to the player.[29] Although he had adapted percussion instruments in San Francisco, this instrument would begin a lifelong love of building his own instruments. The experiment was only partially successful, as the frame had trouble supporting the tension of the strings. Frustrated, he tinkered with a wholly original design, finally completing it in 1953. But the choice to build this instrument was more than just an expedient. "It's a difference between positive listening and simply hearing," he said later. "To a degree you have to listen harder to it. That's the opposite of hearing."[30]

The end of their idyllic coastal interlude in August 1945 began the worst period of Harrison's life, commencing with the horror of the atomic bombing of Japan, which brought an end to World War II and a beginning to the Cold War and decades in which Americans lived in fear of nuclear catastrophe. In the exultation of victory in the long war, few of Harrison's friends fully appreciated the enormity of what had happened when those cities were incinerated—and what it might bode for the future. The fact that the attack killed thousands of Japanese civilians, albeit citizens of a hostile power, particularly affected Harrison, a pacifist whose orientation toward Asia had begun in childhood.

He already foresaw the implications of nuclear warfare. An avid science fiction fan, he had read Lester Del Rey's famous novella "Nerves" and other magazine stories predicting the consequences of an atomic meltdown and war.[31] "So I knew about atomic power, and when the bomb was dropped, I told my friends," Harrison recounted later.

"This monstrous activity—friends of mine were taken away to be trained and so on. I hated it all. When it happened I felt total numbness and incomprehension. It was a defensive reaction, I suppose. It was too much for me."[32]

Shortly after the bombs dropped, Harrison began feeling sharp pains in his abdomen and was diagnosed with an ulcer. His doctor ordered a regimen of baby food, and Harrison soon found himself a vegetarian. However, like most of his friends, he smoked more than a pack of cigarettes a day and, as solace in the face of New York's dispiriting atmosphere, spent many a late night getting drunk, boasting that he could drink Cage and most of his other friends under the table.[33]

Though on that idyllic late summer trip to Maine, Harrison began to relax and even put on a few pounds, once the racket and stress of Manhattan returned, so did the abdominal twinges and intermittent anxiety attacks.[34] Everything felt like it was closing in. Once an inveterate walker and nature lover, Harrison found himself taking the subway for a trip of only a few blocks. Life in the "madhouse" of New York was hardly bearable, he wrote his mother. "I'm afraid I will not be able to write a note in the midst of this noise and confusion."[35]

Since Harrison had arrived in New York, his circle of friends had provided a lifeline to stability. Increasingly, however, Harrison sought comfort: cloistering himself in his dark apartment, working with monastic meticulousness composing atonal works, analyzing Ruggles scores and others, transcribing scores of Ives, and writing reviews. While his gregariousness would eventually return, for the rest of his life, Harrison would be most comfortable composing alone in small, windowless spaces.

Thomson saw "both joy and pain" in the twenty-eight-year-old Harrison and detected inner demons in his protégé's psyche.[36] Thomson attributed some of Harrison's brooding personality to being conflicted about his sexuality. Harrison, even then relatively open about his sexuality, disputed Thomson's diagnosis, viewing his relationship with Edward as long-term and stable. Even so, there were already rumblings from the church hierarchy that McGowan's high-profile civil rights work, not to mention consorting with a white man, could have repercussions. McGowan told Harrison he was worried about their future. One day in the fall of 1945, Harrison was in the newsroom office at the Herald Tribune, trying to write a concert review, but he couldn't seem to focus on the words. He got up, walked around, sat down again. His hands began to shake, his breathing grew shallow—he was in a panic. Virgil Thomson saw his friend struggling and tried to console him. "You're having a tizzy, aren't you?" he said.

He sat down next to Harrison. Everyone is born with three guardian angels, he explained, but there aren't quite enough to go around. So sometimes your guardian angel has to go off and take care of someone else, and that's when you get into trouble. But she'll be back, he murmured, don't worry. That's the reason everything is going to hell, he told Harrison. "You mustn't squirm. You must sit quietly and wait for the guardian angel to return." He gave Harrison some much-needed money and gave him the day off. Harrison spent the afternoon at the Bronx Zoo.[37] But soon, the angels would again prove elusive.

In December 1945, Harrison sat for one of Thomson's celebrated musical portraits, one of 140 Thomson would compose to portray his friends and acquaintances in music. The subjects had to pose as they would for a painting while Thomson composed. Thomson had a gift for capturing his subjects' personalities, and he knew Harrison as well as anyone at this time, when he was surrounded by close friends old and new, as well as a whole network of acquaintances and colleagues. And yet when Thomson has finished his brief, poignant sketch and was ready to inscribe the title on the manuscript, he wrote, "Lou Harrison: Solitude."

12

PRAISES FOR THE ARCHANGEL (1946)

*At every stage the artist will delight in rules.... It is of the essence of art to bring
back into order the multiplicity of Nature, and it is in this sense that he "prepares
all creatures to return to God."*

—Ananda Coomaraswamy[1]

One day in the summer of 1946, Lou Harrison and John Cage were engaged in deep
discussion with a young student newly arrived in New York from India about the
nature and meaning of art, when Cage posed a fateful question.

"What," Cage asked twenty-five-year-old Gita Sarabhai, "is the purpose of music?"

Having completed eight years of study of North Indian music, Sarabhai now
wanted to explore Western music, everything from counterpoint to contemporary
techniques. I know just the teacher for you, the sculptor Isamu Noguchi told her
and called his friend John Cage. Cage agreed to teach her—on the condition that
she repay him by teaching him about Indian music. For the next six months, he and
Sarabhai and usually Harrison (always interested in Asian music) met several times
per week for lessons, dinner, and discussion. Sarabhai's teacher in India had given
her a ready answer to Cage's trenchant question.

"To sober and quiet the mind," she replied, "thus rendering it susceptible to divine
influences."[2]

Harrison was startled, for he had just read almost identical words—but coming
from the seventeenth-century English composer Thomas Mace, as part of his
research of English viol composers: "Those Influences, which come along with
[music], may aptly be compar'd, to Emanations, Communications, or Distillations,
of some Sweet, and Heavenly Genius, or Spirit; Mystically, and Unapprehensibly
(yet Effectually) Dispossessing the Soul, and Mind, of All Irregular Disturbing, and
Unquiet Motions; and Stills, and Fills It, with Quietness, Joy, and Peace; Absolute
Tranquility, and Unexpressible Satisfaction."[3]

And later, when speaking of the encroachment of superficial new fashions into
the tradition of Harrison's beloved English viol music, Mace wrote, "Observe with
what wonderful swiftness they now run over their brave new airs, and with what

high-prized noise, viz., ten or twenty violins, etc., as I said before, to some single-souled ayre . . . and such-like stuff, seldom any other, which is rather fit to make a man's ears glow, and fill his brains full of frisks, etc. than to season and sober his mind, or elevate his affections to goodness."[4]

Harrison's investigation of Indian philosophy was also part of a larger search that increasingly preoccupied him, and shows up in his music, in the years between 1945 and 1947—a spiritual and philosophical search that would also embrace medieval mysticism, myth. and more, as Harrison sought meaning for himself and his music in an increasingly fraught New York existence.

At this critical juncture, two books of Eastern philosophy cast powerful spells on Harrison and Cage. Before she returned to India in December, Sarabhai left Cage a copy of *The Gospel of Sri Ramakrishna* (which Campbell had just helped publish), a lengthy account of the teachings of the nineteenth-century Hindu saint. Cage devoured the book, carrying it around constantly, and he became so enraptured with Indian culture that he acquired the affectation of eating like a native of India, with only the fingers of his right hand, even with ice cream.[5] Ramakrishna's ideas were at once revelatory and familiar to Cage and Harrison. Harrison had studied Vedanta religion (closely related to the philosophy of Ramakrishna) in San Francisco, and these were the same ideas that had enthralled his friend John Dobson. Ramakrishna's attainment of what Indian philosopher Ananda Coomaraswamy called a state of higher reality, often achieved through song, deeply inspired Harrison. Coomaraswamy's *The Transformation of Nature in Art*, recommended to Cage and Harrison by Joseph Campbell, contended that Asian art bridges mundane existence and an ultimate reality that both transcends and is a part of every individual. The book argued for an ideal art as a process of reflecting this transcendent state in ordinary existence, rather than (as in the West) constituting specific objects created by individual personalities. To Coomaraswamy, post-Renaissance Europe had lost its artistic connection to transcendence, creating instead superficially sensuous but ultimately empty reflections of individual egos and a sick society.[6] Inspired, Harrison wrote to Coomaraswamy, who replied with a list of recommended readings.

The correspondence of Hindu ideas of cyclic time with Joseph Campbell's ur-myth of the great journey from darkness to light led to Cage's ballet *The Seasons*, which he wrote in 1947 for the great dance impresario Lincoln Kirstein with sets by Noguchi. Harrison (who suggested the use of an Asian pentatonic scale for one movement) and Thomson helped Cage with the orchestration of his first piece for orchestra.[7] Two years later, Harrison would also create a ballet based on Campbell's ideas of mythic cycles.

Unlike a self-absorbed Romantic composer offering the audience a voyeuristic glimpse of an artist's angst, Coomaraswamy idealized the expression of emotions that transcend individual experience, even to the point of artist anonymity. In the wake of World War II's devastation, many artists sought to objectify their work, wringing from art the controlling egotism that, in their view, reflected the war's horrific attempts to control humanity. According to Coomaraswamy, a work of art should evoke a "flavor," or *rasa*, the timeless affect of the so-called permanent emotions that transcend individual experience.

Cage based his monumental *Sonatas and Interludes* as well as his *Sixteen Dances* for prepared piano on this concept of *rasa*. Harrison heard this concept in the particular expressive potential of modes, and spoke of it—especially in the music of Hovhaness, whom he called "probably the composer whose apt and singularly direct establishment of 'Rasa,' or flavor (immediate and sustained), brings most suddenly to the dance stage an awareness of tonal 'setting.' His approach (natural to him in his concert music as well) is based on the flavor of the modes."[8]

A LAND OF THE HEART'S DESIRE

> *The composers who today wish to imbue their music with the ineffable, seem to find it necessary to make use of musical characteristics not purely Western. They go for inspiration to those places, or return to those times, where or when harmony is not of the essence.*

—John Cage[9]

This confluence of influences from Coomaraswamy, Ramakrishna, and Campbell exerted a profound impact on both Cage's and Harrison's music, first in their mutual disdain for what Cage called harmony, meaning, for him, the traditional march of tonal chords that create grand musical edifices, sonic monuments to Romantic ego: "I now saw harmony, for which I had never had any natural feeling, as a device to make music impressive, loud, and big, in order to enlarge audiences and increase box-office returns. It had been avoided by the Orient, and our earlier Christian society, since they were interested in music not as an aid in the acquisition of money and fame but rather as a handmaiden to pleasure and religion."[10]

If Harrison's music of this period doesn't as strictly avoid direction or rhetoric as Cage's, it frequently evokes stillness and suspended time. In such works as *The Only Jealousy of Emer* (1949), Harrison would often literally avoid harmony, frequently using textures of just a single instrument or melody, prefiguring his later career's wholesale application of the melody-dominated textures of Chinese and other Asian traditional music, when he would become nearly entirely a melodist. Even in his more densely contrapuntal pieces of this period, Harrison never used harmony as a means for propelling listeners toward a big climax but rather as a constantly shifting interaction among members of a community of sounds.

Furthermore, just as Cage replaced the traditional Western emphasis on harmony with an emphasis on the divisions of time, Harrison too experimented with strict formal structures reflecting Coomaraswamy's "delight in rules." Cage found this disinterested cycling of time in the Indian musical concept of *tala*, or rhythmic cycle, and Coomaraswamy used the term for any canon of mathematical proportions in art. In *Symphony on G* (begun 1947) and his *Strict Songs* (in the sketches begun in 1951), Harrison carefully laid out a strict structure of measures even before he started filling in the notes.

Coomaraswamy and Ramakrishna struck another chord with both Cage and Harrison in their disdain for materialism. "Hatred of commercialism is also an absolute essential to any serious American composers, nowadays," Harrison wrote in a 1945 article in *View* magazine.[11] A 1944 letter to Ives decried "the rampant prostitution of a great creative art to purely commercial ends."[12] In a 1948 lecture, Cage called it "sheer materialistic nonsense" when a *Times* article quoted a composer inspired by "the rising crescendo of modern industrialism."[13] Instead, Harrison and Cage regarded music as a way of finding wholeness and peace (for both composers and audiences) within a war-ravaged, capitalist society of shattered, alienated psyches.

As striking as these parallels between the aesthetics of these two best friends were at this time, their differences are crucial to understanding the divergence of their careers and the way that divergence represented a similar fork in the course of American music. To Cage, music was at once a therapy and a philosophical statement, even at times a provocation to awaken a superficial, neurotic culture. Cage came to see all sounds as more or less equal (excepting, of course, the sounds of grand harmony and Europe's musical past), leading him finally to question the need for or wisdom of imposing his own intentions on a piece of music at all.

Harrison, however, never failed to be transported by a lovely tune. Though he agreed that music was "an adventure in time awareness," he also quickly added, "the singlest, most simple route to this beauty is through melody; for herein is form, shape, 'recollection,' surprise, architecture, and the 'take-home-pay' of a memorable tune: for few of us are double or multi-minded, and the old 'song and dance' idea is presently, as anciently, the most rewarding."[14]

They also differed in their views of the usable past. Cage polemicized for a music without a past, stolen from the arms of its birth mother—music, in Harrison's words, "without any reference to 'historicity.'"[15] Cage complained that the neoclassicists "spend their lives with the music of another time, which, putting it bluntly and chronologically, does not belong to them."[16] He even denounced Schoenberg himself as representing not modernism's dawn but instead the final "disintegration" of Romantic harmony.[17]

Although Harrison never adopted the wryly self-conscious return to eighteenth-century academic forms as did Stravinsky and Hindemith, nor the deliberate traditionalism of Walter Piston and Howard Hanson, nearly every piece of this period drew unabashedly (if with great originality) from the music of the past that he loved. "The past in the present creates the future," he wrote later.[18] Unlike Cage, he remained throughout his life an unapologetic eclectic, later drawing from Asian traditions as he then did from Europe's past. Harrison rhapsodized about these passions: "To a composer, of course music is the magic land and reports from its princely towers are wonderful. And the sudden lights within his own practicing are like swinging lanterns before him. He searches and he is led to Cathay and Arabia and he crosses time as well. We each of us develops, as a composer, a kind of land of the heart's desire to which we are primarily attracted."[19]

Along with their divergent attitudes toward the role of the past for contemporary composers, Harrison and Cage also differed in their views about personal expression in art. Unlike Cage's reactions against historical Romanticism, Harrison's compositions of this period can be profoundly emotional, as are the intensely expressive works of Ruggles, but their emotion is introspective, even detached, in the same sense that Coomaraswamy saw emotional expression in Asian art rising above individual ego. While many regarded both Cage and Harrison as representatives of New York's "ultramodernists," the cold objectification of Cage's works anticipated the postwar avant-garde, while Harrison's works drew upon traditions of humanism and even spirituality.

Like Coomaraswamy, Harrison claimed that "Europe suffered a compound fracture of the cultural backbone during the middle crusades," after which Renaissance humanism had shattered Europe's aesthetic parallels to Asian traditionalism.[20] "We shall find that Asiatic art is ideal in the mathematical sense," Coomaraswamy wrote, paraphrasing Thomas Aquinas, "like Nature (*natura naturans*), not in appearance (viz. that of *ens naturata*), but in operation." Cage would later be fond of paraphrasing this quote as, "Art is the imitation of nature in her manner of operation."[21]

To Harrison, the medieval period also defined a very different model of music and of an artist's place in society than in the twentieth century's commercialized artistic market. An artist who sought introspection and deeper meaning in a world swamped by the industrialization of art could be sustained only by a monk-like faith in a higher relevance., "As I see it, the musical 'industry' in the U.S. is rapidly reducing anyone who has a sense of music as a meaningful art to the curious position of . . . at best, a cloistered medieval monk," he wrote in a letter to Ives."[22] To Harrison, like Thomson, a composer was first a craftsman, and if Harrison did not literally live Coomaraswamy's ideal of the anonymous and humble artist, he did spend hours and hours in his own dark hermitage, patiently and meticulously working out scores that represented his own ideals, regardless of their ultimate popularity.[23]

To Harrison, these ideals extended beyond the Middle Ages and represented a perennial battle between art as shallow entertainment and art that served deeper meanings. He wrote of an example from the seventeenth century, when the encroachment of "light and airy music" spelled the end of the great school of Jacobean viol music of Gibbons, Jenkins, and Purcell that Harrison so treasured in his youth.[24] To Harrison, the uncompromisingly profound and self-consistent counterpoint of the seventeenth-century viol composers represented deep human insights, a music of highly personal expression unswayed by the "monstrous waywardness of fashion" in Purcell's day or the deterioration of the arts in modern times: "Ignorance is doubtless to blame this time as well, but not quite the same kind because the state of the composer has so deteriorated . . . that the whole matter stays on a very degraded level indeed, having nothing to do with the taste of kings. Having little to do with taste. Having almost nothing to do with anything but money, which can be had, and in vast quantities, if a man is willing to give himself up to the great American canning racket, success incorporated, and all that sort of thing."[25]

Harrison found inspiration back across the centuries to the Middle Ages, across the oceans to Asia, and within his own artist soul—everywhere, in fact, except the modern technocratic future, where Cage the inventor's son and the modernist composers who would soon dominate postwar music aimed. But Harrison was no Miniver Cheevy who wanted to retreat to the past. He saw that certain modern composers had transcended the degradation of industrial commercialism and brought back the intensely introspective polyphony of what Harrison called "the great flowering" of European music, 1250–1750. One contemporary composer in particular would now become central to his music.

STRUGGLE WITH ANGELS

> *Ruggles, if Ives is the type of the public artist, is the private man; inquisitive, reflective, violent of allegiance, aristocratic, and above all religious. He is the type vested with a fire from heaven. He fuses together without seam the whole person of the separate soul. . . . How distilled and clear a one he is of the kind of man, who having once seen the living word, is from that moment on engaged in a traveling struggle with angels.*
>
> —Lou Harrison[26]

In December 1944, Cowell called up Harrison to ask him for a favor. A composer was coming into town to arrange publication of his work in *New Music Quarterly*. However, Cowell had a conflicting commitment out of town. As assistant editor for *New Music*, could Harrison go in his place? The composer, Harrison was elated to learn, was the one whose music was possibly the greatest influence on the direction his own composition was taking: Carl Ruggles.

Like his contemporary Charles Ives, Carl Ruggles was a crusty Yankee experimenter who saw little value in extending the conservatism of composers like his teacher John Knowles Paine. Instead, during World War I, he struggled with chromaticism, independently recapitulating much of Schoenberg's earlier evolution from chromaticism to atonality, arriving at a unique but still largely intuitive atonal language. In 1917, Ruggles had met the twenty-year-old firebrand Henry Cowell in New York, and in 1920 Cowell introduced him to Charles Seeger and his ideas about dissonant counterpoint.

Soon Ruggles and Seeger were working together, seeking, as was Schoenberg around the time, a way to structure atonality. However, Ruggles's musical personality was very different from that of the Viennese traditionalist. While Schoenberg moved his focus inward, from a concentrated expressionism to near abstraction, Ruggles cultivated an intensely emotional expression of striving, of human struggle. Virgil Thomson described Ruggles's *Portals* as having "high-jutting points to it that might be either Gothic arches or simply man's aspiration" and *Angels* as "quietly ecstatic."[27]

In 1927, when Henry Cowell brought out the first issue of *New Music*, it consisted entirely of Ruggles's rugged *Men and Mountains*. Cowell also published Ruggles's *Portals* in 1930 and *Sun-treader* in 1934 and also that year released two of his songs in the New Music recording series. They showed the teenaged Lou Harrison how expressive atonality could be structured—without having to submit to the restrictions of the twelve-tone method.

As Harrison's move from Los Angeles to New York also represented an emergence from his self-described "Schoenberg period" (though not his commitment to atonal modernism), the profound introspection, consistency, and intensity of the Ruggles style—and even a number of specific techniques—began to pervade his music. By 1943, Harrison was already as immersed in the music of Ruggles as he had been with that of Schoenberg. Although Harrison, characteristically, continued to compose in a variety of idioms in New York, he devoted most of his effort for at least the next six years to this language of concentrated, polyphonic, dissonant atonality.

Harrison's composing always maintained a tension between experimentalism and tonal lyricism. Even in New York, despite the aesthetic split between the traditionalists of the League of Composers (including Thomson and Copland) and the experimentalists of the Pan-American Association of Composers (including Cowell and Ives), Harrison easily navigated both circles. It was not in Harrison's personality to be exclusive about his musical materials. For example, Harrison realized that Thomson's "white-key" music (which would garner him the Pulitzer Prize in music in 1949), so seemingly different from Schoenberg's, in fact represented a system not unlike the atonal master's. "It dawned on me at once that just as serial music is a watertight system, so is the extreme simplicity of Virgil," he said. "They represent polar balances: the clear sharp wit of Virgil's music and the closed system of Schoenberg."[28] After all, Harrison often pointed out, every European period had its diatonic and chromatic sides, and so did he.

But fresh from his study with Schoenberg, Harrison's new allegiance was to intensely atonal expressionism, in part as a reaction, even then, against the shallow commercialization of American culture and the insanity of world war. Harrison found himself categorized, along with Merton Brown and Ben Weber, as one of New York's young atonalists.[29] Harrison's infatuation with his idols Ives, Ruggles, and Varèse even led him at that time to disdain Copland's Americanist music, though the two composers maintained an affable and respectful relationship.[30]

All of his serious "voluntary" pieces during this time were explorations in atonality, although he struggled mightily to find a language that approached his ideal of a transcendent polyphony. During 1943 and 1944, Harrison was filling his notebooks with the twelve-tone string quartet that was to become *Schoenbergiana* and his dark, Rugglesian *Alleluia* for chamber orchestra. The fact that he did not complete the *Alleluia* for over a year (uncharacteristic for the prolific Harrison) suggests that he was so carefully working out this concentrated style that he was recapitulating Ruggles's own notoriously painstaking compositional process.

When Harrison finally had the opportunity to meet the cigar-chomping Ruggles over the lunch that Cowell had arranged, Ruggles and his wife were flattered by the younger composer's attention. "I found him a *very intelligent* and delightful person," Ruggles later wrote Cowell. "We both liked him tremendously."[31] The feeling was mutual. "How wonderful he is," Harrison wrote later, "this little man with his curiously peaked head, his clear blue eyes and gusty, blowing brilliance that seems always to be active in him, moving him one minute to loud pronouncement of the coarsest joke he can think of and in the next to the tenderness and charm that have long endeared him to myriad friends."[32]

A few months later, Cowell, overcommitted with his work as music editor for the Office of War Information, asked Harrison to take over as editor of *New Music* from

Otto Luening, hoping that an energetic young composer would be able to give more attention to the publication. However, Harrison struggled with the new responsibilities. He did manage to get the next issue to press on time, but it consisted of only a single work, Ruggles's *Evocation #4*, a four-page piano score. The issue's brevity occasioned some grumbling among the magazine's subscribers, but Harrison defended his decision, made partly because of a wartime paper shortage. Harrison found the handwritten score "pricelessly beautiful"[33] and thought the effort he'd put into getting Ruggles to publish it so strenuous that it was worth it.

In May 1945, Harrison organized a reception and recital for the occasion, honoring Ruggles with a performance of the *Evocations* and other works by pianist John Kirkpatrick and an exhibit of his paintings that Harrison's and Ruggles's mutual friend Jack Heliker helped arrange. Harrison told Ruggles that he intended to organize a performance of *Portals*, but Ruggles was most excited about Harrison's decision to write a book about him.

ABOUT CARL RUGGLES

While Harrison planned a four-part book that would include a biography of Ruggles and analysis of his works, he completed only the fourth part, an extended essay that analyzes his contrapuntal style and puts it into historical context. Jack Heliker knew a bookstore owner named Oscar Baradinsky, who had published two short works by Henry Miller as part of a projected series on "outcast" artists. He agreed that Ruggles would fit nicely into that theme and brought out the book (actually hardly more than a pamphlet, even with Cowell's generous introduction), dedicated to Brown and Heliker, in March 1946.

The penetrating if rhapsodic *About Carl Ruggles* reveals as much about Harrison's preoccupations of the time as it does about Ruggles's music, in which Harrison discerned the resurrection of a musical idiom that he called "total polyphony," one that persisted from the Middle Ages until the time of Bach. "Each voice is a real melody," Harrison wrote, "bound into a community of singing lines, living a life of its own with regard to phrasing and breathing, careful not to get ahead or behind in its rhythmic cooperation with the others, and sustaining a responsible independence in the whole polyphony of life."[34] Other ruminations in Harrison's notebooks of the period give the impression that Harrison idealized such a symbol of harmonious community because he needed it so much in his own troubled life at the time.

Appreciating such music may require some concentration and commitment, which is why Harrison thought it was disappearing at a time when the industrialization of the arts encouraged fads of shallow entertainment. This argument resembles those made by the intellectual modernists in the twentieth century, such as many of Harrison's New York friends. But Harrison presented it not as a call to elitist self-indulgence but instead as a humanist plea for movement toward depth, reflection, and even spirituality (though he came to dislike that term) in art as in life.

Unfortunately, Ruggles the man turned out to be less impressive than his music. In October 1946, Harrison met one last time with Ruggles, to discuss the publication of his new work, *Organum*. At the Penn Station diner where they met, Harrison was mortified when Ruggles loudly spat racist and anti-Semitic slurs.[35] After that experience, Harrison distanced himself from Ruggles, though he continued to advocate his music.

His essay delineated several devices in Ruggles's music that became prominent in Harrison's own work—and distinguished Harrison, Ruggles, and Brown from nearly all other composers of their time. Before Harrison's book, Ruggles's techniques had been known nearly entirely through an article by Charles Seeger that Harrison had read in Cowell's *American Composers on American Music*. Seeger showed that once Ruggles used a particular pitch in a melody, he avoided it until at least seven different pitches had intervened.[36] Harrison used such a "non-repetition principle" in his 1946 *Motet for the Day of Ascension*, for example.

Along with non-repetition, Harrison adopted Ruggles's approach to dissonant counterpoint, in which he allowed only the most strident of dissonances—minor seconds, tritones, and major sevenths—as resting points, avoiding even the less jarring major seconds or minor sevenths, as in his *Triphony* for piano. Despite its relatively simple texture, a reflection of Schoenberg's parting admonition that he study only Mozart, Harrison to the end of his life found the dark, yearning *Triphony* among the most successful of his ventures into this style. In 1946 he arranged it as his *String Trio*, in which form it was first published.[37]

A third Ruggles technique that Harrison employed is creating a "shadow" countermelody that mostly or exactly parallels the principal melody in fourths or fifths. In *Triphony*, for example, the "leftover" intervals (those not a minor second, tritone, or major seventh) are organized by quintal counterpoint, a technique also found in Ruggles's *Portals*, which appeared in *New Music* in 1930. After discovering it in the San Francisco Public Library, Harrison had composed his own version of this kind of texture thickened by parallel fourths in the baroque form of the concerto grosso.

Ruggles-style dissonant counterpoint also floats through Harrison's *Alma Redemptoris Mater* (1949–1951), in which a baritone voice and violin, mostly in parallel fourths, evoke medieval polyphony while followed by a tack piano, a conventional piano with thumbtacks inserted into the felts of the hammers to change the timbre. An old friend from Mills College, Esther Williamson (now Esther Ballou), introduced him to this instrument backstage at the New York Philharmonic, where it was used as a substitute for the harpsichord, but the instrument's unique sound and smoothly changeable dynamics (which the harpsichord lacks) attracted Harrison.[38] In *Alma Redemptoris Mater*, a trombone joins the tack piano, shadowing the voice's flowing intonation of the Latin text in a dissonant counterpoint canon. The slow, meditative piece also lacks bar lines and leaves a chant-like impression, despite the very disjunct melody, and it creates a timelessness appropriate for its invocation to the Virgin Mary.

Similar contrapuntal writing is the basis for his Fugue, begun in 1947[39] the second movement of Harrison's *Suite No. 2* for strings. Over the course of its two minutes, Harrison gradually transforms one melodicle into others, giving the work a sense of perpetual change, a prose-like rhetoric common both in Ruggles and in

Schoenberg.[40] Following these intricate mutations represented to Harrison the kind of "traveling struggle with angels" he wrote about in reference to Ruggles.[41]

Melodicles such as the characteristic combination of minor second and perfect fifth, as in *Alma Redemptoris Mater* and his brooding *Praises for the Archangel Michael*, became a hallmark of Harrison's New York style, both melodically and harmonically. He saw that a pervasive, if free, use of such small melodicles was the glue that kept Ruggles's pieces together in the face of the restrictions imposed by dissonant counterpoint. "Motivally the work abounds in brilliancies of the composing technique," Harrison wrote of Ruggles's *Evocations*. "His subjects evolve and have their life within an idiom which is at every turn restricting to them."[42] This importance of rigor and discipline to Ruggles, Schoenberg, and Coomaraswamy helped shape Harrison's own ideal of human expression finding form in rational order.

A NEW POLYPHONY

> All the activities of the angels . . . are intellectually emanated; those of men are put forth by conscious effort; therefore it is that the works to be done by men are defined in detail.
>
> —*Natya Sastra*[43]

Angels touched Harrison's mind and music throughout 1946 and '47. They flit throughout his Ruggles essay almost as if in fulfillment of the above passage in the ancient Indian music text the *Natya Sastra*, which Harrison read about in Coomaraswamy. Already predisposed to find comfort in his readings in religion, Harrison's interests were reignited by Joseph Campbell (who esteemed the symbolic power of ancient rituals), by Ruggles's own composition *Angels*, and by his poring through religious texts. Harrison copied into his notebook quotes from these readings—the *Aitareya Brahmana, Sankhayana Aranyaka, Confucian Five Classics, Chuang Tze*—all about harmony and concord, as he struggled to find spiritual and musical harmony himself.[44]

One day Jack Heliker, who shared his rising interest in religious mysticism, invited Harrison to an unusual church he had found. The Episcopal Church of St. Mary the Virgin on West Forty-Sixth Street had split off from the Anglican rite and reintroduced ancient Christian rituals and medieval chant. Its lack of emphasis on dogma appealed to both Harrison and Heliker, whose homosexuality contradicted traditional church teachings. "Smoky Mary"—so called because of its immoderate dosages of incense in rituals—became a cool, stone refuge for Harrison from the city's pervasive noise and stress.[45]

Harrison's emerging preoccupation with Christian mysticism is reflected in the titles of several of his most introspective, Ruggles-inspired works: *Alleluia* (1943–1945), *Motet for the Day of Ascension* (1945), *Praises for Michael the Archangel* (1946–1947), and *Alma Redemptoris Mater* (1949, completed 1951). His notebooks teem with arcane, often calligraphic references to Christian theology, sometimes connecting them (as did Joseph Campbell) to other mystical traditions.[46] For someone who spent most of his later life as an "epicurean" agnostic, some these musings are startling: "A correct and traditional society is theocentric. This is the kind of society of the greatest number of the world's peoples for the longest time. Its members are artists and are called to the operations by heavenly ordinance. Every man has in fact, by nature, a vocation and is responsible for its employment to his own highest exemplar; him in truth, by whom every man and all things are by minute and minute constantly and freshly made, the same within as without."[47]

The idea of a kind of priesthood of artists must have appealed to Harrison, who was then struggling, along with his avant-garde artist friends, in a capitalist society that seemed to place little value on their work or ideas, particularly in the postwar recession that gripped the country. But he continued to compose, if only to work through the radical ideas he was grappling with. One of them involved the nature of time in music.

In the same notebook as his *Alma Redemptoris Mater* (probably from 1949), Harrison connected time and rhythm to spirituality (see table 12.1.).

These different levels of time, all bound through the community of counterpoint, fuel the prose-like rhythms of such works from this period as *Praises for the Archangel Michael*, in which distinct levels of rhythm appear one at a time and maintain separate identities throughout. This dissonant, searching work for organ was apparently prompted by informal organ lessons that Harrison was receiving from Virgil Thomson, who played organ for some years for his family's Baptist church back in Kansas City.

Harrison's time-bending approach challenges conventional rhythm the same way his twelve-tone-derived music challenged traditional harmony. Charles Seeger recognized very early that the regular divisions of traditional rhythms are the rhythmic equivalent of tonality—both represented a dependence on a worn-out hierarchical structure. Just as Seeger proposed dissonant counterpoint to achieve an independence from tonality, he also counseled composers to "dissonate" rhythm through the use of irregular divisions and combinations. Only by creating such self-consistency in all dimensions of a compositions, he believed, could composers achieve a "real independence" of voices and a "new polyphony."[48] In works by Ruggles, Ruth Crawford, Edgard Varèse, and Harrison's friend Merton Brown, this brash dissonance of rhythm obscures the beat and meter just as their dissonant harmonies obscure tonality.[49] Elliott Carter would soon carry these rhythmic layers far further into the complexities of the 1950s avant-garde.

TABLE 12.1. The Levels of Rhythmic Shift[1]

		Into light and sound	
♪	faster	↑	
	2+3 connections	↑	area of heavenly excitement
♪	near heartbeat	♥	area of earth's ecstasy
♩		↓	area of form
	slower	↓	
		Into darkness & silence	

[1] Notebook #45 LHA.

Even though such techniques tend to lead to greater complexity, the textures of such rhythmically "dissonated" works as Harrison's *Praises for the Michael Archangel* are never obscure, and each rhythmically distinct voice somehow cooperates in Harrison's anguished climaxes. This "new polyphony" that Seeger wrote about was to Harrison the same "total polyphony" that he admired in Purcell and Bach, a polyphony that represented community and harmony of spirit.

While community and concord would remain preoccupations for Harrison throughout his life, their representation in the mystical depths of Rugglesian counterpoint would gradually disappear from his work. In 1960 for example, when Harrison used material from *Triphony* for his *Suite for Symphonic Strings* after he moved to California, he realigned all the previously irregular rhythmic divisions so that they corresponded to simple divisions of the beat. While the harmonic dissonances remain, the rhythms cooperate within the meter, losing some of Seeger's "real independence" and their New York angst.

Like the rest of his New York music through 1946, these compositions resided only in his notebooks. But that spring, he seized the opportunity to showcase the pioneering musical ideas he cherished on stage.

13

DAY OF ASCENSION (1946–1947)

Oh that some conductor would discover the Ives orchestral works! Fair warning is here given that sooner or later, someone is going to make his conductorial reputation on the strength of them. . . . Ives' symphonies or suites would be a natural for the audience and might well be received with banners and flower throwing. . . . It is sad that so important a composer should have reached his seventieth birthday and still be unperformed by the leading orchestra of his own city.

—Lou Harrison, 1944[1]

Anyone might have expected Lou Harrison to be nervous as he approached the podium at the recital hall in Carnegie Hall at around 10:00 pm on Friday, April 5, 1946. Still an unknown, under-thirty composer who had never before conducted a full orchestra, he faced players initially resistant to an amateur who had recently criticized them in New York's second-largest daily newspaper. Also, the music he wanted the New York Little Symphony to play—music he had long wanted to hear—was unheard and unheard of.

The path to Harrison's debut as an orchestral conductor began with Harrison's negative review of the New York Little Symphony's December 1944 performance. "The orchestral accompaniment," he wrote in the *Herald Tribune*, "was especially remarkable in that it was so out of tune, and set something of a record in that its well-trained constituents . . . played wrong notes in a simple piece by Handel."[2] The especially harsh review prompted the conductor of the ensemble, Joseph Barone, to seek out the young reviewer and complain in person. Harrison's expectations were too high, he said, for a struggling orchestra whose funding allowed for minimal rehearsal time. If you think you can do better, Barone said, do it.[3]

It was a tempting offer. Ultimately Harrison decided to accept the challenge and program a concert in the orchestra's upcoming 1945–1946 season, not because he harbored any aspirations as a conductor, but so he could hear and publicize music that he knew would not be programmed by any other orchestra. Not surprisingly, first on his list was a previously unperformed work by that most unjustly neglected of all composers of the time, Charles Ives.

When Harrison moved to New York, Cowell enlisted him to arrange and prepare the orchestra and choir version of Ives's *They Are There!*, a wartime commission by the League of Composers. Harrison asked Carol Beals to ship his Ives crate from San Francisco, and by 1945, Cowell had arranged for Harrison to earn a stipend from Ives for copying and editing the old man's scrawls, with an eye toward preparing the scores for publication. At times he had to fill in the orchestration or even do a bit of "internal composition" to complete Ives's manuscript.[4] By then, intimately familiar with Ives's style, Harrison even recomposed, with Ives's permission, missing or incomplete measures in the First Piano Sonata and Second String Quartet[5]—"the high point of American chamber music so far," he wrote, but, like the others, it had not been publicly performed.[6] "I think it is something in the nature of an immorality to allow great music to languish on shelves," Harrison wrote Ives in October 1944. "Some of us are powerfully aware that we have been quite forcibly prevented from receiving our heritage and are determined to stand against this."[7]

Now, thanks to Barone's invitation, Harrison would have the chance to be one of the first conductors to bring this pioneering, long-dormant music to life. The conductor offered Harrison the concert's second half for whatever he wanted to program. For the centerpiece, Harrison chose Ives's Third Symphony, composed in the first decade of the century, a touching evocation of a revivalist camp meeting in a prophetically modernist but unmistakably American style.

Harrison had known the piece for a decade and had recently been corresponding with Ives over his edits. He spent weeks copying out the instrumental parts. But though it was suitable for the Little Symphony's chamber orchestra forces, the score proved daunting for the players, who greeted the music, like their guest conductor, with great skepticism. When faced with Ives's notoriously difficult polyrhythms, some complained that it was impossible to play four beats to the measure while Harrison conducted in three. With his background in percussion, dance, and Dalcroze rhythmic technique, such combinations came easily to Harrison. "Would you prefer," he asked the nonplussed musicians, "that I conduct four in the right hand and three in the left, or vice versa?"[8] Ultimately, Harrison's enthusiasm and skill won them over.

The seventy-three-year-old composer himself was too frail to attend the historic concert, but his wife, Harmony, sat expectantly in the audience. "This first performance," read Harrison's program notes, "presents the work for the original manuscript and in the exact form in which it lay in a Connecticut barn for forty years." Enthusiastic applause and shouts greeted this landmark of American music. "That the symphony of Ives presented on this occasion had to wait forty years for this initial hearing is a sad commentary on the neglect that has been meted out to one of this country's most gifted composers throughout his long career," Noel Straus wrote in the *New York Times*. "It was music close to the soil and deeply felt."[9] Thomson praised Harrison's "loving conductor's hands."[10]

The performance went well, but Harrison had conscientiously spent the great majority of his limited rehearsal time on the Ives symphony. He was less confident about the performance of the next piece on the program, Ruggles's *Portals*, which he'd longed to hear since finding it in *New Music* and which he'd promised Ruggles he would find a way to perform. He was less pleased with the orchestra's handling of the Ruggles, but after the final chord died, the crowd cheered, even after conductor and musicians had bowed, and then bowed again . . . and again.[11]

Finally, Harrison had to turn his back on the audience and wait until they quieted down so they could proceed to the last piece on the program, his own *Motet for the Day of Ascension*, which he had been able to give only minimal rehearsal time. The atonal prose style of the piece, whose title suggests medievalist spiritual devotion, evokes a timeless striving toward ascension beyond earthly reality. One of his most densely Rugglesian scores, this difficult, brooding work's desperate insistence eventually overwhelms its balance and focus. Nevertheless, Donald Fuller's review in *Modern Music* called it "rich yet transparent" and "limpid and expressive."[12] However, Straus wrote in the *New York Times*, "As for Mr. Harrison's motet for seven strings, it failed to place him in as flattering a light as did his baton."[13] It was something of a missed opportunity for Harrison at a time when his music could have broken through to attention on the big New York stage.

The audience reception of the Ives was so enthusiastic that Harrison came back out on stage, as Cowell had done at New Music Society concerts, and announced that they would repeat the symphony. Such an important work, after all, needed more than one hearing. The overwhelming applause affirmed the concert's triumph.

Although preceded by scattered performances arranged by Ives advocates such as Cowell, Nicolas Slonimsky, and pianist John Kirkpatrick, the Little Symphony performance was a landmark evening in American music that marked the long-overdue ascension of Charles Ives into the pantheon of twentieth-century composers. Fortunately, and unknown to either Harrison or Ives, an enthusiastic student at Columbia recorded the radio broadcast of the concert on a large disc recorder. His teacher, the composer Douglas Moore, took the recording across town where the committee charged with recommending finalists for that year's Pulitzer Prize was meeting—and they eventually voted to award the honor to Charles Ives's forty-year-old creation.[14]

Ives, characteristically dismissive of awards and not needing the money, divided the prize between Harrison and the New Music Edition. Ives wrote to Harrison (via Harmony), "As you are very much to blame for getting me into that Pulitzer Prize street, and for having a bushel of letters to answer, and for having a check of $500 thrown over me by the trustees of Colum[bia] Uni[versity] you have to help me by taking 1/2 this (somewhere enclosed) and the rest I'll send to the New Music Edition and Arrow Press," read the letter. "We both feel that if you had not done so much in behalf of the '3rd,' this prize might have gone to Vickey Herbert 'et al.'"[15] Harrison was named an heir of Ives's estate and continued to receive royalties from his music throughout his life.

Harrison received abundant congratulations from new music lovers and requests to borrow his score. "The morning after the concert, I went up to the American Music Center, where all hell had been going on all morning," he recalled. "There had been phone calls and telegrams from all over the eastern seaboard, and Koussevitzky was demanding the score." Rather than exulting in this new attention, Harrison was mostly irritated that other musicians, including Leonard Bernstein and Bernard Herrmann, wanted to conduct the Third again. "But there are three other symphonies," Harrison sputtered. "Why don't they get busy on one of those?"[16]

Within a month the Third was performed again at Columbia University. Later, Harrison and Cowell edited Ives's Second Symphony for a performance conducted by Bernstein, and Harrison continued to work on Ives's manuscripts before donating the volumes he had shipped from San Francisco to the New Music Society.

As another way to express his gratitude for Harrison's premiere of his symphony, Ives offered to pay the publication costs for Harrison's *Motet for the Day of Ascension*. Already harboring misgivings about the piece, Harrison set to work on a revision. As he did, Schoenberg's admonition toward simplicity seemed to be an ever-retreating goal, as the motet became increasingly mired in directionless counterpoint. Finally, utterly frustrated, Harrison ripped the score to shreds, declined Ives's offer, and refused to authorize later performances of it. A month after his Carnegie Hall debut, a triumph for Harrison the conductor but a failure for Harrison the composer, he wrote Ruggles, "Sometimes I wish I didn't write music."[17]

He might have achieved his wish. After Straus so heartily praised his conducting in the *New York Times* review, Barone offered Harrison an associate conductor position with the orchestra and even began planning the next season.[18] But Harrison harbored no ambition to be a conductor, and other events would intervene.

UNANSWERED QUESTION

As he ascended the steps to the midtown Manhattan brownstone, Lou Harrison was excited by what was about to happen. For a decade, he had lived with the music of Charles Ives, poring over the manuscripts in the crate that the old man had sent him in San Francisco, absorbing the techniques and attitude that transformed his own music. Over those years, Harrison and Ives had exchanged letters often—but they had never met, despite the fact that Harrison now lived in the same city. In fact, Ives, who was in poor health and unable to compose, had long refused visitors. According to Cowell, Ives's "nervous condition" gave him trembling hands and a tendency to jump at the sound of the doorbell or telephone.[19] Mostly, the seventy-two-year-old father of American music brooded in his upstairs aerie, dealing with the world through correspondence managed by his aptly named wife, Harmony.

But now, in February 1947, grateful for Harrison's continuing devotion and the attention he'd brought to his long-neglected music at the Carnegie Recital Hall concert nine months earlier, Ives felt strong enough to issue a rare invitation. Would Lou have lunch with him at his home? Harrison eagerly accepted. When he knocked on the door, Harmony greeted him warmly and called up to Ives that his visitor was here. Harrison stood nervously, peering up the stairs. Ives's cane thumped as he haltingly descended the steps—and then, spying Harrison, the rail-thin old maverick seemed to light up.

"My old friend!" he called. Laboriously reaching the bottom of the stairs, he twirled the cane above his head. Harrison ducked. "My old friend!" He was beautiful, Harrison thought, his alabaster skin almost translucent, his piercing blue eyes evoking William Blake's drawings of God the father. Ives became so excited to finally meet the man who for ten years had been one of the few who believed in his music that he had to lie down briefly, weakened by the heart condition that had plagued him for years. Then Harmony ushered them to the table and joined them for lunch.

In person, Harrison's effeminate (to a crusty, old-fashioned New Englander burdened by cultural stereotypes about "sissies") manner might have surprised Ives, who had hitherto known the young acolyte only through his enthusiastic prose. As they were chatting over lunch, Ives suddenly paused. "When I was growing up," he said at last, apropos of nothing previously discussed, "just to be a musician or to think of yourself as a musician automatically meant that you were a sissy." He fixed Harrison in his steely gaze. "But all that seems to have changed now."[20]

Harrison took this to mean that Ives recognized that composers he respected, such as himself and Cowell (who had renewed his friendship with Ives after his scandalous imprisonment), were gay and unashamed of the "sissy" label. In any event, Ives maintained a paternal attitude toward Harrison for the rest of his life, even calling him "Lew Harry Son" in one of his letters.[21]

After lunch, Ives led Harrison to some chairs in front of the house's bay window. Then he paused for a moment. Cowell had warned Harrison that when Ives got excited, he often "went blank." Harrison waited until the old man recovered. What Ives, whose own eyes were failing, wanted to discuss was the possibility of Harrison compiling and editing a complete Ives edition—a monumental task, though one for which Harrison seemed well suited. Not only was he a composer himself and an enthusiast of Ives's music, but also no other American composer to that time had studied Ives's neglected scores more. "I want you," Ives told him, "to be my eyes."[22]

Flattered, and needing the money, Harrison nevertheless hesitated. He remembered a recent incident in which he'd asked Ives for permission to perform the old composer's First Piano Sonata. Harrison had known the difficult work for a decade, and he also understood that it contained depths and peaks that only a truly great performer could attain. Harrison had just the player for it: his friend and "a great virtuoso pianist in the grand manner" William Masselos, a young Juilliard graduate and a well-known specialist in contemporary music who performed works of Cage and Ben Weber, as well as Harrison, at a time when such a specialty was a rarity.[23] Over at Ben Weber's apartment, Harrison showed Masselos his transcription of the Ives work. With Masselos agreeable, Harrison telephoned the Ives townhouse, and Harmony answered. She put down the phone to relay their request to her husband, and down from the aerie came the word: permission granted. Harrison later recounted what happened next.

> So I went ahead, and William Masselos and I went through the whole sonata, working, then I came to a fairly extensive passage in one of the movements that was only written in sketch form, and I had to create it. So I did. . . . [H]e gave them the first performance. It was very well received, and he played it thereafter, and recorded it, and so on. But the minute Ives got the first printing of it, he went through it with a red pencil and started to recompose it. He did this with all of these things.[24]

Harrison realized that trying to prepare definitive editions of Ives's music would be a never-ending nightmare, especially in his own fragile emotional state. "I decided I couldn't do it," he recalled later. "I was much too busy, and I'm glad I didn't, because he never wanted anything finished, you know. He really didn't. I don't know whether it was timidity on his part, modesty, or an aggressive move towards a society which he didn't really quite appreciate or like too much in some senses."[25] While Harrison finished up his edition of the First Sonata, even working on it during his later hospitalization, Harrison's friend Elliott Carter soon took over most of the Ives copying.[26]

Harrison was reluctant to give up the small income the copying job provided, but his life was turbulent enough. Though it paid a pittance, his *Herald Tribune* reviewing grew more intense when his friend Paul Bowles knocked on Harrison's door one day to announce that he was moving to Morocco, where he would give up composition and eventually become a celebrated novelist. He offered to recommend Harrison to fill his reviewing slots in the paper. To cope with the extra assignments, Harrison started writing at his new flat on Prince Street, after he and McGowan bought a Smith Corona typewriter at a pawnshop. Shortly after, the publication *Modern Music* folded and with it, one source of Harrison's income.

FUGUE

The loss of *Modern Music* wasn't the only source of new stress in Harrison's life. At his unpaid position directing the *New Music Edition*, Harrison had formed a board consisting of himself, John Cage, Elliott Carter, and Kurt List, another local atonalist. Harrison brought enthusiasm and good intentions, but his neglect of the business side soon put the publication in even worse shape than it had been under Cowell. "Well, if anybody is less organized about papers than Henry, it's Lou Harrison," Sidney Cowell later said. "So this just added to the general confusion."[27] In late 1946, ill and realizing that he would never be able to handle the work, Harrison gave up the job to his friend Frank Wigglesworth.

Harrison's musical life was no more satisfying: Only a handful of his pieces had been played in New York. In all of 1946, he saw only a performance of three of his *Cembalo Sonatas*, Erdman's performance of his dance *Changing Moment*, a New School performance of his *Trio for Strings*, and the Little Symphony performance of his *Motet for the Day of Ascension*, quite a contrast to the San Francisco years when his music might be played several times a month. The pains from his ulcer had not abated, and Harrison continued to smoke and drink alcohol heavily. Sometimes he would "blank out," his thoughts paralyzed by swirling "mystical notions" and Christian imagery.[28] He told friends that he had seen visions of angels on the walls of his apartment.[29] He was often afraid to sleep, and consequently he was exhausted much of the time, suddenly weeping for no apparent reason.[30] As his anxieties sometimes reached the breaking point, his relationship with McGowan provided one of his few sources of emotional stability.

May 1947, however, Edward delivered shattering news. The AME Church had transferred him out of his Bronx church and to Maryland. To Harrison it was clear that rumors of McGowan's relationship with a white man had finally reached the church administration.[31] Nevertheless, the church was McGowan's calling; he could not refuse to go. Desperate, Harrison wrote the church authorities, pleading with them to reverse the decision, but to no avail. Despite his recent Carnegie triumph, Harrison was broke, beset by noise and stress, struggling to compose, only rarely finding creative outlets—and now, the love of his life was gone. He had come to New York to find success and happiness, and even when he had managed a taste of either, it all turned bitter in the end.

It was a week before his thirtieth birthday, and Harrison was supposed to attend a concert of Renaissance music and write a review immediately afterward for tomorrow's paper. But, he told Jack Heliker, he couldn't do it. He simply was not able to get up and go to the concert. Heliker calmed Harrison down and even accompanied him to the concert and then to the *Tribune* and sat with him while he finished the review. It would be his last for the paper.[32]

A few nights later, while working on another review at the *Tribune* office, Harrison began to shudder. He typed for a little while and then got up and walked around aimlessly, muttering to himself. He grew more and more anxious, and finally he grabbed a trash can and threw up. He rushed out of the office. That night, he showed up at Thomson's apartment—driven by voices in his head—and Thomson ordered him to stay the night, sleeping on the couch.[33]

The next morning, Heliker found Harrison staggering down Fifth Avenue. He tried to talk to him, but Harrison was in a daze. He looked as though he'd been wandering around for hours. Heliker took him to a nearby church and tried to engage him in conversation. But he couldn't do anything. Harrison was having a nervous breakdown.

14

TEARS OF THE ANGEL (1947–1948)

A composer friend of mine spent some time in a mental rehabilitation facility. There the staff encouraged the patients to play bridge. One day my friend's partner criticized him for playing an ace on a trick that had already been won. My friend stood up and said, 'If you think I've come to the loony bin to learn to play bridge, you're crazy!'

—John Cage[1]

John Cage was the first person Jack Heliker called when he found Lou Harrison wandering in a daze on the street. Heliker walked his distraught friend back to his apartment. "Come and get me!" Harrison wailed.[2] Cage came over immediately and took his friend to a psychiatrist on the Upper East Side, who examined Harrison and recommended him for admission to a private psychiatric hospital in Ossining in Westchester County.[3] Eventually, Harrison was admitted to the Psychiatric Institute and Hospital at the Presbyterian Medical Center in New York and assigned a private room, with shared toilets and mess hall.[4]

Harrison's friends and family rallied to help. His parents paid the rent on his apartment, and Cage and other friends looked after it. Unknown to Harrison, Cage slipped a note through the Ives's mail slot, telling him that Harrison was in the hospital. Ives immediately wrote a check that paid for much of the medical expenses.[5]

Although the official diagnosis was a form of schizophrenia, Harrison and friends used the then-popular term "nervous breakdown" to describe his stress-induced anxiety crisis, and at first Harrison felt ashamed to be in the "loony bin."[6] But the hospital's relatively enlightened therapeutic approach and the consciously predictable routine soon calmed him. Harrison's routine included daily meetings with his therapist, three meals per day, exercise walks, and recreation with the other patients. He especially enjoyed hydrotherapy, and he temporarily gave up his vegetarianism in order to adjust to hospital food. As Harrison gradually improved, John Cage wrote to Henry and Sidney Cowell:

> Virgil showed me your letter to him about Lou because I've been seeing Lou and taking care of the things that need to be done for him. There is nothing to avoid in letters to him except things touching on mysticism, but generally that is a private matter anyway.

Most of his physical symptoms (tears, fears of sleep, exhaustion, etc.) have gone and there remain only now-and-then appearing pains and whirling sensations which seem to be common in such a case (which is called apparently, an anxiety neurosis)....Lou's mind is perfectly all right; it is simply his emotions (their state was measured as that of a 2 year old; but since that measurement he has grown miraculously to an adolescent age in a matter of weeks). All of us now are images: Henry and Virgil and Schoenberg are father-images; I am a brother image. Sidney undoubtedly is a mother image.[7]

At first shy when living (and showering) in close quarters with other men, Harrison gradually got along with the other patients: Wall Street types, veterans, academics—the ward held all manner of New Yorkers. He spent time playing whist or contract bridge with the other patients—whereupon a ferocious and unwelcome competitive streak emerged.[8]

Fortunately, his relatively enlightened therapists didn't try to "cure" Harrison of his sexual orientation but instead told him they wanted him to be a happy and comfortable gay man, a lucky break in the days when homosexuality was officially regarded as a pathological condition. The combination of medications, routine, and conversations with therapists gradually stabilized Harrison's condition, though he would suffer flare-ups for the next decade. In contrast to his San Francisco ebullience, "he was a gentle soul" then, Anahid Ajemian recalled later. "He was quiet and lovely and had a beautiful smile."[9]

The therapy's enforced introspection did bring Harrison some new insights that his peripatetic lifestyle during his twenties had never permitted. "I was nasty to people," he remembered much later. "Before the breakdown, it was because I was so oblivious to everybody that I was doing things I wasn't aware of, though people never told me. I lived not thinking about other people very much. Afterward I was coping with my own eruptions."[10]

On the other hand, Harrison's involuntary hermitage brought him to the realization that it was fine to be a nonconformist, in his sexuality and in his identity as an artist. After he'd spent eight months in the facility, Harrison's doctors met to discuss whether it would be safe for Harrison to leave the hospital, and in the course of the discussion, one of them asked him how he conceived his role in society. "I'm not playing a role," Harrison insisted. "This is me!"[11] He would continue to follow his own path, even when that included pacifism during war, environmentalism long before it was recognized as a valuable philosophy—and, soon, writing music that did not fit any of the acceptable categories in postwar American music.

As Harrison gradually rebuilt his identity, he left behind his musical evocations of the shadowy mysticism that had haunted him during his breakdown, but he otherwise claimed no connections between this trauma and his music. Still, it's hard to miss this period's eventual abandonment of intense introspection and expressionism for unwavering drones, translucent textures, and sunny melodies. Like Harrison's mental recovery, the change was gradual, and atonality would always have a prominent place in Harrison's acreage of techniques. But tellingly, two of his pre-breakdown works that he judged to be successes, *Triphony* and *Praises for Michael the Archangel*, he would years later adapt in larger works as expressions of personal grief. In contrast, his next project would reach outward, toward the comforts of strict forms and the solace of loved ones.

ON G

The quiet setting and the absence of deadlines gave Harrison—at last—the emotional space and extended time needed to commence what was to become his most ambitious project to date. His substantial twelve-tone symphony explored different approaches to Schoenberg's method—while finding tonality in a style best known for its usefulness in achieving atonality. Harrison's first model was the piece that so impressed him when he heard it on the radio as a teenager in San Francisco: Alban Berg's Violin Concerto. Berg achieved his kaleidoscopically shifting tonalities through a tone row that features a series of interlocking triads, a technique typically avoided by his teacher Schoenberg.

Although atonality might seem suited for a soundtrack to this anguished point in Harrison's life, the symphony in fact has little in common with the angst of Harrison's earlier atonal New York works. Harrison had come to realize that Ruggles's intense style of "stretching, yearning, pushing outward" would be difficult to extend to large-scale works. "Constant counterpoint of that kind is hard to sustain in that manner," he explained. "To keep the chromaticism in any sense cogent and the texture moving without too many repetitions is a hard one to do."[12] But beyond the practicalities of form, Harrison's decision to find a new direction for his atonal language signaled a new musical outlook.

The vigorous first movement, for example, owes much more to the power of Ives's Symphony #4 or Stravinsky's *Symphony in Three Movements* (premiered in New York the previous year) than to Harrison's earlier dark mysticism. Harrison called its jaunty angularity "uptight and syncopated and a little Stravinsky.... The first movement is chop, chop!"[13] Because Ives, who grew up in a time and culture where heterosexual young men needed to be defensive about any interest in music, characterized this style as "masculine" (a description that Ruggles also appropriated), some writers have applied that description to this movement, even speculating that this style expresses the composer's sexual confusion during the breakdown. Harrison strongly denied such a connection, just as he did later attempts to find "gay markers" in such influences as Asian music. "I think of the musical qualities," he said, "but I don't think of sex in connection with it, or gender, if it's rhetorically excited," and in fact, potent, even gritty dramatic statements inhabit works throughout his career.[14]

For this new symphony, Harrison created a twelve-tone row unlike his earlier ones, which had followed the recommendation for intervallic variety he had read in Ernst Krenek's book. Instead, this row used only three distinct intervals: six minor seconds and four major thirds, which give the symphony a characteristic sound, and two perfect fourths, which, when strategically placed, establish snatches of triads and a bittersweet tonality. While restricting the successive intervals risks limiting variety, this parsimonious approach to intervals provides unity throughout the symphony's nearly forty minutes.

Along with these harmonic choices, Harrison used another device to establish a sense of tonality: an overall plan of tonal form through the movements, using the pitch G as a foundational tone. He initially gave his new creation the seemingly contradictory title (for a twelve-tone piece) *Symphony in G.* Later he began to think that perhaps "in G," with its implication of diatonic keys and harmonies was not quite right, and finally he settled on the more creative title *Symphony on G.*[15]

To emphasize this pitch, Harrison adopted a new device: starting a particular row form at an arbitrary point, not necessarily the beginning. "I began to regard the row as not a fixed twelve positions but rather as a wheel with gears, and you could intercept it at any gear point. And as long as you went around, you could go to any other gear point and go around in any other way as long as you completed the row," he said. "That made a difference in use because it meant I had a number of choices as I was approaching the end of any one group."[16] He needed them because, as in the *Suite for Piano,* his linear approach to the twelve-tone method, one tone after another in all parts, also constrained his choices.

The hospital's influence appears less in the symphony's expressive content than in its careful construction. Just as the strict routine of hospital life helped ease his panic attacks, its predictability made it easier for Harrison to focus meticulously on working out his score. The first movement consists of six sections of exactly thirty-two and a half measures each, plus a short coda. The first two sections constitute the first and second themes of traditional sonata form associated with the opening of symphonies since the time of Haydn. The first theme is based entirely on transpositions of the prime, or original, form of the row, while the second, "a sort of Russian cello song," contrasts not only in its lyricism but also in the fact that it is based entirely on retrograde (backward) versions of the row.[17] This second theme emphasizes the pitch D—the dominant of G, the traditional key for the second theme in symphonies. The next two sections comprise the "development," a contrasting working out of some implications of the row, this time based entirely on inversions of the row. The last two sections, as in a traditional first movement, recapitulate the first two themes.

The brooding second movement immediately contrasts with the dramatic extroversion of the first movement. Composed mostly of woodwind dialogues with soft but colorful commentary by the other sections of the orchestra, it contains some of Harrison's most adventuresome orchestration, often featuring the brittle tones of the tack piano. This unusual tone color ("quite glittery in overtones," according to Harrison) is especially effective when combined with soft, tremolo strings and the harp, often creating delicate atmospheric effects.[18] Harrison would continue to use the unusual combination throughout his career.

In approaching his first big orchestral work, Harrison followed the advice of Virgil Thomson, who advocated what he called the French style of orchestration. "Clarity and brilliance are achieved by keeping the different instruments at all times recognizably separate," Thomson wrote, contrasting it with the weighty German style.[19] Nevertheless, Harrison judged this advice to be "almost the same thing that Schoenberg said—if you assign a note to an instrument and no other instrument is playing it, it will be heard." It was the same lesson he heard in the works of Handel: "Clarity, no big 'German' unisons or tuttis. I always remember that from Virgil and Schoenberg. . . . *Symphony on G* . . . is very sparsely scored."[20]

For Harrison, who throughout his life was most at home writing compact pieces often gathered into suites, the symphony's first two movements represent something of a landmark—expansive statements (the second movement is over ten minutes long) of a kind that he would only occasionally summon even late in his career. The symphony's third movement, though, inaugurates an innovative compromise with his love for miniatures—making the dance movement "scherzo" a kind of mini-suite itself.[21] Harrison viewed the scherzo movement of a classical symphony as a kind of suite because it evolved out of what were (in the baroque era) separate dances. In *Symphony on G*, the four sub-movements are "Waltz," "Polka," "Song," and "Rondeau." The hospital's weekly dances with the women patients (a "co-recreation" therapy) inspired the first two, and he dedicated them to two of those patients, identified only as Leona (the waltz) and Janet (the polka), "a charming girl who enjoyed dancing, especially polkas," he said.[22]

Harrison said the uproarious polka came naturally from his childhood dance lessons as well as Dmitri Shostakovich's polka in his ballet *The Age of Gold*. One of Harrison's most humorous compositions, it features a madly dancing clarinet over oompah chords on the tack piano and pizzicato strings and even schmaltzy trombone glissandos. He jokingly called it the "Great Wind" because the clarinetist can barely take a breath for pages.[23] Here Harrison ingeniously assembled tonal chords from his row to create a kind of off-kilter tonality that expresses the humor he found in dances at "the loony hatch."

In the most memorable sub-movement, "Song," impressionistic arpeggios on the harp accompany a long, expressive melody on the cello high in its range, usually doubled by the plaintive English horn. Here Harrison freely "clumped together" four- and five-note subsets of the row to create triads with softly dissonant added tones.[24] Like Hovhaness, he also established tonality through the use of long pedal tones. The tonality constantly shifts as it follows the row, creating an ethereally floating lyricism. Comparing it with Camille Saint-Saëns's iconic cello solo, the ever-witty Virgil Thomson observed, "It is like 'The Swan' sans Saint-Saëns, Lou."[25] The song's dedication to John Cage, though offered as a kind of love song for his dear friend, is nevertheless mischievously ironic since, as Harrison said, "John could never write a long melody like that."[26] Knowing Cage's admiration of French culture, Harrison cast the song as an impressionistic "French nocturne," its original title.[27] As Harrison emerged from the nightmare of his breakdown, so did his instinctive melodicism.

The "Rondeau" section returns to the atonality of the waltz, but in an elaborate trio for piano, tack piano, and harp, creating what Harrison called "a kind of cadenza for the whole symphony."[28] Harrison, who cherished bright, bell-like tones throughout his career, called this collection of instruments, sometimes together with the celesta or vibraphone in later works such as his Fourth Symphony, his "gamelan section" within the orchestra. The elaborateness of the whole scherzo helps create what Harrison called an "expanding form" for the whole symphony: "The first movement, after all, is not very big and it's a little bit nervous and tense and tight," he said. "Then the slow movement opens up a little bit more. It evolves. Then the scherzo is a real expansion scherzo. It really goes to town."[29]

Harrison left the hospital with his symphony incomplete. Though he had finished the first movement in December 1947, as well as much of the second movement and some of the dances, he still had no finale. He wouldn't be able to return to the massive project until he was free of New York's urban bustle.

THE OPEN ROAD

On a winter day in 1947, John Cage drove Lou Harrison down from the hospital to the house of the parents of the eminent young New York new-music-performing sisters Anahid and Maro Ajemian, whom Harrison had met at a concert of Hovhaness's music. (Maro would give the New York premiere of Cage's *Sonatas and Interludes* for prepared piano the next year.) They joined the two young Juilliard graduates at a table with Cage's partner, Merce Cunningham, and set to work. One drew up a promotional poster, another looked up addresses (sometimes those of friends or professional acquaintances, sometimes those of famous New Yorkers—Helena Rubinstein, Jasper Johns—who, whether or not they knew anything about the music or the people involved, might have an interest in vanguard music or who might be able to help the cause), another stuffed envelopes with the one-page concert announcement that brochure Cage had drafted, and another stamped them. Contrived by Cage, this kind of assembly line for promoting new music was a frequent part of the composers' lives in New York.[30]

For Harrison, the camaraderie during this visit back to the city provided a welcome first step back into society. The occasion was arranged by Cage and Cunningham, who, trying to help Harrison during his hospitalization, offered him a commission for a program featuring Cunningham at Hunter College Playhouse in December 1947. Harrison made another of his tentative trips back into the city to work with the dancers and conduct the program, which also featured William Masselos and Maro Ajemian playing several of Cage's prepared piano works.

Like the symphony, Harrison's contribution to Cunningham's dance *The Open Road* (Harrison's title for the music was *Western Dance*) tried to reconcile his Schoenbergian background with new expressive concerns, albeit in a different and more modest way. This brief but sunny piece lyrically evokes the West's wide-open spaces. "I wrote it in more or less in the Aaron style," he said, but unlike Copland, Harrison created this scene within the unlikely context of floating atonality.[31] Originally written out for piano, Harrison arranged it for the instruments Cunningham had available: flute, bassoon, trumpet, cello, violin, and piano—the last two instruments played by the Ajemian sisters. Its dramatic opening and inviting atmosphere seem to announce a rebirth, and it contrasts strikingly with his earlier Ruggles-besotted compositions.

Although Harrison would sometimes reuse or revise his earlier atonal pieces, he began to realize that he had reached the limits of the style. "When I was doing the Ruggles thing, there were incredible numbers of erasures and changes, and this didn't happen in the other music where I sort of wrote it and imagined it worked. I must have felt a frustration," he explained. "There comes a limit to the Ruggles idiom, and I think I reached it. And the business of constantly pushing out and struggling—for what? Finally it occurs to you that it's for pleasure, and the pleasure finally turns out to be centricity and modality and apprehensibility. Why undertake that amount of stretching and the agony of it all which is implied in all that chromatic struggling, when you could simply relax and enjoy the melody? I was poised when I had done enough of that to enter the monophonic world of Alan Hovhaness. Hovhaness was so very important."[32]

The move toward Hovhanessian lyricism continued in another piece that Harrison composed toward the end of his hospital stay, the haunting little *Air* for solo recorder for his friend Olin Stevens; the piece's pastoral qualities recall his idyllic Maine coast getaway.[33] The mysterious melodicism of this sinuous set of four short variations also echoes his favorite Elizabethan models and points toward the great modal ballets that Harrison would soon undertake.[34]

After some months in the hospital, Harrison was feeling somewhat stronger, though still fragile. He was assigned to dream and to report his dreams and to paint as a form of art therapy. He painted an orchard and other views from his window, a portrait of his family, and other works in an expressionist style. And, away from the constant rumble of the city, he began to sleep better.[35] "I am getting better," he wrote his mother.[36] In early 1948, when he felt ready to attempt a return to society, Harrison was transferred to a private convalescent home upstate. His initial forays back into city life were "scary and tentative," Harrison recalled. "We were given and had the responsibility to take care of ourselves, and part of the therapy itself was making decisions. I had to find out if I could work and in what way."[37]

Although therapy had fortified his emotional condition, Harrison was still emotionally shaky when he returned to his Prince Street apartment in early 1948. Harrison would continue meeting with his therapists periodically, and for the next few years, his emotional state would continue to fluctuate. "I'd have enormous anxieties, melancholies that amounted to manic depression," he recalled. "Sometimes I'd have enormous enthusiasms, and sometimes I couldn't care less."[38]

Along with his piano, his purple wall hanging, and the trunk of musical projects in progress, many of the sources of Harrison's crisis remained. Still impoverished, he was appalled to discover that grocery prices had doubled in the postwar economic upheaval, though his landlady generously kept his rent low. He was unable to return to the stressful, deadline-driven job of a newspaper music critic, even had there been an opening. Edward was gone, and by that summer, so were Cage and Cunningham. They had booked a series of performances at colleges from California to an experimental campus in rural North Carolina called Black Mountain College.[39] Heliker, too, had received an award—the prestigious Rome Prize—and moved to Rome with Merton Brown and Frank Wigglesworth.

But although his closest friends were gone, some welcome news arrived a few weeks after his release: his own award, a $1,000 grant from the American Academy of Arts and Letters. The influential Virgil Thomson likely had steered the prize his way, knowing that the money was sorely needed.[40] The awards ceremony, scheduled for

May 21, 1948, would include a small orchestra to play works by the composers. Harrison set aside his work on the symphony, as well as some cursory sketches he'd just begun for a work based on the romantic myth of Cupid and Psyche, to put together a new piece for this occasion.[41]

Harrison created a five-movement *First Suite for Strings* based largely on sketches that he had been working on during the year prior to his breakdown. Emboldened by his new embrace of his own eclecticism, Harrison kept the even-numbered movements in his slow, searching chromatic style, but the odd-numbered movements are brisk diatonic fantasies, seventeenth-century string *ricercari* translated into a language of quintal counterpoint. This alternation between atonality and diatonicism, echoing some of his San Francisco eclecticism, functions like a baroque composer's alternation between major and minor keys, but even so, the unremitting polyphony produces an overall sameness that increasingly dissatisfied Harrison.[42]

Still replete with sketches, that summer Harrison created a *Suite #2 for Strings* in which he tried to make up for some of the shortcomings of the first suite, settling on a more manageable two diatonic movements sandwiching a fleet atonal fantasia. The middle movement's light, two-part texture contrasts not just with the more densely scored outer movements, but also with the Ruggles-like atonal chorales in the first suite. "Harrison, in common with many men about his age in this country, incorporates elements of both diatonic and chromatic schools into his music," Cowell wrote in a review of Harrison's works for the *Musical Quarterly* in 1950. "Instead of trying to integrate these elements into a single fabric, as is more usual at the moment, Harrison uses them as contrasting material for different movements."[43]

These startling juxtapositions reveal a composer trying to integrate the contrasting sides of his musical personality, just as he was trying to integrate the fragments of his psyche. His release from the hospital after nine months didn't mean that his mental stability returned immediately. For the next decade, Harrison would continue to rebuild his personality, asking himself basic questions about his identity and purpose: "What kind of music are you going to write? What's your attitude toward society going to be? What's the attitude of society going to be toward you? Well, it's going to continue to pound through your head."[44] These reevaluations would take Harrison down a new musical path, one that would ultimately lead him out of the dark intricacies of his New York style and toward a renewed exploration of the foundations of music and sound. "Not everyone has had the advantage of going bonkers," he explained later. "I had a chance to reconstruct a life out of the detritus."[45]

THE PERILOUS CHAPEL (1948–1949)

A lone flute accompanies six women dancing in unison onstage, their movements alluringly integrated, the different colors of their costumes—turquoise, red, blue, more—representing diverse parts of a single personality working together in harmony.

Then, the stage darkens, and a gleaming white and gold abstract cylinder descends, dropping a pair of wings from inside. The music halts, the women stand frozen as the sculpture touches a lone dancer. She collapses, and suddenly, as the music returns, each colorfully clad woman springs to life. The dancer in white staggers around them, hands over her eyes. The women arise, leap, dancing in pairs and groups, then forming a circle and moving in synchrony, whole and harmonious, like the winsome music that escorts them.[1]

The action onstage at the January 1949 premiere of Jean Erdman's ballet *The Perilous Chapel*, at Hunter Playhouse on Sixty-Eighth Street, paralleled Harrison's life at the time. In the program, a passage from the Book of Revelations followed the title: "And I saw a new heaven and new earth: for the first heaven and the first earth were passed away; and there was no more sea."[2] The biblical text reflected the attitude of renewal that accompanied the debut of Erdman's new company, and also Harrison's search for a new start after his breakdown. "In *The Perilous Chapel*," Erdman said later, "the seed idea is of a soul's adventure in the crisis of a life transforming experience."[3]

The Perilous Chapel's beguiling music and mythic themes marked an unanticipated change in direction for the thirty-one-year-old Harrison, whose percussion and dissonant counterpoint seemed very distant from the expressive tonality of this score. Also distant were the concerns of the artists he had grown up around in 1930s San Francisco. The social activism of artists like Carol Beals were out of fashion in postwar New York, a city of abstract expressionists and radical experimenters. The works of Jean Erdman and her husband Joseph Campbell were steeped in symbols and ritual. Erdman, for example, created symbolic categories of movement in a way analogous to Campbell's abstraction of meta-themes from world mythologies.[4] Despite his political concerns, Harrison's love of mythology made him receptive to this approach to art. And when Erdman's call came at this crucial juncture, with all these notions swirling around his still-fragile mind, his score to *The Perilous Chapel* would provide the vehicle to apply all the new ideas he'd been absorbing in the writings of Campbell and two other crucially important thinkers.

AN ALGEBRA OF METAPHYSICAL ABSTRACTIONS

All music is based on the relations between sounds, and a careful study of the numbers by which these relations are ruled brings us immediately into the almost forgotten science of numerical symbolism. Numbers correspond to abstract principles, and their application to physical reality follows absolute and inescapable laws. In musical experience we are brought into direct contact with these principles, the connection between physical reality and metaphysical principles can be felt in music as nowhere else.

—Alain Daniélou [5]

Symbols and underlying profound truths in art and life obsessed Harrison throughout his stay in New York, as in the Christian mysticism that so captivated his creative thinking prior to his breakdown. While Harrison's interest in Christian ritual faded after his return from the hospital, his attraction to mythic symbols intensified. And as always with Harrison, any interest in a subject meant reading about it obsessively, in Robert Graves's *The White Goddess: A Historical Grammar of Poetic Myth* and especially in the works of his friend Joseph Campbell. In 1948, Campbell was just completing the first of his famous series of books on comparative mythology, *The Hero With a Thousand Faces*, which supposes that the commonality of hero myths throughout the world reveals a fundamental human need to describe psychological, social, and spiritual truths that transcend individual cultures. In mythology throughout the world, Campbell identified the common story of a hero encountering a place or trial of great danger and then emerging victorious, bringing back to humanity some gift as a result of the experience.

The musical application of the universal symbols that Campbell discerned became clear to Harrison when he happened upon a book by Alain Daniélou, a French ethnomusicologist, that explored the mathematical and symbolic basis of the scales of many cultures and times in history. When ancient musicians marked off lengths of strings, they found that octaves occur when the string is stopped at its halfway point, again at a quarter of its length, an eighth, and so on. They saw that intervals are defined by ratios of string lengths rather than absolute differences. As one ascends the scale, the frets on a guitar begin to crowd together toward the high end of the neck, halving every octave; that is, a 2:1 ratio. The next simplest ratio less than the octave, 3:2, is the "perfect fifth" so common in musical scales all over the world, and the interval between it and an octave is 4:3, or the "perfect fourth." With these simple relationships between integers one through four, many ancient cultures derived scales, including, according to Daniélou, the Chinese, Indians, and ancient Greeks. [6]

Thus music makes the abstractions of sacred numbers real to our senses—the two of the fundamental duality of heaven and earth, the three of Christianity's or Hinduism's divine trinity, the four of the terrestrial world (four corners of the Earth, four seasons, four elements, etc.). "In ancient times, music was something other than mere pleasure of the ear: it was like an algebra of metaphysical abstractions, knowledge of which was given only to initiates, but by whose principles the masses were instinctively and unconsciously influenced."[7]

A complementary influence in Harrison's musical thinking arrived in 1949, when Virgil Thomson received a review copy of a curious book at the *Herald Tribune*: *Genesis of a Music*. As promised by its title, the book told of an extraordinary evolution of the American composer Harry Partch's singular vision. Central to Partch's ideas was the reinvention of musical scales based on these same integer ratios as in Daniélou's book, a tuning method known as just intonation. Knowing Harrison's growing interest in these matters, Thomson handed him the book one day. "Here, Lou, see what you can make of this."[8]

Harrison had reviewed Partch's League of Composers–sponsored concert a few years earlier for *Modern Music*, and while intrigued by Partch's strange instruments and his outlandish forty-three-tone-per-octave scale, he didn't know quite what to make of it. He found the sounds interesting, but, consumed by counterpoint in those early New York years, Harrison decided that most of the forty-three tones decorated "a fairly simple scheme," missing the implications of just intonation.[9]

These implications of Partch's book would take Harrison some years to fully absorb, and he would not venture into just-intonation composition himself until he had left New York, but then it would profoundly affect his music. For now, though, he went out and bought a tuning hammer (the wrench used by piano tuners) and went to work on his piano.[10] He tried to block out the noise of the city and listen for the subtly smooth sound that told him when a fifth had found its perfect 3:2 ratio. He tuned his piano entirely in these fifths (a tuning named for Pythagoras, its supposed inventor) and was startled to hear what a difference it made to his works in quintal (fifth-based) counterpoint. In order to play in different keys with instruments (especially the keyboard) that are limited to a restricted number of fixed pitches, Western musicians and instrument makers compromised when tuning their instruments, adjusting some of those ratios in a tuning method known as temperament (which Harrison came to denigrate as "tampering") so that a "perfect fifth" was no longer really a 3:2 but instead some other interval slightly smaller, inexpressible as an integer ratio.

Daniélou viewed these compromises, which culminated in the standard equal temperament tuning system of the West, as having betrayed music's connection to spirituality: "The result is that Westerners have more and more lost all conception of a music able to express clearly the highest ideas and feelings. They now expect from music mostly a confused noise, more or less agreeable, but able to arouse in the audience only the most ordinary sensations and simplified images. This is a complete misconception of the true role of music."[11]

Daniélou's and Partch's books weren't Harrison's first exposure to other tunings. Henry Cowell gave an important, if idiosyncratic, explanation of the harmonic series in his *New Musical Resources*, for example.[12] While Harrison wasn't yet ready to abandon his use of the conventional instruments that temperament made possible, nor to adopt wholesale the melodic music of India and China that Daniélou described, the symbolic connections between musical scales and deeper truths that Daniélou described intrigued him. He tried first to find ways that he could adapt the ideas of scale construction he found in the book to ordinary tempered instruments.

Harrison seized upon the scale constructed by tetrachords, a method associated with the ancient Greeks, though Daniélou, who lived in India, thought it originated there or in Egypt. "Tetrachord" literally means "four strings" (of the Greek lyre); that is, four pitches of a scale within the span of a 4:3 ratio (perfect fourth). The beginning and ending pitches are fixed in the 4:3 relationship to each other, but the internal two pitches and the three intervals they define can be shifted around to create a variety of distinctive constructions. The Greeks grouped these possibilities under three categories called *genera*, which include the diatonic, roughly consisting of two whole tones and one semitone; the chromatic, consisting of two semitones and a minor third; and the enharmonic, consisting of two quartertones and a major third. Because on tempered instruments there is only one type of semitone and one type of whole tone (and no quartertones), there are only three possibilities for the diatonic tetrachord: semitone, whole tone, whole tone (STT); whole tone, semitone, whole tone (TST); and whole tone, whole tone, semitone (TTS). Two tetrachords can then be combined, either with a note in common or a whole tone between, to create an octave scale.

In the fall of 1948, while sketching out a third suite for strings, Harrison carefully worked out all of these possibilities—a process interrupted when Jean Erdman asked him to score a new ballet. *The Perilous Chapel* (the title had been suggested by Campbell) metaphorically portrays the "perilous journey" (as Campbell called it) that takes the entranced white-clad dancer into the depths of chaos and out again.[13] Harrison's music for Erdman's production shimmers with occasional sunlight glimpsed through slowly parting clouds. These universal symbols informed more than just the dance and psychological drama of *The Perilous Chapel*; they permeated the music itself, thanks to new methods of composition that Harrison contrived, inspired by Daniélou's and Partch's books.

Although he struggled with his emotional stability and, at one particularly unsteady moment, even suggested that Erdman ask other composers to take over the score, he relented. "I was working without music," remembered Erdman, "developing the structure and the rhythms. Lou came over and took down the counts, then he made the music the way he wanted to, to fit."[14] The result was an enchanting quartet for flute, harp, cello, and drums that also comprised a systematic series of variations on tetrachord construction.

In the peaceful Prelude, the flute's ostinato of an ascending tetrachord of the semitone, tone, tone (STT) type mirrors a lyrical cello melody based on a tetrachord with the same pattern in descending form, working together and then switching roles like the different sides of the soul in Erdman's scenario. After the large, mysterious sculpture descends from the ceiling, the music (based on contrasting TST tetrachords) grows louder and more angular, via Harrison's use of the octave displacement of tones in the tetrachordal patterns. A magical force emanating from the object symbolizes the hero's confrontation with crisis. A "barbaro" movement of secundal dissonances (still based on tetrachords) and drums then accompanies the psychological descent into darkness. The journey reaches a climax in the fifth movement, when the tetrachords combine polytonally into dizzying scales with the onset of chaos.

As the hero returns from crisis transformed, the ballet ends with a peaceful "Alleluia" based on the form of a chaconne. The reassurance of the repeating bass line of this form, which Harrison learned from the baroque composers Lully and Purcell, would make it one of his favorite ways to end multi-movement pieces.[15]

Despite the importance of Harrison's renewed interest in melodic lyricism and pitch relationships, Henry Cowell in his review for the *Musical Quarterly* wisely called attention instead to Harrison's brilliant use of timbre in this small ensemble. His choice of harp instead of piano avoids percussiveness, "making sounds now incisive, now subtle," and the writing for flute creates "the loveliest possible limpid, watery tone. . . . The result is a uniquely flowing tone quality in this perfectionist work."[16]

The ballet also uncannily reflected Harrison's own Campbellian journey from youthful successes to the depths of a mental breakdown. He slowly emerged from the darkness with a reawakened (and increasingly unfashionable) need for sensual beauty and the comforts of strict form. Although he continued to admire many of his atonal works, they bear the scars of a bitter struggle and contrast with the luminous modal melodies of *The Perilous Chapel*.

As Harrison continued his journey, friends were still looking out for him. Cage was now back in town from Paris, where he had begun writing a string quartet that he would finish in 1950 and dedicate to Harrison. Cage had been in contact with the choreographer Bonnie Bird, who was now on faculty at Smith College. She told him of her plans to teach a summer dance class at Reed College, in Harrison's (and Bird's) hometown: Portland, Oregon—and that she needed a composer.

SCENES FROM A MARRIAGE

One Sunday morning, shortly after Harrison's arrival at Reed College, he was shaving in the dormitory bathroom when he heard a call outside the window. He opened the second floor window and looked down to see a beautiful twenty-year-old student named Remy Charlip looking up at him. Charlip had just completed a cross-country trip, hitchhiking the last leg to Portland, but he hadn't counted on arriving on a Sunday, when everything was closed. He was calling up to windows at random. Finally, in one of them appeared Harrison's face, graced with a mustache of shaving cream. "Come on up!" he shouted.[17]

A native New Yorker, Abraham Charlip had recently graduated from the Cooper Union School of Art, but he found that "being a painter seemed hopeless," and he gravitated toward the stage rather than the studio. He applied to Bonnie Bird's 1949 summer program in dance at Reed and received a scholarship. His sunny disposition and eager devotion to theater, dance, visual arts, and poetry immediately charmed Harrison, and the two soon became a couple, despite the difference in their ages and

Harrison's continued moodiness and occasional outbursts. He would become one of the most important people in Harrison's life.

Buoyed by a new romance and a return to his verdant hometown, Harrison relished his tonic summer respite from the pressures of New York life. Working with Bonnie Bird brought back some of the ease and confidence he remembered from San Francisco. The pain from his ulcer, which he had associated with the stress of living in New York, began to wane. He and Remy spent a few days hitchhiking down the coast to San Francisco, visiting Carol Beals and Harrison's old haunts.

On one of the college's bulletin boards, an elegant poster prepared by the college's Scribe Club caught Harrison's eye, and he discovered that a gruff former English professor named Lloyd Reynolds was giving calligraphy classes. Even back in his San Francisco days, Harrison had dabbled in calligraphy, trying out different styles, but without any training. After the class, calligraphy became a lifelong passion for Harrison, who made even casual letters to friends into works of art. The views of the self-taught Reynolds dovetailed with Harrison's in a number of areas—their common appreciation of Asian and Native American art and culture, their democratic instinct about art as something anyone can make, their love of theater (Reynolds made masks and posters for Reed theater productions), their fear of industrialization destroying craft, and more.[18] Harrison bought a calligraphy book at a local bookstore that referenced the calligraphy of English artist William Morris, who shared many of these same concerns.[19] Intrigued, Harrison found an old edition of Morris's poetry, from which, three years later, he would extract the libretto for his first opera.

Two phonograph cabinets stand on the stage. A bouncy overture concludes with a drum roll. A voice from one of the cabinets announces that the audience is on the first level of the Eiffel Tower. The other speaker cabinet notes the appearance of an ostrich, pursued by a hunter who fires at it. A lion appears, scattering the assembled characters and creatures, except for a pompous general who insists it is a mirage and is swiftly gobbled up.

—Jean Cocteau[20]

Jean Cocteau described his hilarious 1921 Dada ballet *The Marriage at the Eiffel Tower* as "a contemporary analogue to the blend of spectacle, ballet, music, chorus and song, a kind of secret marriage between ancient tragedy and the end of the year revue, chorus and music hall number."[21] All action in the play is described by two narrators, inspired by the barkers of the Paris carnivals and enclosed in gramophone cabinets on opposite sides of the stage. The original Paris production used music by members of "Les Six," the young composers that Cocteau championed as the successors to the anti-romantic modernism of Satie.

That original unpublished score was lost until 1956, so when Bonnie Bird produced the dance at Reed in the summer of 1949, she requested a new one from Lou Harrison, who thus became the first single composer to provide music for the entire Cocteau play.[22] Remy Charlip designed the sets and costumes, and Bird and her husband, Ralph Gundlach, a psychology professor, announced the lines from within the two phonograph cabinets.

While Harrison's first composing assignment in Portland didn't afford him the opportunity to continue his experiments with tetrachords and modal symbolism, it proved both delightful and musically successful, reflecting his elation at being back on the West Coast, close to nature and on familiar ground. After the dark, dissonant works of his past few years in New York, the score for *The Marriage at the Eiffel Tower* sounds like the music of an entirely different composer.

As in previous works inspired by Ives, Cowell, Schoenberg, and Ruggles, Harrison drew on the style of another composer he admired—his Francophilic mentor, Virgil Thomson, who moved to Paris in 1921, the year Cocteau wrote *The Marriage at the Eiffel Tower*. In a 1941 essay on the importance of Erik Satie's works, Thomson wrote, "To the uninitiated they sound trifling. To those who love them they are fresh and beautiful and firmly right."[23] He might just as well have been talking about Harrison's score, which sounds like almost nothing Harrison had written before, excepting possibly the recent little New York waltzes. The quick overture evokes all the charm of 1920s Paris and Les Six, spiced up with the occasional polytonal dissonance and shifting meters. When it was performed in New York, Aaron Copland (who had studied in Paris) was astonished that Harrison could have captured the spirit of the time so well without having been there. "Lou, you can't get any more 1920s champagne bubbly!" he said.[24]

Although some of Harrison's *Eiffel Tower* movements share Cocteau's playful sense of mockery, others recall Satie's use of light humor to delight, as in the quintal counterpoint wedding march movement that Harrison dedicated to the marriage of his friends Frank and Anne Wigglesworth that year. But the most striking movement of the set is the "Blues for the Trouville Bathing Beauty," which, aside from bits of *Something to Please Everybody*, is Harrison's only real experiment in composed jazz. In addition to the acknowledged influence of blues pianist Meade "Lux" Lewis,[25] another precedent for Harrison's blues was a similarly tongue-in-cheek movement of Cowell's *Ritual of Wonder*, the "kit" that Harrison had assembled at Mills, titled "Sentimental Blues (Without Apology to 'Porgy and Bess')."

Although Harrison was not attracted to jazz for its own sake, he still remembered his youthful stride-piano lessons and the crash course in jazz from his friend William Russell. In New York, Harrison sometimes accompanied Virgil Thomson in his jazz club slumming, and in 1946 Thomson helped him get a job transcribing recordings for a jazz history book by *Herald Tribune* jazz critic Rudi Blesh titled *Shining Trumpets*.[26] Blesh credited Harrison with abstracting a blues scale on the basis of these transcriptions, which Harrison shows as a five- or six-tone scale with added flat blue notes around the third and sixth scale degrees—the very scale he would use in the "Blues for the Trouville Bathing Beauty."

MUSIC FOR THE FOLDING OF THE CLOTH

The other play Bird staged that summer at Reed College was one of William Butler Yeats's poetic dramas, an evocation of shadowy ancient Irish mythology, *The Only*

Jealousy of Emer, a work Harrison had loved at least since high school. Instead of trying to resurrect ancient Celtic modes, Harrison's score suggests mythic timelessness through a mostly chromatic language—but without the dissonance or tangles of counterpoint of his earlier atonal works. Although Harrison scored *The Only Jealousy of Emer* for piano, celesta, harp, flute, cello, and bass, at no time do all the instruments play together or even in the same movement. The texture is so wispy and transparent that Harrison sometimes notated whole movements on a single staff. As in the lyrical "Song" movement from the *Symphony on G*, Harrison suggested tonality through drones and simple ostinatos, resulting in a dreamlike atmosphere that looks forward to Harrison's 1952 opera *Rapunzel*.

Bird brought both Reed productions to New York the following year and recorded *Emer*. "'Emer' was a decided success," Bird wrote of the professional restaging. "The music was just breathtaking, so magnificently performed and so sensitively right."[27] When it was released on an LP by Esoteric Records in 1951, it would be Harrison's first commercial recording. Pleased, Bird invited Harrison back to Reed the following summer. The music of the ballets Harrison wrote after his breakdown contrast strikingly with the voluntary works that preceded them, and they remain some of his most accessible creations, but they also owe their success—and their diversity—to an insight Harrison reached during his Reed sojourn.

"That may have been when I realized that a fellow didn't need to do only one thing and purvey it for rest of his life," Harrison explained. "He could do lots of things well. It followed a period of confusion when I was doing all one thing or all the other, and then it seems to have dawned on me at Reed: you can do each thing well. . . . [Y]ou could do different things coherently and balance off between the movements—at a certain point now we need chromatic movement, now we need to change mode from the first mode—where each thing is as coherent as I can make it but different from the other thing. I hadn't got that idea during that awful period [before the breakdown]. Once that dawned on me, I went ahead and haven't stopped since."[28]

16

PASTORALES (1949–1950)

Harrison's emergence from the dense thickets of neo-Reformationist counterpoint into textures that finally let sunlight in continued that fall of 1949. Even before his trip to Reed College, he had sketched out some ideas for a score for a film about the recently discovered Paleolithic cave paintings at Lascaux, France, which had been opened to the public after the war, but the film never materialized. When Harrison returned to New York that August, his friend, the cellist Seymour Barab, "a large, cheerful man swinging his cello at the end of his arm,"[1] reminded Harrison of a promise he had made the previous spring to write something for a recital that Barab was giving that fall. Harrison had completely forgotten, but he set to work right away creating a new work based on the Lascaux sketches.

Like Harrison's earlier string suites, the *Suite for Cello and Harp* is an eclectic work, with an opening chorale based on quintal counterpoint (also as in the suites), a dissonant interlude, and a serial "aria" movement, based on the "Song" movement from the *Symphony on G*.[2] This time, the chorale is repeated at the end, depicting an "old man plowing in the ancient manner behind the immemorial ox" in the original Lascaux film.[3] The suite leaves an impression of pensive melancholy and spare, meditative beauty as Harrison returned to New York's urban anxiety.

The *Suite for Cello and Harp* also became Harrison's first recording on a major label. In 1948, Harrison and Barab's friend Anahid Ajemian had married George Avakian, who worked for Columbia Records and would soon become well known as a jazz producer. Goddard Lieberson, the head of Columbia's Masterworks division and himself a composer, proposed a series of LPs recording contemporary American composers, called the Modern American Music series. Probably through Avakian or Thomson, Lieberson chose Harrison's *Suite for Cello and Harp* for the series and recorded it in 1951, although it would not appear until 1954, along with Harrison's *Suite #2* (played by a string quartet) and works by Virgil Thomson.

The second movement of *Suite for Cello and Harp* signals the direction that Harrison's music would move that fall, for it carries the title "Pastorale." Although originally written to depict "the willowed, rivered landscape of the valley of the Dordogne,"[4] home of the Lascaux caves, the movement can as easily be interpreted as an expression of the recently returned Harrison's idealization of the world outside the urban pressures of New York. The cello's melody gently sways in the 6/8 meter that was traditional for the pastorale form from Bach through Beethoven. When two friends, Ellie and David Decker, were married that October, Harrison wrote another lyrical pastorale in their honor, this time for flute, oboe, and two cellos, but again in translucent quintal counterpoint.

While Harrison used quintal counterpoint on occasion throughout his time in New York, these pastorales employ the "open" sound of the fifth for the first time to create a spaciousness in the texture and, as in Copland's works, to suggest the outdoors. Daniélou's spiritual associations with the 3:2 interval of the perfect fifth and its foundational use in musical systems around the world suggested something of Joseph Campbell's mythic transcendentalism.

The form of the pastorale also reflected Harrison's current interest in classical mythology that had led him to Virgil's bucolic *Eclogues* and Alexandrian pastoral poetry. That spring, Harrison wrote two more pastorales in the same style and atmosphere as the first. They were performed, along with the new *Suite for Cello and Harp*, at a Columbia University concert featuring an ensemble conducted by Fritz Rikko, a German-born violinist who taught at Greenwich House Music School near Harrison's apartment, and later at Juilliard. Another pastorale would follow that August and three more the following year (in rural Black Mountain, North Carolina), for a total of seven.[5]

Composing the *Seven Pastorales* proved a therapeutic undertaking to Harrison, as the tranquil, idyllic scenes represented in the form of the pastorale, as in Virgil's work, symbolized the mental and emotional peace he was seeking in the years following his hospitalization. Harrison dedicated its movements to people close to him at the time, and the whole piece represented a symbolic gathering of his loved ones around him: his brother, his mother, John Cage, Ellie and David Decker, Remy Charlip, and Fritz Rikko. Another friend, Robert Duncan, praised the "seven pastorals that Harrison playd" in his poem "Light Song."

The gentle *Seven Pastorales* abandon both Harrison's densely expressionist counterpoint and their prose-like forms for seemingly simple structures that flow effortlessly. The *Pastorales* are almost completely diatonic—that is, without accidentals—but without the pressing insistence of classical Western tonality and its goal-directed phrases. As Harrison continued to follow Schoenberg's advice to simplify and pare down to the essentials, gone too from the *Seven Pastorales* are the drastic contrasts of mood and technique as in the string suites, though Harrison contrived a remarkable amount of variety within the seemingly narrow expressive focus of the pastorale form. Number 3, to Remy Charlip, quietly evokes a thirteenth-century motet, and number 5, for John Cage, is a kind of Virgilian shepherd's flute dialogue. Number 6, for Harrison's mother, imitates a Balinese gamelan scale, which he would also use in his ballet *Solstice* later that year.[6]

The *Pastorales*, with their sometimes nearly static serenity and drones, also reflect Harrison's renewed interest in the classical music of India. Although Harrison had been introduced to Indian classical music by Cowell and had a 78-rpm recording of it he loved, Gita Sarabhai first introduced him to its details in New York, and now he was reading about it in books by Daniélou and Arthur Henry Fox-Strangways. Through them, Harrison began to see in the concept of mode, or *raga* in Indian music, a reflection of spiritual reality that emerged as expression, Coomaraswamy's *rasa*. Harrison's new explorations of the expressive potential of mode would have a great impact on his next works and, ultimately, on his later embrace of just intonation. With the sunny calm of these works that emerged after his restorative trips back West, Harrison may have been conjuring the world he wanted to live in.

SOLSTICE

> At the entrance to a monolithic temple in the Garden of the Sun, the Sun Lion is dancing with a woman to the lilting strains of a sweet flute melody, soon joined by the delicate tones of the tack-piano.[7]

In the fall of 1949, when Harrison was writing his pastorales, Jean Erdman approached him with a commission to score another of her ballets. Like *The Perilous Chapel*, the new ballet, *Solstice*, was another abstraction from Joseph Campbell's ur-myths, though, at half an hour, it was more expansive and elaborate.[8] Reluctant to take on a large commission when he was immersed in his studies in scales and medievalism, Harrison quoted her twice his usual fee, expecting rejection—but Erdman accepted. Then he told her that he would need twice the number of musicians as in *The Perilous Chapel*; that is, eight. Again, she unexpectedly agreed. Cornered, Harrison put aside his pastorales and began work on *Solstice*.[9]

"I was interested in the ways that the abstract language of dance could reveal realms of experience antecedent to words," Erdman said later, and Harrison shared this vision.[10] She remembered that Harrison "always seemed to understand what the dance was about. He's very sensitive to movement."[11]

The myth Erdman devised for *Solstice*, like *The Perilous Chapel*, depicts a Campbell-esque cyclic journey from light to darkness and back again, but here the cycle is that of the seasons. The athletic Merce Cunningham applied his feline movements to the part of the invented mythological beast the Sun-Lion, representing the light of summer in a struggle with the Moon-Bull, danced by nineteen-year-old Donald McKayle. McKayle had a "powerful attack with its rhythmic reverberations,"[12] but Cunningham was a "strange, disturbing mixture of Greek god, panther and madman."[13]

In Erdman's vision, the new year's god of spring doesn't achieve true renewal, because the old year's god of winter isn't so easily vanquished. Suggestions of rape and violent destruction—antithetical to nature—require winter's destruction of all the living, sort of a Noah's Ark scenario. The female, fertile vision of spring restores wholeness and achieves true renewal in this "eternal seesaw of energy."[14] Harrison's "haunting score, wonderfully sensitive to the choreographic rhythms," set out to depict not only this "cosmogonic cycle" (Campbell's term) musically, but also the contrast between light and darkness, summer and winter.[15]

Despite the lack of enthusiasm he originally felt for the project, Harrison began to see in the score new opportunities for experimenting with scales. Although in

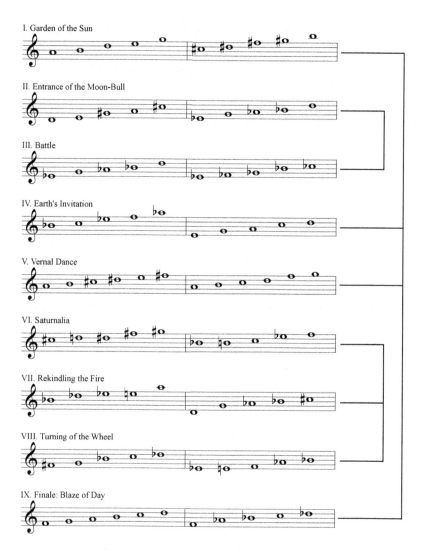

EXAMPLE 16.1. Each movement of Harrison's *Solstice* is based on a pair of mostly pentatonic scales, representative of light (scales without semitones in movements 1, 4, and 5), darkness and chaos (scales with semitones in movements 2, 3, 6, 7, and 8), and a combination (movement 9).

The Perilous Chapel Harrison chose to unify the score through a series of variations of tetrachords, here he chose to split the range of the tetrachord into two instead of three intervals, creating pentatonic modes. Splitting the fourth into a major second and minor third gives some of the most common scales in the world (in China, for example). Harrison decided that the forces of light, of the Sun-Lion, would be represented by these scales with their characteristic lack of semitones. For contrast, pentatonic scales with semitones would then represent the forces of darkness, of the Moon-Bull.

To create the cyclic sense of the turn of the seasons, Harrison mapped out a plan of tonalities and modes.[16] Furthermore, unlike the *Pastorales*, each of which is short enough to hold the listener's interest without departing from a single tonality, the more expansive movements of *Solstice* would need to modulate between scales.

These contrasting tonalities—and the sometimes frequent polytonal clashes when they overlap—mirror the cosmic struggles of the ballet's story. For example, in a light, *Emer*-like texture of flute and cello in double octaves with a celesta ostinato in between, the "Garden of the Sun" melody opens in a bright pentatonic on A. However, disturbingly chromatic pitches then intervene before resolving into a glorious repetition of the melody with the full ensemble, but this time in C#—the chromaticisms were really the result of the overlapping pentatonic scales.

> *Suddenly shadows appear, along with a trumpet fanfare, heralding the intrusion of the Moon Bull, garbed in red and black, and his chorus of horned female followers, bedecked in green dresses. The Bride of Spring leaves the lion and embraces the bull. The lion, resplendent in red and white, confronts him.*

This movement marks a significant point in Harrison's career, because it is his first explicit imitation of the music of the Indonesian gamelan orchestra. However, whereas he would become known for his association with the meditative sounds of the Javanese variety of gamelan, this movement represents the bright and dynamic music of the neighboring island of Bali. Harrison had known of Balinese music through the recordings played in Cowell's class and the gamelan that performed at San Francisco's Golden Gate Exposition, but it was likely Erdman herself who inspired its inclusion in *Solstice*.

Common in multicultural 1940s New York, so-called ethnic dance exerted a palpable influence in the modern dance scene. The Moon-Bull, Donald McKayle, had studied Balinese dance in New York,[17] but Erdman had experienced the magic of this culture at the source. On an around-the-world cruise while still a Sarah Lawrence undergraduate, she traveled to the fabled island, where she studied dance and listened to gamelan nearly constantly. "Nothing that has been written, painted nor sung about Bali has ever described the real thing," she wrote to her then-professor Campbell:

> The refinement, the apparent ornateness and richness which is conveyed by the simplest even limited form—structure and most of all the subtlety is such a far cry from the present state of the "Modern Dance"! Their style is fixed, is rigid! to nth degree and yet there is infinite variation within the crystallized forms. That is characteristic of the music, too . . . they . . . use the sounds of percussion & bells & gongs—which keep them safely away from the sentimental yearning wail of strings . . . In spite of the fact that they use only those kinds of tones with only five notes, their symphonies can stand a lot of study.[18]

Erdman found a sympathetic musician in Lou Harrison, whose *Counterdance in Spring* she had set to a Balinese-inspired solo dance in 1943. That existing score had nothing to do with Balinese musical forms, but in 1949, Harrison read Colin McPhee's landmark summary of Balinese musical practice in the *Musical Quarterly*, which laid out for him details of the music's construction.[19] In 1931 McPhee left behind his promising composing career when what was to be a short trip in Bali turned into a nine-year residency, during which McPhee became a pioneering authority on the island's music.

From recordings and McPhee's articles, Harrison learned that Balinese music used one of the pentatonics with semitones that he had identified and associated with the Moon-Bull. Harrison also used the exciting and intricate interlocking figuration so characteristic of most Balinese music described in McPhee's article in *Solstice*'s celesta and tack-piano parts, though with the interlocking parts collapsed into a single melodic line. At first, the intricate rhythms so confused the dancers that they began to count out loud in rehearsal. "How can you dance with a head full of roaring digits?" Harrison shouted. "Just listen to the music!"[20]

Harrison also represented dramatic tutti strikes of the gamelan (which the Balinese onomatopoeically call "*byong*") and had the contrabass player imitate the gamelan's polyrhythmic drumming by beating the strings below the bridge with a stick (as he had done in *Labyrinth* of 1941). When the Sun-Lion responds to the entrance of the Moon-Bull, his theme from the first movement appears in this scale, but the dramatic gamelan interjections finally drown it out.

Despite the importance of these transcultural influences, Henry Cowell in his review rejected an interpretation of exoticism: "The form is based on the successive use of five Oriental-sounding scales. The scales are used, however, not as exotic impressions but as necessary basic materials. The music is charming and varied, and the suggestion of Eastern materials is woven into a fabric related to the Occidental medieval as well as Occidental modern styles."[21]

> *The battle begins as the two celestial protagonists circle each other as both the stage lights and the music darken, then they pounce, flying over each other, whirling and twisting in a stylized wrestling match to a tense duet between trumpet and flute over a repeating cello and bass patterns and piano interjections. The Moon-Bull retreats, as the women return, lining up with the triumphant Sun-Lion as the music quiets.*

In the third movement, "Battle," Harrison dissonantly combined dueling pentatonic tonalities a semitone apart. Erdman hired a Chinese martial arts expert as a consultant to create the movements for the dynamic battle between the two male dancers. When the Sun-Lion emerges victorious, his pentatonic without semitones returns in the following victory dance, "Earth's Invitation."

> *The playful solo flute line returns with a blue sky as the lion frolics with each of the women, escorting the Bride of Spring back to the temple, as the music melts into the winsome sound of a tuneful summer dance.*

Suddenly, the sky flushes an angry red as the Moon-Bull reappears, accompanied by an ominous and dissonant scale. One by one, he seizes each woman, forcing her to the ground. The wild orgy of violence subsides as Moon-Bull and Sun-Lion (still in the temple) slumber. The Bride of Spring, the lone remaining woman, rises from the floor, accompanied by a single flute. She alone understands that the light of day must be rekindled. The lion and bull awaken and stand back to back, arms intertwined, and then begin a duet, arms akimbo, side by side.

In "Turning of the Wheel," the darkly dissonant pentatonics continue, but the dancers are emerging into the light, not through another battle, but instead through a reconciliation finally marked by cyclic runs up and down the celesta keyboard. In the finale, "The Blaze of Day," the opening scale returns as the story comes full circle. The Bride of Spring descends from the temple and the trio dance together, with the woman now cavorting with the bull, now joining the lion. Finally, she finds a place between them, and both bull and lion thrust her up to the sky.

Although Harrison had only reluctantly undertaken *Solstice*, the score turned out to be one of his finest compositions and one of the loveliest American ballet scores of that rich era. And although New York's new radical arts scene took little notice of Harrison's sweetly tonal pastorales and ballet scores at their late 1940s and early 1950s premieres, their sunny textures and attractive explorations of modes would form a crucial foundation for his later career. Eventually, fashion would catch up with Harrison, rather than the other way around.

THE SWEETNESS OF EPICURUS

His rather rosy-cheeked good looks, and a pair of innocent blue eyes have sometimes caused him to be called "the baby-faced intellectual." But the colourful impression—heightened rather than dimmed by a truly hectic taste in socks and ties and a habit of writing his music in coloured inks on hand-made parchment with illuminated titles—is misleading. These attributes conceal an erudite and scholarly man, and one with an impressive creative talent.

—Peggy Glanville-Hicks[22]

By the beginning of the 1950s, editors at *Vogue* deemed the thirty-two-year-old Harrison worthy of inclusion in Peggy Glanville-Hicks's feature story about New York's trailblazing musicians. Although this notoriety brought no immediate opportunities, the *Solstice* premiere, on January 22, 1950, at Hunter Playhouse, proved financially rewarding, leaving Harrison less impoverished than when he had first emerged from his hospitalization. He no longer had his regular job at the *Herald Tribune* to depend on, but he was glad to give up the constant pressures that came with it.

Instead, he had taken a job teaching piano, counterpoint, and composition at the neighborhood Greenwich House Music School (where Rikko also taught), though he also took students at his apartment and occasionally at Bonnie Bird's dance studio.[23] During this time he composed a few pieces for these beginning pianists, including his brief, delightful *Homage to Milhaud*, the Les Six composer who had joined the Mills College faculty in 1940 (around the time Harrison left) and who would later become a friend of Harrison's and an admirer of his music. One of Harrison's students was his lover from Reed College, Remy Charlip, who had returned to New York and, through Harrison, found a job with Merce Cunningham's dance company. Their relationship was close but complex, veering from devotion to bickering as the mercurial Harrison's moods continued to oscillate.

Charlip decided that he needed to learn music, and so Harrison taught him beginning piano and recorder. He composed a suite for Charlip that he later titled *Village Music*, a charming set in which the pianist hardly has to move his hand position.[24] It begins, now characteristically, with a "Pastorale" without bar lines, followed by a "Quadrille" and a brief "Chorale."

Their romance was interrupted when Harrison returned to the pastoral setting of Reed College for the 1950 summer session. Bird repeated the previous season's two ballets, and Harrison led a symposium on Henry Purcell's opera *Dido and Aeneas* and composed a new score, *Almanac of the Seasons* (spiced with "modernist modal seasonings from Carlos Chávez," Harrison said), for a dance based on a poetic seventeenth-century evocation of the months.[25] This score has since been lost, except for a movement later arranged for the *Suite for Symphonic Strings*, an exhilarating "Round in Honor of Hermes." That movement echoes some of the propulsive dances in *Solstice* but now in frequently changing meters and in Harrison's increasingly favored form of a rondeau, or round, a piece with a recurring theme.

These two restorative Portland summers made a return to the big city all the more depressing. It had been only seven years since Harrison had moved to New York, but by 1950, his social and artistic worlds were in upheaval. The times when Harrison and Cage would go out to dinner nearly nightly were long past. In January 1950, Cage had met the composer Morton Feldman and, soon afterward, a precocious teenager named Christian Wolff. That fall, the three met sometimes daily in Cage's loft, trying out new radical ideas such as graphic notation, which might at times appear more like abstract art than music notation. Not surprisingly, then, the other group Cage and Feldman were hanging around with were radical visual artists, including the founders of the so-called New York School of abstract expressionism. Cage and Feldman were members of the Artists' Club (which they somewhat pretentiously shortened to "The Club"), a group that regularly met in Greenwich Village's Cedar Tavern and included Willem de Kooning, Franz Kline, Ad Reinhardt, and Jackson Pollock.[26]

The new aesthetic represented by these avant-garde artists (and their downtown contemporaries the Beat poets) emphasized a radicalism and spontaneity increasingly distant from Harrison's medievalist studies of the magic of modes and meticulous counterpoint. Often still uncomfortable in social situations, Harrison frequently cloistered himself in his messy apartment, meeting only occasionally with a few remaining friends—Charlip, Weber, Cowell—and his students. One, a young composer named Richard Miller, idolized Harrison and opened for him a door into a new and intense artistic social world, one that revolved around a captivating young actress who quickly set her sights on him.

17

THE WHITE GODDESS (1951)

A big, heavy man, he was reminiscent of the young Orson Welles, with a theatrical, flamboyant personality—always amusing, keeping the conversation going at all times. . . . Lou played his compositions on the piano and on records, then showed me his verse and Noh play. I was overwhelmed by so much Blakean activity. He writes his scores in red and black ink in Gothic script. His work on counterpoint is not a mere textual account but poetic prose, as if Swedenborg or Blake had applied their vision to a textbook. . . . Lou is the nearest thing to a Renaissance man that I've encountered.

—Harold Norse[1]

On Easter Sunday 1951, Lou Harrison awoke amid the familiar surroundings of his Greenwich Village apartment, "the fine grand piano, bits of stained glass, a brass mobile and oil lamp, a photograph of Remy, and the atmosphere of Lou as rich as the world. Powerful, strong, strange."[2] And, also familiar, a stranger sleeping next to him. What was unfamiliar was the fact that this stranger was a woman. After a lifetime of homosexuality, Lou Harrison was exploring another kind of lovemaking, just as he was experimenting with new ways of making music.

He was set to depart for a week in rural North Carolina later that afternoon. But now what would he do with the woman in his bed?

The previous February, Harrison accepted his student Richard Miller's invitation to his twentieth birthday party. Although this party was for Miller, the unquestioned center of it was Judith Malina. Tiny and riveting, the twenty-four-year-old actress radiated a magnetic intensity at the Village's frequent social gatherings with her husband, Julian Beck. Fixtures in avant-garde art and poetry circles, the pair had recently formed the most radical of New York's theater groups, the Living Theater, a reflection of their commitment to political and artistic anarchism that would become one of the most influential artistic groups of the 1950s and '60s. Their marriage was as unconventional as their theater, the bisexual Julian taking male lovers and Judith successively seducing artists that currently infatuated her. Remy Charlip came to value her friendship but remembered her as a gifted hysteric, given to spontaneous crying or inappropriate laughter.[3]

"We were an artistic community, striving to make sense of things" in a period of transition between the old Village bohemia and the one that would emerge with the Beats and then the counterculture, Malina remembered. "Something was cohering then, but it wasn't complete. We all felt we were on the verge of tremendous social change."[4] The writer Anatole Broyard, who moved to a "cramped and dingy" tenement on Prince Street around the same time as Harrison, concurred: "In Greenwich Village in the period just after World War II . . . there was a sense of coming back to life, a terrific energy and curiosity, even a feeling of destiny arising out of the war that had just ended. The Village, like New York City itself, had an immense, beckoning sweetness. It was like Paris in the twenties—with the difference that it was our city."[5]

Their circle included an impressive lineup of the twentieth-century American avant-garde—writers, artists, and choreographers such as John Ashbery, Frank O'Hara, Robert Rauschenberg, Robert Motherwell, Erick Hawkins, Jean Erdman and Joe Campbell, Paul Goodman, and, later, Merce Cunningham and John Cage. They frequented the theater at Cherry Lane, house parties, the Waldorf cafeteria, and Howard Johnson's, "everybody sitting around gloomily, drinking at lousy coffee shops in the middle of the night with the dregs of the city."[6]

Many of them were at Miller's birthday party, including Harold Norse, a poet and friend of Ned Rorem and vanguard American writers including W. H. Auden, Tennessee Williams, and William Carlos Williams.[7] Now studying for his master's degree at New York University, Norse had been Charlip's poetry teacher at Cooper Union. Norse's partner, a young composer named Dick Stryker, had already played some of Harrison's music for Malina before their meeting and would soon become a student of Harrison's.

The group immediately absorbed the charismatic Harrison into its social circle. At another party at Harrison's house a few weeks later, "Lou whooped, gasped, and guffawed, waving fingers adorned with huge rings," Norse wrote.[8] Ned Rorem remembered Harrison then as "tall and big boned but somehow fragile, like Orson Welles on a tulip stem."[9] He recalled that autograph-seekers on the street wouldn't believe Harrison when he explained that he was not Orson Welles. Finally, he would just sign Welles's name for them.

Harrison was intrigued by the artistic intensity of the group, then immersed in rehearsals for *The Thirteenth God*, a play about Alexander the Great directed by Malina. He thought that Norse might be able to provide him with a libretto for his dormant opera project about Cupid and Psyche. Later they worked on an aborted opera based on the story of Abelard and Heloise.

Harrison was also meeting other new friends, including young aspiring composers and Cowell students Burt Bacharach and John Duffy, who accompanied him and Cage to concerts and parties.[10] "Lou had tuned his piano to mean[tone] temperament, new to me, and all about were scores of his music (dance scores he was working on), Frescobaldi, Dufay, and Perotinus," Duffy recalled of one visit. "I loved it there. And I loved Lou's gentle, kind spirit. Often we gathered with Cowell, Hovhaness, the Becks and [Pierre] Boulez, who was conducting for the Barraut company on Broadway, and took a crosstown bus to John Cage and Merce Cunningham's apartment, where we had lots of fun, wine, and good things to eat."[11] Like good Village bohos, they often smoked marijuana at his apartment, where Malina saw Harrison playing some of his music—his *Pastorales*, part of his unfinished mass. "Lou transforms when he plays the piano, and lights up as though from within," she wrote.[12] Making music seemed to give him a refuge from his demons. "I felt him most unbearably desirable when was conducting," Malina remembered, his hands moving "like miraculous birds."[13]

But while Norse and Duffy remembered Harrison the bon vivant, Malina sensed something darker and vulnerable behind Harrison's flashy facade. "He is a quarrel between what his mouth reveals him to be and what his eyes insist he is . . . a man with a sudden smile that vanishes just as one is about to smile back," she wrote.[14] "I also detected the rawness of the open emotional wound he'd suffered in the breakdown," she recalled later. "The very sensitivity that made him so appealing and artistically accomplished left him vulnerable to the catty social scene."[15] It also made him nearly irresistible to Malina, who cast Harrison as a tormented genius, still struggling, since his breakdown, between an idealized world of Platonic beauty and the messy world of human interactions. "Lou charmed me from the first with his buoyant brilliance, his music—and those enchanting looks of terror and turbulence that fleet across his face," she wrote.[16]

After the opening night of *The Thirteenth God*, Harrison rushed backstage to congratulate Malina, who kissed him. Harrison was, surprisingly, receptive, holding her hands close. When he and Charlip joined the cast at a nearby restaurant for their celebratory dinner after the show, Harrison sat with Malina. "People loved him dearly—artistically and sexually," she recalled. "But he couldn't make sense of the world. He was caught in this profound contradiction between the guileless purity of expressing what he saw and felt in a very pure way, and the sophisticated cynicism of the '40s, where we had to sit around a table or bar and say clever things, and he was very good at it. And then sometimes I saw him panic while he was doing it. He'd make clever remark one and clever remark two and then he had tendency to run away in a kind of mental fright."[17]

Since his breakdown, Harrison had begun to explore sex with the opposite gender, first with Leona, the woman he met at the mental hospital dances and to whom he had dedicated the Waltz from the *Symphony on G*. She was a social worker who was giving Rorschach tests at the time of her breakdown, and when they were both released, they had sought each other out. Although his therapists had not suggested it, this experimentation was a part of Harrison's process of rebuilding his shattered personality. Later he realized that immediately after every one of his half dozen affairs with women (all during the few years following his hospitalization), he would go out looking for a man. "The proof," he observed, "in the pudding."[18]

When Harrison woke up that Easter morning with Malina sleeping next to him, only weeks after they had met at Miller's party, he didn't know what to do. Soon Charlip would be coming over and driving down to North Carolina with him. John Cage had suggested that Harrison explore a collaboration with the choreographer Katherine Litz at the experimental Black Mountain College. Panicked, Harrison called Judith's husband, Julian. "Help! Judith is in my bed! What do I do?" he wailed. Unconcerned and accustomed to Judith's affairs, Julian told Harrison simply, "Feed her breakfast and send her home, Lou."

Malina wrote in her diary, "At breakfast, he is suddenly taciturn, distant. In spite of our lovemaking, perhaps because of it, he is afraid. He talks of going to North Carolina that same afternoon, of going to Paris in the summer, of going to California. He leaves me at eleven, angry and depressed."[19]

HESITATION WALTZ

Springtime in the Smoky Mountains of North Carolina must have seemed even more distant than the day's drive from New York. Harrison found himself surrounded by verdant hills and many remarkable artists. Although he and Charlip stayed only the week, the place made a profound impression on Harrison, especially by way of contrast to his noisy, socially unmanageable life in New York.[20]

He agreed to create a "kit," a flexible dance composition, for choreographer Katie Litz—and in turn came away with an invitation to teach at the 1951 summer session. As always after these pastoral interludes, the spirit of nature quickly manifested itself in his music. He began sketching a new work deeply influenced by the college's Arcadian atmosphere.

The following week, at the end of March, Harrison invited Malina and her circle to a performance at Erdman's studio, featuring her dances and his music as well as a percussion *Sarabande* by Richard Miller, whose romantic interest Harrison rather coldly rebuffed in one of those examples of how he remembered mistreating people at the time. "He'd been in some odd way hypnotized on our relationship," Harrison said of Miller. "He sort of got an odd notion of maybe being more than he became.... I did undertake him as a composer and colleague, and that may have been bad."[21]

After the concert, Harrison ("nervous, flighty, unstable," Malina wrote)[22] introduced Malina to several other people who would be pivotal in the development of the Living Theater, including Joseph Campbell (with whom she would also have a brief affair), Merce Cunningham, and John Cage, and off they trooped to a restaurant for some socializing. Norse recited one of his poems, "God Is a Circle," which, contrary to Voltaire's dictum that God's center is everywhere, concluded that the circle's center is the goddess. Harrison looked at Malina. "I favor the goddess," he declared.

But Malina knew she wasn't a goddess, even if Harrison couldn't distinguish her from the character she was playing onstage when they met, the role "in which he knows me. And does not know I'm not, and can never be, the cold white queen," she wrote. "Lou lives in symbols. He sees me as Woman and not as Judith, but with an innocence that would be cruel to betray."[23]

But it wouldn't be Malina who betrayed innocence that spring. It would be Harrison.

A DANGEROUS ANGEL

After the lights went up for intermission at an informal performance of *Marriage at the Eiffel Tower* at Bonnie Bird's studio, Lou Harrison gathered with his friends from the Living Theater, fellow musicians, and Bird and her dancers. I have an announcement to make, Harrison intoned, as his puzzled friends quieted down.

Unlike the others gathered there, Judith Malina and Julian Beck knew what was coming, because Dick Stryker had told Julian the big news earlier. "What is the most surprising thing Lou could do?" Julian asked Judith after Harrison had confided the big news. "Nothing he could do would surprise me," she'd replied.

But she was wrong there. Harrison was getting married, he told the shocked gathering.[24]

Mary Callantine was a dark-haired, stately pianist who grew up on a Montana ranch and struck Malina and her circle as naive. Slightly younger than the thirty-three-year-old Harrison and well educated, new to New York and seeking a counterpoint and composition teacher, she had been referred to Harrison by Henry Cowell. Harrison's friends thought nothing more about it until he made his surprise announcement of their engagement.

"He wanted to shock Remy and me and all the people around him," Malina recalled. "He was trying to say to all of us in that community, 'I can surprise you all and do the thing you least expect: marry a sweet young girl.' We all felt very bad about it. I knew it wasn't going to happen for real."[25] Harrison may have relished the surprise, but he also envied how Cowell's marriage to Sidney had provided friendship, stability, and social acceptance to his mentor's life.

But there was more involved than Malina or their other friends knew. Mary was pregnant. "I got angry at her," Harrison remembered. "She was absorbed in the pregnancy, so eager about this and herself that I realized she was only interested in the child, and that made me mad. I was quite rough about it verbally."[26]

As Malina had predicted, the fantasy wore off, and in April 1951 Callantine boarded a train for Eugene, Oregon, where she had relatives. Whatever shame or responsibility Harrison felt, he did not take care of the woman he had put into this life-changing situation. He didn't even show up to see her off.

Callantine sent a postcard from Oregon explaining that she had miscarried, though Harrison understood this to be a euphemism for an illegal abortion. "Thank heavens!" his therapist said after Harrison relayed this news. "We thought we had lost you."[27]

"You were the greatest of rascals for refusing to come up and go through the ritual of bidding me adieu before leaving the great metropolis of New York," Callantine wrote him. "I had to leave very hurriedly. Please admit to yourself that you are not committed to a state of romanticism with me. But as you know already I do think a great deal of you and would like to keep in touch with you through letters. . . . Since I do think so much of you, it would be a kindness on your part if you would write if you say no more than that you feel like hell and that you hate yourself and all the world. But don't use that excuse for not writing on the grounds that I expect something overwhelmingly personal from you." She wrote again a year later, reproving him for his "stony silence" in not answering her letter.[28]

"He was on a fantasy, but a person was involved who was very hurt when she realized that he couldn't really respond to her or be her husband," said Malina.

"Everybody told her, 'Don't take this as a serious commitment. Lou may not be aware.' But she was a simple kind of person. In her guilelessness, she was a child in a kingdom by the sea. She felt far more deeply about it than he did. He hurt her terribly."[29]

Despite this abundant evidence that the increasingly moody Harrison was in no way able to sustain a relationship with a woman, Malina continued to pursue him. "What can I say Lou is? Half saint? Half beast?" she wrote. "Lou tries to be honest, but he constructs an imaginary world to which he retreats. He understands its illusory quality, but then he encounters demons."[30]

But neither Harrison's music nor the company of his fellow artists could stave off the stress imposed by his return to New York's urban dissonance, and he more and more often descended into the "half beast" side of his fragmented personality. "He was sensitive enough to observe social niceties," Malina remembered. "But when he felt opposed, he'd say 'Fuck you.' He was bold, brazen, very open about himself. He never hid his sexual feelings and inclinations. He liked outrageous behavior. He was startling. He came into a room and would say outrageous things." At one party at Harrison's crowded apartment, he was rude to everyone, especially Malina.

"Suddenly Lou came into the room in which Julian was trying to stir up conversation and said, 'Everyone please go home. I'm tired,'" she wrote. "Dick [Stryker] calls Lou a dangerous angel. Because he inspires love but does not give it."[31] After misbehaving at a party at the Malinas', he sent Beck a contrite, calligraphic note "to thank you for the party, apologize for my none too obscure idiocies & iniquities" and offered a little song in honor of their son Garrick's second birthday.[32]

Another day, Stryker told Malina, "Lou says, with that humor that is only a feint for speaking shocking truths, 'I destroy all my pupils.'"[33] Harrison's cold criticism of Richard Miller, according to Malina, created "a life-shattering trauma that destroyed a very fine musician. There were terrible scenes with Richard . . . and after Lou dropped him, he felt incompetent to put anything on paper."[34]

Ultimately, Malina concluded, Harrison was simply unable at that point in his life to form the kind of relationships that might have kept him in New York's creative community. "Between the episodes of confusions and madness, he just couldn't deal with the incompatibility of the misery of daily life, social life—even the mystery of sexual encounters," she explained. "I don't think he could compute it the way he computed his music. Lou was too sensitive, too much affected viscerally by what was around him. For that reason he maintained a certain distancing from all of us who were so enamored of him."[35]

THE FORESTS ARE GETTING DRESSED

Texture of sable gongs in subtle blue
Of morning tongues—evoke again
For us that halo of soft gold
The clappers of the bells wreathe in the air! . . . Cast delicately, always,
Lou, last magician of the vault
And big rose-windows of the soul, your line,

That choiring melodious spell—O pour
Into the damp, demotic modes of sense
Auras of gold gamelongs,—immense!
—Harold Norse, 1951[36]

Before he headed off to North Carolina for the summer, Harrison participated in several more concerts, including a performance of his *Alleluia* at the Manhattan School and a soon-to-be notorious New Music Society concert. The Society was presenting Harrison's *Canticle #3*, one of the triumphs of his San Francisco years, amidst a forest of pieces—less a formal concert than a fun (and lengthy) sharing of musical jokes and experiments.

However, from the beginning, there were signs of trouble. The German American composer Stefan Wolpe sat in the balcony with his clique, who proceeded to boo every piece that night but Harrison's.[37] The climax of the concert did not come until after midnight (meaning that reviewers from the dailies could not make their deadlines): John Cage's *Imaginary Landscape No. 4* for twelve radios. The twenty-four performers, two to each radio, included Harrison, Charlip, Norse, Malina and Beck, Miller, and Stryker. Dressed to the nines in white tie and tails, "Cage conducted with great seriousness from his score," beating time with a baton, Norse recalled. "The effect was similar to an automobile ride at night on an American highway in which neon signs and patches of noise from radios and automobiles flash in the distance."[38]

The five-minute soundscape of silence and static, punctuated only occasionally by random fragments of broadcast speech and Haydn's music, created an uproar even among new-music supporters in the audience. Even the *Herald Tribune* turned against Cage: Arthur Berger turned in a lengthy excoriation, viewing the performance as nothing more than a neo-Dada stunt.[39] Cage was so incensed at the whole incident and the way it was handled that the day after the concert, he quit the New Music Society.[40]

But even as he participated in one of Cage's first chance compositions, Harrison must have sensed that he and his old friend were approaching an artistic divide. The controversies surrounding Cage and his new circle of friends and Harrison's mixed feelings about his place in it would follow him to North Carolina.

Harrison's own emerging music couldn't have been much more different than his friend's early experiment in what then seemed to be the music of the future. On Harrison's occasional visits to Erdman's studio, where Charlip was designing costumes, he had struck up an acquaintance with the dancer Donald McKayle, who had danced the part of the Moon-Bull in *Solstice*. One day, while McKayle was choreographing a dance based on children's songs and games, Harrison sat to the side, scribbling with his pencil. During a break, he called McKayle over to the piano, where he played sketches in which the motives of the children's songs were transformed into "little studies that shimmered with the sounds of Bali."[41]

These three pieces became the score for a solo dance he choreographed titled *Songs in the Forest*, which he performed that May at Hunter Playhouse.[42] The largely pentatonic movements for the unlikely but attractive combination of piccolo/flute (a single player alternating instruments), violin, vibraphone/marimba, and piano echo their previous collaboration, *Solstice*. However, *Songs in the Forest* is even more weightless in its simplicity, particularly the serene third movement. Its quiet evocation of nature also recalled the inspiring scenery he had experienced in his brief trip to Black Mountain College the previous month—another example of the soothing effect that pastoral settings insinuated into his music. The following year, Harrison would present the score as a concert piece at Black Mountain with his own poems declaimed between the movements.[43]

Also in April, just days after returning from his initial Black Mountain visit, Harrison began sketching a setting of an eleventh-century poem of praise to (of course) nature, celebrating the forests' flowers and fruit, soaring eagles, larks singing scales on the wind. Merging his recent medievalisms with his continuing quintal counterpoint, *Vestiunt Silve* ("The Forests Are Getting Dressed"), like his other pastoral works, seemed both to celebrate Harrison's escape from the complexity of urbanity and dense counterpoint and to portend a new direction in both his music and his life.

18

A GREAT PLAYGROUND (1951–1952)

Lou Harrison walked alone through the forest, inhaling the pungent fragrance of spruce, fir, and mountain laurel as he descended the foothills through the mists that gave North Carolina's Smoky Mountains their name. As he descended toward his cabin, the evergreens gave way to oaks, dogwoods, and hemlocks, whose reds, golds, pinks, and brilliant yellows provided an annual pageant of autumn for locals and visitors alike. Free of the oppressive clamor of the city, Harrison's thoughts turned to Artemis, goddess of wild nature. He pulled out one of his ever-present notebooks and began to write:

> And where is She?
> Her breath stirs shadows here,
> Her undermurmur moves among
>   the humming wind of dusk—
> bats' velvet flutters, owls' down,
>   hoots mild & sly—
> She's in her wisdom
>   here in the trees.[1]

Off Highway 70 in the Smoky Mountains of western North Carolina, the lush forest briefly opens to a small lake whose name, Eden, seemed appropriate for the educational utopia that a handful of idealists brought there. The long, stark building in the Internationalist Bauhaus style of architecture up the dirt road past the lake was the site of the major turning point in American post–World War II arts. Black Mountain College was founded on progressive-era ideals of democracy (initially faculty and students alike voted on college issues), cooperation (students and faculty grew their own food and helped build college structures), and individual freedom (no required courses). While the early professors saw this plan as a renewal of a liberal arts ideal, after the war the college transformed into an arts school that appealed to the experimental spirit of the disaffected Beat generation.

The abstract artist Josef Albers, a refugee from the original Bauhaus in Germany, oversaw Black Mountain's transformation into a unique school of modernist art. Though he left the college in 1949, Albers's legacy lived on in an illustrious, if unconventional, faculty, often expanded through invitations to ascendant representatives of the artistic avant-garde. Cage and Merce Cunningham accepted such an invitation for the spring of 1948 and the following summer session. Cage, who was then, like Virgil Thomson, a devotee of the iconoclastic proto-modernism of Erik Satie, delivered a series of concerts and lectures on the composer, concluding with an attack on what he saw as the opposing side to this aesthetic: Ludwig van Beethoven.[2] His assault on such a cherished icon infuriated many of the faculty, and Cage was not asked back until the 1952 summer session.[3]

When he saw Harrison struggling to adjust to the noise and pressures of New York after his return from the Reed College summer sessions, Cage thought the remote, peaceful setting among other creative people would be just the tonic to help his friend recover.

Harrison's two years at Black Mountain would prove to be pivotal for him, both musically and personally. While the campus's bucolic setting presaged the sylvan serenity Harrison craved, it also pulsed with the edgy energy of the mostly urban artists who taught and created there. Black Mountain would be the scene for some of his lowest moments—and the cradle of one of his greatest creations.

As he and Charlip drove down to North Carolina in the spring of 1951, Harrison's confusion about the previous night's escapade with Judith Malina slowly gave way to anticipation of escaping urban clamor—and to working with the unconventional and engaging choreographer at Black Mountain, Katherine Litz, whom Cage had introduced to Harrison when she performed in New York the previous December.[4] "Certainly one of the most important artists in the field," wrote the *New York Times* dance critic, noting the daring ways in which she would often choreograph in "antagonism" to the music.[5] A veteran of the expressionist Weidman-Humphrey dance company, Katie Litz was right at home at Black Mountain, though her carelessly hitched skirt over tights stirred a mini-scandal at the local drugstore.[6]

Charlip contrasted Litz's free-spirited choreography with Cunningham's rigidity—"more fluid, more magical, a little wilder and spiritual at the same time."[7] To accommodate this flexibility, Harrison adapted his kit method to create an "Adjustable Chorale," much of which, like *The Only Jealousy of Emer*, is written on a single staff. Even though this chorale had a pulse as well, the timings, in deference to Litz's way of working, were not predetermined. Instead, "a more relaxed attitude has been engendered towards the erstwhile, continuous beat-by-beat association of the dance and music," Harrison wrote. "Much time is silently allowed the dancer for the display and feeling of essential motor rhythms undocumented or 'associated' by music's special expressive meanings. This presumes two things: a rhythmic impulse in the dancer imperative enough to carry the life beat of the work, and a new, more pointed staticity of musical materials."[8] Harrison paired "Adjustable Chorale" with a short "Chorale for Spring," and these two *Chorales for Spring* joined *Songs in the Forest* as Harrison's first works whose evocation of nature was inspired by Black Mountain.

The "Chorale for Spring" movement experiments with a technique that Cage discovered in a string quartet attributed to Benjamin Franklin. In this brief but fascinating work, the players play only on open strings, but the strings are retuned (a technique known as *scordatura*) so that conventional harmonies result. Harrison realized that the technique could provide a warm, Satie-like stasis of the type he created in the chorale for his *Suite for Cello and Harp,* but now slowly traversing a small number of chords derived from the possible pitches. As in that Lascaux-inspired suite, this movement evokes "ancient and antique things, the mystery," Harrison said. "It's a very ecstatic piece, surprisingly enough, considering its construction."[9]

The pianist who played it, David Tudor, was a skilled improviser, a foundation of Litz's method. Inspired by his avant-garde spirit and awesome technique, Harrison began work on a piano score titled *Prometheus Bound.*[10] Like the chorales, this reductionist music often consists of just a single line tightly constructed from a series of melodicles, but it also resurrects Cowell's adventurous inside-the-piano techniques. When Harrison returned to New York, he finished the piece as a score for a new dance by Jean Erdman depicting the struggles of the mythical bringer of fire—a favorite symbol in Joseph Campbell's writings. Tudor premiered the work as a concert piece later that summer in Colorado.

The brief visit to Black Mountain lifted Harrison's spirits. He was impressed by the openness to experimentation, the ease with which artists from different disciplines collaborated, the informality. (Cage's well-known habit of wearing a jacket and tie made him nearly unique among the faculty.[11]) "There were so many artists doing so many different things, but it nonetheless levered up critical standards in one's own mind," Harrison remembered. But unlike New York's competitive cliques of artists and critics, "it wasn't in any sense a part of the commercial environment—it was a great playground of fun things."[12] The freedom from the distractions and noise of the city, Harrison reasoned, would give him the time and focus needed to complete several unfinished projects and perhaps improve his state of mind. Other than Remy Charlip, Harrison found little to keep him New York, so he decided to apply for a teaching position. When submitting his résumé to Black Mountain, Harrison laconically accounted for the years 1947–1948 with the entry "Lost mind."[13] And when offered a teaching position for the 1951 summer session at Black Mountain, Harrison happily seized it.

GLYPH

The reality of Black Mountain proved less idyllic than Harrison had hoped. He was paid only $64 a month in addition to the food in the communal dining room and his small room in the Bauhaus-inspired Studies Building overlooking the lake. As the winter approached, the food, which mostly came from the college's struggling farm, became more dominated by eggs and beans. Rides in the college's single pickup truck to the tiny town of Black Mountain, six miles away, were at a premium.[14]

At first, Harrison felt intimidated by the powerful presence of some of the faculty, which in the 1951 summer session included abstract expressionist painters Robert Motherwell and Ben Shahn, and photographer Aaron Siskind. Cy Twombly and Robert Rauschenberg were students. Presiding over the faculty was the iconoclastic poet Charles Olson, who represented a new wind in the development of the arts, one with which Harrison felt increasingly out of touch. "Olson's rebellion against all traditional literary forms, his militant insistence on subjectivity, self-expression, self-exposure—these were the first aspects of his teaching that struck me as revolutionary," wrote a student at the 1951 summer session.[15] This sort of uninhibited dive into the subjectivity of intense personal expression also inspired the abstract expressionists, such as Motherwell, Shahn, and Willem de Kooning, who had been at Black Mountain for the same 1948 summer session that hosted Cage and Cunningham. Franz Kline would come for the 1952 summer session, at which time Harrison would hang one of his paintings over his piano.[16] Litz, who developed her dances through improvisation out of inner necessity, shared this expressive aesthetic, as did the emerging Beat poets, including Harrison's old friend Robert Duncan, who occasionally visited Black Mountain and would teach there after Harrison had left.

However, when Harrison was there, the college was situated at the confluence of another, even more radical current, led by Harrison's dear friend John Cage. Despite his close association with the New York abstract expressionists, Cage sought to purge from his music precisely the sort of (as he saw it) ego-centered emotionalism that they had come to represent. By the late 1940s, his interests in Eastern religions had led Cage to study Zen Buddhism, most notably by attending Daisetsu Suzuki's lectures at Columbia. He began to realize the Zen ideal of suppressing his ego by leaving compositional decisions up to chance. In his piece for David Tudor, *Music of Changes*, all of the elements were chosen by elaborate random processes mediated by the *I Ching*—the Chinese book of wisdom that Harrison had first introduced him to. Though Harrison still felt a close friendship with Cage, he viewed this new aesthetic path and his old partner's New York clique skeptically.

Still, over the summer of 1951, Harrison gradually became friendly with the faculty and collaborated on a new work that sprang from interests he shared with some of them. Olson had studied the glyphs—hierographic pictograms—of the Mayans and was intrigued with the way that this reductionism led to both a symbol and a picture. "Litz recalled that Olson, who had overheard a black boy at an auction exclaim, 'It's like a race,' had been intrigued by the double meaning of the word. He wrote a glyph poem using the word 'race,' which he gave to Shahn."[17] Shahn then invented a "combo of a Mayan glyph and a Chinese character" to be painted on a dancer's body and a background screen. Litz choreographed a dance.

For *The Glyph* Harrison again provided a piano score to exploit the adventurous Tudor, requiring the pianist to press the sharp edge of a long block of wood at the nodal points of the piano strings, producing high harmonics with a muffled percussive quality. Harrison also asked the pianist to play claves and a tuning fork in one hand at times. The score is divided into six sections that closely follow cues from the dancer, allowing a great deal of flexibility. In fact, the third section is entirely improvised, either on the same notes on the piano or with an optional gong. At the performance, Litz, clad in a jersey tube, squirmed out of a burlap bag, which the amused audience accorded "baffled approbation."[18]

Harrison also wrote small occasional piano pieces for Litz and her husband (*A Thought on the Anniversary of Katherine Litz and Charles Oscar*) and Ben Shahn's daughter (*A Portrait of Abby Shahn on Her Birthday*). But aside from his work with

Litz, his initial Black Mountain experience proved tougher than he expected. Harrison soon realized that the *absence* of the ever-present "rumble" (as he called it) of the city was making him more and more nervous. Having made the tumultuous transition from the hospital back to the city, he was now making another passage, into the cold silence of North Carolina's remote hills. "It was terribly shocking, of course, [to] lose your habituated sounds," he said, "and by that time I was at once habituated and had gone mad from them."[19] He spent many nights drunk on liquor from the Asheville ABC store or at Ma Peak's Tavern, the watering hole three miles from school.[20]

"It was, as all artistic milieus are, turbulent and exciting, interesting and troublesome," Harrison recalled; he found himself "very mixed up" and often unable to control his temper.[21] While Black Mountain's pastoral environment proved palliating, Harrison still sporadically suffered aftershocks from his breakdown. He had an affair with a married man on the faculty. But it was a small community, and the man's wife publicly confronted Harrison, slapping him in front of faculty and students. He apologized to her and ended the relationship.[22]

"Things are very black at Black Mountain," Charlip wrote to Judith Malina that August 1951 when he visited Harrison. "Lou is in a stew, drunk (now and mostly), and I don't want to be here when the pot blows off."[23] It didn't take long for the pot to blow. Harrison fulfilled a "lifelong ambition to break a window" when he threw a bottle through one in the studies building. Expecting a cathartic crash, he was actually disappointed by the sound, and after calming down, he replaced the window out of his own tiny salary.[24] Charlip returned to New York, taking a retail job.

As the summer session ended with no new prospects, Harrison accepted the college's offer to stay for the 1951–1952 academic year as the music teacher on the regular faculty. For the next year, he would experience a new and very different way of living than he had for the preceding decade in New York and Los Angeles. And though he cherished the college's intellectual and natural environments, already it was clear that nature's balm alone wouldn't be enough to heal his troubled soul.

WISDOM HERE IN THE TREES

Lou Harrison invited some of us to the gate house to commemorate Saint Cecilia's Day [patron saint of music, November 22]. The gate house had no electricity so we had candles. It did have a piano (of sorts) and so we had music. Lou gave a class in the Round House where we talked about tuning of instruments and the virtues of equal temperament versus just intonation. Then we had to tune. It was so difficult and so ear-opening. He had a series of brass bowls which gave beautiful tones when struck. He also used them upon occasion as bowls to eat from, and once in a while would invite Joe and me up to his apartment in the Studies Building to have peaches and strawberries after supper.

—Mary Fitton Fiore[25]

While his Black Mountain appointment provided Harrison a refreshing return to nature and some stability, it also imposed unexpected stress, as he was single-handedly responsible for what had been rather piecemeal music instruction at the college. He became nearly a one-person music department, responsible for everything from conducting Bach cantatas to teaching private composition students to serving on faculty committees. This sudden responsibility added to his anxiety so much that he telephoned his parents in a panic.[26] The only other music instructor at the time was Johanna Jalowetz, an elderly voice teacher who also ran the bookbinding workshop; Harrison took her course, bound a book, and presented it to Cage upon the latter's return to the college.

Still, Harrison proved a responsible and active faculty member. During his first year, he arranged for his New York friend Bill Masselos to visit and play Harrison's transcription of Ives's First Piano Sonata.[27] In the spring of 1952, Harrison wrote to Ives soliciting start-up funds for a college music publishing venture and received a warm letter and a check for $165 in response.[28]

Most important, Harrison found himself composing, soon more prolifically than he had in all of his years in New York. His works at Black Mountain continue to represent his eclectic interests, as he tied up loose ends of his New York-period aesthetic and explored new ones. He began by going back to projects that had lain incomplete in his notebooks, sometimes for years, including the *Alma Redemptoris Mater* and a similar atonal *Fugue* for piano, which he gave to David Tudor. In the same style of trying to tame his Rugglesian expressionism through strict counterpoint, he also finally completed the brief but complex *Double Canon for Carl Ruggles*.

Perhaps in response to the news that summer of the death of his famous teacher, Arnold Schoenberg, Harrison began a new twelve-tone piece, a sort of suite unified by a common twelve-tone row rather than by consistent instrumentation. He completed only three of the projected pieces for *Group on a Row the Same*, adding another around 1960. Like his tone row for the *Symphony on G* and the later row for *Rapunzel*, this one emphasizes minor seconds and major thirds, with two strategic perfect fourths to allow for the occasional suggestion of tonality. The pieces here are brief and, like his other atonal works of the time, often focus on intricate canons.

Harrison also returned to neo-medievalism in a setting of the medieval Christmas carol "Holly and Ivy," which he discovered while at Reed College the previous summer. He set it in the quasi-medieval quintal polyphony of such works as the second "Pastorale" and *Vestiunt Silve*.[29] Underlining its historicism, he wrote the piece in an elaborate illuminated manuscript, using multicolored inks and the calligraphy he had learned at Reed. He also made headway on the unfinished *Symphony on G*.

Along with these backward gazes, Harrison continued to explore the other side of his compositional personality—the modalism and quintal counterpoint of the *Seven Pastorales*, of which he completed two more in the summer and the last in October.[30] In the same pastoral mood, Harrison composed a *Nocturne* for two violins and tack piano that same month that closely resembles the medievalist third Pastorale that he had dedicated to Charlip the previous summer. Like the dance from *Almanac of the Seasons* two summers previous, the *Nocturne* used the unusual, poignant Locrian mode.

He also sketched out a Kyrie movement for a mass in which he extended the modal consistency and melodic invention of the *Seven Pastorales* to a larger form. As before when exploring more ambitious applications of his experiments, Harrison set himself limits. In addition to restricting the range of the Kyrie's two vocal lines to an octave, he constructed the form out of nine sections, each consisting of nine phrases, with each phrase lasting exactly nine half notes. While he had used precise structures in the *Symphony on G* and elsewhere, here they echo the traditional triple repetition of the three-part plea for mercy of the Kyrie. When Harrison explained its form to Cage, himself no stranger to such rigid structures, his friend joked, "Why, Lou, that's the mass of the straight and narrow path!"[31]

Still another of his pre-breakdown inclinations, Christian mysticism, informed sketches for an oratorio based on texts by the French Christian mystics Charles Péguy and Simone Weil, whose book *Waiting for God* had just been published in English that year. Their spiritual associations with number increasingly converged with his interest in just intonation (though he would later abandon these mystical associations). The beauty of harmonious proportions, like counterpoint, also represented to him the ideal harmony of community and society. This was the lesson Simone Weil saw in the Pythagoreans: "The Incarnation of Christianity implies a harmonious solution of the problem of the relations between the individual and the collective. Harmony in the Pythagorean sense; the just balance of contraries. This solution is precisely what men are thirsting for today."[32]

His music wasn't the only part of Harrison's life influenced by Black Mountain's immersion in natural surroundings. At one of the many informal lectures Harrison attended, he heard a representative of the World Health Organization explain that much of the world's arable land was devoted not toward feeding the starving but instead for feed for cattle or other meat sources, wasting up to five pounds of grain for every pound of meat produced. Having been distressed reading the many news reports of famines in India and China that year, Harrison resolved to return to a vegetarian diet.[33] Except for periodic lapses out of necessity, he would remain vegetarian for the rest of his life.

As the stress of New York gradually evaporated, Harrison's periodic ulcer pain abated. Finally easing into his new rural surroundings, he adopted a shaggy black spaniel and, inspired by ocean explorer Jacques Cousteau's first book, ventured into the lake outside the college, snorkel affixed to a diving mask, to watch the fishes frolic.[34] With so many compositional loose ends tied up at last, his restored energy and focus arrived just in time to fuel the composition of his greatest work so far.

THE JUST BALANCE OF CONTRARIES

In the fall of 1951, Harrison received a phone call from the Ajemian sisters in New York City. They had been offered the rare opportunity to perform at Carnegie Hall that coming January and wanted to commission a new work from Harrison. The showcase performance was important to his young violin- and piano-playing friends—but it was also an opportunity for Lou Harrison, given his limited performances in the past years. Although his previous Carnegie Hall appearance was a triumph for Ives, it had not measurably advanced Harrison's composing career.

As he had when faced with a similar short deadline for the *Suite for Cello and Harp*, Harrison dipped into his inexhaustible stack of sketches, adapting other works for the occasion. As before, the original context of the source, in this case Simone Weil's serene mystic visions, colors the ultimate work, the *Suite for Violin, Piano, and Small Orchestra*, even though her words were no longer associated with the piece. From the oratorio sketches, Harrison had chosen a plangent, tranquil aria originally setting Charles Péguy's poem on the Chartres Cathedral to become the suite's fourth movement and an elegy for the second. As in the *Suite for Cello and Harp*, a serene chorale from the same sketches, incorporating both Asian and European melodic influences, closes the composition.

Like his *Easter Cantata*, the first movement is in the form of a French overture, contrasting a dramatic, deliberate opening with a faster, intricate fugal section, the standard opening movement in baroque orchestral suites. Harrison's dramatic overture heightened the contrast by using two different scales for each section, with the opening astringent scale based on parallel tetrachords juxtaposed with the pentatonic theme of the Carlos Chávez-influenced fugue. Harrison's study of Paul Klee's paintings (no doubt influenced by hanging around all those great painters at the college) directly inspired the pensive second movement, a quasi-pentatonic elegy whose extremely sparse texture makes each small change—a surprising harp run near the end, for instance—flash like a splash of color on a dark canvas.

The small orchestra of the title sacrifices the upper strings in favor of the more colorful woodwinds, spotlighting the violin soloist.[35] As in *Solstice*, one cello plays melodies while a second furnishes a bass line, and as with the *Symphony on G*, the harp, celesta, and tack piano comprise a (now explicitly named) imitation gamelan ensemble within the ensemble. He returns to that sound in two movements, phonetically titled "Gamelon 1" and "Gamelon 2," that contrast with the "European" movements (overture, aria, chorale), reflecting the productive tension between Harrison's old European and new Asian influences.

When he wrote the *Suite*, "my music was changing," Harrison recalled. "I was starting to draw from world resources, collecting them like a magpie systematically."[36] Not only did he have one foot in each culture, but Harrison was also straddling his European-dominated past and his future, when he would compose music in Asian forms for Asian instruments.

Harrison the magpie chose scales more varied than his systematic working-through of pentatonics in *Solstice*. Although the first gamelan movement uses a bluesy, decidedly un-Balinese scale inspired by Roy Harris's Second String Quartet, its dynamism, contrast, and figuration evoke the spirit of the gamelan.[37] The ensemble of *gender wayang*, a quartet of metallophones used in Bali to accompany the shadow puppet drama, inspired the similarly dynamic fifth movement. Harrison's interest in the sound of the Balinese gamelan had also recently emerged in a short piano piece for Katherine Litz that spring, *A Little Gamelon for Katherine Litz to Teach By*.[38]

The *Suite for Violin, Piano, and Small Orchestra* incorporates still another Asian inspiration: the Indian music that had preoccupied Harrison since he had studied Daniélou's book. One of the books he took with him to Black Mountain was Arthur Fox-Strangways's *The Music of Hindostan*, an old but fairly reliable account of the

EXAMPLE 18.1. This excerpt of the piano part from *Suite for Violin, Piano, and Small Orchestra* demonstrates Harrison's *jhala* technique, in which repeated drone pitches are interpolated between melody notes. Copyright © 1964 by C. F. Peters Corporation. Used by permission. All rights reserved.

basics of Indian music theory, which also drew comparisons with European music. One of the techniques Harrison discovered there was the form known as the *jhala* (sometimes spelled "jahla" by Harrison), in which an instrumental soloist such as a sitar player begins to articulate a constant pulse by repeatedly interpolating the drone pitch between those of the melody. Referring to the stock accompaniment figure of the European classical period, Harrison often called the *jhala* "India's answer to the Alberti bass," and as the latter had for European classical composers, the *jhala* became a characteristic technique for Harrison throughout his career. It afforded him a new, propulsive way of handling the drone pitches he had borrowed from Hovhaness's music. It would soon surface often, beginning with another 1951 piece in the style of the *Suite*, the brief, fanfare-like *Festival Dance*, an arrangement for two pianos also evidently drawn from his sketches for the never-completed oratorio based on Peguy's and Weil's writings.[39]

For all of its diverse Asian and European influences, though, it is the *Suite*'s melodic inventiveness and contrasts (which fit together surprisingly smoothly) that really sustain these gem-like movements. The gripping first gamelan movement, for example, contains four elements—the ostinato, a lead melody, a contrasting melody, and interjections from the bass—whose artful variations and memorable melodic phrases maintain excitement and charm throughout. The *Suite* closes with a softly swaying, melancholy chorale that reaches as deep into the heart as anything Harrison ever wrote.

Harrison drove up to New York to conduct the *Suite*'s premiere at Carnegie Hall in the Ajemian sisters' concert of January 11, 1952.[40] Just as with the urban noise that was absent from his Black Mountain existence, the *Suite* is also notable for what's not there. Unlike his New York suites (for strings, for cello and harp), he did not feel the need to whipsaw between tonality and atonality, between angularity and lyricism. His ability to make modal experiments and influences from Asia cohere so tightly and beautifully would define Harrison's best music for the rest of his career. In many ways a culmination of the seductive sound he had been developing in his Erdman ballets (which it resembles), the *Suite* stands as the pinnacle of Harrison's East Coast sojourn and one of the most surpassingly beautiful American musical creations of the 1950s.

Fortunately, someone in the audience that night recognized the magnitude of Harrison's creation. At the reception after the performance, Harrison was approached by his new friend Oliver Daniel, a pianist and music director of the educational division of CBS radio, where he had become an effective advocate for new American music. He had recently become the director of the American Composers Alliance (ACA), an organization Copland, Thomson, and others had founded, where he was able to apply his significant contacts and influence for the support of new music.

Daniel brought Harrison over to meet one of the most famous of those contacts, a musician whose distinctive profile and wispy white hair was already familiar to millions of concert- and movie-goers: Leopold Stokowski. The conductor was so much a part of popular culture that his deified status and conducting style had only two years before been parodied in the Bugs Bunny cartoon "Long-Haired Hare," and of course he had co-starred with Mickey Mouse in Walt Disney's 1940 classic, *Fantasia*. On the conductor's arm was his beautiful wife, the twenty-seven-year-old heiress Gloria Vanderbilt.

Behind the internationalism of Stokowski's affected, vaguely European accent stood a champion of new American works, which he thought essential to a new democracy of the concert hall. As far back as the 1920s, Stokowski had collaborated with the League of Composers in bringing groundbreaking new works to New York audiences. However, his uncompromising advocacy of such works as Schoenberg's *Piano Concerto* and *Variations for Orchestra*, which Harrison had heard him conduct in New York, had contributed to his departure from the Philadelphia Orchestra and the NBC Orchestra.

Although at the time he met Harrison, Stokowski lacked a regular position as a music director, he'd gained a new freedom to champion more new works, including pieces that would not fit into an orchestral program. When he had asked Daniel for ACA scores of American composers, Daniel had given him Harrison's pieces. The following autumn, Stokowski told Harrison, he would be conducting a contemporary music festival at Columbia University—and he wanted to include Harrison's *Suite*.[41] And he was so impressed by Harrison's breakthrough suite that he recorded it, with the Ajemians reprising their starring roles, in 1954.[42]

Despite Harrison's absence from the New York scene, other successes followed. Oliver Daniel offered Stokowski more Harrison scores from the ACA library, and in February 1953, Stokowski chose to perform *Canticle #3* in an ACA concert at the Museum of Modern Art. Stokowski would remain an advocate for Harrison in the 1950s, performing his percussion pieces several times. Most important, in the spring of 1952, Harrison received word that he had been awarded a Guggenheim Fellowship, which would support his full-time devotion to composition for the next academic year.

PRAISES FOR THE BEAUTY

Although he had little tolerance left for living in the city, Harrison's Christmas sojourn in New York offered a chance to reconnect with the artistic world there. A week after conducting his *Suite* at Carnegie Hall in January 1952, he attended the premiere of Erdman's choreography for his *Io and Prometheus*. He saw Malina there, and they were soon hanging out again; she took him shopping and introduced him to her colleague, the poet and playwright Paul Goodman, who had been at Black Mountain the summer session before Harrison. In a February 10 concert at the Living Theater's Cherry Lane Theater home, David Tudor played Harrison's knotty, atonal *Fugue*.

Harrison also met Erdman's colleague, choreographer Shirley Broughton, who sent him back to Black Mountain with a new commission. Its title, *Praises for the Beauty of Hummingbirds and Hawks,* demonstrates an adoration of nature that was beginning to supplant the praises previously devoted to the Christian saints and other mythological figures. The second movement consists entirely of an inversion of the first—that is, the same with all of the intervals reversed. This type of tonal contrapuntal trickery was uncharacteristic for Harrison, and ultimately he decided that the piece as a whole was "awful stuff. It doesn't go anywhere—canons accompanying ostinati that are not connected."[43] Furthermore, in his "haste and false confidence" to replicate the drones and modalism of Alan Hovhaness, Harrison felt he had not fully digested their implications. After its run in New York that spring, Harrison withdrew the work.[44]

After this uncharacteristic false start (following one of his great successes), Harrison decided to salvage some of the useful ideas from *Praises for the Beauty of Hummingbirds and Hawks* in a new piece whose delicate ensemble (two muted violins, flute, celesta, suspended cymbal, and tam-tam, the last two played very quietly throughout) and airy texture seem to calm its atonal essence, as though Black Mountain's Arcadian air was blowing away the noisome New York miasma he had just left behind. Harrison based the enchanting *Praises for the Beauty of Hummingbirds* on a single melodicle, injecting variety by varying the order of the intervals and allowing them to occur in more than one octave. The violins interpolate tremolos around the flute melody that, with the rolled cymbal, suggest the flitting of tiny wings.

Now, as he was recovering from his breakdown and from the rumble of Manhattan, Black Mountain's distance from the clamor and crassness of modern commercialism had finally become not only tolerable for Harrison but indispensable. In a February letter to his friend Frank Wigglesworth in Rome, Harrison confessed to being "personally confused and miserable" and revealed that he had left Charlip a note demanding that he change or Lou wouldn't see him anymore. "I don't know what love is anymore," Harrison wrote. "I am, needless to say, lonely!"

That letter to Wigglesworth also contained a little score. "How wonderful that you are playing piano and guitar!" Harrison wrote, evidently replying to a Wigglesworth letter. "When did you take up the guitar? I'm coocoo for it! A friend of mine, a painter . . . was over during [the] Xmas holidays & played for me. . . . What a pleasure! Those dulcet tones ringing through the house. Oh, I'm delighted you've taken it up!! I'll write some pieces for it soon & send [them] to you. . . . Soon? Why not now? Here goes!"[45]

What follows is a charming, gentle serenade in binary form that sounds remarkably assured, considering that he'd never written for the instrument before. The brief *Serenade for Guitar* represents a return to the modal writing he'd recently found so much success with and contains one additional crucial element. In the letter, Harrison indicates that the modal piece should, if possible, be performed in just intonation and includes the frequency ratios defining the mode of the piece, just like the examples in the books of Daniélou and Partch. At first blush, it seems a pointless instruction. Unlike the viols and lutes Harrison played as a youth, a guitar has frets fixed on the neck in the pattern of equal temperament.[46] Nevertheless, he included the ratios, if only to show the idealized version of this piece apart from the practicalities of performance. This *Serenade* thus became Harrison's first composition in which he specified a just intonation scale and the first work ever explicitly composed for just-intonation guitar. Even in equal temperament, this lovely idyll feels like clouds gradually lifting from his hectic New York interruption.

Finally free of deadlines, financial stress, and noise, Harrison at last had the time and emotional space to return to unfinished projects, starting next on the Mission Period mass with percussion. Of the pieces of Harrison's San Francisco period, this one most fully explored the characters of modes—in this case the diatonic "church" modes—and so it was a natural project to revive. Now, however, distant from his percussion ensemble days and the stark missions of California, Harrison reconsidered. A mass with percussion accompaniment would be unlikely to find performances in sacred settings.[47] And a conventional ensemble would allow him to weave a more elaborate texture around the bare melodies he had sketched out thirteen years earlier.

He decided on an orchestra of trumpet, harp, and strings to accompany the choir, though retaining a transparent texture, with no more than three melodic voices at any one time.[48] The strings often join in quintal counterpoint to the choral melodies, their parts charged with spirited and original countermelodies and interwoven seamlessly into the singers' original tunes. In the yearning Gloria movement, Harrison added his now favorite *jhala* accompaniment on the harp.

As he revisited the Agnus Dei, which he called "the mystical movement of the mass," Harrison was reading a borrowed copy of a novel about the tarot deck, *The Greater Trumps,* by the darkly mystical Christian author Charles Williams.[49] "Fundamentally, it's about God the madman," he recalled. "It's part of the tarot cards you know, the upside down crucifixion. At the end of the Agnus Dei you will notice that the ostinato part starts and keeps doing this while the Lamb of God is sounding. The mode rights itself, as it were; the crucifixion turns right side up, then there's the stab from the trumpet. . . . The mode turns all of a sudden. It's curious, mystical imagery in music, but nonetheless that's what was going on in my mind at the time."[50] This twist gives the conclusion of the movement a sense of calm, earned benediction.

On March 12, 1952, Harrison wrote the final notes of the mass he'd begun thirteen years earlier and then carried with him across the country to New York City, protected by the saint medal given to him by Melissa Blake. Now, in rural North Carolina, he was on another journey from the city to an uncertain future. He thought about the medal and, perhaps contemplating another cross-country journey ahead, wrote a dedication on his new mass: "to St. Anthony."

19

LAKE EDEN (1952–1953)

As the Black Mountain College faculty and students filed into the hall, they noticed that the chairs (each containing an empty cup) were all arranged in a square, divided into four triangular sections, each separated by aisles. A quartet of all-white paintings, freshly created by the not-yet-famous Robert Rauschenberg, dangled from the rafters above, glowing with images created by Nick Cernovitch projected by the college's students from a slide projector.[1]

On the piano outside the square of seats, David Tudor periodically launched into fragments of dissonant works, while Merce Cunningham danced through the aisles and behind the audience, at one point pursued by a dog that had wandered in. Rauschenberg sped up old Edith Piaf disks on a wind-up Victrola record player. And at the center, perched on a ladder, stood the perpetrator of the organized chaos: Harrison's best friend, John Cage, dapper and utterly serious in black suit and tie, declaiming from his Juilliard lecture. The poet Mary Carole Richards and Black Mountain College president Charles Olson himself recited poems, sometimes all at the same time.[2] By the time some of the female students brought coffee from the kitchen and filled the cups, signaling the end of the event, everyone there had earned the distinction of participating in history's first "happening."

Freed by a new Guggenheim Fellowship from the necessity of teaching for the 1952–1953 academic year, Harrison chose to remain in the quiet beauty of Black Mountain, moving into the college's tiny gatehouse, which had a small piano and an herb garden outside. Harrison was elated that Remy Charlip had returned, as well as (on Harrison's recommendation as head of music studies) John Cage and Merce Cunningham. For the 1952 summer session, Olson hired the composer Stefan Wolpe to fill in for Harrison. Although their circles in New York's avant-garde scene overlapped considerably (Morton Feldman and David Tudor were students of Wolpe's), Cage and Wolpe held fiercely opposing views of the arts. Like so many German artists, the fifty-year-old Wolpe had fled Nazism and brought to the United States a passionate belief in the social relevance of art. In an iconoclastic lecture at the Artists' Club in Greenwich Village, he argued fiercely against the aesthetic "purism" of art focused only on rarefied ideas rather than on society.[3] The implication that the postwar avant-garde somehow paralleled the Nazis' love of "purity" infuriated many and seemed to be directed toward one particular attendee: John Cage.

By now Cage had acquired the reputation of being the ringleader of the ultraradical faction of artists, which included Cunningham, Tudor, Feldman, and Robert Rauschenberg. Cage had started working with electronic music, mixing and splicing together recorded sounds according to random processes. But the chance procedures had also evolved through a celebration of natural surroundings to a point of Zen-like reductionism. In 1952, Cage wrote his most notorious piece of all, 4′33″, consisting entirely of silence, just as Rauschenberg was painting his all-white canvases and exhibiting them at the college.

A climax to the Black Mountain College summer session came when, reportedly over lunch the same day as the performance, Cage conceived the new work described above, later given the title *Theatre Piece No. 1* but more famously known as the first "happening," a genre that would later help define the avant-garde of the 1960s. As in many of his compositions, Cage chose a length of time and divided it into random segments for each performer, during which they could perform however they wished, surrounded by silences.

The faculty and students were variously perplexed, excited, or infuriated by the provocative performance. An outraged Stefan Wolpe stormed out. Harrison remembered the performance in good humor, chuckling at the "moderate hysteria" until it became "quite boring." He later expressed exasperation at its self-conscious avant-gardism.[4] Nevertheless, in an article published that fall, Harrison gave a fair and insightful appraisal of Cage and his followers, at least as associated with dance. "Led by the inventive and philosophical John Cage, a new kind of music has been evolving more fantastic than those who have not heard it can imagine; rich in fabulous, unprecedented new sounds and organized in ways entirely new to the art—silence as a plastic material (reckoned with in design), sound of the most violent, lush, bespangled, clangorsome and subtle kind; brought together, seemingly, at the least expected moments. . . . The Cage school, by its adherence to chance and its disinclination to common melodic or rhythmic formulae or to any reference to 'historicity,' is at its best."[5]

On the other hand, Harrison could not resist contrasting this approach with his own increasing personal conviction of the importance of melody and personal expression. "I value melody highly and think of it as melos riding on the crest of kinesis," he wrote. "I believe in more traditional formations, on the grounds that form and expression are accidents of assemblage, and not possible without the first essential, traditional choice. Musically speaking, I would rather 'chance a choice' than 'choose a chance.' . . . I am quite opposed to Frank Lloyd Wright's remark that just as modern architecture has done away with unnecessary cornice adornment of buildings, so has modern music done away with melody."[6]

Melody was at the center of Harrison's Guggenheim application, which proposed what would become his largest work to date—an opera. Although Harrison had been sketching ideas for mythologically themed operas since his return from the hospital, his thoughts now turned to the William Morris volume he had found in a Portland bookstore. Among the poems was a verse drama based on the fairy tale of a woman trapped in a tower.

RAPUNZEL

In a letter to *New Music* editor Vladimir Ussachevsky, Harrison wrote:

> The frogs sing out in Lake Eden—the air is warm and balmy and [the] outside flower-scented. In daylight the dogwood shimmers through the forests and the hills are green and soft and fuzzy. A whippoorwill has just begun its repetitive serenade.... Within a brief time I find that I have completed three acts of a six-act opera, and that I like it very much, and all in all astonish myself thereby.[7]

Harrison had long admired the Victorian poet, craftsman, and artist William Morris, not just for his verse and decorative designs (which had established England's Arts and Crafts movement in the mid-nineteenth century), but also for the way he made art an inseparable part of everyday life, from home decorations to moral behavior. Just as Harrison sought refuge from the city's incessant rumble, so Morris bemoaned the "dull squalor of civilization" and loved medieval legends and folktales.[8]

Harrison credited his reading of Morris during this period for his renewed interest in medievalism in such pieces as *Holly and Ivy*. But despite Morris's evocation of a mystic, shadowy past in his poetry and his revival of medieval crafts, from stained glass to calligraphy, he was no escapist. Like Harrison, he harbored a deep concern for people of his time; he helped found England's Socialist Party. So he also dedicated his creativity to the useful arts—furniture, wallpaper, typography—and lived the romantic ideal of the devoted and meticulous medieval craftsman opposed to the dehumanizing effects of the Industrial Revolution—a role model for Lou Harrison.

The tale of Rapunzel trapped in a tower without stairs, which her captor, the witch, may only access by climbing up her captive's long blonde braids becomes, in Morris's version, a deeply inward psychological fable of roles that imprison us. Her rescuer prince, who should be off at war, is instead a dreamer imprisoned by his own knightly armor, lured to the tower by visions. The poem teeters between the ugly light of reality and the twilight realm of dreams and imagination.

Harrison saw in this dualism not only the turmoil of Morris's imprisonment in an unhappy marriage but also a reflection of his own post-breakdown struggles. *Rapunzel* was "in part self-analysis," he acknowledged, "holding implicit in it some of the problems, tortures, and false rapture that I was myself experiencing."[9]

The opera opens with the three characters (soprano Rapunzel, mezzo-soprano witch, and baritone prince), each isolated but singing in turn, producing a triple soliloquy underpinned by the spidery tones of the tack piano constantly ticking away on a drone pitch. Each scene features several drones or ostinatos of one to three pitches so that the melodic material may actually consist of only the remaining nine or ten notes of the row. Even more tightly constructed than the rows in the *Symphony on G* or *Group on a Row the Same*, *Rapunzel's* self-similar row is divided into six pairs of notes, with the first pitch of each a semitone higher than the second (except in the last pair). Harrison carefully used intervals between the pairs (four perfect fourths and two major thirds) to help establish a sense of tonality. Depending on whether Harrison uses the original form of the row (sung by the prince in act I) or its inversion (Rapunzel in act I), the semitones either fall downward into darkness or rise upward into the light.

Working out the intricacies imposed by the restricted materials, Harrison also cast himself as a Morris-like craftsman, quite distinct from the Romantic myth of the visionary genius that the modernists, for all their putatively anti-Romantic rhetoric, seemed to embrace. In Harrison's opera the graceful floral and arabesque patterns of the Arts and Crafts movement become gentle, repetitive melodic turns, especially in the intricate ostinatos and Rapunzel's arias. The angularity of the *Symphony on G* sometimes lingers, though most often it is relegated to the part of the witch, represented by the strident major seventh and minor ninth (the primary interval of the row displaced by an octave in either direction).

Harrison set Morris's poem faithfully from beginning to end, despite the absence of the main dramatic episodes—the prince climbing up the tower, the couple's escape, the descent of the witch to hell—leaving only the characters' internal monologues and the philosophical dialogue between the prince and Rapunzel.[10] Scene 2 presents the prince's memories and inner conflicts and scene 3 Rapunzel's prayer, in which she adds her wish for her own savior, laden with pre-Freudian symbols for a sexual awakening, as sweet triads bloom from the row.

But while such a psychological focus may be fascinating in book of late Romantic verse, on the stage it presents considerable dramatic challenges. Harrison decided to embrace this atmosphere in his music, to draw listeners into the characters' haunting inner world through floating melodies and tonalities, and transforming Morris's explorations of the psyche into a hallucinatory drama.

The fourth scene, the midpoint of the opera, depicts the two lovers finally together in the tower. Their isolation ended, the characters suddenly gain a new perspective on what had been their world of dreams, as Rapunzel sings, "It grows halfway between the dark and light." The musical perspective shifts as well, and it would seem an ideal place for a shift in the row form as well, just as Harrison had contrasted his first theme in his *Symphony on G* (which used the prime form of the row) with the second theme (which used the retrograde form).

However, when Harrison began composing a new melody with the retrograde, something didn't seem quite right. He had seen this melody before. "Midway through . . . I began to get a little disturbed because I couldn't create as much variety out of that row as I had been doing with the row of the *Symphony* [*on G*] and I couldn't figure it out," Harrison recalled. "Finally I took a very careful look at the row only to discover that it is one of those trick rows. . . . Something I couldn't have created by conscious effort, had I tried, in a thousand years, I'm just not that kind, but my subconscious mind played a trick on me, so I really had exactly one-half the materials. Normally you have 48 forms of any row, but in the opera I had 24."[11]

Harrison had inadvertently achieved an effect that composers such as Anton von Webern had intentionally employed to create more tightly unified twelve-tone structures. They would use a series of intervals that are the same forward as in reverse, or in inversion, or some other combination. As a result, once the composer transformed that "trick" series in a certain way, it resulted in a return to the original series of notes.[12] But while this row's extreme internal consistency gave the opera a strong cohesion, it also limited his materials by half, snaring Harrison in a compositional trap of his own creation. When Harrison realized, after so many hours invested in composing the longest and most complex piece of his life, how he'd boxed himself in, he plummeted into a deep depression. Despite his recent successes, he was still recovering from his breakdown, artistic self-doubt, and indecision about what compositional path to take. This new discovery was too much.

One evening, he reached for the bottle of the "revoltingly sweet" concoction known as Rock and Rye. He'd asked friends who were heading to the ABC store to pick up bottles of the cordial made of rye whiskey flavored with (and intensified by) rock candy syrup.[13] Like the heroine of his opera, Harrison felt imprisoned, but he had built his own prison tower out of tone rows. He picked up the bottle again, filling and quaffing glass after glass. He glared at the intransigent opera score that stubbornly resisted his efforts to wrangle a recalcitrant system into the musical creation he envisioned. In a burst of fury, he ripped the score into pieces.

Now I remember what a most strange year,
Most strange and awful, in the beechen wood
I have pass'd now; I still have a faint fear
It is a kind of dream not understood.

—William Morris[14]

The next day, after the alcohol and anger had abated, an abashed Harrison (with help from Charlip, who had returned to Black Mountain for the summer session and stayed in the fall) carefully reassembled the pieces of the score and taped it together. They also mended a Joseph Fiore painting that Harrison had damaged during his drunken rage.[15] Harrison derived the strength to continue with the project from the model of William Morris himself. Just as a craftsman makes furniture, Harrison finally resolved to piece together his opera. He confronted his taped-up score and sang its troublesome row over and over, relying on his melodic intuition and trial and error to finally make his way through the remaining scenes.

For scenes 5 and 6, he fashioned strangely tonal-sounding melodies woven between gossamer threads of celesta, harp, and tack-piano tones, creating an ominous atmosphere that complicates Morris's happy ending, confusing what is dream and what is reality. The closest parallel in the European opera tradition, Debussy's *Pélleas et Mélisande,* also sets a quasi-medieval folktale by a late Romantic through understatement and suggestion.[16]

An even closer parallel is the highly ritualized classical Noh theater of Japan, whose narratives unfold with glacial deliberateness and indirection, creating an atmosphere of floating timelessness. Harrison, who had been introduced to these Zen-influenced dramas by Henry Cowell and had recently scored Yeats's Noh-influenced *The Only*

Jealousy of Emer, found that he shared an interest in them with several of the writers and theater artists at Black Mountain.[17] His interest in Noh influenced the architecture of *Rapunzel,* which, like a Noh drama, is largely static and evocative, its resolution both sudden and ambiguous.[18]

Harrison's twelve-tone swan song might seem anachronistic, given that his future output would build on the foundation of the *Seven Pastorales* and the *Suite for Violin, Piano, and Small Orchestra.* Yet in 1952, both his personality and his musical language were in flux, and Harrison was coming to accept his eclecticism. Besides achieving an integration of twelve-tone music and a tonal lyricism, *Rapunzel* culminated a remarkably productive eighteen-month tenure at Black Mountain College. Despite some emotional turbulence, Harrison had clearly found in the college's quiet, bucolic surroundings (as he had in his similarly prolific summers at arboreal Reed College) the supportive artistic environment he'd so long craved.

But now he had to go back to New York.

THE POOL OF SACRIFICE

Eastward I go only by force; but westward I go free.

—Henry David Thoreau, "Walking"

The Guggenheim money allowed Harrison to buy a secondhand car in Asheville, the nearest large town, and more easily travel there for occasional explorations of the nightlife. Once the rainy fall of 1952 turned to a frigid winter, the unpleasantness of orchestrating his opera in the drafty, unheated gatehouse and depression over Charlip's absence finally overcame his fear of moving back to New York. So toward the end of 1952, Harrison reluctantly returned to his Manhattan apartment, where Charlip had been living.

He soon delighted in getting back in touch with his New York friends and discussing his new interests in Pythagoras, Confucius, and musical tuning.[19] But most of the time he spent huddled in his apartment trying to concentrate amid the noise, orchestrating *Rapunzel* and sketching out ideas for a new opera about Persephone.[20] In January 1953, he conducted *Solstice* for a performance by Jean Erdman's company at Columbia's Hunter Playhouse and also an excerpt from *Rapunzel.* But despite its success, he resolved to turn down further dance commissions. "I tend to overtheatricalize when I know it's to be for dance," he explained, "and the music loses its integrity."[21]

Yet, as his Guggenheim funds were winding down, Harrison's financial options looked very limited. After paying for the parts duplication, a concert with Stokowski had ended up costing him money, and although Columbia had at last released the recordings of his *Suite for Cello and Harp* and *Suite #2,* his meager royalties covered only the costs of duplicating a score now and then. He was soon reduced to writing his parents to ask for loans.[22] "Life in NY is hell!" he wrote. "The place is so noisy that I simply give up after a while and almost cease functioning at all."[23] Along with cash, they also sent shirts and ties, in exchange for some of the music he'd written for his students for his mother to play.

Knowing his difficulties, Harrison's friend Virgil Thomson again offered him a regular staff position at the *Herald Tribune*, but Harrison knew he could no longer face the pressures of daily reviewing.[24] Likely because of Thomson's connections, Harrison also received an invitation to stay at the MacDowell Colony, an artists' retreat, for the following summer.[25] Again he declined, perhaps hoping for another summer at Black Mountain or with Jean Erdman at her new position at the University of Colorado's summer session.[26] A third offer (instigated by, again, Thomson and Harrison's composer friend Nicolas Nabokov) then arrived, for Harrison to send in a score to be considered for a prize at an Italian conference of twentieth-century music, so Harrison put together an arrangement of one of the arias from *Rapunzel*.[27]

Now habituated to the quiet sounds of the forest, Harrison craved the delicate tones of the clavichord even more, and he resumed building his own so that he could work late in his thin-walled apartment. But as much as he tried to cloister himself, the ugliness of the world continued to intrude. He learned that the red-baiting Senator Joseph McCarthy had called Aaron Copland to testify in Washington. Despite peace talks, the horrors of the Korean War still filled the front pages of the newspaper, along with regular reports of aboveground atomic bomb tests in Nevada.

On May 20, just after his thirty-sixth birthday, Harrison was appalled to read about a miscalculated explosion that showered radioactive fallout on nearby towns.[28] In response, Harrison composed a very short song to his own text, accompanied by harp, viola, and violin drones. *Little Song on the Atom Bomb*'s gentle modal countermelody and musing text form a quiet protest against the violence of nuclear weapons:

> *Both the explosion & the cloud of an atom bomb are beautiful to look at in color movies. The bomb proper, I suddenly realize, I haven't seen; &, of course, wonder what it looks like. My young friend Jeffrey Terulian says that an atom bomb exploded near sandy ground, would, due to its heat, produce a good glass swimming pool & I wonder whether this has been tried.*

As spring arrived and the orchestration of *Rapunzel* neared completion, Harrison received word that the Guggenheim Foundation had turned down his application for a renewal of his fellowship for another year. Harrison approached Charles Olson about returning to his teaching position at Black Mountain College for the next academic term. However, though Olson did not object to Harrison staying at the college through the end of the Guggenheim Fellowship period (which ended that summer), he had decided instead to keep Stefan Wolpe as the regular faculty member in music.

Olson's decision provoked a bitter response—but not from Harrison, who always maintained that his relationship with Wolpe was cordial.[29] Instead, John Cage (whose personal antipathy for Wolpe had not receded) was incensed that his friend Lou could not return to his job as he had been led to believe.[30] Cage viewed Wolpe's hiring as a "usurpation" of the job from "sweet-hearted Lou," engineered by members of the faculty who associated Harrison, mistakenly if true, with the Cage-Cunningham-Rauschenberg circle.[31] Certainly Wolpe had more in common with the largely European-influenced expressionists on the faculty, in contrast to Harrison's eccentric interests in Asian music and tuning systems.

The sudden change in his plans to return to Black Mountain's beauty (and teaching income) left Harrison surly and temperamental, and Remy Charlip bore the brunt. Charlip was attracted to another dancer, a student closer to his age that he had met at Black Mountain; no longer able to tolerate Harrison's inebriated rages, Charlip finally resolved to move out. A terrible argument ensued, and Harrison exploded, "Three Jews have ruined the world: Freud, Einstein, and Schoenberg!" Charlip, who (as Harrison well knew) was Jewish, was stunned. He could not believe, even as much as Lou was drunk and wanted to hurt him in that moment, that he could have hurled such an ugly anti-Semitic slur.[32] Without another word, Charlip walked out the door. He joined Cunningham's new dance company at inception that year. Their friendship would gradually resume from a distance, but they would not speak to each other again for over a decade.

Still desperately seeking nature's balm (and to escape New York's sweltering summer), Harrison returned to Black Mountain without Charlip (and without a teaching job) for the summer session of 1953, continued orchestrating his opera, and contributed music to a reading of a translation of a Japanese Noh play, *The Pool of Sacrifice*. To accompany this sparse, contemplative, and highly stylized Asian drama, Harrison wrote a chant for chorus and solo singers. He also filed the metal keys of a children's toy xylophone to tune it to just intonation for the accompaniment, but unfortunately this music, which prefigures his building of just intonation gamelans, has been lost.[33]

But as the end of summer session (and the end of his Guggenheim money) approached, Harrison faced the unappetizing prospect of returning to the city he could no longer tolerate, with no job prospects; no desire to write music for his only semi-regular outlet, dance; and, although he socialized with musician colleagues, a dwindling number of close friends. He couldn't do it.

"I long to live simply and well and that just isn't possible here," he wrote his mother that winter. "My true musical talent is a very sensitive and easily disturbed and temporarily defeated one and I fully realize now that I must protect it and give it the means of growing.... My plans are taking shape." Nearly broke, Harrison decided to head back to California, where he could at least be assured of a place to live with his parents. He wrote his mother, asking her to retrieve his old piano from Carol Beals in San Francisco and move it to their Redwood City home. "Everything will be all right as soon as I get out of New York," he wrote. "I hate the place."[34]

Once again, Virgil Thomson tried to engineer an opportunity for his friend, asking George Antheil, who was working as a Hollywood composer, to help him out. Antheil, who had met Harrison in New York a few years earlier, graciously offered Harrison a room in his spacious Hollywood home overlooking Sunset Boulevard and introductions to studio music directors.[35]

Harrison was intrigued. He had read Antheil's reports on the "Hollywood scene" in *Modern Music* and his entertaining autobiography, and he had been greatly impressed with his friend Bernard Herrmann's score to the 1951 film *The Day the Earth Stood Still*.[36] Yet it is hard to imagine a composer less suited to the schmoozing so vital to the success of a Hollywood composer, or that Harrison—who had only recently complained about deadlines and restrictions when composing for modern dance—would be satisfied with such a career. In any case, Antheil's well-meaning efforts, which had paid off for other composers, led nowhere.

In 1943, Schoenberg had wished fame and good fortune for Harrison on his journey to the artistic capital of the United States. Now, as Harrison prepared to board a Greyhound bus for the long trip back to where he started, it would have been easy for him to conclude that he had found neither. His modest foothold in the professional musical life of the city had resulted in only a meager number of performances and near-poverty, while the new fashions of the avant-garde had passed him by. Later he noted that he had become first not a composer but a writer in New York and that most of his New York compositions were commissions for dancers.[37] The psychic cost of living in the city was too great, and his youthful ambition to advance his career in this artistic capital had given way to a visceral need to nurture his creativity in the quiet surroundings of nature. Even so, his connections and experience in New York and North Carolina would form an important foundation for the rest of his career, and out of this upheaval had emerged a unique and mature musical voice.

FIGURE 1. Harrison, age two, in front of Silver Court Apartments, Portland. Courtesy of Special Collections, University Library, University of California Santa Cruz, Lou Harrison papers.

FIGURE 2. Buster Harrison, about three years old. Courtesy of Special Collections, University Library, University of California Santa Cruz, Lou Harrison papers.

FIGURE 3. Harrison (second from right) plays bass recorder in a photo from a newspaper article about Eileen McCall's Ancient Music Ensemble at San Francisco State College, April 17, 1936. Courtesy of the *Oakland Tribune*.

FIGURE 4. Sherman Slayback, left, and Harrison in front of their apartment in San Francisco, c. 1940. Courtesy of Special Collections, University Library, University of California Santa Cruz, Lou Harrison papers.

FIGURE 5. Facing top, The percussion concert at Mills College, July 18, 1940, with the set designed by Bauhaus students. The three men are, from left to right, Harrison, John Cage, and William Russell. Photo credit: Mary Edwards and Norman Donant. *Dance Observer* 7, no. 7, August/September 1940.

FIGURE 6. Facing bottom, Recording session of the Cage-Harrison percussion ensemble, 1941. Left to right: John Cage (conducting), Doris Dennison (back to camera), Xenia Cage, Margaret Jameson, Lou Harrison. Elizabeth Hall, playing bass drum, is reflected in the glass window of the studio. Courtesy of Special Collections, University Library, University of California Santa Cruz, Lou Harrison papers.

FIGURE 7. Above, John Heliker (left) and Harrison in New York, c. 1945. Courtesy of Special Collections, University Library, University of California Santa Cruz, Lou Harrison papers.

FIGURE 8. Above, Harrison with Peggy
Glanville-Hicks (right), Henry Cowell (second
from right), and other friends in New York, c.
1949. Courtesy of Special Collections, University
Library, University of California Santa Cruz,
Lou Harrison papers.

FIGURE 9. Left, Mary Callantine. Courtesy of
Hal Callantine.

FIGURE 10. Facing top, Harrison at Black
Mountain College, c. 1952. Courtesy of Special
Collections, University Library, University of
California Santa Cruz, Lou Harrison papers.

FIGURE 11. Facing bottom, Harrison discussing
his score of *Four Strict Songs* with conductor
Robert Whitney at the work's premiere in
Louisville, 1956. Courtesy of Special Collections,
University Library, University of California
Santa Cruz, Lou Harrison papers.

FIGURE 12. Above, Harrison and Robert Hughes in front of Harrison's parents' house in Redwood City, 1961. Courtesy of Robert Hughes.

FIGURE 13. Facing top, At the San Francisco dock before Harrison's departure to Japan, 1961. From left, Lou Harrison, his father Clarence, his mother Calline, his brother Bill. Courtesy of Robert Hughes.

FIGURE 14. Facing bottom, Harrison and guide visiting the Nikko Toshogu Shrine north of Tokyo during his 1961 trip. Courtesy of Special Collections, University Library, University of California Santa Cruz, Lou Harrison papers.

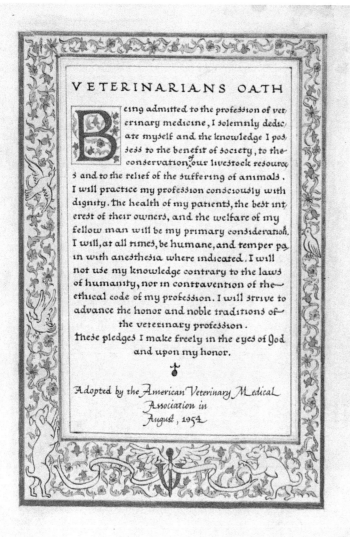

VETERINARIANS OATH

Being admitted to the profession of veterinary medicine, I solemnly dedicate myself and the knowledge I possess to the benefit of society, to the conservation of our livestock resources and to the relief of the suffering of animals. I will practice my profession consciously with dignity. The health of my patients, the best interest of their owners, and the welfare of my fellow man will be my primary consideration. I will, at all times, be humane, and temper pain with anesthesia where indicated. I will not use my knowledge contrary to the laws of humanity, nor in contravention of the ethical code of my profession. I will strive to advance the honor and noble traditions of the veterinary profession.

These pledges I make freely in the eyes of God and upon my honor.

Adopted by the American Veterinary Medical Association in August, 1954

Dear Bob,

I hear from mother and from Richard Vee that you gave two delightful concerts that were well received, and I send my congratulations & why dont you break down and let the "old mandarin" know about it?? Long time no hear from you!! Summer is, as mother says, hotter than the hinges of hell!! maybe soon I take pleasure-boat on the Han river and drift with breeze & I think of you often and am glad indeed that you continue your ebullient and stimulating music-making & I will be back in mid-July with marvels ≡ with love from Lou

FIGURE 15. Two examples of Harrison's calligraphy. Facing top, the Veterinarians Oath from the 1950s; facing bottom, a letter to Bob Hughes from Korea (1961). Courtesy of Special Collections, University Library, University of California Santa Cruz, Lou Harrison papers.

FIGURE 16. Above, Harrison practicing *piri*, 1962. Courtesy of Special Collections, University Library, University of California Santa Cruz, Lou Harrison papers.

FIGURE 17. Facing top, Harrison practicing *zheng* (also known as "psaltery"), c. 1964. On the wall is his Mondrian-like painting based on proportions of the Fibonacci series. Courtesy of Special Collections, University Library, University of California Santa Cruz, Lou Harrison papers.

FIGURE 18. Facing bottom, Harrison playing *xiao* (Chinese bamboo flute) in front of the Buddhist painting he brought back from Korea. His psaltery is in the foreground, and his *erhu* (two-string Chinese fiddle) is on the right. Courtesy of Special Collections, University Library, University of California Santa Cruz, Lou Harrison papers.

FIGURE 19. Above, Harrison on *janggu* (Korean drum) with dancer Lorle Kranzler, c. 1966. Photo credit: Hank Kranzler. Used with permission of Lorle Kennedy.

FIGURE 20. Above, Harrison and Bill Colvig in front of Harrison's original Aptos home, October 1967. Courtesy of Special Collections, University Library, University of California Santa Cruz, Lou Harrison papers.

FIGURE 21. Facing top, Harrison, Richard Dee (seated at *zheng*), and Colvig at a demonstration and performance of Chinese music. Courtesy of Special Collections, University Library, University of California Santa Cruz, Lou Harrison papers.

FIGURE 22. Facing bottom, Scene in King Nicodemus's bedroom with Gaius (left) from the original production of *Young Caesar* (1971). Courtesy of Special Collections, University Library, University of California Santa Cruz, Lou Harrison papers.

199

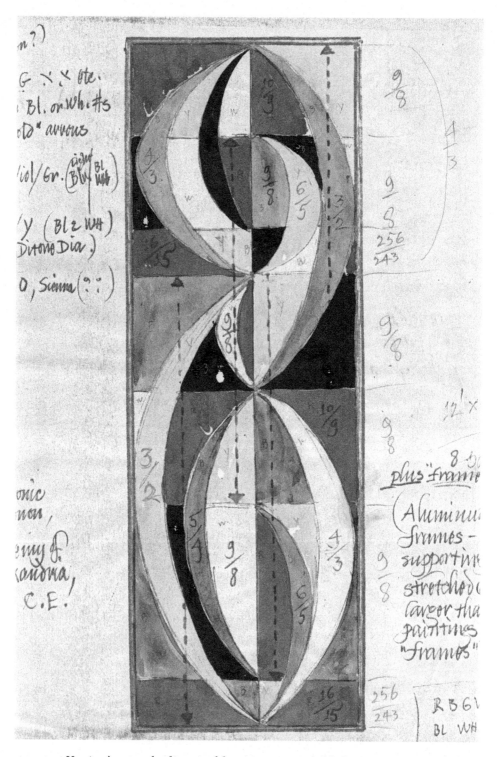

FIGURE 23. Harrison's watercolor diagram of the tuning system used for his American gamelan, Claudius Ptolemy's syntonic diatonic scale. Courtesy of Special Collections, University Library, University of California Santa Cruz, Lou Harrison papers.

FIGURE 24. The American gamelan, later known as "Old Granddad," in a performance of *La Koro Sutro* with the Chamber Chorus of the University of California Berkeley, the Sacred and Profane Chamber Chorus, the University of San Francisco Chorus, and the William Winant Percussion Group at the UC Berkeley Art Museum and Pacific Film Archive in 2012. Photo credit: Peter Cavagnaro. Courtesy of the UC Berkeley Art Museum and Pacific Film Archive.

FIGURE 25. K. R. T. Wasitodipuro, known as Pak Cokro. Photo credit: I Nyoman Wenten.

FIGURE 26. Virgil Thomson with Harrison during Thomson's 1976 visit to California. Courtesy of Special Collections, University Library, University of California Santa Cruz, Lou Harrison papers.

FIGURE 27. Harrison rehearsing with gamelan Si Betty. Courtesy of Special Collections, University Library, University of California Santa Cruz, Lou Harrison papers.

FIGURE 28. Above, A corner of the Ives Room in Harrison's house, with instruments of Gamelan Si Aptos. Photo credit: Bill Alves.

FIGURE 29. Facing top, Colvig and Harrison in front of a metal sculpture caricature of them by Mark Bulwinkle. Photo credit: David Harsany. Courtesy of David Harsany and Special Collections, University Library, University of California Santa Cruz, Lou Harrison papers.

FIGURE 30. Facing bottom, Remy Charlip with Harrison, 2001. Photo credit: Eva Soltes.

FIGURE 31. Harrison's straw-bale house in Joshua Tree, California. Photo credit: Eva Soltes.

PART 4

Full Circle

Lou Harrison's journey from east back west in the summer of 1953 marked a tremendous transition in his life and music, and not just geographically speaking. For the rest of the decade, he would work almost entirely in isolation, not just from the musical maelstrom of New York City, but also from the new tides gradually inundating the avant-garde. Even as he abandoned the method of his teacher Arnold Schoenberg, a new generation of composers took serialism to new extremes, alongside the development of electronic music and the reverberations of chance music of his friend John Cage.

Although Harrison never left behind his modernist curiosity, his blooming passions for Asian music and tuning systems took those explorations down paths at right angles to those of the artistic mainstream. Harrison had learned that conventional measures of accomplishment would not by themselves bring him satisfaction, even if he achieved them. As he reevaluated his life in the wake of his breakdown, the importance of his own peace, stability, and personal satisfaction finally outweighed New York's meager opportunities for professional recognition.

Back in California, Harrison would feel liberated by the ability to follow his own artistic enthusiasms without having to worry about performances to further his career. Unlike the prolific days of his last time on the West Coast, during the 1950s Harrison neither sought nor found regular outlets for his music. Instead, he would use his self-imposed isolation in the forested hills overlooking Monterey Bay to investigate new compositional ideas, particularly the hidden worlds between the notes of the equal-tempered scale. Such explorations could at times be magnified into obsessions by his separation from the professional world and his freedom from deadlines.

His 1950s hermitage also permitted him to begin to heal emotional wounds. Seven years after his breakdown, it had become clear to Harrison that he needed not just nature but also solitude in order to rebuild his personality. By the end of the 1950s, his few friends saw the unstable, sometimes outrageous extrovert of New York transform into a guarded and shy Harrison. This social isolation would also produce intricate, even impractical experiments that contrasted with his earlier Californian music, whose performances with friends had been social events in themselves.

The emotionally damaged Harrison's reconnections with his parents, with a few old friends, and with nature formed sequential steps in the healing process. Gradually, he would also find his way back to the professional musical world and the joys of making music with small groups of friends like those of his early San Francisco years. But for now, trying to sleep with improvised earplugs on the bus heading west, the thirty-six-year-old Harrison was grateful simply to have his own bedroom waiting for him in his parents' house.

20

A PARADISE GARDEN OF DELIGHTS (1953–1955)

At a bus stop, Harrison scrawled in his notebook, continuing around the margins when space ran out:

> As though a nation of deaf, engines of every description run at their noisiest, without acoustic shields. It is as tho none noticed noise, or, if they did, would never imagine it possible that this unbelievable exacerbation could, in almost all instances be stopped. In the name of what do so many rush away from their senses, towards what delusion? Surely it is a collective delusion. (The designers of these vehicles are vulgarians, surely happy in the noise & gas they make, & trusting in the public support that none shall escape their triumphal racket.) One thinks to rest at a rest-stop. I counted 6 automatic motors roaring in one rest-stop, before someone remembered the juke-box. Enforced consumption of anything I do not construe as just, but there is almost no public place left where one is free of what the vulgar consider an inalienable right: foisting a noise &, at the control-box of the juke-box, their taste, on all others; conversation has ceased, enforced consumption takes over & Big Brother is served.[1]

Lou Harrison's return home began unpleasantly, but after a clangorous trip and a tumultuous decade, he was relieved to find refuge in the room his parents had set up for him at their house in Redwood City, south of San Francisco. Although he looked forward to seeing old friends in San Francisco occasionally, he still did not yet feel "socially acceptable" six years after his breakdown. Shaken by his inability to deal with social situations and his obliviousness to friends, Harrison was more comfortable sequestered with a piano—retrieved from his friends Carol Beals and Mervin Leeds—or with a book than socializing.[2]

Without the immediate demands of a job or commissions, he looked forward to reconnecting with his family and to having time to study and plot a course for a new trajectory in his music. First, though, he needed some paying work. While unpacking at his parents' house, he began to send off letters. After some correspondence with Antheil, he realized that composing for Hollywood was not a realistic possibility. He wrote to the science fiction writer Ray Bradbury proposing a collaboration, possibly an opera. Bradbury was receptive but in Ireland working on John Huston's film *Moby Dick*, and the partnership never materialized.[3] Hoping for a more stable teaching position, he sent his résumé to the San Francisco Conservatory and as far afield as

Chiapas, Mexico, and Accra, Ghana. However, many positions were closed to him because of his lack of a college degree.[4]

After months of decompressing by San Francisco Bay, a new opportunity arose—not from Harrison's many letters, but once again via Virgil Thomson. The aria from *Rapunzel* that Thomson had solicited from Harrison had been accepted by an international music festival. Pack your bags again, Lou, he said, you're going to Rome, all expenses paid.

A PANDEMONIUM

Italy is an anarchy conducted as a pandemonium.

—Lou Harrison[5]

The twenty-seven-year-old soprano, just two years from her first opera performance in a student production of Verdi's *Falstaff*, admitted that she was "sweating blood" over the new twelve-tone aria she had been given to learn for the International Conference of Contemporary Music.[6] She would be singing it in a few days before a distinguished audience including some of the world's most famous composers, at Rome's legendary Academia de Santa Cecilia, but the person who had picked her for this prestigious role, Virgil Thomson, knew she was up to the task. So did the composer, as soon as he heard the not-yet-famous Leontyne Price sing his aria from *Rapunzel* in rehearsal.[7]

A few days before the rehearsal with Price, exhausted but exhilarated after his twenty-two-hour flight from New York, Harrison found his way to the Villa Aurelia, a seventeenth-century palace and home to the American Academy, where Harrison and the other American guests would be staying along with the resident Rome Prize recipients. Harrison and his friend Ben Weber were the official American representatives to the April 1954 festival, but other Americans attending included Thomson, Aaron Copland, Merton Brown, Ned Rorem, Elliott Carter, Frank Wigglesworth, and Samuel Barber (who was there with his partner, the Italian American composer Gian Carlo Menotti)—so many that it was almost like going back to New York. But amid the fond reunions, Harrison didn't realize that he was simultaneously entering the cultural front of the Cold War.

In New York, Harrison had been acquainted with the festival's director, Nicolas Nabokov, a charming, gregarious composer with a booming voice and a subtle accent. After Nabokov's aristocratic family (along with that of his famous novelist cousin, Vladimir) fled the Red Army when he was a teenager, Nicolas became a fixture in the artistic circles of Stravinsky, Gertrude Stein, and Virgil Thomson in 1920s Paris. The US military hired Nabokov to advise in cultural affairs in post-World War II Europe, and somehow this led to the directorship of a mysteriously well-endowed organization known as the Congress for Cultural Freedom (CCF). Once on the periphery of Paris and New York artistic circles, Nabokov was now a US citizen and one of the most powerful impresarios in Europe, allowing him to organize an ambitious international music festival in 1954 in Rome. But more than artistic considerations played a role. The CCF's secret funding originated with an organization with an intense interest in Italy: the US Central Intelligence Agency.

As unlikely as it might seem, the CIA found itself in the position of being a secret patron of the arts to counter perceived Soviet propaganda saying that the communist system provided superior support for arts and culture. Such a rebuttal was especially important in Italy, where the CIA had already intervened in an election and continued to fight the popularity of the Italian Communist Party. In this new festival, Nabokov sought to feature "advanced" music of a type that would not be allowed in the Soviet Union, which to him meant primarily atonal music, and to invite as the headliner his fellow Russian expatriate Igor Stravinsky.[8]

Nabokov identified several of the most promising young twelve-tone composers in Europe, and in response to Nabokov's request, Virgil Thomson recommended two similarly "advanced" young composers from America: Ben Weber and Lou Harrison.[9] Two other atonalists, Merton Brown and Elliott Carter, already lived in Rome, Carter because of the Rome Prize. Brown had accompanied his partner, Jack Heliker, when the painter had received his own Rome Prize in visual arts in 1950, and he had remained in Rome after the couple broke up. He had sent Harrison glowing reports of the artistic life there, despite his frequently precarious financial situation.[10] Below his apartment lived Harrison's poet friend Harold Norse, who praised Rome's sensuality and friendliness to gays.[11]

So it was that, courtesy of Thomson, Nabokov, and (unknown to him) America's foreign spy agency—Harrison wound up hearing the rising young singer Leontyne Price rehearse the aria from his still-unproduced opera. She would sing an entire program of chamber works by composers invited to the "Twentieth-Century Masterpieces" competition. The other American representative composer, Ben Weber, was entered into a violin concerto category. Price immediately impressed Harrison at their rehearsal session. "She was marvelous," he recalled. "She was very cordial, very warm, and listened carefully."[12] A few days later, she sang the aria beautifully in the competition concert (which withheld composers' names to give the appearance of unbiased judgments) that pitted it against eleven other works. The audience greeted the *Rapunzel* excerpt warmly, as did that week's review in the *New York Times*.[13]

The April 4–15 festival also included panels and discussions on such topics as "Music and Politics" and "Music and Contemporary Society," where Harrison met and chatted with his European counterparts.[14] Having just completed his own first opera, Harrison had much to discuss with the young German composer Hans Werner Henze, whose new opera, *Boulevard Solitude*, was featured at the festival. The first performance of Henze's opera was a formal affair and also Harrison's first experience of the militancy of European artistic squabbles. An iconoclastic mélange of atonalism, percussion, and jazz, Henze's score seemed a slap in the face of Boulez's serialist purity, and its story was a sordid update of Puccini's beloved *Manon Lascaut*. Before long, a group of provocateurs in the balcony were shouting so loudly that the singers couldn't hear the orchestra.[15] Harrison was indignant. "At least in America we let other people listen," he loudly proclaimed in the lobby at intermission.[16] Soon the uproar rivaled the legendary riot that accompanied the premiere of *The Rite of Spring*.

However, the composer responsible for this historic precedent was not on hand to experience the reenactment. Igor Stravinsky, his assistant Robert Craft, and Nabokov himself had shown up to the performance in lounge jackets rather than the required formalwear, whereupon the doorman refused them entrance, even after receiving a punch in the face from Nabokov.[17] The scandal made the front pages of all the Roman newspapers, where it presumably did little for the cause of Western cultural superiority.

Critics noted the unusual proportion of atonal works among Nabokov's choices; Thomson groused that the festival "suffered from a plethora of overcomplex music."[18] Even Stravinsky, who had a concert to himself, presented a new *Septet* whose angular atonality signaled a new direction in the master's output. Aaron Copland too bowed to the new trend with the European premiere of his atonal *Piano Quartet*. Harrison liked to think he had some responsibility for this piece, as he had earlier tried to persuade Copland to try twelve-tone composition. "But Lou, doesn't this restrict you?" Copland had asked Harrison. "Aaron!" Harrison had replied. "You're old enough to know better. You can make music with flowerpots!"[19] Despite this faith in his and Copland's craft, Harrison admitted to struggling with the strictures of atonality. But the conference's emphasis on atonality signaled the direction in which contemporary classical music was heading—a direction that would veer away from Harrison's own path.

Harrison was less concerned about the competition, concerts, and controversy than with exploring the abundant art and history of the Eternal City, which had beckoned since his high school forays into Pliny, Ovid, and Virgil. On his walks from the American Academy on Giancolo Hill near the heart of the city, he encountered historic sites wherever he turned. Harold Norse gave Harrison an introduction to Rome's gay scene, and Harrison soon found himself out carousing along the banks of the Tiber with Norse and Norse's friend, playwright Tennessee Williams. Harrison picked up an Italian man who spoke little English, so he only gradually came to understand that the man was trying to tell him that the chamber in which they trysted had been one of Michelangelo's studios.[20]

A few days later, after having lingered over breakfast at the American Academy, Harrison and Ben Weber had to hurry to make it to a gathering for the invited guests in a room in the capitol designed by Michelangelo, where the composition prizes were announced. Just after the two composers belatedly hurried in past the statue of Marcus Aurelius astride his horse, Harrison heard the voice of Igor Stravinsky: "Mr. Harrison!"

Lou Harrison had won the festival prize (in a tie with French composer Jean-Louis Martinet). He shook Stravinsky's hand and they chatted, a prize almost as valuable in itself as the $1,200 check he received. It would be over a decade before the irony of a Russian émigré presenting a prize from the CIA to a stalwart leftist and US government critic would become apparent.

After the festival ended, Harrison still had some days for sightseeing before his plane flight home, but misfortunes began to balance his triumph. First, he fell victim to one of Rome's notorious pickpockets and had to begin the process to replace his passport. Then, on a trip to Ravenna with Frank Wigglesworth and his wife, where they visited the Palladio Theater and explored ancient architecture, he stepped backward onto the edge of a grass-covered ditch, tumbling down and breaking his ankle. The Wigglesworths took him back to their hotel in Venice, and Harrison tried to keep his mind off the pain by identifying the overtones of the bells of St. Mark's.[21] Forced to return to Rome for more extensive medical treatment, Harrison emerged with a cast on his lower leg and instructions not to fly for several weeks. Determined to use the enforced extra time to see even more of the city, he learned to amble—slowly—with crutches. He invited the painters at the Academy to decorate his cast, and its colorful saints and flowers soon brought much attention on the street.[22]

Harrison found Rome rather less romantic than the portrait painted by such recent Hollywood movies as *Three Coins in the Fountain*. Less than a decade since the war's end, its streets remained so rough that the only women typically walking them were prostitutes.[23] Few Italians spoke English, and Harrison found his high school Latin useless. When he could, Harrison brought along Merton Brown, Frank Wigglesworth, or some other Italian-speaking friend.

After one particularly frustrating day, Harrison sat and rested at the Coliseum and reflected, as many travelers do, on the languages that divide nations. In this time of conflicting ideologies, simply allowing ordinary people to communicate more easily could help the cause of peace. Then he remembered that there is, in fact, such a thing as an international language. While in high school, he had been playfully passing notes to a girl, a daughter of a Stanford University linguist, in hieroglyphics. At dinner with her family, the topic of invented languages came up, and Harrison recalled the name the professor told him: Esperanto.[24] He resolved to explore it as soon as he got home.

TRUED IN RATIOS

Warm wonderful Harry Partch in recent times
Has made his lovely life's music
Entirely trued in ratios, & has told us
Of these perfections in a book. . . .
Thus we compose continuance from his start
More full than for centuries.
Such history perhaps must follow from him
That tune & tuning shall conjoin. . . .
He grasps & holds us in a sweet reminder
That yes it is our flesh that knows
All these lovely ratios, as we know also
Blooms & loves & tunes & sunlight.
—Lou Harrison[25]

After he returned from Rome, Harrison frequented his old haunt, the San Francisco Public Library. One day in 1954, he spied among the shelves none other than Harry Partch. The eccentric composer had returned to the state he considered home in 1947 and in 1951 had enjoyed a residency at Mills College, which produced the first of his musical theater works, *King Oedipus*. By 1953, Partch had found a building large enough to house his growing instrumentarium among the abandoned World War II shipyards of Sausalito, a short trip across San Francisco Bay. With its large studios and low rents, the city became one of the centers of the emerging Bay Area Beat movement. Many of its most famous personalities, including writer Alan Watts, liked to hang out at Partch's studio, dubbed "Gate Five" after a shipyard sign near the entrance.

Harrison and Partch struck up an enthusiastic conversation, despite the fact that Partch had not forgotten the largely negative review Harrison had written of Partch's League of Composers concert in New York. Now that Harrison finally appreciated just intonation through Partch's book, he apologized for his insufficient comprehension at the time.[26]

His initial puzzlement is understandable. Ask a just-intonation composer for a short definition of the system, and the answer is as likely to disappoint as enlighten, given the expressive, even spiritual power some composers claim for it. While "a system of tuning in which pitches are related by relatively small integers" is correct, it communicates nothing about the sound of just-intonation music, much less explains why this seemingly technical aspect of composition earns such evangelical fervor among adherents like Harrison that other techniques (in rhythm or orchestration, say) don't.

As Harrison's mind and ears quieted down after his New York years, he began to hear (and teach his Black Mountain students) that the differences between tunings like equal temperament and just intonation are not subtle at all. To finally hear the modes of the ancient Greeks, the music of the Renaissance humanists, or the keyboard music of the baroque in the tunings intended by those composers felt like stripping away centuries of grime from the frescos of the Sistine Chapel. As Harrison discovered, when two frequencies, related in a ratio that can be represented by small integers, are played together, the interval resounds with a remarkable purity, a crystalline quality next to which the complex ratios of equal temperament can sound rough and grating.

Why does this seemingly abstract mathematical relationship produce such an audible result? Whenever a taut string is set in motion (or a column of air in a wind instrument), it can vibrate not only along its whole length, but simultaneously also in halves (producing a frequency at twice that of the whole length), in thirds (producing a frequency three times that of the whole length), in fourths, fifths, and so on. What we hear as a single violin tone, for example, is really a complex mixture of sine waves that always fall in this pattern: the lowest frequency (which is the sine wave we associate with the pitch—for example, if the lowest frequency in a tone is 262 cycles per second, musicians call the pitch middle C), two times that, three times that, and so on. Rather than hear these higher sine waves (called harmonics, or, informally, "overtones") directly, we hear a composite sound, in which these harmonics influence the tone quality or what musicians call the timbre of the instrument. Nevertheless, their existence is an acoustical fact. "Just intonation," composer Michael Harrison (another nature-loving erstwhile Oregonian who's no relation to Lou) has said, "*is* nature."[27]

Mathematicians call this orderly sequence of ratios of the divisions to whole string length (1:1, 2:1, 3:1, 4:1, etc.—by convention musicians put the larger number first) the harmonic series. Many of the common intervals of not only Western music but also the music of many cultures can be found in or approximated by intervals in the harmonic series. The interval between the first and second harmonics—that is, a ratio of 2:1 in frequency—is the octave. The interval between the third and the second, 3:2, is the perfect fifth, 4:3 the perfect fourth, and 5:4 the major third.

However, even though Western composers have long idealized this harmonic purity, incompatibilities began to surface as soon as composers of the Renaissance wanted to use a variety of harmonies and to change keys, or modulate—a key to variety and structure in European music. But once a composer chooses a different starting point in calculating ratios (i.e., a new key center or tonic), the resulting intervals may no longer represent simple ratios. Common chords in the new key may sound sour indeed.[28]

Faced with this dilemma, most musicians chose to compromise, or "temper," the intervals; that is, they would choose irrational relationships that split the difference between competing ideals.[29] Like many enthusiasts, Partch and Harrison believed that if two notes are played together and most of their harmonics coincide (which will happen if they are related by relatively simple proportions), we will perceive this sort of harmonic purity. If, on the other hand, the harmonics are close but not coincident (as with tempered intervals), acoustic interference will result, creating a beating (or "wah-wah") effect—a "roughness" of tone. "Real intervals—the ones with whole number ratios—grab you; they're beautiful; they draw you into the music," Harrison explained.[30]

Although few twentieth-century listeners realized it, baroque composers used many different temperaments that moved the deviations from just intervals around in various ways, usually so that the most common keys sounded closest to just and the less common keys somewhat more dissonant but still playable. Harrison came to understand the previously puzzling insistence of musicians of this period that different keys had clearly different characters. Once he had tuned his clavichord in these unequal temperaments, Harrison found that the keys did indeed sound noticeably different—D major much "brighter" than E♭ major, for example. The tetrachords he had read about in Daniélou's book and elsewhere now marvelously came to life in all their Technicolor variety.[31]

By the nineteenth century, European musicians' desire for seamless modulation and chromatic harmonies grew so important that these differences were sanded down to the point that all keys shared the compromises equally. Next to the delightful diversity of earlier tunings, Harrison denigrated the equality of keys in this equal temperament tuning as "industrial gray."[32] In equal temperament, the lovely 5:4

major third becomes quite sharp (almost unbearably so to Harrison), the minor third becomes very flat compared to the 6:5 interval, and all the keys sound identical. Making all keys identical created a circularity that composers such as Richard Wagner exploited in the ambiguity of their chromaticism and frequent modulations. This expressionistic chromaticism made possible by equal temperament led directly to the atonal works of Arnold Schoenberg and, ultimately, to his invention of the twelve-tone method. Harrison declared that it was part of Schoenberg's genius to see that atonality was a logical consequence of equal temperament.[33]

To Harrison, the collapse of the pluralism of baroque temperaments and the nineteenth-century triumph of the single equal temperament resembled the impersonal standardization that became necessary for the contemporary Industrial Revolution's factories to replace the individual craftsmen that he and other devotees of William Morris so esteemed. Likewise, the harpsichordists of J. S. Bach's time, who by necessity tuned their own instruments and were familiar with the theories of tunings, were replaced by a guild of professional piano tuners, many of whom, by Harrison's time, simply turned their hammers in deaf reference to electronic devices. Harrison also deplored the replacement of these idealized composer-performers by musicians who, their ears dulled by urban noise and the ubiquity of equal-tempered roughness, had all but forgotten the existence of alternatives to the rigid standard now implicitly enshrined in millions of pianos and music theory textbooks.

As Harrison's research led him to such writers as al-Farabi, Boethius, and Ptolemy, he found that, to authorities from these other times and cultures, just intonation represented far more than merely a euphonious way of creating music. The tuning reflected, in a sense that was very real to these writers, the beauty of the order of the cosmos made audible. He traced these ideas back through the ancient Greeks and Chinese and even earlier civilizations that associated numerical relationships with esoteric spirituality manifested not just in music, but also in art and architecture. When Renaissance artists and architects rediscovered this fact, they applied the proportions of musical consonances to their paintings and buildings as well.

Always a devotee of architecture, Harrison often carried around a well-worn copy of Rudolf Wittkower's *Architectural Principles in the Age of Humanism*, which details these "musical" proportions in the architecture of the period. Though these ideas of well-proportioned art were somewhat eclipsed with the coming of the baroque era (and temperament in music), Harrison retained a lifelong love of those architects whose buildings continued to reflect this beauty of proportion, including England's Christopher Wren and Turkey's Mimar Sinan. Toward the end of his life, Harrison would base the design of his own house in Joshua Tree, California, on the 3:2 ratios of so-called Pythagorean tuning.

Not that Harrison needed the mystical justifications of numerological esoterica to hear the splendor of just intonation. He had left behind the mystical side of his personality in New York and still associated such thinking with his breakdown. Throughout his life he continued to speak of tuning as an empirically aural experience and remained convinced that the perception of simple ratios, aurally as well as visually, is psychologically powerful. He viewed just intonation as a place where ancient philosophy, physics, and perception converged.

Harrison's research gradually helped him understand that his own compositional vexations of the last decade might have owed as much to the flawed system in which he was composing as to the noise of his urban environment. Since equal temperament created a system in which (in Schoenberg's phrase) tones are related only to one another, any attempt to create a hierarchy on a firm foundation (like conventional tonality) was therefore illusory at best, doomed at worst. Harrison realized that trying to create tonality out of a system that lacks true harmonic relationships and forces all tones into unnatural "equality" led to frustration and circularity in his own explorations.

"I would do a white note piece, all neat . . . whether tonal or not still nothing but the diatonics," he explained, "and then in the next piece I wrote I would permit myself F♯ and perhaps B♭ . . . and so on, until finally I would have to write another serial piece. Well, this constitutes a squirrel cage, you know. You're going around and around and around. And it was Harry's book and actually getting to the reality of intervals that, of course, stopped the squirrel cage, because once you've found that there are perfectly real intervals then, of course, there's no way out of that. . . . But it also opens up . . . a sort of paradise garden of delights, which we never cease working with."[34]

For the next few years, he eagerly, even giddily explored the many fruitful varieties of scales from his new garden of just intonation. To categorize these scales, Partch and others related them to the harmonic series. A just tuning system created by a chain of fifths—that is, the 3:2 or the second and third harmonic partials—is called a three-limit system, also called Pythagorean tuning. Add in just thirds (5:4, 6:5), and now you have a new prime number in the system (five), so the tuning becomes five-limit. Though compromised by temperament, the European diatonic scale and conventional harmonies are essentially five-limit in their conception, but beyond the five-limit, Harrison found delicious and exotic intervals not even remotely approximated in the equally tempered twelve-tone equal scale: seven-limit harmonies such as the natural seventh (7:4) and the small or septimal third (7:6); eleven-limit harmonies such as the eleventh harmonic (11:8, almost exactly between the equal-tempered perfect fourth and the tritone) and the bracing neutral third (11:9, about halfway between major and minor thirds). Beyond the eleven-limit lies increasing complexity and dissonance that Harrison would explore later in his career.[35] He thrilled at the creative possibilities now opened from these previously unavailable (to him) intervals.

"The music sounds better, it just does," he insisted. "Because I'm a sensualist, the hearing of those just intervals just pulls me in, whereas in equal temperament, I feel as though I'm on ice skates. I get vertigo in equal temperament whereas I don't in just intonation. The equal temperaments are particularly displeasurable. They are like whirling down the vortex with no place to rest or no place to hang onto at all."[36] Just intonation represented the same order and stability he craved in his life and the same sensual beauty he found in nature.

Yet despite his increasing fascination with and commitment to just intonation, Harrison composed only two experiments involving the tuning while at Black Mountain: the little guitar serenade he had written for Frank Wigglesworth, in which just intonation was suggested as an option, and in his retuning of a toy metallophone for the Noh play *Almanac of the Seasons*. Actually creating justly tuned music entailed formidable challenges. Most modern instruments by default assume the equal-tempered standard, and even on those instruments that have available pitches within a continuous range (the violin family, the voice, the trombone), to require something outside the standard means asking musicians to counter a lifetime of ingrained training. Partch took the courageous—some thought crazy—route of inventing his own instruments and training his own players.

Harrison came to think of Partch as more of a Romantic than he let on, noting the "nineteenth-century system builder" mentality that fueled Partch's creation of a forty-three-tone-per-octave just-intonation scale.[37] By contrast, Harrison's initial interests in just intonation had grown out of its application to tetrachords and seven-, six-, or five-tone modes. Talking to Partch, Harrison began to be overwhelmed by the possibilities of just intonation, and he would spend much of the 1950s carefully mapping and exploring that new landscape. Not yet ready to make as extreme a commitment as Partch by inventing new instruments, Harrison began to consider other possible methods to realize such tunings, even with a conventional orchestra. It was at this auspicious moment that word arrived of a commission from the Louisville Orchestra.

HERE IS HOLINESS

> *Now arrived home behold me,*
> *Now arrived on the rainbow;*
> *Now arrived home behold me,*
> *Lo, here, the Holy Place!*
> > *Yea, now arrived home behold me,*
> *At Sisnajinni, and beyond it,*
> > *Yea, now arrived home behold me;*
> *The Chief of Mountains, and beyond it,*
> > *Yea, now arrived home behold me;*
> *In Life Unending, and beyond it,*
> > *Yea, now arrived home behold me;*
> *In Joy Unchanging, and beyond it,*
> > *Yea, now arrived home behold me.*

—Navajo chant[38]

In 1953, Louisville Orchestra conductor Robert Whitney teamed with mayor-elect Charles P. Farnsley, who, as Harrison put it, had the radical idea that a city orchestra could make a name for itself commissioning and recording the music of living composers.[39] Whitney approached BMI's Oliver Daniel for recommendations of composers to commission, and one of Daniel's first suggestions was Harrison.

The commission arrived while Harrison was in transition—from equal temperament to just intonation, but also in the midst of his personal journey from New York distress to West Coast solace.

His healing process partly involved reconnecting with his family. By the summer of 1954, Harrison's parents were again living separately. Rather than continuing to stay in his mother's suburban home, where both his late-night composing and his carousing were curtailed, Harrison got an apartment on San Francisco's Haight Street and bought his mother's car with the prize money from Rome. Harrison drove up to see his father in the Northern California city of Arcata, where the elder Harrison ran a sawmill, and paid back the loan that had gotten him to New York for the Rome trip. Harrison had also just gotten word that he had received a new Guggenheim Fellowship, which would finally provide further financial stability, at least for the following year.

Seeing his father apart from the poisonous dynamics that had so polarized the family during his last years in San Francisco made Harrison realize how much he had neglected his dad. "Pop" Harrison, who had recently been working at a mine in Nevada, where Lou's brother Bill and his family lived, seemed suddenly old and fragile. Because of the recent atomic tests in Nevada, Harrison was especially glad that Pop had moved back to California. Harrison newly appreciated his dad's unfailing affability, even when humiliated by his wife.

In bustling postwar San Francisco, Harrison began to face the same problems that had caused such distress in New York: the stress of city life, constant noise, nighttime piano curfews. After just a few weeks in San Francisco, Harrison began to search for a place outside the city. He finally settled on an apartment in the small Sacramento Valley town of Chico, roughly equidistant from Redwood City and Arcata, between his mother and father. Just as he was working to mend his own broken psyche, he wanted to make things right again with his family. Living in a small western town also reignited his fascination with Native American cultures—their connections of families, of communities, and to nature, all of which would influence his next major work.

Daniel knew that Harrison was mostly finished with the *Symphony on G*, and that a commission from the Louisville Orchestra would be the perfect opportunity to get it performed. However, Harrison told Daniel that he had agreed to have the symphony published by Southern Music, whereas the contract with Louisville explicitly stipulated that the piece could not be published.[40] Harrison told the frustrated Daniel not to worry, that he wanted to write a new piece anyway and could have it done on time. Harrison asked the conductor, Robert Whitney, if a choir might be available, but the only one was small and amateur. A nearby seminary, though, had a small group of male singers, some pretty good. Harrison also asked for an unusual subset of the orchestra, with winds represented only by two trombones. Finally, Harrison made possibly the most unusual request Whitney had yet heard from a commissioned composer. Would it be possible to include a retuned piano? And harps?

When Whitney agreed to Harrison's suggestions for retuning the orchestra, Harrison went back through his Black Mountain sketches and pulled out his "mass of the straight and narrow path," as Cage had called it—the first movement of the projected choral work that Harrison had begun at Black Mountain. Although Harrison hadn't explicitly required just intonation, the movement was all pentatonic and modal (i.e., without complicating modulations or bedeviling twelve-tone rows) and thus could be relatively easily adapted to a five-limit tuning with the orchestration he had in mind.

However, the setting of a mass no longer appealed to Harrison as it had during his New York preoccupation with Christian mysticism. As his head and his ears cleared in the natural surroundings of Black Mountain, and now rural California, he wanted to sing praises to the divinity of nature, celebrating his turn to the "natural" tunings of just intonation and his return to the verdant setting of his new home in rural California. He decided to replace the Kyrie text of the mass movement with his own text and to expand the work to four movements.

Instead of Christian scripture, Harrison looked for inspiration to Native American songs, such as those in Burlin's book, where he encountered the Navajo genre of nature praise songs known as *hozhonji*, which he characterized as "make-things-right-and-well-again" songs.[41] "The Hozhonji songs are holy songs, given to us by the gods," said a Navajo source quoted by Burlin. "They protect the people against all evil. A man will often sing a Hozhonji song before starting on a journey."[42] The song thus also became a commemoration of Harrison's journey through the darkness of his breakdown, "making things right" through his renewed appreciation for nature and his place in it. In the examples of *hozhonji* songs given by Burlin, images of nature, especially mountains, represent divine protection.

Harrison's own song reflects his emergence from his breakdown and his return to the West Coast. His first stanza mimics the *hozhonji* song's litany-like repetition, beginning each line with "Here is Holiness," followed by a celebration of an aspect of nature that Harrison cherished: the plant kingdom, animals, minerals, and the cosmos. The "Holiness" stanza is followed by one each of lines that begin, "Here is Nourishment," "Here is Tenderness," and finally "Here is Splendor." "They are emotional," Harrison said of his original texts, "and the verse has to do with my childhood."[43]

For each of these stanzas, Harrison planned a movement that would feature a different pentatonic mode, each emotionally and musically distinct. In his *Music Primer*, Harrison would later write, "5-tone modes . . . constitute every human's most important tonal heritage. Also, still, our subtlest."[44] The mass movement that Harrison adapted for the "Here is Holiness" movement used a pentatonic mode best known for its prevalence in Chinese traditional music, but, like Esperanto, is understood throughout the world and so common that Harrison called it "the Prime Pentatonic, it is practically 'The Human Song.'"[45] Now adapted to just intonation, the mode takes on a brilliance unattainable in equal temperament in the first of what he now titled *Four Strict Songs*.

The "Strict" of the title refers not only to the tuning, but also to the fixed, four-line structure of the poetry, the form of the movements, and the theme of permanence, which is central to the work. Harrison had recently read Thomas Mann's new novel

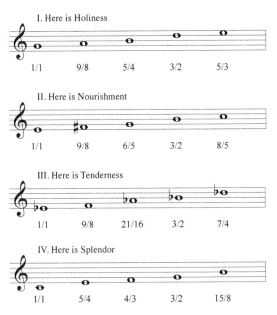

EXAMPLE 20.1. The movements of Harrison's *Four Strict Songs* each use a different pentatonic just-intonation scale. The numbers represent the frequency ratios relative to the first pitch in each scale.

Dr. Faustus, which acquired some notoriety among musicians for its dark portrayal of a syphilitic composer who sacrifices his humanity in his obsession with art.[46] This protagonist makes a distinction at one point between composition in "strict style" and "free style"—the former being "the complete integration of all musical dimensions, their neutrality towards each other due to complete organization." Although Harrison would later use the term somewhat differently than did Mann, who had nothing to say about musical tuning, the book's description of "a sort of astronomical regularity" through "rational organization" fits these songs.[47]

To structure his *Strict Songs*, Harrison adapted Cage's square-root form, where the micro-level structure reflects the same proportion as in the macro-level. The first movement consists of nine sections, each consisting of nine phrases, each exactly nine half notes long (9×9×9). He confined the vocal melodies for the eight baritones to a range of just one octave. Movement two has eleven phrases of eleven half notes each (11×11). Movement three (the one based on ratios of seven in the tuning) is 7×7×7, and the final movement is 5×5×5. Harrison applied the same comfortable and beautiful relationships of number that he found in tuning to the formal structure, though such a strictness of form was hardly new to him. Despite (or perhaps because of) such abstract mathematics, none of the movements comes off as stilted, too long, or too short. Each flows seamlessly with proportions that seem just right. Unlike many "process" composers (including Cage), Harrison always used his methods as a means to an expressive end.

Propelled by the junk percussion (in this case, tuned brake drums) that signals Harrison's return to his San Francisco roots, the exuberant opening bursts out like spring flowers. After this sunny celebration of the divine in nature, the mode of the reflective second movement, "Here is Nourishment," turns solemn, representing the shimmering heat of Harrison's summer in California's rural interior.[48]

The third movement, which Harrison described as "playful," has the set's most startling tuning, based on ratios of the seventh harmonic (thus a seven-limit tuning). The result is five pitches that deviate significantly from equal temperament and that are spread almost (but not quite) equally across the octave, resembling one of the two standard tunings of the Indonesian gamelan known as *slendro*. Harrison realized that brass instruments have the seventh harmonic implicit in their instruments (though they normally avoid it in order to stay in tune in an equal-temperament orchestra) and wrote engaging canons for the two trombones around these intervals between the sung phrases. The percussion rattles suggest a Native American ceremony amid gamelan-like interjections by the piano, harp, and the distinctive sound of tuned waterbowls, an instrument from India called *jaltarang*, which Cowell had shown him.[49] The thirty-eight-year-old Harrison dedicated this "Tenderness" movement to his father.

The glorious last movement, which brings the listener to a sense of repose and home, aptly names things of "splendor," using a common pentatonic form of the other Indonesian gamelan tuning, *pelog*. It brings to mind Harrison's epigraph for the score, a quote from the Indian music scholar Arthur Fox-Strangways: "For, after all, a man sings because it is a splendid thing to do, and because he cannot help it."[50]

Certainly one of the finest creations of his career, Harrison's *Strict Songs* garnered critical praise after its January 18, 1956, Louisville premiere, and so did the subsequent recording on the Louisville Symphony's label.[51] "It was a new way of seeing music," says Michael Zwiebach. With his adoption of modes, Asian influences, and just tuning, "[Harrison] was basically rewriting the rules of Western music ten years before anyone else was doing anything like that."[52] Harrison's *Strict Songs* expands the sublime diatonic style of such Black Mountain works as the *Seven Pastorales* and *Suite for Violin, Piano, and Small Orchestra* into the new dimension of just intonation, and it exalts, and exults in, Harrison's return—to the West, to nature and the ancient principles, to home.

21

FREE STYLE (1955–1957)

On the coast
I see mist-webbing rise
among the pines upon the hill
the storm winds shred this

—Lou Harrison[1]

Harrison's parched summer in the Central Valley town of Chico ended when his mother suggested that she could use her modest savings to buy him a place of his own, which would also be a real estate investment for her. Harrison drove around the Sierra foothills, looking for possible properties, and finally found a place to the south of the Bay Area. The hamlet lay just outside the coastal town of Santa Cruz, a few paved roads then its main concession to civilization. Harrison's parents found a small lot (a former avocado farm) with a house, really more of a cabin, on one of its steep hills, reminding Harrison of his gatehouse at Black Mountain. He loved it immediately, especially the big windows that gazed out into the forest. And for a composer who was about to dedicate the rest of his life to integrating two great streams of human music, East and West, the town had the perfect name: Aptos, which in the language of its original native Ohlone Awaswas inhabitants means "the meeting of two waters."

Viewpoint Road got its name from the occasional glimpses of the Pacific through its conifers, but (ironically, considering the prices that would eventually be offered for those views) Harrison preferred to work with the window shades drawn, cloistered in his tiny bungalow. Its main room was soon stuffed with Asian art and scattered books and manuscripts. He later added skylights, and he converted a shack formerly used to raise chinchillas in the back into a tiny composing studio whose walls (unlike those of his single-plank house) were thick enough to prevent his late-night practicing from disturbing the neighbors—not that there would be many for some years. He installed his upright piano and had a technician drive out to remove the extra strings for each pitch (pianos usually have one to three strings per note), so that Harrison could tune it more precisely.

Cage wrote to him from his new home in rural Stony Point, New York, noting that they had both ended up out in the country after decades of urban life. "If, at the moment, you think of me as musician," Cage wrote, "it must be in terms of birds and wind in the trees, which, when I hear, I think of you."[2]

In comparison to Chico, these hills by the coast were thick and verdant. Fern-lined trails snaked into a state park in one direction, down to the beach in another. Harrison enjoyed the wildlife—a resident fox, deer, raccoons—and they were his closest neighbors. He made several friends among his human neighbors, including an older woman who allowed him to use her telephone because he had none. "People who live in forests are sober and delighted," he wrote in his notebook.[3]

Aptos was so isolated at the time that its main road even lacked a bus stop, but Harrison learned when the buses would come by and could flag them down. He eventually bought a secondhand motorcycle, but he found it easier to take the bus or hitchhike into San Francisco. Harrison often took these trips north on the weekend to visit friends such as Harry Partch, bookstores, or art galleries, but most of all, the baths. Since his early years in San Francisco, much of the gay scene had moved from the beaches and Union Square to bathhouses, where one could meet a lover and retire to a private room. These rooms were available at all hours, so he could stay overnight in the city without the extra expense of a hotel room.

These superficial encounters suited Harrison, particularly in the wake of his ill treatment of and disastrous breakup with Remy Charlip. He wouldn't feel confident enough to approach another long-term relationship for years. At times he suffered intense lonely spells, but just as often these bouts evaporated in a giddy enthusiasm for his latest project. One of those projects would become probably the most radical piece of his career.

DELICIOUS NUMBERS

> Charm me asleep, & melt me so
> With thy delicious numbers,
> Thou being ravished, hence I go
> Away in easy slumbers
>
> —Robert Herrick[4]

During one of his many long talks with Harry Partch, Harrison suggested a different approach to just intonation. One of its traditional limitations, and the reason it had been rejected as impractical, was the impossibility of keeping it consistent with the range of harmonies and modulations that composers wanted—at least, noted Harrison, if one stuck to a limited gamut of pitches. Faced with this limitation, the few musicians who shunned tempered tunings chose simply to expand the number of available keys on their instruments, but experiments such as Nicolai Vicentino's harpsichord with thirty-six keys per octave proved understandably unpopular. Harry Partch himself had designed a keyboard with forty-three tones per octave, but it proved too technically difficult to complete with the funds he had.

EXAMPLE 21.1. In this excerpt from Harrison's *Simfony in Free Style*, two lines exchange a figure of four notes rising, but the intervals between the pitches (represented by the ratios between them) get gradually larger. Courtesy of Special Collections, University Library, University of California Santa Cruz, Lou Harrison papers.

Instead, he retuned an existing reed organ and mapped his forty-three tones onto its standard keyboard.

But Partch's system is still based on a fixed scale and tonal center (the "1:1," Partch and Harrison called it)—a larger tonal landscape to explore but still one with fixed borders. Harrison, though, was impressed with the way that the members of a good string quartet constantly adjust their tuning to accommodate the harmonies at any given moment, suggested a system in which pitches are tuned not according to some fixed or "strict" set of pitches but instead according to whatever frequency was needed in the immediate context. Harrison, again appropriating the term if not the exact meaning from Mann's novel, called such an approach "free style." Partch said thinking about it made him dizzy.[5] Harrison's 1955 experiment with this idea, titled *Simfony in Free Style*, returned to his idiosyncratic spelling of "symphony" to indicate the original meaning of a harmonious "sounding together" rather than a large orchestral work.

Harrison notated each pitch of the *Simfony* on the staff position closest to those he intended, but instead of defining each absolutely, he included precise ratios *between* each succession of notes.[6] Though free style would allow a performer to modulate freely and retain pure harmonies—the dream of Renaissance and baroque composers—Harrison's *Simfony* is still focused on melody. The opening flute theme at first may look like a simple scale, but inspecting the ratios he wrote next to each pitch reveals that each step is a different size (rather than, as in equal temperament, the same sonic "distance" apart), and the intervals get gradually wider by tiny degrees. Harrison then literally transposes this melodicle, keeping the intervals the same. And, as with his flute theme, he used free style to gradually expand or contract intervals, as Schoenberg did, but by tiny degrees. Harrison's experimentation applied to the *Simfony's* temporal dimension as well, through a process called metric modulation, in which an irregular division of the beat (quarter-note triplets, in this case) becomes the regular division of the following section (straight quarter notes, in this case). Therefore the *Simfony's* tempo changes according to the same proportion (3:2) as the melodic intervals.[7]

Perhaps the only aspect of the *Simfony* more striking than this ingenuity is its glorious impracticality of realizing it on conventional instruments. The piano (or tack piano here), bells, and five different harps each have precisely tuned pitches, but even so, they account for only a small fraction of the needed pitches. To fill in the rest, Harrison turned to the Renaissance viols he learned as a student in San Francisco. Unlike its cousin the violin, the viol has frets, and, unlike the guitar, the frets are tied onto the neck rather than permanently fixed into the fingerboard. The players could easily place those frets in the positions needed to play Harrison's specified pitches, though each performer would be required to use between four and six separately tuned viols to cover all the pitches.

Harrison's other choice of an instrument for his free-style orchestra was inspired by a book he and Partch were discussing—*The Greek Aulos*. Although Harrison felt that Partch took author Kathleen Schlesinger's somewhat dubious historical theories a bit too seriously, her attempt to reconstruct the *aulos*, an ancient Greek double-reed instrument, intrigued him. Schlesinger, an Irish musicologist who advocated just intonation as early as World War I, constructed her own *auloi*, drilling the holes at different points on the tube to create different tunings. Harrison built his own *aulos* after Schlesinger's design and would in a few years take up a modern equivalent of this instrument in Korea. Schlesinger further suggested that "cylindrical key-less flutes may be plotted and bored specifically for the *harmonia* [Greek tunings] required."[8]

This passage reminded Harrison of the recent appearance of inexpensive plastic recorders with mechanically drilled finger holes, and he reasoned that these plastic tubes could have finger holes bored at virtually any point. Once he counted up all the pitches, he noted that the score would call for a total of nineteen differently tuned flutes, though Harrison was frustrated by his ambition to procure or build these instruments himself and annoyed at "so vastly rich a land that could not make me flutes to play upon this day in the intonation of the numbers three and two."[9]

Harrison never gave up on making *Simfony in Free Style* a reality, and in 1992 Harrison's friend David Doty created a computer-realized version under the composer's supervision.[10] But in 1955, such a possibility seemed fantastically impractical—not that Harrison, following Charles Ives, who was known for his sometimes outlandish demands, had ever been overly concerned with practicality in his "voluntary" pieces. Moreover, now that Harrison was free of the stressful intensity of the New York art scene and its ready access to musicians, dancers, and others who might be interested in commissioning or playing his music, he had little reason to write to please anyone but himself.

Ives may have been even more on Harrison's mind since, when in Rome, he had received the news that the great American composer had died. Harrison later said it felt like *Götterdämmerung*, the death of a god, and he telegrammed condolences to Ives's wife, Harmony.[11] As the money from Harrison's Guggenheim Fellowship ran out that spring, Harrison saw himself following the model of Ives's life more than his music ("doing the Ives thing," as he put it), although at a much leaner financial margin than the insurance millionaire. Henry and Sidney Cowell's biography of

Ives appeared in 1955 and detailed Ives's idealization of maintaining a conventional profession while composing on the side. One of the few occasional music jobs Harrison found during this period was writing elegant and insightful liner notes for a recording of Ives's violin sonatas.[12]

Ives had assigned to Harrison some of his royalties, but the income from Ives's as-yet-seldom-performed music flowing to Harrison was negligible. In his search for more conventional employment, he circled a newspaper ad that looked especially promising, given his love for nature. The state forestry service was hiring extra men for the summer fire season at the nearby Loma Prieta fire station, on the road between Santa Cruz and San Jose, and Harrison signed up.

Beat writers Jack Kerouac and Gary Snyder wrote about experiences as forestry lookouts during the 1950s, recommending the job as a place for artistic and spiritual contemplation. Although Harrison had some free time to work, unlike Kerouac he was not a solitary fire lookout but instead a working member of a fire crew. The regular forestry employees trained the recruits in firefighting, running drills and practice calls. Soon one freezing morning, they jumped onto their truck and drove to a fire at Big Basin, the first of several calls. Harrison came to greatly appreciate the routine dedication of his fellow firefighters to saving lives, property, and forests, and he regarded living in a dormitory with other males as a way to come to terms with his own masculinity and the camaraderie of men in a nonsexual setting. When not fighting fires, they filled the days with maintaining and cleaning their fire truck and training. After dinner was free time, and the fire chief let Harrison use his office to copy scores. There Harrison finished up the final ink score of his *Strict Songs* as well as a calligraphic score of *Simfony in Free Style* in which he colored the note heads according to their numerical relationships.[13]

When the fire station's cook quit, Harrison was tapped as the replacement, his modest experience cooking for himself making him the most qualified among the mostly young men. His new job meant that he was no longer part of the firefighting crew; instead he spent his days cooking, cleaning, and keeping account of the station's groceries. When the summer ended, one of the regular forestry employees suggested that Harrison stay on. They liked his voice and said that he could get a job as a dispatcher in nearby Scotts Valley.

But although the experience had been good for Harrison, he was ready to get back to his Aptos home, perhaps finding a new job there. He even applied for a job as a janitor, but one day at the state employment office, Harrison came across a listing for the Santa Cruz Animal Hospital. Harrison had always loved animals and on occasion owned a pet, including a dog at Black Mountain. But would the sight of blood bother him, a veterinarian interviewer asked.

"No," Harrison replied, "because I have looked into my nature."[14] He was hired as a veterinarian's nurse. Only one other profession, he often noted, allowed an employee to caress the customers all day.[15] It was difficult to stay depressed, he found, when you showed up to work and were greeted with dozens of wagging tails. He found one friendly bansenji dog so irresistible that he tried taking him home, but the match didn't work out. The dog needed constant attention, and Harrison found himself unable to work. Instead, he fed the neighborhood cats and admired them for their devotion to "holy meditation."[16] At different times, he found himself in his ankle-length apron trying to hold down a golden gibbon for an x-ray, caring for orphaned fox kits, and arm-deep in a cow's birth canal.

Only one aspect of the job really distressed him: the noise. He nearly went mad from the howls of the Siamese cats alone. He set aside a large ward for dogs and cats and redesigned it to cut down on the noise by filling it with baffles of alternating hard and soft material, a trick he had learned from Irving Morrow, his architect friend in San Francisco.[17]

Still, the job provided enough of an income to temporarily ease Harrison's money concerns, freeing up mental and emotional space that he would, characteristically, fill with artistic exploration. Now contentedly ensconced in California with a home in quiet, green surroundings and with paying work, Harrison felt free—liberated not just from the tyrannical constraints of conventional tuning, but also from the practical limitations of writing music for performance, or even writing music at all. As he sought new directions in his life and art, the next few years would be filled with experiments—musical and more.

SHADOW PLAY

For his first few years back in California, Harrison's closest friend was Harry Partch, "a musician seduced into carpentry," who was hard at work with his nascent self-produced label, Gate 5 Records. "Harry and I had a very close relationship which went on for years," Harrison recalled. "He was an affectionate man, who warmly gave and received love and who attained an intellectual majesty that yet included hobos around a campfire. So yes, we exchanged instruments, ideas, and pleasantries—and he made wonderful mint juleps too!"[18]

Lacking the ensemble of players he'd enjoyed during his earlier residency at Mills, Partch bought an early tape recorder and overdubbed all the difficult parts of his music himself. He also showed Harrison, who had experimented with temporal proportions in *Simfony in Free Style*, how to record a track at half speed and play it back at normal speed, doubling the speed and raising the pitch by an octave, or the reverse.[19]

On July 29, 1955 (an "out-of-this-world day," Harrison wrote on his score), Harrison completed a new experiment that channeled his percussion composing days to create a new work that used this new technology, just at the same time when his New York friends Vladimir Ussachevsky and Otto Luening were also pioneering the tape machine as a musical instrument. Harrison used a novel Partchian noisemaker: boobams ("bamboo spelled sideways," Partch explained), a set of tuned drums the older composer had created with Bill Loughborough, a percussionist deeply involved with the West Coast jazz scene, who helped build several of Partch's exotic instruments. Dedicated to Loughborough, Harrison's *Recording Piece* opens with a boobam solo followed by a dizzying sequence of metric modulations worthy of his friend Elliott Carter. Then Harrison combined a boobam solo with that same solo played (in a recording on a tape machine) at double speed, creating a technological realization of what Harrison knew as a mensuration canon, a favorite medieval device in which a melody is combined with itself at a different tempo.[20] However, lacking a tape machine of his own, Harrison was forced to leave *Recording Piece,* like his *Simfony in Free Style,* as an unrealized experiment.[21]

In the mid-1950s, electronic music was still a novelty that had not yet acquired the symbolism that later made it so distasteful to Harrison. In fact, in 1955 when he read that engineers at RCA had created the first programmable music synthesizer, he immediately wrote to the American Composers Alliance, suggesting that this instrument (which required a whole room to house) could be made available to composers under the ACA's auspices. He hoped it would help composers realize any just-intonation system they could dream up, but nothing came of this effort.[22]

Harrison's restless exploration included an abandoned attempt at experimental film, scratching images directly on film emulsion like the Canadian filmmaker Norman McLaren, whose films he had seen in New York. He also attended his visual muse by resuming his lifelong affair with calligraphy, spending hours filling his notebooks with new alphabets of chancery cursive, Renaissance bookend, and Roman rustica. He created one particularly beautiful illuminated page with colored inks and gold leaf that might have come from a medieval prince's psalter, except that its text was the veterinarian's oath, created to be framed in the hospital's waiting room.

For a time, he returned to painting, in which he had dabbled therapeutically in New York and with artist friends at Black Mountain. In the reductive rectangles of Piet Mondrian (whom he had once spied in a New York cafeteria), Harrison perceived the same principles of proportion he admired in just intonation.[23] Harrison started to paint his own Mondrian-esque equivalents of other tuning systems. He liked to point out that one of his favorite artists, the seventeenth-century Frenchman Claude Lorrain, claimed to be able to paint in any musical mode.[24]

On one excursion, he was so amazed at an exhibition of contemporary paintings by a local artist at San Francisco's Legion of Honor art museum that he tracked down Elizabeth Campbell to tell her what an enormous impact her paintings had had on him. Initially wary, Campbell soon came to appreciate Harrison's sincerity and artistic expertise.[25] Sharing interests in art as well as Buddhism, they became fast friends, and she gave him some informal art lessons, sometimes making the day trip down to Aptos for a visit.[26] Harrison developed grand plans for a series of fifteen paintings whose proportions related not only to just intonation but also to the row he had created for his series *Group on a Row the Same.* Like the transformations of row forms, these paintings could be viewed in a series of variations created by rotating them to different positions on a grid. Like many other ambitious projects, he left this one unfinished.

Another unfinished project, though, indirectly led to a lifetime infatuation. Hoping for another Guggenheim grant to fund a sojourn in Mexico, he enrolled in a Spanish class, even engaging a private tutor to help. As he learned, though, his thoughts turned back to the international language he had heard of as a teenager: Esperanto. In San Francisco, he located books on the language and then saw that proprietors of a Santa Cruz motel advertised that they spoke Esperanto. He began to practice the language with them and soon gave up the Spanish class.[27]

Gradually, Harrison met other interesting people in Santa Cruz, including members of the Santa Cruz Symphony. In 1961, Harrison arranged a suite from his *Marriage at the Eiffel Tower* for this small orchestra. He also spent time reconnecting with old friends from San Francisco—Jim Cleghorn, Bob Metcalf, Carol Beals, Elsa Gidlow. And he stayed in touch with some now-scattered New York friends (Cage, Wolpe, Brown, Glanville-Hicks, Weber, etc.) by mail.

His most frequent correspondent, though, was Henry Cowell; he and his wife, Sidney, came to stay with Harrison in Aptos on their way back from an extended around-the-world trip in 1957. Cowell, now subject to frequent health problems, was exhausted and ill. Unknown to Harrison, he had suffered a stroke during the trip.[28] He and Sidney found recuperating in Harrison's isolated cabin for several days preferable to social obligations in San Francisco and Palo Alto, and Harrison treasured the opportunity to spend some extended time with his teacher and soul mate. Cowell promised Harrison his grand piano, which had belonged to Percy Grainger and would become a beloved fixture in Harrison's home.

MEDICINE FOR MELANCHOLIA

When deeply depressed about the fact that I'm in middle age & a capable person I yet realize that no matter how hard I work, nor at what I shall not be able simply to pay my small bills, then I have asked older persons about this matter. From one I received the embarrassed reply that I should "just forget" it & "take things as they come"; from my mother received the news that "everyone has the same trouble." To all such answers I have asked: "Then why are we so proud of civilization?" Certainly the longer I live the more I understand that civilization, though absorbing, is really a "horse-laugh"—a plain horse-laugh.

—Lou Harrison[29]

As he turned forty in May 1957, despite his tentative attempts to return to sociability and his fascinating artistic experiments, Harrison still occasionally sank into grim depression, unable to summon the will to do anything. His meager income from the animal hospital notwithstanding, finances were a constant worry, and the disorganized Harrison often fretted over bills and other paperwork. "When I have completed a composition and return to the world of affairs, I suffer miserably," he confided in his journal. "It feels like the expulsions from the garden of Eden must have felt, and the more so if the work is not performed at once, for somehow my subconscious then seems to decide that society has condemned me for doing it at all and interprets this again as the reason for expulsion, that I was wrong to work. This is a miserable misunderstanding—perhaps."[30]

At other times he would become so gripped by a project that he could not sleep. Although careful not to self-diagnose using a clinical term like manic depression, he recognized that his psychic state still had not healed. He practiced baroque keyboard music on his piano and clavichord obsessively during this period, putting his piano into a certain tuning and trying it out with each piece in his collection. A few months later, he would repeat the process with another tuning. During this period when popular music like jazz and nascent rock and roll seized the imagination of even sophisticated listeners, and "classical" composers veered ever farther from popular tastes, the splendidly isolated Harrison devoted his efforts to the graceful melodies of the French harpsichord composers, the so-called *clavecinists*: the musical equivalents of gilded Louis XV furniture, thick with graceful ornaments and sinuous lines that would also characterize his next composition.[31]

CINNA

After the enlightening but extravagant impracticalities of the so-far conjectural *Simfony in Free Style* and *Recording Piece*, Harrison was ready to focus his creative energies on a project that could more easily find an outlet, even if it was only a local and very personal one. His multi-artistic passions naturally attracted him to dramatic projects. However, his opera *Rapunzel* had consumed over a year of his life, with no performances on the horizon. Conventional opera was extremely expensive to produce, even for a work of relatively modest demands like *Rapunzel*, and opera companies rarely performed new works.[32]

How could he return to the world of theater without the costs, compromises, and constraints of opera? Harrison remembered Pauline Benton, whose performance of Chinese shadow puppetry he had seen at Mills College in 1939. Harrison also knew something of the elaborate art of Indonesian shadow puppetry from Henry Cowell and the articles of Colin McPhee, and he had long enjoyed European puppet theater music, especially Harrison's favorite, Manuel de Falla's 1923 *Master Peter's Puppet Show*, which used a harpsichord. The illusion of puppetry allows extravagant settings and sets that would be fantastically expensive or impossible in a conventional theater. Like Benton, he could create effective dramatic performances with minimal investment and without the need for a dedicated theater.

Harrison asked a cabinetmaker whose shop was next door to the animal hospital to design and build for him a miniature proscenium stage. Although the play he envisioned would never be realized, its musical legacy constituted a remarkable experiment in just intonation. Harrison wanted to stage the tale of Cinna (a Roman official pardoned by Caesar Augustus despite Cinna's plot to kill the emperor) as dramatized by the seventeenth-century French playwright Pierre Corneille, a contemporary of Racine and Molière and of the early *clavecinist* composers who so preoccupied Harrison's musical thoughts at the time. The choice of a seventeenth-century neoclassical play reflected the same impulse toward order and proportion that he found in just intonation.

Harrison scored *Incidental Music for Corneille's Cinna* for tack piano tuned in just intonation, which approximates the timbre of a harpsichord but also allows possibilities not available on the early keyboard. "When you play pianissimo you get just a shimmering little metallic sound with many, many overtones," he said of the tack piano. "And then as you increase the volume it deepens, and the overtone content drops out until it gets almost like a straight piano at the fortissimo. . . . Its principal virtue is in the pianissimo [very soft] and the piano [soft] area, where it has a radiance of overtones that no felt is ever going to give you."[33]

As in earlier pieces, such as the *Prelude for Grandpiano*, Harrison omitted bar lines, letting the music flow without metrical encumbrances, also a nod to the *préludes non-mèsuré*, or unmeasured preludes, written by *clavecinists* such as Louis Couperin.[34] Like the music of those French composers, Harrison's score is replete with ornamentation (or "graces," as he liked to call them), including his favorite, a (somewhat un-baroque) quick alternation between two pitches a third or a fourth apart. The suite ends with a rondeau, a form favored by both Harrison and the French baroque composers.

As with the modal *Strict Songs*, Harrison wrote *Cinna* for a fixed gamut of pitches, but here in a kind of tonal chromaticism. Harrison specified a mostly five-limit tuning, providing sweet major and minor triads. However, two of the pitches, B♭ and F, he tuned to startling seven-limit ratios (7:6 and 7:4 respectively, relative to the tonic, G), providing triads nowhere approximated in equal temperament—a delicious "subminor" triad on G and a "supermajor" triad on B♭. The whole piece revolves around these various triads, contrasting the seven-limit and the five-limit, interlocking and shifting through them in various surprising ways, often spicing them up with added seconds and fourths, creating a kaleidoscope of quickly changing tonal relationships. The tonal structures of the movements reflect the same relationships of a third found in the triadic harmonies. Pedal points (drones) often teeter between notes a third apart. The tunings afford a range of emotional nuance despite the single-instrument sound; almost every gesture in the twelve-minute suite seems to suggest more than one mood, with undercurrents of darkness tinting even the brightest tunes, as appropriate for a tale replete with intrigue and shrouded motivations.

Cinna stands apart in its approach to just intonation, not only from Harrison's *Simfony in Free Style* but also from his modal *Strict Songs*. Little in these chromatically shifting triads and tetrads suggests modality at all, somewhat resembling Harrison's chromatic but tonal experiments from New York, such as parts of *The Perilous Chapel*. Yet *Cinna* is unique—perhaps some of the most distinctive music of Harrison's career. Responding to a recording Harrison made of the score, his friend Robert Duncan wrote back, "Your theater music still haunts our ears. Processionals of a puppet's imaginary Rome, they prepare for beauty, & your inventions are weddings of deliberation and spontaneity."[35]

His experiments in just intonation placed Harrison in a tiny, esoteric niche; except for Partch, hardly anyone else at the time was exploring microtonality. But his *Cinna* music, complete by May 1957, represents a first glance out of his sealed cocoon and toward performance as a social undertaking, even if the envisioned puppet play would never be realized. Harrison could also play it himself, with each of its five movements (alternating fast and slow, lively and majestic) functioning as entr'actes between each of *Cinna's* five acts.

Just as *Cinna* signaled Harrison's readiness to gradually emerge from abstract experiments to undertake actual productions, it also looks outward in its theme. Every day in the newspapers, Harrison encountered contemporary echoes of Corneille's story of politics and divided loyalties in ancient Rome. The story's ending, with the would-be sinner Cinna receiving mercy rather than revenge, surely appealed to its pacifist composer's social concerns. As Harrison increasingly turned his attention from what was going on inside his imagination to what was happening in the world outside his isolated, art-drenched Aptos existence, where he had enjoyed a couple of years exploring colorful, hitherto unthinkable dimensions in his art and his life, he could no longer hide from the bleakly reactionary politics of Cold War America.

22

WILD RIGHTS (1957–1961)

The heavens are filled with smog
& have a geiger count as well
so does the sea;
to hell with creature comforts,
We need a bill of rights for simple creature safety: fresh air
Fresh rain & sea
& land un-DDT'ed

—Lou Harrison[1]

On one of his trips into San Francisco during the mid-1950s, Lou Harrison revisited the famous Japanese Tea Garden in Golden Gate Park for the first time since he had returned to California. He was appalled to find that much of the serene natural space had been demolished or left to decay during the anti-Japanese hysteria of the war, its Japanese American caretakers sent to internment camps. When he discovered one new feature in the now-renamed "Oriental Tea Garden," tears sprang into his eyes. A nine-thousand-pound Lantern of Peace had been installed in 1953, a gesture of friendship paid for with contributions from Japanese schoolchildren.

He had ample reason to wonder whether the light of peace would soon be extinguished. The memory of the atomic bombs dropped on Japan and the ever-present specter of nuclear Armageddon haunted Harrison. "John Cage once said that he thought that maybe humankind's purpose here on earth was to make a nova of it," he wrote in his notebook. "It is certain that if humans continue as they are going that it is exactly that which will happen."[2]

The Cold War's chilly tendrils reached close to home. In 1954 the House Un-American Activities Committee held hearings on the supposed communist infiltration of San Francisco, focusing on Depression-era organizations such as the now-defunct Young Communist League, which Harrison had known in his youth chiefly for its tiresome taste in music ("All in G minor," he remembered).[3] In the wake of Aaron Copland's interrogation by Joseph McCarthy's committee, the House Committee on Un-American Activities targeted Henry Cowell and Wallingford Riegger, though neither would be prosecuted, as well as a poet acquaintance in New York who would later become Harrison's collaborator, Kenneth Rexroth.[4] Month after month reading about artists forced to hide their beliefs to protect their livelihoods made Harrison regret the closeted life he had led in New York. "Senator Joe McCarthy was the one who resolved me never to hide in any closet about anything ever again in my life," he later said. "When you get to the point that you don't know what's in your mailbox, the only counter-power you have is to live an absolutely open life."[5]

Harrison worried that the alarmingly expanding national security state endangered not only fundamental liberties but even life itself. He was shocked to read a *Life* magazine story about scientists working to treat the effects of fallout radiation rather than decrying its existence. "The question of how many H-bombs may safely be exploded is irrelevant," the article quoted one researcher as saying. "To remain free we must develop powerful nuclear bombs."[6] One heartbreaking photograph showed an irradiated beagle in a measurement chamber, looking out with the same sorrowful hope that Harrison saw daily at the animal hospital. He wrote an outraged letter to the editor, which was never published.

With nuclear tests regularly exploding on the other side of the Sierra Nevada a few hundred miles away, Harrison's concerns about radiation were hardly abstract. His brother Bill and his family lived in Reno, often upwind from the Nevada Test Site. Lou bought a Geiger counter in Santa Cruz and observed its frequency rise and fall after each nuclear explosion in Nevada—audible refutation of the government's insistence that these tests did not spread dangerous radiation. He wrote an angry letter protesting this radioactive fallout to President Eisenhower, but Ike did not respond.[7] To Harrison, these tests constituted a government violation of the most basic of human rights, what he called "Wild Rights, final rights."[8]

All these government transgressions jolted Harrison out of his splendid creative isolation. He religiously tuned in to Berkeley's liberal public radio station, KPFA, where he heard programs attacking McCarthyism, including a weekly program hosted by his friend, the influential Beat mystic Alan Watts.[9] A later investigation into "communist affiliations" at the station prompted Harrison to write to Cowell, "How disgusting can these morons in Washington's 'noble Senate' get?"[10] In his notebook of the time, he decried warmongers "who use state power to tax for private interest . . . and compel belief and punish dissent by secret police, congressional committees and the like inquisitions."[11] He joined the National Committee for a Sane Nuclear Policy (SANE), founded in 1957 by one of his favorite writers, Norman Cousins, the editor of the *Saturday Review*, with whom he corresponded.[12]

Now a regular writer of letters to editors, Harrison sent a furious letter to Washington, saying that since the government had breached the social contract, it was no longer due his taxes. Not long afterward, two visitors from the Internal Revenue Service showed up at the animal hospital, took Harrison to a room, and began to question him. Harrison was glad to have a chance to debate his position, a harangue that the IRS agents endured for some three hours. Finally, they conceded the rationality of Harrison's point of view but warned that if he refused to pay his taxes for any reason, he would go to prison. For the rest of his life, Harrison wrote the words "under duress" under his signature on his checks to the IRS.[13] He liked to note that government "war scares" often occurred in April, when those checks were due.[14]

In 1957, when the Soviets launched Sputnik, the first man-made object in space, Harrison was elated: "All of a sudden," he said, "it became clear that the power to leave the planet was a greater one than the power to destroy it." To many science fiction-reading optimists of the period, the opening of space to the human race represented a safety valve for a dying planet, and Harrison immediately wrote a poem describing this "little moon's exquisite silver arcs" in the nighttime sky.[15] On further reflection, however, he reasoned that an invasion of the domain of space by this species that had ravaged its planet and made war with atomic weapons could alarm any extraterrestrial observer. So convinced was Harrison of this possibility that he fashioned a tube, one end of which could be attached to the tailpipe of his Volkswagen and the other end affixed in the van's window—a painless suicide method in case of a *War of the Worlds*–style invasion.[16]

Typically, one of Harrison's reactions to what he considered fundamental abrogation of the role of a just government was to research political history, reading Plato, Aristotle, Confucius, and other classics of political philosophy. What would emerge would be his most ambitious artistic vision to date, but it was one that he would ultimately fail to realize.

POLITICAL PRIMER

In 1958, Harrison set out to write a fundamental analysis, a "primer," on politics and set it as a large-scale oratorio for singers and orchestra. The unlikely (even for Harrison) notion reveals both the depth of his passion and his conviction that such spirit must be guided by rationality—a word that, he liked to point out, originated in the Greeks' organization of musical scales by ratios, so that art itself is spirit structured by reason.

In accord with America's founding fathers, Harrison wrote that governments are inventions of people and exist to serve them. They fail when one group (Eisenhower's "military-industrial complex" for example) is allowed to "unbalance the variety of interests usual to Human Persons; indeed to encroach on these [rights] and begin to consume them."[17] Harrison proposed that in the same way that the separation of church and state ended the tyranny of religion over citizens, a "separation of war and state" could do the same. A government, he suggested, could set aside battlegrounds for those people who feel the need for warfare ("a great many persons do enjoy war, some not undistinguished"), where they could pursue their pleasure safely apart from the rest of the population.[18]

Harrison's musical structure stemmed from the fact that governments historically filled offices by three methods: birth (monarchy), election (republic), and lottery (democracy). He argued for this original, ancient Greek definition of democracy, for, he wrote, quoting Virgil Thomson, "more than half the troubles of the world come from not calling things by their right names." The three types of government then became the basis for a three-part structure of the piece, each part to consist of an orchestral overture, then Harrison's didactic text divided into an aria and a chorus, and finally Harrison's editorial commentary, set as a recitative. Including an opening dedication, this large piece would boast thirteen movements.

To give readers worldwide access to his ideas, Harrison began by translating his text to Esperanto, itself a major undertaking. He found help from a linguist in Santa Cruz named Bruce Kennedy and then crafted the recitatives that constituted his commentary on the didactic text, setting them similarly to the recitatives of *Rapunzel* but now with versions in both English and Esperanto. And, in accord with his current musical interests, he composed them in free style, with just-intonation intervals specified between each successive interval in the melody. Although they avoid the exotic and complex intervals of *Simfony in Free Style*, the recitatives still wander, like Harrison's thoughts, around the tonal landscape, unrestrained by a fixed scale.

Next Harrison set to work on the orchestral interludes or *uverturoj* ("overtures"). Since his experiment with orchestral just intonation in the *Strict Songs* had turned out so well, Harrison chose a similar orchestra for the *Political Primer*, using instruments able to continually adjust their tuning—trombones and the violin family— plus percussion, harp, piano, two tack pianos, and celesta[19] (for a total of four keyboards on stage). "I early on adopted the use of the word 'gamelan' for all the 'pretty' instruments of the symphony orchestra! Harps, pianos, celestas, and so on," he said.[20] These instruments, which had already appeared in the *Symphony on G*, add a sparkling tintinnabulation to Harrison's orchestral works.

Unlike the pentatonic *Strict Songs*, these overtures are freely diatonic (seven-tone "white note" scales) with very few accidentals, and they eschew the exotic seven-limit intervals of *Cinna* or the third *Strict Song*, using only relatively familiar five-limit ratios. At a time when most of his contemporaries were delving ever more deeply into chromaticism, Harrison created endless modal and contrapuntal interest entirely within these seven diatonic pitches, a style for which he acknowledged his debt to Mexican composer Carlos Chávez.[21] Each opens with a distinctive, captivating tune, which becomes the subject of a fugal opening (a double fugue in the case of one), followed by a contrasting texture frequently thickened with drones and *jhalas*.

He never completed the projected choruses and arias between these overtures that would have provide some contrast, but even so, for all its ingenuity, it's hard to imagine how the *Political Primer* would have succeeded dramatically. Conventional opera choruses or arias, such as *Rapunzel*'s, set a limited amount of text in verse form, but setting paragraphs of didactic prose as songs or even recitatives would pose an enormous challenge to composer and audience alike; just getting through all the text would take several minutes each. Could even the most engaging of didactic essays be turned into a compelling musical performance?

Still, the unfinished *Political Primer* was a landmark for Harrison. The overtures represented his first purely orchestral composition since the *Symphony on G* and the first time he had adapted his evolving tonal, diatonic style to such large forces. They would provide precedents for much of his later orchestral music.[22] In both orchestration and politics, Harrison's unfinished *Political Primer* reveals his passionate, if eccentric, idealism. American society had a word for such an oddball way of looking at hard reality.

CRACKPOT

I myself am bold to say that I am a crackpot. I am a vegetarian, a frank admirer of other races, and a speaker of the international language Esperanto. I'm a polypolitical logician and an economic stabilitarian. For example: If debt were paid at the terminal value, would there be inflation? I'm a promoter of population restraint and sexual freedom. I'm a writer of letters to the editor and a reader of science fiction. Indeed I know that we shall voyage to the flaming stars. I'm a calligrapher and not last of all I'm a living composer. Yes, I'm a fairly thorough growing crackpot and I'm delighted so to be.

—Lou Harrison

Harrison recorded some of these political ideas in an impassioned little essay that he was invited to read on the air at KPFA in 1959. He called it his "Crackpot Lecture" because of its thesis: "There is then to civilization more than a touch of the crackpot if that be felt through the feelings of the present common man. Surely we should allow fools but we should I think encourage crackpots."

He praised the play of children because that play becomes civilization itself and it is the crackpots who move civilization forward. "The theme knowledge of my generation is of the exhaustibility of things. No earlier generation has had to learn that," he wrote. "It grows increasingly wondrous to me in the plain view of the scientific overthrow of any possibility of war that that antediluvian and unemployable class, the military, is now already separated from the state.[23] Later he railed, "'Modern Life' is high-decibel chaos, in smog. The civilization which invented it is clearly bent headlong to suicide, and I profoundly mistrust anything in it that is regarded as 'First Class' or 'First Rate.' Brand X is more likely to be for Life and Love. There has never been a 'big, First Class' civilization that was not founded on slavery. Question: Do we need 'big, First Class' civilizations??"[24]

Ironically, at the time, Harrison himself was actually under the spell of what composer Laurie Anderson would later call "Big Science." He had seen psychoanalysts since his breakdown in New York, but the suggestion that medication might help his current bouts with "melancholia" (as he sometimes archaically termed it) led him to see a doctor in Santa Cruz. The doctor suggested boosting his thyroid levels and suggested the first available antidepressant drug, Iproniazid, a monoamine oxidase inhibitor or MAOI. Doctors at the time did not know the full effects of this antidepressant, which can produce dangerous reactions. On Harrison, it had an unusual side effect—he needed only two or three hours of sleep a night. Suddenly he was able to work all day at the animal hospital and then obsessively fill his nights with his latest creative passions.[25]

"Oddly, I'm in a most productive phase, & am up to the forehead in various fascinating projects," he wrote Cowell. "Rather, I should say, expectably, for I'm enjoying the continuous use of the fabulous drug 'Iproniazid,' & I have the sensation that it fills my most important 'deficiency,' resulting in a continuous source of splendid energy, along with a wonderful 'well-why-not-ness' in connection with whatever interests me at the moment."[26] After about a year, finally wondering why he was subjecting himself to this unnatural regime, he stopped taking the drug.

Harrison's process of reintegrating his identity after his breakdown paralleled his search for a new creative voice. "I was healing myself out here," he remembered about this period, "trying to reorganize my life."[27] In the six years since he had moved back to California, Harrison had, despite periods of manic creativity and fascinating experimentation, completed fewer works than at any other period in his career. Unimpeded by performance opportunities or deadlines, he could work on large-scale projects (including the *Political Primer* and the unrealized production of *Cinna*) and less practical explorations (the *Simfony in Free Style* and *Recording Piece*). Even if he had been inclined to compose performable new works, Harrison's musical aesthetic would have seemed quite distant (either old-fashioned or eccentric) from the regnant modernism propagated by Cage, Pierre Boulez, Elliott Carter, and their disciples, or the popular music that dominated the airwaves and the recording industry. Isolated in rural California, Harrison may have seemed to have fallen off the musical map, but he was hardly forgotten. Professional recognition was slowly coming to the veterinarian's assistant.

One day in 1959, his old friend Anahid Ajemian called to commission a new violin work for her upcoming Carnegie Hall concert. Searching through his old notebooks, Harrison located his unfinished 1940 *Concerto for Violin and Percussion Orchestra*, which he sometimes Esperantized as *Koncherto por la Violono kun Perkuta Orkestra*. He simplified the ornamentation and meters and changed some of the percussion instruments, but otherwise he left the original two movements alone. He then "summoned up that [early] period" to compose a fitting third movement.[28]

Around the same time, his old Los Angeles friend Peter Yates put together a concert devoted to Harrison's work at the prestigious Monday Evening Concerts series he had founded (under the name Evenings on the Roof), and another of his Los Angeles friends, Ingolf Dahl, conducted his *Mass* there. (Music from the *Mass* was also included in a 1959 NBC program about religion.) William Kraft, a Los Angeles percussionist whose own work as a composer would be indebted to Harrison, conducted several of Harrison's percussion works at the Los Angeles concert, including the new *Concerto for Violin with Percussion Orchestra*. "All the sounds, whether produced by maracas or flower pots, are so well integrated that you forget that they're exotic," Kraft said later. "It's the music of a real composer."[29] Harrison flew down to assist with the rehearsals and reconnect with old friends, including Dahl and composer Gerald Strang, and new ones, such as film composer David Raksin.[30] The same concert included an experimental film by Ed Emshwiller that used Harrison's *Canticle #3* as its soundtrack.

Emshwiller's choice had been prompted by a New York percussionist named Paul Price, whose 1959 Urania Records LP, *Breaking the Sound Barrier*, included works by Cage and Cowell, along with Harrison's *Canticle #3*. After Stokowski had revived Harrison's *Canticle #3*, Price began unearthing then-obscure (now considered classic) percussion ensemble works by these composers, alerting or reminding the music world of Harrison's pioneering role in the history of the percussion ensemble.

But the most exciting development in Harrison's professional life was the news that his opera *Rapunzel* was finally going to be realized. Still another old friend, Peggy Glanville-Hicks, had written a one-act opera of her own and raised the money for the production of her and Harrison's operas at New York's Lexington Avenue YMHA.[31] The forty-two-year-old Harrison made another rare foray from his hermitage and was delighted with the performance and the art nouveau–style sets.[32] "His ear is so fastidious and he handles his voice with such tact and the orchestra with such economy and allusiveness that his atonalism is not in the least forbidding," declared the *New York Times* review, after criticizing its libretto's lack of drama. "There are places in 'Rapunzel' that sing with a freshness that is quite magical."[33]

Along with these and other performances, the number of recordings of Harrison's works also swelled. In addition to the percussion LP, a 1955 Fromm Foundation award subsidized the recording of his *Mass to St. Anthony* by conductor Margaret Hillis and the New York Concert Choir. Then in 1957, Composers Recordings Incorporated, a new label started by the American Composers Alliance's Oliver Daniel and others, finally released Leopold Stokowski's recording of the *Suite for Violin, Piano & Small Orchestra*.

Harrison's earlier recording of the *Suite #2 for Strings* on Goddard Lieberson's Modern American Music Series on Columbia, caught the ear of a graduate student composer at the University at Buffalo in New York. Robert Hughes listened to all twelve of the LPs in the Columbia series and was impressed by Harrison's work most of all. He quickly located Harrison's other recordings. "It was just astounding," he recalled. "Having heard only three of his pieces, [I knew] that this was a major, fresh voice that nobody was doing anything about."[34] A recent major gift to the university had endowed a composer residency, then occupied by Mills College professor Leon Kirchner. Hughes knew that the relatively unknown Harrison would be unlikely to win this prestigious position, but he suspected that sufficient funds existed to bring Harrison out for a week or so.

Hughes's youthful enthusiasm won over his department chairman, and Hughes set out to contact Harrison. But how? Hughes got a phone number from Oliver Daniel, who had recently profiled Harrison in the ACA newsletter, but when Hughes tried it, he got an animal hospital in California. Puzzled, he asked for Harrison, and in a moment another voice answered. Hughes told Harrison the good news and asked when he could be available to come out. To his surprise, Harrison was guarded and equivocal.

Hughes didn't realize that his invitation had revived all of Harrison's terrible memories of New York and of his disastrous reintroduction to social life after his breakdown. In California, he had finally found stability. Although Hughes was not proposing to send him back to the New York City pressure cooker of noise and ambition, just the suggestion that Harrison would leave his comforting routine and reenter the world of professional music, even for a short time, rekindled that old anxiety.

But Hughes was persistent. After more phone calls, Harrison finally accepted, and Hughes asked him for new scores beyond what was on file at the ACA. After some thought, Harrison suggested a series of recitatives from an oratorio he was working on. Elated to present a world premiere, Hughes sought out one of the best singers there, a baritone named Herbert Beattie. Then the score arrived—and Hughes frowned, perplexed by his first experience with the notation for just intonation. Between the pitches appeared what looked like fractions.

"Dear Mr. Beattie, I am most fortunate that you will sing these 4 recitatives!" Harrison hastily wrote in a note at the front of the score. "Do not be frightened by the numbers—here is the explanation (which, I hasten to add, I send along only in the event that you are not already 'numerate' as well as 'literate')."[35]

Hughes met the slightly portly Harrison at the Buffalo airport in May 1959, helping him carry a bizarre instrument consisting of clock coils attached to a guitar resonator. Harrison's shyness and awkwardness around the music department faculty—all of whom were cordial, though few, perhaps none, had ever heard of him—surprised Hughes.[36] To advocates of the serialist orthodoxy, Harrison's exploration of Asian simplicity and justly tuned tonality must have bordered on, to use Harrison's proud term, "crackpot." While Harrison continued to revere Schoenberg, he grew increasingly dismissive of what he called the "standard mannerism" of 1950s serialist complexity.[37]

The faculty nevertheless admired Hughes's program, which, along with music by Stravinsky, Chávez, and Webern, included two arias from *Rapunzel*, selections from *Solstice*, and the premiere of the recitatives from the *Political Primer*, with interpolations from the clock coils and other percussion as well as Harrison's amplified Geiger counter. In the middle of the movement, the conductor dramatically turned and addressed the audience:

> The accompaniment which you hear is that of an amplified Geiger counter. This is not a recording. Most of the clickings are the sounds made by the expirations of cosmic rays in the Geiger tube. These are coming into this building from the far splendor of the universe. Some, though, are the sounds of class D poisons from nuclear tests, slowly settling down over the planet. (Pause, to listen.) This is wrong! "I feel it in my bones," as Dr. Asimov said.[38]

The concert also featured Harrison's new *Concerto for Violin with Percussion Orchestra*. The composer especially appreciated the personal congratulations of Syracuse University music professor Louis Krasner, the violinist whose premiere recording of Alban Berg's Violin Concerto had inspired Harrison to compose that very piece.

The directness and attractiveness of Harrison's music also impressed the skeptical faculty. "Here was a kind of modern music that spoke of nature and wonderful things in clear sounds and rhythms," remembered the poet Calvin Harlan, then at the university. "It had none of the strident display of so-called experimental music. Its form and texture were crystalline, and through them one could see Himalayas and skies and forests." As the new music of Cage and Boulez had dominated recent critical discourse, Harlan asked Harrison if his music might be moving in that direction. No, in the opposite direction, Harrison protested. "The difference, as I see it, is between a long musical line allied to a poetry of wonder and affection," Harlan explained, "and the choppy, bird-song line and fragmented rhythms of an avant-garde but doctrinaire aesthetic."[39]

Almost as soon as Harrison returned to California, another letter from Hughes arrived, informing him that the music faculty had unanimously selected him as the next academic year's composer-in-residence. This position would allow Harrison to once more be a full-time teacher and composer, as he had been at Black Mountain—but now also with a handsome salary and a school full of talented musicians.[40] The position also came with a commission or two. It was a stunning offer for possibly the most prestigious such academic position then open in the United States.

Harrison tentatively accepted, but before signing the contract, he hesitated, ruminated. Now, back in his forested hermitage, he slipped easily back into his routine amid the overcast June mornings of the Central Coast: ordering food at the tiny Aptos grocery store, preparing for the laundry woman, feeding the neighborhood cats. Each weekday, he traveled down the road to his job, and he devoted his nights to the delights of baroque keyboard music and his latest creative project, charting his own path without obligations to musical trend makers or others' ideas of a conventional career. Accepting the job would mean pulling up the roots he'd so recently planted in California, roots that were now sprouting with a sense of comfort he had not known in decades.

The more he imagined a future back east, the more anxious he grew, his stomach churning in that old familiar way. The thought of reentering the institutional music establishment rekindled Harrison's resentment of a supposedly rich society that expected artists to "always accept the occasional job here, there and yon," he wrote, "without any stable reliable background behind it. I further found that even well known adults do expect so to live. I am astonished."[41] Harrison valued teaching interested students who came to him, but he remained deeply distrustful of the academy as an institution. In contrast, his spare, simple life gave him a sense of wholeness—holiness, tenderness, nourishment, splendor—that he had never known when cobbling together a living by teaching and writing in New York.

By the end of the week, the music department chair received a letter. Harrison expressed thanks for the offer of the residency—and he turned it down.

IN ARCADIA

For there is little doubt, I believe, that, if the strings decline, then there would scarcely be left a "Western" music, for the string orchestra I regard as the basis of our tradition.

—Lou Harrison[42]

Harrison's rejection of academic employment didn't slow his gradual return to national attention. In 1960, the performing rights organization to which Harrison belonged, Broadcast Music Incorporated (BMI), was celebrating its twentieth anniversary by commissioning composers. BMI's Oliver Daniel had previously recommended Harrison to the Louisville Orchestra for the commission of the *Strict Songs*, and so when this opportunity arose, BMI commissioned Harrison to write another work for the same orchestra. Daniel might have expected him to continue the experimental course he had set out in the *Strict Songs*. The obvious choice was the overtures he had recently written for the *Political Primer*, at least two virtually complete, which used an orchestra not all that different from the one in *Strict Songs*.

Instead, as he had just done with the *Violin Concerto* for Anahid Ajemian, Harrison resumed his career-long cycle of following a period of looking forward with another that looked back, a pattern that seemed to recharge his batteries for his next new idea. The *Suite for Symphonic Strings* is important not just because of its sprawling, nine-movement length, but *also* because it's one of what he called his "taking stock" pieces—a career retrospective, an acknowledgment of the importance of his new ideas in the context of his quarter century of creative growth, and the culmination of the series of works (including his first symphony and *The Perilous Chapel*, among others) whose creation helped him understand and come to terms with his breakdown, his healing, his life to that point.

As Harrison sifted through his trunk for pieces he could adapt, he concentrated on works from Black Mountain (which wound up in three of the movements) and Reed College (from the play *Almanac of the Seasons*). The middle movement became a radical revision of his New York–period *Triphony* for piano. For another movement, he reached all the way back to a fugue he wrote at age eighteen or nineteen. He wrote only three new movements of the nine movements finally used, though he substantially revised most of the others from their original versions. Taken together, they represent a retrospective of his career and a symbolic narrative of life itself, perhaps an autobiographical one.

Harrison's decision to write only for strings reflects a calculated austerity going back to his beloved seventeenth-century viol consort. He had lamented the demise of that tradition of serious, contemplative music and feared the same thing happening in the twentieth century. Despite the homogeneity of an all-strings ensemble, Harrison saw abundant opportunity for orchestral color. At different points in the *Suite for Symphonic Strings*, players beat the strings with the wood of the bows (*col legno*), pluck with guitar picks, beat the bodies of the instruments, pluck below the bridge, play without vibrato, and use other innovative techniques.[43] He thought his careful divisions of the sections so important that he deliberately inserted the word "symphonic" into the title, so that no one would be tempted to adapt it for a chamber group.[44] Harrison's meticulously specific instructions also reflect his admiration for the subtlest techniques in Chinese *erhu* music. "The melody should be minutely inflected in the manner of 'decorated' Greek or Oriental melodies," he instructed the players of the fourth movement.

Though the suite's strings have no fixed reference to tune to, such as the piano or harp used in the *Strict Songs*, Harrison's experience with that performance as well as with the New Music Quartet, which had premiered his String Trio in 1947, convinced him that players can naturally adjust their intervals to just intonation, even in very chromatic movements. "A little lowering or raising here and there, a little listening,

TABLE 22.1

Movement	Title	Source	Description
1	Estampie	Newly composed	Modal, fast
2	Chorale: Et in Arcadia Ego	*Chorales for Spring*, 1st mvt. (1951)	Slow, static
3	Double Fugue: In Honor of Heracles	*Double Fugue* (1936)	Chromatic
4	Ductia: In Honor of Eros	Newly composed	Modal dance with drone
5	Lament	*Triphony* (1945)	Atonal chromatic
6	Canonic Variations: In Honor of Apollo	Newly composed	Modal, majestic
7	Little Fugue: Viola's Reward	*Fugue for David Tudor* (1952)	Atonal chromatic
8	Round: In Honor of Hermes	*Almanac of the Seasons* (1950)	Fast diatonic dance
9	Nocturne	*Nocturne*, mvt. 1 (1951)	Modal

and the melodies flowed and the sonorities easily settled," he told the players in his score. "Certainly Equal-Temperament is 'wrong' here, as elsewhere."[45]

As in his previous string suites of 1948, chromatic movements alternate with contrasting diatonic ones, but now influenced by his just-intonation ideal. Harrison went so far as to include a table of pitch ratios, but he added, "I do not give these ratios in order to 'trounce' fellow musicians and conductors. I give them only because, if you do play these movements in best tune, by ear, then these are the ratios that you will be playing; and I think it not out-of-the-way to let you in on the matter."[46]

Each movement fits neatly into a musical and narrative plan: three dances, three contemplations of death, three fugues/canons, and four odes to the gods of the palaestra, the school or athletic grounds of ancient Greece. Harrison ingeniously arranged the movements to offer contrast in many different dimensions while retaining the overall sense of a narrative. The suite opens with a newly composed movement based on a dance form from medieval France that, along with the *jhala*, would become one of Harrison's favorite forms—his version of the Romantic scherzo—the estampie.[47] Breathlessly fast melodies in three (though often enlivened by polyrhythms) whirl past in this tumultuous dance.

"In this delightful form each of five or seven melodies is repeated—but at the first ending a 'half-cadence' is used, and at the ending of the repetition a 'full-cadence,'" Harrison explained in the *Music Primer*. "These cadences are complete little melodies, the 'half' called '*overt*,' the 'full' called '*clos*'—and, furthermore, these two formulae remain the same throughout the composition, though the main melodic material of each strophe is, of course, fresh."[48] Each melody appears twice, the first time ending with an inconclusive motive (open or *overt*) and the second time with a firm one (closed or *clos*). The motives used for each of these endings are common to the entire sequence of melodies, tying the tsunami of tunes together.

Also unifying the movement is a drone chopped up into rapid repeated notes and a "percussion section" created by the string players tapping their instruments or strings, a technique Harrison frequently used in estampies throughout his career. Likely inspired by Cowell's *United Quartet* of 1936, this kind of percussive accompaniment reminded Harrison of "the bumps and thuds of imaginary dancers dancing to the music."[49] The kinesthetic physicality of his dance scores was never far from Harrison's mind. This estampie, in addition to unleashing a breakneck opening to a long suite, also represents the energy of life (it is marked "molto vigoroso") as the narrative of the suite unfolds.

The next movement, the first of the Black Mountain *Chorales for Spring*, bears the subtitle "Et in Arcadia Ego" (Even in Arcadia Am I), which comes from Virgil's *Eclogues*. This famous epitaph suggests that death finds its way even into idyllic Arcadia and establishes the suite's primary tension: between life and death. For practicality's sake, this version does not follow the original concept of using entirely open strings, but the music nevertheless achieves the same eerie stasis, thanks to its severely restricted palette and wide leaps. Yet, he judged it "a very ecstatic piece, surprisingly enough, considering its construction."[50]

"I used the antiphony of a true melody with wide spread octaves to suggest the cave of the heart, the Lascaux Caves (because I was going to write a movie on that)," he recalled of this chorale. "That was my suggestion of ancient and antique things, the mystery, with that extremely widespread octave way at the top and then way, way, down. Then in the middle, more of the chords and the melody, ending with that kind of resigned chant on the cello."[51] Appearing after the lively dance of the estampie, the tune represented to Harrison the introduction of death into the Garden of Eden.[52]

Different perspectives on mortality return in the middle of the suite (the lament) and at the end (the nocturne), establishing a frame around which Harrison offers further perspectives on the stages of life. His inspiration for the organization of this journey came from his discovery, through recent reading, that the palaestrae were surrounded on four corners by statues of Herakles (Hercules), Eros, Apollo, and Hermes. "They were the Four Patrons of the Palaestra, and I am presently persuaded that they represented four worthy kinds of manly integrations."[53] To Harrison these four patrons of the training of young men "represented the four maturities of a man, four different routes, or ways, or integrations, four kinds of primary integrations of a man."[54]

For the third movement, Harrison chose a piece written in his own youth in which he worked out an intricate and knotty contrapuntal problem with all the ingenuity and self-confidence of its dedicatee, Herakles, completing one of his twelve labors. For the next movement, Harrison intended "a kind of adolescent dance, a round dance of erotic quality" to suggest "erotic integration with the motive force of the world. After all, Eros is co-terminal with the universe . . . the desire, the gravity that holds the universe together, you know—the conjunctive, the attractive, the magnetic."[55] As in the opening movement, Harrison represented this affirmation of life with a medieval sectional dance with drones and percussive ostinatos, this time a ductia, a form like the estampie but shorter and not in triple meter. Instead, Harrison creates a seductive but decidedly un-medieval alternation of meters. The violins play an elaborate, almost ecstatic melody in the bright Lydian mode that suggests the highly ornamented improvisations of Eros's own instrument, the ancient Greek *aulos*.

But just as the excitement of youth ended in Harrison's depressing New York period, so does the suite arrive at the renewed contemplation of death, in an anguished cry of grief. For this "Lament," Harrison adapted his *Triphony* for piano, making it more cohesive and simplifying the complex combination of different rhythmic levels—perhaps reflecting the orderliness that he now idealized. Gone is the wandering sense of a prose form, but not the Rugglesian sense of striving, even in the face of grief.

Modal and based on quintal counterpoint, the next (sixth) movement returns to the patrons of the palaestra with a newly composed set of canonic variations dedicated to Apollo. The noble classicism of its intricate polyphony reflects Apollonian wisdom in its appreciation for the subtleties of the art of which Apollo was the patron. "When young he was cruel to other musicians, / yet he became the Muses' master," wrote Harrison in a poetic tribute to Apollo and perhaps to the role of counterpoint in his own creative evolution.[56]

The seventh movement, titled "Little Fugue" and based on the atonal piano fugue Harrison had written for David Tudor at Black Mountain, here spotlights the viola, whose distinctive timbre was a favorite of Harrison's. Nevertheless, in the *Strict Songs*, he had often consigned the viola to a mere carrier of the drone, leading one of the Louisville violists to tease Harrison about their lack of activity. Here he pays tribute to this underappreciated section, subtitling the movement "Violists' reward."

Adapted from the otherwise lost score to the Reed College play *Almanac of the Seasons*, the eighth movement honors fleet-footed Hermes—whose phallus, Harrison recalled, gave directional signs at crossroads—with a fast, sectional diatonic dance: a round comprising contrasting sections that always return to a central tune. The movement's quick, circular motives certainly evoke the messenger of the gods, whom his worshipers credited with inventing the modes and music itself.[57]

In the final movement, the contemplation of death returns, but now with resignation and poignancy rather than grief or apprehension. Harrison wrote the original version at Black Mountain (and retained its title of "Nocturne") in the inherently unsettled (because it has no perfect fifth above the tonic) Locrian mode.[58] As a result, the suite's musical journey through life concludes with neither the consolation of a firm and familiar tonal foundation nor the unsettled chaos of atonality, but rather with a wistful sigh in the fallen night.

This narrative reflected Harrison's own life course, which, thanks to such recent opportunities as this commission and the trip to Buffalo, was beginning to change. Slowly, Lou Harrison was emerging from his seeming exile and finding his way back into the world of professional music-making. The catalyst for this transformation would be that devoted young student from Buffalo.

STICKY WICKET

In January 1961, Bob Hughes found himself on the bus to Watsonville, California, after having been told that the driver could drop him off on Highway 1 somewhere in the vicinity of the hamlet of Aptos. Hughes had intended to make this trip immediately after Harrison's visit to Buffalo, when Hughes had decided that he did not want to study with anyone else. But those plans were interrupted by the arrival of a prestigious grant to study in Italy for two years. With six months still left in his grant period, Hughes could no longer tolerate European serialism and wrote Harrison, saying that regardless of the rules of the grant, he was taking the remaining funds and moving to California.

The bus left Hughes at an unmarked stop, where there was little except a roadside café with a curious name: the Sticky Wicket. He gathered his luggage and walked in. Hughes met the owners, Victor and Sidney Jowers, and asked about the composer Lou Harrison. Of course they knew him, as he had become a regular shortly after the combination restaurant and bookstore opened in 1959 a mile and a half from Harrison's house by car, just a half-mile hike via the trail up the forested hill. The Jowerses, who lived below the restaurant itself with their two young children, soon became fast friends with Harrison, cooking his vegetarian meals several times a week. Harrison and Vic Jowers, an enthusiastic Englishman with a hearty handshake and a passion for cricket (hence the curious name of his establishment), could quaff copious amounts of alcohol when they stayed up chatting after closing time.

Sidney, a Vassar graduate with refined tastes in art and poetry, hung paintings of local artists and lined the restaurant's bookshelves with classic literature and philosophy alongside works of local writers. The Sticky Wicket quickly became the unofficial meeting place of the region's meager bohemian community. A local folk-singer entertained customers every weekend.

Hughes met Harrison up at his small cabin, bringing the pieces he had been working on with serialist composer Luigi Dallapiccola while in Italy: short works in the style of the prevailing European avant-garde. Each had been a struggle, and all Hughes could think of while composing them was moving to California to study with Harrison. Now Harrison took them and politely praised the melodic invention of the first few bars, but he quickly pointed out that "as Virgil Thomson said, 'if all of music consisted of eight bars, or sixteen bars, the whole world would be composers.' Anybody can do it. Where you fall apart, Bob, is your antecedent phrase." Hughes called his compositions from his period in Italy "constipated." Harrison laughed, "What you need is a cathartic."[59]

Where Dallapiccola made Hughes rigorously study Mahler and Webern, Harrison began by having him play games with music: create a melody entirely from a seven-note melodicle but lasting seven beats, and then group seven such phrases together, for example. It was like a crossword puzzle. "Eventually what he was able to do was to divorce, in the composition lessons, a feeling of a deep psyche having to manifest itself in music," Hughes recalled. Instead of tense thickets of serialism, composition became "a play, like dolphins in the water."[60]

Hughes spent a couple of weeks sharing Harrison's tiny cabin, cluttered with music manuscripts, books, and hanging lanterns from Chinatown. "I was sure I was in his way, because he [was] doing his projects and so forth. But always he was the kindest person imaginable and . . . he was a gourmet cook," Hughes remembered.

"He was into spices, particularly Asian spices, but he was in the heavy drinking stage too."[61] Hughes soon rented a tiny cabin next door to the Sticky Wicket, from the Jowerses, who also put him to work at the café.

Harrison immediately assigned Hughes to tune Harrison's single-string upright piano: first the octaves, listening for the telltale beats that indicate when the tuning is just or not. Then the fifths, until he could reliably tune the piano in Pythagorean tuning. As a professional bassoonist before he began studying composition, Hughes was accustomed to adjusting his pitch by listening for beats but never before so systematically and carefully. After the fifths came the thirds and learning to discern the subtle difference between a 9:8 major second and the 10:9 major second, both required in five-limit tuning. As he worked his way up the harmonic series, Hughes eventually reached the seventh harmonic, the interval so striking in Harrison's *Cinna*. Hughes and his new mentor also collaborated (as had Harrison and Cage in *Double Music*) on a quintet titled *Ritmicas* in honor of the Cuban percussion composer Amadeo Roldán, in which Hughes composed parts for flute, horn, and piano while Harrison handled clarinet and bassoon.

Hughes soon began getting occasional jobs playing bassoon in the area, and one of the musicians he met was a talented young violinist. "Lou's been out from New York however many years, and he really doesn't have very many friends," Hughes told Richard Dee. "I think he could really use somebody like you for a friend."[62] Hughes arranged for Dee to come visit the cabin, and soon he was playing baroque violin sonatas with Harrison and trying out different bowings for the *Suite for Symphonic Strings*. As Hughes had foreseen, a friendship soon developed. Hughes felt that Harrison's loneliness also stemmed from the fact that he had largely ceased to be a performing musician, bereft of the gratifying feeling that comes from constantly connecting with fellow musicians and with an audience, even if just a few people. Hughes knew just the place to get him restarted: the Sticky Wicket.

The Jowerses and Hughes decided to build a performance venue larger than the tiny space in the restaurant: a small outdoor theater next to the little café. Hughes told them that they needed a concert series there and that it made sense to invite their friend up the road. The Wicket stage provided an entry point for Harrison's return to public performance, sometimes simple baroque works, sometimes little pieces of his own (rescued from that vast trunk of compositions) that he could play. Harrison had at last, it seemed, found an ideal setting: a quiet home, next to a forest, in which to study, think, experiment, compose, and otherwise create, along with an intimate, unintimidating place to play music.

But then a letter arrived that would dramatically alter Harrison's life and creative direction. Nicolas Nabokov, the CIA-funded impresario who had organized the Rome conference in 1954, was putting together a new conference—and he offered Harrison a $3,500 grant to attend. This conference, however, was not in the Old Country but in the part of the world whose influence had since childhood found its way into his mind and music. Harrison, at last, was going to Asia.[63]

PART 5

Pacifica

*It is as though the world is a round continuum of music. Perhaps here a
particular kind of expression is at its most intense and perfect. Then by gradual
and geographic degrees we move to some other center with a special expression.
Anywhere on the planet we may do this—always by insensible degrees the music
changes, and always the music is a compound, a hybrid of collected virtues.*

—Lou Harrison[1]

On March 25, 1961, Lou Harrison arrived at the San Francisco docks and gazed out to
sea. Before him beckoned Pacifica, the ocean connecting him and California to Asia.
As he looked westward, his view also stretched forward in time, for he was about to
embark on the journey that would consume the rest of his musical life.

Harrison's parents, his brother Bill, and Bob Hughes were there to see him off on
his trip to Tokyo by freighter. They carried a bon voyage basket of oranges and snacks
and his trunk up the gangplank and snapped some photos. By 1961, most visitors
crossed the Pacific by air, and the generous grant he had received to support his trip
to the East–West Music Encounter and subsequent study would have paid for the
plane fare. But since flying to Rome in 1954, Harrison's lifelong distaste for air travel
had grown along with his girth. Besides, he had plenty of time for a more leisurely
mode of transportation, as he had quit his job at the animal hospital, though with
some hope that he could return to it if necessary.

"If you leave Atlantica, you're very much aware of it," Harrison said of his reconnec-
tion to the Pacific Rim after escaping New York. "I'd had the previous experience of
Chinese opera and music and Japanese music, so it was like returning to a quest or a love
that I had missed in New York. And that [connection with Asia] was coming back. It
came from hunting around the world in every place but the dodecaphonic corners. And
I reunited with things that I had known in the past and admired and loved, and found
that I really didn't need the pretty grim concert apparatus of . . . Manhattan anymore."[2]

Harrison's pilgrimage to the other side of Pacifica also represented a voyage away
from the last few years of gazing inward, exploring his own emotional scars and
conflicts as well as his musical obsessions. Now he would be looking outward, to the
world's music—and the world's problems.

23

THE HUMAN MUSIC (1961)

As he began his voyage west, Harrison sat down with the new first volume of the monumental *New Oxford History of Music*, devoted to "Ancient and Oriental Music." It provided concise references for the different Asian countries represented in the conference—Japan, India, Thailand, etc. Harrison studied especially carefully the chapter on Chinese music written by the well-known ethnomusicologist Laurence Picken. Chinese scales have five tones per octave but without any notes close together—the configuration found on the black keys of the piano and known to musicologists as anhemitonic pentatonic tunings—a perfectly absurd name, according to Harrison. He found in the chapter on Java that musicians there used a much simpler term, "*slendro*," for pentatonics without semitones, and so he resolved to use this "perfectly good term."[1] Harrison spent his ocean voyage systematically working out the tunings for various pentatonic scales. "Five-tone modes are spread planetwide, alike in highly 'civilized' & in 'primitive' cultures," he wrote later in his *Music Primer*, where he reprinted the list. "They constitute every human's most important tonal heritage."[2]

With his new friend, violinist Richard Dee, in mind, Harrison resolved to create a new piece similar to his *Concerto for Violin with Percussion Orchestra* using these *slendro* modes.[3] Inspired by his beloved baroque concerto grosso, with its pattern of back-and-forth solo and ensemble (*ripieno*) sections, he wanted an orchestra that could answer in the same modes, not just the unpitched percussion he had used in the violin concerto and throughout his San Francisco years. So for his *Concerto in Slendro*, Harrison chose an ensemble of two tack pianos, a retuned celesta, and two percussionists playing an array of metal trash cans, washtubs, gongs, and various sizes of triangle.[4] "I had been studying Picken, Vivaldi, and Corelli," he explained, "and you put them all together, and you get *Concerto in Slendro*!"[5]

The concerto's propulsive opening does recall a Vivaldi concerto (albeit with trash cans). Harrison used the three keyboards solely as melodic rather than chordal instruments, playing single melodies that weave around each other in quintal counterpoint and occasional imitation.[6] The violin alternately joins them or plays with only unpitched percussion accompaniment, like the solo and *ripieno* sections of a concerto grosso. But instead of imitating the standard baroque form—a single consistent theme tying together all of the orchestral returns—Harrison's concerto presents an ever-morphing mosaic of melodicles. Like modern editors of Renaissance pieces, Harrison placed the bar lines, constantly alternating between twos and threes, between the staves rather than through the staff lines, finding a compromise between modern music's tyranny of the bar line and the visually unimpeded flow of notes he valued from the Renaissance. In these ways, the first and last movements of the concerto resemble his other through-composed melodicle tapestries, such as the "Monarchy" overture of the *Political Primer*, the first of the *Seven Pastorales*, and the opening of the *Suite for Violin, Piano, and Small Orchestra*.

The baroque structure continues in the serene middle movement's contrast with the two energetic outer movements. The movement's duet between the violin and tack piano, floating above spare, cicada-like interpolations from quiet gongs, metal pipes, and wooden claves, evokes the sparsity, stillness, and exquisite slowness of much traditional Japanese music. To suggest random night sounds, Harrison distributed the notes of those instruments according to a series of prime numbers. For example, the number of eighth notes between the successive clave strikes are seventeen, eleven, two, twenty-nine, twenty-three, three, nineteen, five, and so on. The pipe hits come in the same series but are offset in time, creating what Harrison called "an infinite canon in prime numbers."[7]

It all evokes the poignant tranquility that Harrison might have felt while staring up at a dazzling night sky on his freighter en route to Japan. The dancing closing movement joyously heralds Harrison's exuberant anticipation of the musical and other discoveries that awaited him just over the horizon.

EAST–WEST ENCOUNTERS

All of our music is hybrid, one way or the other. . . . And I think this is important to realize, that we still are members of the human race.

—Lou Harrison[8]

Approaching Japan, the freighter slammed into a typhoon, which Harrison, apparently immune to motion sickness, found immensely fun, reading and composing as the oranges from his gift basket rolled about his cabin floor. After two and a half weeks at sea, Harrison finally disembarked in Tokyo—and found, to his surprise, a welcoming committee. Before leaving, he had written ahead to an Esperanto society in Japan, hoping to find time to connect and converse with Japanese in a neutral, mutual language. These hospitable Esperantists, though, took his visit very seriously, and they arranged for translators, tours, and help with his stay.[9]

In bustling modern Tokyo, the Japanese *kanji* characters on street signs excited rather than frustrated Harrison, and he soon learned enough of them to find his way around. While other conference attendees spent their days at the hotel, Harrison boarded buses and subway trains, remembering his stops by counting lampposts or by identifying landmarks. He befriended a traditional painter and ended up staying overnight at the man's house. He loved the food. "There is growing life here in the

Orient—real, bright life," he wrote Bob Hughes. "The Occident seems a corpse in comparison."[10]

At the hotel, Harrison happily reconnected with Virgil Thomson, Henry Cowell, Elliott Carter, music critic Alfred Frankenstein, and other friends he had not seen for years. He also seized the opportunity to meet and exchange ideas with scholars he knew only from their writings: Alain Daniélou, the Indian music authority whose writings on just intonation had so influenced Harrison; Mantle Hood, who just two years earlier had started America's first Javanese gamelan performance program at the University of California Los Angeles; Peter Crossley-Holland, a specialist in Central Asian music; and Colin McPhee, whose writings on Balinese music had also been so important to Harrison.

But for all the conference's friendly trappings, Harrison was about to find himself enmeshed in both Cold War and ethnomusicological conflicts that would affect his subsequent explorations for decades. And he would experience an insight that would guide his musical values for the rest of his life.

The East–West Music Encounter inaugurated the newly completed Tokyo Metropolitan Festival Hall, a sleek monument of rectilinear concrete representative both of Tokyo's five hundredth anniversary that year and its place in internationalist modernity. Eager to establish itself on the world stage and demonstrate its cultural parity with the West, the resurgent postwar Japanese government and corporations lavishly funded the conference and festival, as did (via Nicolas Nabokov's Congress for Cultural Freedom) American institutions such as the Rockefeller Foundation, which financed Harrison's participation in the conference and a period of post-conference research in East Asia.

Intercultural egalitarianism was on display from the opening ceremony, which paired music by Italian Renaissance composer Giovanni Gabrieli with the ancient Japanese court music known as *gagaku*. Western ensembles included the Juilliard String Quartet, the United Kingdom's Royal Ballet, and the New York Philharmonic—whose conductor, Leonard Bernstein, enchanted the audience when he turned and addressed them in Japanese.

But Harrison craved traditional music, which the festival supplied in abundance, including Kabuki and Noh performances in the Festival Hall and court music and dance at the Imperial Palace.[11] A performance by a *zheng* zither specialist from Taiwan especially impressed him. "I fell instantly in love with Chinese music, with Liang Tsai-Ping, with the cheng."[12] Harrison prevailed upon Henry Cowell to introduce him to Liang, who agreed to Harrison's request to study with him in the future.

After reading the description of Thai music in his new book, Harrison was especially eager to hear the Royal Ballet and Orchestra from Thailand, and he decided to study in Thailand after the conference. Though Thai court music includes the gongs and xylophones that characterize gamelan music in nearby Java, Harrison soon discovered, to his dismay, that the scales differ considerably. The Thai scale approaches an equal seven-tone division of the octave—and Harrison had just fled the twelve-tone version of equal temperament. He heard in the Thai music performance the same kind of circularity that just intonation had freed him from. Because of the symmetry of equal scale steps, the melodies cycled up and down and up with no obvious foundation. "It nearly drove me up a wall!" he wrote.[13] He would have to find another tradition to study.

HYBRID MUSICS

Music is no language: it is Sound beautiful, Thought direct, Idea moving, and Feeling evident.

—Lou Harrison[14]

The East–West Music Encounter aimed "to find some way to preserve the traditional musics of the East, which, unlike Western music, are endangered by modern industrial society, both capitalist and Communist," Nicolas Nabokov announced to the press. But skeptical critics noted that the festival depended on the financial support of corporations, conservative foundations, and other "money Nabokov has collected in the cause of anti-Communism."[15] A festival, funded by Western interests, about "Third World" Asia in Japan, even with Nabokov's lineup of Japanese participants, smacked of cultural colonialism.[16] Leftist Japanese composers and scholars boycotted the conference, as did communist countries.

On April 18, participants convened in the large new conference room of the Metropolitan Festival Hall to hear readings of papers mostly devoted to surveying Asian traditions and genres. Nabokov's stated preservationist agenda appeared explicitly in or between the lines of many presentations. In a paper that must have resonated strongly with Harrison, Alain Daniélou made powerful arguments for protecting traditional modal, melodic music in contrast to Western polyphony. "The lifeless skeleton that remains when [modal music's] basic tenets are transgressed," he insisted, "cannot give us any idea of the fascinating beauty of pure modal music."[17]

Nabokov (whose upper-class Russian family had fled the Red Army) recognized that many Asian civilizations at their height created art at a level equivalent to the great monuments of European culture. As a corollary, he harbored a deep mistrust of "middlebrow" culture of any country and regarded the communist leveling of social class as a defeat of great art by populist mediocrity.[18] Though hardly an anti-communist (he had joined Socialist Party in April, just before leaving for Asia),[19] Harrison too preferred to survey the music of other cultures from the perspective of refined, courtly art—the kind hanging from the walls at the Silver Court. His coming study in Asia would focus on such genres to the near-exclusion of folk and popular traditions, as would the college courses in world music he would later teach.[20] He agreed with the (then new) argument for equality of high art traditions throughout the world and likely would have sympathized with Mantle Hood's student Robert Garfias's denunciation of Western modernism's erosion of Japanese traditional music at the conference.[21]

But then Peter Crossley-Holland took the lectern. "The assimilation of Eastern music to Western music in its lighter forms robs the former of most of what is valuable, obscures or destroys its native color and, though a certain charm may remain, produces, at best, a variety of ill-begotten forms," he declared. "This process may also be observed at a more serious level, where composers with an insufficient cultural background can produce hybrids at least superficially more plausible."[22] Crossley-Holland's argument went beyond recognition of the threat posed by Western cultural domination, to speak out against Asian music's hybridization with other traditions. It was Harrison's first experience with the erection of artificial cultural barriers, a purism he associated entirely with (no doubt well-intentioned) Western ethnomusicologists desperate to protect traditional music's imagined virginal purity from the depredations of Western commercialism.

Though Harrison had long inveighed against capitalism's vulgarizing effects on art and artists, this either/or attitude contrasted sharply with his emerging inclusive philosophy. "It was about then that I was studying the history of Western music too, to the point that I realized that the farther you got back, the more you were in world music," he said. "And I began to formulate the idea which I still maintain, that Northwest Asia is just a part of world music."[23]

Later that afternoon, Henry Cowell presented an eloquent refutation, from the standpoint of a creative musician rather than that of an ideologically inspired theoretician:

> I felt strongly that other composers should be exposed to the exciting variety and fertility of [Oriental] music, so beginning in the spring of 1932 at the New School for Social Research in New York I gave a course of lectures and demonstrations: "Music Systems of the World" and "Primitive and Folk Music of the World." I approached all this music as a composer, and everything I learned I tried to use.... But I never believed that a composer in the 20th century, particularly in the United States, should limit himself to musical ideas drawn from those developed only in Europe, and only during the last 350 years.[24]

The moment was a powerful one for Harrison, and directly led him to formulate the bedrock belief that would guide both his music and philosophy ever after. "Henry Cowell made a plea in behalf of hybrid musics, pointing out that combinations of the kind have often proved new & stimulating," he wrote later. "Out of my respect for him, I took his remarks at face value (& 'on faith' as it were) until a little while later when I realized that the full idea was: 'don't underrate hybrid musics BECAUSE THAT'S ALL THERE IS.'"[25]

Harrison's own presentation came on the fifth day of the conference. After paper after paper on the current avant-garde,[26] Harrison stood to give a paper on "Refreshing the Auditory Perception," which he had personally experienced since moving from urban New York to rural California. A culmination of many of his musical musings over the past few years, it inveighed against equal temperament's recent dominion over ancient "natural" tunings:

> I feel strongly that the way through musical satisfaction now lies in the Orient, no longer in the Occident.... European musical theory is presently less interesting than the Navajo, for while lacking reason it also lacks metaphysic. Indeed, most of my Western friends calmly leave one of the loveliest labors of our art to that "little man" who is telephoned at times to come to tune the piano.... When the "tuning man" has done his work, the unisons are good again, and the 2:1s are accurate as well. Every other interval is false. What bowellish trust! What a prudery, really! I hear that some of my

colleagues from the Indian and from the Sino-Japanese musical traditions are adopting this Western custom, and I am appalled! Equal temperament . . . absolutely preclude[s] lyric graces or any necessary subtlety of intonation or expression.[27]

Urging more than just the cleansing of ears through a renewed sensitivity to musical tuning, Harrison's polemic implicitly abjures the then-common abstract mathematics of serialism, with its unquestioned loyalty to equal temperament and skepticism of notions of beauty. Instead he calls for connecting the precision of reason with sensitivity of perception: "Thank heavens Ganesha is sober if Saraswati is drunk!" Harrison told the audience. "We must keep our ears and minds alert, and, more importantly, connected."

Though invited to deliver only one paper to the conference, Harrison also brought another, available both in English and Esperanto copies for each of the participants. Even less "academic" and more opinionated, it reveals Harrison's increasing determination, since leaving New York and emerging from his self-imposed exile, to directly address social and cultural concerns—a broadening of the understandably more self-centered view he took while grappling with stress, mental illness, and recovery. We are, he told his fellow conference participants, the keepers of the music rooms on the "large spaceship" that is this planet. While our species faces war, overpopulation, and the noise and stress of urban life, musicians cultivate and protect their rooms, and it is to our mutual benefit to connect them in conferences such as this one. Then Harrison moved from metaphorical rooms to a proposal for a real one to unite all cultures, perhaps under the auspices of UNESCO. To house the planetary wealth of musical modes, his proposed institute would include a "Mode Room" furnished with metallophones, harps, and zithers tuned to different modes.[28]

In just two weeks, Harrison's East–West encounter had opened his eyes and ears to the music of the world as never before, as well as to the political and cultural complexities involved in creatively embracing it, and he was ready to turn from a broad survey to deep study. Each night, after the papers were done, the conference composers and scholars gathered in each other's hotel rooms or meeting rooms for impromptu listening sessions, playing tapes and records brought by the participants. One of them, Dr. Lee Hye-Ku of Korea, came bearing new pressings of traditional Korean music unavailable outside the country. When Harrison played them on a record-store turntable, he knew at once where he was going to spend the next few months. He took out his datebook and crossed out the words "Hong Kong" and "Bangkok" in the spaces labeled May 1 and May 3. The next day, after making arrangements, on the line for May 4, he wrote. "Seoul."

THE WIND FROM HEAVEN

Korea . . . has beautiful palaces that sit on great granite terraces, banquet halls and pavilions that rest in lotus pools, or poise over waterfalls. Audience halls, there, stand like disciplined forests, in whose leafy ceilings dragons curl—golden among silver clouds. On the terraces, before brilliant walls, orchestras still play that are long since lost to both Chinas. The wind from heaven blows across giant melodies, and as they breathe flutes flutter down. Jade chimes and bronze bells resound in ancient Confucian music played nowhere else on earth.[29]

In classical Chinese music, Harrison heard an exquisite subtlety emanating from Confucian moderation. In Japanese music, he found unique melancholy, earthly imperfections transformed into Zen transcendence. But Harrison most adored the "very intense, noble lyricism" permeating the strikingly extroverted, deeply and unabashedly expressionist music of Korea. "It's from the heart," he marveled, "very intense, ravishing."[30]

In 1958, composer Peggy Glanville-Hicks had written Harrison, proposing a grant that would send him to Korea "as a kind of musical missionary" to teach young Korean composers.[31] Instead, Harrison wanted to learn from the Koreans about this captivating type of music unknown to him until hearing the recordings of Lee Hye-Ku: the large ceremonial court music of flutes, double-reeds known as *piri*, zithers, large drums, and radiant percussion instruments including bronze bells, stone chimes, and iron slabs. These ancient orchestras (divided into sub-genres called *tangak*, *hyangak*, and *a-ak*, the last sometimes serving as an umbrella term) had died out in dynastic China but survived in all their austere nobility in Korea and (in a different form) in Japanese *gagaku*, which Harrison had heard at the Imperial Palace.

Both *gagaku* and *a-ak* are extremely slow and based on a single melody that thickens as each family of instruments plays what Harrison called simultaneous variations, a chorus of melodies striving toward the goal tones but each with its own voice, ornamentation, and path. "When a change of notes comes in one of these big orchestra pieces," he explained, "it shudders through the whole orchestra." At a time when techniques of increasing complexity dominated the European avant-garde, he valued Korean music's surface simplicity and "intensely emotional" expression, which were absent from the more austere *gagaku* tradition. "Oh! I could not believe there was such beauty," he said of Lee's recordings. "I was breathtaken. So I had to go there but fast—and I did."[32] The same day he heard those recordings, Harrison arranged a visa and bought a plane ticket.

Lee happily arranged for Harrison to come to Seoul National University, where he was on the faculty. Within days, as Harrison's flight descended into Seoul, the sight of the fields and the old buildings beside the new ones presented a confusing first impression of Korea. Not even eight years had passed since the end of the war, and Harrison saw signs of deprivation and rebuilding everywhere. Taxis (surplus jeeps) shared the road with bicycles and hand-drawn carts, and beggars pulled on Harrison's sleeve when he ventured onto the streets.

Harrison located a small, comfortable hotel in the city's "entertainment district" and found his way to Seoul National University. Many of its professors and historic treasures had been lost in the war, and its buildings were in need of renovation. The country was also riven by political unrest; two weeks after Harrison arrived, Korean military officers overthrew the democratically elected government. That night, the curfew made Seoul eerily quiet, except for the mournful sound of a *danso* flute that Harrison heard someone playing for hours in the darkness.

But the coup and short-lived martial law proved no obstacle to Harrison's immersion in Korean culture, as the letter he wrote to Bob Hughes (excerpted above) demonstrates. "If you're gay, you can quickly find friends," Harrison said, and within days of his arrival, he had picked up a graduate student in English literature with the almost-too-perfect name (for Harrison, at least) Hwang-Suk Dong.[33] Harrison impishly delighted in pronouncing the full name, with honorific, at every opportunity, including in his merry correspondence with stateside friends.

Hwang became his translator, lover, and guide as they explored the turmeric-scented open market with its giant clay jars of kimchi. They visited one of the magnificent Buddhist temples and marveled at the famous ceremony of lanterns celebrating the Buddha's birthday: "over a thousand glimmering candle-lit paper lanterns, handsome young priests smiling, leading chains of people while chanting and beating beautiful temple blocks and burning incense."[34] With Hwang's able assistance, Harrison bought alluring Buddhist paintings and musical instruments, all at very cheap prices.

At the US embassy, Harrison befriended the American cultural attaché, who took him to dinner and introduced him around. The embassy also helped him retrieve recordings that he had brought from Tokyo and that had been seized because they were Japanese. Soon Harrison was a minor celebrity, giving interviews to local newspapers whose editors took pride in having a famous American composer studying their own traditional music. He was given an awkward translation of one of these articles:

> Mr. Harrison, wearing a white no-tie shirt and a black single, was very impressive with his big eyes and broad forehead. . . . He says frankly that he is hearing [the] most beautiful music that he ever heard before in his life. During the interview, he smoked "Arirang" cigarettes. . . . Mr. Harrison likes to go anywhere with our Korean white rubber shoes, and he says he does not like the noises of the street, and he goes on the street with his ears closed except when necessary to hear them. And then he laughed a sound laugh. . . . He says his impression of Korea is the kindness and gentleness of the people. . . . He does not have a watch or a camera that every foreigner in our country have as accessories. And when I asked why is he a bachelor still, his right forefinger pointed [to] me and said, this question is the same one to those who have got married why have they got married. "It's just the same," and burst to laugh.[35]

Harrison found the music he had heard on Lee's records by accident, when he asked a taxi driver to take him to the Classical Music Institute and wound up at the Court Music Institute instead. "There were 4 orchestras; 2 on the terrace, & 2 on the ground below," he wrote to Sidney and Vic Jowers. "The front of this great throne chamber was opened—processions & dancers moved up the middle, the throne in the middle, of the hall."[36] The sound captivated him. "There really does exist here another kind of music," he wrote to Hughes, "rare, special, probably from the rings of Saturn, certainly (to the musical ear) from some part of heaven."[37]

Lee, a musicologist and scholar, met with Harrison daily to help him study the history and theory of Korean music. Ever the hands-on musician, Harrison wanted to learn to play the music, and Lee introduced him to the traditional music faculty at the university. Harrison tried out the *gayageum*, the Korean zither, a relative of the Japanese koto and the Chinese *zheng* but uniquely Korean, "much more murmurous and emotional,"[38] and the *daegeum*, a mammoth bamboo flute whose "languid, elegant" timbre entranced Harrison but whose playing technique hurt his neck.[39]

Finally, Harrison decided on the *piri*, a small, cylindrical double-reed instrument, the Korean version of the ancient Greek *aulos*, which he had just read about in Kathleen Schlesinger's book. Playing the piercing, unwieldy instrument demands precise control of the air pressure, which can greatly affect the pitch, providing an intonational flexibility that naturally appealed to Harrison. Harrison began taking daily lessons, struggling to discern the extremely slow beats of the Confucian orchestral music until he noticed subtle cues from his teacher and learned to adjust to the new conception of musical time. Outside his lessons, he discovered that an analogous concept of time applied to everyday interactions such as changing money, which might take an entire afternoon.

Gauze windows glimmer & the yellow nightingale twitters.
In the fireplace some fire still lingers.
Silk curtain & tapestry hold me warm from Spring's cold.[40]

Lee took Harrison to the library, whose centuries-old books described in great detail the court orchestras of earlier dynasties. Unable to read the Chinese characters, Harrison did learn the notation of the ancient Confucian ceremonial music. With Lee's help, Harrison transcribed many melodies from their ancient sources and recordings held in the university.

He arranged a realization of one of these ancient melodies, *Nak Yang Chun* or *Spring in Nak Yang* ("unquestionably [one of the] masterworks of orchestral literature" of the world, he wrote) for European instruments, copying the ornaments and techniques as closely as possible.[41] "The celesta, harp, & [piano] are used to give some kind of sound similar to the combined effect of jade chimes & bronze bells," Harrison instructed.[42] The celesta follows the melody with sparkling chords moving in parallel, a distinctive Harrison technique that goes back to the clusters of Henry Cowell rather than an Asian source.[43]

Reversing the process, Harrison also wrote an original composition for Korean instruments, in the style of *tangak*, the ancient Chinese melodies that formed the basis for the classical court orchestra tradition in Korea. He named the piece *Moogunkwha* after the delicate national flower of Korea (known in English as the "Rose of Sharon rose," which Harrison used as an alternate title), which he saw everywhere that spring.

Harrison was delighted to learn that, unlike the tradition-bound *gagaku* ensembles of Japan (or orchestras in the United States, for that matter), these groups were open to new compositions. "The classic music here is absolutely booming!" he wrote Cowell. "New works, many young composers & performers rising, the Classic Institute renovated almost into a palace, government prizes for new works, etc., etc.—it is very exciting!"[44] Unlike some of his conference colleagues, perhaps, Harrison saw his contribution to this boom of new music not as cultural encroachment, nor even as a self-conscious fusion of traditions. As his presentation to the East–West Encounter suggested, he looked at it from a composer's perspective, not an academic's. "When I encounter something that is beautiful to me, my natural reaction is one of greed," he said. "I have to have it. I have to do it. I have to make it. . . . It's just plain greed, that's all. I'm making no intellectual fusion of cultures or anything."[45]

NOVA ODO

Armed now with the confidence to embark on a new large-scale project, Harrison decided to set to music a poem he had written in the form of an ancient Greek ode, whose traditional sections—the strophe, antistrophe, and epode—would correspond to the projected three movements. Resembling an oratorio, this "new ode" included a large European orchestra, *piris*, and both a singing and a reciting chorus.

Like the *Political Primer*, *Nova Odo* (its Esperanto title) begins with a recitative in free style, this one announcing a prohibition against the work's performance by any government that "poisons the earth atomically." Then, against a backdrop of militaristic percussion ostinatos, snarling reeds spit out repeated dissonant chords. Their rhythmic pattern turns out to spell, in Morse code, "CLASS STRUGGLE BETWEEN CHURCH AND STATE WAS WON; WILL LAYMAN WIN STRUGGLE AGAINST MILITARY?" Suddenly, all but the percussion ends, and the reciters assume the voices of children in texts speaking about living under the specter of the atomic age. Then begins the through-composed unison cry of a melody, composed with chromatic interval controls, setting Harrison's Esperanto text:

> The Witch who lives in the Mushroom Cloud
> has ashen falling hair that glitters & kills[46]

The movement continues amid the chaos of pounding dissonances (specified to be in equal temperament), hammering percussion, sirens, and reciters shouting ("monstrous!" "vile!") as though in a protest march against the evils of destructive technology. Strings and trombones swoop around in siren-like sliding tones, an innovation Henry Cowell had recommended in *New Musical Resources* and to which he returned in his own orchestral works of this period.[47] To structure his ode, Harrison used the simultaneous variation form that he was learning in this country so recently threatened with atomic attack.

Less blatant than the first movement's text, the contrasting antistrophe in the second movement idealizes a renewed connection to nature and asserts that those turning away from Mars will find love and peace in man's primal nature. This movement imitates the austere nobility of the classical Korean orchestra and its simultaneous variation form, marrying the sliding tones of a *piri* section with European strings, which combine with the voices in a gravely beautiful procession. In a later lecture in Korea, he pointed out that in some classic Korean orchestral pieces, "the 'Prolongations' of the flutes and bowed strings across the ends of the phrases are sufficiently lengthy to give the impression of large-scale antiphony with the piris. . . . Such large-scale alternations were much developed, too, in Baroque Europe, leading directly to the Concerto Grosso form."[48] Baroque-like alternations of three instrumental families—*piri*, Western strings, and percussion—structure this movement, and the "prolongations" of the strings create background chords reminiscent also of the *sho* mouth organs in Japanese *gagaku* court music. This serene and floating texture, so attractive to Harrison the melodist, would become a signature sound for several subsequent compositions.

The text of the epode, the third movement, takes an unexpected turn to the optimism of utopian science fiction:

> Beyond our solar ken, to speed in toward the center of
> suns—meet other intelligence there, there join with
> neighbors among the lights:
> From then, eventually unshackle time,
> & traverse galaxies.[49]

The music of this last movement (completed only in 1968) leaves behind not only the Earth but also the deliberate dignity of the Korean orchestra for a spry melody in Chinese style. As before, the mode is basically pentatonic but with frequent decorative tones outside the mode. In his manuscript on Korean music, Harrison called these pitches outside the mode "innocent tones," and they "can become startling indeed."[50] However, the form is a decidedly un-Chinese rondo, like the finale to the *Symphony on G* that he was working on around the same time.[51]

Although it received only two performances in Harrison's lifetime, *Nova Odo* is a pivotal work of this period, an ambitious amalgamation of his studies in Asia and his resurgent political and social concerns.[52] The first major work in which he fused Asian and Western classical forms and orchestral forces, it set the stage for Harrison's world music innovations to come.

In July 1961, much sooner than he would have liked, the forty-four-year-old Harrison's grant-funded stay in Asia ended. He shipped back a box stuffed with instruments and paintings and made his way back to Tokyo to catch a freighter home. His Korean sojourn had given him a new panoply of compositional possibilities but had also revealed just how many more thrilling frontiers remained for him to explore across the Pacific. After four months away, he was looking forward to returning to his own house, his friends, and his neighborhood, but now something had changed. Even as he was leaving, he couldn't wait to return to Asia.

24

PACIFIC ROUNDS (1962–1963)

I feel strongly that the way through to musical satisfaction now lies in the Orient, no longer in the Occident, except insofar as the occidental concept of experiment and enquiry favors just such a path.

—Lou Harrison[1]

Back in Aptos, Harrison glowed with a renewed sense of purpose. Energized by his new engagement with the world and with new performing partners at hand (Hughes and Dee), he was ready to end his long exile from the concert stage. Bob Hughes's initiative and encouragement would help clear a new path for the older composer into not only a world of performance but also a renewed sociability that would mark his distinctive personality for the rest of his life.

While Harrison was in Asia, Hughes had arranged summer concerts in the outdoor theater at the Sticky Wicket café. Broadcast live over the local radio station KSCO, the last one featured both Harrison's and Hughes's music and had to be amplified to reach the crowd of 250. In 1962, he arranged Santa Cruz and San Jose performances of Harrison's music, including the premiere of *Concerto in Slendro* plus older works like his award-winning *Rapunzel* aria, *Solstice*, *Song of Quetzalcoatl*, *Schoenbergiana* (which he arranged from Harrison's sketches), and *Suite for Violin, Piano and Small Orchestra*. Hughes also encouraged Harrison to write new, small pieces that they could perform themselves at the Sticky Wicket. Harrison's pioneering world music journey would commence at an unprepossessing little café in a California coastal backwater.

Harrison started with a *taryung*, a Korean form that Lee Hye-Ku had suggested could be adapted polyphonically.[2] To Harrison, the traditionally solo melodic structure sounded very much like the European ductia, a genre that in the twelfth century was sometimes written in quintal counterpoint. Envisioning a duet for himself and Hughes, he wrote a *Quintal Taryung* for two vertical flutes (the Korean *danso* and *tungso* for those with access to the instruments, or European alto and tenor recorders otherwise) and optional Korean *janggu* drum.[3] Harrison then added a short *Prelude for Piri and Reed Organ* for himself to play, with Hughes accompanying on a small pump organ he had found. Harrison began teaching *piri* to Hughes (a trained double-reed player), so each could play either part. The organ's sustained pentatonic chords form a background canvas for the *piri* melody Harrison had used in the second movement of *Nova Odo*. Like the strings there, the organ imitates the Japanese *sho*, a mouth reed organ that plays similar chords to form a luminous scrim in *gagaku*, Japanese court music.

Not only did Harrison learn to play the instruments—he learned how to make them as well. With the help of Morris Reynolds, the Santa Cruz carpenter who had built his puppet stage when Harrison had been planning a production of *Cinna*, Harrison built an instrument on the model of a Chinese *zheng* zither. To underline the instrument's trans-Asiatic ubiquity (and the fact that this version was native to California rather than China), he preferred to call it a "psaltery" after the medieval European version of the zither. In homage to the *zheng* player he had met in Japan and his soon-to-be teacher, Liang Tsai-Ping, Harrison composed a short *Psalter Sonato* (or *Sonata for Psaltery*) for the instrument, though its engaging rhythmic combinations of twos, threes, and fours are neither medieval nor Asian.

Harrison wanted to create an "album" that would include pieces such as this for all different varieties of Asian psalteries (for example, the Chinese *zheng*, the Korean *gayageum*, the Japanese koto),[4] though he usually realized them on his own psaltery. Hughes and Harrison performed the new pieces in November 1961 concerts at the Sticky Wicket and down the coast at a resort in Big Sur where Harrison's friend from his Los Angeles days, Melissa Blake, now worked.

As the joy of making music for local performances with friends—something he had missed since he left San Francisco twenty years earlier—returned, so did (ever so slowly) Harrison's open, more gregarious personality. While in Korea he had envisioned establishing an Asian court orchestra of his own in California, but that ambition would eventually transform into the establishment of a smaller chamber ensemble with a few friends. Harrison began training more players and, faced with a shortage of *piri*, began to make his own out of Lucite plastic tubes, harking back to his self-assembled percussion ensemble of the 1930s.[5] "For myself it is necessary to regain instruments that permit a wide range of artistic uses, as well as to regain vocal techniques which in the Occident have been destroyed by the use of instruments designed by engineers during the early industrial revolution," he wrote. "The occidental 19th century much admired engineers, and with delight accepted instruments from them which were fully committed to the false tuning of equal temperament and which absolutely preclude lyric graces or any necessary subtleties of intonation or expression. Engineers will not undo their work, so that artists must."[6]

The impulse to create his Asian orchestra actually extended back even further than his San Francisco days. "The whole impulse was, I guess, the marvel of growing up with Mother's home of Asian art," in Portland, he remembered. "This dream world, this being close to the Jade Emperor, and the whole richness of Asia and the Orient. 'Could we do it here in modern America?' was my thought immediately. And we do this. It's the same thing I have said about all of these things: 'Me too!' So I came back and started designing *zhengs* and the *piri*. Yes, we *could* do them."[7]

But Harrison knew he needed even deeper understanding of these ancient musical traditions. Given the success of Harrison's first Asia visit, Virgil Thomson had suggested that the Rockefeller Foundation might be open to a follow-up, and the foundation quickly accepted Harrison's proposal to return for more study in Korea, together with a trip to Taiwan to study with Liang Tsai-Ping. The grant also funded a visit to California for his teacher, Lee Hye-Ku, to collaborate on a book about the history of Korean music, a history then largely unavailable in English.

After the grant came through, Lee joined Harrison early in 1962, happily sharing his small Aptos cabin, where they worked closely on their manuscript. In their collaboration, Lee would explain what he and their reference works knew about a given topic, and then Harrison would rough out an outline of the information. Then Harrison would commit the information to his own distinctive English prose, often inserting editorial asides, and would finally write out a final copy in ink, much as he did with his music manuscripts. Harrison also contributed the perspective of a practical musician to many of the topics, drawing on his own research to discuss the tuning of instruments and modes, for example.

The idiosyncratic, unfinished forty-six-page manuscript begins with an overview of Buddhist music and then moves to a more conventional chronological survey that focuses on court music and religious music. This focus, slighting such subjects as folk music and dramatic music, is understandable, considering Harrison's interests, Lee's background, and the fact that, as in most countries, most historical evidence comes from such literate traditions. After forty carefully inked pages detailing the changes in the court and ceremonial orchestra traditions, the instruments, and their repertories up through the eighteenth century, there follows a hurried synopsis of the modern period and other traditions. Lee had to leave before they could complete a full manuscript, which Harrison ever after spoke about finishing—but, to his great disappointment, never did. He was always more interested in writing music than writing about it.[8]

FROM THE DRAGON POOL

> Mountains he loves, & mountainous
>   his art & his music
> rise in memory around us.
>   He lifts us cups of tune
> sung full fresh from fountains worldwide
>   of the human music.
> —Lou Harrison[9]

On his return trip to Korea in June 1962 (flying this time), Harrison stopped for a few days at the University of Hawaii's East–West Center, where his old friend and "brother Sinophile" Alan Hovhaness, who happened to be composer-in-residence there that year, introduced him to the music faculty.[10] Harrison gave a lecture there and, perhaps again inspired by Hovhaness, grew his distinctive Van Dyke beard.

Hovhaness's recent career had mirrored Harrison's. He too had received a Rock-efeller grant, which took him to India, where he composed and lectured on "Eastern Influence on American Music," playing the "First Gamelon" movement of Harrison's *Suite for Violin, Piano, and Small Orchestra* for the Indian musicians.[11] Harrison and Hovhaness had kept up a lively correspondence about these shared interests, discussing Asian traditions, instruments, tunings, and other topics.[12] Harrison encouraged Hovhaness to write him a *piri* work, and Hovhaness composed his Sonata op. 171 for *hichiriki* (the Japanese equivalent of the *piri*) and Japanese *sho* mouth organ, which closely resembles Harrison's own *Prelude for Piri and Reed Organ*.[13] "We are both auletes now," Harrison wrote Cowell, referring to the ancient Greek name for players of the *aulos* double-reed instrument.[14] "These instruments have changed my life," Hovhaness wrote to Harrison, asking him to pick him up a *piri* in Korea.[15] Harrison also persuaded Hovhaness to use his Rockefeller grant to come to Korea while he was there.

Once back in Korea, Harrison met up again with friends at the university, and he resumed his friendship and romance with Hwang-Suk Dong as well as his studies and collaboration with Lee. But he and Lee were so busy—Harrison eagerly attended concerts and gave lectures, interviews, even a radio broadcast—that Harrison began to despair that their collaboration on the book would ever be completed. This return to his hectic, pre-California urban lifestyle took its toll: After having invested so much time and effort in the project, Harrison finally succumbed to panic attacks of the type he used to have in New York. He periodically suffered from dysentery and constantly cursed the un-mufflered noise of the busy city of Seoul, never venturing onto the street without improvised earplugs. Soon, Harrison's fear of social situations returned. "Am now in that condition of dazed acquiescence in which I'm not sure of anything," he wrote Hughes, "and my social responses are strange, even to me."[16]

Finally, Hwang took Harrison for the first time out of the city of Seoul, and the two lovers spent a refreshing vacation in the quiet countryside. They found traditional Korean accommodations in the east coast city of Gyeongju, where they saw the ancient royal burial mounds and the eighth-century bell of King Seongdeok, which Harrison and Lee had written about in their book. With Lee, they traveled up the coast to a Buddhist temple at picturesque Seoraksan, where Harrison worked on his *Nova Odo* score by candlelight because there was no electricity.[17]

When Hovhaness arrived in Seoul, Harrison introduced him to the *a-ak* court music he was studying; characteristically, the prolific Hovhaness responded with his Symphony #16 for solo *gayageum* zither, bronze bells, Korean drums, and European strings. The university orchestra premiered the work in a concert broadcast nationally. The same orchestra and the university choir performed the newly completed second movement of Harrison's *Nova Odo*, and students read through his *Moogunk-wha* for traditional orchestra.

"Korean music seems to me ever more beautiful," Harrison wrote his parents, "aristocratic, elegant, noble and lyric."[18] His experiences in the country confirmed his new direction. "Korean music reveals new paths for western composers—the revelation that musical form is melody—that the form of a piece can be one giant melody, evolving as melodies beautifully do, and accumulating lovely decorations as it goes. . . . I feel young composers should begin to learn to compose such great basic melodies and . . . learn also to enrich and ornament those into full compositions. There is no reason that the classical revolution cannot be achieved by the single composer."[19]

Harrison's pursuit of traditional Asian music—and, unfortunately, his dysentery—persisted as he left for Taiwan that October. Like Tokyo, Taipei was a busy urban center, reminding Harrison more of Brooklyn than Chinatown, but beneath the surface Harrison found a fascinating stratum of traditional Chinese life. Liang Tsai-Ping represented the old literary, intellectual tradition—of elegant painting, calligraphy, poetry, and music—now extinct on the mainland. One of the most well-traveled Chinese musicians of his day, Liang had lived in the United States and given many concerts there in the 1940s.[20] He insisted that Harrison come stay at his small house, where every evening Harrison and Liang's family were served dinner by the family servant, an old woman who was treated as a member of the family herself. And according to tradition, Harrison became an honorary member of that family as well.[21]

The most famous twentieth-century exponent and teacher of the eighteen-string *zheng*, or *guzheng*, zither, Liang had published the first instruction book for the instrument in 1938 and collected compositions from many different traditions. After moving to Taiwan during the Communist Revolution, he founded the Chinese Classical Music Association to renew China's declining classical music traditions. Harrison began daily lessons on the *zheng*, and Liang connected him with many other Chinese musicians, government officials, and journalists.

The musically ravenous Harrison soon was also studying the *guan* (a Chinese relative of the *piri*), the *sheng* (Chinese mouth organ), and the *erhu* (two-string fiddle). At Liang's invitation, Harrison arranged his *Nak Yang Chun* for Chinese instruments and heard it performed by Taiwan's classical Chinese orchestra.[22] In a letter to Hughes, Harrison recounted his busy schedule: "5 radio broadcasts, 2 tv shows, 3 lectures, daily lessons, . . . public performances on piris, . . . meetings with government ministers, foundations, record companies, Chinese musicians."[23] Harrison brought back from his 1961–1962 Asian journeys not just some lovely artifacts, but also a newly confirmed worldview.

PACIFIC ROUNDS

I have been bold to try several of the ways in which I think classic Asian musics might of themselves and together evolve in the future, and have combined instruments of several ethnicities directly for musical expressions.
—Lou Harrison[24]

One hot and humid afternoon in 1963, Frederic Lieberman knocked on the door of Lou Harrison's Honolulu apartment. A young master's student studying Japanese music, Lieberman had been assigned to help Harrison, who had been appointed composer-in-residence at the East–West Center at the University of Hawaii, a scholarly outpost in the strategic Pacific established by the US Congress as another bulwark in the cultural Cold War. In 1962, after visiting its first composer-in-residence, Alan Hovhaness, Harrison had stopped by again on his way back from Asia and kept in contact with the faculty. The Center's festival director, pianist Marian Kerr, invited Harrison and Filipino composer Lucrecia Kasilag to be the next composers-in-residence in that steamy spring of 1963. Harrison enjoyed learning about music of the Philippines from "King" Kasilag (her informal name), and she arranged for Harrison the purchase and shipping of a *kulintang* ensemble, a set of gongs related to the Indonesian gamelan, although much smaller and more affordable. It was the first of Harrison's metallophone ensembles, although, preoccupied with Chinese instruments, he would not make immediate use of it.

After weeks of lectures and meetings with students, the residency culminated with a series of public concerts in support of the trans-Pacific ideals of the institution. Along with the debut of *Concerto in Slendro*, the program included another Harrison premiere: his *Majestic Fanfare*, a dramatic canon for three trumpets with percussion that Harrison wrote for the dedication of the new Fine Art Department of the San Francisco Public Library, now directed by his old friend James Cleghorn.

Another Harrison premiere during his Hawaiian residency originated in his 1960 trip to Los Angeles for the Monday Evening Concert devoted to his works, where Peter Yates introduced Harrison to some unlikely fans—the sisters of Immaculate Heart College in Hollywood. After returning to Aptos, Harrison returned to his love of religious ritual long enough to compose an unusual two-part piece for them, his *A Joyous Procession and a Solemn Procession*, both using hexatonic modes and cyclic vocal melodies accompanied by trombones in just intonation and percussion ostinatos. Rather than specifying lyrics, Harrison's score invites the performers to provide their own text so that these functional pieces may be adapted to any religious or secular occasion. Harrison stipulated that a great gong (joyous) or bass drum (solemn) be transported in a carriage with (as he himself illustrates) many bells, jingles, and wind chimes. "Somewhere in the world, at every minute, a solemn song is being sung," he wrote. "Every people, every culture, sings some serious chant either of instruction, magic, praise or ecstasy."[25]

But the major Harrison work on the program, scheduled for the third concert in the series, turned out to be a milestone in his career. For his commission for the Center, Harrison might have completed the *Nova Odo*, which lacked just the last movement. But he decided instead to channel his impulse to protest into a different sort of combined East and West orchestra without text or chorus. Instead of the somewhat expansive, symphonic movements of the *Nova Odo*, Harrison planned short, jewel-like movements for an ambitious, style-spanning suite that would take listeners on a symbolic tour of Pacific cultures. The Esperanto title, *Pacifika Rondo* (translating to *Pacific Round* or *Pacific Circle*), simultaneously invokes the Pacific Rim, that set of coastlines encircling the great ocean; "round" in the sense of a journey around these cultures; and the cyclic structure of the whole piece that ties together these different cultures.

It was an ambitious concept, and for his comparably formidable orchestra of combined Western and Asian instruments, Harrison asked the faculty for the use of their collection of Asian instruments and added his own instruments, carefully packed for the ship voyage: *sheng* (Chinese mouth organs), a *gayageum* (the Korean zither), a *janggu* (a large Korean drum), a *daiko* (a large Japanese drum), a *zheng* zither, his *piri,* and elephant bells and other instruments from his percussion collection.[26]

Now, with the concert (which would also include a work by Kasilag on Philippine instruments) only weeks away, he was faced with hurriedly concocting a new kind of piece for an unprecedented collection of instruments. But when Harrison opened the door and welcomed Lieberman into his non-air-conditioned apartment, the nervous young student was surprised to find the sweaty composer in his boxer shorts—with music manuscripts spread out across a coffee table and around the floor. Not only was Harrison not finished with the work, but it didn't look like he was anywhere close to completing it.

Harrison assured him that now that the planning was done, the rest would follow quickly, and he began to explain what seemed to Lieberman an unexpectedly rigid, even mathematical approach to composition. First, Harrison laid out the movements (see table 24.1.).

Harrison explained to Lieberman that the odd-numbered movements were variations on the same form. As in the *Concerto in Slendro,* he chose a sequence of prime numbers, but this time just four numbers: two, three, five, and seven. He then laid out the melodies of each movement in phrases of these lengths, but in any order and with an extra "breath" at each cadence. For example, the first phrase of the first movement consists of seven quarter notes, followed by a quarter note breath, then three quarter notes, breath, then five, and finally two. The next section has phrases in the lengths of two, three, five, and seven quarter notes with breaks in between, and so on. Although the staves on his scattered manuscript pages mostly lacked notes, Lieberman saw that Harrison had already marked out the measures according to these patterns.

Yet instead of producing a sterile and arbitrary form, the kind Harrison associated with the mathematical processes of his serialist contemporaries, this structural strictness instead undergirds a form both resplendent and satisfyingly proportioned,

TABLE 24.1

1. *La familio de la regha korto* ("The family of the court")	Orchestral simultaneous variations (Korean court music style)	D, prime pentatonic
2. *Ludado de l'delfinoj* ("A play of dolphins")	Chamber trio for *sheng, zheng, gayageum*	E, "minor" hexatonic
3. *Lotus* ("Lotus")	Orchestral simultaneous variations	E, "minor" pentatonic
4. *En sekuoj-ombro* ("In Sequoias' shade")	Chamber duet for *jaltarang* and violin with *zheng, gayageum* ostinato	E, "minor" hexatonic with leading tone alterations
5. *Netzahualcóuotl fabrikas piramidon* ("Netzahualcóyotl builds a pyramid")	*Piri* and piccolo duet with percussion ensemble and drones	D, prime pentatonic
6. *Malamo pri la malpuregaj bomboj* ("A hatred of the filthy bomb")	Orchestral, Western instruments	Atonal, equal temperament
7. *El la draka lago* ("From the dragon pool")	Orchestral, simultaneous variations	A, pentatonic

resembling more the carefully balanced forms of Handel. Lieberman also noted that, unlike many other composers, who would make a point of describing their mathematical processes in program notes, Harrison told him that such "shop talk" was just for fellow composers, not for audiences.[27] For Harrison, formal means were precisely that—means to an emotional end aimed at non-insider listeners, not other members of the club.

Pacifika Rondo's slow and solemn first movement imitates both Korean court music and the drone chords of Japanese *gagaku*. For the benefit of his Western musicians, Harrison painstakingly notated all the ornaments, staggered rhythms, slides, and other simultaneous variations that trained court musicians would render without notation. The movement's languid melody describes a very long arc in the form of a modified palindrome: the second half of the melody mirroring the first half.[28] The "family of the court" in the movement's title evokes not only a silk painting-like image but also the heritage shared by China, Japan, and Korea in this form of court music.

"Dolphins are people, who have language, and who sensibly use their very large brains only to invent elaborate and good natured games," Harrison (a Jacques Cousteau fan) wrote, and *Pacifika Rondo*'s second movement depicts the sea mammals at play.[29] The chamber music trio's (*zheng* zither, *gayageum* zither, and *sheng* mouth organ) delicate texture contrasts with the expansive first orchestral movement and is structured according to the *terza rima* form—that is, phrases in the pattern A-B-A', then B-C-B', then C-D-C', and so on—creating an interlocking form patterned after Dante's innovative rhyme scheme.[30] He called the result "mid-ocean music" in which "the sound of the psalteries suggests the movement of waves and the dancing of dolphins."[31]

The plangent third movement resembles the first, but instead of the slow court orchestra weaving around a single melody, two melodies intertwine in close canon (that is, a "round"), separated by the interval of a fifth. Although the quintal counterpoint of their combination can be found in East Asian music, as Harrison knew from his first studies of the technique, this type of canon is not. "I have been bold to try several of the ways in which I think classic Asian musics might of themselves and together evolve in the future, and have combined instruments of several ethnicities directly for musical expressions," Harrison wrote in explanation of his approach to musical hybrids.[32]

Harrison's program note explains that the middle movement, "In Sequoia's Shade," refers to "California, particularly its colonial days," but the form comes from the European Middle Ages. The form of this duet is a ductia, the medieval dance structured in paired phrases, like its cousin the estampie. The *zheng* and *gayageum* return, this time in an interlocking canonic ostinato to support a duet by a violin and *jaltarang*—the tuned ceramic bowls Harrison had used in his *Strict Songs*.[33] The delightful combination of plucked strings, bowed strings playing one of those irresistibly poignant, unfurling Harrison melodies, and bell-like bowls evokes a cool repose in the forests near Harrison's home.

The next movement alights in another Pacific Rim country, Mexico, evoking its pre-Columbian heritage in a way indebted to its dedicatee, composer Carlos Chávez.

Harrison named it for the fifteenth-century Mexican ruler Nezahualcoyotl, a philosopher and poet who built a pyramid temple in which no blood was to be spilled. Like Harrison's scores for the Aztec-themed *Conquest* and *Canticle #3* (from his earlier "Mission Period"), this one imitates the percussion and flute instruments of Mexico's past. Unusually for Harrison, he asks for players of three small fipple flutes (Harrison brought tin whistles for this purpose) to improvise appropriate melodies, resulting in a birdlike cacophony. The main melody, which returns to the prime pentatonic mode of the opening, alternates between a *piri* and a piccolo.

For all its musical and natural beauty, the Pacific was nevertheless the site of American atomic tests through the 1950s, which destroyed verdant islands, produced massive radioactive fallout, and displaced and poisoned indigenous people. For *Pacifika Rondo*'s startling penultimate movement, "A Hatred of the Filthy Bomb," Harrison specified only European instruments playing in equal temperament and resurrected his facility with the twelve-tone method, which he called "an intrusion of common 'Atlantic' modernism."[34] Unlike his earlier, expressionistic twelve-tone works, though, this one opens with hammering bells, pizzicato strings, and piano over eerily swooping string slides (as in the similar "protest" in the first movement of *Nova Odo*). A mad atonal march brutally intrudes from the brass and percussion, surging to a furious climax that ends in a blood-chilling male scream. Harrison's use of the twelve-tone method to depict violence is perhaps unique in his output, but his placement of his most contrasting section as the penultimate movement is typical of his suites throughout his career.

The majestic last movement, "From the Dragon Pool," returns to the court orchestra texture of the first movement but now even slower and in a different, placid mode, supplying a cool and refreshing antidote to the terror of the previous movement.

Pacifika Rondo was a landmark not just in Harrison's creative journey, but also in the twentieth century's integration of the European classical tradition with other traditions around the world—not for the sake of novelty or cultural tourism, but in the Cowell-inspired conviction that deep and respectful hybrids ultimately enrich all traditions. Cowell himself strove for this ideal in his orchestral works of the 1950s, as did Colin McPhee and Alan Hovhaness, but never before in such a convincing synthesis (or on such a large scale) as *Pacifika Rondo*. In a few years, the term "world music" would proliferate through record stores and academic circles, and if one had to choose a single date for this new movement (based on an old theme), the May 26, 1963, premiere of *Pacifika Rondo* at the East–West Center's Orvis Music Auditorium is as plausible as any.

Some years later, Harrison's friend from his New York days, composer and writer Paul Bowles, received a tape of *Pacifika Rondo* when he was living in Tangier. He wrote back to his friend Peter Garland, "You'll be interested to know that one Moroccan on hearing the first tape of Lou Harrison's music couldn't rest until he'd copied it. He came by yesterday to report the reactions of various friends: Senegalese, Iraqis, and Nigerians, all of whom expressed more or less the same thought—that it was music which described Paradise of one kind or another. (I wonder what Lou would make of that.) The Moroccan himself speaks of it as *'música escrita por un diós.'*"[35]

Harrison's Hawaiian sojourn—appropriately, midway between the Asian and American mainlands—produced a great synthesis that could serve as a convenient marker for the birth of his musical identity as the Pacific composer. But the supreme reward of Harrison's residency and the premiere of *Pacifika Rondo* came from the presence of its dedicatees: his elderly parents. Recognizing that their health was declining, Harrison spent his small honorarium as composer-in-residence to bring them out to the tropical paradise. Neither had been overseas before, and they were thrilled both to vacation and to see their boy celebrated at concerts of his music. As he headed home to California at the end of his residency, he would realize just how precious their attendance had been.

25

THE FAMILY OF THE COURT (1963–1966)

I remember
his patient kindnesses
my nightly childhood homework was
with him—
he drove
me each Monday
many miles, at night, to
class in Gregorian chant and
singing.
The wood
he had kiln-dried
for me so that I might
construct a redwood harpsichord
to play—
Sawdust's
aromatic
smell surrounded Dad's mill
and the pond, splashed and rippled with
timber.
He liked
plucked instruments
and wanted to help me
make a factory for Chinese
psalteries.
Talking
with friends Dad would
speak his interest with
"you don't say," "by George," "feature that,"
and more.

—Lou Harrison[1]

A decade back in California gave Harrison a new perspective on the dynamics of relationships within his family, which had reached such a tense level in his teenage years that Harrison had been eager to move out. He was cast in the role of the comforting son to his emotional, sometimes hysterical mother—hysterics that hindsight revealed as power plays against his often humiliated father. After Harrison's departure, his parents sometimes separated, as they were when Harrison returned to California, where he reconnected with his now graying, overweight, but ever affable father.

Though supportive, his parents evinced little understanding of Lou's career or professional standing, but they had become increasingly impressed with seeing his name in newspaper reviews, magazine articles, and long-play records. Although they rarely heard his performances when Harrison was still living in San Francisco, his parents were proud to attend a Harrison concert that Bob Hughes organized at the Sticky Wicket while the composer was still in Asia. When Lou constructed his Chinese *zheng*, Pop Harrison, who knew woodworking and could see how the instrument was put together, enthusiastically if impractically proposed that they could start a business building and selling Chinese *zheng*. His mother asked, "Lou, why did you become a Chinese musician?" Harrison replied, "Well, that's the risk you took when you raised me in a household of Asian art!"[2]

Yesterday, his eyes were bright,
today they lack all life . . .
it's hard to bear,
to feel no father there.
—"Caesar's Aria" from Harrison's *Young Caesar* (1988)

One day in July 1963, two months after Lou returned from Hawaii, Sidney Jowers climbed up to his cabin. She had received a phone call. Clarence Harrison had gone to bed, and he never woke up. "My father!" Harrison wailed. Harrison recalled his smiling father saying, "When you're dead, you're dead!" Harrison would remember this "sensible remark" as he began to consider his own mortality, years later.[3]

In the wake of his father's death, Harrison composed a memorial for his symbolic musical father, Charles Ives—what the French call a *tombeau*. Like many of the works of the uncompromising New Englander, *At the Tomb of Charles Ives* concedes little to performance practicality, calling for two psalteries, two dulcimers, three harps (all these plucked strings tuned to different just-intonation scales), alto trombone, tam-tam, and Western strings, tuned to a just-intonation scale that is mostly five-limit, but with a single, savory seven-limit B♭. Like the querulous trumpet in Ives's *The Unanswered Question*, a distinctive alto trombone (or, Harrison suggested, its medieval predecessor, the sackbut) plays a short pentatonic tune a few times over the course of the piece, with each repetition answered by stepwise psaltery melodies that descend as if into the grave. Yet the trombone returns each time, unbowed.

A proliferation of plucked strings continued in another lament. When Harrison heard about the 1964 death of the famously silent Marx brother, he composed an *Elegy for Harpo Marx*—an equal-tempered chromatic fantasy based on a single melodicle and arpeggiated chords for, fittingly, three harps.

The exhilaration of Harrison's Hawaiian success now gave way to grief. Around the same time as her husband's death, Calline Harrison became very ill, and her son Lou moved into the Redwood City house to care for her. Perhaps reflecting on his own mortality in the wake of these events and the surgeon general's 1964 report on the health effects of cigarettes, Harrison, formerly such a heavy smoker that his fingernails were stained yellow with nicotine, quit smoking cold turkey.[4] For solace, he brought to his mother's house his *zheng* psaltery and another renewed interest that he had brought back from Asia.

But this lord, who is the universe,
sustains, endures, rescues & disappears
Like the piper at the gates of dawn
& Pan, he gives the gift of forgetfulness
to whom he helps
he releases,
allows,
& vanishes.

—Lou Harrison[5]

After he returned from Asia, Harrison began immersing himself in the sutras and other Buddhist literature, even signing his manuscripts by the Buddhist rather than Christian reckoning of years. However, he was less interested in the Zen sect, which had so inspired writers Jack Kerouac, Allen Ginsberg, Gary Snyder, and of course Harrison's friends Alan Watts and John Cage, with its rejection of logical causality and fetishizing of spontaneity.[6] "Abstract Expressionism, Happenings, Tacheism, etc., were all aimed at revivifying single states or events," he wrote. "I myself was miserable during that period—for it almost neglected the inter-compositional relationships that, to me, constitute Art and made The Relationship to be only between oneself (as person) and some thing or event (paint, sound, etc.). I am happy now to notice in Society a return toward relational and/or mensurating art—Planned Art."[7]

Harrison kept in his house a small shrine to Amitabha, the Buddha of the Pure Land sect, which, contrary to Zen, envisioned a world of harmony where the Buddhas and bodhisattvas reside. A large painting of the Buddhas that Harrison had brought back from Korea dominated a wall of his home for the rest of his life. However, Harrison stopped short of calling himself a Buddhist and would never give up his ecumenical appreciation of the pacific and humanistic aspects of many religious traditions. He only occasionally visited the nearby Buddhist temple in Watsonville, such as during its celebration of the Buddha's birth.

To commemorate this holiday, known as Wesak or Vesakha, he wrote music in late 1964 for the psaltery (i.e., *zheng* zither), employing the traditional Chinese number notation he had learned from Liang Tsai-Ping rather than Western staff notation. The delightful *Wesak Sonata* retains traditional *zheng* idioms and ornamentation but discards Chinese form and meter in favor of Harrison's characteristic free combinations of twos, threes, and fours; and, of course, it specifies just intonation for the pentatonic mode. It melds a Chinese atmosphere and Harrison's own voice much more organically than the delicate, earlier *Psalter Sonato*, composed just before his study with Liang.

Buddhism inspired another late 1964 psaltery piece, *Avalokiteshvara*, named for the bodhisattva who listens for the cries of unhappy beings in order to help them.[8] In contrast to introspective traditional *zheng* pieces, *Avalokiteshvara* is a life-giving, propulsive dance, accompanied (like his 1939 *First Concerto for Flute and Percussion*) by two cycling bell ostinatos and filled with engaging combinations of twos and threes. It resembles most of all the second "gamelan" movement of the *Suite for Violin, Piano, and Small Orchestra*, but to Harrison it represented the transcendence of the bodhisattva's compassion that he wrote of in the poem excerpted above.

About the same time as *Avalokiteshvara*, Harrison composed (and dedicated to Hughes) a companion psaltery piece, *The Garden at One and a Quarter Moons*, its enigmatic title and mysterious mood inspired by an abstract etching Harrison had bought.[9] Its leisurely tempo and serene mode contrasts with the exuberant *Avalokiteshvara* but retains its metrical freedom. These three pieces, combined with the earlier *Psalter Sonato*, comprise Harrison's new repertoire for psaltery, all composed within two years of his study with Liang Tsai-Ping. "Now when I want to play a little," he wrote Lieberman in 1963, "I reach for a psaltery—no longer a piano."[10]

In addition to writing his own pieces, Harrison often transcribed traditional Chinese pieces from his notebooks, printed books, or recordings, sometimes in Western notation but frequently in Chinese notation, in which Arabic numbers correspond to the melodic tones. Gradually, he, Hughes, and Dee put together a regular repertoire, and their small ensemble performed at the Sticky Wicket, schools, and other small venues in the area. Their shows might include Dee declaiming a Chinese poem to an improvised musical accompaniment, or Harrison's mini-lectures on the instruments, the musical tradition, or the next work in the program.[11]

THE CABRILLO FESTIVAL

During his teacher's travels, Bob Hughes had remained a tireless advocate for music in his adopted community. His increasingly elaborate Sticky Wicket music series caught the attention of local music lovers, and Hughes soon became active in the nearby Watsonville Concert Association.[12] He connected with local patrons and musicians, including the music faculty at the newly opened Aptos campus of Cabrillo College, a small junior college just up the road. Ted Toews, the choir director there, and the energetic Hughes ambitiously proposed that the community expand the outdoor series into a regular music festival with a full orchestra, beginning that summer of 1963. Members of the Concert Association volunteered to house the musicians in their own homes, a tradition that remains.

Although still invested in the community, Hughes found it too difficult to make a living as a bassoonist in Santa Cruz and reluctantly moved to the Bay Area. Even after he found a job with the Oakland Symphony, Hughes continued to travel down to see Harrison and help organize the festival. He brought a list of possible music directors to the festival organizers, and to their credit, the organizers agreed that they wanted someone who would program new and adventurous music—passing up the opportunity to offer the position to Arthur Fiedler. Instead, they offered the job to Gerhard Samuel, the music director of the Oakland Symphony.

On August 21, 1963, the German native ascended the podium in Cabrillo College's theater, in front of an audience of three hundred, to conduct music by Hindemith and Stravinsky. Harrison, still grief-stricken in the wake of his father's death a few weeks earlier and preoccupied with taking care of his mother during her illness, missed the inaugural festival that he'd helped inspire. "It was a bold and interesting idea of Samuel, who is general director of the festival, to open with a program of contemporary masters," wrote Alfred Frankenstein in the *San Francisco Chronicle*. "But it is hard to understand why another contemporary composer, Lou Harrison, the most distinguished citizen of Aptos, is not represented on the festival programs at all. In Europe, a man of his standing would have been commissioned to write a dedicatory piece for the opening concert."[13]

Frankenstein's review genuinely dismayed Samuel, who took Hughes aside for advice on how he could make amends. Fortunately, the inaugural festival's success resulted in an invitation to bring Samuel back the next summer, and Samuel soon met with and befriended Harrison. For the 1964 festival, he programmed Harrison's long-neglected *Symphony on G*. Harrison got to work on the still-unfinished finale, casting it in the form of an elaborate chaconne and fugue. He avoided the traditional ending form of the rondo in order to avoid abutting the immediately preceding section, a similar rondeau. However, at the premiere, after such a dramatic setup and increasingly expanding form, this strict contrapuntal approach to the last movement came off as "laborious and pointless," in the words of critic Alexander Fried.[14] Harrison agreed and wrote another movement, this time embracing the form of the rondo to produce an electrifying finale—a "primal scream, a big drama"—which Samuel premiered with the Oakland Symphony Youth Orchestra in February 1966.[15]

Another disappointment followed that second Cabrillo Music Festival, when its cradle, the Sticky Wicket café, closed in the fall of 1964, a victim of the Cabrillo Highway's conversion to a modern freeway, leaving the café invisible to travelers. Harrison remained close friends with the Jowerses, but Aptos lost an important focal point for local arts.

By then, Hughes had found another establishment open to local performers—and yet another nearby outlet for Harrison's gradually reemerging music. At San Francisco's Old Spaghetti Factory, an eccentric North Beach landmark, beatniks, writers, actors, and various artists dined on cheap, overcooked spaghetti beneath chairs and piñatas and a giant turtle sculpture, all suspended from the ceiling. On his visits, Harrison often strolled down Grant Street, through Chinatown, made his way through the ivy-covered garden patio to the entrance, and ordered an Anchor Steam beer for a quarter and a meal for $2.[16] Owner Freddie Kuh had built a stage for local performers, including folk singers such as the Kingston Trio but also a weekly chamber music series organized by Donald Pippin. Pippin, a local pianist and conductor, had followed his high school friend, composer Ben Johnston, to California to study with Harry Partch, eventually ending up in North Beach.[17]

Pippin performed some of Harrison's piano works and happily turned over other Old Spaghetti Factory concerts to Harrison, Hughes, Dee, and their friends. In addition to recent works, Harrison's group performed and often premiered pieces that had moldered in his trunk, including *Praises for the Beauty of Hummingbirds* from 1952, the 1940 song "Pied Beauty," and another composition from that year, *Jephthah's Daughter*, which Harrison revised for an Old Spaghetti Factory performance. It was repeated at Cabrillo with choreography by his old friend Carol Beals. A 1964 profile in the *Chronicle* noted the previously reclusive Harrison's reintroduction to the local music scene.[18] Near-annual performances of Harrison works became much-anticipated features of Cabrillo Festivals for decades, eventually giving Harrison visibility and even power within the world of professional classical music.

Unable to live in New York or other urban centers of the professional music world, Harrison now had the Cabrillo Festival to effectively bring the professional music world to him. It expanded his little Aptos "family" into a much larger musical community that would both enrich his life and help spread his music around the world. Most important for his emotional and artistic health, he was playing music again with his friends, as he had in San Francisco with his percussion ensemble and dance buddies, when he had been happiest.

REFLECTIONS IN MOTION

Predominant practice today is for dancers to use disks and/or tapes while teaching classes, and for accompanying concerts as well. This is Bad Practice—for it trains in lifeless (un-inter-responding) rhythm, and it increases the popular belief that Machines are Holy. It is part of the same thing that causes us to housebreak our children and allow our automobiles to spew their waste-products all over us. The dancer who uses disks or tapes in concert (unless the music is originally "Electronic") is not an Artist but a Hack.

—Lou Harrison[19]

Since his father's death, Harrison had needed to take care of his mother. Driving up to her Redwood City home precluded taking any jobs outside of the area, and Harrison even turned down a teaching opportunity at York University in England.[20] Finances remained precarious, and Harrison had gone back to work at the animal hospital and borrowed money from his mother. He complained that no one else would hire him because he was openly gay.[21] His fortunes changed in late 1964 when he received a phone call from a dancer, Lorle Kranzler, who taught classes in Palo Alto.

Fortunately for Harrison, Kranzler still insisted on live accompaniment in a time when nearly all other dance instructors had come to depend on the new technology of tape recorders. Choreographers liked the ability to choose any musical piece in a performance that was precisely repeatable without having to hire expensive musicians. Harrison argued that this very repeatability, a product of the Industrial

Revolution's mass production, had produced a "general Bourgeois Tedium."[22] Faced with what he saw as the destruction of a vital collaborative art form, Harrison wrote a furious article for the contemporary dance journal *Impulse,* excerpted above.

Seeing nothing creative in dance students "hopping along" the same dance steps in response to a fixed recording, Kranzler needed an accompanist who could improvise, allowing her to create a constant interaction between the musician's and the dancers' improvisations.[23] Harrison, who had become an expert improvising dance accompanist a quarter century earlier at Mills College, perfectly suited her needs. His new job enabled Harrison, at age forty-eight, to finally quit "clipping poodles."

Twice a week, Harrison would pack his van with his collection of percussion instruments, flutes, Asian psalteries, and inexpensive wind chimes (from local import stores) dismantled to make rhythm sticks for the students. Spread out on a blanket, these instruments surrounded Harrison as he improvised an accompaniment for each class. Sometimes the kids would play the instruments as well as dance. One dance might require a Bartók-like piece played on the studio piano, the next a fantasy for woodblocks and flowerpots, the next a languid melody on the *xiao* bamboo flute. Kranzler insisted that students bring their parents to the class when possible, so that the kids would take the dance seriously, and accordingly, even Harrison sometimes brought his own mother to the class.[24]

He would work all day, sometimes eight or nine classes in a row, and then repair to a Palo Alto gay bar he knew, order a pitcher of beer, and later drive to his mother's house to sleep.[25] The steady income was welcome, but it made working on other compositions difficult. "Since improvising 18 hours a week exhausts my modest musicality, I am painting, making mobiles, & learning etching for creative pleasure now," he wrote to Cowell.[26]

Harrison and Kranzler's collaboration proved so successful that they attracted invitations to give performances and master classes, including one at UCLA in 1966, where Harrison was delighted to discover the composer Carlos Chávez in residence.[27] Once, Kranzler took her teenage dancers and Harrison to a dance conference in Monterey, where, in the middle of the performances, the power went out. Their group was the only one able to go on with the concert, because every one of the other dance companies used recordings for their accompaniment.[28]

In 1966, San Francisco's public television station, KQED, filmed a program of three of Kranzler and Harrison's collaborations for broadcast. Harrison (on piano) and Dee (on violin and strumming, Cowell-like, inside the piano) improvised the first two pieces. After some discussions with the technical staff, Harrison designed the third piece so that his on-camera improvisations would be supplemented by overdubs of special tapes that Harrison and Dee made at his home, a tape of bells and gongs, one of "heartbeat" drums, and one of melodic fragments and sliding tones on recorder or violin. Harrison carefully designed the tapes so that they could fit on top of the existing meterless improvisations without interfering with the mode or character. "It was an interesting way to work," he said, and it was unique in his career. However, to Harrison's frustration, the technicians at KQED could not make it work, and the tape was broadcast as it was.[29] That same summer, choreographer Norman Walker set music from Harrison's *Suite for Violin, Piano and Small Orchestra* at Massachusetts's famous Jacob's Pillow dance center, the first of many times his music would accompany dance there. His old muse, dance, helped Harrison's music avoid obscurity during the 1960s.[30]

Despite his new role improvising interplays with dancers, Harrison nevertheless eschewed Cage/Cunningham-style chance as an antidote to repeatability. He recognized that impulse within the avant-garde as a reaction to the increasing regimentation of modern life, symbolized by the Vietnam War-era draft. "I was distressed by the frequently aleatory procedures of many of the Young until it dawned on me that in a very real sense they were being realists and realistic," he wrote. "As the population grows (world-wide) and decadence grows socially in the U.S.A., and as the only socially undisciplined class (the Military) can actually thwart any plans of youth, or kill it off for that matter—then youths certainly can't plan their lives, let alone plan their art! Why should they? Why should Society ask them to plan their art?"[31] As the war intensified, Harrison's *Peace Pieces* felt even more relevant; Hughes programmed recitatives from them, along with his own *Vietnam Elegy*, in an April 1967 concert at California Hall.

Freedom and experimentation quickened in the foggy air of the Bay region, and Harrison's improvisational skills led to more classes with a colleague of Kranzler's named Chloe Scott, an English native who was hanging out with a group of artists over in Menlo Park that included writer and psychedelic prophet Ken Kesey, LSD researcher Richard Alpert (later Ram Dass), and Whole Earth Catalog founder Stewart Brand, all of whom were in Scott's class for which Harrison provided music.[32]

On January 22, 1966, Kesey's group organized one of their legendary "Acid Tests," formally known as the Trips Festival, a psychedelic circus of rock bands, light shows, films, live video, theater, and anything else the organizers could stuff into San Francisco's Longshoremen's Hall. For those still awake at 11:00 the next morning, the handbills advertised a "side trip" provocatively titled "Worship Service" for the Sunday morning, with Chloe Scott, "dancemistress," and Lou Harrison at the San Francisco Tape Music Center. The Tape Music Center was a growing avant-garde nexus in the city, though this time, the outpost of electronic music hosted a defiantly acoustic, goateed, forty-nine-year-old technophobe driving up in a van jammed with exotic and ancient instruments. When Harrison and Scott arrived that morning, they found the facility double-booked with a light show. After some negotiations, the performances merged.[33]

The following September, Scott and Harrison created another event at Stewart Brand's Whatever It Is Festival at San Francisco State (also known as "the last of the Acid Tests"). Other acts there included the Grateful Dead, synthesist Donald Buchla, and light shows in one gym and a "Sensory Awareness Seminar" in the other, with Scott's dancers leaping to strike objects dangling from wires in the ceiling. Soon dancers mixed with leaping, cannabis-fueled audience members (including Merry Pranksters Kesey and Ken Babbs) as Harrison provided music.[34]

Harrison, himself an original Bay Area countercultural rebel, admired the psychedelic light shows and viewed the emerging hippie scene in San Francisco with an outsider's fascination. Although he admired the baroque-like melody and harmonic movement of the Doors' "Light My Fire," he remained on the whole unsympathetic to the new popular music.[35] Once, his visiting friend Carlos Chávez asked for a tour of this scene he had read about, so Harrison and Hughes took the Mexican composer slumming around the Haight-Ashbury district. When the three of them peeked into the Fillmore West as a band was getting set up for a concert, Harrison was shocked and offended to see one of the guitarists tuning his instrument to the equal-tempered piano. Later, he railed that the "Hippy high-volume movement . . . aimed consciously at the destruction of hearing."[36]

Overtaken by this countercultural wave, Harrison found his social circles expanding again. But none meant as much to him as another community he rediscovered in 1966. That year, the gay organization the Society for Individual Rights (SIR) opened the first gay community center in the United States, and Harrison often drove up for Saturday night dances, classes, and special interest group meetings. A SIR audience warmly received a concert presented by Bob Hughes and Harrison of early music and their own compositions.[37] In SIR, Harrison found a welcoming community that would further expand his life beyond his Aptos cabin.

"I cannot tell how much relief, pleasure, conviviality, interest & warmth SIR—the Society for Individual Rights brings me," he wrote. "When I first joined I told my friends that I felt like a member of a successful slave revolt & this delighted triumphant feeling still comes with any SIR activities. It is wonderful to enjoy a public & comradely commitment with other friendly homophiles to the internal and mutual betterment of our lot. . . . Until SIR I had not really had any estimate of how lonely socially I have felt nor how wonderful was the remedy."[38] Engaging with SIR stirred in Harrison what would soon be called gay pride. "Homosexuality is not a disgrace," he wrote in his journal the next year. "On the contrary—it is a proud blessing."[39]

Harrison enjoyed working with dancers again, but with so much of his creative energy focused on hours and hours of improvisation and his continued study of Asian music and Buddhist literature, his "planned art" amounted to little during those years, and most of that was related to existing pieces: his revisions of the *Symphony on G* finale and the completion of his *Easter Cantata*, begun in 1943 and now resurrected for a residency with Kranzler at Hartnell College in Salinas, where it was performed along with his *Mass to St. Anthony*, another artifact of his earlier spiritually influenced music.

Like many mid-1960s Americans, Harrison had expanded his horizons. But although he had renewed his expertise as an improviser, by mid-1966, Harrison was finding that his work for dance was growing stale, as it had for him in the early 1940s in San Francisco, and again in the early '50s in New York. Regardless of the money involved, he knew it was time to quit. "When you already know what you're going to do . . . by the formula that's gone on too long, that's the time to stop," he explained. "It was the same thing with reviewing in New York. It got to the point where the minute a concert would start, I was thinking what I was going to write and not listening to the music anymore. For a composer, that's a no-no."[40] When a letter arrived, asking whether he would accept a fellowship from the Phebe Ketchum Thorne Foundation, Harrison quickly replied.

He would.

EVERYDAY PAGEANTRY

While the culture of the United States still remains as open, as vital, and as extensive as it was before, nevertheless, from its neighbor to the south there can come into it, if men are wise, a quickening of the imagination and the spirit, a deepening of the sentiments and the emotions, a heightening of the sense of beauty, and a seriousness, vitality, integrity, and realism in architectural, political, and religious forms and practices that are desperately needed.

—F. S. C. Northrop[41]

In 1965, Francis Thorne, a composer and heir to a New York banking fortune, established a foundation to help support other composers. Named for the family matriarch, the award came with a $300 per month stipend, no strings attached, for three years. The foundation did not reveal how it chose the composers, but the list (which included Harrison's friend Ben Weber) once again suggests the influence of Virgil Thomson. The stipend replaced Harrison's dance income, allowing him to focus on a new large project. However, his life in Aptos, once a remote hermitage, had become increasingly busy and complicated, and Harrison searched for a retreat free from distractions.

The solution came from Harrison's New York friend Ross Parmenter, a well-known critic for the *Times* and Harrison's frequent concert-going companion during his New York years. Recently retired from the paper, Parmenter now spent most of his time in the southern Mexican town of Oaxaca, renowned for its cultural and architectural heritage, where he had become an authority on Spanish period architecture. He invited Harrison to meet him there.

When earlier passing through New Mexico, Harrison had been fascinated by the "combination of Pueblo and Spanish" culture, but Mexico itself remained for him an unexplored quarter of the Circle of the Pacific. Harrison's collaboration with Lester Horton had earlier stoked this enthusiasm for the romance of Mexico's past (which once included California), when it emerged in such pieces as his percussion quartet *Song of Quetzalcoatl*. After the war, he had been influenced by the internationalist ideas of the philosopher F. S. C. Northrop, whose *The Meeting of East and West* had a chapter on "The Rich Culture of Mexico," quoted above.[42] Harrison also knew that, thanks to Carlos Chávez's encouragement, Aaron Copland also regularly retreated to Mexico to work, and Parmenter himself was researching D. H. Lawrence's inspiring sojourn in Oaxaca.

Retaining only a few phrases of Spanish from the class he had enrolled in ten years earlier (and knowing no Mexican Esperantists), Harrison nevertheless decided to drive the 2,500 miles himself in the hot summer of 1966, after the Cabrillo Festival. For customs, he prepared a declaration of all the belongings he stuffed into his van, a list that paints a portrait of his varied enthusiasms of the time: "16-string chinese cheng, 1 nan hu (2 str chinese viol), 1 shiao, 1 mbira, 4 piris, 4 Esperanto books, 3 Greek translations, 1 Piet Mondrian, 1 abstract painting (senphor, Abrams), 2 Albers catalogues, 1 Plays of Kuan Han-Ching, 2 [books of] poetry, 1 Byzantine music and Hymnography."[43] And he attached to his van a 1963 Honda motorcycle for excursions.

This meandering journey allowed Harrison some time to explore Mexican villages and the countryside. Seeking links to Mexico's rich past, he marveled at the cathedrals of Mazatlán and Puebla, where he also explored the seventeenth-century vaulted library and the splendid tilework, and in tropical Oaxaca the neoclassical architecture and the "everyday pageantry" of the indigenous Zapotec cultures.[44] One day he happened upon a religious procession marching down the cobblestone street for the feast day of St. Cecilia (patron saint of music), complete with icons of the saint and marimbas suspended from the musicians' shoulders.

However, most of his time was set aside for work, including an oratorio for choir and percussion on poetry of Robert Duncan. Perhaps the pressure to create during the uninterrupted period of his retreat magnified the challenges of working with Duncan's complex text, but Harrison's frustration mounted.[45] Instead, his oratorio unfinished, he turned his attention to another project—a book.

Ever since his youthful discovery of Henry Cowell's *New Musical Resources*, Harrison had appreciated its uniqueness. Most college music theory textbooks concentrated entirely on old European classical harmony and forms. While still in prison, Cowell wrote a modest corrective in the form of a book on melody and planned to follow it with a book on rhythm.[46] Hardly any books offered composers such practical help in such areas. Topics like the use of motives (melodicles) or dissonant counterpoint seemed like trade secrets, passed around by composers in the know but otherwise inexcusably inaccessible to students.

Cowell's wisdom had been on Harrison's mind since the day at the end of 1965 when, shopping at a grocery store with his mother, Harrison glanced at *Newsweek* magazine and saw that his old mentor and friend had died in New York. (He would inherit the 1871 Steinway piano owned by his teacher, who had received it from Percy Grainger.) Heartbroken, Harrison immediately wrote a letter of condolences and memories to Sidney, recalling how Cowell had encouraged him to write up his ideas on composition and even to include examples and exercises, like conventional textbooks.

As he had become more of a teacher since Greenwich House Music School and Black Mountain College and especially while teaching Bob Hughes and others in California, Harrison began jotting down his pedagogical thoughts in his enormous collection of spiral notebooks. The nonlinear result reflects its author's magpie mind: Rather than presuming to impose anything like a graduated course of study on a student's creativity, Harrison instead simply collected these ideas for students to peruse and pursue as they liked, as a "primer" for composing music. More terse and delightful than Cowell's book, its closest model, Lou Harrison's *Music Primer* is structured as a series of these "items," imitating a style used by the old Chinatown newspapers, "in which the reader, not the editor, is free to assign a hierarchy of importance to the items gathered on the page," wrote Harrison's friend, composer

Daniel Wolf.[47] Dedicated to "my fellow students," the irresistibly idiosyncratic little volume more resembles the diverse packing list he provided to customs officials (and together, they offer a portrait of his mid-1960s life and thoughts) than a formal textbook—Harrison's "vast acreage" of toys, scattered across fifty hand-calligraphed pages between soft covers, compact enough to carry around like the books of poetry and art that Harrison always toted.

The *Music Primer*'s practical items include items on "Composing with Melod-icles," melodic and rhythmic permutations, prime number proportions in forms (with examples from *Pacifika Rondo*), just intonation, free and strict style, square root form, simultaneous variations, twelve-tone composing, interval and duration controls, rhythmic modes, musical forms, modes, *jhala*, and other techniques that Harrison had picked up during his long career.

Harrison couldn't resist including occasional thoughts about various musical tra-ditions around the world and some of his favorite invented aphorisms: "The Knowl-edge of Madness (i.e. that we are mad), & the Vision of Reason (imagination in the light of the former)—the one is Humor, the other is Art. These are the essen-tials." The deliciously quirky compendium also collected some of what Ned Rorem called his "thrillingly indignant" views of the composer in society[48]—"[the public] seems to fancy that our greatest desire, even Need, is to Please it!"—and proclaimed Harrison's original credo: "Cherish, Conserve, Consider, Create." His work on the primer constituted Harrison's primary original creative output in 1966.

From the start, Harrison envisioned publishing his *Music Primer* in calligraphy and to that end spent many of his days in Oaxaca preparing elaborate test sheets of his texts in various colored inks. Ultimately these plans proved impractical, and it would be five more years before the *Music Primer*, in lovely but less ambitious cal-ligraphy, would be published.[49] Harrison then submitted it to the editorial board at Peters, but company officials were reluctant to establish the precedent of the music publisher releasing a textual book—especially, one supposes, one as eccentric as the *Music Primer*. However, the owner, Evelyn Hinrichsen, at Mills when Harrison was there and a supporter of Harrison's ever since, insisted.[50] His primer's homespun look evokes William Morris's individualistic handcrafting more than the West's industrial music factories.

Harrison's exegesis of his long-gestating thoughts on pedagogy came at an opportune time, because he would be putting them to daily use after his return from Mexico. Harrison's student Richard Dee, now studying at San Jose State College, had recommended Harrison to his teacher, violinist Gary Beswick. As the baby boom generation reached college age and swelled the ranks of applicants, many schools were willing to open the faculty to a greater range of experience than that represented by the degrees that Harrison lacked. A general education course on music from around the world, still an unusual course (though not quite as unheard of as when Harrison had studied with Cowell), would both attract enrollments to the department and look good on an upcoming accreditation report. After an interview, the school hired Harrison to teach world music during the spring 1967 semester.

He had mixed feelings about joining the academy. Eight years earlier, he had firmly told Brooklyn College that he had "gone on a teaching strike" because of his resentment of society's expectation that artists should support themselves by such means.[51] Virgil Thomson had warned, "I sometimes think the worst mischief a composer can get into is teaching."[52] Nevertheless, Harrison respected his own teachers such as Cowell and loved sharing his knowledge with students such as Bob Hughes. Practically, too, he had few other prospects for a steady paycheck once the Thorne Fellowship was complete. Although he continued to consider himself an independent artist, he later wrote a friend, "Nonetheless and ironically too, I've been institutionalized!"[53]

Harrison's San Jose State appointment letter arrived while he was still in Mexico. Toward the end of his stay in late 1966, Harrison's sister-in-law Dorothy and her new son accompanied Harrison's mother as they flew down to Mexico City. Harrison drove up to meet them and guide them around. When he visited, Remy Charlip, who had corresponded with but not seen Harrison since their disastrous falling-out in 1953, found Harrison a very different person from the one he had walked out on in New York. Gone was the dark, moody, and temperamental Lou, often unable to handle social situations, especially when drunk. Charlip saw emerging the sunny personality that would be so familiar to those who knew Harrison in his later years. "Really for a great deal of my life I was an awful prig," the older version of Harrison reflected. "I suppose I still look back on things that simply shock me that I said and did, the way I behaved."[54] Their friendship repaired, they remained close (with occasional eruptions of the old tensions) for the rest of Harrison's life.[55]

Another old New York friend came to visit San Francisco in November 1966, shortly after Harrison drove back to California. Composer Ned Rorem arrived to attend the premiere of his new *Water Music* that Bob Hughes, now the director of the Oakland Youth Symphony, had commissioned.[56] Harrison excitedly introduced his old New York friend to his gay community, even teaching him to Charleston at one of the SIR dances. Early in 1967, Hughes also arranged for the two old friends to perform together at the Old Spaghetti Factory, where he wanted to conduct William Walton's *Façade*, a blithely biting setting of Edith Sitwell poems for speaker and ensemble, in the restaurant's capacious performance space.

Across the room, packed with members of the Youth Orchestra and the audience both sitting and standing, Harrison spied amid a group of his acquaintances a man about his age with a pioneer's beard and an outdoorsman's build.

"Oh," he sighed, "isn't he beautiful?"

26

STARS UPON HIS FACE (1967–1969)

The footwear was a dead giveaway. It had been a long time since Lou Harrison had gone on a serious hike, which probably explained the utterly impractical sandals he was wearing when he showed up for this expedition. As much as he'd expressed his love for nature in music and poetry, his rambles through the hills of Marin County with his teenage lover John Dobson lay three decades behind him. He had only just given up smoking, a habit so heavy it had left his fingers yellowed from nicotine stains. Yet here he was, sandal-shod, carrying only the dozens of extra pounds he'd acquired in the intervening years and his Chinese dizi flute. Within a few miles, his companion Bob Hughes could see that Harrison was struggling to keep up with his knobby-kneed, hiking-booted companion, but the portly composer refused to slow or give up. "Lou was a bull of willpower," remembered Hughes.[1] At the end of the day, an exhausted Harrison smiled to the beautiful, bearded hike leader and began to play Chinese melodies on the dizi. Other hikers ambled by, doffed their backpacks, and listened to the pentatonic tunes echoing over the Sierra foothills.

Bill Colvig was born into a heritage of both trailblazing and music. His grandfather was a storied pioneer in Southern Oregon, and his father was a school band director. His uncle "Pinto" Colvig, a musician and vaudeville performer, became more famous as the voice of Walt Disney's Goofy and other characters. Like Harrison a native Oregonian, Bill was born in Medford in Southern Oregon and raised on the other side of Mount Shasta in Weed in far northern California. He grew up in a musical household where he learned piano, euphonium, and tuba and focused on trombone. Several of his five siblings became professional musicians, and one of Bill's brothers had even played with Harrison in the early music ensemble at San Francisco State.[2] Bill received a music scholarship to the University of the Pacific in Stockton.

Although he loved music, Bill was the Colvig who had an inclination for things mechanical. Around the household, he tinkered with gramophones, radios, and of course the family cars. In Stockton, he began taking more courses in electrical engineering than music and soon transferred to the University of California at Berkeley to continue his studies. During World War II he served as an electrician for the Army Signal Corps and, returning to the Bay Area after the war, took it up as his profession.[3]

It was a job ideally suited for Colvig's lifestyle, which focused on three passions: music, traveling, and the outdoors. An expert backpacker and a well-known guide for the California Sierra Club, he developed a routine of working as a contract electrician long enough to save up a few hundred dollars and then disappearing on a trip overseas or into the Sierras for as long as the money held out. It was on a Sierra Club outing in 1955 that Harrison's composer friend Ingolf Dahl met Bill Colvig, perched on a boulder, playing tunes by Francois Couperin on his recorder.[4]

Although an experienced mountaineer, having grown up climbing in the Alps, even Dahl had never met anyone quite like Colvig, who had a reputation for being such an energetic leader that he might leave a lagging group behind. Dahl was instantly attracted to his rugged physique, love of classical music, and endless collection of plaid flannel shirts. Although neither man wanted an exclusive relationship (Dahl was married), they became summer hiking partners, backpacking for weeks at a time in the Sierras. Through Dahl, the friendly and personable Colvig soon got to know a circle of composers and musicians, and the two continued to correspond affectionately when apart, discussing everything from family to aesthetics.

By the time Harrison caught his eye in the Old Spaghetti Factory in January 1967, Colvig, like Harrison, was just a few weeks shy of his fiftieth birthday. Both Ned Rorem and Harrison introduced themselves to the handsome man with the bushy beard. "The question," Rorem remembered, "was whether Bill was going home with Lou or with me."[5] That night, it was Lou. Even so, Rorem continued to make a play for Colvig after he left, via correspondence that spring.[6] By then, though, Harrison was in love.

Colvig was living on Francisco Street in San Francisco, and he mentioned that he had a room for rent. Harrison asked how much it was and showed up one day and paid him a month's rent. Colvig at the time was working on a contract for a new audiovisual system in San Francisco's War Memorial Opera House, and the two men traveled back and forth between Aptos and San Francisco to see each other. Although Colvig had never been one to settle down, Harrison persuaded him to come live with him in Aptos when his contract was complete.

"One reason I broke off my electrical career was that I was disgusted with the whole way things were going in our society, building armaments and all," said Colvig. "And I was part of that, even though I wasn't working on any so-called defense work. I felt better about getting into artistic pursuits. Lou seemed to need someone to help him. We were both tired of living alone and thought we each had something to offer the other."[7] Even though Harrison was teaching in San Jose only two days a week, the part-time salary, combined with the remaining years on the Thorne grant, gave the couple a welcome stability. Colvig found Harrison's cabin a mess and within days was busily putting up shelving, repairing the structure, and reorganizing the household.

When Harrison introduced Colvig to his mother, they got along famously almost at once. While Colvig set out to fix something, as he often did during their weekly visits, she waved her cigarette at Harrison. "It's great to have a man around the house again!" she said, oblivious of the irony. Later, his mother took Harrison aside and broached "the subject." In response, "I gave her the unconcealed & unblushing 'works,' including 'what do you do's'! History, morality, etc., a long talk."[8] Colvig's family accepted Harrison just as readily; several of his siblings lived in the Bay Area, and he often joined them for family music-making.[9]

To outsiders, Harrison's partnership with Colvig may have seemed like it was meant to be, given their complementary skills and interests, but Harrison's journals of the time reveal plenty of turbulence in their early relationship, which continued to flare up throughout their long and mostly happy lives together. Like any new marriage, their partnership didn't lack tensions. Harrison liked the network of mom-and-pop stores that he knew in Aptos, while Colvig preferred the convenience of the new chain stores that were beginning to take over the region. Harrison might spend whole days cloistered against the sunlight while absorbed in a score or other project, but Colvig would go crazy if he didn't get outside for hours every day. Colvig was quick to deflect Harrison's mercurial outbursts of temper and overreactions. Harrison worried that he was sometimes assuming the "hysteric" role his mother played in his parents' sometimes-fraught marriage (as he had with Charlip), with Colvig sometimes passive-aggressively staging what seemed to Lou to be power plays involving sex, flirting with other men and more. "It was a rocky, tempestuous thing from the beginning," Richard Dee remembered. "Bill was wild, untamed, and they had terrible arguments."[10]

Yet as Dee, Hughes, and other friends noted, the pair proved both complementary and compatible. "When I first met [Bill] I was in another period of hating music," having given up dance improvisation and remaining stuck on his large oratorio project, Harrison remembered. "Then Bill got me reinvolved because he comes from a long musical family."[11] In social situations where Harrison was the center of attention, Colvig graciously stepped out of the spotlight, but he refused to give up his own independence or distinctive identity. Yet they played, loved, and worked together, making history—by making instruments.

TO SUMMON THE FUTURE

> To make an instrument is in some strong sense to summon the future. It is as Robert Duncan has said of composing, "A volition. To seize from the air its form." Almost no pleasure is to be compared to the first tones, tests & perfections of an instrument one has just made. Nor are all instruments invented & over with, so to speak. The world is rich with models—but innumerable forms, tones & powers await their summons from the mind & hand. Make an instrument—you will learn more in this way than you can imagine.
>
> —Lou Harrison [12]

Another crucial and historic dimension to their relationship began when Harrison showed Colvig some of the instruments he had built or experimented with: his Lucite *piri*, his homemade psaltery, and an *mbira*, an African instrument of plucked metal tines. Immediately, Colvig's mechanical mind saw how they could be improved. He began to experiment with designs for a monochord, an instrument that, although it might have more than the single string of its name, has been used since the days of Pythagoras as a standard for measuring tunings.[13] Colvig designed it so that the distance between the two bridges was exactly one meter, enabling them to slide an intermediate stopping point to an exact place along a meter stick to get a particular ratio. Harrison worked out the math for various tunings and copied them onto paper guides to be laid out next to the ruler. They could then transfer the pitches to the strings of a homemade metal-strung harp they therefore called a "transfer harp."[14] Although Harrison couldn't bend pitches on it as he could his psaltery, he had always loved the sound of the harp.

Harrison featured other Colvig instruments in a new piece for San Jose State violinist Gary Beswick that spring. Colvig built several versions of an *mbira*, including a *marimbula*, an Afro-Cuban bass version mounted on a large box resonator.[15] The fourth of Harrison's chamber violin concertos, *Music for Violin with Various Instruments, European, Asian, and African*, in some ways resembles his recent *Concerto in Slendro*, including its three-movement structure, but opens with a form resembling a mixed-meter estampie.[16]

The multicultural accompaniment to the violin consists of Harrison's reed organ (occasionally used as a percussion instrument with Cowell-esque clusters), drums, and an Asian psaltery (the *zheng*). The accompaniment of the middle movement consists entirely of drones from the justly tuned organ, as in his *Prelude for Piri and Reed Organ*. Harrison asks for the otherwise chromatic violin to tune certain notes to the seventh and eleventh harmonics of the droned key center, resulting in startling pitches quite distant from their tempered counterparts. In the final movement, the three accompanying musicians all take up Colvig's *mbiras* to create cascades of bell-like tones from the metal tines, providing an entrancing backdrop for those unforgettable Harrison violin melodies.

As Harrison's stamina grew, he joined Colvig on hikes throughout the region, often up to nearby Fremont Peak but as far as Northern California's Mt. Lassen—"days filled with hikes and instrument making," he wrote.[17] Eventually they developed a routine of hiking on one weekday per week when Harrison wasn't teaching. Harrison even co-led some of Colvig's Sierra Club hikes. More frequently, Colvig would disappear on his own or with a Sierra Club group. Harrison jotted in his notebook,

> Weary,
> But light of pack,
> The mountaineer comes back,
> With air & light & stars upon
> His face.[18]

MUSIC FOR BILL AND ME

The first thing the audience saw as it filed into the auditorium were colorful screens behind three music stands, each bearing a folder emblazoned with ornate patterns. The music in each folder sometimes looked like conventional Western music, with the usual little black notes hand-drawn on staffs, but more often just rows of numbers. Next to the music stands stood instruments that looked strange to 1967 Americans: the beautiful wooden box of Harrison's *zheng* zither, the forest of pipes in

Colvig's *sheng* reed mouth organ, the *yangqin* dulcimer up on a stand with its dozens of strings and delicate hammers, and a small table with delicate brass cymbals, a bamboo flute, small wooden slats tied together, and other exotica.

Just as unusual were the musicians who strode onstage: a slim, mustached thirty-something man sporting a white shirt topped by a large gold pendant; a rangy, bow-legged, long-haired, bearded man in striped shirt and black pants; an Asian woman elegantly clad in a black Chinese silk dress with a white pattern; and a stout, goateed, middle-aged man wearing an old-fashioned Western bolo tie, a red and yellow Chinese shirt (handmade from silk fabric), black slacks, and sandals. After the first piece, he began to explain the strange but beguiling music the audience had just heard.

Just as Harrison was drawn into Colvig's passion for the outdoors, his new boyfriend immersed himself in Lou's activities and gradually became a full creative partner in playing the music and ultimately in making the instruments themselves. Harrison taught Colvig to play Chinese instruments, but instead of the psaltery, the former brass player gravitated to the wind instruments. Colvig specialized in the *sheng*, an instrument that requires a fair amount of lung power. Harrison showed him what he could, and then they received further lessons from David Mingyue Liang (the son of Harrison's teacher Liang Tsai-Ping), who was by then a graduate student in ethnomusicology at UC Berkeley. Later, Harrison wrote an extensive ethnomusicology article about the history and dispersal of these Asian mouth organs.[19] Thanks to his new position at San Jose State, Harrison invited Liang Tsai-Ping himself to give a concert there when he came to visit in May 1967.

With Hughes busy as a professional musician in San Francisco and Oakland, Harrison, Dee, and Colvig more often formed a trio, with outdoorsman Colvig reluctantly acquiescing to long pants instead of his usual hiking shorts and boots. They were often joined by Lily Chin, a student from China who had initially sought out Harrison at San Jose State. An accomplished singer of European music, Chin wanted to learn about the traditional music of the country she had left behind when fleeing the Maoist regime. Harrison taught her *zheng*, and she soon became an accomplished player on several instruments. She also helped by translating the Chinese characters of Harrison's collection of manuscripts and books.

Harrison's ensemble began to play more and more frequently around the area at colleges, community centers, women's clubs, and public schools, to audiences ranging up to two hundred or more people. All told, this ensemble would give more than three hundred concerts throughout the Bay Area (and even one gig in New York) in the late 1960s into the '70s.[20] Harrison's ample collection of instruments allowed them to create programs up to an hour and a half long, with a variety of chamber realizations in simultaneous variations, solo works, or melodic pieces with simple percussion accompaniment. The second half of the concert often consisted of new works—not only Harrison's compositions for the instruments, but also an occasional piece by Dee or Colvig, as Harrison had encouraged them to compose for their instruments. Harrison and Colvig also designed and constructed the colorful screens and music folders.[21]

Harrison and Colvig tuned those eye-catching porcelain bowls to their specific pitches by pouring water into them, and they played them with chopsticks, creating the Chinese version of the Indian *jaltarang* that Harrison had used in his *Strict Songs*. (On many a visit to shops in Chinatown, Harrison received quizzical looks when he set about tapping on the kitchenware on display.) Once, at a gig at a restaurant, the group set up their instruments and tuned the porcelain bowls using an eyedropper for precision, and then they sat down to enjoy a pre-concert dinner. When they performed, however, they were startled to hear, instead of the characteristically delicate, bell-like tones from the bowls, dull, pitchless "thunks." It turned out that, over time, a layer of bubbles had formed between the water and the bowl, dampening its resonance. They learned later that a layer of glycerin would keep the bubbles from sticking to the underwater surfaces, but Harrison wanted to find a permanent solution.

Then he remembered that the ancient Korean orchestras used an instrument of tuned metal bars called a *banghyang*. These bars also made bell-like sounds but only had to be tuned once, with little risk of going out of tune or losing resonance. Bell-like sounds had always been a central and characteristic color in Harrison's palette, from his affinity for metal instruments in his percussion works to the celesta in the orchestra. Once, when inspecting Harry Partch's collection of invented wooden and string instruments, Harrison had suggested that he use metal as well. "I like wood and bamboo," Partch replied. "Why don't *you* do metal?"[22]

Now, years later, Harrison followed his advice. Colvig started experimenting with cutting aluminum tubes out of one-inch conduit. At first they tuned them by ear, but Colvig the electrician thought of another solution and ordered a $90 oscilloscope kit. The device allowed him to display waveforms generated when the tubes were struck and precisely compare them to the desired frequencies. For this instrument of aluminum tubes, which they simply called "bells," Harrison decided on a just-intonation diatonic scale in D, a five-limit major scale that opened up many possibilities.[23] "I was aware that I was reaching toward Asian practice within a diatonic set-up from Europe and the Mediterranean," he recalled, "[and also trying] to find how many of those Asian . . . schemas would be possible within the basic diatonic system. It was a conjunction idea—a larger tuning from the West which could be found in a perfectly presentable Asian style."[24]

They mounted the tubes on a rack by threading cord through holes in the tubes, like the bars of a vibraphone. Next, Colvig began experimenting with aluminum bars to get lower pitches. Harrison called these instruments *gendèr* (pronounced with a hard "G"), after a similar-sounding Javanese metallophone. Born out of necessity, this move to invented metal instruments would soon herald a new direction in Harrison's music.

One instrument Harrison bought with his salary from San Jose State at that time was a small Lyon & Healy diatonic harp that lacked the complicated system of chromatic pedals—and many of the strings—of the familiar large concert harp and had nylon strings rather than the metal strings of his transfer harp. The first piece he wrote for his new instrument was *Music for Bill and Me*, a slow and tender pentatonic melody, easily played by novice harpists such as Harrison and Colvig. One evening Harrison, Colvig, Hughes, Harrison's friend Beverly Bellows (who happened to be a concert harpist), and other friends squeezed into Harrison's cabin after a concert, Harrison eager to show off his new instrument. He proposed a party game: that each of them write a little piece for the troubadour harp. Harrison, in about half an hour, sketched out *Beverly's Troubadour Piece*. Like *Music for Bill and Me*, it is pentatonic without bar lines, but its invigorating dance rhythms resemble his *Avalokiteshvara*, and as in that earlier piece, Harrison later added a percussion ostinato.[25]

In the fall of 1967, Colvig took his savings from his opera house job and made plans for a visit to Harrison's cherished Oaxaca, Mexico. Meanwhile, Harrison's chairman at the San Jose State music department was so pleased with his Music in World Cultures class that spring that he offered to continue Harrison's contract, so Colvig traveled solo. While he was gone, Harrison ruminated about how much his life had changed as he reached the half-century mark. By late 1967, the fifty-year-old Harrison was finally beginning to settle down, at least by conventional standards. He had found a creative and romantic partner and moved in with the love of his life, established a regular performing ensemble, mastered yet another form of Asian music, and secured stable employment teaching music. In a poem to Ned Rorem, Harrison called his fiftieth year the "finest yet of all I'd lived."

> the year in which we know we've likeliest not
> another half to live, & thus impatient,
> proud to live at last most as we want to, &
>   slough off false duty.[26]

One night, he took out his pen and carefully began a letter to his lover.

> I review in my heart some of our beautiful lovings—I see the beauty of your person—I smell the incense of you, I remember sweet warm hair and flesh—your manhood your lovely face and eyes and smiles and kisses, the odd bouncing bow-legged way you walk— your melodious voice and much else and I am warm and happy and I remember you close and I anticipate and wait your return. Ingolf and others are right, I think, we very likely were made for one another. This house feels our house, with you temporarily absent.[27]

That fall, Harrison was composing a letter to Colvig at his desk at San Jose State, when through the ventilation system wafted the acrid smell of tear gas.[28]

UP RISING

> Bill has convinced me of the permanence and the reality of evil and I think
> that evil is non-empathy, an unwillingness or even inability to want to help the
> happiness of another [and instead] want to get solely one's own relief.
> The pressure is on us all;
> It is unremitting.
> We are not responsible for it.
> We are responsible to know of it
> & to help one another in its
> remission & relief.
> —Lou Harrison, December 17, 1967[29]

In November 1967, Harrison's good friend, the back-slapping English owner of the Sticky Wicket, Victor Jowers, died. Officially, the cause was aplastic anemia, an inability to produce blood cells. Although no one could know with absolute certainty, Harrison knew that this disease had one obvious cause: atomic radiation. In his *Political Primer*, Harrison had raged against radiation from atomic tests then blanketing the western United States, turning those deadly particles into music with his Geiger counter, and now Victor Jowers, who had witnessed atomic tests close up during his work as a journalist, was another victim of those particles. (Marie Curie died from the same illness.) The government's poisoning of its own people was no longer an abstract injustice to Harrison—now it was heartrendingly personal. For the memorial service, Harrison wrote his poignant *In Memory of Victor Jowers* for clarinet and piano.

Jowers's government-caused death was just the latest political outrage to infuriate Harrison, and he was hardly alone. By 1967 it looked as though the seams of the country were unraveling. In the so-called Long Hot Summer of that year, the inner cities of Newark and Detroit and scores of other urban ghettos exploded in flames. Protests against the war in Vietnam were spreading too, including a huge demonstration in San Francisco in April. In October, tens of thousands of marchers converged on Washington DC and were met with fixed bayonets.

Many protesters targeted Dow Chemical, makers of the horrific, skin-searing explosive napalm. On October 18, police beat and teargassed dozens of students at a University of Wisconsin sit-in protesting Dow recruiters on campus. At Harrison's employer, San Jose State College, word went out that those same recruiters would be on campus on November 20, the day after Jowers's memorial service. As picketers surrounded the San Jose State administration building, just up the street from the music building, 150 police officers moved in, wielding billy clubs and tear gas. To Harrison they resembled "Buck Rogers storm troopers."[30] California governor Ronald Reagan threatened to fire any faculty supporters of the protesters.

Just as he focused earlier outrage into his *Political Primer*, Harrison now directed his creative energies outward, toward a society that he and many others viewed as lethally misdirected. "My personal reasons for composing the works that I have of the 'war & peace' kind are that there are some times when one wants to stand and scream aloud—'This is not right' . . . or 'This is all wrong' and personal frustration led me to express my rage in music," he wrote.[31] When Harrison and Gerhard Samuel met to discuss programming the 1968 Cabrillo Festival, Harrison suggested that the time was right for the long-delayed premiere of his protest oratorio, *Nova Odo*. In fact, Harrison proposed an entire program of his "peace pieces," including two not yet composed, and Samuel agreed.

Harrison's first *Peace Piece*, at least in name, was his 1953 *Little Song on the Atom Bomb*, which he began to revise for the summer's concert.[32] To it, he added a choral setting of "An Invocation for the Health of All Beings," a cherished Buddhist text from the Mettā Sutta, a sutra devoted to benevolence. Rather than venting his anger about the state of America's military-industrial complex and the deadly government policies it controlled, that consoling, encouraging spirit permeates Harrison's oceanic *Peace Piece #1*. Harrison set the section, for unison chorus, much as he had the texts for the *Nova Odo*, accompanied by returning high trombone melody, as in *At the Tomb of Charles Ives*, and filigree patterns on harps and percussion that foreshadow Harrison's future gamelan-like textures. He finished it just in time for an April concert arranged by Bob Hughes at Berkeley's First Unitarian Church. Then, just three days before the concert, came the word that Martin Luther King Jr. had been assassinated. In shock and grief, Harrison added a dedication to the civil rights leader.

His next *Peace Piece* was not so gentle. His friend Robert Duncan had arisen from bed late one night and, unable to contain his fury at Lyndon Johnson and the Vietnam War, grabbed a sheet of paper and wrote the poem "Up Rising," a single-sentence cry of anger. As in *Little Song on the Atom Bomb*, Harrison, to focus attention on the ferocious words, sets them as an unmeasured recitative, accompanied only by sustained string drones. At the Cabrillo Festival in August 1968, Duncan's fiery poetry nearly scorched the listeners:

> the burning of homes and the torture of mothers and fathers and children,
> > their hair a-flame, screaming in agony, but
> in the line of duty, for the might and enduring fame
> > of Johnson, for the victory of American will over its victims,
> in terror and hatred of all communal things[33]

The piece ended, and the stunned audience sat silent. An audience member finally voiced a "boo!" One of the bass players immediately glared at him and responded, firmly enough to fill the silent auditorium, "Shame!" The crowd exploded in such applause that the critics gave the victory to the "doves" at Cabrillo.[34]

Harrison's 1968 Cabrillo triumph proved to be Gerhard Samuel's last hurrah at the festival. The conductor's ambition and budget demands created tensions with the local board. In particular, Samuel had a weakness for producing operas whose expensive productions finally led to a budget crisis in 1968, forcing cancellation of the festival's final week. Harrison continued to support his friend Samuel and was irate when the board could not come to terms with him. Suddenly, the board had to find a music director for the next season. Desperate, they offered the job to Bob Hughes, who declined.[35]

Finally they hired the conductor at nearby Santa Clara University, Richard Williams, who, however, had his own orchestra—meaning the musicians of the orchestra Samuel had built up would not be asked back for the 1969 festival. Incensed, Harrison sent a letter to the local newspaper, publicly renouncing his lifetime festival membership.[36] (Nevertheless, Williams performed Harrison's *First Suite for Strings*.) Although the scaled-back festival allowed the organization to recover its stability, the board recognized the need to find a new permanent director. One especially prominent name came up that Hughes and Harrison endorsed immediately: Carlos Chávez.

Harrison had become reacquainted with Chávez during his 1966 trip to UCLA, and he greatly admired the distinguished Mexican composer. Like Samuel, Chávez recruited a local orchestra but demanded an especially high degree of professionalism.

He brought to Cabrillo international contacts and a professional stature even greater than Samuel's—and an abiding respect for Harrison's music.

FOR JOHN CAGE

Another reunion with an old colleague, however, didn't go so well. Just as he found himself at odds with US government policy, Harrison also opposed the prevailing trends in contemporary music. Not only had the tonal melodicism he and Chávez championed gone out of fashion, such styles were being actively attacked. "These days," he mused to his student Kerry Lewis, "people think a piece of serious music can't possibly be of any significance unless it's profoundly unattractive."[37] It didn't help that the standard-bearer for the most radical composers, and the one to gain most national attention, was none other than his old friend John Cage. Although Harrison consistently composed for the first performance, rather than fads or posterity, and would become a model of a maverick artist, he bristled at the success of Cage and of other composers whose new aesthetic he could not bear.

To Harrison's dismay, not only had Cage stubbornly stuck to compositional chance procedures, but he also entered a phase of designing extravagant circuses of artistic chaos, successors to the infamous theater piece that Harrison had laughed off at Black Mountain in 1952. Now Cage's work abandoned not just a cherished style but even the very idea of what it meant, to Harrison, to be an artist: making aesthetic choices, crafting coherent creations. "John doesn't really write what you call music anymore," Harrison told Lewis. Cage's monumental 1969 multimedia extravaganza *HPSCHD*, which grabbed headlines in *Time, Newsweek,* and the *New York Times,* bore more than a passing resemblance to San Francisco's 1966 Trips Festival and similar psychedelic happenings, and a cynic might have sniffed opportunism in Cage's artistic path.

In the fall of 1969, Cage moved to a residency at the University of California Davis, a couple hours' drive from Santa Cruz. Toward the end of his stay, Cage drove down to see Harrison and another old friend, Norman O. Brown, who had invited him to the University of California Santa Cruz, where Brown was a professor of humanities. Harrison's friend Charles Shere recalled "seeing them, both guests of honor at a party in Olive Cowell's house, sitting all evening on either end of the fireplace like bronze Chinese lions, not speaking to one another,"[38] and Harrison's journal suggests that this reunion with his old partner didn't go well either: "Item: I am, of course, fearfully (& somewhat justly) inferior. In my dreams, for example, I labor towards being 'with it' (sexually, artistically, & socially)—& in them I am surrounded with 'meaning ful' activity which to me is without meaning. Well, I am the Loser, tho I wonder what 'reality' it is that I actually lose. Therefore Fuck John Cage, if need be . . . he is a prude (with Norman Brown) about pot (they have a pact together never to touch such stuffs without a mutual permission)."[39]

At a time when popular culture enjoyed a greater cultural cachet than ever in American history, Harrison's own aesthetic gravitated toward the classical, the (Silver) courtly, and the esoteric. And even in his niche of music, he was an outsider, ignored by Cagean experimentalists and dissonance-drenched serialists. "I refuse to be held back by our own culture," he defiantly told an interviewer, "and in this sense, I regard myself as experimental and avant garde."[40] Yet Harrison's insecure side couldn't help fretting about whether his lack of "success" on Cage's level made him a loser. Elsewhere he wrote, with envy but also with a genuine concern for his art, "Item: John Cage tells the young, over and over again in various ways, that they don't have to know anything. It is a good way to become popular—it always has been—and Mr. Cage is quite popular indeed in certain circles. Up to a point customers are best left ignorant, he tells you, and he has the customers to back it up."[41] Their complex, sibling-like relationship would later relax, and Harrison would value Cage's friendship for the rest of his life.

"I myself am glad that I was not born a moment later," he wrote in his journal at the zenith (or nadir) of '60s musical modernism. "The period from Pythagoras 26 centuries ago thru Ptolemy 18 centuries ago (even Porphyry?) is surely the most wondrous time of music anywhere, of intelligent beauty, of loveliness enabled in Apollo's rules (regulations)—the inner furies just barely contained by the form without."[42] Although Harrison was one of American music's great innovators, unlike Cage he never rejected the vast acreage of music's past. He had happily confessed to being "a Fuddy Dud" about old treasures he could use to make new music.[43]

MUSIC OF THE PEOPLES OF THE WORLD

Harrison had his own platform for propagating his démodé ideas about music back on campus. At San Jose State, Harrison's world music course proved increasingly popular as word spread, pleasing the administration. The class focused on art music traditions, principally from Asia, but had little time for folk traditions.[44] He lectured, demonstrated instruments, and played sound examples from records. Enrollments were large enough that he was able to convince the department to fund Richard Dee as his teaching assistant and to tolerate the occasional absences necessitated by Harrison's composing career.

Like his own teachers, Harrison accepted individual composition students, although he wasn't paid extra to teach them. Like Schoenberg, Harrison would ask students to bring in whatever they were working on, in any style, and offer them advice. Harrison relied less on exercises like those Cowell had given him, although he would sometimes assign students to write melodies in different modes or tunings.[45] Instead, he freely distributed his *Music Primer*, which advised his students, "Always compose as if there's plenty of paper," and "Write out your music with space in & around it for changes," and "Compose Rhythm & Tune—these are the important things."[46]

"Every time I came in to see him, I was inspired about how open things were and how being a composer allowed you the opportunity to think about everything in the world," remembered composer David Lang, who studied with Harrison at age seventeen when Harrison filled in for a year at Stanford in 1974–1975. In his classes, said Lang, "the definition of what I was able to get into a piece of music grew much larger. When you study music, it's who gets your soul that counts. And when you learn you can be experimental, that's a big revelation."[47]

"Lou ... looked at the first draft of my first composition for *degung* and gave me a lesson on writing that has stayed with me my whole life," remembered student Jon Siddall. "The main melody I was working on had some good qualities but was not well focused. He counseled me to look at the best part of the melody, study it and let the melody tell me where it wanted to go."[48]

"A visit to Lou was always an inspiration," said his student David Doty, "not merely because of the beauty of his music, but because of his enthusiasm and his eagerness to share his latest ideas and discoveries."[49]

Harrison's success led to more classes. Soon he was teaching orchestration and a course in American music. In a proposal perhaps designed to maximize enrollment, the administration even asked him to teach a course on music and sex. Harrison found that the students of the free love generation came to him knowing almost nothing about sex, and Harrison by necessity became their sex-ed instructor before he could ever get to the music. (The course failed to attract the hoped-for enrollments and was discontinued.)

Although behind his back, some students and faculty grumbled about his outspoken antiwar politics and gay advocacy, Harrison also found common ground with other members of the faculty.[50] In addition to his *Music for Violin and Various Instruments* for violinist Gary Beswick, he wrote his short *Haiku* for the choir director, William Erlendson. For Erlendson and the director of the percussion ensemble, Tony Cirone, Harrison finally completed his large-scale work for chorus and percussion, setting to music the poetry of his friend from New York and Black Mountain, Robert Duncan. Duncan was now teaching poetry classes at the SIR community center and San Francisco State College; after setting Duncan's antiwar screed for his *Peace Piece*, Harrison returned to the oratorio on Duncan's poetry that he had begun while in Mexico.

Harrison had chosen Duncan's "A Set of Romantic Hymns," a typically Duncan-esque whirlwind collage of sometimes-obscure images, here representing ebullient beauty (symbolized by the underworld-defying power of Orpheus's lyre) amid the ever-shifting dance of life. Like Harrison, Duncan was fascinated with the secrets of life unlocked by modern science, and he depicted the recently discovered mechanisms of DNA as an intricate ballet: "The dancers cross over to the other side, / change places and again divide."[51] Harrison thus envisioned an elaborate work that alternated singing and choreography, all accompanied by a large percussion orchestra of fifteen players and over a hundred instruments; he titled it *Orpheus: For the Singer to the Dance.*

Harrison set the first of Duncan's hymns, a celebration of the power of beauty, as a powerful unison pentatonic melody, as he had in the recently completed last movement of his *Nova Odo*. However, he departed from that model in his innovative setting of a stanza depicting an intimate romantic scene, in which a soloist sings over an a cappella chorus, which hums unsynchronized melodic fragments that Harrison dubbed "tunelets" and whispers fragments of the text. A unique beehive texture emerges beneath the solo line that shows that, for all his disdain of Cage's aesthetic direction in the 1960s, Harrison was not above choosing chance when it suited his expressive purposes.

Harrison set the following hymn to a darkly chromatic interval-control melody and the next in a majestic Indonesian *pelog* mode (like the final *Strict Song*). For the fourth hymn, half the chorus takes the place of the resting percussion orchestra, rhythmically speaking and shouting in their role as the nagging memory of a reincarnated Orpheus. The soloist sings in a strangely chromatic mode while the chorus tells of how Orpheus "turnd anew the keys, the strings / shadowd, the rays of Apollo's mode / alterd."[52] The refreshing pentatonic mode from the opening returns for the final hymn, but now with newly colorful chromatic alterations here and there, for a powerful climax with images of the eternal dance of chromosomes. In the quietly dying end, Orpheus the musician, perhaps like Harrison himself, laments that he has "only this song to send / to take my place among the dancers."[53]

For the choreographic interludes between the choral hymns, Harrison resurrected, like Orpheus himself tried to do with his lover, Eurydice, the never-performed 1941 *Labyrinth* for percussion orchestra. He retained the original movement titles, with their evocation of a youthful mysticism connected with the earth, ancestry, and the labyrinth within our own "brainmeat" (Duncan's term): "Ode," "Passage through Dreams," "Seed," and "Image in the Soil."

With a text much longer than that of *Nova Odo* or *Strict Songs*, the eight-movement, forty-minute *Orpheus* is a challenging score with sometimes awkward juxtapositions of his youthful and mature styles. Harrison has to hurry through much of Duncan's often elliptical imagery, and its complex language and themes are difficult for an audience to follow. *Orpheus* is nevertheless a colorful work of striking drama that includes some of Harrison's most innovative choral writing. It finally premiered at San Jose State in 1969, and Harrison would continue to find a way to make the medium of chorus and percussion work, including in his first film score.[54]

NUPTIAE

Another local countercultural institution Harrison found via Robert Duncan was the Poetry Center at San Francisco State College, where Harrison met the poet Kenneth Rexroth and the writer and filmmaker James Broughton. (He had previously met Broughton a quarter century earlier, after one of his percussion concerts.) Harrison had seen Broughton's controversial experimental film *The Bed* when it brought a lively, anarchic celebration of sexual freedom to underground cinemas during 1967's Summer of Love. Although a gay activist, Broughton had married artist Suzanne Hart in a self-designed three-day outdoor ritual presided over by Alan Watts and filmed by legendary avant-grade filmmaker Stan Brakhage. In 1968, Broughton began to turn Brakhage's footage into the short film *Nuptiae*, which contemplated roles of the sexes and Jungian dualities. Knowing that the film would have no dialogue, he considered a musical soundtrack essential and so sent a letter to Harrison, asking him to score it.

Since the days of working with film students at Black Mountain and his brief flirtation with a Hollywood job, Harrison had wanted to compose a film score, as Antheil, Thomson, Copland, and other friends had done. For this meditation on marriage, Harrison envisioned a soundtrack with many bells and also a chorus, for which he wrote his own text. Since the instruments would be restricted to whatever he could bring to the recording studio, Harrison chose the Philippine *kulintang* ensemble he had purchased during his trip to Hawaii's East–West Center in 1963: a rack of horizontal gongs and some larger hanging gongs similar to the instruments of the Indonesian gamelan, and with a tuning also related to the pentatonic *slendro* tuning of Indonesia. Harrison's tintinnabulous composition, though, bears little resemblance to either traditional Philippine music or gamelan music. When the chorus comes in, the singers are accompanied by overlapping percussion ostinatos, as in his *Joyous and Solemn Processions*.

But as lovely as his music for the film turned out, this wedding of music and images, so like so many first marriages, didn't work out so well, at least for Harrison. When he, Colvig, Richard Dee, and Hughes showed up to record the soundtrack at a San Mateo studio, Harrison worked carefully to "hit" or synchronize certain music events to images in the film. However, because of Broughton's preferences, inattention, reediting, or (most likely) limitations of the equipment available, Harrison was disappointed at the film's premiere to find virtually all such efforts to have been futile. "[*Nuptiae* is] when I learned that if you want something to happen at a given place, [and] you write for that, then it won't be put there," he said. "I was just writing music to the images. That's when I learned that isn't the way the filmmaker thinks. The filmmaker thinks in units. So, after that I made wallpaper music for films, and it worked perfectly well."[55]

Still, the screening of *Nuptiae* at the San Francisco Museum of Modern Art that May, along with productions of his *Orpheus* and the long-awaited second performance of *Pacifika Rondo* conducted by Bob Hughes with the Oakland Symphony Youth Orchestra around the same time, betokened Harrison's growing recognition in San Francisco. He soon received invitations to performances of his music in New York, Pittsburgh, and elsewhere. But while Harrison's growing network of friends and colleagues fueled a burst of productivity of small works, Harrison hadn't created an entirely new large-scale piece since 1963's *Pacifika Rondo*. The demands imposed by his study and performance of Chinese music (and before that, his improvised dance accompaniment), his new teaching and other faculty duties, and of course his new relationship with his life partner, Bill, had enormously enriched his life and his musical palette but had left little room for the long stretches of concentration needed to create ambitious productions.

But there was more to it. "The older I get and more complex life becomes," he said in a forum with Virgil Thomson at a 1968 conference at the University of Pittsburgh, "writing for solo instruments in a simple fashion is more pleasurable than writing very large scores for a great number of players that [necessitate] very expensive and difficult rehearsals. And I wonder if this isn't also because of my contact with the Asian cultures," he added with a laugh, "because it does seem that all overpopulated cultures eventually wind up with chamber music!"[56]

One large-scale genre, though, continued to haunt his thoughts: opera. Certainly he was not the first composer to feel compelled to add a major dramatic form to his list of works. "Most composers will agree that opera is a risky medium," Aaron

Copland once said. "However, the reward for writing a GOOD opera is so great that the temptation is to forget the problems and barge ahead. To have the courage to cope with opera regularly, the urge has to be so strong that little else in music attracts you. I am not such. For me opera was a really problematical form—*la FORME fatale*—as I called it after my experience with *The Tender Land*."[57]

Harrison's next work would become the *forme fatale* of his career, perhaps his greatest love and his bitterest disappointment.

27

YOUNG CAESAR AND OLD GRANDDAD (1969–1974)

Go Gaius—
  at the court of Nicomedes
  there are chances,
  there are riches,
  there are many many many many loves
—Lou Harrison[1]

One day in the 1930s, while Lou Harrison was working as a dance accompanist at Mills College, he witnessed a group of young San Franciscans pull up to the college theater in their car. An older woman directed them to unload some pieces of wood from the back of the car—and within minutes, it magically metamorphosed into an enchanting window onto a mythic world.

This was Harrison's introduction to the Red Gate Players and their entirely portable production of Chinese shadow puppetry. The medium fascinated him even then; one of his favorite works was Manuel de Falla's charming setting of the puppet scene from *Don Quixote, El Retablo de Maese Pedro* (*Master Peter's Puppet Show*). Ever since, he had wanted to make his own puppet opera. His 1960s investigations of Asian music revived that notion: The ancient puppet dramas of China and Indonesia could represent far more elaborate settings and events than were practical to stage in conventional opera.

And now he'd have the chance, thanks to a commission from the Encounters new music series in Pasadena. He proposed a puppet opera, which, unlike his one-act *Rapunzel*, would be a full evening production. The organization agreed, arranging for more funding from the Judith S. Thomas Foundation to cover the production costs. Harrison's first idea was to adapt a Native American story for the kachina puppets that the Hopi use as sacred representations of natural and supernatural forces—but, as he told Colvig one night, not long after one of their trips to the city to attend a SIR function, he couldn't find a suitable story.

"Why don't you do a gay subject?" Colvig replied.[2]

What a splendid idea, Harrison thought, and he searched his memory. He'd already used a story from the historian Suetonius's chronicles of Rome about Julius

Caesar's father-in-law, Cinna, as source material for a dramatic production. Now he remembered another Suetonius story about Caesar's dalliance with the king of Bithynia, long before he became emperor. As with Cinna, the ancient story suited the times. At the height of the Vietnam War, Harrison's puppet opera would recount the tale of a young citizen of a powerful, militaristic Western kingdom, expected by society to fulfill the roles of husband, father, and soldier. Yet first he is assigned to go and confront the king of a province of the sensual East, where he encounters beauty and love. Without abandoning his duty, Gaius (Julius Caesar) gives himself openly to these pleasures and suffers the contempt of Western society as a result.

As Harrison delved into the history, though, he realized that the story posed dramatic challenges. For audiences to understand the significance of the opera's events, the libretto would have to explain unfamiliar history at the risk of overshadowing the characters' conflicts and motivations. When Harrison composed *Rapunzel*, he had a libretto ready-made: Morris's dramatic poem. Not here; creating a libretto for this exposition-heavy story required a skilled writer. He wrote to playwright Jack Larson, who had written the libretto for Virgil Thomson's 1958 opera *Lord Byron*, asking whether he would be willing to take on *Young Caesar*. He wasn't willing, but he put the word out among writers, and one of his friends, Robert Gordon, approached Harrison at a San Francisco performance of a Satie puppet opera and volunteered to take on the tricky task.

Gordon began by conscientiously and carefully researching the story and the period—maybe too carefully, because the first draft he sent Harrison read less like a libretto than a historical novel and was the size of the latter. At Harrison's insistence, Gordon whittled at the text over and over, down to fourteen scenes (each, Harrison estimated, the size of his complete *Rapunzel* libretto), but resisted cutting any further.[3]

Next, Harrison had to find someone to make the puppets and puppeteers to realize a production about a gay love affair—decades before such themes were commonly accepted on the concert stage. An artist friend began work on the puppets, but when the work dragged, Harrison enlisted an art director at San Francisco's public television station, KQED, Bill Jones, to help create a set of over twenty rod puppets, which ultimately required seven puppeteers to manipulate. At least two puppeteers that Harrison contacted to direct the performance pulled out, and several of the final group had never been puppeteers before.

Colvig helped out by building the stage and lighting, and as the increasingly elaborate project progressed, Harrison found himself painting the moving backdrops as well as composing. Harrison's do-it-yourself method, reminiscent of his old days in San Francisco making instruments from junk and rounding up dancers to play them, turned out to have downsides as well as advantages. Instead of simplifying the production, this puppet opera wound up entailing more work and maybe even more expense than if he had relied on a conventional opera company. As expenses approached the budget limit, a worried Harrison met with the organizers of the commissioning organization, and to his relief, they proved so supportive of his concept that they even increased the budget. Harrison personally paid Gordon $150 a month, enough to live on at the time, while he worked on the libretto.[4]

For months through 1970 and stretching into the next year, *Young Caesar* consumed Harrison, with Gordon's libretto proving especially knotty. To give the audience the complex background and context needed to understand the action, he proposed a narrator. After experimenting with using a male chorus to provide narration, Harrison decided to make the narrator a central solo role, patterned after the *tayu* storyteller of Japanese *bunraku* puppetry, who not only sets scenes but also describes action happening onstage. Narration also helped overcome another limitation: the puppets' limited movement capabilities. An action as simple as Gaius picking up his infant son had to be described instead of acted, and at times the narration would crowd out the characters' dialogue.

With so much explaining to do and an entirely prose text, Harrison realized, conventional arias, which generally use poetic texts to allow characters to express their emotional states, wouldn't work. To get through the prose exposition as quickly as possible, Harrison relied almost entirely on recitatives (which sometimes obscure the opera's most alluring musical moments), often modeling them on the psalmody of the Gregorian chant he had learned as a teenager. As in a chanted psalm, each line would have many rhythmically free syllables chanted on a central psalm tone or "tenor" surrounded by an introductory intonation motive and a termination motive.[5]

Harrison added another exotic element to narration and dialogue that he remembered from the Chinese operas he had seen as a youth: punctuating the vocal melodies with percussive woodblock sounds.[6] Harrison also applied the lesson he learned from Henry Cowell's incidental music for *Fanati*, where percussion ostinatos bubbled under the onstage action, a technique in turn inspired by Japanese Noh drama. In *Young Caesar*, those ostinatos add texture and depth to the recitatives and sometimes suspense to the scenes.

But the opera still lacked what Harrison called the audience's "take-home pay" of such a work: beautiful arias. "When I wanted to make an aria, I had to extract sentences and repeat them, take a phrase and make an aria out of that, and so on," he remembered ruefully. "It was a very hard libretto to work with."[7] Even the few places where Harrison dwelled on the text long enough to grace it with snatches of lyricism—Gaius's lullaby for his daughter, his sorrow when he learns of his betrothal, Nicomedes's confrontation with the financiers—hardly qualify as full-fledged arias.

Harrison (rather jokingly, given his antipathy for Wagner) compared this crucial aspect of his opera to *Parsifal*, where the prose speech also flows in non-repetitive melodies.[8] Yet such a superficial comparison ignores the ways in which Harrison's phrases follow both speech patterns and the necessary proportions of musical form. "My problem with Wagner is that he again has no fenestration, no time to breathe," Harrison said. "It goes on and on and on. Cadences, I think, are important. All the concerti grossi of Handel, they're all placed at just the right moments, but they're irregular. . . . There's a man who knew how to breathe and open windows and who had a public sound. J. S. Bach is so internal, and Handel was public, always."[9] In these ways, Harrison's work bears comparison to his hero's opera on the same character: Handel's *Giulio Cesare*.

Without typical Harrisonian modal lyricism, it is left up to the central pitches (or "psalm tones") of the recitatives to establish a tonic and mode and thus unify each scene. The characters firmly associated with Rome—Gaius's aunt Julia, the tutor Gniphos, General Thermus—sing on diatonic scales, the class of modes used in classical Rome. These scales were supported by the new metallophones that Colvig had begun to build for Harrison's Chinese ensemble using conduit tubes and aluminum bars cut to the lengths of a five-limit just-intonation diatonic scale.

In contrast, the scenes depicting the despair of Gaius's spurned fiancée Cossutia and Caesar's escape from the dictator Sulla use the equal-tempered octatonic scale, popular with Russian modernists such as early Stravinsky but then unusual for Harrison. The scale's alternation of half tones and whole tones creates a tense ambiguity appropriate for these painful moments without being entirely chromatic. The characters associated with Bithynia and the East use colorful non-diatonic scales often associated with the Middle East. For these scenes, Harrison decided to build a new set of metallophones tuned to the harmonic series, and when the scene changes to Rome's client kingdom of Bithynia in Asia Minor, they ring out the surprising sounds of harmonics seven and eleven.[10] Gaius himself, the Roman who falls in love with the East, partakes of both types of scales.

West and East also collide in other instrumentation that Harrison collected for the production, for which he relied almost completely on the instruments in his own large collection: his Chinese *zheng* zither, *sheng* mouth organ, flutes, and various percussion; Korean *piri* and drums; percussion orchestra instruments including metal trash cans, cymbals, woodblocks, various bells, rattles, and rasps; European harp, violin, viola, and organ. Much of the score's colorful character stems from these delightfully distinct and unusual timbres: the breathy sound of the syrinx (Greek panpipe) as sixteen-year-old Gaius processes to his manhood ceremony; the haunting ocarina and weird slide whistle accompanying his delirious dreams; a ram's horn for the courtly procession; the sweet sensuality of the *zheng* together with an Indian *ektara* (plucked lute) and elephant bells as Gaius moves in wonder through the Bithynian palace.

The set pieces played by these colorful instruments use forms similar to the miniature works Harrison had focused on during the 1960s, especially his lovely miniatures for harp and for psaltery. A sensuous psaltery piece, "Palace Music," accompanies Gaius's wonder at the Bithynian opulence, with idiomatic slides but a very un-Chinese scale. The funeral procession (done in shadow) is set to a solemn melody on harp and violin with spare percussion ostinatos.

The episodic story that Gordon distilled from several years of Julius Caesar's life lacks a conventional dramatic arc, juxtaposing several incidents in the first half and then showing the trip to Bithynia in the second. Caesar first appears in his manhood ceremony at age sixteen; then he hatches political schemes after the death of his father, and he reappears next with his new wife and daughter. Unfortunately, the real drama doesn't begin until he defies the dictator Sulla and appears as a soldier preparing to charge a besieged city. Harrison's scrolling backdrop mechanism depicted these grand settings.

Gaius is saved from this battle by orders to collect an overdue tribute of ships promised by the elegant and handsome king of Bithynia, Nicomedes. Overwhelmed by the opulent palace and the flirting king, the adolescent Gaius is treated to a lavish banquet, followed by entertainment of dancers to a "Whirling Dance" for violin, harp, and gongs in the form of an estampie, and then acrobats accompanied by a thrilling melody on the *sheng*. The celebrations intensify to a climactic "Eroticon" dream ballet in which Western strings and Eastern winds entwine lines in a sensuous musical intercourse.

"Here we find a young Roman noble of conservative and upper class parentage confronting, for the first time, an elaborately Asianized court by which he obviously found himself dazzled," Harrison later described the scene[11]—which sounds very much like the similarly teenaged Lou Harrison first encountering Chinese opera in San Francisco. Determined to unflinchingly represent this (historically accurate) orgy, Harrison advertised the production as an "opera for X-rated puppets."[12] His concern that conventional opera-goers would object proved unfounded in the case of one older woman in the audience, who afterward expressed her adoration of the "butterflies"—actually shadow puppets of phalli flying around the puppet banquet.[13] The flying phalli nevertheless so upset two of the original wealthy funders, Gordon said, that they withdrew their support.[14] Still, Gordon discreetly handled the ensuing love affair between Gaius and Nicomedes. Gaius's dalliance at the court creates a scandal, but the future emperor faces up to gossipers, and in the end, by force of love instead of arms, he gets his ships, which cross the Mediterranean (to Harrison's rousing barcarolle) at the final curtain.

Harrison intended to give trial performances before the official premiere in Pasadena, but he wound up spending so much time on production issues like painting the backdrop and training puppeteers that he couldn't complete the score in time for the summer 1971 Cabrillo Festival as planned. Harrison and his company of five singers and five instrumentalists (including his Chinese music ensemble with Dee and Colvig) performed only seven of the fourteen scenes there and at the Old Spaghetti Factory. Finally in November, Colvig packed all of their instruments, puppets, and the 8' by 4' stage into their camper, and they headed south on the daylong journey Pasadena.

The audience at the California Institute of Technology, intrigued by such an unusual production, greeted the hourlong *Young Caesar* warmly, on the whole.[15] After returning north, the troupe put together another performance, directed by poet Paul Mariah, in the auditorium at the Palace of the Legion of Honor museum in San Francisco.

The show did boast some virtues, presenting a contemporarily relevant, too-little known true tale featuring positive and historically accurate portrayals of homosexuality, peace, love, and intercultural understanding—along with some of Harrison's most compelling dramatic music. Thanks to the homespun instruments and puppets, and occasional humor, despite *Young Caesar*'s ambitions, it retained an appealing intimacy lacking in such large-scale works as his symphonies.

But performances in front of audiences revealed some unforeseen weaknesses. The unexpressive puppets often made Harrison's attempts to express love, sexuality, and other emotions clumsy or even unintentionally comical. And by devoting the first half of the opera to exposition of history, rather than the central drama (which really doesn't ignite until Caesar meets Nicomedes, the natural starting point for a classic heart-versus-head conflict), the original *Young Caesar* spends too much time in chattering explanation and not nearly enough in singing and action.

Worse, "the crippling weakness of 'Young Caesar' is its precious, self-indulgent libretto," wrote critic John Rockwell in the *Los Angeles Times*. While praising Harrison's music and the singers, he noted that traditional Asian puppet theater works precisely because of its acceptance of its mythic assumptions, whereas Gordon's realism produced only a "pervasive, embarrassing ennui."[16] In trying to make the story more approachable to contemporary audiences (by using colloquial language and realistic—for puppets, anyway—action), the production vitiated the suggestive power of its mythic theater origins.

More important than these dramatic failings, though, is the sheer audacity of *Young Caesar*. In the year that Richard Nixon was on his way to a landslide reelection, serial complexity was the new norm, and neither "world music" nor "gay rights" had entered the popular lexicon, Harrison had brought to a mainstream stage a homosexual puppet opera with unheard-of instruments and sensual melodies. But such an accomplishment, inconceivable by anyone but Lou Harrison, could not overcome *Young Caesar*'s fundamental flaws and practical difficulties. Its failure crushed Harrison, who had devoted two and a half years of his professional life—and some fine music—to a story he cherished. Like a father who refuses to give up on a problem child, Harrison continued to pursue opportunities to rehabilitate his beloved work for the rest of his life.

MOVING STAINED GLASS

On the white screen appeared wondrous figures of the most enchanting beauty and splendid colors. Their movement was as subtle or as robust as that of living actors and the stories were of serene, mystic richness. This performance went directly into my heart and was permanently impressed there.

—Lou Harrison[17]

Harrison's experience with *Young Caesar* revived fond memories of the Red Gate Shadow Players, the group whose Chinese shadow puppetry had so impressed him at Mills College back in October 1939. The puppets were made of various translucent materials that, when projected on the screen, looked to Harrison like "moving stained glass."[18] Through the *Young Caesar* puppetry contacts, Harrison discovered that, remarkably, the woman behind that company was still alive—and living down the coast in Carmel. Now Pauline Benton worked part time in a Carmel mineral art shop and gave occasional lessons in shadow puppetry at San Francisco's Chinese Cultural Center.[19]

Harrison drove down to Carmel with Colvig and Richard Dee, where he visited "the sweetest generous and very elegant little lady" at her modest cottage, surrounded by Japanese and Chinese art and artifacts.[20] The elderly Benton had long since retired from puppetry, after Americans grew hostile to Chinese culture in the wake of the Communist takeover of China in 1949. Confronted by Harrison's persistence and enthusiasm, Benton, initially cool, finally smiled and led her visitors to a battered trunk, in which she had long ago packed away her marvelous puppets. Some of them were stuck together, but even in their somewhat decayed condition, seeing them here vividly reminded Harrison of his thrilling, three-decades-old experience at her shows. Ecstatic, he proposed then and there that they revive the old theater and bring her out of retirement to perform with his Chinese ensemble. The septuagenarian Benton was skeptical but finally pulled out a dusty script called *The White Snake Lady*.

At Harrison's insistence, she agreed to a performance. Harrison examined her yellowing copies of William Russell's decades-old arrangements of traditional Chinese music for *The White Snake Lady*, but ultimately the group, by now experienced in playing Chinese music, decided to improvise their own. They soon began rehearsing with Benton, who insisted that the music appropriately accompany the puppets' action.[21] They performed several times in concerts arranged by the Chinese Cultural Center and others, with Harrison playing *xiao* flute and other Chinese instruments and Colvig playing the *sheng* and percussion, while Dee played the string instruments, sang, and voiced all the male roles. Along with *Young Caesar*, *The White Snake Lady* scratched Harrison's decades-long itch to perpetrate puppet opera.

Harrison gained another performing partner in 1971, as his Chinese ensemble sometimes paired half a concert featuring Benton's shadow puppetry with a half featuring the great Beat poet and bohemian San Francisco institution Kenneth Rexroth, who had published two popular books of imagistic translations of classical Chinese poetry that mightily impressed Harrison. "Rexroth had reimagined the poems as the work of someone on the other side of the Pacific Rim, speaking in a plain, natural-breathing, neutral American idiom" and emphasized the poets' affection for the wilderness, which resonated with Harrison's (and Rexroth's) own.[22]

When the composer approached the poet for permission to use these translations at their concerts, Rexroth volunteered to read them himself. Although Richard Dee's theatrically trained voice had previously declaimed poems in their performances, Rexroth's bardic yet unaffected baritone, tinged with a wistful longing for an imagined ancient era, brought the exotic old tales alive. "He always paused / just a breath-pause / at the end of / lines, thus making / meaning's own line / often doubtful," wrote Harrison of Rexroth's method of audibly defining the forms of the poems.[23] The group's music (one member would accompany each poem with a solo improvisation), woven in through and under the lines, heightened the poetry's evocative power.

"Kenneth was a real camp," Harrison remembered. "He enjoyed telling us about what perfume J. Edgar Hoover wore that day at a luncheon and things like that. He was argumentative, but you know he was very entertaining."[24] Rexroth's notorious grumpiness prompted Robert Duncan to nickname him The Terrible Tempered Mr. Bangs.[25] At one performance in Santa Cruz, Rexroth offended women in the audience by introducing his "Japanese paramour." To those who hissed the following performance, he snarled, "I was a feminist before most of your mothers were born."[26]

Unfortunately, the collaborations didn't last long. In 1971, Gerard Samuel invited Harrison's group, Benton, and Rexroth to perform at Southern California's Ojai Festival, which Samuel had just been appointed to direct. Unknown to Harrison, the venerable puppet mistress was suffering from brain cancer, and Dee sometimes had to cover Benton's otherwise inexplicable pauses.

Their concert at Ojai also occasioned a memorial performance. Harrison's friend and Colvig's one-time lover Ingolf Dahl, who had been Ojai's director in the 1960s, had died unexpectedly. In memory, Colvig played a moving solo on the *xun* (clay ocarina), an ancient Chinese song depicting two old friends sharing wine at a mountain pass, where one is to cross over, never to return.[27] After Ojai, Rexroth and Harrison's ensemble played at the prestigious Mark Taper Forum in Los Angeles. Harrison characteristically spent his considerable fee on some sumptuous Iranian tiles he found as they passed through Santa Barbara, which decorated his home ever after.[28]

Like the percussion ensemble that preceded it three decades earlier, Harrison had created, through infectious enthusiasm and force of personality, his own community of musician friends to play his music and the music he loved. The Chinese ensemble continued to perform through the mid-1970s, but his decade-long direct involvement with East Asian music was drawing to a close. Just as he finished the performances of his opera and *The White Snake Lady,* another opportunity arose for still another ambitious creation.

THE HEART OF THE MATTER

One of Harrison's most beloved Buddhist texts is familiarly known as the Heart Sutra, which he had studied soon after his first trip to Asia reawakened his enthusiasm for Buddhist thought. It elegantly distills the hundred thousand lines of the "Perfection of Wisdom" literature down to just fourteen verses. "It's called that because it's the heart of the matter," Harrison explained. "It concentrates all of the paradoxical beauty of this whole area of philosophy into a very brief, sharp space."[29] In 1969, after setting a different Buddhist sutra for his *Peace Piece #1,* Harrison felt that the Heart Sutra would be ideal for another Peace Piece, although necessarily on a larger scale to accommodate the longer text. Harrison's concern for the universality of the message led him to commission an Esperanto translation from his linguist friend Bruce Kennedy.

Harrison maintained his involvement in the international language and the community surrounding it, attending meetings in the Bay Area and corresponding with Esperantists worldwide.[30] Toward the end of *Young Caesar*'s run, Harrison got word of a perfect opportunity to present an Esperanto musical sutra. The Universala Kongreso, or World Congress of Esperanto, had chosen Harrison's hometown of

Portland for its 1972 meeting. Some of Harrison's contacts among the local Esperantists suggested a concert. Although it was impractical to take a large performing group up to Portland, after the meeting, many of the visiting Esperantists would be coming down on an *ekskurso* to San Francisco State, which offered an annual summer Esperanto course. Harrison asked Vahé Aslanian, the choir conductor at Hartnell College in Salinas who had premiered his *Easter Cantata*, if he would be able to assemble a chorus for a performance that summer at San Francisco State.

Harrison's experience with *Young Caesar* inspired him to compose a piece featuring the metal instruments he and Colvig had constructed, which could fill out a complete ensemble from bass to soprano with homemade metal bars and tubes. They built four instruments of metal tubes, each covering a range of over two octaves in a just D-major diatonic scale.[31] Two of the instruments sound an octave higher (called by Harrison "soprano bells") than the other pair (made of slightly wider conduit and called "tenor bells"). They fashioned each instrument in each pair from different metals—one aluminum, which produces a deeply resonant, mellow timbre, and one steel, for a louder and brighter sound.[32]

The baritone instrument consists of large aluminum bars arrayed in the same configuration as the tube instruments. The large bass instrument proved the most troublesome: The lowest bars required resonators over five feet tall. When faced with this problem on his bass marimba, Harry Partch made a platform for the player to stand on. Instead, Colvig elected to separate the lowest three notes onto a different rack, making the majority of the bars more accessible and the instrument as a whole more portable. Colvig built the resonators out of large steel cans of the kind that restaurants typically discard by the dozens, welded together to achieve the correct length.[33] Harrison also wanted to find some practical large bells. After some experimentation, Colvig chose large steel gas canisters. With their bottoms cut off and suspended from a crossbeam, these tanks emitted a bright, satisfying bell tone when struck with a large mallet or baseball bat.

Harrison called their homemade metallophone ensemble an "American gamelan," after the traditional orchestra of mostly metal instruments in Indonesia.[34] Because different regions there have their own versions—a Javanese gamelan, a Balinese gamelan, a Sundanese gamelan—Harrison proposed theirs as an American version. However, Harrison and Colvig didn't model this set after any traditional Indonesian instruments, unlike the ensembles they would later build. The scale and instruments differ considerably from their Asian namesake, so the works Harrison composed for it, including his setting of the Heart Sutra, cannot be realized on any other instruments. Later, after having built several other gamelan, he and Colvig sentimentally referred to this first effort as "Old Granddad."

The text of the Heart Sutra, rendered in Bruce Kennedy's Esperanto translation as "La Koro Sutro," occupies fourteen lines, divided into seven sections he called *paragrafoj*. To these Harrison adds an opening invocation and an epilogue, for a total of nine movements. This suite-like approach to a large piece resembles the form of *Pacifika Rondo*, and *La Koro Sutro* has a similar large-scale plan unifying the keys and modes of the work.

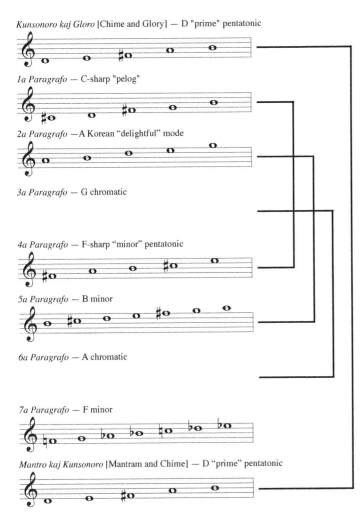

Kunsonoro kaj Gloro [Chime and Glory] — D "prime" pentatonic

1a Paragrafo — C-sharp "pelog"

2a Paragrafo — A Korean "delightful" mode

3a Paragrafo — G chromatic

4a Paragrafo — F-sharp "minor" pentatonic

5a Paragrafo — B minor

6a Paragrafo — A chromatic

7a Paragrafo — F minor

Mantro kaj Kunsonoro [Mantram and Chime] — D "prime" pentatonic

EXAMPLE 27.1. Harrison mapped out a large-scale plan of tonalities and just-intonation modes for the movements of *La Koro Sutro*, though the relationships shown here reflect connections in more than just the scales. Paragraphs three and six have no fixed scales.

The opening invocation on the sacred syllable "om" recalls the "superfluous number of bells" Harrison had envisioned for the Gloria movement of his *Mass* (which Chávez had performed at Cabrillo in 1970). However, this time the bells—including the big gas canisters, large ranch triangles, deep Chinese gongs, and a Balinese-style bell tree—ring out not to the glory of God but to the "Blessed, Noble Perfect Wisdom."[35] The reed organist holds down all of the keys in the scale, and this "radiant chord"[36] creates a *gagaku*-like background; as in the *St. Anthony Mass*, the chorus sings in unison, creating variety as the different sections of men and women take over in different combinations. The long melodic lines with many notes on a syllable recall the Alleluia of the mass and open *The Heart Sutra* in a thrilling, celebratory mood.

The atmosphere suddenly changes in the second movement, as a darker pentatonic with semitones eclipses the bright mode of the opening.[37] The tubular metallophones play a long, delicately haunting melody in octaves, with a single repeated pitch in between each of the melodic tones—Harrison's adaptation of the Indian *jhala* technique, but where in an Indian performance these interpolations often happen dazzlingly fast, here they tick away deliberately. Above this repeating melody, the chorus sings gravely of the bodhisattva Avalokiteshvara, who "saw that in their nature all Five Aggregates are void and empty." In Buddhist literature, the "Aggregates" (matter, feeling, perception, impulses, and consciousness) refer to the phenomenological world of human perception that we identify with Being. The haunting melody sets up the opening mystery: that all of these aspects that make us human are in fact empty and illusory.

In the second *paragrafo*, Avalokiteshvara reveals to Shariputra, an original disciple of the Buddha, that emptiness is form and form is emptiness. This movement, like the third of Harrison's *Seven Pastorales*, pays homage to the early thirteenth-century conducti of Perotin, in which interlocking voices weave a rich tapestry of sound. Harrison's reed organ now plays the role not of a Japanese *sho* but instead of a medieval European organ, whose drones formed earthly foundations to fill Gothic cathedrals.

The brief *paragrafo* that follows features nearly all unpitched percussion, gently cycling through ostinatos while the chorus sings a chromatic unison melody. Neither serial nor even atonal, the different tetrachords always hover above a stable key center, a distinctive device that retains tonality and unity in a chromatic context. The harmonic ambiguity reflects the text's insistence that dharma (or all earthly phenomena) is "neither tainted nor yet spotless, neither lacking, nor completed."

In the mesmerizing fourth *paragrafo*, *La Koro Sutro*'s balancing point, the deep bass *gendèrs* resolutely sway back and forth between the tonic and the fifth, providing the eternal stability of wisdom, even as the meter of the *jhala* melody shifts above them—linking the movement to the other *jhala* melody of the first *paragrafo*, which revealed Avalokiteshvara's first insight. This midpoint, the heart of the Heart Sutra, gives us the central paradox of Buddhism: if the phenomena of our lives do not exist in the void, neither does suffering nor the attainment of nirvana itself.

Suddenly the clockwork *jhala* melodies end, and the chorus alone sings a diatonic chorale in quintal/secundal counterpoint like the one in the recently resurrected *Easter Cantata*.[38] The chorales surround a mellifluously flowing unison melody that sings how the bodhisattva is indifferent to the attainment or non-attainment of nirvana. In the same way that Harrison connects the first and fourth *paragrafoj*, he also links the sixth and third *paragrafoj*: both have similar chromatic melodies with unpitched accompaniment. As before, shifting tetrachords create a chromatic melody without compromising the tonal foundation, a melody that sings how the perfection of wisdom has awakened all Buddhas of all time.

The last *paragrafo*, which might be expected to bring a comfortable return to the opening tonality, instead launches into the startling realm of F minor, a tonality not at all related to *The Heart Sutra*'s prevailing D major, as if the wisdom of the sutra has provided a new view of the world.[39] When Harrison realized the necessity of the key, rather than asking Colvig (who was off leading a Sierra Club hike) to build a new set of instruments for this single movement, Harrison decided to include a harp.[40]

Only the organist and the harpist (who is otherwise silent through the performance) accompany the choir's polyphonic fantasia on the transcendental wisdom of the following mantra (sacred repeated formula).

Without pause, the choir strikingly modulates back to the home prime pentatonic and the epilogue. The *gendèr* instruments announce a gently repeating pattern that underlies the final passage's concluding chaconne (a favorite Harrison ending form). To Harrison, the movement represented "the smile on the face of the Thai Buddhas. There are kind of alleluias in the air."[41] The bells reemerge into a resplendent texture as the choir sings the final mantra: "Going, going!"—that is, going over the sea of human suffering. *La Koro Sutro* ends with another superfluity of radiant bells and the joyous chorus exulting, "Awake, all hail!" Harrison said, "The final mantra is written in the spirit of a Russian folk song! I had no idea why, but it works, musically, is the point."[42]

Despite the difficulty of performing with a unique set of homemade instruments, the glorious *La Koro Sutro* would become one of Harrison's best-loved compositions, embracing some of his most characteristic passions: peace, universality, homemade instruments, just intonation, bell sounds, Asian influences. Somehow, Harrison had taken a text that counsels indifference to desire and created a gripping paean to peace.

Although it presents few of the difficulties associated with complex modernist pieces, *The Heart Sutra*'s deceptively challenging vocal parts require a sensitivity to tuning and texture found in few other choral works.[43] And the fact that it can't be performed on anything but Harrison's American gamelan would seem to doom it to obscurity. Yet so many of those who heard *La Koro Sutro* (especially after it was recorded) recognized it as one of the great sacred works of the twentieth century that by the end of Harrison's life, copies of the American gamelan would be constructed so that it could be shipped to all the choirs wanting to perform it.[44]

MORE DOUBLE MUSIC

Lou Harrison had relied on his friend Richard Dee for assistance in teaching and making music. Now, he wanted to encourage Dee's own creativity. To fill out the August 1972 concert at San Francisco State's Knuth Hall where the half-hour-long *La Koro Sutro* premiered, Harrison asked colleagues at San Jose State to perform, and he, Richard Dee, and Colvig played some of their traditional Chinese works. But there was still room on the program for another piece. Harrison could have programmed another of his own. Instead, characteristically, he turned to Dee. "Why don't you compose a piece on an Esperanto text?"

Dee could think of a couple of reasons. First, he told Harrison, he didn't speak Esperanto. Second, he had taken only beginning music theory classes and lacked experience with voice-leading and harmony, the central topics of conventional music courses.

"You don't have to know harmony and counterpoint," Harrison scoffed.

"Really?" asked Dee, still uneasy.

"Yeah! All you have to do is write a melody," Harrison told him. "The rest can be simultaneous variation."

Dee finally set one of Harrison's own poems on the Greek gods of the palaestra with violin obbligato. Still, the program was a little short, and Harrison wanted a way to feature his new instruments apart from the choir. Again he turned to the skeptical Dee with a new proposal.

"A chaconne?"

"That's right, a chaconne." Harrison said. "I don't have time to write it myself, so I want you to help. I want you to cooperatively write it."

"I don't know how to do that," Dee replied. "Who does? I've never heard of such a thing."

"Oh, I'll explain it to you," Harrison said breezily.[45] Already planning to end *La Koro Sutro* with a modest chaconne, he thought a more expansive one would work well in the program, perhaps pairing a violin with the American gamelan. Although Dee would not be performing the piece (one of Harrison's faculty colleagues would), he was an accomplished violinist and already had a good grasp of what worked well for the instrument.

Harrison had written at least two other pieces in collaboration with other composers, *Double Music* with John Cage and *Ritmicas* with Bob Hughes.[46] However, those pieces had been split up horizontally; that is, each composer wrote the individual parts for a certain number of players for the entire length of the piece, and they were then played together to form the finished composition. A chaconne, which depends on a sequence of melodies over a repeating bass line, demanded a different approach to collaboration. Perhaps mindful of the precedent of the round-robin composing he had done with friends in New York (and which Hughes had recently arranged as *Party Pieces*), Harrison proposed that the two of them compose alternate sections of the violin melody; the rest of the gamelan accompaniment could come later.

Harrison first composed the nine-beat bass melody whose repetitions on the low metal-bar instruments form the underpinning to the piece. Then Harrison composed the first melody for violin, an expressively rising tune in quintal counterpoint with the bass ostinato, and turned it over to Dee, who contributed a melody consisting of a contrasting series of mostly eighth notes, largely derived from a step-down, skip-down melodicle (suggested in the *Music Primer*).[47] Then Dee turned it back over to Harrison, who introduced other contrasts: sixteenth notes soaring into the very high range of the instrument, while the gamelan reprises the original melody. Dee next added a variation with virtuosic violin string crossings and octave jumps, and he suggested that the first melody return again, this time in glorious octaves, creating a kind of rondeau form within the chaconne. As Dee had little experience with gamelan instruments, Harrison worked out most of the accompaniment, completing their *Chaconne* just in time for the concert.[48]

Harrison was pleased with the result. Some months later, when the San Francisco Chamber Music Society commissioned Harrison to write a piece, he took the opportunity to create an entire suite, again in collaboration with Dee, concluding with the existing chaconne. The two sat down with a piece of notebook paper to plan out the work.[49] Harrison said that they first needed to know the form, the tonality, and the length of each movement and suggested beginning with a rhapsodic prelude that he would write alone on an unsettled drone of C♯, moving on to an estampie in F♯. An estampie, like a chaconne, consists of a series of linked melodies, so they agreed to write it the same way, alternating sections. Harrison wrote the consistent pair of ending phrases used in estampies, an open (or *overt*) ending for the mid-point and a closed (or *clos*) ending for the end of each phrase. Once again Harrison wrote the first melody, and they alternated writing the seven sections from there. Following the estampie, Harrison proposed a movement in the form of a baroque air, composed by Dee.

For the B minor air, Dee appropriated part of the melody from his Esperanto song. Despite Dee's distinctive compositional voice, he adopted Harrisonian ornaments and climactic thickening of the violin line with parallel fourths (a technique borrowed in turn from that of the Chinese *sheng* mouth organ).

Following the air, Harrison proposed a "mosaic" piece in which they would collaboratively string together elaborate variations of a melodicle, transformed just as in a twelve-tone piece, and in a foreign key, just like the dramatic last *paragrafo* of *La Koro Sutro*. In the end, however, they collected a mini-suite (as the scherzo movement of the *Symphony on G*) based on the *jhala* technique. Dee agreed to write the violin part and Harrison the gamelan part of the first *jhala*. The second *jhala* would be Dee's alone, and Harrison would compose the third *jhala*, for gamelan alone. "Cooperative composition is fun," Harrison said, "if the rules are set up and nobody cheats."[50] Their *Suite for Violin and American Gamelan* premiered in December 1974, Harrison sharing the spotlight with Dee with characteristic generosity.[51]

Harrison was not finished with Old Granddad, and he began composing a new work further ruminating on the tuning system, completing only a slow, contemplative *Solo* for tenor bells, dedicated to San Jose State percussionist Anthony Cirone. Harrison chose a B minor mode, knowing that in this tuning system, the E would be dissonant (a "wolf") with respect to the tonic B. At the end of the score, Harrison showed how such details were central to his compositional process: "N.B. The tuning must be in 'Just' D Major, otherwise the tension of the 'false B Minor' will be lost, & the 'narrow escape' (tonally) in the climax section will disappear, & thus the point of the piece be lost." The climactic phrase settles on an E, which on the bells will set up interference beats that impart a visceral tension that Harrison then cleverly works out (the "narrow escape") as he returns to the smooth just intervals of the home key. It was the latest in a series of successful Harrison pieces using just intonation in the early '70s. But he would soon put on hold his continued fascination with the "paradise garden of delights" of just intonation, thanks, in part, to Tony Cirone.

28

ELEGIES (1973–1975)

One day late in 1972, the San Jose State organist, Philip Simpson, asked Harrison if he would consider composing a piece for him. Just a couple of days later, at a reception at the home of percussionist Tony Cirone, came another request, this time from Cirone for his percussion ensemble. The college's accomplished percussion ensemble had already performed several of Harrison's works, including the ambitious premiere of *Orpheus* in 1969. As Harrison thought about both requests from his new friends on the faculty, he noted one commonality: "Well, they can both make a lot of racket, let's put them together and see what happens."[1]

Concerto for Organ with Percussion Orchestra proved an abrupt departure for Harrison, veering away from the Chinese- and Korean-influenced sounds that pervaded the last decade of his music, and away from the just-intonation Old Granddad instruments that had preoccupied him for the last four years. Now he was heading back to the worlds of equal temperament (because the organ could play only in equal temperament) and unpitched percussion.[2] Harrison responded to the fixed tuning of the organ with a return to atonality and tone clusters. His score asks the organist to fashion an "octave bar," a device (invented for pianists to play Ives's *Concord* sonata) used to mash down all the keys within the range of an octave.

Even as he added more of Colvig's new inventions to his percussion orchestra, the shotgun marriage of the sustained, fixed-pitch organ to unpitched percussion proved more of a problem. His 1959 violin concerto provided one model of combining a sustained, pitched instrument with the more "abstract" (as he called them) percussion instruments. But whereas the violinist's alternately lyrical and dramatic single line balances the percussion ensemble, the organ is like an orchestra in itself, and Harrison came to feel that using unpitched percussion as the only foil to the organ was insufficient for such a large conception. Instead, he added another set of percussive, fixed-pitch instruments—glockenspiel, vibraphone, tubular chimes, celesta, piano—to mediate between the sustained, pitched organ and the drier, unpitched percussion instruments. This middle-ground section operates like what Harrison termed his "gamelan section" of the orchestra, which had already surfaced in works such as the *Symphony on G* and the *Political Primer*. These three large sections (organ, pitched percussion, unpitched percussion) provide a wide terrain of timbral possibilities to encompass Harrison's grand vision.[3]

Harrison also considered the classic three-movement concerto form (as in his 1959 violin concerto and *Concerto in Slendro*) to be insufficient for this enlarged vision. Rather than structuring the work as a suite of small, intimate movements, as he had in his most recent American gamelan pieces, he compromised by sandwiching two shorter interludes between three extended movements.[4]

The first movement provides the promised "racket"—loud organ clusters (almost making the organ a percussion instrument itself) alternating with a dramatic mosaic of percussion melodicles. When melody comes to the organ, it erupts in brash clusters tumbling up and down the keyboard—Harrison had learned from Henry Cowell that clusters can themselves "thicken" a melody.[5] When the gamelan section dramatically enters, the piano and celesta also play the melody in great, clangorous clusters, over explosive snare-drum bursts.

Harrison repurposed his atonal *Double Canon for Carl Ruggles* of 1952 as a brief, pensive interlude in the form of a siciliana for organ solo. The jolting middle movement, which uses the melodicle from the *Double Canon*'s countermelody as a springboard for an extended fantasy, kicks off with another contrapuntal puzzle of a canon in augmentation (the melody combined with itself at different rhythmic levels). Much of its melodic material uses the octatonic scale that Harrison had previously used for the "Cossutia's Despair" scene of *Young Caesar*.

The next interlude, "Canons and Choruses," shares its intricate counterpoint with the second movement, but now in a pentatonic mode. According to Harrison's score, it should sound like "a 'classical' landscape—distant shepherds' flutes, faint bells." When the gamelan section of the orchestra enters to accompany the organ canon, it uses the same pentatonic mode transposed one step up. This curious polymodal conflation, an experiment Harrison never repeated, results in a euphonious layering of the melodies.

The melody of the boisterous finale has a similar kind of polymodality, this time reconciling chromaticism and tonality by conflating two different pentatonics above a common key center (a similar technique to the one he used in the chromatic second *paragrafo* of *La Koro Sutro*). These two scales, a *slendro* (scale with no semitones) and a *pelog* (scale with semitones), achieve both the bite of chromaticism and the stability of tonality, spurring his concerto to a rousing finish.[6] The *Concerto for Organ with Percussion Orchestra* confirmed that, despite his well-known advocacy for just intonation and his openness to Asian cultures, Harrison was never a purist. Unlike many composers, he would happily revisit and draw upon tools from any point in his career when he felt the situation demanded it.

After its premiere in San Jose, the *Concerto for Organ with Percussion Orchestra* received a repeat performance at the 1974 Cabrillo Festival, where a new director had taken over. After the departure of Carlos Chávez, the festival board hired the twenty-nine-year-old, long-haired Dennis Russell Davies, whom Harrison remembered roaring into town on a Harley-Davidson, stripped to the waist. "At first I have to tell you, I didn't really get it," Davies later admitted. "I didn't really, in my heart and in my approach to the festival, think it was extremely important to have [Lou] all that involved. Well, it didn't take me long to figure out that that was not only stupid, but just not very enlightened."[7]

Davies's accession continued the dramatic evolution of the festival, started on a shoestring by Hughes, Harrison, and others a decade earlier, that was becoming one of the nation's beacons of contemporary music. In the 1960s, Gerhard Samuel "balanced modern music by composers residing in California and on the West Coast with older repertoire," Hughes explained. Chávez (who directed the festival from 1970 to 1973) incorporated Latin American music, with the enthusiastic support of Harrison, who had treasured it since his youth.[8] Davies brought to the festival a new sense of informality and an adventuresome spirit, inviting jazz pianist Keith Jarrett and relatively non-establishment composers such as William Bolcom and John Cage. Harrison would steer Davies toward the pan-Pacific sounds he had been exploring himself.

Davies quickly appreciated Harrison's significance and would become one of his most devoted champions, at Cabrillo and beyond, including his prestigious posts in Europe. Harrison, who had benefited so much from advocates like Cowell, Thomson, Yates, Daniel, and Hughes, and had in the past few years accumulated a congenial new coterie of creative colleagues, would now have a new partner to advocate his music.

DRUID HEIGHTS

The organ and percussion concerto's origin in friendship suggests how rapidly the one-time hermit was expanding his social circles in the 1970s. In 1973, the fifty-six-year-old Harrison received one of the most illustrious of his many life-time honors: induction into the National Institute of Arts and Letters. The trip to the New York ceremony gave him the chance to connect with old friends such as Virgil Thomson and Vladimir Ussachevsky, who was also being inducted. He informed the Institute that "Mr. Colvig" would be coming too, and so organizers reserved a place at the table for him.[9] At the luncheon they met the novelist and fellow honoree Kurt Vonnegut. However, two of the inductees, his old friend Joseph Campbell and sometime acquaintance Allen Ginsberg, could not make it to the ceremony.

Harrison sometimes saw Ginsberg at the Marin County home of another old friend, poet Elsa Gidlow, who had created a small community of artists and intel-lectuals on a six-acre property on the slopes of Mount Tamalpais, north of San Francisco. Harrison sometimes would drive the two hours up to what Gidlow dubbed "Druid Heights," the last mile a steep and rocky dirt road under the boughs of eucalyptus and Monterey pines. By the 1960s, the remote assortment of handmade houses became a frequent meeting place for North Beach jazz musicians and Beat writers, including Kenneth Rexroth, Gary Snyder, and James Broughton (whose *The Bed* was filmed there).

Residents of the Druid Heights community included Gidlow's partner, Isabel Quallo (Harrison had introduced them during his New York days), feminist Margo

St. James, and Beat mystic Alan Watts, who lived in a hermitage on the property until his death in 1973. Gidlow's price of admission to Druid Heights was a keen intellect and fascinating ideas, an appreciation that Harrison reciprocated. "Elsa, you are a great conversationalist!" he once exclaimed. "This is not a game we play alone," she replied sharply. "What of you?"[10] The septuagenarians Gidlow and Watts would occasionally take LSD as a sacrament, but Harrison declined anything stronger than alcohol and cannabis, which he had been consuming for years. Gidlow also cultivated an enormous organic garden and introduced Harrison to the region's edible mushrooms.

Gidlow's many parties or "festivals," often celebrating a solstice or a full moon, featured poetry readings and music, sometimes provided by Harrison. Once he took up an ensemble to perform selections from *Young Caesar*. Still interested in his earlier idea of a dramatic work based on Native American mythology, he told Gidlow the story of Payatamu and the Corn Maiden from the Zuni people of New Mexico, a tale of the simultaneous divine revelation of corn and of sacred music. Intrigued, Gidlow wrote a dramatic retelling of the myth and gave it to Harrison to set to music.

Perhaps feeling that he could not improve on Gidlow's declamation, or reluctant to set a long narrative after his experience with *Young Caesar*, Harrison set only the opening processional as a song. Instead, dances portray the action described in the poem, as in his 1942 *In Praise of Johnny Appleseed*, another story that praised the Earth and indigenous cultures. The small ensemble for *Payatamu and the Corn Maiden* includes viola, harp, and a single percussionist, but its expressive heart is a flute, the god Payatamu's instrument. At one point the flutist switches to a sopranino (very high range) recorder, an instrument similar to the flutes Harrison used to evoke Native American culture in *Pacifika Rondo*. The brief but charming chamber piece was performed with the giant puppets instead of dancers in March 1974. The artist, Kathleen Roberts, was Alan Watts's niece and Gidlow's friend. Other plans to perform the work elsewhere and with dancers apparently fell through, and Harrison abandoned it.[11]

Payatamu's part for harp did not specify a tuning, although presumably the part would have been played on Harrison's own troubadour harp in just intonation. Harrison had been adding to his repertory of "voluntary" tuned harp compositions around the same time, including a *Jahla in the Form of a Ductia to Please Leopold Stokowski on His Ninetieth Birthday* and *Little Homage to Eratosthenes*, in the tuning of the librarian of ancient Alexandria.

The singer that Harrison had brought to Druid Heights to perform excerpts from *Young Caesar*, his student Randall Wong, was both a countertenor and a harp student of Beverly Bellows. Harrison wrote for him a short, austere, quintal-counterpoint piece that they could either play together or as a solo. *Sonata in Ishartum*'s title refers to a mode from perhaps the most ancient record of music theory known, found on a cuneiform tablet from the eighteenth century BCE.

Harrison had been excitedly following the scholarly work of translating and reconstructing musical texts from nearly four-thousand-year-old Sumerian cuneiform tablets. At the center of the controversy of their interpretation stood an archaeologist at UC Berkeley, Anne Kilmer. The consensus interpretation of this tablet was that it described diatonic Pythagorean tuning (long before Pythagoras) and different diatonic modes.[12] The home mode, called "Ishartum," corresponded to the diatonic mode that musicians now know as Phrygian. Harrison introduced his San Jose State students to these modes to show the antiquity of these important musical concepts.

Harrison's intellectual community extended far beyond the thinkers at Druid Heights, and their ideas would seep into his music. Around this time, he met a postdoctoral genetics researcher at UC Berkeley named John Chalmers, who also shared his interests in tuning systems. Chalmers would drive down to Aptos on a weekend, have lunch with Harrison, Colvig, and often Richard Dee, and then spend the afternoon resurrecting the ancient sounds of Archytas's enharmonic, Eratosthenes's chromatic, or Ptolemy's equable diatonic scale. After tuning his harp in one of these scales, Harrison would improvise until the distinctive character and musical possibilities of the scale began to sink in.[13] In 1974, Chalmers founded *Xenharmonikôn*, a photocopied journal that connected the small community of composers, musicians, and theorists devoted to other tuning systems. Harrison eagerly looked forward to each issue of tuning esoterica and contributed several articles and scores of his own.

One of those scores was *A Phrase for Arion's Leap*, a miniature, like his *Haiku* from 1968, that referred to the myth of the famous musician who, when threatened by pirates, sang his supposedly last song and leapt overboard. He was safely brought to shore by dolphins that had gathered to hear his magical singing. Just about thirty seconds long, this unusual work nevertheless requires two specially tuned harps, three specially tuned bowed psalteries, and percussion. It is another example of "free style" just intonation, written without reference to a fixed scale. Harrison, Colvig, and Dee recorded it one afternoon, but it remains otherwise unperformed.[14]

DANCE OF LIFE

> —dear Bill
> *You are more beautiful than the dreams I have*
> *In which I have translated*
> *Into webs of pearls your waving silver beard,*
> *Your long swinging silver hair.*
>
> —Lou Harrison[15]

Of course, Harrison's closest relationship in the '70s—and ever after—remained Bill Colvig. In the late 1960s and early '70s, the pair enjoyed visits from old friends (including Harrison's old New York friends such as Jack Heliker) and often socialized with friends from the Society for Individual Rights, particularly at their weekly same-sex dances. "There really is a kind of 'Dance of Life,' I think," Harrison wrote in his notebook after one of the dances, "and it is very beautiful to be with you, Bill, as we 'take our place among the dancers.'"[16]

They marched together in San Francisco's first Gay Freedom Day in 1973, an event that drew tens of thousands (and would later become the San Francisco annual

LGBT Pride Parade). Marching downtown to the Civic Center, Harrison unabashedly waved to San Jose State students he spied among the spectators. Thrilled at how much San Francisco had changed since his youth, Harrison made a point of thanking some of the police who helped the event run smoothly and peacefully.[17]

Harrison and Colvig were very close politically, and Colvig tuned into the liberal KPFA nearly all day (often to Harrison's annoyance) and contributed to progressive causes, though they reserved their personal involvement for their busy artistic pursuits. "Politics is toward the establishment of power," Harrison wrote in his journal around this time. "Art is toward the establishment of order. Ultimately, power is violence. Ultimately, art is beauty."[18]

They lived their ideals, too. "He was such a generous individual," his student Kerry Lewis recalled of Harrison. "He gave me a number of pieces of music. He gave me scores of his own music. He gave me recordings. He gave me all this copy work to do when I was studying with him and for a while after I'd done my master's. I was a newlywed at the time. We didn't have much money. It was very much appreciated, having that income. He was an extremely large-hearted individual."[19] When the royalties Ives had willed to him swelled during the Ives centennial of 1974, Harrison sent the extra $1,000 to Peter Garland's Soundings Press and Partch's foundation.[20]

Like most married couples, Colvig and Harrison occasionally squabbled, Colvig often stoically firm in response to Harrison's tantrums. After, Harrison might contribute a poem to their tender reconciliations. Thanks in part to his relationship with Colvig and in part to his musical maturity, in retrospect Harrison judged that his fifties were the best decade of his life. "You know what you want to do, you know how to do it, and you still have the energy," he wrote Ned Rorem.[21] Their companionship provided needed comfort, because while Harrison was gaining new friends, the year 1974 brought some terrible losses.

Harrison was still in touch with that other pioneer of just intonation, Harry Partch, who in 1972 moved with all of his instruments to San Diego. On the cusp of the release of a new edition of Partch's landmark book, *Genesis of a Music*, the book that had set Harrison down the path of just intonation, Harrison took Colvig and Richard Dee to visit the ailing, alcoholic Partch, who insisted on making them his famous mint juleps, consisting of a liberal amount of whiskey poured over crushed fresh mint leaves and sugar.[22] However, by the time Harrison began writing a review of the new edition in 1974, he received word that Partch had died. As his review turned into a eulogy, Harrison wrote, "The loosely assembled democracy of the Americas is doubtless a fine place for a variety of intonations to develop and thrive, and it is part of the import of Harry Partch that he has opened the gate to a humanist musical paradise. It is a beautiful, various, real, and infinite one too, in which the sources are whole-world and the riches free for the doing."[23]

Partch's death in September was one in a serious of losses for Harrison in 1974. His collaborator Pauline Benton died in November, a year after his friend Alan Watts. In his eulogy, Harrison called Benton "one of the most important artists of the century."[24] And the year produced one more great loss.

Oh, Mother! Just see how my Mother has gone, just as a breath of wind would carry her off. This separation cuts my heart like countless swords. Oh, my Mother! Oh, my Mother![25]

"It's time," his mother's doctor told Harrison, "that you gave her more alcohol and less morphine."[26] Calline Harrison was dying. Alcohol may have been prescribed now, but Harrison attributed his earlier problems with alcohol to his mother, who also abused it. But he recognized that she had also bequeathed him many, more positive inheritances. Calline Harrison was a strong woman raised in an Alaskan log cabin; she loved cars at a time when few women drove. Bob Hughes, who knew both Harrison parents, judged that Lou had inherited his determination and iron will from her.[27] From her too came his love of beautiful finery, of being surrounded by art.

Harrison always thought of himself as a mother's boy and felt that he had much of his mother in him, so her loss felt especially painful. Just as he had taken care of his mother during the decade since his father's death, he and Colvig stayed by her side during her last illness and put her affairs in order. It was a familiar role for Harrison, who, looking back, understood that he had played the part of the willing servant to his mother in childhood. He realized he was recapitulating that role with Colvig, often taking on the responsibility of housework and other little favors for his partner.[28] As their relationship matured, though, this solicitude became a loving gesture freely given, rather than a response to emotional manipulation, as it may have been earlier in his life.

> *she lay, across from my room,*
> *audible in her illness*
>
> *Kind nurses tended her, and*
> *wakened me when she had died*
> *most early in the morning.*
>
> *And then I saw that she had*
> *disappeared, looked like a flea*
> *curled up and small and wizened.*[29]

Her death at her house in Redwood City, early in the morning in March 21, 1974 at age eighty-three, plunged Harrison into despair, and he recalled writing much of the *Suite for Violin and American Gamelan* in an alcoholic near-stupor.[30] "I was reaching into the depths, heading for the bottom of the bottle," he recalled, "near to oblivion."[31]

When the Koussevitsky Foundation approached Harrison to commission a new orchestral work, he decided to express his grief over the year's many losses in an *Elegiac Symphony*. The conductor Serge Koussevitsky had been a champion of many American composers, including Harrison's friends Aaron Copland and Leonard Bernstein, and 1974 was his centennial.[32] The symphony turned out, like several other works of this period, to be a look backward, as Harrison followed his usual pattern of following a period of innovation (*Young Caesar, La Koro Sutro*) with another of retrospection. Losing parents and lifelong friends occasions reminiscence, and for this, Harrison's second symphony (following the first one by more than a quarter of a century), he would take an approach similar to the one he had for his *Suite for Symphonic Strings*—to adapt old works to a new expressive program. Even though four of the five movements recycle versions of previous pieces stretching back over thirty years, the combination results in one of Harrison's most moving compositions.[33] Sorrow, despair, anger, and pain arise throughout the *Elegiac Symphony*'s intense thirty-five minutes before some light finally emerges by the end.

Like the earlier *Suite*, this repurposing of works separated by decades results in a sometimes-awkward eclecticism, but at the same time, a common, nearly unrelenting emphasis on counterpoint holds the movements together. Most sections feature from two to four distinct polyphonic melodies at a time, sometimes together with drones, necessitating a somewhat different approach to orchestration than in his first symphony, the *Symphony on G*. To distinguish the distinct polyphonic lines, Harrison combined multiple instruments to carry each melody, an approach similar to what Virgil Thomson disdained as the "German" school of orchestration. But instead of a Brucknerian layering of instruments, the orchestration of the *Elegiac Symphony* resembles the concertos of his beloved Handel, whose careful combinations of instruments never obscure the clarity of the polyphony.

The first movement, "Tears of the Angel Israfel," an extensive reworking of the poignant second overture from Harrison's unfinished 1958 *Political Primer*, retains the distinctive colors of his now-standard "gamelan section" of glockenspiel, vibraphone, celesta, piano, tack piano, and two harps. However, in a concession to practicality, he does not insist on a justly tuned orchestra and so admits woodwinds and their tempered finger holes, which he'd banished from the *Political Primer*. Harrison named this version after a traditional Islamic archangel. "The angel of music, Israfel ('whose heartstrings are a lute'—Edgar Allan Poe), stands with his feet in the earth and his head in the sun. He will blow the last trumpet. Six times daily he looks down into hell and is so convulsed with grief that his tears would inundate the earth if Allah did not stop their flow."[34]

The second movement, the only relatively fast one among the five, originated in the sketch titled *Canticle* that Harrison was working on when he moved from San Francisco to Los Angeles in 1942. Resembling the neoclassical *Gigue* that he wrote for dancers in Los Angeles, in this context the movement projects a much angrier tone.

The newly composed, ruminative third movement shares the same title as the first and takes a different perspective on some of the same ideas. Unable to restrain his impulse toward just intonation, Harrison featured intertwining melodies for harmonics on two solo double basses, Serge Koussevitsky's instrument. Of all the string players, the bassist can most easily play natural harmonics—that is, pitches of the harmonic series of the open string—by touching lightly at corresponding nodes on the length of the string, even up to the eleventh harmonic and other pitches far outside of equal temperament. Up in this range, bass harmonics have an unearthly tone, unique but comparable to the viol timbre Harrison had so admired in his youth.[35]

When it came time to write the dramatic climax of the symphony that would express a son's grief at his mother's departure, Harrison unflinchingly reached back to his own moment of greatest anguish, the year of his breakdown, and adapted his dark organ work from 1947, *Praises for Michael the Archangel*. That fourth movement's fiercely atonal language sets it apart from the other, mostly tonal movements. The Catholic requiem mass identifies Michael as the angel who leads the souls of the departed into heavenly light. In this orchestration, Harrison turns the introspective counterpoint of his New York years into a cry of torment. Besides Ruggles, the other angel hovering above this fourth movement is Charles Ives, whose aesthetic can be heard in the rhythmic independence of its angular lines and in its uncompromising dissonance. The year of the symphony, 1974, was also the twentieth anniversary of Ives's death and the centennial of his birth.[36]

The final movement, "The Sweetness of Epicurus," could represent the heavenly destination of the archangel Michael's journey; it ends Harrison's *Elegiac Symphony* on a note of resigned acceptance of grief. As with the second movement, Harrison adapted a movement from a 1942 orchestral sketch. After the dissonant cries of the previous movement, the final movement's repeating bass line, in the form of a baroque passacaglia, reassures and consoles.[37] Composed around the time when Harrison first met Copland in Los Angeles, its meandering quintal polyphony finally gives way to an almost Copland-esque climax, but the ending, like Harrison's grief, remains unresolved.

Still depressed and beleaguered by his joint teaching appointments at San Jose State and Stanford (for a single year as a temporary replacement), Harrison scrambled to finish his symphony in time for its December 7, 1975, premiere at Oakland's Paramount Theatre. The musicians of the Oakland Symphony Youth Orchestra arrived that day for the final dress rehearsal to find fifteen new measures of Harrison's new symphony stapled to their orchestral parts. The performance of the first four movements went so well that the audience applauded between them, but not surprisingly, that first performance of the last movement went so roughly that conductor Denis de Coteau turned to the audience and announced that, despite the exhausting program they had just endured, the orchestra would repeat that last movement and do it justice. As the loud and sustained applause (after an extended silence as the final notes faded) demonstrated, they did.[38] "It all sounds of one voice, one spirit," wrote critic Heuwell Tircuit in the *San Francisco Chronicle* two days later.[39]

For Harrison, his symphony provided a cathartic purging of his year of accumulated grief cushioned by love, friendship, and music. In his score he appended an epigraph from Horace: "Bitter sorrows will grow milder with music."[40] And now, with so many figures from his old life departed, he was about to discover a new path that would lead him to the greatest balm of all: the music that would enchant him like no other.

PART 6

The Great Melody

We come together
Eagerly at Manila
In music's domain
and will bear homeward new notes
New hearts & bright memories.
—Lou Harrison, "Go Planetary!"[1]

In October 1975, Lou Harrison returned to Asia for the first time in over a decade to present a paper at the third conference of the Asian Composers League, which aimed to establish a regional identity and cooperation for these composers independent of Europe or North America. Greeting the delegates in the embarrassingly extravagant Cultural Center of the Philippines were First Lady Imelda Marcos and Harrison's friend, the composer Lucrecia "King" Kasilag, now president of the National Music Council, who had organized the conference and invited Harrison.[2]

Harrison's presentation, "Asian Music and the United States," summarized the history of Asian influences on American composers such as Cowell, Hovhaness, and Partch; rather optimistically, it predicted the spread of cultural egalitarianism in music education in the United States. The paper took deliberate aim at postwar serialism, which he labeled the "international atomic style," connoting not only its reductionist and pointillistic techniques but also an association with the dehumanizing elements of the atomic age.

Harrison contrasted this music, "often promoted by huge electronic firms," with the music of younger composers and openly expressed his support for the emerging minimalist style, whose origins he detected in Asian music. "Thus, the music of Terry Riley, Steve Reich and Philip Glass, to name only three prominent [young composers], explores repetitive and shifted patterns (we used to call all this permutations in my day—they call it 'phasing' now) which are regularly rhythmic and clearly melodic and tonal as well and which often sound gamelan-like," he said. "La Monte Young has been exploring extended listening to single ratios—but they are real ones, for example seven to six—and not the surds of equal temperament."[3] (He grudgingly forgave Reich and Glass their use of equal temperament).[4]

Harrison had been a supporter of minimalism since he heard Gerhard Samuel conduct Riley's proto-minimalist masterpiece *In C* in Oakland in 1969. The piece nearly caused an audience riot, but Harrison sought out the young composer and pronounced the piece "splendor torn from the heart of the sun."[5] Riley, at first confused by the effusive old man, later became fast friends with Harrison, and by this point in the 1970s, he had also adopted just intonation. "I feel very close to him musically and always considered him a loving older brother in this wonderful community of musicians we have here on the West Coast," Riley recalled. "I feel blessed to have known him."[6] The two often found themselves programmed together and held up as America's West Coast mavericks.[7] Of special interest to this conference, Glass's, Young's, and Riley's music owed much to their Indian mentors, and Reich drew from his studies of African music and Balinese gamelan music.

At his presentation, Harrison played recorded excerpts from *Pacifika Rondo*, including the movement "Hatred of the Filthy Bomb." A brief argument broke out on the panel, with one participant stating, "[Harrison's] Chinese music was better than that of a lot of Chinese composers." Others considered the excerpts "only superficially Chinese."[8] One delegate challenged Harrison's implication that interest in Asian music would eclipse the "international atomic style." Harrison responded, "It is my personal belief that all of us living in the aftermath of the European explosion around the globe increasingly find our inner tempo dictated more by locality and less by international atomic style. Contrary to what we thought before, Europe, now we all know, is ethnic like the rest of us. I feel that Asian music is bound to prevail in the long run."[9]

Cowell and Harrison bore much responsibility for the profound shift in American attitudes toward Asian music, represented by the young minimalists and Harrison's presence at the conference. This generation of composers, now coming of age at a time when non-Western traditions impinged on the popular consciousness, was picking up the threads that Harrison had first unspooled around the time they were born in the 1930s. At that time, Asian music, if considered at all, was most often a vague source for musical plunder and superficial exoticism. But now Harrison's argument that Asian traditions were equal members of the larger family of what he called "the human music" no longer seemed eccentric. Nearing age sixty, Harrison was already beginning to be recognized as one of the progenitors of the trend that the popular music industry would soon call "world music."

By the mid-1970s, mostly healed from his New York travails, Harrison returned to an active role in music and Bay Area culture; his music increasingly appeared on concert programs and recordings (despite their unusual demands and instruments). He looked forward to retirement from teaching, and many artists would have been content with having achieved the status of éminence grise in American classical music. Although he appreciated the professional recognition, creating beauty with friends remained his life's principle pleasure. "I've really never been overmuch impressed with the grandeur of it all—opera houses and symphony orchestras and so on," he explained. "Making music with friends was the important thing. What we were doing was the important thing."[10]

Harrison now seemed likely to carry these musical interests into his retirement, but as he returned to California from Manila, he was about to enter an unexpected new phase. Just at the time when many artists find comfort in the cushions of their established style, Harrison would plunge deeply into yet another form of Asian music, the sound that would be his lodestar for the rest of his life—one that ultimately allowed him to bring together all of the many influences he'd assimilated over the decades into his greatest musical hybrid of all, and the culmination of his composing career.

29

GOLDEN RAIN (1975–1977)

For myself, I cannot imagine how it would be possible to be an American musician and not have an interest in world music. . . . [A] young composer can (and often does) conclude that he is "on his own," and may develop a lasting distrust of the old European "back home." In the great supermarket of the record store, and in some universities, he may encounter the musics of India, China, Japan, Java and Bali, or Africa. He may decide then, that after all European music is just one more ethnic music. . . . Our young composer . . . may realize that he is heir to more than the local symphony propounds, may suspect that the latter is mostly a foreign propaganda machine, or even a museum-church as well, but that "outside" a beautiful big world awaits him—the neighbors! Is there something a little incestuous, beyond a certain age, in too constant and exclusive an interest in the parental world? Then there is the sensuous aspect. Is there any large orchestra anywhere on the planet so beautiful of sound as the Javanese or Balinese gamelan? No, there isn't. The Overtone Series is the Rule, World Music the Font. Cherish, conserve, consider, create.

—Lou Harrison[1]

Despite his series of new works for conventional instruments, Lou Harrison's fascination with Asian music was undiminished, and he soon had more allies in the Bay Area. One of the scholars whose work on ancient Sumerian music had inspired Harrison's *Sonata in Ishartum* was the vastly talented and energetic Robert Brown. Brown had been one of the first students of the pioneering ethnomusicologist Mantle Hood at UCLA and had inherited his advocacy for what Hood called "bimusicality," the idea that an educated musician should be conversant in more than one musical tradition.[2] One of the new generation of participatory ethnomusicologists who rejected old armchair theorizing, Bob Brown brought his ideas to Connecticut's Wesleyan University in the 1960s, where he also brought masters of musical traditions from around the world.

There, with the help of his friends Luise and Samuel Scripps (Samuel being the arts-loving heir to the founder of United Press International), Brown created the

American Society for Eastern Arts (ASEA) to bring together masters and students of Asian music and dance. At Mills College he established a summer program and later convinced Scripps to purchase and import to California Kyai Udan Mas, a beautiful Javanese gamelan set of instruments whose name means "Golden Rain." Soon the ambitious Brown left Wesleyan, renamed ASEA the Center for World Music (CWM), and expanded it to a year-round institute based in Berkeley. In the fall of 1973 alone, the CWM presented at least six Javanese gamelan concerts, including shadow plays and dance, plus a Balinese shadow play, concerts of music from South India, China, Iran, and Japan, and a concert by program alumnus Steve Reich and his ensemble.

Harrison learned about the CWM early on and made the 160-mile round trip from Aptos to CWM performances as often as he could. He eventually joined the center's board of directors. While working on the *Elegiac Symphony*, Harrison managed to attend many events at the 1974 summer session, which brought more than forty musicians and dancers from India, Japan, China, Ghana, Java, and Bali, culminating that August in the first Berkeley World Music Festival: two days of continuous performances with workshops and booths showcasing international foods, arts, and crafts.

But Brown's expansive vision (which included buying a historic church to house the center) was beginning to outstrip financial reality, and as a downturn in the economy put pressure on Sam Scripps's ability to support the society, he and Brown began to bicker, with Harrison and other board members caught in the middle. Harrison had come to be good friends with Scripps, but Brown convinced Harrison to ask Sam Scripps to leave the board. By year's end, Scripps had resigned his position but also withdrawn his support, and Harrison, bitter and guilty about his role in Scripps's departure, also resigned from the board.[3] Devastated by the loss of Scripps's funding, Brown canceled the spring concert series and laid off most of the staff, but he went ahead with his plan to move the Society and its gamelan into the church buildings and planned another ambitious summer Center for World Music program.

Despite their differences, Brown asked Harrison to be the next summer session's composer-in-residence (as Steve Reich had been the previous summer) and to teach a course. Harrison chose "Intonation in World Music" as the topic.[4] Brown assigned Harrison an upstairs room, and he and Colvig moved in with their turntable, monochords, harps, metallophones, and tools.

About twenty enthusiastic students, mostly college age, crowded into the un-air-conditioned room early that hot summer of 1975, and Harrison handed out a syllabus. Among the students were the young composers David Doty (later a founder of the Just Intonation Network), Barbara Benary (who would later establish the Gamelan Son of Lion in New York), and Daniel Schmidt (also an important West Coast instrument builder). Starting with the music of ancient Sumer, Harrison next introduced Pythagoras and the Greeks, and then he moved on to the tunings of Korea, China, and Indonesia. Harrison included contemporary music (including his own) and used the new edition of Harry Partch's *Genesis of a Music* as the course textbook.

Rather than just assigning readings and playing recordings, he insisted that the students tune the harp and learn the concepts by listening and practicing. "I recall

Lou going to his harp and tuning up a couple of Greek scales and improvising little pieces," remembered student Jeff Abell (later to be professor at Columbia College). "One of them had an oddly bluesy quality, and he noted that this was the scale that Plato had denounced as 'degenerate.'"[5]

To teach Indonesian tuning, Harrison brought the students downstairs to experience a Javanese gamelan for themselves. A complete gamelan, such as Kyai Udan Mas, has not one but two tuning systems and so two sets of instruments. Harrison demonstrated the pentatonic *slendro* tuning system, whose nearly equal scale steps, he proposed, were very close to the just intervals 7:6 and 8:7. The seven-tone *pelog* system, on the other hand, has both larger and smaller unequal scale steps. Although *pelogs* can vary somewhat from one gamelan to another, Harrison maintained that the *pelog* of Kyai Udan Mas replicated the series of harmonics 10, 11, 12, 14, 15, 16, 18 and so could be described in just intonation, "give or take a cycle or so."[6]

Brown strongly objected to this hypothesis, accusing Harrison of imposing a concept alien to Javanese culture. Although Harrison did not necessarily hold that all gamelan tunings were based on just intonation, he considered just intonation to be a foundational musical concept that transcended culture. It wouldn't be the first or the last time that his notions of musical universals would raise hackles.

Even though his class met only one day a week, Harrison and Colvig frequented the CWM grounds, watching rehearsals, meeting with students, and building instruments. And Harrison spent a lot of time talking with a slight old man with thick spectacles and a disarming smile. He would guide Harrison down the path that would largely define the rest of his career.

GENDING PAK COKRO

His full Javanese name was Kanjeng Raden Tumenggung Wasitodipuro, but everyone knew him as Pak Cokro.[7] One of the twentieth century's great masters of the Javanese gamelan, Wasitodipuro had just started teaching at the new California Institute of the Arts (CalArts) in Valencia in Southern California when Brown invited him to participate in ASEA summer workshops. Pak Cokro's daughter, the dancer Nanik, and her husband, Balinese musician and dancer I Nyoman Wenten, were also at CalArts and in residence at Mills in 1972 and later at the Center for World Music. Here was a perfect opportunity for Harrison, who had sought mentors from Henry Cowell to Arnold Schoenberg to Virgil Thomson to Liang Tsai-Ping, to learn this most ravishing music from as close to the source as possible.

Yet at first, Wasitodipuro respectfully declined to be Harrison's teacher. They were both revered professionals, and, to the Javanese way of thinking, for Cokro to take Harrison as a student would be an insult, a demotion of his relative status. But Harrison persisted, and finally Cokro decided that they could converse as equals about music theory and history. Harrison began meeting with Pak Cokro when he could, learning the basics of the music theory of Javanese gamelan. In intermittent studies lasting about a decade, he came to adore the gentle old man, behind whose modest manner and halting English lurked a formidable musician and composer.

Already legendary in Java for his facility on all the gamelan instruments in a variety of regional styles, Pak Cokro couldn't escape the poisonous politics of the developing nation. At times he received government support, but he composed contemporary gamelan works obliquely critical of government inattention to poverty (*Sopir Becak*), corruption (*Kuwi apa kuwi*), and environmental degradation (*Lancaran Penghijauan*). Purists disdained Cokro's compositional innovations, including choral harmonies, triple meter, combining techniques from different Javanese gamelan traditions, and even adding Latin American rhythms to gamelan compositions. Harrison detected in him a kindred spirit who shared a love of musical hybrids, radical politics, and "a rebellious creativity." Harrison recalled, "My lessons with him were wonderful; they'd wander off into general conversations about culture."[8]

Most of the Center for World Music courses, including Javanese gamelan, culminated in public performances at the Festival of World Music that August 1975, and Harrison invited the students in his class to compose new pieces for his American gamelan that they would perform as a final public concert.

Compose for gamelan? To many of the ethnomusicology students studying there, the combination of new compositions and gamelan (even if it was not an Indonesian gamelan at all) seemed oxymoronic, if not heretical. The preservationist agenda that Harrison had experienced in Tokyo had intensified into a sensitivity to postcolonial cultural imbalances, leaving many ethnomusicology students deeply suspicious of incursions into the ancient traditions they revered. To Harrison these attitudes only reinforced a fictional purism, while he viewed art as changing via perennial hybridization. The students often cliquishly associated themselves with different courses—the Javanese gamelan students, the sitar students, the Indian dance students, and so on. Some objected to Harrison's use of the Javanese term "gamelan" to refer to his own set of homemade instruments.

Yet, however innovative, Harrison and Colvig's set of metallophones wasn't even the only "American gamelan" built during this period, and other experimenters with such instruments included the very students in his class. Barbara Benary had already begun building a set of iron instruments in New York modeled after the Javanese gamelan. David Doty and co-conspirators calling themselves Other Music had began gathering junk that would become the basis for their American gamelan. After having earlier seen the Harrison-Colvig instruments, Daniel Schmidt had begun experimenting with using flat bars for gongs.[9] Creating instruments like these felt natural to students coming from backgrounds in experimental music and its tradition (established in part by Harrison in his 1930s percussion ensemble) of nontradition.

The 1975 Festival concert would be the first concert of American gamelan music on the West Coast, launching a new generation of composers for the medium, including Schmidt, Benary, and Doty. Despite the controversy, the concert "gave us the belief that we were a 'movement,'" said Schmidt.[10] Schmidt alone that summer navigated both the circles of the experimentalists and of the Javanese gamelan students (though Benary was also a trained ethnomusicologist). The Javanese gamelan students regarded the bell sounds emanating from the upstairs rehearsal room with suspicion. To Harrison these musical traditions were neither pure nor static and indeed were stronger for their "impurity," the way blending copper and tin made an alloy (bronze) stronger than either of its constituent ingredients.

Even so, he always maintained that composing for the Javanese gamelan itself did not occur to him that summer. "It's a whole world of sound out there, and we're a part of the world, so it's also part of us," Barbara Benary remembered Harrison saying then. "Every classical composer has borrowed from lots around them. Everybody borrows from everybody, but that doesn't mean that they are trying to injure anybody thereby. It's just what it is."[11] Most of the students in his class, aware of the controversy, shared Harrison's defiance of ethnomusicological orthodoxy and set about enthusiastically preparing for their concert. "He kept his ego out of the way and let us produce that concert," Daniel Schmidt remembered. "We felt very much that we were doing it together as a group."[12]

The admiration was mutual. "I adore these young people to whom anything is possible (and who do so) because they were born into an affluent and confident country and can have no conception of what it is to have grown up when there may never have ever been any legitimate paying work for one," Harrison wrote in his notebook from the time. "They can play my *Fugue for Percussion*, for instance; no one has told them it is impossible to play. They compose splendid long pieces in which we hear (in extended joy) all the permutations of some sensible lovely figure of music."[13] Perhaps his students' youthful enthusiasm and refusal to accept limits inspired the nearly fifty-eight-year-old Harrison to become a student again, as he embarked on the final and most satisfying musical learning experience in his long search for new artistic horizons.

PLAINT

We all complain, at least a little.

—Lou Harrison[14]

Harrison's part-time position at San Jose State gave him a valuable platform for his career, even as it gave the university more national exposure.[15] In 1975, while working with the Center for World Music, he was also hatching big plans for his university. For the next year's United States bicentennial, the university approved his ambitious proposal for a celebration of American music in collaboration with the San Jose Symphony. For the 1975–1976 season, Harrison planned an "American Music" course and a series of university and community residencies for the most prominent American composers, including Virgil Thomson, Alan Hovhaness, John Cage, and Carlos Chávez. Aaron Copland and Martha Graham came out to recreate their famous production of *Appalachian Spring*. Only later did the university administration suddenly decline to fully fund the series after all. Plans for what would have been a historic second production of Harry Partch's *Delusion of the Fury* were canceled.[16]

Harrison's old friends had already made all their travel arrangements when the news came, and Harrison felt he had no choice but to pay the visiting composers out of his own pocket. Thomson's trip alone cost him $535. Harrison assigned blame for these and other perceived injustices squarely to the university administration. "You have demeaned our faculty and shamed yourself in a Nixonian manner," he thundered in a furious letter of protest to the (politically liberal) university president, dropping about the most scurrilous possible epithet at that time and place. "You will have transformed our music department into a college of sopranos."[17] San Jose State further infuriated Harrison when he discovered that the administration had been unfairly denying him retirement benefits for more than a decade.[18] Harrison vowed to quit after the end of his current contract; however, concerned about finances, he would end up staying for several more years.

Nevertheless, Harrison was happy to see his old friends, none more than Virgil Thomson, who conducted a performance of his celebrated opera *Four Saints in Three Acts* that April. Thomson insisted that Harrison, Colvig, and Dee accompany him on a road trip down to Los Angeles and offered to pay so they could stay in fine hotels and eat in elegant restaurants, rather than the more rustic accommodations that Harrison and Colvig were used to. "Virgil was as always stimulating," Harrison remembered, "lots of fun, very dear and totally exasperating in restaurants, where he takes evident delight in creating great scenes about the state of his bacon or the unfreshness of his vegetables."[19]

Later that winter, Thomson returned the favor, hosting Harrison when he came out to New York for a performance of his version of *Marriage at the Eiffel Tower* with the two of them as utterly charming narrators. The occasion was the fortieth anniversary of the American Composers Alliance, with Harrison's great ally Dennis Russell Davies conducting in Lincoln Center's Alice Tully Hall.[20] Harrison met with publishers, appeared on the radio, and gave talks.

The successful return to the city he had left in despair nearly a quarter century earlier signaled Harrison's growing recognition as one of the elder statesmen of American music. Invitations followed for residencies at the Eastman School of Music and the University of Illinois, talks at performances in St. Paul (led by Davies) and other cities. He and Colvig shipped their American gamelan to Illinois for a performance of the *Suite for Violin and American Gamelan*. This piece even became the theme for a weekly gay-oriented radio program on KPFA.

Despite his increasing national repute and the success of his existing style, however, Harrison began a new chapter in his creative life when he accepted an invitation from philanthropist Betty Freeman. Freeman had been a piano student and later a collector of modern paintings, but she didn't discover the world of contemporary experimental music until 1961, when she was approached to bail La Monte Young out of jail (on a marijuana charge). His music captivated her, and she became America's leading angel of contemporary music and soon of Harrison's. Freeman underwrote the premiere of Harry Partch's last theater piece, *Delusion of the Fury*, and virtually supported him until his death in 1974. Her salons hosted some of the best contemporary music in the country, and now she wanted to present Lou Harrison and Pak Cokro in concert in her hometown of Los Angeles.

Students trucked the gamelan over to Freeman's Hollywood home, where half the program would be devoted to gamelan compositions by Pak Cokro and the other half to Harrison's non-gamelan music. As they waited to perform at a little pre-concert party, Harrison and Pak Cokro chatted—and Harrison received a second, much more fateful invitation. "You should please write for gamelan," Pak Cokro told him.

Harrison was stunned. Even though he had composed for his own American gamelan, "it didn't even vaguely occur to me to compose for [Javanese gamelan]," he often said. "You could have knocked me over with a piano!"[21]

HONEYED THUNDER

Harrison had fallen in love with the gamelan. The subtleties of its intricate melodies, its textures that ingeniously reconciled his love of counterpoint with his love of melody, its "ravishing" ringing timbres, all conspired to make Harrison swoon.[22] Although he had not started playing in the ensemble during the CWM session, he never missed an opportunity to hear Pak Cokro lead the bronze orchestra at the summer and fall concerts. The music's indirectness and frequent ambiguities reflected the subtle ways in which Pak Cokro could make a point without ever telling a listener directly what he meant. His soft, melodic speech, even in rehearsal, echoed the gentle waterfalls of tones of the gamelan.

But the future of the Center for World Music and its Javanese gamelan, Kyai Udan Mas, was uncertain; Bob Brown understood that its only realistic hope for survival was to become a part of an academic institution. Of course Harrison immediately thought of San Jose State, where he could then keep gamelan in his musical life. Brown and Harrison proposed to the music department, the dean, and the university president to bring the Center for World Music permanently to the university. Brown wanted a position on the faculty, space for the gamelan and other groups, and a budget for bringing visiting artists, among other things. Negotiations continued, and the university administration agreed only to a temporary arrangement for the spring 1976 semester.

The deal brought the Kyai Udan Mas gamelan from Berkeley to San Jose. Pak Cokro would teach the gamelan with his assistant, Jody Diamond, and Cokro's daughter Nanik and son-in-law I Nyoman Wenten came up to teach Javanese dance. Brown taught a class in Indonesian music with Wenten as his assistant. Harrison took the course and completed all the assignments just like any other student.[23] "The gamelan lived just outside my door," remembered Harrison, "so I spent many an hour (when not occupied with my pupils) studying its special composition, tuning, and powers."[24]

That spring, Harrison joined the Javanese gamelan and for the first time learned to play the music that had so beguiled him forty years earlier. Like the other students, he progressed through the different instruments, becoming familiar first with the relatively easy core melody instruments of the gamelan. Theorists conventionally divide up the melodic instruments of the Central Javanese gamelan into three roles—the core melody or *balungan* instruments; the colotomic instruments (which regularly interpunctuate the melody, creating a series of graduated pillars that form the framework for the cyclic forms); and the "elaborating" or faster melodic instruments. Only after playing the core melody would Harrison have graduated to the colotomic instruments, which may seem technically easy (how hard can it be to hit a gong with a mallet?) but ideally require a deep knowledge of the structural and metrical concepts of Javanese gamelan compositions. Harrison continued to learn of these concepts, as well as modal theory and history, with Pak Cokro when he could.

But the biggest question facing Harrison was how to approach composing for Javanese gamelan. He had written for American gamelan just as he would any other set of percussion instruments, and other American gamelan composers (Schmidt, Doty, and Philip Corner, among others) had done the same. That approach would not be possible with a Javanese gamelan, first for the very practical reason that many of the players simply didn't read music in Western (staff) notation. The Javanese notate core melodies through a system in which numbers indicate notes, known as *kepatihan* or cipher notation, but players of the faster melodic instruments create their own, unnotated melodies based on this core melody.

Apart from this obvious impracticality, Harrison had begun to realize that the Javanese had developed their elaborate musical system after centuries with these instruments and that he could benefit from respecting the wisdom already inherent in this tradition. Harrison thus began to approach the problem of composing for this set of instruments by fashioning a middle path between Javanese tradition and his own instincts as an American composer. It was a path he would follow for the rest of his life.

CLASSIC ORDER

Harrison began, as he usually did, by finding a melody in the mode, but now he wrote it down in cipher notation as the *balungan*. The next step was to find a way for the gongs and various colotomic instruments to divide the melody up in a way that made musical sense to Harrison. He modeled, in a general way, the typical Javanese doubling and halving of the metrical cycles and the interpunctuations of the colotomic instruments. However, he made little pretense of duplicating traditional Javanese forms. Harrison's first gamelan melodies have fragments that resemble the modal motives typical of Javanese melodies, but their discursive nature makes them more similar to the free-form melodies he wrote for other media throughout his career, where he would write in bar lines only after the fact. Although still a Javanese gamelan novice, he did not make these choices out of ignorance, just as he could compose engaging asymmetries in his *zheng* compositions while still regularly performing the steady duple meters of traditional Chinese music.

"My problem was, of course I didn't really know how to deal with classic form at that point, so I used a kind of Whitmanesque free verse form," he explained. "Also I didn't know how really to deal with the colotomy [gongs], the measuring off-ers. What I did was to make a list to myself of the 'weight' of each one of them, how they felt as weight. Then I used that in connection with the sort of free verse thing to mark it off according to the weight system I needed . . . I balanced all of these."[25]

Harrison named the first piece in honor of his teacher, the one who suggested that he write for Javanese gamelan, *Gending Pak Chokro* ("*gending*" is a generic Javanese term for a composition).[26] The elder Javanese master must have found the notes very confusing. Harrison did not realize that players of the faster melodic instruments rely on traditional structures and modes to help guide them, markers that were absent in Harrison's earliest gamelan compositions. Players of instruments such as the *bonang* kettle-gongs or *gambang* xylophone would know what to do when moving from one tone to another over a four-beat phrase in a traditional mode and style, but what to do in a six-beat phrase? Or when a gong suddenly appears in the middle of the phrase?

Harrison did not realize it, but he was putting Pak Cokro in a difficult social situation. According to Javanese social tradition, he and Harrison were peers, both highly respected musicians in their respective countries. Pak Cokro could share with Harrison information on gamelan theory, as two equal scholars can converse, but to criticize Harrison's composition directly or even to offer suggestions would be, for a refined Javanese man like Pak Cokro, almost unthinkable. Presenting him with the composition also put Pak Cokro in a difficult situation in regard to the ensemble. He could not see how he would be able to teach the gamelan to play this eccentric work, but neither would social etiquette allow him to say no to his friend. Instead, he quietly deflected his friend's inquiries about the piece while the ensemble rehearsed traditional works for an end-of-semester concert.

Oblivious to such cross-cultural subtleties, Harrison continued to compose. While *Gending Pak Chokro* uses the pentatonic *slendro* tuning system, another of his "free verse form" pieces, *Gending Samuel* (dedicated to Sam Scripps) uses the seven-tone *pelog* system. Instead of choosing one of the traditional Javanese sub-sets and modes of *pelog*, Harrison invented his own six-tone mode consisting of pitches 1, 2, 3, 4, 5, and 7, an innovation certain to raise eyebrows among Javanese musicians.[27]

Finally, Pak Cokro figured out a solution for the status dilemma—by removing himself from the fraught equation. He took Jody Diamond aside. "Why don't you go help Lou?"[28] With Diamond's help, Harrison finally decided that his next piece would adopt a traditional Javanese form. Although he would feel free to periodi-cally return to "Whitmanesque" forms, Harrison came to understand the internal logic of the Javanese structures for the gamelan orchestra, which appealed to him for many reasons. "First of them all is order—classic order," he said. "I love the structural shapes of the music, like the harmonic sense of classic architecture. I spent many years studying architecture, and the classical styles always appealed. There's that element and formal sense in a Javanese gending: it can be thought of as classically formulated—section A, section B and so on are like pillars and walls and arches."[29]

The temporal structures that create this architecture reflect the cycles of Hindu cosmology, in which eternity is divided into the rise and fall of days, seasons, years, lifetimes, and civilizations. In gamelan, the primary cycle is the one punctuated by the great gong (*gong ageng* or simply *gong*), a cycle thus known as a *gongan*. The *gongan* is divided into halves or quarters by strikes on the *kenong*, and those phrases demarked are themselves halved by the sound of the smaller hanging gongs called *kempul*. In between the *kempul* strokes sounds a yet smaller horizontal gong known, with typical onomatopoeia, as *ketuk*.[30] This hierarchical framework is always built on divisions or groupings of two, reflecting Hinduism's great cosmic dualism. Thus *gongan* are nearly always made up of a power-of-two number of beats, typically 16 or 32, but sometimes 64 or even 128. Like much of the other Asian music Harrison already loved, these Javanese structures contrast with the insistent, goal-directed forms of Western music.

The first Javanese form that Harrison attempted was the relatively simple sixteen-beat structure called *bubaran* for his *Bubaran Robert*, named for Bob Brown. Rather than using staff notation, Harrison notated the piece as a Javanese composer might, with number or cipher notation:

T		T	N		T	P	T	N		T	P	T	N		T	P	T	N
5	6	6̶6̶	6		5	6	3	5		3	5	5̶5̶	5		3	5	2	3̂

EXAMPLE 29.1

The numbers indicate the scale degrees in the *slendro* tuning system,[31] and the letters above represent the colotomic instruments *ketuk* (T), *kempul* (P), and *kenong* (N). The phrase ends with the *gong suwukan* (represented by the vertical parentheses). The slashes through the numbers indicate hitting the bar while holding it to get a damped sound, and the lines above the pitch numbers indicate a halving of durations.

The Javanese hear the gong as ending the cycle rather than beginning it, so that the metrical stress is inverted from the convention in the West; that is, the stress appears on the "upbeat" rather than the "downbeat." Thus the important structural points are at the end of each four-beat section (known as a *gatra*), in this case where the *kenong* strikes. Yet to think of these periodic gong strokes just as supporting pillars for a melody is only part of the story. The *kempul* and *kenong* are not single instruments; instead they are sets that usually include all or most of the notes of the scale, and the player will usually hit the one that is the same pitch as the coincident note of the core melody. (For example, in the first measure or *gatra* above, the fourth pitch in the *balungan* melody is pitch 6, which means the *kenong* player strikes the pitch 6 *kenong* pot.) Therefore, the *kempul* and *kenong* together form another melody inside the one played by the *balungan* instruments, one that can be found by taking every other note of the above melody. (The dot represents a rest):

	N		P	N		P	N		P	N
.	6		6	5		5	5		5	3̂

EXAMPLE 29.2

This new melody, in a sense an "abstraction" or "reduction" of the *balungan*, shows the inner structure of the phrase—a stair-step descent from pitch 6 to a resolution on pitch 3. The pattern becomes even clearer by taking the process even further and looking at only the *kenong* pitches:

EXAMPLE 29.3

Harrison came to understand that a good melody for the gamelan must make sense at each of these levels.

The instruments that play more rhythmically dense ("faster") melodies are sometimes called the "elaborating" instruments, but that word, with its connotation of inessential decoration, can be misleading. These melodies are often compared to the intricate woodcarvings on the instrument racks or the lace-like holes in the flat shadow puppets (*wayang kulit*). Although the skeleton of the puppet may give it form, like the core melody in gamelan, the elaborate filigree surrounding it is not simply ornamentation—it is the very life of the artwork.

In the same way that the *balungan* melody can be heard as a denser version of the sequence of tones in the *kenong* gongs, so these faster melodies weave yet more intricate melodies around the core tones of the *balungan*. Normally, players of these instruments create their melodies extemporaneously based on their knowledge of the *balungan* pitches, form, mode, and style, and the idiomatic melodic frameworks (known as *cengkok*) of that instrument, but sometimes they (or composers) might want to plan those parts in advance. Jody Diamond's first meeting with Harrison aimed to figure out a part for the set of small horizontal gongs known as *bonang*. The melody she and Harrison worked out carefully fills around the important tones of the *balungan* melody being played at the same time:[32]

bonang melody: 5 6 5 6 2 3 5 6   5 6 1 6 3 5 6 5   3 5 3 5 1 2 3 5   3 5 6 5 2 3 5 3

balungan melody: 5   6   6 6 6   5   6   3   5   3   5   5 5 5   3   5   2   3

EXAMPLE 29.4

Although the *bonang* melody has more notes in the same amount of time, its pitches correspond with those of the *balungan* on the "strong" beats of each of the pair of *balungan* notes (enclosed in rectangles above). The most common pattern here is a simple back-and-forth repetition of each pair of tones, a technique called *pipilan* or *mipil*. This stock form of elaboration would soon have a featured place in Harrison's acreage of toys, and he would apply it to Western instruments as well. Such patterns at higher pitches would be denser yet. However, gamelan players' freedom to diverge from the *balungan* tones would be inversely proportional to the metrical stress at that point. All instruments must sound together on the gong and probably the *kenong* tones, but in the passages between those notes, the players of the elaborating instruments have some latitude to create a melody with a pleasing contour appropriate to the style, mode, and form—a stylistic issue that requires considerable study for players to appreciate. Harrison recognized that he had a lot of work ahead of him.

The Javanese call this process of creating progressively denser versions of a melody *kembangan*, literally the "flowering" of the melody. The gamelan melody exfoliates its skeletal form into elaborate filigrees that fit together, fractal-like, in different rhythmic strata. What emerges from this sonic weft and warp is polyphony based on principles completely different from those of European counterpoint. Instead of distinct, independent voices forming harmonies, a single melody blooms into many that alternately wander and converge but are always moved by the gravitational attraction of the core melody.[33]

Harrison next composed *Lancaran Daniel* (named for Daniel Schmidt) in a traditional Javanese form.[34] In both *Lancaran Daniel* and *Bubaran Robert*, Harrison for the first time attempted to write a melody in a particular Javanese mode or *patet*. This one, *patet manyura*, has a "tonic" or stressed tone on pitch number 6, but Harrison would later discover that, unlike Western modes, much more than the scale defines a *patet*. Nevertheless, Harrison called *Lancaran Daniel* "one of the first pieces I considered a well-done gamelan piece. . . . I felt it was a successful piece. It set me out on a journey that I've been on ever since."[35]

Harrison was, so far, alone on this journey. Among the other composers who wrote for American gamelan, none had written works that drew so directly from the Javanese tradition. Doing so required the courage of becoming a novice student in a tradition that many study for decades. Yet continuing his journey required access to gamelan instruments—and that access was about to disappear.

In the spring of 1976, administrators decided that SJSU could not afford to keep the Center for World Music, a move perhaps not unexpected given the intemperate tone of Harrison's earlier letter to the university president, and Bob Brown accepted the invitation of the University of Wisconsin to move it there.[36] The gamelan Kyai Udan Mas, which Harrison had enjoyed daily access to for months, would move to UC Berkeley in the fall. Determined to continue playing and composing through his last summer with the instruments in San Jose, Harrison turned to Schmidt and asked him to teach a summer session of gamelan. Despite the bad news, Pak Cokro's absence as gamelan director proved an advantage for Harrison, because for the first time, Harrison was able to try out his compositions in rehearsal. Gradually, with Schmidt's help, he devised ways to realize his nontraditional compositions.

Continuing his habit of naming his pieces for his friends, Harrison wrote *Gending Jody* for Jody Diamond, another *slendro* melody with an irregular "free verse" form. When Harrison's friend Peggy Glanville-Hicks contacted him about providing music for an art exhibition, Harrison visited the San Francisco studio of the sculptor, Pamela Boden, and was greatly impressed. The free form of Harrison's resulting gamelan work *Music for the Turning of a Sculpture* mirrors the dynamic asymmetry of Boden's *Mountain Torrent*, a cascade of gracefully curved wooden planks. However, the summer session was too short to prepare a public concert, and that August they packed up the instruments in a truck for the long drive back to Berkeley.

Harrison feared not only losing regular access to the gamelan but also losing the circle of young people, including many from the Center for World Music, whose enthusiasm and ideas he found so stimulating. Harrison let it be known that one

Sunday each month, he and Colvig would host a brunch at an Aptos or Berkeley restaurant to continue discussions of instruments, tunings, gamelan, and anything else that came up. Among those regularly attending were Daniel Schmidt, David Doty, Henry Rosenthal (a collaborator of Doty's), and a pair of percussionist brothers, Gary and Rick Kvistad. The brunch and talking would last for hours, with Harrison picking up the tab for everyone who came. For the few years they lasted, these informal seminars inspired a new generation of composers and instrument builders.[37]

As their dialogue continued, Schmidt concocted another scheme to perform Harrison's gamelan pieces. In fall 1976, while assisting Pak Cokro and Jody Diamond in teaching the Javanese gamelan in Berkeley, he met the young composer Paul Dresher, whom he spied surreptitiously measuring the instruments in gamelan class. As he suspected, Dresher, like Schmidt, was experimenting with building his own American gamelan instruments. While Schmidt was constructing metal bar instruments low-pitched enough to imitate the sounds of gongs, Dresher (who, influenced by Partch's book, had made instruments since high school) had been building the higher metallophones. They quickly conspired to merge their instruments into a new American gamelan with instruments based on Javanese models.

Schmidt and Dresher and other friends finally premiered Harrison's first gamelan works with these instruments at a concert in honor of Harrison's sixtieth birthday in May 1977 in Berkeley. Harrison's composer friend Peter Garland, pianist Rae Imamura, and Bob Hughes put together a three-and-a-half-hour career retrospective that included his 1940s percussion and chamber music and 1957's *Cinna* in addition to the gamelan works.[38]

The success of these first performances of his gamelan pieces inspired Harrison to continue composing, even though he lacked regular access to any gamelan. He sometimes made the drive up to Berkeley to see his friend Pak Cokro, but once again he found the elder composer reluctant to answer questions when the conversation turned to Harrison's own compositions. Gradually, Harrison came to understand Pak Cokro's perception of a social barrier that prevented him from speaking to Harrison as he would another student.

Pak Cokro could, however, offer advice to the student Daniel Schmidt, since they were not of the same social status, and the young man regularly studied with him. Harrison hatched a plan and began asking Schmidt to relay his questions as his own; then Harrison would call Schmidt and ask what the master had said. For a while the subterfuge worked, until one day after practice, as they ate at Pak Cokro's favorite Berkeley restaurant. When Schmidt casually asked a compositional question, Pak Cokro's eyes narrowed. "That's a question from Lou, isn't it?" he asked.[39]

It's hard to imagine another composer at the height of his career who would become a beginner again, but Harrison did so in an entirely different musical culture, determined to learn its fundamentals and nuances from the ground up and make them his—all without violating the cultural origins of that music. Although it felt perfectly natural to a musician whose entire career represented a constant process of exploring and learning, few artists had so fundamentally reinvented their style at age sixty.

But Harrison could hardly apply his new knowledge without much more frequent access to gamelan instruments than he could get at Berkeley, often a two-hour drive from his Aptos home. Then he learned that an ethnomusicologist at UC Santa Cruz, David Kilpatrick, had brought to that university a gamelan from Sunda in West Java. Closer, yes, but Harrison needed one of his own to work with. Kilpatrick had brought a young Sundanese musician, Undang Sumarna, to teach the ensemble. Could he help, Harrison asked Sumarna, purchase a gamelan for San Jose State?

30

PLAYING TOGETHER (1977–1979)

Even as their relationship settled, Colvig and Harrison's neighborhood around View-point Road was changing considerably over the nearly twenty years that Harrison had lived there. Attracted by the scenic views of Monterey Bay, newcomers were moving in, and houses sprouted over the bluffs, separating him from his old neighbors and trailheads. An elderly couple that lived up at the very end of the street, in failing health and annoyed about the changes to the neighborhood, confided to Colvig one day that they had finally decided to move. Their cabin was not much bigger than Harrison's, but it was on a double parcel and in a wonderful location. Colvig returned home and walked in their cabin door and over to Harrison. "How soon can we move?" he asked.

Harrison, for the first time in his life, had a reliable though hardly bounteous income, and Colvig received a small electrician's pension. With some savings as a down payment, Harrison borrowed $25,000 to buy the property—the first time that he had ever borrowed money, except from his parents. Having grown up in the Depression, he was always nervous about finances and didn't even have a credit card. "I'm a cash-and-carry man," he often said.[1]

Needing the money, he stuck with his job at San Jose State, despite his threat to quit over the bicentennial program fiasco. He also took on a class at the University of Southern California, flying down to Los Angeles every Monday and back, and Harrison earned enough to pay back the loan in only two years. Just one year after having bought it, he was offered $60,000 for half the property, which he declined. Ever enthusiastic about architecture, Harrison commissioned an architect friend for a design and got back a proposal for a beautiful two-story Japanese-style house. However, once the reality of their financial prospects sank in, he had to reluctantly accept a more affordable option: prebuilt modular structures trucked in from Sacramento.

They certainly needed the room to expand that the double lot afforded. "Once, he took me into his storeroom, where he had shadow puppets and all kinds of instruments and books and manuscripts, God knows what else," recalled his student Kerry Lewis. "I'd been in there two or three times with him when he was looking for things before I realized there was a full-size grand piano underneath a bunch of that stuff. It was so packed with things." Lewis remembered similar clutter at Harrison's campus office: "a full-size troubadour harp in there and Balinese masks and puppets and various instruments and things sitting around or hanging on the wall."[2] Annoyed by the buzzing fluorescent overhead lights, Harrison brought in some battered lamps, suffusing his office with a distinctive golden glow.[3]

The house Harrison and Colvig lived in for the rest of their lives displayed the same improvised, homemade quality as many of their instruments. A main living and dining room, spangled with Korean paintings, a Buddhist shrine, and Harrison's Iranian tiles at the entrance, connected to modest bedrooms and a tiny kitchen. In the kitchen they established the tradition of keeping a simmering pot of soup on the stove, into which they would dump any leftovers and the occasional hot pepper. They maintained this soup literally for years, during which time it turned into a disgusting purplish mess, which Harrison called their "thousand-year-old" soup.[4] The young Berkeley composer Daniel Schmidt, invited to "family soup" one afternoon, remembered the house "covered in sunshine and a cascading green of plants."

Colvig initially constructed a space for himself by laying corrugated fiberglass over trellises in back. "Plants twined all around the workbench, the radio and the oscilloscope."[5] Colvig eventually built his workshop in the backyard, whose interior was a chaos of scattered tools, half-built instruments, electronics, and an out-of-date beefcake calendar.

They attached another prefab module to the main house, creating what Harrison called the "Ives Room" because it was essentially paid for by the royalties Ives willed to Harrison for his Third Symphony.[6] Colvig constructed bookshelves that would eventually cover most of its circumference, except for spaces for Harrison's reed organ and paintings. Bedsheets formed improvised covers for trunks and boxes and more boxes of papers and manuscripts. The room finally afforded Harrison sufficient space for his grand piano, which had belonged to Cowell and Percy Grainger, but otherwise teemed with harps, monochords, and piles of whatever percussion exotica Harrison happened to be working with at the time.

However, Harrison did not usually compose in the cluttered music room. After their camper finally broke down, Colvig and Harrison converted the shell into a tiny room off the garage where Harrison did much of his composing, sealed off from the spectacular views of Monterey Bay just yards away—a quiet and dark hermitage insulated from the ringing phone and Colvig's putterings. "I can't be anywhere near any public connections," he insisted. "I absolutely cannot even be in the same building with a phone or anybody. Doors have to be locked and so on. I fear the interruption, 'cause it's my lifeline. It's my real therapy. That's my real way of adjusting to life."[7]

Over the years, they added an entryway trellis, soon covered in vines and an often-empty fountain. "No garden is complete without a muse," Harrison would say, pointing out the classical-style statue in its backyard niche.[8] Their gravel drive and curbless, unmowed lawn fronting a faded wooden fence soon set their property apart from the expensive houses that came to dominate the road. Their new neighbors paid enormous sums for two-story views of the Pacific, but Harrison and Colvig's house, set back from the road, had few windows. After some deliverymen were reluctant to come through the gate to their front door, they added a sign: "Please enter—There is no dog inside."

SERENADE

Sweet as the domes and garden flowered light
of the mosque of Mirimah, oh Sinan, the
blossoms red and white rest on your covered tomb
in lovely homage.

—Lou Harrison[9]

While utterly infatuated with the gamelan, Harrison never lost his equally sensuous love of plucked strings—psaltery, harp, guitar. "The first thing I like about [the guitar] is its extraordinary harmonicity: the body of the instruments, and the strings—it's like the harp in that sense, it also is a very harmonic instrument," he told guitarist John Schneider. "The whole body vibrates, and [it's] all of a piece. For reasons that I do not understand, the guitar's sound and body are simply marvelous for intonation studies and other things."[10] Harrison lamented only the fixed steel frets of the guitar that, unlike the movable frets tied onto the fingerboards of viols and lutes, force players into equal temperament.

Like Harrison, the guitarist and luthier Tom Stone, an instructor at the San Francisco Conservatory, wanted to free the guitar of its reliance on equally tempered frets. He dropped by Harrison's house one day with a prototype instrument that was fretted to play harmonics 16 through 32, which Harrison adored. However, Stone didn't want to lock the guitarist into any single tuning system. His ingenious solution was to create a system of interchangeable fingerboards, each of which could be swapped out and locked to the neck of a single guitar. With a few snaps, he showed an astonished Harrison how the same guitar could now be fitted with a fingerboard for another tuning. In fact, Stone could make many fingerboards, one for any tuning he wished.

Harrison was so excited that he immediately conceived a plan to compose five suites for refretted guitar, one in each of five tunings. A single performance could even feature them all, mixing corresponding movements from different suites simply by switching out the fingerboards between each movement.

By 1978, Harrison completed the first of these suites, and it became one of his most appealing and accomplished creations of the decade. His *Serenade for Guitar* uses a quirky eight-tone scale that resembles the octatonic scale that Harrison used in his *Concerto for Organ and Percussion*, except that it is in just intonation.[11] Although steeped in gamelan music at the time, Harrison easily drew upon familiar toys in his repertoire. Harrison's beloved baroque period flavors the two movements that bookend the suite, beginning with an urgent "Round" or rondeau, spiced with Harrison's favored *jhala* technique, and ending with a "Sonata" movement with a clear debt to the harpsichord sonatas of Domenico Scarlatti. The sultry second movement, "Air," suggests a lyrical baroque movement, although its thirteen-beat phrases are punctuated by gong-like low strings. The "Infinite Canon" pays homage to the "Canon perpetuus" from J. S. Bach's *Musical Offering*, and like that baroque classic, its end seamlessly aligns with its beginning, producing a musical Möbius strip.

In naming the fourth movement "Usul," Harrison referenced yet another culture, for this title refers to the rhythmic patterns of traditional Turkish music. This movement's cycle of 3+2+4+2 beats is Harrison's own, and the optional percussion—finger cymbals and drums—effectively evokes the atmosphere of a Near Eastern procession. Turkey represented to Harrison a bridge between Europe and Asia, much like Harrison himself, and he noted how Turkish melodies and rhythms found their way into the works of eighteenth-century European composers. Harrison dedicated this movement to Mimar Sinan, the sixteenth-century Turkish architect of Istanbul's Suleiman Mosque, whose buildings use the visual equivalents of just-intonation ratios.

Satisfied with his first guitar suite, Harrison set to work on a second, this time using three-limit tuning, conventionally known as Pythagorean tuning. Harrison, though, noting the Sumerian tablet that described the tuning some twelve hundred years before Pythagoras, preferred to use the term "ditone tuning," referring to the fact that thirds in the tuning are composed of two "tones," that is, 9:8 whole tones. The tuning of the *Ditone Suite* thus exclusively uses factors 3 and 2 in its ratios, which makes it well suited for counterpoint based on the fifth (3:2) and the major second (9:8), in stark distinction to the chromatically colorful *Serenade*.

"By proving to us that the guitar's fingerboard is really nothing more than a proverbial *tabula rasa*, whose pitches and colors can be chosen at will the way that painters select their pigments," Schneider wrote later, "he has helped change the face of the guitar forever."[12] But Harrison's next composition intended for guitar ended up being scored for a different medium. During his medievalist researches in New York, Harrison found in the newly published *Historical Anthology of Music* a song by the thirteenth-century composer Walther von der Vogelweide. Although he wrote this song ("*Nu alrest leb'ich mir werde*," but widely known as the "Song of Palestine") to encourage enlistment in the Crusades, Harrison's variations on this solemn tune create a sense of timelessness and perhaps irony. The middle variation is set to a Middle Eastern–style rhythmic pattern (like the Turkish *usul* or Arabic *'iqa*), and the movement ends with a coda in the style of a *taqsim*, a rhapsodic contemplation on a mode often played on the *'ud* (the Arabic cousin of the guitar). His pairing the European call to war with the beauties of the invaded region suggests an ulterior political commentary, especially given its composition at a moment when the Middle East was convulsing with new violence.

Harrison completed another expressive, chromatic movement with the medievalist title of "Plaint," a cognate of "complaint" and "plaintive." Impatient with Tom Stone, who was late supplying the necessary fingerboards, Harrison tuned his harpsichord to that tuning so that he could work on it. He threatened to turn the piece into a harpsichord suite if Stone did not get back to him soon; he even tried, with Colvig's help, to refret an old flea-market guitar.[13] When a commission from the Canada Council suddenly arrived, Harrison, lacking the financial stability to turn away commissions, felt that he couldn't wait any longer for Stone, so he abandoned writing for the guitar and began to adapt the completed movements into a piece for Toronto's Orford String Quartet.

He completed a "roughneck and Breugelish" estampie,[14] in which, like the estampie in the *Suite for Symphonic Strings*, the cellist becomes a percussionist, tapping on the instrument body and strings. After the fifth-based austerity of the first three movements, the blossoming of third-based counterpoint in the following neo-baroque rondeau sounds suddenly and satisfyingly sweet. The texture in the final movement reverts to a single melody, like in the final movement of the *Serenade*, in the form of the Turkish *usul*, this time repeating a 6+6+4+4 rhythmic pattern.

One of Harrison's major works, the *String Quartet Set*, also constitutes a somewhat awkward collision of this most polyphonic of ensembles with Harrison's uncompromising melodicism, so characteristic of this point in his career.[15] This singular melodic focus (the "Estampie" and "Usul" movements are entirely monophonic) contrasts sharply with Harrison's intensely contrapuntal earlier works for strings: his 1944 *Schoenbergiana* quartet and his two 1948 string suites.

"Lou Harrison's piece, you feel it, you really feel it," the composer Laurie Anderson said at the emotionally affecting *String Quartet Set*'s California premiere, "and it's a physical sensation and intellectual all at once." Music like Harrison's has a distinct power to move an audience, she observed. "You see very few people crying in art museums."[16]

REDISCOVERING KOREA

In 1978, San Francisco's Asian Art Museum was organizing an unprecedented tour of the treasures of the National Museum of Korea called "5000 Years of Korean Art." The exhibition included a companion book and film, and the producers wanted to know if Harrison would be interested in scoring the film, to be titled *Discovering the Art of Korea*. The music would have unusual prominence in the hourlong film, as it would provide nearly continuous underscoring to the narration.

As Harrison knew from the ethnomusicological vitriol that had erupted over his Asian/Western hybrids, an American composer accompanying the visual display of icons of another culture's long tradition could raise hackles. Rather than directly imitate Korean traditional music, Harrison sought to apply the techniques and spirit of those traditions to his own modern interpretations, much as he did his gamelan music. But like his gamelan music, respect for and knowledge of the tradition formed the foundation for his modern hybrids. The film score became Harrison's most ambitious homage to the culture that had so enthralled him since the series of Korea-inspired works that followed his initial trips there. Harrison and Colvig recorded the score themselves, improvising acoustic isolation by piling mattresses along the walls of a small room in their still-under-construction new Aptos home.[17]

To accompany the opening of the film's chronological survey of art, Harrison appropriately used one of China and Korea's most ancient instruments, the haunting clay ocarina known as the *xun* in China and *hun* in Korea, in a characteristically Korean pentatonic mode.[18] The silky tones of Korea's very low-pitched *daegeum* bamboo flute, with its characteristic wide vibrato and copious grace notes, soon arrive, followed by the bell tones of the American gamelan instruments, this time fulfilling the role of the *banghyang* bronze bars from Korean Confucian orchestras.

To accompany the film's depiction of later, more elaborate artworks, Harrison used his troubadour harp, the *sheng* mouth organ, the *pak* (wooden slats, also from Confucian orchestras), and a variety of percussion, including Chinese gongs, tam-tam, and the low *janggu* Korean drum. Drums and cymbals erupt at the mention of martial themes in the narration, but the ostinatos are unhurried, like much of the music from the region. Harrison also performed on one of his Korean *gayageum*, a loose-stringed psaltery with wide pitch bends compared to its Chinese cousin, the *zheng*. Even with the duplication of parts through editing, Harrison wrote close to an hour's worth of music for the film.[19]

Surprisingly, the Korean instrument he studied the most, the *piri*, appears only once, for the main title cue. He might have worried that its bright and penetrating timbre would overshadow the accompanying narration, but he might not have made the choice. Harrison had evidently forgotten his vow to avoid trying to precisely compose to film after his failed experiences trying to synchronize his score to Broughton's *Nuptiae* a decade earlier, and he spent hours "spotting" *Discovering the Art of Korea* (i.e., writing down all the timings of the film's shots and the narrator's words). Harrison and Colvig drove down to Hollywood with their tapes, where they spent hours in a studio lining up the score to the film.

When the movie came out, however, Harrison was appalled to discover that, once again, the score had been completely reedited without his knowledge. At times, the editor took single phrases of an existing cue and simply repeated them until the next section. Nearly all the cues simply fade out or cross-fade into the next, and much of Harrison's music was simply jettisoned. Nevertheless, Harrison's score constitutes a major work and his last that draws so directly from East Asian styles.

For Richard Dee, who helped perform the score with his partner, Clifford Porazynski, the project was bittersweet. He missed the days of regularly performing Chinese music with Harrison, who had not had time for the ensemble for several years.[20] The Chinese ensemble, still in demand, became a project entirely organized by Colvig with Dee and Lily Chin. It turned out to be a welcome change for Colvig, a chance to develop a part of his creative life unconnected to Harrison. Sometimes several times a week, Colvig would pack up the camper with their instruments, go pick up Dee and Chin, and drive out to an area elementary school or other venue for a concert and demonstration. Dee saw instead a new circle of friends become prominent in Harrison's life, all connected to his new romance with gamelan. And with his new set of instruments available, that music was about to consume even more of his time and attention. But first, he had one final fling with his former Korean flame.

ANGEL OF THE UNTHINKING

> *Progress*
> *Is the name*
> *Of the Angel*
> *Of the unthinking.*
> —Lou Harrison[21]

In the fall of 1978, Harrison traveled to Korea to address the Asian Arts Symposium, his first time back in that country in sixteen years. He was happy to reconnect with old friends, including Lee Hye-Ku, and he had not yet given up on completing their history of Korean music. His address restates his increasing exasperation with the current path of musical modernism and with another old friend:

> I have noted, recently, that the "media" as they're called—that is to say the access to electronic distribution tools—has created a new kind of musician. He borrows from the Rock world a sense that he is a public phenomenon and he enters a part of the celebrity world. Often in the United States, the doing of this is attributed to John Cage; indeed, I am astonished to realize that John Cage's career, in a way, parallels that of the rock stars. . . . They do not bear with them the sense of traditional culture and, in fact, offer themselves and their works as a substitute for traditional culture. John Cage, for example, has been accused by some of having but one criterion for excellence, and that is innovation. . . . Now, science embodies its past as it goes and carries it all on out—to Mars and beyond. I believe that Art must too, if it is not to be simply frivolous.[22]

Harrison's defense of musical tradition demonstrated just how marginalized he and many other composers of his generation—even those, like Harrison, once regarded as "ultramodernist"—had become. That year, his longtime music publisher, Peters (whose owner, Harrison's old friend Evelyn Hinrichsen, had insisted on the company publishing his unconventional *Music Primer*), lost interest in his unfashionable music. "The editorial committee in the '70s changed," one of its veteran employees, Don Gillespie, remembered. "Most promotion by Peters went to uptown composers such as [Milton] Babbitt and [Charles] Wuorinen. They leaned toward serialist music and didn't like Lou's stuff. They said it was 'just too pretty.' After that, Lou pulled away from Peters."[23]

Peters's editorial board's move reflected the dominance of serialist music on the one hand and Cage-inspired experimentalism on the other, leaving little room for lovers of melody and sheer sonic beauty like Harrison. "Proper music today," Harrison groused to a friend, "must not have an overt melody; it must not have any form of consistent harmonic or contrapuntal bondings, and, of course, it must never repeat or have recognizably functional sections. In short, what is being sought is simply moderately personal ways of wandering through twelve tones."[24] In another letter to Peter Garland, he resigned himself to being a perpetual outsider to what he called "the Musical Industrial Complex," understanding serialists with their loyalty to the European tradition "in the same way that I understand conservative Republicans."[25]

In addition to the new prominence of academic modernists, electronic and computer music had moved from the periphery to a central and well-publicized place in contemporary music. Although these technological tools may not seem to demand any particular musical style, "electronic music" had become nearly synonymous with the atonal, non-metric soundscapes recently institutionalized by Pierre Boulez in Paris's Institut de Recherche et Coordination Acoustique/Musique (IRCAM). "Everything they're doing at IRCAM is high-tech, imposed from above," Harrison grumbled in a letter to Schneider. "It has little to do with any generality or any common observation of people on a simple level from their ears."[26]

A couple of over-amplified concert experiences made Harrison wary of attending plugged-in shows, and he brought ear protection on the rare occasions he did, such as at the 1977 Cabrillo Festival. The adventurous Dennis Russell Davies had invited Cage for a residency and also included electronic music composers such as Laurie Anderson and San Jose State's Allen Strange. The Cabrillo concert of the previously radical 1930s–1940s percussion music of Harrison and Cage must have seemed almost quaint in comparison.

However, it's simplistic to label Harrison a technophobe. He was quick to point out his admiration of the technology of Javanese gongsmithing, Tom Stone's interchangeable guitar fretboards, and other examples of innovative instrument building.[27] He would later be intrigued by the possibility of using computers to help him create everything from fonts to otherwise unrealizable tunings.

But his disdain for Cage's aesthetic didn't interfere with the gradual rewarming of feelings between the two great twentieth-century composers. Cage brought and "seeded" some tasty mushrooms in a tree stump in front of Harrison's cabin, and for Harrison's sixtieth birthday in 1977, Cage wrote him a mesostic comparing Harrison's music to a river opening into its delta. "Listening to it," Cage ended his tribute, "we become ocean."[28]

Instead of composing music as a sixty-fifth birthday present for his old colleague that year, Harrison wrote him a poem.[29]

> You, John, are a loved, romantic man
> So multiple of image that Each
> Designs another one about you
> Who conceives you in his dart of mind,
> And so adds facet to your being
> Such that often All seem equally
> Reflected

The two affectionate poetic tributes demonstrate how deep the two great composers' aesthetic differences ran. Cage's poem complimented the transcendent effect that Harrison's music has on a listener, a potential power of personal transformation that Cage so valued in art. By contrast, Harrison, for all his own inclinations toward new tunings and such, most valued making music together with friends, as they had in their percussion ensemble.

And now he would have the chance to do so again—his new small gamelan had arrived from Java. "We have done it up like Cleopatra's barge with six resident *nagas* [decorative serpents common in gamelan woodwork] in gold leaf," he excitedly wrote.[30] He would finally have his own ensemble at San Jose State, and from this set would spring Harrison's first masterpieces for gamelan.

A COMMUNAL MUSIC

> My pleasure in and advocacy of Javanese gamelan arises from several
> sources. First, a fine gamelan is the most beautiful sounding orchestra on the

*planet. Second, its classic repertory is enormous and ranges in expression
from the thunderously grand to a lyricism of spider-web delicacy. Third, it
is a communal music practiced by villagers and courtiers alike, and indeed
oftentimes together. Fourth, in a gamelan there is something to do for almost
anyone, from singing, or simply counting and feeling one's way to the striking
of a gong, to elaborate and difficult performance at speed, on highly refined
solo instruments. The array of musical forms in gamelan music is the most
developed of any music and is enough to dazzle or benumb anyone who has only
Europe as background. You can import or build a gamelan in different metals.
You can play classics or compose new music. You can never again be bored.*

—Lou Harrison[31]

This sense of gamelan as egalitarian, communitarian music elated Harrison in a
way he hadn't felt since his early 1940s performances of percussion music and early
music with his friends in San Francisco. For decades after, he had followed the usual
model of writing pieces and turning them over to professionals for performances,
distancing himself from communal music-making until the 1960s, when his Chinese
ensemble marked a step back toward music as an intimate creative activity among
friends. Now gamelan provided an experience in which even larger groups collaboratively created a community of sound. Players from beginner to expert must feel
the gong cycle, respond to the drummer, and fit in with the group so as to achieve a
community goal.

The title Harrison gave to his next work reflects the importance of this ideal to
him. He called it *Main Bersama-Sama*, which means "playing together." The Indonesian word for play, "*main*," has the same double meaning as in English: to manipulate
a musical instrument as well as to participate in games. "Children are very busy, very
absorbed in their play," Harrison declared in his 1959 *Crackpot Lecture*. "Play is the
only really solemn thing. When we grow up, we continue this solemn play and it is
civilization."[32] To Harrison, the shared, focused play of community music-making
echoed the communal cooperation needed to build a civilized society.[33]

The motivation for *Main Bersama-Sama* had come, like several of his pieces since
taking his teaching position at San Jose State, out of friendship, from a faculty colleague (this time French horn instructor William George) asking for a piece to perform. Harrison knew that horn players can reach notes outside the equal-tempered
system by adjusting their fist inside the bell of the instrument and bending pitches.
Harrison's idea to combine the gamelan with a Western instrument was an important
and fateful innovation, but it had the precedent of Harrison's many works for solo
melodic instrument and percussion ensemble, dating back four decades to his *First
Concerto for Flute and Percussion*.

Harrison kept George's request in mind when he and Colvig finally received their
gamelan *degung* from West Java. Harrison called this sort of ensemble a "chamber
gamelan" because it supported a maximum of about eight players, whereas the more
famous Central Javanese version often accommodated twenty or more. Harrison and
Colvig not only tuned the instruments to each other but also set about "rationalizing"

the tuning: adjusting each of the instruments so that the pitches corresponded to just intervals.[34] Patiently, Colvig used a machine grinder to shave off metal from the end of a bar (to raise the pitch) or the bottom (to lower it). The pitch of the large gong, much harder to retune, lay between scale steps, an unusual pitch that nevertheless allowed the gong to harmonize with different modes. Therefore, the gamelan eventually acquired the name Sekar Kembar, literally "paired flowers" or "twin songs," for the way the gong forms a bridge between different scales.[35] It might also represent Harrison and Colvig themselves—and, it would soon turn out, the paired American and Indonesian cultures whose music it would soon carry.

Although he retained ownership, Harrison installed the small gamelan at San Jose State and began teaching some of the traditional Sundanese repertoire he had learned from Undang Sumarna. He also began composing for the ensemble, beginning, as he did with most of his pieces, with the melody. He came up with a simple but ravishing tune in two repeated halves. These would become the part for the horn, alternating with Harrison himself playing the *suling* bamboo flute—Western and Asian instruments "playing together."[36]

In Harrison's works for Central Javanese gamelan, the free form of his melodies sometimes frustrated even skilled players of the elaborating instruments, accustomed to crafting improvisations based on binary forms and traditional modal structures. But in the gamelan *degung* repertory he was learning from Undang Sumarna, Harrison instead found it more straightforward to create these "elaborating" melodies himself, rather than leaving them to the players' constrained improvisation in traditional style. During his study of traditional gamelan *degung* melodies, he wrote out the parts for the various instruments in Western staff notation and figured out how to derive the elaborating instruments' idiomatic patterns, which became the basis for the instrumental parts of *Main Bersama-Sama*. For the first time, Harrison wrote out the parts for all the instruments in Indonesian cipher notation rather than Western staff notation.[37] Presenting written-out elaborating parts might have offended traditional gamelan players, who took pride in their ability to derive the most appropriate pattern based on a given core melody, but Harrison now had his own ensemble, selected from friends and students at San Jose State.

Ethnomusicologists would continue to argue about the tradeoffs in the use of notation in this tradition. "Notation becomes at once stultifying and liberating," wrote Harrison's student Jarrad Powell, a composer who later directed Seattle's Gamelan Pacifica. "It takes the emphasis away from group process and places it on individual decision making. Enter the composer. Notation allows manipulation of musical ideas free from the context of performance. At the same time, a notational system may engender constraints of its own, by establishing a perceptual bias or emphasizing parameters of the music."[38]

In *Main Bersama-Sama*, notation made possible what may be the most fundamental departure from traditional practice in the piece. In traditional gamelan works, the elaborating instruments typically anticipate the core tones and gong tones, reflecting the Javanese sense that those tones end or complete metrical cycles. But in Harrison's work, the faster melodies reflect the *preceding* core tone, implying, as in Western harmony, that the following pitches are part of the same harmony.[39] In composing for gamelan, Harrison was no more enslaved to traditional practices than he was to Western tunings or forms when he wrote for Western instruments. But he did draw on traditional Indonesian forms when it suited his expressive purposes. Like the tuning of the gamelan *degung*, Harrison's melody has been "rationalized" compared to his earlier, metrically free forms. This melody fits within a traditional Indonesian binary structure, in particular the Sundanese form known as *sekar alit* ("short song"). As before, Harrison carefully crafted the melody so that its core tones reflect, on multiple levels, the query-and-resolution structure that the Javanese call *padang-ulihan*.[40]

Harrison's fascination with the way that binary structure permeates all levels of Javanese forms inspired his next piece, initially titled *Main Bersama-Sama II*. What if, he reflected, he created a piece in which all metrical levels were related by threes instead of twos? The medievalist Harrison knew that in the fourteenth century, such a meter would have been called *tempus perfectum prolatio maior*—that is, all divisions and groupings by threes (the "perfect" number to the Trinitarian Christians).[41] Harrison intended no Christian symbolism, but it became for him a creative puzzle. Instead of the AB structure of the Javanese *padang-ulihan*, Harrison created an AAB structure for each of the three phrases of each gong cycle; then he divided each of those phrases into three parts, also in AAB form (the two-thirds point colotomically marked not by a gong but instead by a Balinese bell tree and *bonang* flourish). The three different gong cycles (named A, B, and C) follow the same pattern: AAB AAB CCB. Of course this grouping of the gong cycle creates, again, an overall same-same-different structure for the entire composition.

To introduce some variety into this especially consistent form, Harrison added a simple melodicle—down to a neighbor tone and back—to his AAB pattern. With these simple building blocks and his usual transpositions and inversions, Harrison's self-similar architecture seems perfectly proportioned rather than mathematically contrived—but he was not done. Around this *balungan* he wove a rhapsodic viola melody in quintal counterpoint to the carefully crafted *balungan*.[42] Unconstrained by frets, a violist can (with practice and a careful ear) match the pitches of the gamelan. Shortly after performing the new work, much more melancholy than the sunny and delightful *Main Bersama-Sama*, at the 1978 Cabrillo festival, Harrison learned of the death of his friend and the former Cabrillo music director, and he named what turned out to be the presciently poignant piece in his honor: *Threnody for Carlos Chávez*.

Although this chamber gamelan brought many joys to Harrison, and fine compositions from him, he still missed the "thunderously grand" sound of the full Javanese gamelan with its expanded community of players. The gamelan *degung* sated his craving only temporarily. Soon he was scheming for a way to bring a full gamelan back into his musical life.

31

SHOWERS OF BEAUTY (1978–1982)

*We were rehearsing, and I was playing along with the demung [metallophone]
part. . . . There's a point where the gerongan [male chorus] rise up in
volume and the gong ageng [great gong] came. All the hair on my body
stood up, my tears ran, I didn't know where I was, what I was doing,
and I had to put my beater down, collect my wits, stop the tears, rub
down the hair, and find out where I was before I could start again.*

—Lou Harrison[1]

One day, not long before Pak Cokro left San Jose State, Lou Harrison was sitting
in his office at the school, playing one of Colvig's metallophones, which they had
tuned to the harmonic series. Harrison's experience with Tom Stone's guitar fretted to harmonics 16 through 32 had taught him "the surprising gentleness of higher
ratios."[2] Whenever he had a little downtime, Harrison explored different combinations of these harmonics. Amid those sounds, he was searching for a particular scale,
a version of the Javanese *pelog* scale that Harrison thought could be found in the
harmonic series. Intrigued by a particularly enticing combination, he was startled
by a knock at the door.

He opened it, and there stood Pak Cokro. "What are you doing?" the old man
asked, politely.

"I'm hunting for a *pelog* in the upper overtones," Harrison replied.

"Play the last one that I heard," Wasitodiningrat said, and Harrison repeated it.
His visitor paused, thinking.

"It's a good *pelog*," he finally allowed. "What's more, it would be good to sing with."

Harrison smiled politely, but he was skeptical. No way would it be easy for Americans trained in equal temperament to sing harmonics 12, 13, 14, 17, 18, 19, and 21. Still,
he made a note of the sequence, just in case.[3]

Now, in 1978, his thoughts turned back to the scale. He couldn't use it with the
degung set, which was already tuned. But he had been thinking about acquiring
another set. His gamelan *degung* class at San Jose State was proving too popular.
He had enough instruments to accommodate only about eight players, including
himself. Recognizing that the state university's budget constraints made importing

a full Javanese gamelan unlikely, he envisioned building a new set of instruments. Unlike his earlier American gamelan, this much larger ensemble would be based on the Javanese model, with *pelog* and *slendro* tuning and counterparts to all of the Javanese gamelan instruments necessary to play traditional works, though Harrison was already hatching new compositions. However, even a homemade gamelan would cost more than the music department or Harrison himself could afford. Finally, Harrison asked the new music patron he had met in Los Angeles, Betty Freeman, if she would fund this new venture. She did.

The first requirement for Harrison's new gamelan was to find a tuning, or rather two tunings, since Harrison wanted versions of both Javanese *pelog* and *slendro* scales. For the former, he remembered the scale that had so beguiled Pak Cokro. Although the Javanese master had judged it to be a "good *pelog*," some of these intervals would be quite unusual in a Javanese gamelan.[4] They nevertheless provided, to Harrison's ears, some beautiful relationships that, when reinforced throughout the range of gamelan instruments, made the sound of a just-intonation gamelan a striking visceral experience.

But one pitch was especially distant from a Western scale and thus worrisome if Harrison wanted to combine the instruments with Western instruments and singers: the second pitch of the scale, tuned to the thirteenth harmonic. "But there is a problem with pitch 13 when used with instruments," he admitted. "Western ears don't like that, and so it proves to be a problem. For the recording, I switched the tuning a little bit to accommodate Western ears, and then I decided no. The *pelog* had lost its majesty. So we retuned it back . . . and when you hear the piece as a classic *pelog* kind, it has that majesty again. And it's just that one little pitch. But it makes all the difference, and that's true of tunings. It's either there or not there." And when, despite Harrison's doubts, he asked singers to match those overtones for a recording, "it was like falling off a log," Harrison found to his relief.[5]

The Javanese *slendro* scale proved somewhat more of a challenge. On average, the *slendro* scales of various gamelan divide the octave into five equal parts, each step being between a major second and a minor third. However, if each *slendro* gamelan were really equally tempered, it would have the same sort of circularity that Harrison disliked in both Thai and European equal-tempered music. Instead, the scale of each set of Indonesian gamelan instruments has unique deviations from this average that give that set its own characteristic sound. "Pitch variations are treasured realities in Indonesia," he said.[6]

Harrison noted that the scale steps in the Javanese *slendro* tuning system often approximate the just ratios 7:6 and 8:7. The *slendro* scale he first experimented with was based on harmonics 16, 18, 21, 24, and 28 (these scale steps translate to 9:8, 7:6, 8:7, 7:6, and 8:7).[7] Harrison's crucial creative choice was using a 9:8 *slendro* step; rarely found in Java, it allowed 3:2 perfect fifths above pitch numbers 1, 5, and 6, enabling Harrison to establish tonal modes based on those key centers as he had earlier done with his modal music. It was in fact the same tuning he thought he had invented for the third of his *Strict Songs*, but he later realized that Claudius Ptolemy in Alexandria had described such a scale a couple of millennia earlier.

For this new venture, Colvig immediately grasped the utter impracticality of creating a gamelan in bronze, the traditional alloy used in Java; unaffordable, it also had to be cast and then forged, a process that required a foundry and voluminous doses of skill, patience, and laborers. Iron, though cheaper and sometimes used in Java, also required casting and forging. A few years before Harrison and Colvig's American gamelan, Vermont composer Dennis Murphy, a student of Bob Brown's, had made his own American gamelan out of steel and found objects. However, steel is very hard and much more difficult to work with than Colvig's preferred metal, aluminum. Colvig experimented with aluminum bars to find just the right thickness and proportions for the various keyed instruments. Harrison worried that the Javanese would deplore their use of aluminum, finding it a "cheap" substitute.[8] He was relieved when Pak Cokro not only approved but also judged aluminum to be second only to bronze in sound quality.[9]

Horizontally mounted gongs, initially shaped by casting, proved to be more of a problem. After some experimentation, Harrison and Colvig discovered that flat octagonal plates created timbres very similar to those of the *bonang* and the *kenong*. The hanging gongs called *kempul* posed another challenge. Forging these larger gongs in Java involves an even more labor- and time-intensive skilled process than that used for the horizontal gongs. However, Colvig knew from their experience creating the American gamelan that aluminum bars of the right dimensions could reach those low tones, so he created a set with five-foot-tall resonators hidden within attractive wooden cabinets. He added a central raised boss to help imitate the timbre of round gongs.[10] However, they did try their hand at forging when it came time to build their first large gong. To do so, they needed hot sand, and Colvig knew just the place. For years, he had led friends on a lovely hike down the hill from their house to the beach and back. This time, he and Harrison toted a sheet of metal, a blowtorch, and hammers; with the help of local metal sculptor Mark Bulwinkle, they came back with finished instrument.

Harrison named the gamelan Si Betty, in honor of its benefactor, "Si" being an honorific in Java. And the piece he wrote and recorded to thank her and her fiancé, *Serenade for Betty Freeman and Franco Assetto*, featured another cheerful melody similar to the one in *Main Bersama-Sama*, this time played by Harrison himself on the *suling* bamboo flute. In a rather un-Javanese six-beat meter, its melody seems to have one certain downbeat until the gong comes in on another beat and reorients the listener, a favorite trick of Harrison's.[11] He sent Freeman a cassette recording of the *Serenade*, and when she and Assetto married in Las Vegas a few weeks later, they played it for the ceremony.[12] Because Si Betty was still under construction, Harrison wrote the *Serenade* for his smaller gamelan *degung* (which he moved to his house).

For the wooden cases and racks that held the bronze gongs and keys in Betty Freeman's namesake instrumentarium, Harrison designed an attractive red and gold twin-flower pattern on a blue background as the gamelan's decorative motif, which appeared on a front panel of each of the sitting instruments. (Javanese instruments do not have these panels.) Although he expected the group to play mostly traditional pieces, Harrison wanted to distinguish it in other ways as an American ensemble.

He liked the Javanese custom of wearing traditional batiks, though, and so he had his players, men and women, dress in sarongs. Instead of batik fabric, he chose blue bandanna cloth to match the gamelan's colors.

To prepare for teaching his new ensemble after two years immersed in the Sundanese variety, Harrison arranged for refresher lessons in Javanese gamelan from Daniel Schmidt.[13] That year, Harrison's gamelan class using Si Betty became so popular that his assistant, Trish Neilson, was able to informally continue the original gamelan *degung* ensemble as well. Harrison allowed all interested students into the class, as long as there was room, even non-musicians. However, he set the same high expectations of his students as he had for professionals playing his pieces. "If we were just doing general rehearsal music, it was okay," Neilson remembered, "but if we were doing a piece by him, it got a little bit more intense. He was very particular about how he wanted it performed." When a performance date approached, Harrison's temper could sometimes erupt. Rehearsals were "tense, especially getting closer to a concert," remembered his student Daniel Kelley, laughing, "especially if Bill was there and some instrument wasn't working right." Nevertheless, his students adored him. "I loved working with him. I really did," Kelly said. "Lou was just such a special guy, always encouraging, always kind."[14]

Harrison encouraged his students to compose for the gamelan and envisioned this repertory feeding the beginning of a West Coast tradition of American gamelan. Harrison and Nielson would later collect these compositions and privately publish them as *Gending-Gending California*. Other groups arose. A concert that Harrison organized for the 1979 Cabrillo Festival included no fewer than five different American and Javanese gamelan. Within a couple of decades, the United States boasted nearly two hundred gamelan ensembles, a development for which Harrison deserves much credit.

Harrison was excited to install his preferred orchestra of instruments just outside his office. But as important as Si Betty was to his teaching and to proselytizing the gamelan gospel, it was about to prove even more vital to his composing. The expanded forces allowed Harrison's music to achieve the overwhelming sonic richness that only a full Javanese gamelan could create. "The sensuous response is enormous, and I've only seen it to a minor degree in Western music," he said. "I think it's the most beautiful music on the planet, and it has no counterpart in the Western symphony orchestra."[15] Comparing gamelan to Western orchestras, he explained, "I do regard the two entities as sort of alternate traditions. Neither is above the other for me. But the actual sound of the gamelan is more appealing to me than that of a symphony orchestra. In fact, I don't think I've ever had an actual raising of hair and pouring of tear with the sound of a symphony orchestra, where I have had that with gamelan, because of its sheer sensuous beauty."[16]

Along with its sensuous sonorities, the Javanese tradition especially played to his dance-derived love of melody and rhythm. "The gamelan is the world of melody, and that's what I'm most interested in," he said. "Harmony, the simultaneous combination of different tones, doesn't bother me at all. Rhythm I'm interested in, and of course the gamelan has plenty of that."[17]

Harrison was beginning to believe that he would never have to compose for any other ensemble again, that the gamelan held more than enough possibilities to satisfy his creativity for the rest of his life. Now equipped with a new, extensive set of instruments to realize his expanding musical vision, as the 1980s began, so did a new chapter in Harrison's creative life.

MUSIC AT MILLS

One Destination, Many Roads
—Mills College motto

In 1980, Harrison received a phone call from Susan Summerfield, the chair of the music department at his old employer, Mills College in Oakland. Summerfield explained that the college had recently established the Darius Milhaud Chair in music composition in honor of the famous composer and former Mills faculty member. A visiting composer would hold this chair for a fixed term, and they wanted the inaugural holder of the chair to be Lou Harrison.

The overture was well timed. Harrison was growing increasingly concerned about his position at San Jose State. In 1978, California voters passed Proposition 13, which drastically limited property taxes, the foundation of the funding for the state's public education system, including San Jose State. Harrison knew that when the budget axes began to fall, his part-time position would be among the first on the chopping block. Given his history with Mills (a private college unaffected by the financial turmoil in public education wreaked by Proposition 13) and his concerns about San Jose State, Harrison was happy to accept, though, hedging his bets, he didn't yet quit his San Jose State job, taking a year's leave of absence instead, which also allowed him to travel.

Harrison found his position at Mills refreshing and stimulating; even its motto reflected his own belief in fusions from diverse ingredients. He could teach his advanced "Intonation in World Music" course in the graduate program, while at San Jose State he taught general education courses such as his world music survey. And the school maintained "a kind of vortex or center of fine musicians,"[18] including composer Terry Riley, also there in a visiting chair position. The San Francisco Tape Music Center had moved to Mills and become the Center for Contemporary Music. The small women's college (the graduate school was coeducational) had become one of the national centers for new music, and now Harrison was once again part of it. Even though it had been over four decades since his previous employment at the college, Harrison felt right at home.

Also in residence at Mills was San Francisco's Kronos Quartet, whom Harrison had met at the 1978 Cabrillo Festival. Soon to become famous for commissioning and recording new music from all over the world, Kronos found a kindred spirit in their fellow West Coast global visionary. "Lou had such an open and inquiring spirit about influences and allowing his imagination to freely roam the world of music," Kronos leader David Harrington said.[19] After Harrison showed Kronos his *String Quartet Set,* the soon-to-be-famous quartet recorded it for an LP on the CRI label.[20]

Harrington recalled that Harrison was so happy with their recording session that he baked the group a cake.

But despite Mills's many attractions and creative community, Harrison focused on his true passion. With the funds supporting the chair position, Harrison proposed establishing yet another gamelan at Mills and negotiated the hiring of Jody Diamond to teach it. With Colvig and a new assistant, percussionist William Winant, Harrison set out to build another gamelan, this time named for Milhaud and his wife—the *slendro* set of instruments became Si Darius and the *pelog* set Si Madeleine.

Though he kept the new sets' tuning the same as the *pelog* and *slendro* sets in Si Betty, Harrison applied some of the lessons they had learned in making that earlier gamelan to create an even more ambitious set of instruments. "He really went hog wild," observed Daniel Schmidt, who would also teach the Mills gamelan class. He and Colvig built many more *kempul* hanging gongs (again large aluminum slabs in paired octaves), shaping the bars to soften the attack sounds, and developed a new version of *kenong* from "a triangle of thick aluminum, and they actually work pretty well," said Schmidt.[21] Colvig deserves recognition for devising entirely new forms and materials for instruments that had stayed pretty much the same for centuries. Students helped in the construction, but Harrison and Colvig built the big gong, "ball-peening it into shape" after Pak Cokro, hearing their initial effort, said, "More beating, more beauty."[22]

Now Harrison was regularly participating in and composing for two performing gamelan ensembles (Si Betty at SJSU, and Si Darius/Si Madeleine at Mills), both much larger than San Jose's Sekar Kembar gamelan *degung*. As he had done half a lifetime earlier in San Francisco, Harrison often put up posters advertising their concerts, sometimes hand-calligraphing them, and he even made costumes for the players: elegant lace blouses for the women, Javanese-style hats and shirts for the men. The complex ways in which traditional Central Javanese players would realize their parts were also very different from the performance practices of *degung* players in Sunda. However, Harrison applied two crucial lessons from his experience with the gamelan *degung* to his new compositions for the Central Javanese variety.

First, Harrison learned new stereotypical patterns for the faster melodic instruments. The mellow *gendèr* metallophone, whose soft, bell-like sound must have appealed to longtime harp lover Harrison, was the most forbidding of these instruments, because the performance practice in the Central Javanese tradition required the detailed knowledge of dozens of complex two-part melodies (one played independently by each hand), each appropriate for different goal tones, modes, rhythmic densities, styles, and other factors. However, an ethnomusicologist at UC Santa Cruz, Richard North, had shown him the *gendèr* technique from a different tradition, that of the Javanese city of Cirebon. In this city (tellingly, halfway between the Sundanese and Central Javanese regions), *gendèr* players need only memorize a single pattern that they transpose for each corresponding pitch of the *balungan*. These patterns form the basis for the serene beginning of Harrison's *Philemon and Baukis* for gamelan and violin. In its opening passages, only the different *gendèr* metallophones and gongs accompany the languid, heartbreaking violin melody.

EXAMPLE 31.1. This excerpt from the opening of Harrison's *Philemon and Baukis* shows his use of melodic formulas (*cengkok*) from the Cirebonese tradition to elaborate the core melody (*balungan*, played by the *slentem*). The violin melody is related to the *balungan* by counterpoint of the *kempyung* (four scale steps, approximating a Western fifth). Courtesy of Special Collections, University Library, University of California Santa Cruz, Lou Harrison papers.

These more tractable approaches to the faster melodies also meant that Harrison could more easily put together a student ensemble without needing experts to take over the more difficult instruments. Even so, Harrison regularly sought out Jody Diamond's help and often wrote out the melodies they arrived at. As his understanding of Javanese gamelan grew, so too did Harrison's confidence in departing from the traditional models. Once, for example, he asked Diamond's help in realizing his version of interlocking, hocket-like parts called *imbal*.

"I want it to go really fast," he told Diamond.

"Lou, that's really not the idea of it," she replied, urging him to slow it down in traditional Javanese fashion. "It's supposed to be a layer of decoration."

"Don't pamper the *imbal*!" Harrison exclaimed.[23]

Similarly, traditional Javanese music gradually morphs through layers of rhythmic density, stretching out the notes of the core melody two, four, or even eight times their original length, a concept called *irama*. Harrison instead handed Diamond a score that abruptly shifted from one level to the next.

"Lou, you're giving up one of the most beautiful things about Javanese gamelan, which is slowing down, expanding the form, and then the structural instruments going twice as fast, but not quite twice as fast, so then the elaborating instruments are going faster."

"No," he insisted. "This is what I want."[24] While respectful of Javanese tradition, Harrison unapologetically trusted his own creative instincts first.

As he studied more music from different traditions, Harrison realized that he preferred one of the two major Central Javanese styles, and the reasons for that preference reveal an important aspect of his compositional aesthetic. The two major styles in Java come from two old Central Javanese capitals located only forty miles apart. Musicians stereotype the style of the city of Surakarta, also known as Solo, as the more refined and elegant, while the Yogyakarta style is rather more dynamic and unafraid of dramatic climaxes. Although the former style gained precedence outside Java, in part because of a preponderance of Solonese teachers abroad, Harrison preferred the latter. "I'm not as fond of the kind that sits back, and I think basically that's why I'm not too fond of Solonese music, because it seems to me they're preceded by a series of paroxysms which then sort of idle off," he explained. "It doesn't go there—that's the point; it just has a paroxysm, dribbles off, which is very different than building a climax to a goal. He had the same preference in choreography, which explained his disaffection for Martha Graham's tension-and-release style. "I'm a go-to-goal man—that is to say, instead of *bum*-pa, *bum*-pa, I think ba-*bum*, ba-*bum*, and the same thing rhythmically: everything goes to the goal, and to cadences."[25]

Harrison quickly composed a whole series of new Javanese gamelan pieces in the following years, often dedicated to figures of classical Greece and Rome or to his friends. In 1981 alone, he wrote *Gending Alexander*,[26] *Ladrang Epikuros*, *Gending Hephaestus*, *Gending Hermes*, *Gending Demeter*, and *Gending in Honor of the Poet Virgil*, and he also revised earlier works, including *Gending Samuel*, which became *Ladrang Samuel* when reconciled to a traditional form. That year he added an optional, stirring trumpet part (that his hero Handel would have envied) to his 1976 *Bubaran Robert*, used for years as the graduation processional at Mills College.

That new trumpet line reflected Harrison's second breakthrough: realizing he could effectively add new melodies on top of existing *balungan* compositions. In Java, composers and singers sometimes create new vocal melodies to existing *balungan*—not all that different from Harrison's earlier works in octaval or quintal counterpoint and sharing many familiar contrapuntal techniques: anticipations, suspensions, passing tones, and so on. Although the interval separating two tones that are three scale degrees apart in Javanese modes, called a *kempyung*, is not exactly a Western fifth, it is a special interval in Javanese practice that, to Harrison, resembled the use of the fifth in quintal counterpoint.[27]

The possibility of adding a new melody atop the *balungan* with this technique opened up a new dimension to his gamelan compositions, and his compositions for gamelan plus another instrument became some of his most popular works. And it allowed him to meld his great gift for crafting memorable melodies, developed over a half century, with his fondness for the sonorities of the gamelan.

THE GLASSES OF BLUE AND RED AND GREEN

For one of his first compositions with this technique of adding layers, Harrison wrote a set of songs inspired by the twentieth-century Alexandrian poet Constantine Cavafy, with whom Harrison shared significant characteristics: both were gay artists with a taste for finery who sometimes wrote nostalgically about the faded glories of Greece and Rome. However, instead of setting Cavafy's poems, Harrison composed his own texts about Cavafy composing his poems, a metapoetic conceit that allowed Harrison to make the lyrics at once more opulent and more distant.[28] You can almost smell the incense in Harrison's seductive setting of his paraphrases of Cavafy's evocative poetry, drenched in history and eroticism, two of Harrison's favorite subjects.

The first of Harrison's *Scenes from Cavafy*, based on the poet's "Of Colored Glass," becomes not just an obscure image of the fading of the Ottoman Empire, but also a story of the poet lost in this false world, where glass has replaced the royal jewels.[29]

In the manner of the Javanese *gerong*, or male chorus, the choir sings the refrain in between verses sung by a dramatic baritone, both melodic lines undergirded by the haunting *pelog balungan* that he called "Gending Cavafy."

In the second song, based on Cavafy's "The Next Table," Harrison turns Cavafy's brief sigh of lost youth into an extended memory of the poet's long-past romantic encounter. Appropriately, Harrison dedicated this movement to his own romantic partner, naming it "Gending Bill," and, as with the other movements, allowed for performances of the single movements as stand-alone pieces without the voice.

Although the middle movement is in the contrasting *slendro* tuning system, the final song, "Gending Ptolemy," returns to *pelog* in a nontraditional mode for his poem about Cavafy's "God Abandons Antony." Instead of Cavafy's images of the night before Marc Antony's fateful defeat in 31 BCE, Harrison imagines the poet (also in Alexandria) writing in anticipation of his own death, "when Dionysius and the music leave him." In this movement (named for the ancient scholar Ptolemy, another Alexandrian, who was the most important source of information on tunings of the ancient world), Harrison used non-Javanese percussion ostinatos (as in *Young Caesar* and other works) with the clatter of Balinese *ceng-ceng* cymbals. Harrison freely included non-Javanese instruments in the other movements as well, including a harp and *yazheng* zither in "Gending Bill." After its premiere at San Jose State, Harrison presented the *Scenes* (gay poetry and all) at the 1980 Cabrillo Festival.

HOMECOMING

The audience members turned to look back over their shoulders as the doors at the rear of Evans Auditorium opened. As the musicians of the Kyai Guntur Sari ("Venerable Showers of Beauty") gamelan ensemble began to play their century-old instruments, which had arrived at the college a few months earlier, four young college students entered, bearing a canopy that loomed over the guest of honor and artist in residence, Lou Harrison, and his host (and ensemble leader), music professor Vincent McDermott, who had composed the simple processional to accompany their stroll down to the stage, where they joined the ensemble and began the show. That February 1981 concert represented the completion of a circle: It took place at Lewis & Clark College in Harrison's hometown of Portland, Oregon, which he'd left more than half a century earlier.

Harrison's leave of absence from San Jose State allowed him to accept short residencies in Portland and at Seattle's Cornish College of the Arts (known as the Cornish School in 1938 when John Cage had created his percussion ensemble there on Harrison's recommendation). Cornish had hired former Harrison students Janice Giteck, Jarrad Powell, and Paul Dresher as part of the school's transformation from a Eurocentric to a world music model that was explicitly indebted to Harrison's philosophy and teaching. Dresher and Daniel Schmidt had built a gamelan there. Harrison also refreshed his long friendship with his fellow traveler Alan Hovhaness, who now lived in Seattle, and he and his wife, Hinako, reciprocated with a two-week stay at Harrison's new Aptos house the following summer. At Harrison's urging, Hovhaness even wrote a piece for gamelan—another way that Harrison tried to spread the word about his new muse.[30]

That's the piece that appeared on the program at Lewis & Clark the following February, along with Harrison's *Bubaran Robert, Lagu Socsecnum,* and his new *Gending Hermes. Hermes* was Harrison's most ambitious gamelan work so far, an expansive piece in the style of a Javanese *gending ageng*—a large-scale, usually ceremonial composition—but with un-Javanese phrases alternating four and six beats and with subtle modal shifts. After learning that McDermott was a composer too, Harrison encouraged him to write a piece for the concert as well—*A Stately Salute (For a Man of Substance),* the processional for prepared piano and gamelan dedicated to Harrison. Harrison and Colvig played Javanese *suling* flute and *gambang* xylophone respectively.

With McDermott's acquiescence, Harrison and Colvig set to adjusting the tuning of the school's gamelan set to just intervals. To accommodate McDermott's preference for the Solonese style, Harrison chose a tuning with a slightly larger interval between the third and fourth pitches in the scale, a pattern that, according to Pak Cokro, characterized tunings from that city.[31] Harrison even spent hours (with Colvig) making wooden music stands for the players, after realizing that they had to awkwardly read their scores in their laps while playing. "It is undignified," Harrison declared, "to play music while staring at one's crotch!"[32]

"Lou was so generous and supportive in so many ways," McDermott recalled. "He didn't want special attention paid to him. The students loved him."[33] As he did so often, Harrison wrote a new piece, *Gending Vincent,* for McDermott, and later he had a star named after him by paying a fee to the International Star Registry, another common practice that Harrison adopted during the 1980s, resulting in many of his friends' names populating the heavens.[34] After seeing other friends in Oregon (in Eugene and in Colvig's old home of Medford) and California (their respective childhood homes in Woodland and Weed), Harrison also visited and lectured at the University of British Columbia. He would return to his hometown to work with Venerable Showers of Beauty and other groups in his native Northwest several times.

PAIRED FLOWERS

As Harrison began teaching on Si Darius and Si Madeleine in 1981 and into 1982, his orgy of gamelan writing continued with several small pieces suitable for teaching beginning gamelan students. Harrison named his *Gending Claude,* a *slendro* sixteen-beat melody, for his beloved painter Claude Lorrain. *Gending Pindar,* a *pelog* tune named for the Greek poet, starts in a similar sixteen-beat form but then adds two surprising beats to the end of the second gong cycle. *For the Pleasure of Ovid's Changes* honors the ancient writer through a form that expands the length of the *gongan* from sixteen to thirty-two to forty to forty-eight beats (and back again), creating an aural equivalent of the transformations depicted in Ovid's stories ("the best short stories ever written," according to Harrison[35]). The namesake of *Gending Dennis* was the Cabrillo Festival music director, Dennis Russell Davies, who stayed in Harrison's house with his family every summer for the festival. Davies's wife, Molly, a film-maker, was commemorated in *Lancaran Molly.*

During their stay in the summer of 1981, Molly Davies asked Harrison to score her film *Beyond the Far Blue Mountains*. This experimental and poetic work consisted of three simultaneous projections, the center screen usually showing black-and-white scenes of an immigrant girl wandering a bleak and unfamiliar urban landscape, while the outside screens showed a full-color world of imagination, where the girl dreams of life outside the city. Harrison's score consists nearly entirely of his existing gamelan works recorded that spring: *Serenade, Gending Demeter, Gending Claude, Gending Pindar, Gending Dennis*, and, of course, *Lancaran Molly*. Harrison's ringing aluminum becomes a major character in the dialogue-less film, which Davies showed at Paris's Pompidou Center in June 1982 and then at Cabrillo College later that summer.

Harrison also recorded a gamelan score for his second collaboration with filmmaker James Broughton, this time for his film *Devotions*, a tender celebration of male-male love. Harrison and Colvig also appear in the film, playing a recorder duet conducted by Virgil Thomson. Harrison would dedicate a new gamelan composition to Broughton and his partner, Joel Singer: *Gending in Honor of James and Joel*.

Although none of these new works for the Mills College gamelan included Western instruments, Harrison's experience with *Scenes from Cavafy* suggested new directions. The relative ease with which the singers were able to sing in tune with the gamelan made Harrison think that an extended combination of fretless strings with the gamelan could work. He had poignantly combined viola with his gamelan *degung* in *Threnody for Carlos Chávez*, but the five-limit tuning of that set, Sekar Kembar, did not require as extreme adjustments by the soloist as Western musicians would face in a combination with the tunings of Central Javanese gamelan (including the Mills college gamelan), whose pitches are often much farther away from those of equal temperament.

As so often happened throughout his career, Harrison's next step forward stemmed from a request from a friend, Mills faculty member Kenneth Goldsmith, who approached him for a piece for his piano trio, the Mirecourt Trio. In the midst of writing for gamelan, Harrison found it difficult to summon any enthusiasm for once again writing for an equally tempered piano. Instead, he sent Goldsmith a cassette of *Scenes from Cavafy* to demonstrate how other musicians could join with the gamelan, leading to a commission for violin, cello, and gamelan.[36] In effect, the gamelan orchestra would replace the piano in the trio's texture.

On a 1982 visit to Los Angeles, Harrison sat in on a rehearsal of the Javanese gamelan at UCLA and handed out the notation for his *Ladrang Epikuros* and *Gending Hephaestus*. However, he invited in a cellist and violinist to try out two new parts he had just written to be added to these *balungan*. Despite the rehearsal's bumps and tuning difficulties, Harrison left convinced that it could work.[37]

These two pieces, one *pelog*, one *slendro*, became the outer two movements of Harrison's *Double Concerto for Violin, Cello, and Javanese Gamelan*, one of his most frequently performed gamelan compositions and one of the high points of his '80s output. Unlike the dueling soloists of double concertos of the European tradition, here the violinist and cellist combine to sound like a single instrument. Each movement's solo part comprises a single melody, most often played in octaves or double octaves between the two instruments, creating a sound powerful enough to soar over a full Javanese gamelan playing in loud style. Harrison creates further variation by alternating the instruments or with sections of octaval counterpoint; that is, where the two parts play mostly in octaves with only temporary digressions, creating a sound similar to the simultaneous variation textures of his Chinese- and Korean-inspired pieces.

"Melody," Harrison wrote, "is the grace of music, and the beauty of its work,"[38] and he marked his score (in contrast to the predominant modernism of the period) "ben cantabile" ("sing out"). The violin and cello play over the slowly repeating *balungan*, effectively creating a variations form, though not a self-conscious manipulation of an obvious theme. Instead, the variation shows the different ways in which the *Double Concerto*'s long melodies—instantly captivating and expressive to the point of extravagance—can artfully combine with the *balungan* in quintal counterpoint—or more accurately, counterpoint of *kempyung*, the version of the fifth in gamelan tunings.

For the propulsive middle movement, Harrison created a vigorous estampie with accompaniment only by the drums and gongs. This spare instrumentation allowed him to use a contrasting scale unavailable in the gamelan: the tonally ambiguous octatonic scale. "It has the advantage of sounding chromatic although it uses only eight tones," Harrison explained, "which would provide a distinct difference from the traditional tunings of the outer movements, and still not allow a full encampment of Westernism in the central section."[39] Propelled by the explosive drumming, the strings erupt into a frenzied, feverish, gong-punctuated dance. The third movement's soaring, majestic string melody, one of the most heartbreaking melodies Harrison ever composed, reveals more than any of his words the depth of his devotion to the music of Asia in general and Java in particular, yet he gives the last word to the gamelan ensemble alone. After the concerto premiered at a Mills concert in honor of the composer's sixty-fifth birthday, violinist Goldsmith likened performing with the big gamelan to playing inside Big Ben.[40]

For the same concert, Harrison solicited a pentatonic melody from his old mentor Virgil Thomson and then fashioned it into a wryly jolly *slendro* gamelan piece complete with a vocal melody in which Jody Diamond sang fragments of Thomson's well-known bons mots.

Another nod to the past was Harrison's completion of his *Tributes to Charon*, the cross-metric patterned percussion piece he had begun in San Francisco for John Cage in 1939. Harrison threw a party in the honor of John Cage's seventieth birthday at the residence where he and Colvig had been staying on campus (to avoid having to commute from Aptos constantly). At the party, Jody Diamond met her future husband, Mills composer Larry Polansky, who shared Harrison's interests in microtonality (though not his disdain for computer music). Harrison and Colvig "thought of me and Larry as their children," said Diamond. "We were the kids. When we were at Mills, they'd have us over for a spaghetti dinner each Tuesday."[41]

Once a week, Diamond led the gamelan rehearsal, often trying out new Harrison compositions alongside traditional works, and she and Polansky helped Harrison in another way. Frustrated that American composers had to plead to get a very few works published and rarely made much money from their publication, Harrison decided to follow Harry Partch's example, bypass the establishment, and release his music (as well as unpublished works, available via mail order from his home address) under his own imprint, which he called Hermes' Beard Press. In 1984, Diamond and Polansky offered to sell Hermes' Beard works within a nonprofit collective they had set up called Frog Peak Music. Although the enterprise never made (and never was intended to make) a profit, it provided a centralized source for the distribution of otherwise unpublished scores and recordings of Harrison and other composers.

Harrison's evolving technique of layering new melodies above *balungan* also made possible another attempt to scratch his long itch to create puppet dramas. Since getting involved in the Bay Area puppet community via *The White Snake Lady* and *Young Caesar*, he had hosted meetings of the San Francisco Bay Area Puppet Guild in Aptos. He had befriended local artist Mark Bulwinkle, whose chosen medium was cut metal sheets that turned out to be ideal for making shadow puppets and would also eventually grace Harrison's publications and home. Fulfilling a long ambition, Harrison made a three-foot-deep pit in the Ives Room so that puppeteers could stand in this home theater. The contractors who made the pit in the slab "opined that maybe the space was intended for pet alligators or the like."[42] Harrison also enlisted a writer friend, gay activist Carter Wilson, to adapt a short verse drama by English writer John Masefield based on the folktale of Richard Whittington.

This simple morality tale (in Masefield's version, suitable for children) tells the medieval story of a poor boy upon whom fortune finally shines, thanks in part to his cat. Atop *Ladrang Samuel,* Harrison added an aria for the character Fortune and set narrations as recitatives, like those in *Young Caesar.* Richard and his love Alice sing a duet based on a newly composed *balungan,* appropriately titled for the goddess of love *Gending Aphrodite.* Harrison's friend the ethnomusicologist Mantle Hood admired this melody by itself, with its nontraditional mode, and suggested that it would work well with multiple voices. After some thought, Harrison added a unison choral part on his own text calling on Aphrodite's love as an antidote to this "Mars worn, suiciding world."[43] *Richard Whittington* is not without its charms, but perhaps the story was too slight to support the large forces of Si Betty, and Harrison abandoned the piece after a few performances.[44]

In just the few years since he had been introduced to gamelan, Harrison had adapted his singular voice to an entirely new musical genre, moving from small experiments to much more ambitious multi-movement creations that combined Javanese and European instruments and musical forms.[45] Distanced from the reigning American classical music institutions, Harrison had simply built his own, in which he could play the music he loved with his friends. At an age when most people look forward to retiring, Lou Harrison was just getting started.

32

PARADISAL MUSIC (1982–1984)

I regard the writing of a symphony as, at least in some part, the creation of a world, and one that to my mind needs the balance of humor, seriousness, and both drama and lyricism.

—Lou Harrison[1]

Despite Lou Harrison's singular music and unusual life trajectory, certain lessons from his professional career would be familiar to many twentieth-century American composers. He spent his youthful apprenticeship composing for and performing with friends; and then, full of ambition and energy, he immersed himself in the center of professional musical life. The mainstream music world rewarded Harrison's enthusiasm and innovation with only sparse performances, little professional notice, and poverty.

In a letter to the conductor Gerhard Samuel, Harrison expressed his frustration with the stodgy tradition of the symphony orchestra, which rarely deigned to play new music anymore. In contrast, he wrote, "When I go to my gamelan class I realize that like Haydn and other old European composers, I have my own orchestra and it is a very beautiful one, indeed."[2] Instead of playing the time-consuming, usually fruitless game of sending unperformed scores to uninterested conductors, Harrison could now create heavenly music often just through rows of numbers handed out to his gamelan class, and play it immediately with friends. "No more little ants on paper!" he said. "I don't see why I should compose for any other ensemble ever again!"[3]

Yet Harrison couldn't resist when the mainstream classical music profession finally began to recognize and accept him. As the twentieth anniversary of the Cabrillo Festival approached, musical director Dennis Russell Davies knew that he wanted to commission a major Harrison work, and perhaps only one form in the Western tradition possessed the gravitas for such an occasion. Davies led a campaign to raise the money for the commissioning fee for what would become Harrison's Third Symphony, and many local patrons, including Harrison's friends, contributed. "It wasn't just the money," Bob Hughes remembered. "He composed it because, there was a side of him that, until his very late years, he felt he had to prove himself, still, in the music scene, and a symphony did that. It was an accepted modicum of greatness, to compose a symphony and have it played."[4]

Thus it was with mixed feelings that Harrison put aside his gamelan composing to create another large-scale, equal-tempered work. Harrison wove this patchwork musical quilt, as he had with his *Elegiac Symphony* seven years earlier, by plundering fragments scattered along the vast acreage of his past and substantially reworking pieces he had composed, in some cases, decades earlier.

The symphony is bookended with new versions of two of the overtures from the *Political Primer* (the remaining overture he had used in the *Elegiac Symphony*). The first of the *Political Primer* overtures, for the "Monarchy" section, becomes a sparkling finale to the symphony, while the last overture, "Democracy," becomes the symphony's energetic opening. When adapting this last overture to this new use, Harrison said, "It flatly refused to become a symphonic sonata shape." Although the movement has the requisite contrasting themes of sonata form—a powerful and virile (according to Davies)[5] first theme and a quiet and serene second—each is presented in an extended contrapuntal fantasia. In effect, each theme encapsulates its own development section, making a separate development superfluous and making the form a simple and firm ABA. Like the other *Political Primer* overtures, it is entirely diatonic—that is, with no accidentals—but it has plenty of inventive modal variations and quintal counterpoint.

The second movement returns to the idea of a dance movement consisting of a mini-suite of short sub-movements, each dedicated to a friend, as in the *Symphony on G*. The first resurrects Harrison's *Reel, Homage to Henry Cowell* (now titled "A Reel in Honor of Henry Cowell"), written in 1939, back when friends were working for Cowell's release from prison. The orchestral setting allowed Harrison to indulge in a panoply of textures: a percussion ostinato of spoons and drum, a rough and gritty Irish fiddle solo, and a transfer of Cowell's famous clusters to divided strings. For the second part of the little suite, Harrison repurposed a waltz he had contributed in 1976 to a piano album on the invitation of Evelyn Hinrichsen, the owner of the music publisher Peters. In its delicate orchestration, this deceptively simple tune becomes one of the most heartrending moments in Harrison's entire output. The last sub-movement uses one of Harrison's signature estampies, this one adapted from an organ work he had written for Susan Summerfield at Mills College.

For the third movement, Harrison adapted another piano piece composed during his youthful studies with Cowell. The "spacious" sound[6] and mysterious polytonal atmosphere of his *Largo Ostinato* retains the stamp of Ives's influence on the young composer, but Harrison extensively revised its searching melody, expanding its rather simple 1937 form into an elaborate baroque fantasy.[7]

The symphony's finale hews close to its source, the *Political Primer* "Democracy" overture: an entirely diatonic extended canonic fantasia. Although it abandons the earlier version's just intonation, the glittering ostinatos of the "gamelan section" of tack piano, celesta, vibraphone, and harp remain—like "jingle bells," said Harrison. The way Harrison layered different instruments onto the contrapuntal lines resembles the "German"-style orchestration that also characterized the *Elegiac Symphony*.

However, contrasting passages featuring soloists from different sections emerge amid the sparkling bells, and Harrison characterized these sections as "kind of little soloist things as though you're walking through villages. The villages get a little bigger and more formalized until finally it climaxes in a big thing, and it's as if a boat had been launched—a big sea-going boat. Then the ocean waves are slightly irregular through the coda, and the horns are in their glory, and so on."[8]

ELEGY

At the same 1982 Cabrillo Festival where Davies premiered the *Third Symphony*, Harrison received some shocking news. Calvin Simmons, one of Gerhard Samuel's successors as music director of the Oakland Symphony, had died in a boating accident at the age of thirty-two. A supporter of Harrison's work, he had also been the first African American conductor of a major US orchestra and one of the youngest. When the news reached Davies on a Sunday, he asked if Harrison could provide a memorial for the concert the following Friday, and Harrison agreed. However, though he had often composed the core tones and melodies of his gamelan pieces in just days, composing a new work for European orchestra would be especially challenging, even for the prolific Harrison. "Since my subconscious composes Javanese pieces, I felt, 'let it go.' I'm not going to worry."[9] Why not compose a gamelan-style elegy for that orchestra?

Harrison began by writing the core tones, the *balungan*, in the Javanese form known as a *ketawang*; that is, a sixteen-beat gong cycle divided in half by the *kenong* gongs. Although Harrison brought in his own gong to join the orchestra (supplemented by double basses), he assigned the punctuating role of the *kenong* to a harp arpeggio and horn tone. The strings in octaves play the *balungan*, a mostly pentatonic, *slendro*-like melody that, crucially, also includes a semitone just above the tonic, permitting Harrison to use the falling semitone that in the baroque period represented grief. The melody embodies a tension between a pentatonic calm and the mournful semitone.[10]

As they approach the second gong, the melodic instruments suddenly double the length of the core melody tones, triggering a shift in what the Javanese call *irama*, or level of rhythmic density. In this more expansive *irama*, the harp and other strings shift to an elaborating countermelody using the Javanese technique known as *pipilan*, an alternation between pairs of *balungan* pitches. Unsure at first how a technique associated with the *bonang* kettle-gongs would sound when transferred to the instruments of the European orchestra, Harrison was pleased with the results, and he used this technique in his Fourth Symphony and other later works. At this point in the elegy, a plaintive oboe enters in quintal counterpoint, giving a singular, sorrowful voice to a short piece that contains several inspirations that Harrison would later use to bridge his parallel lives in the worlds of gamelan and of mainstream classical music.

Completed in just two days, *Elegy, to the Memory of Calvin Simmons* was slow and simple enough for the orchestra to learn in just a couple of rehearsals before the Friday night concert. The concert, which included many members of the Oakland

Symphony who had played under Simmons, came off very well. As the last gong echoed in the Cabrillo Theater, the audience sat in silence for the memory of its lost leader.

Harrison's return to the mainstream musical world represented by the Cabrillo Festival showed that this professional attention had already compromised his resolve to focus entirely on playing gamelan with friends. His attempts to simultaneously satisfy both his great ambitions—to compose for professional recognition and to compose for himself and friends—led to an inability to say no to any new project. As the paperwork and projects mounted in his terminally disorganized home, one day he picked up the telephone and called a young woman he'd met years earlier.

"Hello, dear," the deep, jolly voice boomed. "Glub glub glub, I'm drowning in papers. Can you save me?"[11]

JOURNEY TO JAVA

Harrison's increasing success and rising profile in the professional music world translated to many travel opportunities, arranged around his Mills and San Jose State obligations. Harrison traveled to festivals and residencies at Cal State Sacramento, the University of Delaware, SUNY Buffalo, and the University of Michigan (where he was delighted to play the gamelan). In his keynote address at the American Society of University Composers conference in Seattle, he suggested a tax on popular music to pay back classical composers for all their ideas that pop composers had stolen.[12] He enjoyed seeing Virgil Thomson on a trip to New York and seeing Peter Garland when in Santa Fe.

When Harrison and Colvig traveled to Paris to see Davies, Madeleine Milhaud, and other European acquaintances, Davies took Harrison to a performance of Boulez's Ensemble Intercontemporain featuring the great jazz pianist Keith Jarrett, who had impressed Harrison in Cabrillo Festival performances of Harrison's *Suite for Violin, Piano, and Small Orchestra*.[13] Admiring Jarrett's "kinetics" and inventiveness as an improviser, Harrison casually suggested that Jarrett write a concerto for himself. In the spring of 1983, Jarrett phoned Harrison and explained why he didn't want to compose a concerto for himself, and the two talked about the possibility of Harrison writing a concerto for him. The idea appealed to Harrison, but he would not have time to begin work on such a project for another year.[14]

Harrison's hectic schedule hardly abated when he was home; his and Colvig's datebooks bristled with performances by the San Jose State and Mills gamelan, rehearsals, and meetings with musicians, composers, students, and artists. Harrison's increasingly frantic schedule took its toll. His ambitious hikes with Colvig diminished as his girth grew. His increasingly frequent visits to the doctor produced a frightening diagnosis: the precursor to diabetes. Then, on one of his many long commutes on highways between Mills College in Oakland and Aptos, Harrison's car overturned.

Harrison and Colvig escaped serious injury, but Harrison's damaged right wrist would continue to bother him for years, and his famous calligraphy (used even on casual correspondence) never entirely recovered. The crash shook up the sixty-seven-year-old Harrison and caused him to confront his own mortality. If he had died in the accident, Bill would have faced a house stuffed full of scattered manuscripts, artworks, pieces of instruments, misplaced contracts, and more. As it was, Harrison staggered under the pressure of an increasingly chaotic home and work life bursting with bags of unanswered correspondence, notes written on scraps of paper, and piles of unorganized records.

That's when he called the young woman he had met at the 1974 Center for World Music summer session. Eva Soltes was studying classical Indian dance with the famed dancer T. Balasaraswati, and on leaving dance practice, she often passed a room in which two bearded men worked on strange but beautiful-sounding percussion instruments. A local concert producer as well, she asked Harrison to speak at a Charles Ives centennial event. Soltes recognized the respect that the charismatic polymath Harrison commanded even then. "When you were in Lou's presence," she recalled, "you'd stand straighter or sit taller or listen a little better."

Busy producing one hundred concerts a year at Berkeley's chamber music organization, 1750 Arch Street, Soltes now stood before the garage of the grand old maverick of American music. "His scores were everywhere," she remembered. "It had all been eaten by rats. It was all in really, really, really bad shape. I knew something had to be done."[5]

Despite loathing paperwork and already having a full-time job, her appreciation for Harrison's historical significance impelled her to help. She arranged for Mary Hill, on staff at the Mills Music Department, to help sort through shopping bags stuffed full of unanswered correspondence. Soltes also began to help him with his many travel arrangements. Where Harrison had never known how to broach the sensitive question of asking presenters to support Colvig's travel with him to concerts, residencies, and lectures, Soltes was happy to apply her management and concert production experience.

Soltes also sought help from musician Charles Hanson with putting Harrison's large art collection into shape, and had it appraised. Gradually, Hanson's duties expanded beyond that role to that of archivist and assistant. Soltes also stayed in Harrison's orbit for the rest of his life, playing a crucial role in his rise to fame by producing concerts around the world for him and bringing much-needed order to the chaos of his burgeoning career.

One of Soltes's first jobs was to help Harrison with an application for a Fulbright grant. This flagship program of the US State Department funded overseas residencies and exchange positions for American scholars and artists. Among the many composers Harrison had befriended, he felt a special kinship with New Zealand composer and ethnomusicologist Jack Body, a lecturer at Victoria University of Wellington in New Zealand who composed for a Javanese gamelan there. Soltes put together a proposal that included a three-month residency in Wellington and other residencies elsewhere in New Zealand, which would also provide Harrison with a leaping-off point for a trip around the world. Harrison and Colvig would leave behind their

California home for a full year, and on their itinerary was what would be another life-changing visit to Asia—this time to the cradle of gamelan itself.

JOURNEY TO JAVA

The warm, open-air airport in Honolulu was Harrison's first stop, at the end of May 1983. Familiar with the city and university from his residency two decades earlier, he welcomed its recent acquisition of a gorgeous Javanese gamelan, directed by Harja Susilo (known as Pak Sus), who gave Harrison a lesson. Harrison also reconnected with his ethnomusicologist friend from Santa Cruz, Richard North, a specialist in the gamelan styles of the Javanese city of Cirebon; he gave Harrison valuable contact information and suggestions for a trip to Java.

On June 1, Harrison and Colvig descended into the rainy antipodean winter of Wellington, New Zealand. Almost as soon as they moved into the small, comfortable cottage that composer Jack Body had arranged for them, Colvig was off exploring the green mountains surrounding Wellington Harbour. Harrison lectured at Victoria University and began playing in the university's gamelan, even performing in a *wayang kulit* (shadow play). The performance was led by a young eleventh-generation puppet master (*dalang*) named Widiyanto S. Putro (known familiarly as Midiyanto or Pak Midi). Harrison invited Widiyanto to California, and the master puppeteer and musician would eventually make the West Coast of the United States his second home, teaching at UC Berkeley and Porland's Lewis & Clark College, among others.

Naturally, Harrison began to compose works for the university's gamelan, which originated in Cirebon: *Ketawang Wellington, Lagu Lagu Thomasan* (dedicated to local ethnomusicologist Allan Thomas, his wife, Jennifer Shennan, and their children), and *Lagu Victoria* (named for the university—"*lagu*" means "song" or "tune"). He was especially fascinated with the tuning, and he found that by selecting a nontraditional set of pitches (as in *Ketawang Wellington*), he could make a *slendro*-like scale emerge from *pelog*.

When not socializing with the musicians at the local Mexican cantina, Harrison might be found under a favorite big tree in the nearby botanic gardens. He began speaking to the tree, since he had left behind his weekly therapy appointments in California. "This seems to be working just as well," he declared, "and he's cheaper!"[16] Colvig, meanwhile, built some instruments and tuned the gamelan. Harrison also visited and lectured at three other New Zealand colleges.

In December 1983, the Fulbright grant ended, but Harrison and Colvig were just getting under way. The next stop on their around-the-world tour, just in time for summer Christmas, was Sydney, Australia. They met the well-known Australian composer Peter Sculthorpe and left their host—Harrison's friend from his New York days, Peggy Glanville-Hicks—with a gift of a chandelier for her house.[17]

Harrison's first sight of his long-revered country of Indonesia was not of Java but instead of the neighboring island of Bali, the source of his first gamelan inspirations in such works as *Solstice* and *Suite for Violin, Piano, and Small Orchestra* from the early 1950s. Harrison met friends including I Nyoman Wenten and his wife, Nanik, who escorted them down many narrow, rice-paddy-bounded roads, to rituals, temples, and the so-called Monkey Forest. Harrison and Colvig commissioned a performance of a *wayang kulit* shadow-puppet play from the renowned Balinese *dalang* I Nyoman Wija to provide good luck for the rest of their trip. Unfortunately, the spiritual powers responded with a devastating thunderstorm.[18]

Harrison loved the way that art was so deeply integrated into the everyday life of the people in this complex Hindu society, but on the whole he was unmoved by the music. Instead of tuning the instruments to eliminate acoustic beats (as in just intonation), Balinese musicians deliberately detune pairs of instruments to create these same acoustic beats at precise frequencies. In his *Music Primer*, Harrison contrasted the "clangorous" sound of the Balinese gamelan to the "paradisal" Javanese version.[19]

A few years hence, in response to a request from his friend JaFran Jones, an ethnomusicologist at Bowling Green State University in Ohio, Harrison would try his hand at composing for this flashier, more dynamic set of instruments. However, he was out of his element composing *Round for JaFran Jones*, and he left to her the determination of the ensemble's characteristic intricate figuration, what Harrison called the "flowers."[20] Despite his respect for Balinese artistry, his real love originated on the next island over.

Their first experience of Javanese gamelan in its native habitat came in the East Javanese city of Surabaya, where they were invited to a performance at the local radio station. The next stop took them to the very center of the refined Central Javanese tradition, the city of Solo (or Surakarta), where they stayed in a hotel just outside the Mangkunegaran, one of Solo's two palaces and a focal point for this famous gamelan tradition. They explored the city by *becak* (pedaled taxi) and visited a gong foundry. Harrison was fascinated with the tuning of the "breathtaking and majestic" gamelan Kyai Udan Arum, one of the most famous gamelan in the country.[21]

Thanks to referrals from Vincent McDermott and his other contacts, Harrison and Colvig met with scholars and musicians of the Akademi Seni Karawitan Indonesia (Indonesian Academy of Traditional Musical Arts), among them the legendary gamelan teacher and theorist Martopangrawit.[22] The ASKI faculty, honored by Harrison's visit, arranged for an impromptu concert, reading through several of Harrison's gamelan compositions, followed (as was typical) by a question-and-answer session. Fascinated that their tradition had extended its roots to a distant country, the Javanese asked Harrison many questions. Then Martopangrawit, perhaps the foremost authority on Javanese music theory, stood up. He pointed to one of the scores they had run through, Harrison's *Bubaran Robert*, and noted that the score indicated that it was in *patet manyura*. *Patet* is a concept sometimes translated as "mode," but it implies many nuances regarding the way the melody lies in the scale. For example, Harrison knew from Pak Cokro that *patet manyura* emphasizes pitch 6, deemphasizes pitch 5, and favors certain four-note patterns, such as 3-2-1-6. Why, Martopangrawit asked, had Harrison decided that this melody was in *patet manyura*?

Harrison paused. He had presumed that he could apply this elusive concept of *patet*, which his esteemed questioner had spent his lifetime studying, to his own music.

"Ignorance," he finally answered. "Purely from ignorance."[23]

Harrison thereafter ceased indicating the *patet* of his compositions on the scores. After all, he was not Javanese and had no desire or pretensions to copy their traditions, only to respect them as he invented his own compositions. Just as he often had no misgivings about creating unique, nontraditional forms in his compositions, he in essence created his own modes that sometimes differed sharply from those traditionally used in Java.

Harrison and Colvig next visited the other center of the Central Javanese gamelan tradition, the city of Yogyakarta, a larger and vibrant town that is the site of the Sultan's Palace and the Pakualaman court, where Pak Cokro had made his career. Every night brought another performance: gamelan, *wayang kulit*, *wayang wong* (a drama performed with people rather than puppets), dance dramas. Harrison splurged on puppets, batik costumes for him and his gamelan musicians, books and cassettes, instrument parts, and even gold paint for the instrument cases. They visited Pak Cokro's home and the magnificent ancient Buddhist monument Borobudur outside the city.

Harrison and Colvig were introduced to a gamelan maker named Pak Daliyo who made inexpensive gamelan out of iron (rather than traditional but expensive bronze) salvaged from oil drums discarded by the national oil company, Pertamina. Harrison immediately commissioned a small *slendro* set, to be named Si Aptos, the last of the gamelan he would own.[24] Although modest in size, gamelan Si Aptos had its own unique timbre and charm, enabling Harrison to play *slendro* gamelan at his home, now that his other gamelan remained housed at Mills and San Jose State. In celebration of the event, Harrison composed a new piece, *Ladrang in Honor of Pak Daliyo*.[25]

Harrison and Colvig arrived in the city of Cirebon bearing introductions from Richard North and Allan Thomas, both ethnomusicologists with long associations with the court there. Harrison was introduced to Pangeran Haji Yusuf Dendabrata, more commonly known as Elang Yusuf, the palace arts director and second in line to the sultan, who arranged for Harrison to have some lessons in Cirebonese gamelan style. Then one day at their hotel, Harrison and Colvig received a gold-engraved invitation to attend the ceremonial circumcision of the princes. Their visit happened to coincide with this extraordinary royal event, and to be invited was a great honor. Despite the honor, Harrison was a bit appalled by the ritual. "Here were these poor guys, princes sitting on their thrones, waiting to be circumcised with an audience of about fifty to a hundred people. A whole-day festivity, you know—terrible!"[26] Feeling very ill, Harrison and Colvig made what they thought was an unobtrusive exit, which, unknown to them, turned out to be a major faux pas, and Elang Yusuf himself came to the hotel to find out what had happened. Perhaps by way of an apology, Harrison composed a piece, *Lagu Elang Yusuf*, in his honor.

HEAVEN'S BENEFICE

> *one cannot*
> *well tell whether domes are rising*
> *here to heaven, or whether the*
> *heaven's benefice flows down these*

arches into us; for it is
       a kind of open paradise,
and song flows through it openly.
       —Lou Harrison[27]

After Indonesia, the couple visited Singapore, where Harrison recuperated and composed. In Bangkok, despite his antipathy toward the tuning of Thai *piphat* ensembles, Harrison delighted in Thai arts. Then Harrison and Colvig visited classical sites in Jordan and the architectural wonders of Istanbul, home of his beloved architect Sinan. Inspired by his mosque for Sultan Suleiman, Harrison composed the above verses in his honor.

In April, they visited the Acropolis and other ancient Athenian glories. But Rome, so changed since Harrison's visit thirty years before, they hated almost from the moment of their arrival, when Colvig was injured by one of the city's notoriously reckless motorcyclists; they later had to fight off a robber on a public street. In Naples, they found Virgil's tomb under a highway overpass, closed. "We need not worry about the destruction of civilizations by superpower wars," he wrote in his diary, disgusted by commercial and industrial degradations of European civilization's cradle. "The same is being done daily and joyously all over the planet under the aegis of 'multinational companies' and by the common man with the tools given him by the industrial revolutions: cars, spray cans, guns, posters, television, loudspeakers, bombs, poisons, computers, movies, plastics, airplanes and other such. Surely the industrial revolution was humankind's worst mistake, as it is in all probability the last."[28]

Finally, in the summer of 1984, they continued to several cities in the Netherlands and Germany, where Davies led performances of Harrison's three symphonies and more. They continued to Switzerland and London, seeing old friends at many stops, before heading to New York for a week and returning home by July.

Happy to be at his own house after 414 days abroad, Harrison spent some days recovering while Colvig headed off to his familiar local hikes. Harrison wouldn't rest long, however. He had compiled a mental list of new compositional projects and ideas after a year of absorbing an enormous influx of artistic influences on his journey, including the piece that would become perhaps his most successful work for Western orchestra.

33

STAMPEDE (1984–1987)

When I heard at the close of the day how my name had been receiv'd with
  plaudits in the capitol, still it was not a happy night for me that follow'd,
And else when I carous'd, or when my plans were
  accomplish'd, still I was not happy,
But the day when I rose at dawn from the bed of perfect health,
  refresh'd, singing, inhaling the ripe breath of autumn,
When I saw the full moon in the west grow pale and dis-
  appear in the morning light,
When I wander'd alone over the beach, and undressing bathed,
  laughing with the cool waters, and saw the sun rise,
And when I thought how my dear friend my lover was
  on his way coming, O then I was happy . . .

—Walt Whitman, "When I Heard at the Close of the Day," set by Harrison in
  his *Three Songs*

One day in 1985, Harrison received a letter from the man who'd perhaps been his first
great love: Edward McGowan.

"Do you remember me from the 1940s when you lived on Bleecker Street?" asked
his old boyfriend, who'd just retired after forty-six years as a Methodist minister.
"You were responsible for helping me understand great music. I listen to the Good
Radio Station and hear your compositions."[1] The two old friends exchanged information about their lives after they'd been forcibly separated. McGowan had hastily
married the year he left New York, he wrote, and now had grandchildren.

Harrison's bitter memory of the social forces that had separated them contrasted
with the stability of his current relationship, and he was inspired by the open acceptance of the Portland Gay Men's Chorus (PGMC) on one of his visits to his hometown. When the director approached Harrison to ask for a piece, Harrison thought
of the song he had written for McGowan at the height of their passionate affair in
1946, his setting of one of Walt Whitman's homosexually charged *Calamus* poems.
During a visit to England in the summer of 1985, he orchestrated the song, adding

strings and organ to the original piano and dividing the chromatic melody between tenors and basses.

Harrison added another song from the period, *King David's Lament for Jonathan* from 1941, which laments the loss of a brother whose love "surpass[ed] the love of women." Its diatonicism, Cowell-period clusters, and sorrowful descending bass lines contrast with the *Calamus* setting. During the same trip, he composed a new Whitman setting, "When I Heard at the Close of the Day," in which the narrator (perhaps speaking for Harrison himself) finds happiness in his (male) beloved rather than in society's acclamations. It is set mostly as a free recitative over orchestral drones, much like his earlier *Peace Piece #2* setting of Robert Duncan's poem. It ends not with a loud finale but instead with a whisper, as an affirming C major triad fades like Whitman's happy moment.

Whitman, who had seen so much suffering while a nurse during the American Civil War, was on Harrison's mind. As he had been preparing for his around-the-world trip in 1983, reports had swirled through the news of a mysterious disease that targeted gay men. While Harrison was abroad, the Department of Health of San Francisco, one of the plague's epicenters, closed down the city's famous bathhouses. Since taking up with Colvig, Harrison visited the baths only infrequently, sometimes with Bill. Nevertheless, the gay world he knew was changing quickly.

"How much I hate the AIDS plague days!" he wrote. "In past years we could just go to the Baths for happy release and relief from tensions that now pile up to prison miseries."[2] As the seriousness of the epidemic became clearer, Harrison could count several personal acquaintances who had succumbed to the disease. Half of the commission he earned for the *Three Songs* he donated to AIDS research. Nevertheless, and despite his guilt about working on the songs instead of the concerto he had promised Keith Jarrett,[3] Harrison was moved by hearing his *Three Songs* sung by the Portland Gay Men's Chorus that September (in the same church where he and his brother had attended Sunday school as children) and being "treated royally by 80 fine and handsome men" in the PGMC.[4]

As usual when he was in Portland, Harrison worked intensively with Vincent McDermott and the Lewis & Clark College gamelan, the Venerable Showers of Beauty. Harrison contributed his new *Gending Vincent* (named for McDermott) to the group, a large (but nontraditional) form, with plenty of room for the very refined expansive sections that McDermott admired in the Solonese style. Harrison also met up with Widiyanto, the master Javanese puppeteer and musician from New Zealand, who had taken Harrison up on his offer to visit. Harrison had sent him on a bus ride to Portland, where he became McDermott's assistant and, after McDermott's retirement, his replacement.

While in Portland, Harrison and Colvig were tuning the Venerable Showers of Beauty instruments ("he was always talking about tuning ratios," McDermott recalled) when they had one of their frequent (and frequently commented on by friends who knew them) spats. Colvig had mistakenly hammered the boss of a gong (a no-no), and Harrison erupted, criticizing his partner's negligence and storming out. A few hours later, Widiyanto recalled, Harrison returned—bearing a dozen roses and (as always happened in these situations) no remnant of anger.[5]

FAUST MEETS HAMLET

> *Now I have taught for many years*
>   *& have grown to need young people,*
> *so that I panic after all*
>   *in thinking that soon I might not*
> *grow & debate in daily hours*
>   *among the young & beautiful.*

—Lou Harrison, 1984[6]

In April 1985, Mills College threw a retirement party for Lou Harrison, who, at age sixty-eight, was stepping down from his Milhaud chair at the college. In order to replenish his bank account after the expensive global journey, Harrison had decided to continue teaching at Mills, half-time, for another year before fully retiring. After a farewell gamelan concert in which Harrison and Colvig played with real enthusiasm, he turned the gamelan program over to Jody Diamond. He had cherished his relationship with the school since his first experiences there nearly a half century earlier, but he wouldn't miss commuting two hours each way to and from Oakland.

And his life had become so hectic that he barely had time to teach. Although Harrison and Colvig had been happy to return home after more than a year abroad, Aptos offered little respite. Honors (his 1985 election to the Percussive Arts Society's Hall of Fame, for example), invitations for appearances, and requests for scores continued to accelerate. The long-indifferent San Francisco Symphony played his increasingly acclaimed *Suite for Violin, Piano and Small Orchestra*, though consigning it to a new-music-only concert, causing Harrison to lament to Hovhaness that little had changed in the classical music world since their struggles to get contemporary music performed half a century earlier.[7]

Despite his world tour and subsequent travels east and north over the ensuing year, his unflagging efforts to spread the gamelan gospel, and the flurry of other activities back home, "I am in a composing mania these days," Harrison wrote to a friend at the end of 1984.[8] Often, to get away from the phone and other distractions, he and Colvig would pack up the camper and drive up to Fremont Peak, where Harrison would compose while Colvig hiked.

Though he was grateful for the opportunities to compose—and get paid for it—Harrison worried that his compulsion to say yes to commissions stemmed from a deep-set insecurity about his finances and future and that it might crowd out his more enjoyable voluntary compositions. "I've always had the feeling that there would never be any work for me, I would never be part of society as a productive, money-earning person, because I came under the job market when people were diving out of windows, 1929, and so formed this notion that there was never any place for me in society," he remembered telling his therapist. "I'm constantly worrying, and I'm overworking at commissions because of that to try to get enough ahead. Of course, when you're old, too, you have operations or the hospital—all this sort of thing, it all adds up."

"I've heard this from every person of your age," his therapist replied. "It was a major trauma to any person at that time, and it stays with you. It's like going through a war or something."[9]

Now returned from his travels and creatively reenergized by them, and at last having assimilated his gamelan influences and found his compositional voice in that music, Harrison was ready to embark on the most fruitful stretch of his long career. Typically, he faced not one but two compositional agendas: the commissioned works now rolling in (topped by the piano concerto that he and Keith Jarrett had discussed), and "voluntary" pieces he wanted to write for his own enjoyment, though these projects would pay little (or might even end up costing him money). Beginning in the fall of 1984 and into 1985, he worked on projects in both categories simultaneously.

Topping the list of new projects for his own enjoyment was a new puppet drama. After witnessing several *wayang* performances and other dramas in Indonesia and New Zealand (where he had performed a *wayang* with the puppet master Widiyanto), Harrison's old ambition to produce dramas himself reemerged. He hoped that the example of the Indonesian dramatic tradition might help restore the West's declining bardic storytelling tradition, and he contemplated making a company of archetypal shadow-puppet figures (for example, a king or villain) that he could use in various dramas based on myths from ancient cultures.[10] It was the same impulse that had led to *Young Caesar* and *Richard Whittington*, but now Harrison had in mind a collaborator.

In 1980, Harrison and Vincent McDermott had attended a rod-puppet performance by Kathy Foley, a UC Santa Cruz faculty member, scholar, and riveting performer who specialized in Southeast Asian puppet theater, and in particular the Sundanese *wayang golek* style. As the two composers were the only members of the audience that night, it was easy to strike up a conversation, which led Foley to collaborate with McDermott on the puppet opera *The King of Bali* in 1982. Now Harrison—a Westerner just returned from Java—asked her to help him create an "American *wayang*," presenting Western myths and stories in the puppet theater format that was such a crucial aspect of Javanese arts culture.[11]

Harrison first suggested staging Ovid's massive *Metamorphoses*, but Foley realized it would be too elaborate—think how many puppets would need to be created for all those characters. They discussed two seminal stories of the Western canon, *Faust* and *Hamlet*—and suddenly realized they could combine the two. In this *Faust*, the title character is an aloof professor at the University of Wittenberg where Shakespeare's Hamlet is a student. (Sometimes in the Indonesian *wayang* tradition, favorite characters will also find their way into stories from other sources.)

Faust takes on the role of the evil god, a role familiar from the Indonesian *wayang*, but instead of speaking in archaic Javanese (which divine *wayang* characters traditionally use, even though it's a language not usually understood by contemporary Javanese audiences), in Foley's drama he speaks the Western equivalent,

Latin. That leaves the clown puppets, here represented by the Shakespearean characters Rosencrantz and Guildenstern, to interpret the speech of the master, while throwing in a few improvised topical jokes and slapstick (like the *punakawan* or clown-servants of the *wayang* tradition). Harrison and Foley adapted the American poet Randall Jarrell's translation of Goethe's *Faust* into their mostly comic take. Unlike *Young Caesar*, but like the Indonesian *wayang*, a single puppeteer, Foley, manipulated all the characters, voiced all their lines (scripted and improvised), and narrated. Separate singers would sing for the characters and function as a chorus.

For this marriage of traditions, Harrison composed music for both his gamelan and a Western chamber orchestra. For the witches' sabbath scene on Walpurgisnacht Mountain, he created a diabolical estampie. Faust's beloved and innocent Gretchen sings a spinning song in a poignant non-diatonic mode, accompanied by cycling harp and strings (which bear some resemblance to Schubert's setting of the same scene). A joyous Easter procession sung by the chorus sparkles with harp and bell ostinatos. For various points in the play, Harrison created harp dances, recitatives, and (as in *Young Caesar*) percussion ostinato backgrounds.

"Lou's mood songs were just right for puppets," Foley recalled. "I believe it is this ability of puppets—to be pure truth for emotion otherwise too raw—that caused Harrison to gravitate toward the puppets, build his gamelan, and teach people how to play for shadows or figures. . . . Puppets were just closer to that world he could envision."[12]

Their *Faust* script was timely, aimed at the 1985 summer Shakespeare Santa Cruz Festival on the UCSC campus—the same summer the festival was staging both *Hamlet* and Tom Stoppard's ingenious *Hamlet* spoof, *Rosencrantz and Guildenstern Are Dead*. Unfortunately, Foley was unable to build all of the puppets in time, so they performed *Faust* in a conventional stage version. And unable to fund the chamber orchestra Harrison had composed for, the production dropped half the music, using only Harrison's gamelan.[13]

However, Faust did spawn one of Harrison's greatest hits. One of the new gamelan pieces Harrison wrote for the production accompanied a scene in which Ovid's characters Philemon and Baukis, the humble peasants who were rewarded for giving hospitality to gods in disguise, find their way into the drama. In Goethe's *Faust*, Mephistopheles kills the pious old couple when they resist Faust's new urban empire. The lyrical opening of Harrison's *Philemon and Baukis* combines the *rebab* (the bowed fiddle of the gamelan) with the soft *gendèr* metallophones, which play Cirebonese patterns above a flowing *slendro balungan* melody. In 1987, when Harrison adapted the movement as a standalone piece with violin instead of *rebab*, *Philemon and Baukis* became one of his most successful marriages of a Western soloist and gamelan. The second half accelerates into an energetic fantasy in which the *balungan* has expanded to an asymmetrical thirty-six-beat structure. As in the *Double Concerto*, the violin plays a series of variations that weave around the repeating *balungan* in quintal counterpoint, but unlike that earlier piece, the form is periodically interrupted by a contrasting section that seemingly halts this busy melody in moments of serene stasis.

Philemon and Baukis kicked off a series of mid-1980s masterpieces that constitute the climax of Harrison's long and prolific career.

CHORDS LIKE BELLS

Upon his return from England and Portland, Harrison faced a deadline for his piano concerto: October 20, 1985, at a Carnegie Hall anniversary concert for the American Composers Orchestra, conducted by Dennis Russell Davies. Harrison's initial impulse was to write a three-movement piece, each movement in a different tuning, just as the *Double Concerto* began in *pelog*, moved to an octatonic middle movement, and ended in *slendro*. Jarrett was intrigued by the idea, but ultimately Harrison realized how impractical it would be to require three pianos for a touring pianist like Jarrett. Instead he selected the second temperament described by Johann Philipp Kirnberger, an eighteenth-century composer and a student of J. S. Bach.

The choice of a temperament may seem quite un-Harrisonian, as just intonation, with its pure intervals, is the antithesis of temperaments, with their compromised, irrational relationships. However, Harrison understood that the great variety of baroque temperaments offered an equal variety of possible expressive palettes (unlike the gray sameness of equal temperament), with some keys close to just and others more dissonant. Kirnberger #2 is unusual among eighteenth-century temperaments in that almost all of the intervals are just. Kirnberger modified the wolf interval created in Pythagorean tuning by splitting the "leftover" interval or comma between two fifths instead of leaving it to one "wolf fifth." So instead of having to work with only a medievalist three-limit tuning, as he had in his *Ditone Suite* for guitar, this innovation allows for three sweet five-limit thirds (otherwise absent in Pythagorean tuning). However, it does mean that the two fifths that do include the tempered tone, A (D-A and A-E), are still pretty dissonant—Harrison called them "gutsy" fifths and used them strategically through the piece.

Noting the presence of three-limit, five-limit, and tempered intervals, Harrison said, "This astonishing tuning contains almost the whole history of 'Western music' from Babylonian to the mid-part of the last century, for its flat series produces perfectly tuned 4ths and 5ths (the whole Middle Ages) and the white keys are, with the exception of a very slightly raised pitch A, in perfect Renaissance and Baroque just intonation. The 'cross-overs' between the two series are of fascinating character and the expressive powers of the forms in this tuning are, to me, very attractive."[14]

In preparation for the concerto, both Harrison and Keith Jarrett tuned their pianos to Kirnberger #2, so that they could get the sound of it in their ears and understand its particular characteristics. As he had in the *Strict Songs*, Harrison selected an orchestra that could tune to the piano—strings, harps, and trombones, plus unpitched percussion—hence its unusual name: *Piano Concerto with Selected Orchestra*.

As Harrison discovered, changing the tuning on his home instruments whenever the inspiration moved him was one thing, but requiring it in the great temple of music known as Carnegie Hall was quite another. At first, the piano technician refused to follow Harrison's instructions, until Harrison threatened to withdraw his piece—and himself—from the concert.[15] After the piano was finally retuned, Jarrett headed over to the New York Steinway factory to check out the instrument. A fretful-looking company representative pulled Jarrett aside. "Mr. Jarrett," he said gravely, "you have to tell us about this piece."

"What do you mean?" the pianist replied.

"Is it going to give us a bad name?"

"What?"

"Well, it's tuned differently, isn't it?" Steinway honchos, he confided, were worried about this concert. The nonstandard tuning might make audiences and reviewers think there was something wrong with their company's piano.

"I had to keep saying, 'It's okay, it's okay,'" Jarrett recalled. "Don't worry."[16]

Keith Jarrett remembered that the string players of the orchestra did not like having to tune their A string differently. "I mean, it's worse than dealing with an audience. The audiences are probably more open than the orchestra."[17] Harrison later said that this experience taught him that "concert grand pianos are not instruments at all—they are symbolic fetishes, just this side of the Holy Grail!"[18] When the night came, the Steinway personnel "crossed the street in force,"[19] including the company president. As it happened, the president loved the performance.[20] "At times in the piece," Jarrett observed, "whole chords sound like bells."[21]

Harrison had often combined soloists with an orchestra, but the magnitude and tradition of the piano concerto presented new challenges, and his response to them makes this concerto one of his least typical—and most conventionally "Western"—pieces of this period. Momentarily setting aside his rejection of Romanticism forty years earlier, he commenced his concerto with dramatic octaves over a thundering bass drum roll, recalling the opening of Brahms's first piano concerto.[22] The *pipil* (gamelan) elaboration throughout also recalls baroque harpsichord writing. In contrast to his typical use of short movements in a suite format (even in his symphonies), the first three of Harrison's four movements are some of the longest and most profound of his career. However atypical for Harrison, the nearly twelve-minute first movement's sonata form, complete with a titanic Beethovian development, suits the Romantic cast of this piece. Unlike the intensely contrapuntal movements from earlier in his career that he adapted for his second and third symphonies, this movement is entirely melodic, one long melody almost throughout its length.

Also like Brahms, Harrison adds a dance as a second movement to this concerto. Where Brahms had a scherzo, Harrison inserts a "Stampede"—the longest and most complex version of the many incarnations Harrison gave the form. Instead of long, whirling sequences of eighth notes, so familiar from pieces like the *Suite for Symphonic Strings*, the piano concerto's "Stampede" starts off sounding like one of Harrison's percussion pieces. The pianist plays a long duet with a drummer (instructed to stand next to the piano onstage) and becomes almost as a percussionist himself when wielding an octave bar to slam down tone clusters that interrupt fragmentary melodies.[23] In this way, the movement resembles the crashing opening of the *Concerto for Organ with Percussion Orchestra*, but the pianist goes on to play hair-raising double-octave clusters with a forearm. Before the piece was written, Jarrett had warned Harrison that he was having trouble with his shoulder and asked him not to write anything percussive. "Then he turns around and gives me the 'Stampede' movement, which is not just banging with the octave bar but putting it down and picking it up again." Harrison's unsympathetic advice: "Don't get muscle-bound."[24]

The "Stampede" makes a thrilling ride, but critics bestowed most praise on the following "magically serene and perhaps healingly holy"[25] slow movement and its sense of luminous stasis. Its chords of stacked seconds and fourths originate in Harrison's counterpoint of the 1940s, but perhaps the more significant precedents were the hymn-like interludes Jarrett often played in his famous free improvisations. Knowing Jarrett's fame as an improviser, Harrison also found a place in that movement for an optional cadenza, and Jarrett responded with a different cadenza at each performance.[26] "Everything about it speaks of the fact that it was written with Jarrett in mind," judged one jazz critic.[27]

The brisk final movement resembles the ending movement of Ravel's vivacious Piano Concerto in G, both in its brevity in proportion to the rest of the piece (Harrison's movement is only three minutes) and in its sparkle. The mode has a bright raised fourth but a bluesy lowered seventh.

"No other American piano concerto, I think, is its equal," wrote *Los Angeles Times* critic Mark Swed. "It was half an hour of heaven."[28] Author, critic, and classical music historian Joseph Horowitz wondered "if there is a more formidable American piano concerto."[29] Beauty, it seemed, was in again in classical music, and a new generation of critics recognized that Harrison had led the way for decades.

For all the acclaim his first piano concerto garnered, though, that's all it earned initially. When Jarrett had suggested the concerto and they had talked about it at length, the subject of money never came up. Harrison claimed that he told Jarrett that he had only to ask a foundation or raise money from various patrons, as Davies had done for the Third Symphony. When he didn't hear anything, he let Jarrett's business manager know that the normal commission fee for a project of this scope was $20,000. The reply he received was, "There was no contract, was there?" as though the honor of composing for Keith Jarrett were enough. Harrison was furious. He had spent months on the project, including copying parts, and had assumed that their long phone calls discussing the piece amounted to a verbal contract between equal artists. Although it was a sizable amount of money that Harrison could not afford to lose, he was also bitter about what he perceived as a lack of respect for what he did. "It felt to me like a castration," he wrote in his notebook.[30]

Betty Freeman ended up supporting the copying of the instrument parts. "When he didn't get paid for his piano concerto, Lou was so mad," Jody Diamond remembered. "He was furious, because of all this respect that he had been assuming and he wasn't getting. So he came back, and he said, 'I'm only writing pieces for my friends from now on.' That's when he wrote the piano concerto for Javanese gamelan."[31]

Not long after Harrison learned that he might not be paid for his acclaimed piano concerto, he was commiserating with his friend Belle Bulwinkle, a pianist at Mills College and wife of artist Mark Bulwinkle, whose work would form the covers of several of Harrison's CDs. She understood his frustration, she confided to Harrison, because she had just lost out on a gig herself. Still smarting from the contretemps with Keith Jarrett, Harrison decided that he would write her a concerto himself. Composing for Belle Bulwinkle might not result in prestigious performances like writing for Keith Jarrett, but if he was not going to get paid either way, Harrison was determined to take on the project that gave him the most pleasure—and that meant working not for an orchestra of strangers but instead for an ensemble of his friends: the gamelan. Thus inspired, he would produce another masterpiece fully the equal of its much-praised predecessor.

MUSIC FOR FRIENDS

> *The orchestra is a glorious noise. But the heart and soul of our music lies elsewhere. We're the ones who form our own ensembles, make our own tunings, build our own instruments and create our own musical worlds. We're the 'Do It Yourself' school of American music!*
> —Lou Harrison[32]

Still at the height of his powers, Harrison now poured his overflowing creative energy into writing a new piece for the homemade orchestra he loved. "Writing this work is a catharsis, a renewing self proof, and an adventure into the obvious-that-is-now," he wrote in his diary. "My own motives are double: to renew my confidence in being able to compose again in my older and most continuous way, i.e. affording it myself—and, too, to cheer up a dear friend who is suffering in a way the same thing that I am—the feeling of professional diminishment. Perhaps our performances will help us both."[33]

As with his earlier combinations of solo instruments with the gamelan, Harrison began by writing the tune, the *balungan*, of the gamelan part. The first and last of the three movements are in *slendro*, named respectively "Bull's Belle" and "Belle's Bull." The piano is retuned to match the gamelan, a far more radical retuning than necessary for his earlier piano concerto. The instrument often takes on the familiar role of playing a single-line melody (in octaves) with the *balungan*, though now often elaborated and filled in. In the most ambitious of Harrison's gamelan works since *La Koro Sutro*, the piano also often echoes the Romantic concerto, as did Harrison's other piano concerto. Following Beethoven's example, the concerto begins with the piano alone, with forceful octaves, before the long, spinning melody with *bonang*-like elaboration (also like the first movement of the other piano concerto). The movement ends with a piano solo again, this time a wistful and spare postlude (known as a *patetan* in Javanese practice) that explores the character of the tuning of the Mills College gamelan.

In the darkly contemplative *pelog* middle movement, the instruments of the gamelan, rather than playing a conventional *balungan*, independently sound over-lapping ostinatos of different lengths. Such polymetric layers formed percussion backgrounds for several of Harrison's pieces, including the metallophones he used for the film score *Nuptiae* and (transferred to voices) in *Orpheus*. The piano part swells ever more expansively and expressively, with soaring Romantic arpeggios and broken octaves.

In the joyous finale, the piano returns to its simpler role as carrier of the melody, and for the end Harrison writes in the score "full imbals," meaning that all parts are to play the exciting interlocking patterns at breakneck (and somewhat un-Javanese) speeds, with the piano part expertly woven into the gong cycle so that the piano and gamelan phrases periodically come together in immensely satisfying detonations. In a typically Javanese closing accelerando gesture, the music resumes its canter till it rushes to an exuberant end. Like the *Double Concerto*, Harrison's *Piano Concerto with Javanese Gamelan* reflects the composer's rich personality in his seventh decade—irrepressibly exploratory, sometimes melancholy, playful, overwhelmingly joyful—and it shows how much he valued making music with his friends.

THIS MAGICKER

Having completed two late-career masterworks, Harrison next turned to the rest of the items on his dual lists, and in 1986–1987 he polished off a prodigious number of them. Given Harrison's post-piano concerto disinclination to write for anyone other than his friends, as well as his decades-long abandonment of Christianity (and especially his aversion to the Catholic Church's anti-birth control stance), his acceptance of a commission to write a mass dedicated to the "St. Cecilia Society" seems unlikely. But the organization's full name, "The St. Cecilia Society for the Preservation and Restoration of Gregorian Chant and Peking Opera and Other Endangered Things of Beauty," reveals an origin in Santa Cruz's ever-colorful counterculture rather than a religious institution. Founded by artist and Santa Cruz coffee shop owner Frank Foreman in the early 1970s, Santa Cruz's St. Cecilia Society was mostly an excuse for Foreman and his friends to gather to drink coffee and sing Gregorian chant straight from the four-line staves of the Catholic Church's *Liber Usualis*, which seemed endangered in the period following the Second Vatican Council and its abolition of Latin chant in most masses. Their reverence extended to Peking opera, then likewise endangered by China's Cultural Revolution. Harrison, when told the full title of the organization, immediately understood this point of commonality between the Chinese Communist Party and the Roman Catholic Church.[34]

One of this circle of friends approached Harrison to ask for a piece to honor the memory of her late husband, Charles Gordon. Although the couple was Jewish, she saw no contradiction in commissioning a Catholic mass, thinking of it not as a religious statement but as an "endangered thing of beauty."[35] And though Harrison had long ago left behind his flirtation with Christianity and (despite an admiration for Buddhism and other traditions) organized religion, he retained his teenage love of chant, which he had sung at San Francisco's Mission Dolores.[36] "As I think it the responsibility of the Pacifist to do something for the Military," he wrote, "so I, an atheist, here do something for the Religious. These chants may, of course, be used in secular manner too."[37]

After rejecting the suggestion that he write a requiem mass ("Mozart died before completing his"),[38] Harrison named the piece for the patron saint of music and this society, St. Cecilia, whose feast day Harrison sometimes celebrated (in strictly secular fashion) with friends. For his *Mass for St. Cecilia's Day*, he chose eleven texts from the traditional service for her feast day, November 22. His inclusion of texts from the "proper" liturgy of that day, as well as the conspicuous absence of a Credo movement (the assertion of belief), distinguishes it from his earlier *Mass to St. Anthony*.[39]

Like his earlier mass, this one is an exploration of modes, but this time they are six-tone modes rather than the *St. Anthony*'s diatonic "church modes." Two seven-tone scales are the "parents": a diatonic scale on E that originated in some of his experiments with *pelog*, and a non-diatonic scale on F, which he also used in the last movement of his *Concerto for Piano with Selected Orchestra*.[40] Variety comes from changing the tone deleted from the set of seven, as well as from the relationship of the *finalis* (or ending pitch) to the scale. Harrison provides, but does not require, drones and harp ostinatos to relieve the austerity of the lovely but bare melodies, and these textural thickenings sound more like classic Harrisonia than medieval plainsong. The penultimate hymn to Cecilia, recounting her grisly martyrdom, also deviates from strict single-line chant by separating into two parts in quintal counterpoint resembling thirteenth-century polyphony.

Harrison accepted the commission just before leaving on his around-the-world trip in 1983 and finally completed it in 1986 it after fulfilling his obligations to the piano concerto and other works. Like a good medievalist, he wrote the score as an illuminated manuscript, with gold and red ink, calligraphy, and abstract florals and arabesques. Perhaps with a bit of relished irony, given the Catholic Church's dogma on contraception, Harrison, long concerned about overpopulation and its environmental impact, donated the commission fee to Planned Parenthood.[41]

The rest of the music Harrison wrote during this fertile 1986–1987 stretch consisted mostly of "voluntary" works for friends, as he had vowed after the Jarrett kerfuffle, beginning with a gamelan piece for the Foremans, with the idea that the Indonesian ensemble could accompany text in the form of chanted psalm tones. As in *Young Caesar*, any prose text could be adapted to such Gregorian-like formulas with their framing intonation and termination motives and a central chanted "tenor" pitch. When the Si Aptos ensemble was invited to play on a series at the St. John the Baptist Episcopal Church in Capitola, Harrison (inspired by Dan Kelley's shadow play on the same concert) looked for an appropriate text from Native American cultures, finding it in tales of Coyote as a trickster, fool, and divinity.[42] Setting them in the form of psalm tones gives the humorous stories an ironic atmosphere of ritualistic reverence. (One of the tales relates how Coyote ignores the wise man's warning that if he eats sacred berries, his ass will fall off. In the score, Harrison decorously replaced "ass" with "behind.") The *Foremans' Song Tune* becomes the prelude and postlude and the basis for interludes between the *Coyote Stories*, which Harrison would later adapt for his Fourth Symphony.

From the medieval period, Harrison moved forward into the baroque era for his next gift, a solo keyboard work for his friend Susan Summerfield, the harpsichordist who had hired him to his happy post at Mills when she chaired the college's music department. Harrison used modal quintal counterpoint in the *Summerfield Set*'s vigorous outer movements and adapted his 1938 chromatic quintal counterpoint experiment, *Ground*, for the middle movement. Harrison affixed the score's epigraph,

Lucretius's paean to peace honoring Venus, in the aftermath of eight years of belligerent foreign policy perpetrated by the Reagan administration—making the title of the last movement, "Round for the Triumph of Alexander," ironic, for Alexander was the name of Susan and Harry Summerfield's energetic new baby boy.

To showcase his next gift, to the dancer Eva Soltes, who had become his indispensable manager for his increasing number of appearances and travels, Harrison looked to Indian music. Soltes was an expert in the deeply spiritual tradition of bharatanatyam, the ancient dance of South India, with its complex vocabulary of subtly liquid movements, hand positions, and percussion of ankle bells. He based his flute and percussion duo accompaniment to her dance on a myth—not from one of the great Indian epics, but instead the Greek myth of Ariadne, who rescued her lover Theseus from the deadly, confusing Labyrinth, just as Soltes had saved Harrison from the maze of paperwork and other non-musical obligations in which he found himself ensnared.

The music appropriately draws on Indian music's division of performances into a rhythmically free modal introduction and a cycling metrical section with drums. The *alap*, or first section, depicts the heartbroken title character abandoned on the island of Naxos by her betrothed, Theseus. The mode revealed is octatonic, now a favorite scale when Harrison wanted a section (such as the middle movement of the *Double Concerto*) that could alternate between chromatic ambiguity and tonality.

The second section depicts Ariadne's rescue by Dionysus, the only one of the Greek gods said to have gone to India, from which he was returning when he found her.[43] Harrison made this movement a kit, inviting both flutist and percussionist to choose from seven phrases (or silence), each lasting exactly one cycle of the *tala* (or metrical pattern, here of 12+3+8+3+6+4+8), in any order and with repetitions. In the heyday of the avant-garde, such a structure would have been called "mobile form," but Harrison was not experimenting with Cageian chance procedures or the type of improvisation found in Indian classical music. Rather, he was employing a creative solution to a practical artistic challenge, just as he had when assembling Cowell's kit *Ritual of Wonder* some fifty years prior.

Still another friend, Santa Cruz saxophonist Don Stevens, joined the parade of requests. Harrison had written for sax only once before, in his abandoned 1942 orchestra work *Canticle #6*, then admonishing the players (in that jazz era) to play without vibrato and to avoid the instrument's "reedy" qualities.[44] When he adapted these movements for his *Elegiac Symphony* in 1974, it was sans saxes. Nevertheless, he admired the instrument's intonational flexibility (like the Korean *piri*) and thought its sinuous qualities would make a good match for his gamelan piece *Lancaran Samuel*. For that piece he had invented a nontraditional *pelog* mode that included pitch 4, which lies, like a blue note, in between the diatonic fourth and fifth of the scale. Written in 1987 while in residence at Seattle's Cornish College of Arts, he named this version *A Cornish Lancaran* for the school.[45]

Possibly the closest Harrison ever got to minimalism was the 1987 soundtrack he wrote for another of his friend James Broughton's films, *The Scattered Remains of James Broughton*.[46] Ostinatos on harpsichord and percussion cycle back and forth under a sinuous, unending *balungan* melody played on one of Colvig's metallophones. Having learned his lesson from previous unsuccessful attempts to synchronize music precisely with film, he instead provided Broughton with music so static and repetitious that it could be faded in and out without too much damage to the sense of the music. Harrison later orchestrated it as *Air for the Poet*. The filmmaker must have appreciated Harrison's work and friendship, calling him in a poem "this magicker" and hailing "harmonious Lou . . . a priest of praises . . . a guardian of jubilance . . . a polyphonic fountain . . . Blissmaker Lou . . . our Saint Harrison."[47]

For a musical gift to Willie Winant, the percussionist who had been Harrison's assistant at Mills and who helped to build the Mills College gamelan, Harrison decided to write him a piece that would include his friends pianist Julie Steinberg and violinist David Abel. Not wanting to be left out, he added parts for himself (on harp) and Colvig (on bells). Instead of piano, Steinberg played a virginal (a type of small harpsichord) tuned with the harp to the metal tube "bell" instruments Colvig had built. The diverse styles of the suite's movements, like the heterogeneous instrumentation, suggested its title: *Varied Quintet*.

Although he enjoyed playing it in this form, Steinberg and Abel wanted a version that they could take on tour with them, and Harrison understood from the beginning the impracticality of bringing or finding a harpsichord, harpist, and bell player at every venue. After its premiere at a March 1987 early birthday concert at UC Berkeley that also included *Gending Aphrodite, May Rain* (for old friend Elsa Gidlow), the *Suite for Violin and American Gamelan*, and more, Harrison recast the quintet (with Steinberg's help) for equal-tempered piano, violin, and percussion. In this form it became one of his most popular chamber works: the *Varied Trio*.[48]

In the first movement, titled "Gending" (the Javanese word for gamelan piece), the pianist's left and right hands and a vibraphone weave three levels of elaboration around a twelve-beat pentatonic *balungan*. A deep fifth on the piano takes the role of the gong, and other chords act as *kenong* and *kempul*. Above these bell tones floats another heart-melting Harrison melody on the violin, serenely surfacing on each repetition of the *balungan*. The mischievous second movement is a virtuosic solo for the *jaltarang*, the Indian instrument of tuned porcelain bowls (played with chopsticks) that he had earlier used in *Strict Songs* and *Pacifika Rondo*. The violin and piano play a colotomic role, interpunctuating the delicate melody not with gongs but instead with sprinkling pizzicato notes on the violin and isolated piano tones. In addition, Harrison, like his teacher Cowell, turns the pianist into a percussionist, knocking on the piano's wooden frame with a mallet. The third movement, a chromatic "Elegy," puts the violinist in the spotlight. As in *Ariadne*'s alap, he asks the fiddler to play "with great liberty" but based on interval controls rather than a fixed scale.

A cousin to the neo-baroque fourth movement of the *String Quartet Set*, the *Varied Trio*'s fourth movement, a French rondeau, pays sumptuous homage to Jean-Honoré Fragonard, echoing the eighteenth-century French artist's sweet sensuality and playfulness. Its trio-sonata-like counterpoint (the percussionist does not play) is based on the quintal-secundal stacking of fifths and seconds that Harrison had first used in New York, and it offers still another unforgettable string melody. The exuberant final movement is a dance in which drums, tambourines, and baker's pans accompany a piano and plucked violin melody. The scale is nearly octatonic but has a distinctive bluesy character that ends the suite on a lively note. Like most of the other movements, this dance has a rigorous consistency of materials and character of baroque suites but, like the *Air for the Poet*, also reflects the post-minimalist musical language that had become prominent in the 1980s, in part thanks to former Harrison students such as Janice Giteck and Paul Dresher.

The last of his mid-1980s masterworks, the *Varied Trio* marked a splendid conclusion to Harrison's sixth decade. None of these "voluntary" projects proved especially remunerative, but they paid in the currency that Harrison valued most: friendship with his fellow musicians and other artists.

In May 1987, Mills hosted a seventieth birthday concert (one of several presented in various cities) for Harrison that included the premieres of *Varied Trio*, *Ariadne* with Soltes dancing, and the *Concerto for Piano with Javanese Gamelan*, plus other gamelan pieces. Just as important as the musical quality—these are some of Harrison's finest works—was the number of friends participating, including Bulwinkle, Abel, Steinberg, Winant, Bill Colvig's brother David (on flute), Diamond, and more. Other friends, including Dresher and John Adams, attended the preceding gala dinner, and the event was broadcast on KPFA (with Harrison interviewed) by still another old friend and advocate, Charles Amirkhanian. Surrounded by his musical friends and homemade instruments, it was a peak moment in Harrison's mountain range of a life.

34

NEW MOON (1986–1990)

The transition from a beautifully eccentric, retuned *Varied Quintet* to an eminently practical, equal-tempered *Varied Trio* reflected Harrison's increasing concessions to the world of professional classical musicians, of the sort he had formerly reviewed for the *Herald Tribune*. Even as he continued to prefer just intonation and bell-like gamelan timbres, he prided himself on his workaday composer's ability to adapt to available forces, much as he was forced to do early in his career. Increasingly less willing to turn away commissions that would result in many performances, Harrison drew liberally from his vast acreage of techniques, often responding to equal temperament with chromatic movements based on his 1930s technique of interval controls. Nevertheless, these equal-tempered suites are sustained by alternations between the modal and the chromatic, the lyrical and the kinesthetic—an approach that resurrected similar contrasts in such pieces as his string suites of 1948. Although they stole time from composing for his beloved gamelan music and "voluntary" experiments, performances and recordings, of more conventional commissions proliferated.

One of these commissions returned him to the world of modern dance, this time with the pioneering American choreographer Erick Hawkins. Hawkins and Merce Cunningham had been Martha Graham's leading men (and Hawkins her husband) when Harrison was in New York, and Hawkins had already commissioned Henry Cowell, Alan Hovhaness, and Virgil Thomson for his company. Now, in 1986, the seventy-six-year-old choreographer wanted a new score from his old friend, and patron Betty Freeman provided the commission. Unusually for a late-twentieth-century choreographer, Hawkins insisted on touring with musicians to provide live music, and their forces dictated Harrison's instrumentation: flute, clarinet, trumpet, trombone, violin, bass, and percussion.

Hawkins proposed no subject or story to Harrison, merely a total length, so Harrison "simply composed out of my vivid memories of his choreographies and his visual stage presence."[1] *New Moon*'s dances include an "Usul" (based on an invented 5+4+5+3+3 pattern), a lightly swaying "Barcarolle" (gondolier song, as in *Young Caesar*), and a free clarion-type trumpet solo called "Bright Call." The slow and deliberate opening "Alabado" recalls Harrison's early "Mission Period," as it refers to praise songs sung in California's Spanish missions.

Once Harrison had created the basic score, he and the New York–based Hawkins worked on merging it with the choreography via letters and phone calls. Harrison made adjustments, dropping a "Song" movement and even adding another movement, "Epilogue," at Hawkins's request. At first unsure what to title his new dance, after seeing Harrison's score, Hawkins recalled a poem of E. E. Cummings, which supplied the title. "Every time I saw the new moon, I thought: 'That's life. You have to begin again,'" Hawkins told the *New York Times*. "That's what great art can do. We all see the new moon all the time. But he put it into a form I could remember and that was vivid."[2]

Despite Harrison's ability to adapt his language to Hawkins's instrumentation, when Carleton and Julie Clay of the Catskill Woodwind Quintet offered to pay Harrison for a piece, he "searched my inner head and could not for the life of me find a woodwind quintet." As when offered a commission for what became the *Double Concerto*, he returned a counterproposal. "I began to hear passages for trumpet and the French horn," he wrote, and to these he asked to add not only percussion and harp—typical Harrison instruments—but also mandolin. The Clays agreed to this more unusual sort of quintet.[3] The first movement ("Song") resurrects the bittersweet sound of the first scene from *Rapunzel*, but this time with early Schoenbergian nine-tone unordered pitch sets instead of an ordered twelve-tone straitjacket. In another of the movements, the brass instruments become muted chanters of a Turkish bagpipe. Mostly, though, Harrison casts the brass as carriers of lyrical melodies, leaving the ostinatos, interjections, and *jhalas* (in the last dance) to the plucked strings. The result of this experiment in heterogeneous instrumentation is quirky at best, and *The Clays' Quintet* often fails to gel.[4]

In 1988, Dennis Russell Davies arranged for the Cabrillo Festival's first commission for Harrison since the Third Symphony, this time for a chamber work for himself and violinist Romuald Tecco. In response, Harrison declared, "Dennis, I'm going to write you a polka!" As promised, a rollicking polka concludes Harrison's *Grand Duo* for piano and violin—a somewhat mischievous ending for what is otherwise a weighty and Romantic piece (the title coincides with Schubert's work for the same instruments). Like the polka of the *Symphony on G*, the vigorous movement recalls Harrison's childhood dance lessons. He used interval controls in the mysterious opening "Prelude" (similar to the *Varied Trio*'s "Elegy") and the haunting "Air" fourth movement. A long "Stampede" second movement, like the middle movement of the *Double Concerto*, uses an octatonic scale and (like the "Stampede" from his piano concerto) tart, crashing octave tone clusters.[5]

Just as the *Varied Trio*'s "Rondeau" movement provided sweet relief from the dark "Elegy," the *Grand Duo*'s "A Round," the middle of the five movements, is a simple, diatonic island in the long, mostly chromatic work. Harrison wrote its original version when visiting Davies in Stuttgart in 1983, for his daughters, Annabel and April, to play on two recorders (like the occasional pieces he used to write with Cowell).

Despite the near naivety of the movement, the *Grand Duo,* which concludes with that demented dance, amounts to a showpiece written for and dedicated to professionals.

In 1989, another request came from the Mirecourt Trio, for whom he had written the *Double Concerto,* but this time they wanted a conventional piano, violin, and cello trio. Harrison's *Trio* mines the romantic vein of the *Grand Duo,* especially in the majestic first movement. Here Harrison uses the *jhala* as only one of several devices to fill out the textures around the long melodies, built up by augmenting phrases through the interpolation of new notes and variations, freely resembling the way gamelan musicians stretch out melodies. The elegiac tone of the second movement represented Harrison's response to the news he had received during its composition that his mentor and friend Virgil Thomson had died in New York at ninety-two.

A "mini suite" of dances (as in the *Third Symphony*) then gives each player a solo in turn, beginning with the violin's fiddle dance on a six-tone mode, followed by an octatonic piano solo and a liltingly lyrical cello "song." The last movement reunites the instruments in a bright rondo that, though not directly borrowing Javanese techniques, evokes the bell-like tones of the gamelan over evocative cello lines.

Gamelan gestures echo throughout these equal-tempered suites but in hybrids that go beyond the translation of the gamelan structures to orchestra in *Elegy, to the Memory of Calvin Simmons.* One of Harrison's most important innovations during this period was the application of gamelan techniques and structure to chromatic melodies that he often used with equal-tempered instruments. The "Alabado" movement of *New Moon* and the *Clays' Quintet* "Song" and a dance movement incorporate the *pipil* elaboration technique of the gamelan's *bonang* instruments, even within the chromatic context of interval controls. The *Trio's* elegy for Virgil Thomson also uses interval controls but exfoliates the chromatic core melody in three different densities, like versions of the *cengkok* patterns of elaborating melodies used in gamelan. In *New Moon's* rejected "Song" movement, Harrison pulls off a neat trick by casting its chromatic melody within the colotomic structure of gamelan music, a structure that otherwise relies on the roles of tones within the modal system of Javanese melodies, somewhat like the first movement of his *Symphony on G,* in which he adapted the twelve-tone system to the grand tradition of the tonally based sonata form. This new direction would inspire Harrison's next large-scale work and his last symphony.

ARM IN ARM

By the time of his seventieth birthday in 1987, Lou Harrison's burgeoning career seemed to ensure that he could finally write only for himself and friends. His friend Peter Garland, composer and editor of the Soundings Press in New Mexico, was going to publish the first book on Harrison, a compendium of bits of his own writings, memorabilia from his life, and tributes from friends, to be called *A Lou Harrison Reader.* The filmmaker Eric Marin interviewed Harrison and Colvig for a half-hour documentary on Harrison that he called *Lou Harrison: Cherish, Conserve, Consider, Create,* after Harrison's personal motto.[6] CDs of Harrison's music were now appearing regularly, including *La Koro Sutro* and *Suite for Violin and American Gamelan* on a new San Francisco label whose name, New Albion (Francis Drake's initial name for the Pacific coast), promised to deliver unexplored territory—often meaning new tonality and post-minimalism—largely from that same region. Its founder, Foster Reed, would issue several Harrison discs and became a great local supporter.

In 1986 alone, Harrison and Colvig traveled for lectures, honors, or residencies in Florida, Louisiana, Toronto, Albuquerque, Stanford University, Seattle (at Cornish), Portland, Vancouver, British Columbia (for gamelan concerts at that year's international exposition), Arcata (in far northern California), Santa Barbara, Los Angeles, San Francisco, San Diego, Cincinnati, and, to close the eventful year, back to New York to receive the American Music Center's Distinguished Achievement Award at Lincoln Center.[7] The peripatetic 1986–1988 period also included trips (usually involving residencies and/or performances of his music) to Michigan, Los Angeles, Buffalo, Syracuse, Houston, Dallas, Colorado, Philadelphia, Boston, and Illinois, along with several trips to New York (which occasioned a performance with Cage of their percussion music with the Manhattan Percussion Ensemble in honor of their deceased director, Paul Price, who had revived Harrison's pathbreaking percussion music), and even Great Britain.

Although he sometimes lost money on these trips,[8] Harrison's frenetic activity, like his acceptance of commissions, was partly motivated by financial concerns. For all these successes, Harrison was still beset by memories of how his family lost their Portland home and the Depression-era fragility of their income as Harrison's father moved from job to job. His retirement from teaching meant the loss of his only stable income stream aside from Social Security checks.[9]

Harrison quickly proposed to nearby Cabrillo College that he could teach a gamelan class there, this time using the small iron gamelan at his home. His ability to keep regular gamelan rehearsals in his life (and now without driving long distances) more than compensated for the community college's modest salary.

But the new freedom proved fleeting. "I accepted too many offers thinking I'd have time in retirement," he wrote his old friend, choreographer Marian Van Tuyl. "Now I have no time and need to retire from my retirement."[10]

To Harrison, retirement did not mean an end to composing; it meant the freedom to compose according to his own wishes. He wanted to do much more, such as spending more time on his poetry, taking up painting again, and reading books, but he concluded that his brave resolution to only write for his friends was premature. His real retirement would come tantalizingly close in the last years of his life but, perhaps because of his deep-set feelings of inadequacy and responsibility, would never be fully realized.

But he still had some projects devoted to friends. For a separate birthday concert in Watsonville, near Harrison's Aptos home, Harrison planned a reunion with another old acquaintance—and love. Remy Charlip, who had not seen Harrison since their 1966 reconciliation, had moved back to San Francisco from New York, where he had found success as both a choreographer and a children's book author.[11] His new children's book about sign language, *Handtalk*, delighted Harrison and would later help inspire him to learn American Sign Language. Harrison asked

Charlip to choreograph a dance to accompany his new version of *Philemon and Baukis* for violin and gamelan in a planned tour of the concert with the gamelan Si Betty.

Unfortunately, the collaboration rekindled not just old memories but also old resentments. Soon they were bickering about money from the project, rehearsals, and publicity, with Charlip's stubbornness colliding with Harrison's volcanic temper, which grew more volatile as a performance date approached. Finally, Charlip accused Harrison of "hogging all the time" for the music rehearsal and crowding out the dancers onstage.[12] Just as he had almost forty years earlier, Charlip walked out, furious. He wrote to Harrison, "Are you so self involved you can't be civil to your friends and lovers? Your anger is not with me. You make it seem like you don't know who your friends are."[13]

After that incident, the two never again collaborated. Despite this, or maybe because of it, they patched up their friendship, which lasted until Harrison's death. In 1998, with the appearance of the new edition of Charlip's children's book *Arm in Arm*, Harrison was charmed by a vignette introduced with the words, "Ladies and Gentlemen, Old Snake is going to dance!" Old Snake then asks for music for his show of amazing shapes, and Harrison decided to write that music. A solo for oboe (the snake charmer instrument) and percussion in an "exotic" non-diatonic mode, the charming and humorous *Music for Remy* ends with a lullaby coda for Old Snake as he, worn out from his performance, falls asleep.

FAIL CAESAR!

Another disappointing reunion with old friends followed. When Harrison heard his friends in the Portland Gay Men's Chorus—whom he visited during his frequent trips to his hometown—premiere his *Three Songs* in 1986, it occurred to him that they might provide the opportunity for a rehabilitation of his opera *Young Caesar*. Harrison had long understood that no opera company was going to put on puppet opera, least of all one that requires an outlandish orchestra of Asian and invented instruments, not to mention one with a then-controversial homosexual theme. He had also been mulling over the weaknesses of the original production: its difficulty in expressing emotion through puppets, its lack of conventional arias, its overreliance on recitatives. Some critics had proposed that the core of problems lay in its libretto, with its voluble prose texts and its lack of a dramatic arc. Even though Harrison agreed that the recitatives were a challenge to work with, he remained devoted to the text and refused to change it without permission from the librettist, Robert Gordon.

The director of the Gay Men's Chorus, David York, agreed that the group would take on this ambitious project, and Harrison spent a good deal of 1987 and 1988 revising his opera. With the assistance of Robert Hughes and Kerry Lewis, he reorchestrated the entire work for conventional equal-tempered instruments.[14] The harp takes over the part of the psaltery and so loses the characteristic pitch bends. The *sheng* becomes a trumpet, and the flute variously plays the roles originally voiced by ocarina, *xiao*, syrinx, and bamboo flute. Although now accessible to a professional orchestra, the new version grays out much of the original's charm, replacing the radiance of the American gamelan instruments with a rather clangorous ersatz gamelan of vibraphone, celesta, and marimba.

Somewhat later, Harrison also tried out a similar imitation gamelan of piano and Western percussion to set an ancient Greek poem, "Now Sleep the Mountains All," but, perhaps sensing the loss of the original ensemble's radiance, Harrison withdrew the work after its premiere. "In revising [*Young Caesar*], I've lost a lot," Harrison admitted. In reference to his earlier self-production, he said, "I'm just getting too old for all that."[15]

On the plus side, with real actors now available to dramatize the actions previously described by the narrator, and with PGMC's surplus singers forming a chorus that could "narrate" in song, he could cut some of the narrator's lines. And he added new choral parts over existing instrumental pieces, allowing them to reflect on the action without lengthening the plot.

The Portland Gay Men's Chorus (with the help of philanthropist Betty Freeman) raised an unprecedented sum to be able to mount such an ambitious production, and Harrison had to confront the limitations of writing for volunteers, accepting that the performance would not be up to the standards of a professional company. However, once again the opera's nonmusical aspects proved the weak link. "A drearier work would be difficult to imagine," sighed the *Oregonian*'s classical music critic, David Stabler. "'Young Caesar' was utterly lifeless. Scores of missed opportunities plodded dimly past. At no point did the drama take off. Not even during the orgy scene that had nearly naked men walking politely back and forth while everyone else appeared to be at a political fund-raiser."[16]

Despite the convenience of human actors, Harrison's *Faust* collaborator and puppeteer Kathy Foley judged that the mythic scale of a puppet drama became merely melodramatic when transferred to human actors. "Those puny singers on stage could hit all the notes but they looked maudlin as they cast themselves to the floor to portray that pathos of youthful first passion or longing for other worlds. Puppets would have been truer to the piece."[17] Nevertheless, Harrison remained convinced that with further revision, this new conventional version would be a success, and he returned to the score toward the end of his life.

DEAR EARTH SUSTAINS US

> *That my*
> *angiogram,*
> *in which I saw my own*
> *heart beat, was done by the doctor*
> *Poisson*
> *I knew*
> *and then found it*
> *wondrous to have Doctor*
> *Fishman to operate inside*
> *my chest*
> *So like*

Beckmann's magic,
as in some triptych scene
the Lords of ocean guide willing
subjects.
Kind drugs
dimmed me downward
as the gurney rolled on
toward appointment with whatever
should be.
Is it because I know that my heart
was stopped that I think of those hours
as deaths?

—Lou Harrison, 1989[18]

Harrison frequently felt exhausted and ill, and his own mortality may have been on his mind following the recent deaths of his friends Joseph Campbell, Jim Cleghorn, and Robert Duncan. Nevertheless, it was typical for him to respond to his doctor's urgent diagnosis with a request to postpone open-heart surgery until he had completed a residency at Arizona State University at Tempe and performed in concerts of his music on April 23 and 24, 1989.

Early in the morning of April 25, Colvig drove him to the AMI Community Hospital's Santa Cruz Heart Institute. The seventy-two-year-old Harrison underwent a triple bypass operation in which arteries from another part of his body were grafted onto his carotid artery, which was otherwise 95 percent blocked. Because Harrison's heart was literally stopped as part of the operation, he came to look upon his life after as his "third life," analogous to the second life given to him after his emergence from his breakdown.[19]

Colvig sat by for days as Harrison drifted in and out of painful consciousness in the intensive care unit, "enmeshed with tubes like a science fiction cyborg lying prone." For half a day, Harrison reported, he was convinced he was in Holland, "desperate to understand such gross displacement at all."[20] Doctors declared the operation a success and sent Harrison home to a solicitous Colvig with help from their assistant Charles Hanson. One unexpected, though fortunately temporary, effect: "I'd been doing spoonerisms like 'I don't want to work and work and die in my salad' instead of 'saddle.'"[21] His increasing concern about the fragility of communication as he aged later led to an interest in American Sign Language, another relatively universal language like Esperanto (although other sign languages also exist). The surgery heralded a year of hard news that also seemed to shadow his music.

As Harrison's strength returned, Colvig was determined to get him some exercise by walking, and so he blazed an easier path from their house at 7121 Viewpoint Road down the hill. They had begun to refer to the main house as their "West Holding" and the older property as their "East Holding." When Colvig led an unsteady Harrison to the path at West Holding, Harrison's first walk outdoors since the operation, nature seemed to have acquired a new and deeper beauty. "I'd not / seen, before my / operated heart could / lift me, the lovely beauty of / these woods."[22]

It felt like a new life. By summer's end, Harrison felt recovered and newly invigorated by a metronomic heartbeat and the rush of oxygen to his cardiovascular system. He accepted an invitation to Chicago's Ravinia Festival and in the fall began introducing his Cabrillo College class to the visceral joys of gamelan. Then on the afternoon of October 17, 1989, another demonstration of the power of resonant frequencies jolted Harrison: the 6.9 Loma Prieta earthquake. The epicenter of the tremor was less than five miles away from their Aptos home, in the Forest of Nisene Marks State Park, where Colvig often hiked. However, because of the region's geology, the shaking collapsed structures in faraway San Francisco and Oakland. Harrison's house escaped serious damage, thanks in part to its prefab modular rooms and lack of a chimney, but books, papers, and knickknacks littered nearly every inch of the floor. The lid on Harrison's 1871 grand piano (which he had inherited from Cowell) cracked in half, and their stovepipe had to be repaired. Despite the best efforts of Charles Hanson and others, some disarray persisted for years, particularly in Colvig's notoriously messy workshop, a no-go zone for Harrison and Hanson.

Mother Nature's rage set the theme for Harrison's next commission, a welcome return to gamelan after a series of equal-tempered works. Peter Poole, an engineer at MIT who had grown up with a great interest in the arts as well as environmentalism, had found Harrison's recordings when an undergraduate at Cornell, visiting the gamelan there and learning Japanese flute amid his engineering studies. His girlfriend at the time was the daughter of a prominent Indonesian diplomat and well-known advocate of human rights and the environment, Soedjatmoko.[23] The young engineer wrote Harrison, offering to commission a piece to honor her family and her father's legacy.

Harrison found an appropriate text in the *Ramayana*, the Hindu epic that serves as a basis for so many *wayang kulit* plays and other Indonesian dramas.[24] The first movement tells the story of how the hero, King Rama, becomes swayed by false rumors against his wife, Sinta, and how she flees to the forest and the protection of his brother, Laksamana. The text, set to an unsettled, nontraditional *pelog* mode, depicts the earth itself trembling at this injustice (just a couple of months after its literal trembling in California). Instead of a conventional melody, the choral part is accompanied by freely improvised patterns on the mode played by the *balungan* instruments, a technique Harrison had also applied in *Coyote Stories*.

The contrasting middle segment, dedicated to Poole's friend Isna, is a tranquil *slendro* melody representing the peace that Sinta finds raising her new children in the forest. Here Harrison's environmentalist statement comes to the fore as the *pesinden* (female vocalist) sings the ravishing long melody with elaborate Javanese ornamentation, "Dear Earth sustains us / mother of flowers and birds, of deer and ferns / dear Earth sustains us." One of Harrison's most "Javanese" passages, "Isna's Song" also remains one of his most seductive.

The last movement returns to *pelog*, this time using a nontraditional set of all seven of the pitches, and recounts Rama's violent attempt to find Sinta, who is protected by "the good Earth mother." Rama's fury threatens to destroy all, but the god Siva restrains him. In this parable, the colonialist destroyer of the environment is stopped. Poole and the Soedjatmoko family were very pleased with the result, which premiered at Portland's Lewis & Clark gamelan in January 1990. Whether due to the added oxygen after his bypass surgery or his return to the glittering Asian world he'd craved since childhood, the set pulses with a revived passion.

After warm end-of-summer residencies at Ravinia and then the University of Miami, Harrison and Colvig went to the opposite extreme in November 1989: a residency in Fairbanks, Alaska, where Harrison and Colvig brought Si Betty to perform in a new music series sponsored by the Fairbanks Symphony, thanks to the efforts of Alaskan composer John Luther Adams, who had long viewed Harrison as a role model for how a composer "could live in an uncompromising way without bitterness or regret." According to Adams, "The music of Lou Harrison was a very powerful model for me and other composers of my generation," giving them a sort of permission to make music that was both "intellectually airtight and unabashedly beautiful."[25]

During their weeklong visit, which included a pair of concerts of Harrison's music, his mentor provided still another lesson when Adams programmed one of his favorites, the *Suite for Violin, Piano and Small Orchestra*. At the first rehearsal, Adams conducted the first movement and turned to Harrison, clad in his warmest lumberjack shirt, for comments.

"John Luther, you remind me of John Cage, but more kinesthetic," Harrison told him. Adams, flattered by the comparison, eagerly waited to hear more.

"Whenever John used to conduct," Harrison went on, "he wanted to hear every little detail and nuance and would try to show everything, every little twist and turn—and it would slow down."

Briefly deflated, Adams took a deep breath. "Instantly I recognized that I was doing the very same thing," Adams recalled. "At the next night's concert my conducting was leaner, crisper and steadier in tempo—a style I've tried to maintain ever since. This lesson from Lou was not just about conducting. It was also a lesson about teaching. Lou was fond of recalling that his teacher Henry Cowell would often begin a sentence by saying 'As you know' and then impart some wonderfully unexpected pearl of wisdom. In his own teaching Lou employed this technique brilliantly, using the gentle touch of flattery to prepare receptive minds for the gifts of learning."[26]

At a post-concert party at Adams's woodstove-heated cabin in the woods, the temperature dropped into the minus-40s. Harrison suffered the cold with forbearance, but Colvig (who had brought his suitcase still unpacked from his last Alaska visit decades before) was, according to Adams, "in his element."[27]

But despite the happy Arctic interlude, more bad news followed. In the summer of 1990 came news of the death of Peggy Glanville-Hicks, and then of Leonard Bernstein in October and Aaron Copland in December. In the same month as Copland's death, Harrison received word of the passing of another good friend from his New York days, Oliver Daniel, the indefatigable supporter of new music in his roles as administrator for the American Composers Alliance, Composers Recordings Inc., Broadcast Music Inc., and finally the American Composers Orchestra, which Dennis Russell Davies conducted. He was the one who put Harrison's scores in front of Leopold Stokowski, among others. The very next day after Daniel's death, Harrison had completed a *Threnody for Oliver Daniel* for harp in the dark Phrygian mode and tuned to Ptolemy's "soft" diatonic, a tuning related to the *slendro* he had used in his gamelans but with small, mournful semitones. Although written for Daniel and dedicated to his partner, Donald Ott, its stoic phrases betoken an enduring grief from a time in Harrison's life when the loss of old friends had become a regular occurrence.

VERY LAST SYMPHONY

In 1990, Dennis Russell Davies was appointed music director of the Brooklyn Philharmonic and took the opportunity to commission yet another symphony from his old friend. When they first discussed the idea, Harrison panicked. Another commission? "I didn't know whether I had another symphony in me or not."[28] Harrison agreed to do it, but impishly he decided initially to title it *Last Symphony* to forestall any future such commissions. When finally published, it was with the more conventional title Fourth Symphony, perhaps because Harrison was tired of the inevitable question from interviewers, "But what if you write another?" He would reply, "Then I suppose I shall have to call it the Very Last Symphony!" Of course, the original title did prove apt.

Harrison's Fourth Symphony continued his mix of chromatic and modal styles on the one hand, and European and Javanese forms on the other, that so characterized his commissioned works of his last decades, but here arranged much more deliberately through the movements. The first and third movements are chromatic, based on interval controls, while the second and fourth movements are modal.[29] He used Javanese forms for the first two movements, European for the last two. (He would later switch the second and fourth movements, making the outer movements Javanese and the inner movements European.)

The symphony's beginning adapts a rejected movement from *New Moon* and extends its distinctive combination of interval-control chromaticism and Javanese-style elaboration to the whole orchestra, mixing not just Europe and Asia but also Harrison's own past and present. Low strings take on the role of colotomic gongs, asymmetrically dividing the sixty-four-beat *balungan* melody. As in his *Elegy, to the Memory of Calvin Simmons* and the "Gending" movement of the *Varied Trio*, the lyrical *balungan* melody blooms with multiple layers of *pipilan* elaborations as the movement shifts to an expansive *irama* (rhythmic level). However, beginning with the second repetition of the *balungan* in the slower *irama*, the core "gamelan" ensemble of harp, celesta, tack piano, and vibraphone also provides a new and more elaborate succession of *cengkok* (melodic patterns) that coalesce into a sparkling cloud following the core melody.

Like the equally long estampie of the *Concerto for Piano with Selected Orchestra*, Harrison's thrilling "Stampede" second movement here sustains its length by giving the audience a quiet respite in a middle section, featuring solo strings, and by bringing back a celebratory, brass-filled climax. One of his most elaborate versions of his favorite dance, the movement is also one of Harrison's most polyrhythmic. Harrison dedicated the vigorous movement to Colvig, who, laid up after knee surgery, "was despondent and needed energy and encouragement."[30]

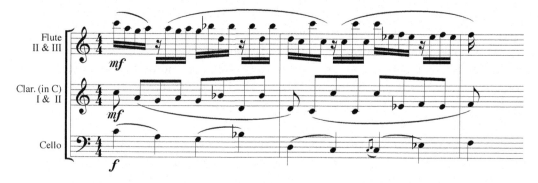

EXAMPLE 34.1. This excerpt from the first movement of Harrison's Fourth Symphony shows his adaptation of the *pipilan* technique of gamelan elaboration. The *pipilan* woodwinds alternate at different rates between each pair of pitches in the core melody (*balungan*, here on the cello). Copyright © Peermusic Classical. International copyright secured. Reprinted by permission.

Harrison's application of Javanese textures to his version of European chromaticism succeeds in part because his technique of interval controls is linear, generating only a single-line melody. During his first experiments with this method in the 1930s, he tried similarly restricting harmonic intervals. However, ensuring that multiple interval-controlled melodies combine so that only those same intervals exist in the resulting chords became so complicated that he gave up the attempt.

Now, over half a century later, he revisited this challenge for his symphony's slow third movement. With few exceptions, every instrumental line in this movement progresses by intervals of a minor second, minor third, or perfect fifth, with all harmonies constrained to the same intervals (or their inversions). "The point was to move them in such a way they make an interesting and 'speaking' texture," he explained.[31] Despite the occasional glitter of the "gamelan" instruments, the ruminative, often contrapuntal movement revives the 1940s Ruggles-like style of intense introspection—a "mood of tense but resigned pessimism."[32]

Harrison's most innovative movement in the Fourth Symphony adapts his *Coyote Stories*, complete with narrator, to the orchestra. As in the first movement, the orchestra becomes a gamelan in Western guise: low brass, basses, and bass drum replace the gong; oboes and tack piano function as a punctuating *kenong*, and horns supply the complementary *kempul* punctuation; the elaborating *bonang barung* part goes to the flutes, clarinets, celesta, and harp, while first violin plays the faster *bonang panerus* part and the remaining strings play the *balungan* core melody. A percussionist takes the role of the *dalang* puppeteer, who brings in the orchestra by rapping on a box, and Harrison in fact included instructions for the construction of a *keprak*, or Javanese woodblock, for this purpose. These boisterous but brief interludes, representing "Coyote's Path," separate three stories, two sung in chant tones, like those of the earlier *Coyote Stories*, while the "gamelan section" of vibraphone, celesta, and harp improvises over given tones (like the "tunelets" of his 1966 *Orpheus*). In contrast, the narrator speaks the middle story rhythmically with percussion accompaniment. This story does not appear in the original *Coyote Stories*, but Harrison found this version by Daniel-Harry Steward in a recently published anthology of gay American Indian writings.[33] Instead of the fool deity, Coyote is the powerful shape-shifter who confronts the volcano god Tehoma in the form of a man. Their wrestling contest turns into lovemaking, until the volcano explodes and Tehoma rises in the form of cinders in the night sky.

The success of the symphony depends in large part, therefore, on the narrator-singer, and the Argo record label, which had agreed to release the California Symphony's recording of the symphony, cast jazz singer Al Jarreau in the part, both for his talent as a performer and his draw as a star. When the Coyote movement was placed second, like his earlier multisectional dance movements, and the exciting "Stampede" as the finale, bringing a star performer onstage for the middle of the piece and then finishing without him seemed awkward. Harrison agreed to swap the second and fourth movements, and the work ends with the delightful stories rather than with a thunderous symphonic climax.

Although Harrison was initially reluctant to take on this large commission, it came at an opportune time. For the first time in Harrison's life, royalties became a substantial part of his income. When asked in 1992 when it was that he finally knew he could survive as a composer, Harrison told the startled interviewer, "About two years ago. . . . I'm not kidding—when my income from BMI and my publishers began to make up what I was losing from not teaching. I was very leery about giving up teaching from Cabrillo [College] because those monthly checks counted."[34] Although Harrison looked forward to a true retirement, when he could work on whatever projects suited his interests, the relative stability afforded by the increasing frequency of his orchestral and other performances allowed for periodic diversions into voluntary, but not always musical, works.

35

BOOK MUSIC (1991–1995)

Although Lou Harrison achieved worldwide acclaim as a famous composer, words had always been as much a part of his life as music. He often spent his days sitting in front of his bookstand, reading the latest issue of *Scientific American*, the *Journal of American Music*, his newest book of art, or a new translation of Boethius. Disturbed by the ringing phone (but a fan of the less intrusive fax machine), he regularly retreated to his messy camper shell to work on his latest music commission, painting, or poem. "A house is a cave," he explained. "I don't like people seeing me, and I don't like to look out. It's protection. Plus the sun would burn up all the precious things I want to preserve—paintings and furniture."[1]

Over the years, he had built up quite a stack of his own poetry, which only occasionally found a public hearing, as with the poems in the new version of *Songs in the Forest*, which he completed in March 1992 for the Black Mountain College retrospective concert. In performances like this, he presented his poems in a manner reminiscent of James Broughton's film *Scattered Remains*, in which the director reads his poetry during pauses in Harrison's score.[2]

Harrison's poems often share the wryness and sexual openness of Broughton's poetry but are imbued with the elegant (sometimes archaically formal) language and classical allusions of Robert Duncan.[3] Harrison generally shunned the Whitmanesque tradition of modernist free verse, preferring, as he did in much of his music, the boundaries of strict structure, and specifically forms in which the numbers of syllables structure the lines, forms he had found in Chinese, Japanese, Indonesian, and Syrian verse. "I was surprised to discover the planetary extent of this probably earliest kind of versing and the elegance of control that it imposes on poetic composition," he wrote, "especially surprised since my discoveries have been haphazard, episodic, and unstudied."[4]

He began to prepare a collection of his poetry for publication, with the help of UCSC librarian and writer Rita Bottoms. Ideally, Harrison thought, such a book would be calligraphed, like the *Music Primer*. However, since the 1982 automobile accident that had injured his right wrist and since the onset of age-related tremors in his hands, Harrison had long given up any ambition to write his poems in calligraphy. He had started using larger and larger staves and paper for his music writing.

At a post-concert reception, Harrison approached his friend Carter Scholz, a writer and just-intonation composer, and asked whether computer technology might offer a solution. Scholz agreed to help, and soon Harrison was mailing him examples of lettering styles that he had developed back in the 1950s. Scholz copied the shapes into font creation software and regularized their lines.[5] Harrison used the first font they completed, Pluma Book ("pluma" being Esperanto for "of the pen"), along with his Uncial Commoncase, to set his book. Later he and Scholz brought out others, including Aptos Uncial, Rotunda, Lou Casual, Lou Titling, and Federov (after Russia's first printer and type designer).[6] Harrison later wrote *Ladrang Carter Scholz* for gamelan in his honor.

Impressed by Scholz's use of a computer to do typesetting in different fonts, Harrison bought a Macintosh computer for his own word processing and proudly pointed to it as evidence that his reputation as a Luddite was unfair (though his facility with the gadget was rudimentary at best). After searching for a publisher willing to print his book in his chosen fonts, Harrison got in touch with his old Black Mountain friend, poet Jonathan Williams, whose Jargon Society press finally brought out Harrison's book, titled *Joys & Perplexities*, in 1992.[7]

Harrison was sometimes invited to give readings from the book, and he soon envisioned performances in which his readings would alternate with music, as in *Songs in the Forest*. He composed a series of short pieces for this purpose that he collectively titled *Book Music*, consisting of a prelude and a postlude for gamelan (the "bookends," similar to those he had created for the *Coyote Stories*) and lovely interludes for *suling* (bamboo flute) and a new just-intonation metallophone Colvig had built, of sixteen tones per octave; Harrison called it the Ptolemy Duple.[8] Although these performances never materialized, Harrison would continue to find ways to creatively combine his literary and musical obsessions.

MUSICA PACIFICA

What was so amazing about Lou and his writing of music was the variety
and quantity of it. I think, now that he's older, he's more devoted to what
I think we could call, with all of its meanings, a music of the Pacific.

—John Cage[9]

All the early-1990s activity involving fonts and poetry may have reignited Harrison's inclination to connect texts and music. Over the next two years, a combination of inclination and opportunity would prompt him to produce new combinations of contemporary words and music. The first arrived from one of his favorite sources of ideas.

From the time he had moved back to California, Harrison had been a faithful listener to KPFA, known as Pacifica Radio, and he appeared on the station multiple times as a guest, guest host, and even commentator, delivering his "Crackpot Lecture" on the air around 1960. Harrison had known several of the musical hosts over the years, including the station's longtime music director, composer Charles

Amirkhanian. When the station moved to its new, state-of-the-art facility on Berkeley's Martin Luther King Jr. Way in 1991, Amirkhanian and the Wallace Alexander Gerbode Foundation commissioned a new piece from Harrison for the occasion. Because the request came with few restrictions, allowing Harrison to return to writing for gamelan and for friends, he cheerfully accepted.

Homage to Pacifica honors the politically liberal voice of the airwaves with movements celebrating people who embodied the station's principles. After a robust *gangsaran* (traditional Javanese gamelan's loud, repetitive introduction), the gamelan accompaniment expands into a long *gending* form with a soprano singing the words of "We Shall Overcome" in the elaborate style of a Javanese *pesinden* (solo female singer), followed by a litany of the Pacifica radio stations' call signs—KPFA, KPFK etc.[10]

The next movement (which, like the others, can be played independently) paid homage to one of Harrison's musical heroes, George Frideric Handel ("the greatest composer of us all"[11]), often called "the divine" for decades after his death. Harrison also wrote "In Honor of the Divine Mr. Handel" for one of his friends who played in the gamelan, harpist and ethnomusicologist Henry Spiller, and so quoted the baroque composer's famous harp concerto, but now for harp accompanied by a Javanese gamelan. Harrison's delightful concerto recalls both the baroque concerto grosso form and its tonic-dominant relationships even within the gamelan's tuning system.

In one of Harrison's favorite books, Howard Zinn's *A People's History of the United States*, he found a quote from an article by Mark Twain, whose eloquent sarcasm skewered the 1902 US invasion of the Philippines. However, none of the radio station's regular listeners would have missed the relevance to the 1991 US invasion of Iraq that Harrison deplored: "We have pacified some thousands of the islanders and buried them, destroyed their fields; burned their villages, and turned their widows and orphans out-of-doors; furnished heartbreak by exile to some dozens of disagreeable patriots: subjugated the remaining ten millions by Benevolent Assimilation, which is the pious new name of the musket. . . . And so, by these Providences of God—and the phrase is the government's, not mine—we are a World Power."[12] Harrison set Twain's words as a *pelog* melody for choir, accompanied by overlapping gamelan ostinatos of different lengths, as he had in the middle movement of his *Concerto for Piano and Javanese Gamelan*, though here forceful gong and drum interjections act as Harrison's exclamation points for the text.

The middle movements feature his friend's Bob Hughes's plaintive bassoon, together with the Ptolemy Duple metallophone.[13] The interlude is interrupted by a dramatic declamation of one of Harrison's angriest poems, a protest in the form of a Horatian ode, titled "Ode on Bravo 20," the code name of a patrol that entered Iraq in advance of the US invasion just as Harrison was writing *Homage to Pacifica*. Remembering Iraq as the cradle of civilization and the center of the golden age of Islamic scholarship, Harrison wrote,

> The "untied snakes of america" drive down
>   with stinking speed-and-gleam to pierce sweet ancient things,
>   to pain earth's elders' bones, to leave red poison pools—
>   school buses shattered.

Another Harrison poem follows the interlude, this time a "Litany" of the names of Native American peoples, spoken rhythmically to the accompaniment of a powwow drum. The punch line: "SCREWED!"

The final, cleansing *slendro* gamelan movement used a passage that had become famous that year when it was included in the best-selling children's book *Brother Sun, Sister Moon*, noting that our planet does not belong to humanity, but the other way around, and that in the web of life, "all things are connected," so that injury done to Earth harms its people.[14] After the chorus's inspiring and dramatic entrance and a quick, asymmetrical unison passage, the gamelan blooms in a comfortingly symmetrical *ladrang* form to accompany the choral melody. With its placid music alternating with ferocious texts, Harrison's *Homage to Pacifica* is as much a plea for his long-cherished pacifism as it is a tribute to a radio network and a region.

Poetry and ancient things also sparked Harrison's next 1992 composition, commissioned by his pianist and good friend Rae Imamura as a part of a project to provide modern settings for hymns used in the services of the Japanese Buddhist Church.[15] Harrison's contribution, perhaps reflecting his own preoccupation with mortality during this time, was a setting of the text "White Ashes," a commentary on life's fleetingness that observes that in the morning, we may be healthy, but "in the evening we may be white ashes." Harrison's setting, for amateur voices and equal-tempered piano, is in an austere but touching counterpoint of fifths and seconds, sometimes with an accompaniment of a simple ostinato suggestive of eternity.[16]

The reminder of life's fleetingness made Harrison's seventy-fifth-birthday concerts—in Aptos, CalArts in Southern California, and elsewhere—even sweeter. He and Colvig served as grand marshals of the Santa Cruz Gay Pride parade. However, the most enjoyable celebration was a symposium at Seattle's Cornish College that he shared with Alan Hovhaness and John Cage (it was Cage's eightieth birthday). Any sibling-like animus between Cage and Harrison had long disappeared, and the two old friends greeted each other excitedly. At a panel together they talked, laughed together, and corrected each other's reminiscences. Just eight months later, while making tea for himself and Merce Cunningham in their New York apartment in August 1992, Cage suffered a stroke; he died the next day, making Harrison's *White Ashes* setting sadly portentous.

Even with his aching, increasing familiarity with the loss of longtime friends, Cage's death hit Harrison especially hard. "Now there's just me and Hovhaness," he told Jody Diamond when she phoned.[17] A few days later, at the Cabrillo Festival, the orchestra performed Harrison's arrangement of Cage's *Suite for Toy Piano*. Harrison also honored Cage's longtime partner with his *An Old Times Tune for Merce Cunningham's 75th Birthday*, in which he turned a sketch for piano made when he was first experimenting with *jhalas* at Black Mountain (when Cunningham was also there) into a brief but energetic work for piano and string quartet.[18] In 1993, he similarly revived part of his San Francisco percussion piece *Canticle #5* for *Canticle and Round in Honor of Gerhard Samuel's Birthday*. For this version, he added a "Round" for solo *gendér barung* accompanied by gong and other percussion.

Another brief instrumental distraction from Harrison's current devotion to words and music came in response to a request from Santa Cruz choreographer Tandy Beal: an uncharacteristic tango, which alternates his clever counterpoint with Piazollian dramatic block chords and big bass octaves. Harrison wrote *Tandy's Tango* on his piano, still tuned to Kirnberger #2 temperament, giving it a dimension unheard when played in equal temperament. It seems to begin in the key of A with an uneasily dissonant fifth in the Kirnberger temperament. However, the home key of E becomes apparent by the end, when the harmony resolves to the coolly smooth fifth in this key.

THE LOVE OF ANCIENT THINGS

> Praise the love of ancient things
> Laud the lure & charm
> that draws from within this concept.
>
> —Lou Harrison[19]

But these brief instrumental gifts to old friends were mere distractions from his text settings of this period. In 1992 Harrison received an unusual proposal from Toshiro Kido, director of the Music Division of the National Theatre of Japan, who was leading a project reconstructing eighth-century musical instruments discovered at the former Imperial Depository in Nara, Japan. Instead of attempting to reconstruct the actual music these instruments played, Kido and his colleagues decided to commission and perform modern compositions on reconstructions of these instruments. Would Harrison like to participate?

Soon after he accepted, a large package arrived at Harrison's house. In it was a reconstruction of a *haisho*, an ancient Japanese panpipe that had been extinct for centuries before its rediscovery.[20] Along with a quartet of the ancient instruments and two percussionists, Harrison's *Set for Four Haisho and Percussion* calls for a speaker to declaim Harrison's dedicatory poem in the third movement in the style of a Noh drama, just as Harrison inserted readings of his poetry into *Homage to Pacifica* and the revived *Songs in the Forest*. Despite the multiple *haisho*, the piece overwhelmingly consists, like the *String Quartet Set* and so many other Harrison works, of single-line melodies.[21] Harrison knew that because it is difficult to connect notes smoothly on panpipes, especially when the melody skips, players in panpipe traditions in the Andes and elsewhere use alternation playing; that is, splitting up a melody between multiple players. Harrison used his kit method in the second movement, asking the players to choose from a set of phrases to play in any order or octave, and giving the percussionists similar freedom, as in his dance *Ariadne*.

The scheduled July 1993 premiere of *Set for Four Haisho and Percussion* in Tokyo coincided closely with the Pacific Music Festival in Sapporo, then directed by a fellow Californian, conductor Michael Tilson Thomas. A Los Angeles native who would soon become a crucial supporter of Harrison, Thomas (or MTT, as Harrison called him) had performed a version of the *Suite for Violin and American Gamelan* arranged for violin and strings by Harrison's former student Kerry Lewis. Now, though, MTT wanted the real thing. When Harrison pointed out that the gamelan instruments were in poor repair and that their current boxes would not survive a transatlantic airplane flight, the festival promised to pay for new shipping containers and to give them time to work on the instruments in Japan. By then, the increasingly venerated Harrison had also received invitations to Europe for the same summer, and so he and Colvig prepared for another circumnavigation of the planet.[22]

Their journey began in England, where Harrison was invited to teach at the Dartington International Summer School of Music. The school obliged Harrison by bringing a Javanese gamelan to the hall. "Bill and I would get up," Harrison reminisced, "and have a wonderful British breakfast, marmalade and all, and then we'd go directly for two hours of gamelan playing. It was heaven!"[23]

For their performance Harrison resurrected another text-based "ancient thing": his Latin song *Vestiunt Silve*, begun when he was writing his pastorales in the early 1950s. Now he completed the setting of the eleventh-century text about nature in a luminous version for soprano, flute, two violas, and harp. Harrison also wrote a new gamelan piece for the occasion, named *Dartington Hall* after their venue, and another piece after the town where he went to visit his friend, poet (and publisher of *Joys & Perplexities*) Jonathan Williams. *A Dentdale Ladrang* rather startlingly alternates between a *slendro* section and a *pelog* section.[24]

Then he and Colvig were off to the continent, where Dennis Russell Davies was conducting Harrison works, including a revival of another wordy oldie, *Rapunzel*, in several cities. They traveled to Amsterdam, Switzerland, and Prague, where Harrison gave a lecture at the European Mozart Foundation in the opulent Dobris Castle, though his notebook reveals that Harrison was less interested in the formerly communist city's small Mozart museum than its gay culture.

In Tokyo, Harrison met Eva Soltes, who single-handedly had brought the entire Old Granddad gamelan, in new huge rolling crates, on the flight and through customs. The festival arranged for Harrison and Colvig to stay at a cottage, where they would have some uninterrupted time to get the instruments into shape, after Colvig and Soltes figured out how to find Tokyo hardware stores and the materials they would need. Performances in Tokyo and Sapporo were very well received, and Harrison began what would become a fruitful relationship with festival director Michael Tilson Thomas. Typically, Harrison spent a considerable chunk of his fee on a twelve-volume edition of the complete works of Japanese woodblock artist Munakata Shiko, whom he regarded as one of the twentieth century's finest artists. For the rest of his life, he carried a small volume of Munakata images wherever he traveled.[25]

Harrison's further travels that fall included a visit to New Hampshire to see Jody Diamond and Larry Polansky (who had recently joined the faculty of Dartmouth College) and then across the border to Toronto to visit the Evergreen Gamelan Club, founded by Harrison's student Jon Siddall. Back in 1983, Harrison had helped Siddall arrange for the purchase of what would be the EGC's first gamelan. Now, for its tenth anniversary, the group premiered Harrison's *Ibu Trish*, written in honor of Trish Neilsen, who had taken over as the gamelan instructor at San Jose State.

Then Harrison set to work on one of his biggest music-meets-words pieces of the decade.

Harrison's 1990s cycle of words and music concluded with, appropriately, another KPFA commission. In 1994, Harrison's friend Erik Bauersfeld, the station's drama director, asked him to score the incidental music for the Bay Area Radio Drama production of Eugene O'Neill's *Lazarus Laughed*. In this play, one of the oddest products of the great playwright's career, O'Neill imagines what happened to Lazarus after Jesus raised him from the dead. Once Lazarus has been freed from the fear of death, he preaches that death is a fiction, that beyond life is only the universe echoing with the eternal laughter of God. Crowds of his followers, mesmerized by his contagious joy of life, trouble Tiberius Caesar and Caesar's heir Caligula, caught between the cruelty of their nature and Lazarus's infectious love.

The score begins with an ominous bass pedal tone and a rising chromatic melody on strings and trombone, a theme that recurs at scene changes, but whose darkness is balanced by tranquil harp ostinatos, bells, and modal flute melodies. By the second act, these fifth-based ostinatos become sprightly melodies leaping between vibraphones and harp, producing what Harrison called a "musicalized laugh," following O'Neill's request for music that would seem as if it "sprang from their laughter, went along with it, dominated it, and finally became pure music."[26] This duality of dark chromaticism and light, fifth-based bell tones continues throughout (and echoes a similar dualism in *Rapunzel*), depicting the human struggle between joy and fear, between life and the specter of death. O'Neill wrote huge scenes with large, masked choruses that interject quasi-poetic chants; Harrison set these scenes in a variety of ways—as rhythmic speech (like his "Litany" in *Homage to Pacifica*), rhythmically chanted on a single tone, or sung to a simple melody—and Harrison's familiar percussion ostinatos also color the dramatic action.[27]

A joyful percussion ensemble and then a flute-led "Round Dance" (similar to the one in the *New First Suite for Strings* he was also working on at the time) accompany the celebration of Lazarus's resurrection. A slow, lyrical theme accompanies the scene when Lazarus must face the death of his wife, Miriam; when Lazarus himself is immolated, the string melody floats up and up as his ashes fly up to the stars and the laughing universe. Many of these cues take the form of kits to give the director the maximum flexibility when combining them with the drama. Despite this Harrisonian approach, *Lazarus Laughed* was probably the closest he ever came to a conventional narrative film score, with themes (if not leitmotivs) for different characters and a large-scale pattern of tonal centers and scales carefully mapped onto the dramatic action.[28]

In spite of all the music-and-word combinations he created in the 1990s, Harrison still craved the space and time to create poetry and visual art, both of which he believed he had neglected in favor of the constant demand (from within and without) for his music. If only, he thought, he could find a place to get away from all the pressures—for new music, for his time—that kept him from creating poetry and art.

AN EDEN OF MUSIC AND MOUNTAINS (1995–1997)

The rich
ancestral trails
we share—sinew & nerve
alike to beach & bloom, will help
us well.

This man,
with whom I've lodged
& loved for a quarter
century in troubled pleasure,
endures.

> *Though now*
> *his age (as mine*
> *does) turns up streaks of pain,*
> *& sometimes communication*
> *lapses,*

Still Bill
& I enjoy
our continued living—
complaints & quarreling, mooning,
hugging.
—Lou Harrison[1]

Harrison's own Pacific Coast domain continued to evolve as he enriched it with artifacts acquired abroad. "Their home was bursting with drama, color, and life, just like they were," remembered Ralph Jackson, director of the classical music division of Broadcast Music Incorporated, Harrison's performance rights organization, after an early-'90s visit with his partner. "We were both struck by the incredible sweetness between them and the sheer joy of their lives together."

Then they all climbed into in Harrison's car to go to his favorite Aptos Mexican food restaurant. Colvig complained about Harrison's sometimes erratic driving, and "Lou responded with growing fury. Every stop, turn and lane change brought a crescendo of harsh words between them, until at one point Lou turned to Bill (taking his eyes off the road while approaching a hairpin turn) and roared 'SHUT UP!'" After they arrived at the restaurant, though, their sweetness returned as if nothing had happened.[2] In his personal life as well as in his music, it seems, equal temperament came to Harrison only with great difficulty.

Still, by then, their relationship had calmed down compared to the tempestuous days in the early 1980s when, after a neighbor complained about noise at one of their late-night parties and Colvig apologized, Harrison exploded. "Don't you ever apologize for me again!" he said and smacked Colvig in the nose, sending him to the hospital. That (or the heart surgery or the diabetes diagnosis) might have been a turning point; he stopped drinking alcohol soon after.[3] Now his hissy fits (over transgressions such as the parsimonious Colvig turning off the heat or absent-mindedly plopping his shod feet on the couch) happened less frequently, and less intensely. Colvig had learned how to defuse them with a chuckle (or well-timed temporary hearing loss or a walk in the woods), and the flare-ups were as likely to be followed by Lou tenderly combing his partner's silver beard and mane. "I thought Lou liked me for my legs," the knobby-kneed Colvig cracked on one such occasion, "but it turns out it was for my hair!" and Harrison agreed.

They were true partners in music as well as romance, and in interviews, liner notes, and program notes, and at any other opportunity, Harrison always carefully credited Colvig's role whenever he was asked about any piece that used his partner's instruments or ideas, which was most of them. "As for my own work, I am very happy that it is being well received and I enjoyed doing it with my partner, Mr. William Colvig, who has helped me to make most of my large works and who is a musician, an instrument builder, and a courageous artist," he told the audience when accepting a 1998 Gay & Lesbian Music Award.[4]

Most of the household tensions originated externally, as, beginning in the 1980s, Harrison suddenly found himself (for a modern composer) famous. Papers and books continued to accumulate, along with commissions and other invitations and obligations, although Charles Hanson had finally imposed some order on Harrison's music manuscripts, uncovering in the process several pieces Harrison had forgotten about or presumed lost.

The house artifacts reflected Harrison's colorful personality, travels, and enthusiasms, including the statue of two embracing nude men that graced the entryway. Harrison would grin mischievously when directing new visitors to the bathroom, whereupon they discovered that it is named the Tchaikovsky Room after Harrison's own full-length nude portrait of the Russian composer on the inside door. The Ives Room boasted gamelan instruments everywhere on rugs, surrounded by stuffed bookshelves; hanging drums and other Asian and African instruments that Harrison demonstrated in his world music classes; art by Harrison, his friends Ben Shahn and Robert Rauschenberg, and others, including a woodcut of Ives himself; and a reed organ that Colvig tinkered with. Colvig had built a small loft for more storage, under which rested Harrison's Steinway piano, still tuned to the favorite Kirnberger #2 temperament that he had used in the *Concerto for Piano with Selected Orchestra*. Nearby stood an Italian virginal and a full-size harpsichord. For many years, the household lacked a television, until Harrison finally bought one and a VCR so that he could watch videotapes sent by friends.[5]

Outside, natural beauty teemed as abundantly as the cultural artifacts within. Over the years, agapanthus and other flowers had grown in nicely, and vines covered the trelliswork. Harrison took to cultivating rosebushes, both for their beauty and for the taste he had acquired for rose tea and rose petal jam while in Istanbul. For gardening chores, Harrison and Colvig had hired a friend of theirs, another septuagenarian, named George Smith. Widowed twice, he had been looking for a place to stay when Colvig and Harrison offered him a room in exchange for gardening, carpentry, and other household help. At other times, Smith loved carving little wooden animals.[6]

Similar changes occurred outside the ramshackle house. By the 1990s, the neighborhood had changed considerably since Harrison had moved in some four decades before. Next to the expensive houses that now lined every available plot along Viewpoint Road, their gravel driveway and homemade carport stood out. In the carport squatted Harrison's old BMW with the vanity license plate CMPOSER1 (a gift from Colvig).[7]

Still, the couple tried their best to hang on to their pleasures. Harrison strove to maintain his voluminous reading and tried to squeeze in the occasional poem, sketch, or gamelan session whenever the press of commissions and the other intrusions of relative celebrity permitted. And even though Colvig's knee surgery and other health concerns had slowed him down, he rarely missed what he called his "tree-sea" hike along a path that he had blazed from their backyard all the way down to the beach, a steep couple of miles along trees and ferns and frequently shared with deer.[8] Harrison no longer joined him, because the hike back up the hill was too steep. At one point, Harrison purchased electric bicycles that would charge their batteries going down the winding road and then bring him back up on electric power. For longer excursions, he also threatened to obtain something called a "power parachute" ultralight aircraft.[9] "As Gertrude Stein said, no matter how old we are, we still consider ourselves to be mature youth," he said.[10]

Then an incident one evening in Oakland in 1994, seemingly minor at the time, signaled what would be a major change in their lives. As Harrison, Colvig, and Charles Hanson were walking to the theater to see Remy Charlip's latest dance, Colvig kept walking off in the wrong direction, even though they had been to the venue many times before. As it would turn out, it was one of the first signs of Colvig's encroaching dementia.[11] In Aptos, Harrison sometimes worried when Colvig went out hiking without telling him where he was going or how long he would be gone. Given his recent health problems, Harrison feared the worst, and finally Colvig sighed and marked out on a map the three most common hikes he took. Harrison tacked up the map on the wall.[12] The precaution proved prescient.

Every week, if possible, several people would arrive at the Colvig-Harrison house, sit down in a circle in the living room or in the garden, and smile—and the household bustle would give way to uncharacteristic silence, occasionally punctuated by outbursts of group laughter. The conversations at these gatherings in the 1990s were conducted entirely in American Sign Language and became a cherished part of Harrison's life.

This latest enthusiasm of Harrison's hatched at a birthday-celebration concert in Portland. When the Portland Gay Men's Chorus sang Harrison's *Three Songs*, he was delighted to see that the performance included a sign language interpreter for the songs. "You know, it's a whole big body thing," he said of the signing. "[It's] beautiful, I discovered."[13] At a March 1992 San Francisco Legion of Honor performance of artists associated with Black Mountain College, Remy Charlip danced a solo to Harrison's *May Rain*. Harrison was deeply moved when he realized that Charlip's choreography included signing the song's text.[14]

Beauty and practicality merged as Colvig's and George Smith's hearing deteriorated, making communication more and more difficult, with Harrison forced to speak in low-pitched tones for Bill to hear him. At six o'clock when the KPFA news came on, everything stopped, as far as Colvig was concerned, even if dinner was ready. As Colvig turned up the radio louder and louder, "it was physical agony for me," said Harrison, "because he couldn't hear unless the highs were up to the point that it was an agony. I sometimes would have to leave, they were so loud." Harrison found a class in American Sign Language at Cabrillo College and immediately signed up the three of them.

Harrison took up study of this new near-universal language with all the enthusiasm and determination that he had brought to his earlier study of Esperanto. But to Harrison's annoyance, Colvig dropped out during the second week.[15] Smith progressed enough to be able to understand spelling and rudimentary phrases but usually resorted to writing on a marker board to communicate. Nevertheless, Harrison continued to study, even hosting weekly meetings for the members of his class when the course ended.

Participants in these meetings rarely spoke except in sign language, so that their gatherings were nearly silent, except for periodic outbursts of laughter that might confuse visitors unaware of the source. To Harrison their meetings were islands of blissful relief. As an auditory person, he was always concentrating on sound. "For example, I used to get a milkshake at a confectioner's counter, and you'd touch it to the counter, and it would make this lovely sound. You can't find those anymore. I guess it was the bubbles in the milk. I'm ears, ears, ears. That's why I take sign language, to relieve that."[16]

Besides the sign language group and Harrison's fellow musicians and artists, one of the mainstays of Harrison and Colvig's social life was the local Gays Over Forty group that would meet twice a month at a restaurant in nearby Capitola and sometimes for a party at Harrison's house. Harrison treasured these relaxing times with Colvig and friends. However, Harrison continued to worry about his partner. "Bill's in bad health," Harrison wrote in his notebook in 1995, "and will not take prescribed help. Don't know what to do and feel guilty to enjoy life myself."[17]

Colvig's forgetfulness was also steadily getting worse, and Hanson and others often had to help out. "I must say that they were in pretty good shape up through about 1994," remembered Hanson, "and then things really started falling apart, health-wise. That did not stop Lou from working, of course. He kept writing. But it did sort of take it out of Bill. It made it hard. When Lou wanted to compose, he had to close the door and compose, and somebody had to make sure that Bill was okay."[18]

Some of Colvig's treatments were not fully covered by their insurance, and bills began to mount. Harrison had little choice but to accept more commissions and put aside gamelan pieces and other voluntary projects, including another puppet opera based on a favorite play, Goethe's *Iphigenia in Tauris*.[19] Fortunately, commissions continued to arrive—and one of them came from a source he'd long treasured. It would commence a series of musical journeys back through Harrison's past.

A PARADE

As San Francisco's Chinatown coalesced in the mid- to late nineteenth century, its population transferred their celebration of the lunar new year and other holidays to that most American of institutions—the parade. By the time the teenage Harrison saw these colorful festivities in the 1930s, they represented an exuberant patchwork of different traditions, much like Harrison himself. The members of Chinatown clubs might don traditional dress but form Western ensembles, often brass bands and, as Harrison remembered, groups of the brilliant mobile version of the glockenspiel known as the bell lyra.

All of those memories came rushing back in 1995 as Harrison considered yet another commission offer—from a most unexpected source. Harrison privately expressed annoyance that the closest major orchestra, the San Francisco Symphony, had largely ignored him since playing his *Trojan Women* overture more than half a century previously. "In fact, I was just about to tell all my publishers not to allow any performances by the San Francisco Symphony," he claimed.[20]

All that changed in 1995 when Michael Tilson Thomas took over as music director. For his very first concert opening the 1995 season, Thomas wanted a new work from Harrison, a great fanfare to inaugurate the season and his tenure, and he encouraged the composer to think big: "Use anything you want—a boys' choir, a gamelan, whatever, and, of course, the San Francisco Symphony."

Harrison, whose musical textures seldom deviated from a decorated single line at this point in his career, was a bit intimidated by such "largesse," but "I finally summoned courage and committed a little tune," he remembered. "It did not want to be a fanfare but rather a parade march such as I had heard in my youth in S. F. splendidly stepping along with a 'bell-lyra' group. I somehow remember Chinese women playing the hip-borne bell-lyras long ago."[21]

In depicting the jubilant chaos of a parade, Harrison channeled the idol of his youth, Charles Ives, who did the same in such pieces as "Putnam's Camp." Many of Ives's works lovingly depict scenes from his childhood and youth, and now at age seventy-eight, Harrison made a similar nod to nostalgia, evoking the wonder and excitement of his youthful discovery of cultures in collision. It would lead the parade of last compositions into his past as Harrison's compositional career came full circle toward the end of his life.

The orchestra for *A Parade* (later renamed *A Parade for M.T.T.* in Thomas's honor and dedicated to the San Francisco Symphony) is the most enormous of any in Harrison's career: four each of winds, six percussionists (playing a large battery of instruments including Javanese gongs, his oxygen tanks, ranch triangles, and a Balinese *gentorak*), celesta, piano, harp, and strings. Yet when Harrison first heard it in rehearsal, he decided that it needed one more thing: the huge organ of Davies Symphony Hall. The organist, like the other keyboard players, sometimes uses octave bars to create clusters for "a variegated brilliance," according to Harrison.[22] The resulting multitude consists of ninety-nine players (an even hundred with the conductor), which may explain why the relatively brief work has been rarely performed since.

A Parade opens with the "gamelan section" of piano, celesta, vibraphone, and glockenspiel imitating the bell-lyras with an enthusiastically rising triad. This theme returns, like marching bands, several times in this rondo-like form, accompanied by the band's drums and cymbals. Harrison thickens contrasting themes with his usual acre of techniques: *jhalas*, clusters, quintal counterpoint (though not gamelan figuration). "This in turn led to a more singing passage and then my early hearing of Japanese Gagaku in S. F. emerged," Harrison wrote. "I could see that my S. F. memories were passing as a parade and so I celebrated that for Michael's arrival." This suddenly atmospheric *gagaku* section (like the dream segment of "Putnam's Camp") finds its way back, in an arch-like form, to the opening theme. After an overwhelming, glorious noise, the piece ends with the marching band percussion slowly fading out as the parade passes. Much pleased, Thomas took the piece on tour with the orchestra during the following season.

The SFSO played Harrison's music again that fall when Davies led a performance of his Third Symphony, and again the following winter when Thomas conducted *Canticle #3* around the same time the San Francisco Contemporary Music Players revived his *Perilous Chapel*. And MTT brought Harrison back the next summer when he instituted the San Francisco Symphony's American Mavericks Festival. He featured Harrison's *Concerto for Organ and Percussion Orchestra* on a marathon program shared with members of San Francisco's iconic and long-lived rock band the Grateful Dead. Their fans, the Deadheads, packed Davies Symphony Hall and cheered Harrison's noisy and rollicking concerto. With these and other performances in 1995, including his and Charlip's *Ludwig and Lou* with the Oakland Ballet and Mark Morris Dance Group performances of his music in Berkeley, finally the prophet of world music was receiving honor in his own homeland.

ROUND DANCE

> *People say: "You're a composer. You can't retire." The hell I can't! People want a Fifth Symphony out of me. Look, Ives wrote four, and so did Brahms, so that's enough.*

—Lou Harrison, 1997[23]

A Parade triggered memories of Harrison's past, which proved handy because still more commissions had arrived for Western instruments, and as usual, that drove him back to his old scores and notebooks in search of suitable ideas. For a Portland concert, he provided a new, expanded version of the slow movement of his *First Suite for Strings* from 1948, his "reflections on Jenkins, Coperario, Frescobaldi, and other of the earlier Baroque," as he put it. Harrison had never been quite satisfied with the piece, first assembled from yet earlier sketches when he was reassembling his own life after having just been released from the New York hospital.

The success of the new slow movement "persuaded me that I was on the right track."[24] In 1994, he tossed out the somewhat pedantic neoclassical passacaglia movement and replaced it with an invigorating "Round Dance," whose non-diatonic melodic focus provides a break from his earlier preoccupation with contrapuntal textures.[25] Harrison also composed an entirely new finale on his now-favored ending form of a chaconne. The chaconne's texture is light and airy, often with just one expressive melody over the repeating bass line. The difference between it and the earlier densely contrapuntal passacaglia demonstrates how Harrison's musical voice had evolved in nearly five decades. Harrison reasoned that he could not call this piece by the same name after such drastic revisions, so he gave it the somewhat oxymoronic title *New First Suite for Strings*.

Harrison's eighth decade had become one of the busiest and most successful of his life. He was receiving more commissions, offers of residencies, and offers of other engagements than he could reasonably handle; after having lived for so long on the edge of poverty with little recognition, he felt reluctant to say no to any opportunity.[26] But he had other interests besides writing music. "My current range of commissions causes me to [overwork], and I don't like it," he grumbled. "It means that I haven't time to paint or write much verse and so on. I still have another book of poetry to come out—24-hour work on scores is not my idea of paradise.... I'm having to ruthlessly write. It's very hard on me. This constant concentration on music makes me hate the art, so it's rough," he told an interviewer.[27] "I need a break from putting black dots on paper," he told another.[28] And the work, the travel, and the pressure were taking an increasing toll. "I've had four commissions this year. After this, no more!" he insisted. "Or at least not any commissions with deadlines anymore. I'm too old for that kind of pressure! ... But all this work was too much—I ended up in the hospital with pneumonia."[29]

Harrison's pneumonia was only the latest of his respiratory problems, which were frequently aggravated by Aptos's damp, cool weather. While recuperating, he thought once again of retirement now that this last series of commissions helped cover his bills. As much as he loved Aptos, though, he began to envision a place where he could get away from the constantly ringing phone, the many visitors, and other demands—perhaps someplace where his lungs could dry out.

On his way home from a residency at the University of New Mexico in 1995, Harrison and Colvig stopped by the tiny hamlet of Joshua Tree in California's Mojave Desert to see their friend, just-intonation composer George Zelenz. The three clambered into Zelenz's truck for a tour around this stark terrain, dotted with the bizarre treelike cactus for which the town is named, brush, and the occasional jackrabbit or roadrunner. The colors seemed all the more vivid in this isolated, sun-drenched landscape surrounded by rocky hills. The heat and the wind can be brutal, Zelenz said, but the people are friendly. It reminded Harrison of the dry desert vistas of the Four Corners area that he regarded as the "real America," and of the picture of the shimmering Southwest of the early European settlers and Native Americans that had so enchanted the young Harrison when he moved to California from Oregon.

A couple of days after Harrison and Colvig returned to Aptos, Zelenz got a phone call. Harrison wanted him to buy them a plot of land.[30] It would be the site of Harrison's last great "composition," and instead of a refuge from turmoil, it would become a source of it.

VAULTING AMBITION

One of the many volumes in the ever-occupied bookstand next to Harrison's favorite chair was the Egyptian polymath Hassan Fathy's 1973 book *Architecture for the Poor,* which advocated building using sustainable, local materials, in his case including mud bricks. Harrison read it around the time a very old building method was undergoing a revival among environmentally conscious North Americans: straw bale construction. Farmers discarded enough baled straw (not hay or grain, but the non-edible byproduct) each year to house the country, according to Harrison. Once baled and packed tight, straw becomes a well-insulating, fireproof, inexpensive building material. Typically covered in stucco, the bales give some straw bale houses the look of adobe abodes. Harrison appreciated its inexpensive materials and "nonproprietary and low-tech" methods," he said. "A core of very practical people, like farmers, have built more straw bale than anyone else."[31]

Harrison's discovery of straw bale housing quickly joined his frequently and wistfully voiced dream of acquiring a getaway cottage, where he would finally get to those projects, musical and non-, that he wanted to focus on—no longer beholden to commissions, no longer pursued by the phone that rang more and more often as the 1980s turned to the '90s. He imagined that Colvig could build a very small gamelan to keep there, and he had in mind a new *pelog* tuning to try out.[32] Motive, method, and money (thanks to those swelling commissions) in place, the final element appeared when George Zelenz sent him pictures of a 1.25-acre plot just outside the main village of Joshua Tree, California, for $8,000. That's what I want, Harrison said, seizing the opportunity, and arranged the purchase.

Even more than the bales' sustainability, another feature most appealed to the noise-sensitive Harrison. "The bales are enormous insulation, at least two feet thick, and also they're sound-impervious," he said. "When I have an unfinished project, I want to take it there and do it without interruption."[33] Harrison engaged a firm specializing in green construction and impressed the architects with his knowledge of architecture and his firm idea of what he wanted.

Sound would play a major role in his new sometime home. Harrison knew from his studies, particularly of the European Renaissance, that harmonious architectural proportions arose from the same ratios as he found in just-intonation tuning.

Humanist architects, following the example of the great Roman architects Vitruvius and Pliny the Younger, created their buildings with ratios of two, three, and four—the same numbers that create Pythagorean tuning and Plato's cosmos in the *Timaeus*. Harrison sat down and drew a three-by-three grid of squares. The northmost column of twelve-by-twelve-foot squares became a kitchen, a bathroom, and a bedroom. The southmost column became a porch divided by three buttresses, giving a view of the barren, rocky hills that border Joshua Tree National Monument to the south. The middle column would be a single long room, what he called his Great Room, capped by a sixteen-foot vault, or arched ceiling.

"He thought of it as being made up of modular pieces in the way that gamelan music is modular," said Harrison's artist friend Chris Daubert. "Traditional gamelan pieces are short and repetitive, and then embellishments are added to the simple structure. In that way, you can think of the house as starting out with nine modular pieces, almost like a tic-tac-toe board."[34]

Harrison knew how the Romans famously perfected vaulted designs and how they used them to create soaring ceilings over their halls and basilicas, in configurations so stable that they lasted for centuries. The architects, who shared Harrison's interest in applying this ancient technique to straw bales, drew up the plans and submitted them to San Bernardino County to apply for a building permit. Then they waited.

And waited. Finally, months later, the county responded. A vault? Of straw? Such a thing had never been permitted in the county (nor, according to Harrison, anywhere in the United States). The county wanted more assurances that a vault was stable. The architects went back to Harrison with the bad news. To keep it remotely within his budget, they would have to have a different roof for the Great Room.

No. Harrison was adamant that the room must have a vault. He was thinking about not just the architectural aesthetics but also the acoustics. A flat ceiling would create so many standing waves that playing music would be compromised, recording impossible. (The harmonious proportions of Renaissance rectangular rooms created a kind of literal harmony, because their halls would resound in the very intervals they had built, due to the resonances created by these parallel walls.) An adobe arch would create a smooth reverberation for the space. If he couldn't have the vault, the project was dead. So the architects hired an engineer, who recommended building a full-scale test structure, one bale wide, so that its properties could be tested to the county's satisfaction.[35]

In May 1998, engineers, builders, architects, and some neighborhood children gathered to watch the structure absorb increasingly large jolts from a hydraulic jack. The bales absorbed the vibrations so well that the crew was unable to collapse the vault, and the children went home disappointed.[36] Harrison, who had originally imagined that an inexpensive "house of straw" would cost no more than $50,000 to build, saw his costs soar. The engineers gathered more data, wrote up a report, and finally submitted a new application. Then the waiting began again.

Months later, perhaps due to heightened concerns following the 1999 7.2 Landers earthquake, the county still wasn't convinced, infuriating Harrison, who suspected not just bureaucratic inertia but even a capitalist conspiracy against affordable housing that would deprive homebuilders of unjustified profits. "It's maddening!" he sputtered. "I wanted to learn how to make letter bombs!" Next, to Harrison's dismay and dwindling bank account, lawyers got involved. "I fear that I've become somewhat a martyr for the straw bale cause around the world," Harrison said ruefully.[37]

When the approval finally came, after nearly three years of battling, Harrison was convinced that the process was ultimately arbitrary. "And apparently it's pure whimsy, because this last time we went in for it . . . the guy said, 'Oh, you people have been waiting long enough.' Boink," he added, imitating a rubber stamp. "I asked the architect, is all this purely opinion, whimsy? And he said yes! Here you're bleeding your life out. Oh! Ghastly."[38] But Harrison would have his home, and, he hoped, the precedent set by his battle and demonstration of safety might open the door for others to build sustainable housing too—a public service and a legacy.

RHYMES WITH SILVER

Onstage, before a painted backdrop of wavy chartreuse and crimson lines, a dancer moves with exquisite grace that belies his relative bulk and age (forty), his long, curled, black locks whipping around behind like a kite's tail, while a cello weaves sinuous melodic lines. Although fifteen other dancers have been onstage in other sections of the nearly hourlong dance, now only one other stands—still, skinny, silent. Suddenly, the moving dancer stops and claps his hands, and the thin man extends his fingers. Finally, the large man collapses with haunting elegance and pushes himself into the wings.

A decade before this performance, Lou Harrison received a phone call from Seattle. The Seattle Gay Men's Chorus had asked one of the city's most renowned native sons, Mark Morris, to choreograph a piece for them, and the piece he wanted to use was Lou Harrison's *Four Strict Songs*. "I heard the Louisville Orchestra record, and I lost my mind," Morris recalled. The chorus director Dennis Coleman knew Harrison—"if you're gay, you know Lou," Morris said—and wanted him to arrange his music for the chorus's 120 voices.

Delighted, Harrison came to Seattle (toting his own mixing bowls for the percussion part and Saran Wrap so they would stay in pitch) to work with Morris and the chorus for several days during a weeklong residency at the University of Washington. The pair hit it off immediately, despite the fact that Colvig fell asleep (which happened often) during their dinner with the world's hottest young choreographer. "He supervised the tuning, delighted in the rehearsals, and we became friends forever," Morris remembered.[39]

That's no surprise: the two great twentieth-century, Northwest-born artists found an uncanny number of parallels between them. "Both are wryly passionate about their work," wrote *New York Times* dance critic Jennifer Dunning. "Both create art that is deceptively simple, filled with a knowing innocence and a complexity that only gradually reveals itself. Each makes use of a wide range of materials ranging from classical to folk and popular influences for the creation of what is obviously meant as high art. Both are exuberantly outspoken about being gay. And despite their reputations as renegades, solid recognition has come to Harrison and Morris."[40] The two brash, bulky, demonstrative, voluble, long-haired, and proudly gay artists also cherished one composer above all others: Morris loved and choreographed the music of Handel. "He taught me everything I know," Morris said.

Unlike many choreographers, Morris is a skilled musician, able to work from a score and even conduct orchestras, and he performs with live musicians, qualities that Harrison especially admired. By the 1980s, Morris had earned the reputation as the most musical of choreographers, his dances somehow embodying music more than accompanying it—the opposite of the sundering of the link between the two art forms that Harrison's friends Merce Cunningham and John Cage had perpetrated, to Harrison's regret, two generations earlier. Morris often developed dances from a limited number of movement motives, just as Harrison created music from melodicles, and both artists preferred to work within the boundaries imposed by such structures.[41] Then based in New York, Morris was already fascinated with maverick American classical music, choreographing works by Henry Cowell, Harry Partch, Conlon Nancarrow, and Virgil Thomson. But no contemporary composer spoke to him like Lou Harrison. "What *isn't* fabulous about his music?" enthused Morris. "It is irresistible."[42]

Morris visited Aptos in 1995, while his company was performing *Grand Duo* and a dance called *World Power* set to "In Honor of the Divine Mr. Handel," "In Honor of Mark Twain," and *Bubaran Robert* in Berkeley. Morris told Harrison that he had found support for a new commission. He wanted Harrison to write him a new score.

"What's the instrumentation?" Harrison asked.

"I don't know, you decide, you're the composer."

"Is there a text?"

"I don't know. Let's talk about it."

"Do you choreograph it first and then I write the music, or do I write the music and you choreograph?"

"Well, if you want I'll make something up, and then you write music to it, but I've never done anything that way."

"No, okay . . . don't do that. I'll write the music . . . Does it have to go on tour?"

"Uh, yes, it'd be good."

"How long is it? "

"I don't know, you make it up." Finally Morris burst out, "It could be eight harps and a boys choir and percussion if you want! Or it can be cello solo, or it can be anything."

"Hmm . . . okay . . . all right—I'll write a piece for you," Harrison responded, "but don't ask me about it."[43]

Despite his professed flexibility, Morris planned to tour with an ensemble that included cello virtuoso Yo-Yo Ma, together with other strings, piano, and percussion, so Harrison worked with that instrumentation.[44] Considering how to structure the work, Harrison remembered that Morris had earlier responded to the suite-like *Grand Duo* with discrete, tightly structured group dances, though he also chose to delete one movement for the sake of the overall dance form. If Harrison was going to write the music first, he decided to give Morris the same flexibility by creating many short movements that could be ordered in any way, like a "kit" of short pieces. The collection also included two kit movements, themselves of variable length.

One by one they arrived in Morris's mailbox, finally totaling twelve movements lasting some fifty minutes. Six movements form a traditional dance suite, which can be excerpted as a standalone piece: a "Gigue and Musette" (adapted from the piece he wrote for the UCLA dance class in 1942), a "Romantic Waltz," an uproarious "Fox Trot" (which, like the *Grand Duo's* polka, combines memories of childhood dance lessons with a quirky scale and exuberantly crashing piano clusters), "Threnody" (not a dance at all but instead an introspective string solo in a *pelog* mode), "In Honor of Prince Kantemir" (another cross-cultural homage, this one for the eighteenth-century Romanian aristocrat who was seduced by Turkish music, appropriately in the form of an *usul* cycling Turkish rhythm), and "Round Dance" (or rondeau, with a *jhala*-like hexatonic theme).

Four movements are a "Set for Cello" (also independently extractable) featuring soloist Yo-Yo Ma: a moving "Prelude" (performed without dance), a "Scherzo" (using the term as it appears in baroque suites as a duple meter "joke," this one being on the cellist, who becomes a percussionist on his instrument), a "Five-Tone Kit," and a searching and emotive "Chromatic Rhapsody" that freely uses interval controls. "I did some risky things for Yo-Yo in the first music that I sent him and there was no problem," Harrison said. "So from there on I just thought, well, here we go!"[45]

Despite the gulf in geography and age, the co-creators worked together smoothly. When Harrison sent Morris the "Romantic Waltz," based on a relic retrieved from one of his 1940s notebooks, the choreographer thought it beautiful, but he hesitated. "Lou, it seems not quite somehow to cohere," he said. "It doesn't sound done." Two weeks later, Harrison sent another copy. "It was actually, like, five or six bars shorter, but it completed itself," Morris remembered. "He finished it by tightening it up, just making a tiny little click, and it was like, 'Of course—that!'"[46]

Morris decided to call the full dance *Rhymes With Silver* as a tribute to Harrison's uniqueness, represented by his non-rhyming middle name. It premiered in 1997 to positive reviews in an all-Harrison program that also featured Morris's previous settings of Harrison's music. "You're not sure what the story was," wrote the *Wall Street Journal's* Joan Acocella, "but you think you may have dreamed it once."[47]

Critics often referred to the score with mention of its "Asian tinges," now as much of a cliché in Harrison reviews as the adjective "avuncular." Despite his reputation, though, few explicit Asian sounds actually inhabit Harrison's late-period suites for equal-tempered chamber groups. Glittering *pipilan* ornamentation occasionally thickens single melodic lines but ends up sounding more "impressionistic" (Harrison's description) in their new context than Indonesian. Likewise, *jhalas* adorn many movements, such as in his 1995 *Suite for Cello and Piano*, but sound as baroque as Indian.[48] His love of bell-like tones ties together his gamelan and later work, but such tintinnabulous timbres had also become commonplace in the 1980s and '90s scores of composers such as John Adams. "I've been influenced by Asian music since I was a kid," he explained. "But I keep my styles separate. I don't put everything in a blender."[49]

Many gems of movements sparkle in these late-period, equal-tempered suites— *New Moon*, the *Clays' Quintet*, the *Grand Duo*, the *Piano Trio*, *Suite for Cello and Piano*, *Rhymes With Silver*—built up from acres of toys, eclectic techniques collected over a lifetime. Yet Harrison developed the most prominent of those techniques—modal melodicles, interval controls, tone clusters, expressive chromaticism, European dance forms, percussion techniques—in the 1930s, and they are not Asian at all. When faced with commissions for conventional equal-tempered chamber music, Harrison summoned up the modernist craftsman part of his personality, which was much indebted to his teacher Cowell and to his experience composing-to-order for San Francisco choreographers and Mills dramas. "I don't have a 'lifeline' attitude about composing," said Harrison. "To me it's a craft, a skill, and a pleasure."[50]

If Harrison could crank out estampies with the same facility that Bach possessed for writing fugues, it doesn't mean that these forms were routine (in either case). At the same time, *New York Times* critic Paul Griffiths complained of an eightieth birthday concert, "Three of the four long works played here included stampedes (or 'estampies,' to use the more formal title), two of them ended with a chaconne, and all of them had at least one elegy."[51] These commissions rarely gave Harrison the room to experiment, and though each one interested him creatively, he did not treasure those opportunities as he did his "voluntary" pieces.

GRAND OLD MAVERICK

Like the Joshua Tree house, *Rhymes With Silver* showed Harrison designing large-scale structures that encompassed many of the beauties he had long cherished, but the celebratory reception and West Coast sounds of the New York birthday concert prompted a dissent. "Every piece on this program seemed to have a nice day and wish us one, too," wrote the *Times*'s Bernard Holland. "Harrison's music doesn't pander or try to ingratiate; it is naturally considerate, indeed so nice that at moments of saturation one wants to give it a kick." Harrison often associated these continuing modernist suspicions of anything attractive with the East Coast. Holland also sniffed at the music's "crossbreeding" and accused Harrison of "expropriating a musical way of thinking that will never truly be his, for, copy and study all one will, there are about 1,000 years of genetic absorption that simply do not arrive over the space of half a century."[52]

Harrison had long experience with those who would police the propriety of composer influences, but sensitivity to cross-cultural exchanges had become even more acute since Harrison had first encountered it in Tokyo in 1961. "Though on paper he may have required more specific knowledge of musical traditions than Cowell," wrote John Corbett in *Western Music and Its Others*, an anthology generally critical of Western "appropriation" of non-Western styles, "Lou Harrison too created works more notable for the craft of their panglobal exotic referentiality—using Indonesian scales and orchestras consisting of both Western and non-Western instruments in rather forced, lushly arranged East–West cultural grafts—than for their intellectual innovation. Unlike Cowell, Partch and Cage, who were stimulated by non-Western musics to come up with something conceptually and/or sonically original, Hovhaness, McPhee, and Harrison tended to pay homage with the sincerest form of flattery—cheap imitation."[53] More generous critics called Harrison's defense that hybrid music is "all there is" "naive" or "utopian."[54]

But to paint Harrison as a cultural colonialist and "appropriator" of artistic resources is itself a naive moral judgment. Harrison was all too aware of the dangers of power differentials, but not between the artists of the West and those of the East. Rather, the borders he perceived were between transnational corporate greed and the needs of disenfranchised people throughout the world, between urban alienation and human community, between oppressive industrial grayness and sublime beauty, between those who would destroy and those who create. As a gay man, he sympathized with victims of bigotry, including those subjected to colonialism, and he identified with people marginalized by society.[55]

"I call it the 'Bali-er than thou' syndrome," Jody Diamond maintained. "You know, the only ones who care about such things are the Americans. No one in Indonesia thinks there's an issue of appropriation. . . . You'll never have a Javanese yell at you, but you'll have plenty of Americans saying, 'You have no right to be writing this music.' But I learned one really important thing from [Harrison]: that it's the essential nature of human beings to be creative, and that we're going to be creative with whatever we have contact with. . . . We can add to their sources but shouldn't say that we don't want human beings to be creative, because they have to be. That's who we are. That I learned from him."[56]

However, such debates represented a minority discourse during a period when enthusiastic reviews of Harrison's works appeared regularly in the mainstream press. Continuing celebrations of Harrison's career, including one in Vienna, plus a 1997 *New Yorker* profile and other media attention, attested to his late-career critical and popular respect. A Harrison quote—"Everything comes to an end . . . even the twentieth century"—even graced the back cover of a 1999 Sonic Youth album.

As the world caught up to his once-eccentric ideas about global culture, the one-time fringe figure suddenly found himself an éminence grise, a beloved leader of the tribe of American Mavericks honored by Michael Tilson Thomas at the San Francisco Symphony's festival of that name. While grateful for the honors, Harrison never thought too much of his newfound celebrity. "I'm having my fifteen minutes," he said, referring to Andy Warhol's aphorism about celebrity. "It's been hot and heavy and wall-to-wall. It's surprising, really, because a lot of people live over eighty."[57]

37

ASIAN ARTISTRY (1997–2002)

Amid the concerts for Harrison's eightieth birthday, he celebrated other anniversaries no less important. Bill Colvig also turned eighty in 1997, and he and Harrison also celebrated their thirtieth anniversary of that fateful meeting at the Old Spaghetti Factory. Colvig's birthday presents included a new prosthetic for his knee. "I saw it through the X-ray, and it looks beautiful," Harrison said. "Just like a Brancusi." After knee surgeries rebuilt those joints and straightened his legs, said Harrison, "not only is Bill no longer bowlegged but he is now taller."[1] For awhile, his medical assistance enabled Colvig to recommence to his relatively spirited outdoor life, but he and Harrison both were accumulating medical bills along with their years, which *Rhymes With Silver* and other commissions helped pay for, along with the increasingly expensive house-to-be in Joshua Tree.

Some months later, Colvig's lower right leg developed lesions from sarcoidosis, all but incapacitating him. Caregivers came by the house periodically to give Colvig his medications, change the dressing on his legs, and bathe him. Once the caregivers left and Harrison went out to the camper to work, someone else, usually Charles Hanson, had to be around to look after Colvig. Such helplessness was especially difficult for the normally vigorous Colvig to bear, but as his legs began to heal, he began to hobble outside to his paths. His hearing had worsened, and Harrison was both worried for him and annoyed that he willfully avoided studying sign language.

When Harrison had a sign language group meeting at his house, Colvig often fell asleep (or feigned sleep, Harrison suspected). When Harrison had a visit one morning from Don Springfield, the laboratory teacher for the Cabrillo College sign language course, Colvig disappeared outside and down his trail. Harrison enjoyed informal sign language conversations such as this, a chance to learn and have a couple hours of blissful silence. He was so caught up in the conversation that he was surprised when his visitor looked up and asked what time it was. Harrison answered. His friend signed, "Bill's been gone too long."

Harrison was frantic. Fortunately, he now had his map of Colvig's most common hikes, and he and Springfield immediately set out to search for Colvig. Springfield finally found him on the short trail to the other property, bloodied and crawling on the ground, trying to pull himself up the trail. His head was at an odd angle from the fall he had taken. It so happened that they had a doctor's appointment that afternoon, and the doctor cleaned him up and sent him for X-rays. Finally they headed home. When they arrived, though, the hospital called. Colvig was to return immediately. He had broken his neck.

Doctors braced his neck and sent him by ambulance to another hospital, where a neurosurgeon carefully wired Colvig's vertebrae back together. Colvig had very narrowly escaped paralysis or death in his fall. For the next three months, he was constantly in a neck brace, unable to hike. "It was hard on Bill, who's so physical," wrote Harrison in his notebook.[2] Colvig's doctor, suspecting that a small stroke had precipitated his fall, warned of the possibility of further strokes. In 1999, medical expenses (including a pacemaker for Harrison) forced Harrison to sell his mother's house in Redwood City. Fortunately, Harrison had more commissions to help pay the mounting expenses. As he neared the end of his career, it was fitting that they would allow Harrison to look, as he had from his childhood days at the Silver Court, back to Asia.

A BIT OF PLUCK

One commission came from Japanese musician Akiko Nishigata, a virtuoso on the Japanese three-string lute instrument known as the shamisen or *sangen*, which reminded Harrison of "long-lutes from elegant old Egyptian paintings, from Persian miniatures."[3] However, Harrison had only occasionally borrowed from Japanese traditional music, and even then, his main interest was in *gagaku*, the court orchestral music, rather than the solo, song, and chamber music traditions associated with the shamisen. Working with Nishigata's recordings and with information about the shamisen brought back fond memories of his previous encounters with the instrument at New York concerts and the *bunraku* puppet theater in Japan.

The melodies in *Suite for Sangen* often emphasize the semitones so characteristic of the instrument's traditional *in* mode but without directly imitating it.[4] Although the slow traditional shamisen music, as sparse as a Japanese ink painting, invites Zen-like contemplation, Harrison was more drawn to the Javanese aesthetic of filling in all available space, especially given the brittle and dry timbre of the shamisen. In the opening "Prelude" and parts of the last movement, the *jhala* technique keeps a drone sounding. It wasn't until after the first movement was complete that he realized that the *jhala* section melody resembled the well-known traditional gamelan piece *Bima Kurda*, but he decided to leave it as it was. "And it was like, if a hymn tune came up in Ives, why cancel it?" he explained. "After all, it's a part of my background."[5] He used a similar drone in the slower third movement ("Adagio"), which employs interval controls rather than a mode. The brisk second movement, "Estampie," shows that his cultural pollination spreads both ways.[6]

A superficially similar commission arrived from Dennis Russell Davies, who suggested a concerto for Chinese *pipa* virtuoso Wu Man—reversing Harrison's earlier process of pairing a Western solo instrument with an Asian orchestra. "I am plucking my way through the year!" he said.[7] But although both plucked-string instruments have dry timbres, the shamisen tradition differs from the *pipa*'s dramatic, extroverted showpieces, a character more in keeping with some of Harrison's recent works. Harrison owned a *pipa*, and though able to extract only the most rudimentary melodies from the instrument, he was able to understand what types of fingerings and chords would work.

"Well, I'm not going to write anything like *pipa* traditional repertoire, a lot of virtuoso kind of a style," Harrison told Wu Man.[8] Nevertheless, Harrison worked closely with Wu Man to adapt his work to the idiomatic idiosyncrasies of the instrument. "Do I do tremolo here?" she asked, describing their collaboration, "or do I do bending notes, do I do vibrato? You know, how can I make the piece more vivid, how can I put more sauce in this piece? Right now, it's just linguini, or the notes."[9] In the end, impressed by Wu Man's artistry, Harrison allowed her considerable interpretive latitude for her solo part.[10]

"What I often do in organizing a suite is to balance off modal and chromatic movements," Harrison explained. "I started off the *pipa* concerto with that in mind, fundamentally, and then retracted because it didn't seem too *pipa*-esque. Or *pipa-gemütlich*. The sound of the *pipa* and its fretting system did not feel right—those silk strings, they don't sound right chromatically."[11] Instead, the *Concerto for Pipa with String Orchestra* is an exploration of six-tone modes, which Harrison frequently favored in his late works, just as he had favored pentatonic modes earlier. The extra tone, while not appreciably altering the character of the pentatonic parent scale, offered the composer new and "charming" possibilities, he thought.[12]

His concerto's first movement followed the traditional *pipa* music pattern, using Chinese pentatonics with occasional substitute tones. However, he structured the movement's lyrical middle section like a Javanese *lancaran* eight-beat form, with the high violin and *pipa* melody set against a repeating bass melody in quintal counterpoint. The other movements use transpositions of a quirky six-tone mode that allowed Harrison to slip between a sense of tonality and more ambiguous sections.[13]

The second movement, another of Harrison's "mini-suites" called "Bits and Pieces," this time comprises four sub-movements. In the first, "Troika," the *pipa* assumes the role of a Russian balalaika in a woozy sleigh-ride dance, complete with (non-diatonic) oompah chords.[14] A sort of percussion ensemble sub-movement follows, called "Three Sharing" because a cellist, a bassist, and the soloist share a set of seven rhythmicles played entirely by striking the body of the instrument or hitting the strings with the wood of the bow, turning them into percussionists as he had the cellist in *Rhymes With Silver*. In the middle section, Harrison arranged the rhythms as a fugue for the instruments, as he did as far back as his 1937 percussion ballet, *Changing World*. He dedicated the next evocative miniature to the composer Liu Tianhua, who played a central role in bringing the techniques of Western theory and orchestration to Chinese traditional instruments in the early twentieth century, in the same way that Harrison had brought Chinese techniques to the West. Harrison's use of the *pipa* to evoke lute-type instruments around the world continues in the last section of this movement, a romantic Neapolitan song with the *pipa* now in the role of a tremolo-ing mandolin.

The mood darkens in the slow movement, a "Threnody" (Harrison's alternative name for an elegy, common to many of his suites), this one dedicated to the memory of San Francisco's best-known AIDS activist, Richard Locke, who had died the previous September.[15] Unlike Harrison's mostly chromatic late elegies, this modal one sounds uncharacteristically sweet and wistful, though it ends on a chord as unresolved as the AIDS epidemic. The bright *pipa* sound, so well suited to the jocular earlier movements, would sound intrusive here, so Harrison restrains it to a few notes, letting the grave string melody set the melancholic mood. The dramatic finale rides another Harrisonian estampie to a surprisingly aggressive climax.

Like the *Suite for Sangen*, the *Concerto for Pipa with String Orchestra* contrasts with Harrison's early pieces for Chinese and Korean instruments from the 1960s, where he more explicitly retained the traditional character of the instruments—the expressive pitch bends of the *zheng*, the slow slides of the *piri*, the simultaneous variations of the Confucian orchestra. In his long series of suites from the 1990s, Harrison used Asian instruments (and all instruments) more freely within whatever form he had plucked from around the world. In this last of his great Asian–European fusions, and his last completed work for orchestra, Harrison again contrived a creation from seemingly incompatible forces that feels different from any other music yet simultaneously seems not only natural but even inevitable. Before the *Concerto for Pipa with String Orchestra*'s 1997 premiere at Berkeley, a journalist asked Wu Man, "What style of music is this? Is it Chinese music?"

"It's Lou Harrison music," she replied.[16]

TIME PROPORTIONS

> *[The gamelan's] size, its interconnections and what you can do are breathtaking, that's all I can say. I will never, for the rest of my life, be bored as long as there are gamelans and players around. And writing too. If I write now, just out of my head, there are only two things I really like to do. One of them is harps and other tuned instruments playing modes, usually from the antique world but sometimes made up. And the other is gamelan compositions.*
>
> —Lou Harrison[17]

Even as commissions demanded more of his creative energy, Harrison's ardor for gamelan never abated. He looked forward to his Cabrillo College rehearsals as blissful islands in his week, until time pressures forced him to give them up, and he continued to fill his notebooks with sketches of *balungan* melodies that he would try out on occasion. *Gending Moon* is a setting of his own poem that pays homage to "the holy man with face of white" who "has taught us time." Harrison knew that the same quest for understanding of cosmic cycles that produced calendars also created musical scales in ancient societies, a connection later expressed by Plato's "harmony of the spheres." The thirty beats of *Gending Moon*'s first *gongan* rationalizes the days in a lunar cycle. The subtlety of the *slendro* melody and the complexity of its colotomic interpunctuations inaugurated what might be termed a late style of Harrison's gamelan compositions, marked by complex, irregular forms and introspective melodies.[18]

Perhaps the height of this style of melodic nuances and irregular time honored the artist whose work Harrison most admired, Japan's most renowned twentieth-century woodblock artist, Munakata Shiko. "He's been a passion of mine and comes up violently sometimes," Harrison said. "I even went so far as to buy a couple of prints by a pupil of his in Kyoto once."[19] Munakata's expressionist style bears comparison with another of Harrison's favorites, German artist Max Beckmann, whom he had also recently honored with a similarly ruminative gamelan composition. Instead of East meets West, in Harrison's *In Honor of Munakata Shiko,* his last major work for gamelan, East greets East: an American composer writes a piece inspired by Japanese aesthetics for a Javanese orchestra—a quintessential example of Harrison's Pacific Rim aesthetic.

Harrison had read about the architecture of Japanese Buddhist temples organized by bays (or *ken*); that is, the spaces between columns. The proportions of what he called the "Japanese order" can be much more complex than the Platonic systems of the European Renaissance, and so the rather lengthy structure of *In Honor of Munakata Shiko* progresses from seven to nine, ten, sixteen, and finally twelve *gatra* phrases. These characteristically Japanese (and un-Javanese) dynamic asymmetries mirror those of Munakata's striking woodblock prints, which Harrison thought could be projected during performances. The piece had languished in Harrison's notebook because he noticed that the opening melody resembled the sentimental turn-of-the-century song "Oh Dry Those Tears," which he had sung as a boy soprano. Finally he decided to leave the reference (perhaps obscure to anyone but him) and completed the piece. *In Honor of Munakata Shiko* is one of his longest yet most contemplative, even abstract gamelan compositions, elusive to both Western and Javanese ears.

Munakata was only one of Harrison's lasting passions. A book by environmentalist David Brower recommended pulp from the kenaf plant over trees as a more sustainable means of paper production, so Harrison immediately ordered some and used it for the rest of his life. He read about people using waste cooking oil from restaurants as an alternative to gasoline in diesel engines and immediately bought an old diesel Mercedes and, although he knew little about engines, enlisted friends to help convert it to biodiesel.

While telling his friends of these pro-environmental projects, he recommended the book *Bonobo: The Forgotten Ape* by Frans de Waal and Santa Cruz photographer Frans Lanting. "They're on our family tree, and we share 98 percent or more of our genes with them," he said. Unlike the warlike groups of their cousins the chimpanzees, he said, "it is a society entirely run by matriarchs who are lesbians. . . . They don't fight. The whole glue of the society is sex. All kinds without discrimination to sex or age."[20]

Harrison's voluminous reading always included books on science and frequently on politics from a progressive point of view. But as angry and even despondent as he could get over his nation's increasingly belligerent and conservative politics, he remained "an intellectual pessimist but a glandular optimist" who, by the time he reached his ninth decade, struck most of the people he met, including Wu Man, as a kind of hippie Santa Claus.

Still another permanent Harrison passion was the baroque keyboard music he often played for pleasure on his harpsichord. Near the eve of the year 2000, amid apocalyptic warnings about the Y2K bug that coincided with Harrison's own distrust of computer technology, Harrison received a request from UC Santa Cruz music professor Linda Burman-Hall for a work for harpsichord, the instrument he wrote for in his *Cembalo Sonatas* (1934–1943) at the very beginning of his career. As in the earlier work, the first movement of the *Sonata for Harpsichord*'s binary form in a non-diatonic scale allowed him to alternate aggressively dissonant semitones with fourths and fifths. The other two movements also reflect familiar Harrison gestures: an "Arioso" in gentle quintal counterpoint followed by a closing vigorous estampie, complete with sections of octave tone clusters, with the glittery timbre of the harpsichord. The movement's Hispanic, perhaps flamenco-like, flavor again echoes the early *Cembalo Sonatas*.[21]

Once Harrison drew the final bar line of his *Sonata for Harpsichord*, he took a moment to relax and look forward to the completion of his house in Joshua Tree. To an interviewer, he repeated his vow to retire, meaning "no more commissions with deadlines, because that's what gets me."[22] However, once again, this resolution would prove premature. Something even more powerful than music soon occupied most of his attention.

TEARS OF THE LONELY NIGHTS

> And his absence brings tears of the lonely nights.
>   Unasked for, in the middle of the nights
> I wake and want to touch him, cross-town in his
>   bed. Too far to reach, but on tomorrow and
> on further days I'll go there to his caress
>   maybe with some flowers—but surely with love.

—Lou Harrison[23]

At a 1999 family reunion with Colvig's three brothers (all of whom lived in the Bay Area) and sister, Bill and Lou enthusiastically played music and laughed along with the family, who had long regarded Lou as one of their own.[24] That would be the last time they'd all be together.

Although affably quiet in social situations around his booming, gregarious partner, Colvig was known to his friends for his impish wit and mischievous laugh. "He delighted in springing puns and punch lines on the unsuspecting," remembered his and Harrison's friend, composer, guitarist, writer, and conductor Phil Collins. "He had a puckish quality, or maybe a little bit of coyote. But Bill spoke his mind unflinchingly. He would be tactful, but never false."[25] In his element, hopping among mountain rocks even while playing baroque recorder, he was a marvel of life energy.

But one night, Colvig fell from his bed and was unable to lift himself back onto it. Harrison also was unable to lift him until he had help from a neighbor the next morning. The incident frightened Harrison, who realized that despite the regular visits from caregivers, Colvig might need more assistance than was available at home. In 2000, they agreed that Colvig should move into a care facility. In hopes that he could return home, Harrison and Hanson painted Colvig's room in their house in bright Mexican colors, while bringing Mexican art and artifacts to decorate his room at the care facility—along with, of course, the radio via which he could tune into his beloved Pacifica broadcasts. As they did often at home, he and Harrison would frequently read to each other aloud from favorite books.

In his bed at the Santa Cruz hospice facility, Colvig was transformed. Finally robbed of his woods and open sky, he smiled but seemed suddenly ancient. Doctors delivered more bad news: cancer. Then pneumonia set in. Harrison sat at his bedside, "holding his hand in mine, and often he would lift my hand to his lips, and I would hold his head and his shoulders." Bob Hughes and Charles Hanson arrived the next day.

> We watched
> his chest breathing
> slower and then lighter,
> propped up a little in his bed:
> eyes closed.
> He had two separate violent spasms,
>   he fell to rest, and at the last, in his neck
> the slowly weaker pulse of breathing came to end.
>   His passive face, still beautiful,
> no longer moved;
>   and his hands no longer trembled
> or sensed my touch.
>   The great vital nature of him
> went up and out.[26]

Harrison told his friend John Luther Adams, "It was a peaceful death. He was so beautiful. Like a beautiful animal returning to Nature."[27]

Bill's passing left an abyss in Harrison's life. Fortunately, there followed the distractions of some welcome events. In June 2000, Michael Tilson Thomas devoted an entire concert of the San Francisco Symphony's American Mavericks Festival to a "Salute to Lou Harrison," including his Third Symphony and Concerto for Organ with Percussion Orchestra. After the final chaconne from the Suite for Violin and American Gamelan died away, the spotlight lit up Richard Dee and the bolo-tied Harrison; after their bows, Harrison accepted the standing ovation by signing "I love you" to the audience.

Harrison received an award from the American Humanist Association and a Gay and Lesbian Music Award, and in August he traveled to New Hampshire to receive the prestigious MacDowell Medal, whose previous composer recipients included Bernstein, Copland, and Thomson. "In choosing Lou Harrison," the MacDowell committee chair said, "the search committee recognizes his gentle and generous spirit, as well as the very personal and multi-faceted way in which he is and will continue to be a major presence in American and world music."[28] Harrison addressed the august gathering of intellectuals with his own brief disquisitions on everything from politics to environmentalism to quantum physics, speculating that advances in string theory might someday affirm Pythagoras's "music of the spheres" and ideas about the innate appeal of natural tunings.[29]

Yet the outpouring of awards and honors bestowed on Harrison could not fill the emotional void left by Colvig's death. "I begin seriously to believe that 'fame' is a form of 'castration,'" Harrison wrote in his diary around this time. "One feels more and more isolated, 'pedestalized' and untouchable."[30]

As he gradually emerged from his grief over the loss of his life partner, Harrison pushed back against the isolation with help from his friends in the Gays Over Forty social group. A pianist friend offered to share a room at a Gay Seniors convention in Miami, where among over a thousand men, Harrison met "old friends from England and Australia and new ones from all over."[31] He began spending time with someone he had known for some time: Todd Burlingame, a sometime artist and puppeteer working at odd jobs around Santa Cruz. The forty-four-year-old Burlingame, a relatively new member of the over-forty group, had recently lost a partner, and the two found mutual solace after their losses.

Burlingame thought that their relationship "was good in a lot of ways for Lou. He needed to be simply accepted as Lou Harrison and loved."[32] Although uncomfortable getting caught up in Harrison's social wake, Burlingame was soon accompanying Harrison to events and meeting his large circle of friends, even helping around the house.

Charles Hanson welcomed the help, especially as Harrison's medical problems mounted. Bouts of trigeminal neuralgia would unexpectedly cause an upwelling of great pain in his jaw. During a conversation, he would sometimes halt mid-sentence, close his eyes and furrow his brow for thirty seconds or a minute, catch his breath once the pain subsided, and start speaking again. Burlingame began to bake him edible marijuana to help with the pain, and he suspected that Harrison was becoming dependent on a powerful prescription sleeping pill called Restoril.

Despite the relationship with Burlingame, the eighty-four-year-old Harrison continued to find solace, as he had in New York, in more casual sexual encounters. "Lou also had that open exploration of sexuality thing in his late years," said Burlingame. "I got driven up a wall by it. We had an open relationship, except it wasn't open on my side. I was monogamous, because I just didn't want to deal with a lot of it."[33] Burlingame reasoned that Harrison's creativity was closely connected to his sexuality. "I do not go along with the pseudo-Freudian notion that sexual frustration, or sublimation, is a help to creative processes," Harrison said. "I think, in fact, exactly the reverse. Unless you have plenty of love, plenty of sex, plenty of affection, it just gets in your way if you're trying to do creative work."[34]

BENEATH HIS ROBES

And that crown of his.
Beneath that crown his eyes,
beneath his robes a King,
beneath his crown a King,
beneath his robes a man.

—Scene IX aria from the revised version of Harrison's *Young Caesar*

At Harrison's eightieth birthday celebration at New York's Ninety-Second Street Y, Eva Soltes had spied John Rockwell, the *New York Times* music critic who had recently been appointed as the first director of the Lincoln Center Festival. He and Soltes had already corresponded about including Harrison in the festival, and she had just the work in mind. "Lou's only [full-length] opera, *Young Caesar*, has never had a professional production," she told him.

An early fan of Harrison's music, Rockwell knew all about it; as a young critic for the *Los Angeles Times*, he had reviewed *Young Caesar*'s premiere in Pasadena. "I was already interested in doing the opera, and Eva corroborated that we should do it," Rockwell said.[35] Since its unsuccessful last production in Portland in 1988, Harrison had tinkered with the score and developed ideas about improving it. ("When do you know a piece is finished?" an interviewer asked Harrison. "When it stops itching," he replied.)[36] Dennis Russell Davies had offered a production in Stuttgart, but translating the libretto into German proved too difficult and expensive. Soltes continued to work behind the scenes, and in 1998 Rockwell called with the good news. Lincoln Center wanted to commission a new version of *Young Caesar* for its festival.

Harrison already had it on his plate of projects that he wanted to get back to, possibly when the Joshua Tree house was finally complete. But funds from the commission would help pay for that house, and he hoped that with new revisions and a professional production, his problem child of an opera would be rehabilitated.

He had another motive. Who knew how many years he had left? "It is important to me to leave a work of art of music, serious classic music, on an overtly gay theme," he told the audience (remotely) at the Gay and Lesbian Music Awards. "Not as suggested as in the Britten opera [*Death in Venice*, which premiered in 1973, two years after the original *Young Caesar*] but an overt scene, historically founded as the real thing. I think that's important and it is that that I am working on now."[37]

His determination to write this musical statement for New York's pantheon of high art required expanding a project conceived for an intimate setting into an elaborate production involving a capacious stage and substantial instrumental and vocal forces. Nevertheless, for the third time, he set to work on *Young Caesar*.

Struggling with increasing age-related central tremors, Harrison laboriously revised the score in shaky handwriting on extra-tall, one-inch staves. He began the process of reorchestrating it for the large orchestra available, and with Gordon's permission he cut narrated descriptions that were now obvious from the stage action.[38]

Most important, Harrison added new arias and expanded others. Through artful repetition and some lovely new melodies, Harrison made the prose texts less awkward. Gauis's recitative complaining about his impending marriage to Cossutia becomes a powerful aria questioning conventional ideas of masculinity: "What is so fine about becoming a man?" A new eulogy for his father helps the audience see a tender side of Gaius (and perhaps Harrison's grief for his own father). While these new arias lengthen the opera, whose plot already plodded, they give the audience time to reflect on the action, which Harrison had rushed through in the first version.

The seemingly jinxed composition quickly encountered new bumps. Rockwell had engaged an enthusiastic Mark Morris to direct it, but soon Morris's touring commitments forced him to bow out, causing Rockwell to postpone the production. Then Rockwell, Harrison's principal supporter and architect of the commission, left Lincoln Center for an editorship at the *Times*. Rockwell's successor, Nigel Redden, an arts administrator and director of the Spoleto Festival, signed up another of America's greatest choreographers (and another outspoken gay rights advocate), Bill T. Jones, to take Morris's place.

Then Harrison got a call. Redden was troubled by the libretto and wanted to get Harrison, librettist Robert Gordon, and Jones together to discuss major revisions. As negotiations continued, Harrison finally refused Redden's idea to bring him to New York City to work with the director. Harrison so disliked flying that he insisted on taking the train everywhere. He simply could not bear the idea of cross-continental travel and an extended stay in the noisy city. "I think the people in big cities are deaf," he growled. "They rev up music to the point where it's terrible pain to me."[39]

Soon a package arrived in the mail. Redden had unilaterally had the libretto revised himself. Harrison was appalled, not so much because he thought the libretto was perfect as it was but because he felt passionately that an artist's (in this case Gordon's) intentions ultimately had to be respected.[40] Harrison's moral indignation collided with Redden's interpretation of the producer's legal rights to the words and his judgment about the libretto's suitability. "He said we could change it if we wanted," Redden said, "but that if we did, it wouldn't be *Young Caesar* anymore—it would be *After Young Caesar*. This became a bit of an issue."[41]

Finally in the fall of 2001, Harrison got a phone call thanking him for his work and saying that unfortunately the production was canceled. At first, Lincoln Center was evasive about the reasons, citing the uncertainty about funding in the aftermath of the terrorist attacks in New York that September. In the industry, rumors swirled that it was being killed because of its overt treatment of homosexuality.[42] However, Redden said, "The program is always in flux until it's finally announced, and in the fall of this year it became apparent that there were going to be financial restraints and we cancelled what were then the two most expensive projects. Unfortunately *Young Caesar* was one of them." He declined to say what else had been canceled.[43] Soltes recalled that Harrison wasn't so much bitter as he was "deeply disappointed and depressed."[44]

Harrison refused to give up on *Young Caesar*. Not long after Lincoln Center reneged on its production, he approached another old ally, UCSC conductor Nicole Paiement. She had already made the premiere recording of his first opera, *Rapunzel*, which Marin Alsop, Davies's successor as director of the Cabrillo Festival, staged in 2001.[45] Although his and Alsop's musical tastes diverged—she favored hard-edged composers from her native East Coast over West Coasters such as Harrison—Alsop wanted to recognize Harrison's importance to the festival and the community. Harrison called it the best-ever performance he'd seen of his opera, and at the end, Santa Cruz's old and new musical heroes embraced onstage.

That left only *Young Caesar*. "Lou," Paiement replied. "I will do this opera."[46] She agreed to take on the difficult job of raising funds for a star-crossed show and persuading Gordon to trim his text. Harrison resumed work on what would now be a fourth version of his problem child, a chamber opera (twenty-one musicians) production that evoked some of the original's color and intimacy.

Even so, critics remained unconvinced by the libretto. "The truly intractable problem with 'Young Caesar' is that it boasts neither a real protagonist nor a compelling dramatic course," noted the *San Francisco Chronicle*'s Joshua Kosman of the version's later premiere by Paiement. "As a narrator reminds us in the opera's opening moments, the title character is neither the soldier, nor the politician, nor the lady's man nor the stabbing victim so well known to history. What that leaves, unfortunately, is a wide-eyed boy of no particular interest . . . a will-less cipher who accedes with equal blankness to the political machinations of his Machiavellian aunt in Rome and to the seductive caresses of Nicomedes."[47]

The September 11 attacks upset Harrison for reasons beyond their role in aborting the Lincoln Center production. "As I get older, and nearer my natural limit, I become more irritable about the increasing global stupidity," he wrote his old friend Sidney Jowers, noting that he was still dealing with issues regarding Colvig's estate that never would have arisen had American law allowed the long-term partners to marry.[48] In the fall of 2001, Harrison's distress about the September 11 terrorist attacks and subsequent invasion of Afghanistan may have brought to mind the numbness he felt in 1939 when he first heard that Germany had invaded Poland. At that time he had begun composing the melody for his modal mass, originally wanting to create a modern version of the hybrid masses of voices and Indian percussion performed in the eighteenth-century California missions. When he turned these sketches into the *Mass to St. Anthony* in 1952, he had abandoned that idea for a more conventional orchestral accompaniment. Nevertheless, people kept asking about the original version, including, memorably, the sisters of Immaculate Heart College in 1962. When Charles Hanson located the original tiny music notebook Harrison was carrying around in his pocket on that day in 1939 "in a rats nest of a box in the shed," Harrison decided to give it another look.[49]

In the dark Kyrie movement, Harrison replaced the string accompaniment with explosive percussion, a cry for mercy in the face of the terror of military invasion, led by a snare drum and a mad, fife-like piccolo. The Gloria movement rings out in a grand superfluity of bells not available in the 1952 version: vibraphone, glockenspiel, celesta, and chimes, among other instruments. Perhaps thinking he would get back to the project in his retirement in Joshua Tree, Harrison then put aside the mass, though these two movements, later recorded on their own, offer a tantalizing taste of what the whole could have been in this beautiful, strikingly different version.[50]

Harrison's late-life excavation of fragments of his past, including the mass, *Young Caesar, Rhymes With Silver* and new versions of his *First Suite for Strings, Canticle #5*, and *Songs in the Forest*, paralleled Hanson's laborious process of archiving his compositions. Now, one final project arrived that would take him all the way back to childhood, back to the Silver Court.

While our mothers were playing mah-jongg, my friends and I listened
to the radio. Everywhere you dialed, you heard this wonderful
Hawaiian slack guitar music. I am attempting to recapture that
sound I've been carrying around all these years in my head.

—Lou Harrison[51]

David Tanenbaum was getting frustrated. A supporter and performer of Harrison's music for a quarter century, the San Francisco Conservatory guitarist had at last secured a commission for a new Harrison piece for his instrument, thanks to Charles Amirkhanian's Other Minds new-music festival and Betty Freeman. It seemed like an ideal opportunity for the music festival and the composer, who, fifty years before, had declared himself "coo-coo" for the guitar.

Yet Harrison hesitated. His experience with his 1978 *Serenade for Guitar* had not been entirely positive, and not just because he had to wait for justly tuned fretboards to be built. As much as he loved the timbre of the guitar and admired Tanenbaum's skill, he was dissatisfied with the quiet tone and lack of sustain in the conventional classical guitar, and he was no fan of the obvious solution, artificial amplification.[52] It was hardly a new problem. When Harrison was a boy, in the era before electronic amplification, dance bands voiced the same complaint about the lovely but weak-toned guitar.

Tanenbaum and luthier Kenny Hill loaded a station wagon full of different guitars and drove to Aptos. Harrison listened politely to Tanenbaum playing each one—and each time said no. After having exhausted their collection of instruments, Hill thought of a Santa Cruz street musician he knew who used an old metal-body instrument called a resonator guitar because it has inside constructions a little like speaker cones that vibrate with and amplify the sound. It is also known as a "steel guitar," not because of its body or strings but because it is often played with a tubular slide, called a steel, on the player's left hand. The two guitar experts headed to Santa Cruz's main drag (where students strolled to the big bookstore, the vintage movie theater, and the record stores) and tracked him down. Could they borrow his guitar? A negotiation ensued, and finally, in exchange for lunch money, they loaded up the resonator guitar and drove back up the hill to the palace of the mage of Aptos. The idea of a composition for such an instrument seemed impractical, but Tanenbaum nevertheless plucked a few lines on the street busker's resonator guitar.

"Yes!" Harrison exclaimed after hearing Tanenbaum play the street steel. Tanenbaum was glad that Harrison would finally accept the commission, but "I wanted most of all for the world to hear his music," Tanenbaum remembered. "In seeking an ideal sound he was probably saying goodbye to hundreds of performances that he would surely have if he wrote for classical." Think practically, he urged Harrison.

"I don't care," Harrison replied. "If you play the piece once beautifully the way I want to hear it, I'll be satisfied."[53]

Harrison imposed still another impractical requirement. He wanted the guitar to be tuned in just intonation, in particular a six-tone mode tuned to pitches six through twelve in the harmonic series.[54] This requirement presented more of a problem, since no such resonator guitar with just-intonation fretting existed. Harrison's friend and student Bill Slye, a guitarist who had written a thesis at UCSC on microtonal guitars, contacted Don Young, the CEO of National Reso-Phonic Guitars, the makers of the National Steel Guitar, the successor to the original Reso-Phonic instrument of the 1920s. Its factory just happened to lie only a few hours south in San Luis Obispo. Young agreed to build an instrument (actually five copies) with frets especially for this project. Slye and others worked out a tuning that expanded Harrison's hexatonic scale to twelve pitches, so that the "Harrison model" National steel would be available to other composers and performers after the work's premiere.[55]

Two central inspirations shaped the three-movement *Scenes from Nek Chand*. First, like Ives's many nostalgic works, it represented memories from Harrison's own childhood, when the sound of the Hawaiian guitar dominated popular music he had heard on the family's crystal set radio at the Silver Court in Portland. The swooping twang of the National steel guitar reminded Harrison of that sound, though it also sounded at times a bit like a *sarod*, a instrument from India whose fretless neck makes possible long pitch slides.

The other inspiration was visual. Harrison had just been reading about the Indian artist Nek Chand Saini, who over years transformed junk and discarded building material from his town of Chandigarh into a magical garden with hundreds of fanciful sculptures of animals and people. This act of artistic and humanistic rebellion offended the power brokers of India's planned city, which had been largely designed by modernist architect Le Corbusier, known for his use of irrational proportions and poured concrete, producing what critics saw as sterile, alienating cityscapes. When the local Chandigarh government discovered the unauthorized structures—"a wonderland, a bit of beautiful chaos in tidy Chandigarh"—and threatened to demolish the secret garden in 1975 to build a parking lot and roads, the local population protested, and the site was eventually turned into a public park that drew thousands of marveling visitors each year.[56]

When Harrison discovered Nek Chand's colorful work in a book on outsider artists, he immediately recognized the artist as a fellow maverick, a kindred spirit, and one of the greatest artists of the era. A warm, organic, artistic sanctuary from cold, capitalistic modernism, Nek Chand's garden echoed Harrison's music and philosophy. Harrison swapped the book with Tanenbaum for a National steel guitar, so that composer and player could learn what they needed. Tanenbaum worked on the realization with Harrison, and he even visited a New York gallery that housed one of Nek Chand's many colorful terracotta sculptures of water-gathering women.

The statue's name, "The Leaning Lady," became the title of the opening movement of the spare *Scenes from Nek Chand,* which glistens with the pared-down purity of so many composers' final works. Harrison asks the guitarist to use a steel (a glass or metal tube over the left pinky finger) to effect graceful slides, like the Hawaiian guitars of his youth but also his psaltery pieces of the 1960s, which, aside from the striking tuning, *Scenes from Nek Chand* also resembles.

In a departure from the typical fast-slow-fast format, Harrison follows the contemplative first movement with a quick bar-line-less tribute to the "Rock Garden" of Nek Chand, similar to his *Avalokiteshvara* and similar pieces with their engaging, shifting meters. He named the last movement (an estampie, naturally) "The Sinuous Arcade with Swings in the Arches." "The arcade is two-sided," explained Harrison. "That is to say, there are arches, and a roof with banisters so you can promenade on the top. In every arch there is an iron-chained swing for two people. It's just beautiful."[57]

A magical garden of music and dance for friends was Lou Harrison's paradise. Harrison dedicated the composition, his last, to his longtime friend and advocate Charles Amirkhanian, his wife, Carol Law, and Tanenbaum.

A BALERAISING

As Harrison contemplated the junk architecture of the artistic sanctuary of Nek Chand, preliminary construction continued on his own sanctuary and oasis, what he called his "straw cave" in the Mojave Desert. Bills continued to arrive, and the unnecessary delays imposed by the head-in-the-desert-sand bureaucracy meant that costs continued to rise. When Harrison's funds ran dangerously low, Hanson told the contractor that construction had to stop.

"I just don't know what to do," he told Hanson. "Should I just scrap the whole thing? Right now it's not even a foundation. It's just some PVC." Hanson suggested that he should consider the possibility. By cutting his losses now, he would have a nice cushion of money for his future, maybe even enough to go around the world again.

But Harrison didn't want to go around the world. He wanted his desert haven and, after hashing it out with Hanson, determined to press ahead.[58] By the time Harrison had accumulated the money to resume construction, the delay had driven the price still higher. Weather and vandals damaged what had already been finished.[59] The costs rose to over $200,000, even with the elimination of the domes intended to cap the three smaller rooms.

Finally, in February 2002, it was time for what aficionados called a "baleraising." Volunteers, who included Harrison's friends and even strangers in the straw bale community who just liked the fun of putting up an environmentally sound house, converged on Joshua Tree for this modern version of a barn-raising party. Harrison drove down with Burlingame, Eva Soltes, and Remy Charlip. After previous baleraisings for the walls and other parts of the structure, it was time to finally top off the great room's magisterial vault. All day the volunteers baled straw and lifted the bales with pulleys onto the wooden frame. Harrison sat, tying bales when he could, enjoying it all. "You have something that can feed you and house you," he said of the materials. "It grows up out of the ground; it's right there! It makes sense."[60]

As the desert sun sank behind the rock hills on the second day, the last bale was set in place. Within days, plasterers were covering the two-foot-thick walls with stucco and finishing the interior. The finished structure was much more fireproof and earthquake-resistant, more efficient and sustainable, and better insulated against desert temperature extremes than standard construction—and, even more important to the pacifist Harrison, much quieter.

By the following month, seven years after having bought the property, Harrison finally started to move in. The east wall of the Great Room (a somewhat grand name for the modest hall) is entirely glass, looking out toward desert sunrises. Harrison knew that in the sunny Middle East and India, such open windows were often shaded by a *mashrabiya*, a wooden latticework screen. Although these screens can be elaborate in traditional architecture, Harrison opted for a simple pattern of triangles— reflecting the Pythagorean triple proportions of the rest of the structure. The lattices also shaded the other windows in the walls, which stretched up sixteen feet to the vaulted ceiling, sometimes offering a handy nesting spot for cactus wrens.

When Harrison started furnishing the thousand-square-foot house, Bob Hughes accompanied him and brought down his bassoon. For their first test of the space, Hughes recorded Harrison's *Group on a Row the Same*, and they were impressed with the acoustic warmth of the Great Hall.[61] One item he did not bring: Although he had spoken of getting a phone for safety reasons, Harrison preferred insulating himself from all distractions, and the house initially lacked a landline.

"Like his music, it is a hybrid built of unexpected materials," wrote *Los Angeles Times* critic Mark Swed of Harrison's newfangled yet extremely old-fashioned house. "Like his music, it takes, with fancy and fantasy, from East and West. Like his music, it is designed with a craftsman's sense of exactitude. Like his music, it exults in the warm beauty and hospitality of the world he lived in. Like his music, it, too, is music."[62]

A month after the baleraising, Tanenbaum premiered *Scenes from Nek Chand* at San Francisco's Other Minds Festival.[63] The following fall, guitarist John Schneider came out to Joshua Tree to record *Scenes from Nek Chand* on the newly available Harrison National steel guitar. Since then, despite the difficulty of obtaining an appropriate guitar, other composers, including Terry Riley, have composed for the instrument. It provided further inspiration for Harrison as well, and he accepted a commission from conductor Nicole Paiement for another piece for the instrument. "After many years of inventing six-tone modes," he said, "I suddenly realized that nature's own is between [harmonics] 6 and 12, and it's beautiful, too."[64]

Harrison had a whole list of projects, not necessarily musical, in mind for his getaway cottage, projects he had been wanting to get to for decades in some cases: finishing his new book of poetry and gamelan scores, called *Poems and Pieces*; making a transcription of Cowell's late *Second Koto Concerto* for harp; perhaps completing the percussion version of his mass; and getting back to his long-abandoned book on the history of Korean music. He also looked forward to painting and to continuing to feed his voracious appetite for book reading. As he passed his eighty-fifth birthday, Harrison's retirement had finally arrived, and it promised to be as rich and colorful as the lifetime that had preceded it.

38

WHITE ASHES (2003)

"Nothing
to fear in God,
nothing to feel in death;
good can be attained and evil
endured"—
so carved Epikuros'
friend Diogenes on
a gift wall for Oenanda, his
city.
. . .
The doves
of home are on
the wing, they land and feed
take flight and vanish in the trees
again.
Before
we begin is
exactly like our end—
absence and nothing—unknowing
ever.

—Lou Harrison[1]

In the cold, dank January of 2003, Charles Hanson drove Lou Harrison and Todd Burlingame to Emeryville, where they would stay overnight before a train trip to Chicago and then Columbus, Ohio. When composer Donald Harris at the Ohio State University had proposed a Lou Harrison festival over a year earlier, Harrison had enthusiastically agreed to attend. The event would include a program of his percussion pieces, a concert of his gamelan works, yet another of chamber pieces, and a finale concert by the Columbus Symphony—the largest celebration of his career yet. He had yet again revised his Third Symphony for the festival and was looking forward to hearing it in what he now considered its final version.

But now, on the train platform early the next morning, Harrison felt exhausted and unwell. He asked Hanson what he would be doing while he was away, and Hanson told him he would be taking the proof pages of Harrison's new book of poetry and gamelan scores to the publisher. Melancholy, Harrison told Hanson how much he would rather be doing that than riding in a rocking train compartment for days over a winter-draped countryside.

Harrison was pleased that all the work to produce his book *Poems and Pieces* was finally at an end. "We worked long and hard to complete the book, and believe that it will prove to have been worth the effort," he wrote to his friend Joel Sachs in New York. "Very likely it will be my last full book—after all I am pushing eighty-six."[2]

The book held musings and memories, of his family, his life, and especially Bill Colvig, interspersed with scores of Harrison's late gamelan compositions. To casual poetry readers, these simple sequences of numbers might not have held much meaning, but to Harrison, they resounded from the pages as islands of blissful contemplation. The book was to be his last collection of beautiful artifacts since he was ejected from the childhood Eden of the Silver Court apartments and his mother's collection of Asian finery. "My little drama is to recover my childhood riches," he told Eva Soltes.[3]

One of the new gamelan pieces in the book he titled *Orchard*, after those bits of ordered nature he explored when his family moved to California and which covered Aptos hillsides when he first sought refuge there. Harrison called this introspective *pelog* piece a *gending lampah*, or "walking" piece, in which the *balungan* wanders around the sometimes asymmetrically ordered rows of colotomic gongs. "I painted an orchard which was largely sort of pink and white and green across," he recalled, remembering his art therapy in the sanitarium in 1947. "I don't know where the orchard is in my life, but there it is."[4] A little while before he was to leave for Ohio, he had asked Hanson to try to find that painting, but it hadn't turned up yet.[5]

Yet the past, for Harrison, was not a source of morose nostalgia. Just as it makes us, so we also make it. In the book, this thought acquires a characteristically cosmological perspective:

> *The past is not a residue;*
> *we know it as facts of*
> *bifurcation uncountably*
> *numerous, unpliable as rock.*
> *Our present runs full-blast*
> *at clock speeds from*
> *geologic to transatomic.*
> *And the sum of our past*
> *we now know is of our own devising,*
> *reckless, cruel and partly abomination.*[6]

Then it was time for Harrison and Burlingame to board the *California Zephyr*. "He and I were never really demonstrative," Hanson said. "We didn't hug a lot or anything, but as I said good-bye to him, he did grab me and hug me and said thanks for all your help."[7]

The next day was scenic as the train climbed the Rocky Mountains, but then, at the frigid apex of the trip, the train slid off the rails. No one was hurt, but as everyone reached for their cell phones to report the delay, Harrison, concerned about the phones interfering with his pacemaker, began having a panic attack. Seeing that he was having trouble breathing at the high altitude, Burlingame gave Harrison oxygen and calmed him down. As they sat on the tracks for six hours, the admittedly superstitious Burlingame thought he saw something in the snowy mountains outside the window. "I started seeing Bill hopping in among the rocks in the mountain, which really surprised me."[8] He did not mention the apparition to Harrison.

Finally, that Sunday evening, the train pulled into Chicago's Union Station. The Ohio State school of music had sent two graduate students in the university van to pick them up and drive them back to Columbus, a five-and-a-half-hour trip. Harrison was polite but exhausted. He smiled quietly and held Burlingame's hand for the trip.

After a couple hours, Harrison asked if they could stop somewhere. On the interstate highway in the middle of Indiana, they did not see very much, but finally they saw a sign for a Denny's restaurant in the town of Lafayette. Harrison stood up to exit the van but slipped on the icy pavement. Burlingame and the students caught him before he fell to the ground, but Burlingame told him that they should use the wheelchair they had brought. Burlingame chatted away as he wheeled Harrison inside and into the men's room. Once there, he looked down and saw that Lou had stopped breathing, his dilated eyes open. "He was gone," said Burlingame.[9]

TURNING OF THE WHEEL

"Sevens on the Passing of Lou Harrison"
The great redwood has fallen.
Light streams into the forest.
The sound will reverberate
for generations to come.
—John Luther Adams[10]

They immediately called paramedics, who arrived quickly and worked on Harrison for several minutes. As the ambulance drove away, Burlingame called Hanson from the Denny's pay phone, and then he and the students followed to the hospital. There, Harrison was pronounced dead at around 9:00 PM on February 2, 2003. "His flesh smelled sweet when I kissed him goodbye," said Burlingame.[11]

After spending the evening in the emergency room, Burlingame checked into a hotel and fixed himself Lou's mother's favorite drink, a concoction of milk and gin that Harrison called "mother's milk." Fortunately, Harrison had made plans for his passing with the Neptune Society, a cremation service. While Burlingame made arrangements with the coroner in Indiana, Hanson called up the society, and within days, Harrison's ashes arrived back in Santa Cruz.

The festival in Ohio became an elaborate memorial, where stunned friends and fans of Harrison enjoyed the music in subdued reverence. Festival director Don

Harris choked up when a box arrived carrying scores and other items Harrison had shipped, including one of his signature red corduroy shirts.

Although the newspapers were full of the news of the *Columbia* space shuttle disaster, which occurred the day before, obituaries began to appear, by John Rockwell in the *New York Times*, Mark Swed in the *Los Angeles Times*, Alex Ross in the *New Yorker.* California senator Barbara Boxer read Joshua Kosman's obituary from the *San Francisco Chronicle* into the Congressional Record.

Memorial performances, including a Berkeley gamelan concert led by Jody Diamond, proliferated throughout the country. At that summer's Cabrillo Festival, Harrison's old friend Phil Collins led the *Concerto in Slendro* and Dennis Russell Davies played piano in Harrison's *Grand Duo* and his 1938 *Third Sonata.* Hundreds attended memorials at Mills College and UC Santa Cruz, where friends recounted that, at least toward the last part of his life, Harrison considered himself an "Epicurean" in regard to questions of death and the afterlife. An epigraph to his *Elegiac Symphony* quotes the philosopher: "Where Death is, we are not; where we are, Death is not; therefore, Death is nothing to us." Or, as Harrison's father (who had passed away just as suddenly) put it more bluntly, "When you're dead, you're dead!"

Harrison's capacious circle of friends shared memories, images, and his music at the memorials, at various events in his honor over the ensuing months, and on a web page set up by Other Minds, where John Luther Adams's poem above appeared; Adams later wrote a large-scale composition, *For Lou Harrison*, in tribute to his fallen mentor. "*For Lou Harrison* was not commissioned," he wrote. "I composed this work because I was compelled to do so in response to the passing of one of the most important figures in my life. Amid the daunting realities of today's world, Lou Harrison and his joyful ecumenical life and music seem more vital and more pertinent than ever."[12] Adams's 2014 Pulitzer Prize–winning composition *Become Ocean* drew its title from Cage's seventieth-birthday mesostic to Harrison. Michael Tilson Thomas dedicated his *Island Music*, written after an Indonesian vacation, to Harrison, Colvig, and Dahl.

Until he met Harrison, his teacher during his freshman year at Stanford, composer David Lang "had imagined that a composer should be dark and moody and troubled and introspective. [Lou] thought a composer should live a good life. And he did."[13]

"When I asked why he thought we'd been put here," Charles Shere remembered, "[Harrison replied,] 'We're here to entertain one another with stories, on our common way to the grave.'"[14]

Said Mark Morris, "Either you've never met Lou Harrison or you're his best friend."[15] At the memorial services, the mood was remarkably joyous, as old friends reconnected and remembered Harrison's joyous energy, ferocious appetite for knowledge, generous philosophy, and contagious ardor for art, science, history, life.

Though his prodigious energy and mental sharpness to the very end made it hard to imagine that either could ever vanish, his death at such an advanced age, much older than other men in his family, couldn't have been a surprise. And as much as his friends felt his absence, the mode of Harrison's death—so quick and painless, occurring on his way to a festival of his music, just after writing a last piece that symbolized his recapturing of his long-sought childhood treasures and at the end of a rich and rewarding life—mitigated the sense of tragedy. Many friends mentioned that he'd enjoyed the kind of long, rich, creative life everyone wants to live. He had suggested as much in his own oft-stated, deliberately prosaic obituary: "Lou Harrison is an old man who has had a lot of fun."[16]

In his will, Harrison left his house to Bob Hughes, Hughes's wife and Harrison's copyist, Margaret Fisher; Jody Diamond, and Larry Polansky. The Joshua Tree house, which Harrison had the chance to enjoy about five times before his death, went to Remy Charlip. His percussion instruments were willed to William Winant, his Asian art to Chris Daubert, and his furnishings and cars to Eva Soltes. His papers, scores, recordings, and other artifacts went to his archive at UC Santa Cruz, financed from grants from foundations set up by members of the Grateful Dead, facilitated by Harrison's old friend and biographer, UC Santa Cruz music professor Fred Lieberman.[17] The "East Holding" property of his original Aptos cabin went to Charles Hanson, who became his executor. On the first anniversary of his death, Harrison's friends scattered his ashes just outside the big east window of the Joshua Tree house, where he finally found his desert place of rest.

BECOME OCEAN

Harrison had won wide recognition only late in his life, and it only continued to increase, along with performances and recordings of his music, after he died. Naturally, many were spearheaded by friends and colleagues—Dennis Russell Davies, Nicole Paiement, John Adams, Michael Tilson Thomas, and Mark Morris, who as music director of the 2013 Ojai Festival programmed over a dozen Harrison works over the three days, plus John Luther Adams's *For Lou Harrison*.

Harrison's immediate legacy—his over three hundred compositions—seems more secure than ever, as his works are performed regularly around the world. "Musicians, audiences and writers in major centers around the world respond enthusiastically to [Harrison's] music," Dennis Russell Davies said. "They relate to a voice that expresses, in an original and authentic way, devotion to the great masters of the past, combined with an open, inclusive, and inquiring spirit expressing truths that artists all over the world believe in."[18]

"Unlike so many of his congenitally embittered ivory-tower colleagues, he not only accepted his marginal status in the nation's culture but reveled in it," wrote *New Yorker* critic Alex Ross. "Yet he was, in many ways, an imposing figure—at once the prophet of the minimalist movement and the last vital representative of the mighty populist generation led by Aaron Copland. His music was so spare in design as to seem naive, but it was not simple, and he was not a simple man. . . . There was much merriment in Harrison's work, much hummable song and rollicking dance; but there were also dark, questing rivers of chant, machinelike ostinatos, erupting dissonances, enveloping silences. He had a rumbling, visionary side."[19]

Appreciation for Harrison's contributions has only intensified in the years since his passing. "I learned to respect creativity from Lou, because it was so strong in him," Jody Diamond said. "He so clearly delighted in it. That was the joy of his life, to have the privilege of being able to create things."[20] Diamond inherited his gamelan

Si Betty and brought it to Harvard University, where it became the Viewpoint Composers' Gamelan.

Two of the major projects that lay unfinished at his death found realization afterward. Paiement finally brought Harrison's *Young Caesar* to the stage four years later, in February 2007. It contained much lovely music and moments of beauty and somewhat redeemed the orchestral version of the opera from the disastrous 1988 production, although the dramatic story still needed work.

The other major project Harrison left unfinished, his book *Poems and Pieces*, turned out to be too expensive to produce, given the money available from his estate. Instead, Charles Hanson decided to publish the poetry (set in Harrison and Carter Scholz's Rotunda typeface) separately from the gamelan scores with Santa Cruz's Cafe Margo Press in 2013, under the title *The Path at West Holding*.[21]

No one promulgated and perpetuated Harrison's legacy more than his indefatigable one-time assistant Eva Soltes. Her long-incubating documentary, *A World of Music*, premiered in its final version just before Harrison's ninety-fifth birthday at San Francisco's Castro Theater, and she accompanied it to screenings and festivals around the country, bringing his colorful story to thousands of viewers. She also preserved many of Harrison's possessions after his Aptos home was torn down by new owners, and she took charge of the straw-bale house from Remy Charlip. Soltes helped care for Charlip, who lived near her in San Francisco, after a severe stroke disabled him in 2005. He died in 2012 at eighty-three; John Dobson died in 2014 at ninety-eight.

Soltes has turned Harrison's Joshua Tree house, now called the "Harrison House," into the site of performances and residencies by dozens of artists, dancers, and musicians. Harrison's stubbornness in creating the unique straw-bale construction has also provided a legal and engineering precedent for people around the world who may never hear his music. "We proved that you could make housing appropriate for areas with high seismic activity for very low cost—maybe $4 a square foot in parts of the developing world," said the structural engineer David Mar. "More than 400 of these houses have already been made in China. Lou would be so proud."[22]

THE TRIUMPH OF DIONYSOS

I wish I had one hundred lifetimes. I still could not get everything done.

—Lou Harrison[23]

Beyond his own music's continuation, an explicit debt to Harrison emerges in many of today's compositions for gamelan or just intonation, and though such pursuits (for all Harrison's optimism) remain outside the mainstream, they are far more numerous now thanks to his trailblazing. When Harrison's friend John Chalmers started his journal *Xenharmonikôn* in 1974 and when Harrison's student David Doty and others started *1/1: Journal of the Just Intonation Network* in 1985, there were just a few dozen subscribers for each. Following in the path first tamped down by Harrison, Harry Partch, Ben Johnston, and a handful of others, the numbers grew into the hundreds on microtonality e-mail lists and, later, news groups and Facebook groups.

And although the idea of Western composers writing for gamelan can still be controversial among ethnomusicologists, CDs of new gamelan compositions now emerge regularly, and some groups encourage composers to write for them or play only newly composed music. The idea of building one's own instruments, pioneered by Partch and followed by Harrison and Colvig, is no longer as outlandish as it once was, though much construction has moved to software rather than hardware. "I am struck by how much I and my colleagues two and three generations removed are indebted to Lou for many aspects of our musical language which we take for granted today but for which there was no precedent 50 years ago," wrote Harrison's student, composer Paul Dresher.[24]

Harrison is often called the godfather of the world music movement. In truth, the "globalization" of music, for better and worse, that began toward the end of the twentieth century would have happened regardless of Harrison, but it's fair to say that Harrison led the way in his respectful and studied fusion of Western and Asian classical artistry, an ideal of beauty he first glimpsed at the Silver Court. It was fitting that he returned there, metaphorically, in one of his last compositions, but of course he had been there for most of his career, in one way or another.

More revolutionary was Harrison's model of the composer who does not need to depend on the musical establishment for performances and exposure. Harrison's and Cage's percussion ensembles and self-produced concerts anticipated by a couple of decades those by New York's downtown composers of the 1960s. At age twenty-five Harrison, like Cage, left San Francisco feeling that he had outgrown its isolated arts community. Yet by the time he had reached middle age, he had come to idealize the artistic companionship and do-it-yourself participation he had experienced during those early years.

The remainder of Harrison's career struck a balance between the joy of making music with friends and the need to fulfill a more conventional model of professional success. Many of what may prove to be his most lasting and characteristic works are not necessarily those for conventional ensembles but instead those for percussion, Asian instruments, homemade instruments, and gamelan. His turn back to these media, the sociability of performances on them, and the democratization of music-making they permitted, helped to shrink the gap that widened in the twentieth century between professional performers and listeners. And it followed the rebuilding of Harrison's social self after his breakdown, when he gradually transformed from an isolated, sometimes self-absorbed, and emotionally unstable personality to the mirthful Buddha figure that friends knew in later years, one who not merely appreciated but craved social interaction and playing together as much as he did beautiful art.

Sometimes an artist's imprint on culture is easily identifiable. Aaron Copland's Americana style is an iconic sound in American culture. John Cage opened the door to chance in art, leaving a lasting impression that the avant-garde arts still keenly feel. But Harrison's most lasting contributions may have come not from his vast acreage of techniques (which he seized and discarded and sometimes reused, one after the other, with a child's glee) but instead from the permission he gave to artists in the late twentieth century to unabashedly embrace beauty. As a younger generation rediscovered tonality, meter, and a planetary music in the 1970s and after, there was a musician who had been there all along, someone who refused to relinquish his ideal of expressive spirit molded by rational order.

Wisdom is a place apart,
and central everywhere;

Because life's an accident
enjoy each minute of it,
and know that heaven is now.[25]

"Cherish, conserve, consider, create."

—Lou Harrison's motto

APPENDIX A: GLOSSARY OF MUSICAL TERMS

A-ak—Traditional Korean orchestral music, used for Confucian rituals.

Alap—The unmetered introduction to a North Indian improvisation in which the musician gradually reveals the characteristics of the melodic structure or mode (*raga*).

Alberti bass—A conventional accompaniment pattern in late eighteenth-century music in which the notes of the chord are played in succession.

Anhemitonic—A term adopted by ethnomusicologists to refer to scales in which each scale step is greater than a semitone, as in the pentatonic scales of China, for example. Harrison sometimes preferred the Indonesian term *slendro*.

Aria—A lyrical solo song in an opera, oratorio, or similar form.

Atonality—Atonal music defies the listener's ability to identify a particular pitch as the tonic; often associated with dissonance and the musical avant-garde of the twentieth century. Composers have sometimes, though not necessarily, achieved this effect through the use of Schoenberg's twelve-tone method.

Augmentation—A technique in which the durations in an established rhythm are lengthened by a fixed factor; for example, by doubling.

Aulos—A double-reed (oboe-like) instrument used in ancient Greece, sometimes mistranslated as "flute."

Balungan—The core melody in a Javanese gamelan composition, played by the *saron* family and *slentem* instruments.

Banghyang—A Korean instrument consisting of a set of tuned metal slabs, used in Confucian ritual orchestras.

Barcarolle—A Venetian gondolier's song.

Bar line—A vertical line in music notation used to demarcate measures, usually of a consistent length of beats in the meter.

Baroque—A period of European arts; in music, the dates are conventionally given as 1600–1750. Associated with such composers as J. S. Bach and G. F. Handel.

Bell lyra—A very high and bright metallophone, essentially the same as a glockenspiel but mounted on a lyre-shaped frame so that it can be carried in a marching band.

Bianyin—Pitches outside the main tones of the traditional Chinese scale that are occasionally inserted into melodies.

Binary form—A structure of a musical piece that consists of two optionally repeated halves, a common form in baroque dances.

Bonang—A Javanese gamelan instrument that consists of two rows of small bronze gongs set horizontally on cords in a wooden rack. The upper-octave version is the *bonang panerus* and the lower-octave version the *bonang barung*. Both usually play simple elaboration patterns around the core melody.

Bubaran—A Javanese gamelan form that consists of sixteen beats per gong stroke and is usually in a loud style.

Bunraku—Japanese theater in which elaborate, lifelike puppets are accompanied by a dramatic narrator and samisen lute.

Canon—A musical form in which a melody combines with itself offset in time.

Cantata—A musical form that combines several vocal pieces, often with choir, with instrumental accompaniment and a single, unifying text.

Cantus firmus—A melody that is used as a foundation for a polyphonic composition when other melodies are added on top of it, a common technique in early polyphony (twelfth to sixteenth centuries).

Cengkok—A melodic formula used as the basis for improvised elaboration in Javanese gamelan.

Chaconne—A musical form with a repeating bass line or harmonic structure, usually associated with the baroque period in European music.

Chance music—Music in which some elements are deliberately random, an innovation developed by John Cage in the early 1950s.

Cheng—See *Zheng*.

Chromaticism—The widespread use of tones outside those of the nominal key, often associated with late Romanticism and expressionism.

Cipher notation—Also known as *kepatihan*, a system of notating melodies with Arabic numbers used in Javanese gamelan music.

Clavichord—A small, quiet keyboard instrument of the European baroque period in which metal tines hit the strings.

Cluster or tone cluster—A sonority in which adjacent notes in a scale are played together, for example by simultaneously pressing down a range of keys on the piano.

Colotomic form—A cyclic musical form in which different divisions of the cycle are demarcated by musical events, usually gong strokes in gamelan music.

Concerto grosso—A musical form of the European baroque period in which a soloist or small group of instruments alternates with a larger orchestra, often with a returning theme.

Conductus—A sacred vocal form of the twelfth and thirteenth centuries, sometimes for a single voice but better known as a form of early polyphony.

Consort—A name for a musical chamber ensemble in the sixteenth and seventeenth centuries, often but not necessarily of instruments of the same family.

Counterpoint—The compositional art of combining melodies, often so that the melodies retain independence and interest while combining into desired harmonies.

Dada—A European art movement, most active between 1915 and 1930, that emphasized provocation, nonsense, and humor, often to protest artistic egotism and reflect the insanity of society.

Daegeum—A very large bamboo flute used in Korean traditional music ("taegum" in the old spelling used by Harrison).

Daff—A circular Arabic frame drum often used to accompany singing and Islamic chant.

Daiko—A large, cylindrical Japanese drum.

Dalang—The puppeteer and storyteller who performs an Indonesian *wayang* shadow puppet play.

Degung—A small set of gamelan instruments from West Java.

Demung—A thick-keyed metallophone in the lower octave of the *saron* family in the Javanese gamelan.

Diatonic—A set of pitches that form the pattern of steps found, for example, on the white keys of the piano keyboard. Various diatonic scales, such as major and minor, can be derived by choosing different pitches within the set as the tonic.

Diminution—A technique in which the durations in an established rhythm are shortened by a fixed factor.

Dissonant counterpoint—A technique in which melodies are combined to produce dissonant harmonies. First named and described by Charles Seeger, but associated with other American modernists, especially in the period between the world wars.

Ditone tuning—A tuning system derived by the successive multiplication of 3:2 ratios of the perfect fifth, also known as Pythagorean tuning. This system creates 9:8 ratio whole tones and major thirds that are two whole tones (81:64), from which the term "ditone" comes.

Dodecaphony—Another term for the twelve-tone method of composition invented by Arnold Schoenberg.

Drone—A very long unchanging pitch.

Ductia—A fourteenth-century European dance form with a series of melodies in couplet form, one ending in an unresolved cadence (open) and the other resolved (closed). It thus resembles the estampie, but Harrison used the term "estampie" or "stampede" for a quick triple-meter dance and "ductia" for similar dances in other meters.

Electronic music—In the 1950s through the 1970s, this term specifically referred to music that included analog synthesizers or manipulation of magnetic tape.

Elephant bells—Bells from India, generally made of brass and a few inches tall, consisting of a hemispherical top above inward-curving tines, or a "claw."

Equal temperament—A tuning in which the divisions of an octave are precisely equal. In order to achieve this equality, the intervals must deviate somewhat from integer ratios of frequencies (except for the octave and multiple octaves). Twelve-tone equal temperament was generally adopted as the standard tuning for pianos by the beginning of the nineteenth century, allowing ease of modulation and combinations of instruments.

Erhu—A two-string bowed instrument used in traditional Chinese music.

Estampie—A medieval dance form in a quick triple meter, with a series of melodies in couplet form, one ending in an unresolved cadence (*overt* or open) and the other resolved (*clos* or closed).

Ethnomusicology—A branch of music scholarship that studies music in culture. During much of the twentieth century, it was synonymous with the study of music of non-Western cultures.

Expressionism—An arts movement in the late nineteenth and early twentieth centuries that emphasized intensity of emotion, the role of the Freudian subconscious, subjectivity, and often the dark side of the human mind. In music, it is associated with dissonance, the rise of atonality, and composers such as Schoenberg and Richard Strauss.

Fipple flute—A wind instrument (such as a recorder) in which the stream of air is directed through a duct to a sharp edge, known as a fipple.

Fret—A construction raised above the fingerboard of a string instrument so that the player can press down behind it and shorten the vibrating length of the string to that point.

Fugue—A musical form, mostly associated with the European baroque period, in which a short theme is treated in polyphonic imitation.

Futurism—A European art movement, active from about 1909 to the 1920s, that emphasized love of technology, speed, dynamism, and modernist revolution.

Gagaku—An ancient Japanese orchestra known for extremely slow and refined repertories.

Gambang—A soft-sounding wooden xylophone used in the Javanese gamelan.

Gamelan—An Indonesian orchestra mostly characterized by its gongs and metallophones but which can also include bamboo flutes, drums, zithers, and a wooden xylophone. It is the most famous representative of the classical music tradition of the islands of Java and Bali.

Gangsaran—A form of gamelan music, often used as an introduction, that features a loud, repeating single pitch.

Gatra—A musical phrase in Javanese gamelan music, usually four beats of the *balungan*. It has therefore been compared to a Western measure.

Gayageum—A Korean zither consisting of twelve strings stretched over inverted-V bridges on a curved board, related to the Chinese *zheng* and Japanese koto. Harrison used the old spelling "kayagum."

Gendèr—A quiet Indonesian metallophone with thin bronze keys and individual tube resonators, played with a two-hand technique.

Gending—Generally, the Javanese name for a gamelan composition; more specifically, an expansive Javanese form of more than thirty-two beats per gong. Harrison used the term in a general sense to refer to his pieces that were not in another standard Javanese form.

Genus (pl. genera)—A way of categorizing tetrachords (four-note scales in the range of a perfect fourth) in ancient Greece. The diatonic genus divides the fourth into two tones and one semitone. The chromatic genus divides the fourth into two semitones and a minor third. The enharmonic genus divides the fourth into two quartertones and a major third. The precise tuning of each of these divisions may vary.

Gerong—A small chorus of singers (traditionally male) in the Javanese gamelan.

Gigue—A dance of the European baroque period in a quick compound meter (where the beats are divided into threes).

Gong or gong ageng—The largest of the Indonesian hanging gongs, used to demarcate the longest cyclic structures in gamelan music.

Gongan—A section of a gamelan composition defined by the period between gong strokes.

Gregorian chant—A category of medieval European Christian chant adopted and standardized by the Roman Catholic Church. Gregorian chants are single-line, diatonic melodies and traditionally are sung in a free meter by a chorus of men.

Ground bass—A repeating melody in the bass line, used to underpin European forms such as the chaconne.

Guqin—See *Qin*.

Haisho—An ancient Japanese pan flute.

Harmonic—A sine wave component of a complex sound wave whose frequency is an integer multiple of the lowest pitch (the "fundamental"). The sounds of string and wind instruments consist nearly entirely of harmonics. We usually don't perceive these sine waves individually; they instead blend to form the characteristic timbre of the instrument. We associate the pitch played with the fundamental.

Harmonic series—The mathematical pattern of wavelengths of sine wave components produced by wind and string instruments: 1, 1/2, 1/3, 1/4, and so on, relative to the longest (fundamental) wavelength.

Harmonium—A small reed organ from Europe but also used in South Asia.

Heterophony—A musical texture in which more than one instrument play together the same basic melody, but with different variations and ornamentation. Also known as "simultaneous variation" texture.

Hexachord—A set of six pitches, a construction sometimes important in twelve-tone music.

Hexatonic—A mode, scale, or tuning system with six pitches per octave.

Hichiriki—A small, loud double-reed instrument used in the Japanese *gagaku* orchestra.

Hun—A Korean ceramic globular flute (ocarina).

Ictus—An attack or beginning of a note.

Imbal—A technique of interlocking two instrumental parts, used in Javanese gamelan.

Impressionism—In music, a style associated with French composer Claude Debussy in the late nineteenth and early twentieth centuries that emphasized instrumental colors, lack of pronounced rhythm, ambiguous harmonies, and diaphanous textures.

Interval—The distance in pitch between two tones.

Interval controls—Harrison's technique in which he would limit the intervals between successive melodic notes to a certain set of preselected intervals. The technique could therefore unify a melody without a reference to a tonal center and offer more choices at each juncture than the twelve-tone method.

Inversion—The inversion of an interval is found by raising the lower pitch of the interval by an octave. For example, the inversion of a perfect fifth is a perfect fourth, and the inversion of a major third is a minor sixth. Inverted intervals are often treated as functionally identical to the non-inverted versions.

Irama—In Javanese gamelan practice, the level of rhythmic density relative to the beat, or the ratio of the most frequent notes to the least frequent.

Jaltarang—An instrument from India consisting of a set of tuned ceramic bowls played with light sticks.

Janggu—A large hourglass-shaped drum used in Korean traditional music, spelled "changgo" by Harrison.

Jarabe—A Mexican folk dance that features an alternation between compound duple and simple triple meters.

Jhala—A technique found in classical Indian performance, usually on plucked strings, in which a player will interpolate a drone pitch between the notes of a fast melody.

Jinghu—A small, bowed string instrument from China, especially associated with Beijing opera.

Just intonation—A method of tuning in which intervals are related by relatively small integer ratios.

Kabuki—A classical Japanese theater form, originating in the eighteenth century, that features singing with multiple musical ensembles, stage spectacle, and expressive acting.

Kembangan—The process of extrapolating more elaborate melodies from a basic melody in Javanese gamelan practice—literally, the "blooming" of a melody.

Kempul—A medium-size hanging gong in the Javanese gamelan.

Kempyung—An interval that spans four notes of an Indonesian scale. Harrison saw parallels between its use and the use of the perfect fifth in Western music, although *kempyung* vary in size from about a tritone to a sixth.

Kenong—A tall gong suspended horizontally in the Javanese gamelan.

Kepatihan—Also known as cipher notation, a system of notating melodies with Arabic numbers used in Javanese gamelan music.

Ketawang—A form of Javanese gamelan music with sixteen beats per gong and eight beats per *kenong*.

Ketuk—A small horizontal gong in Javanese gamelan music.

Kit—Harrison's term for a collection of melodies and rhythms that can be combined in different ways at any given performance, an innovation of Henry Cowell.

Koto—A Japanese zither consisting of thirteen strings stretched over inverted-V bridges on a curved board, related to the Chinese *zheng* and Korean *gayageum*.

Kulintang—An ensemble of gongs from the Philippines.

Ladrang—A form of Javanese gamelan music with thirty-two beats per gong.

Lagu—The "inner melody" or conceptual tune behind a Javanese gamelan composition, not heard directly but represented in a skeletal form by the *balungan*.

Lancaran—A form of Javanese gamelan music with eight beats per gong, sometimes used as an introduction to a larger piece.

Limit—In just intonation, the largest prime factor in the interval ratios. For example, ditone or Pythagorean tuning consists of all combinations of 3:2 and therefore is a three-limit tuning. Renaissance-era just intonation specifies thirds of 5:4 and 6:5 in addition to the 3:2 fifths and so is a five-limit tuning.

Locrian mode—A diatonic mode whose scale can be found by playing on the white keys of the piano from B to B. It is an unusual mode because the scale does not include a perfect fifth above the tonic.

Lute—A term originally referring to the Renaissance-era European plucked string instrument but which is used as a general category of string instruments in which the strings are stretched over a neck with a resonator at one end, such as the guitar or violin.

Mbira—A Zimbabwean instrument of plucked metal tines. Similar instruments with other names are found in many African countries and in Cuba.

Metallophone—A musical instrument consisting of a set of metal bars, rods, or tubes, often mounted above resonators.

Metric modulation—A compositional technique where subdivisions of one beat become different subdivisions of the beat in a subsequent section, resulting in a change in tempo.

Microtonality—Originally music based on tuning systems with step sizes smaller than a semitone, but the term is often used now to refer to music in any tuning system aside from twelve-tone equal temperament.

Minimalism—In music, a movement originating in the 1960s that emphasized very gradual change, repetition, audible processes, radical tonality, and often a steady, constant beat. It is especially associated with American composers Terry Riley, Steve Reich, Philip Glass, and La Monte Young.

Minor pentatonic—The anhemitonic mode that features a minor third between scale degrees one and two. On the black keys of the piano, this mode can be found beginning on the pitch E♭.

Mode—A melodic framework in tonal music that includes at least a set of pitches and a tonic within that set, often represented as a scale. Thus there are seven traditional diatonic modes (one for each possible tonic within the seven-tone diatonic set). However, such frameworks in non-Western cultures can include characteristic motives, ornamentation, and ranges.

Monochord—A zither string instrument used to measure off string lengths in order to find precise pitches for tuning other instruments.

Monophony—A musical texture that consists of only a single melody.

Motive—A recognizable melodic fragment repeated or varied.

Musette—A French baroque dance that imitates a bagpipe.

Neoclassicism—A mid-twentieth-century compositional style in which composers applied modern techniques to old, often eighteenth-century, forms. The style is associated with Stravinsky (post-1920), Hindemith, and many tonal American composers.

Noh—A Japanese dramatic form that includes four musicians and a few masked performers, often in dreamlike, stylized, and Zen-influenced stories.

Octatonic scale—A tonally ambiguous scale created from an alternation of semitones and whole tones, resulting in eight tones per octave. Often associated with early twentieth-century Russian and French composers but used elsewhere too.

Octaval counterpoint—Harrison's name for counterpoint that admits only octaves at places of rest or stability.

Octave—The fundamental interval of music created by a 2:1 ratio of frequencies and represented by the eighth note in a diatonic scale.

Oratorio—A large-scale composition for choir, solo singers, and instruments in multiple movements.

Orchestration—The art of combining instrumental timbres in a composition.

Ostinato—A constantly repeated motive.

Padang-ulihan—The Javanese term for a compositional principle of pairing sections so that the second provides resolution for the first, also called *ding-dong* or "question-answer."

Pak—(1) A Korean instrument that consists of several small wooden slats tied together and that can be brought together suddenly to create a sharp percussive sound. (2) A shortened form of *Bapak*, an Indonesian title for a respected man.

Parlando—Italian term for a rhythm that is free or in imitation of prose speech.

Passacaglia—A baroque form consisting of variations over a repeating bass or harmonic structure.

Pastorale—A European musical form that evokes the countryside.

Patet—Javanese term for a melodic framework or mode, characterized by distinctive motives and certain melodically emphasized tones within the set of pitches.

Pedal tone—A long bass note, so called because it was often played by organ pedals.

Pelog—A seven-tone tuning system in Indonesia.

Pentatonic—A mode, scale, or tuning system with five pitches per octave.

Perfect fifth—The interval that consists of seven semitones; in just intonation, the ratio of 3:2 between the two frequencies. It is a fundamental musical interval in many musical systems around the world.

Pesinden—A female singer in the Javanese gamelan.

Pipa—A Chinese lute-type instrument with four strings and a dry timbre.

Pipilan—A Javanese technique of elaborating a melody by alternating between pairs of melody notes.

Piri—A small, cylindrical double-reed wind instrument from Korea.

Pizzicato—An indication to pluck rather than bow a string instrument.

Polymetric—Describes the simultaneous use of multiple meters or time signatures.

Polyphony—A musical texture with multiple melodies of more or less equal focus at the same time.

Polyrhythm—Multiple simultaneous meters or starting points within meters.

Polytonality—Music with multiple simultaneous tonics or keys.

Préludes non-mèsuré—A rhapsodic form without bar lines or meters, associated with French harpsichord composers in the period of about 1650–1750.

Prepared piano—A piano that has been altered by the insertion of objects into the strings or hammers, invented and named by John Cage in the 1940s.

Prime pentatonic—Harrison's name for the pentatonic mode that is represented by pitches 1, 2, 3, 5, and 6 of the diatonic major scale, or by the black keys on a piano beginning on F♯.

Psaltery—A medieval European zither. Harrison adopted this term to refer to zithers from other regions in the world.

Pythagorean tuning—See Ditone tuning.

Qin—An ancient Chinese seven-string zither with no intermediate bridges, also known as the *guqin*.

Quadrille—A nineteenth-century European ballroom dance in duple meter.

Quartertone—A very small interval, half the size of the interval between two adjacent keys on the piano.

Quijada—A South American percussion instrument that consists of the jawbone and teeth of a donkey.

Quintal counterpoint—Harrison's term for counterpoint in which perfect fourths, perfect fifths, and octaves may serve as points of rest or resolution, but not thirds or sixths.

Raga—The melodic framework for classical music of India, which includes concepts of a scale (different in ascending and descending forms), characteristic motives and ornamentation, stressed pitches, and extramusical associations such as times of day and poetic symbols.

Rasa—South Asian term for "flavor" or the emotional connotations of a particular *raga* or other aesthetic style or performance.

Recitative—A song with prose text in free meter, usually used in operas or oratorios.

Retrograde—A transformation of a melody or tone row so that it is backward.

Ricercare—A seventeenth-century form of imitative polyphony.

Romanticism—A broad term for a mostly nineteenth-century aesthetic style that emphasized individual emotional expression.

Rondeau—A baroque form in which a central melody returns multiple times.

Rondo—A musical form in which a theme returns multiple times, with other varied themes in between. Similar to the baroque rondeau but generally of a larger scale.

Row—In the twelve-tone method of composing, a predetermined ordering of the twelve pitches within an octave, such that each pitch appears exactly once. Later, serial composers generalized this concept to use rows of different numbers or compositional resources, such as dynamics.

Sangen—Another name for the *shamisen*, a Japanese long-neck lute-type instrument.

Saraband—A baroque dance form in a slow triple meter.

Saron—A thick-key metallophone in the Javanese gamelan; also the name for the family of such instruments tuned to different octaves.

Scherzo—In the baroque period, a lively duple meter dance. In the classical and Romantic periods, a sectional piece in a very quick triple meter.

Secundal counterpoint—Harrison's name for counterpoint in which seconds and sevenths are used at points of rest or resolution, similar to dissonant counterpoint.

Semitone—A small interval, represented by two adjacent keys on a piano.

Serialism—A generalization of Schoenberg's twelve-tone method associated with avant-garde atonal composers of the 1950s through the 1970s.

Set—Harrison's term (borrowed from Ives) for a suite or collection of relatively short movements.

Shakuhachi—A Japanese bamboo flute.

Shamisen—See *sangen*.

Sheng—A Chinese reed instrument with multiple pipes, also known as a mouth organ.

Sho—A Japanese version of the Chinese *sheng* reed instrument, used to create a background of sustained chords in *gagaku*.

Slendro—An Indonesian pentatonic tuning system in which the intervals between scale steps are roughly equal.

Slentem—A low, thin-keyed metallophone of the Javanese gamelan.

Sonata—In the Renaissance period, an instrumental piece. In the baroque, a composition in binary form. After the baroque period, a multi-movement extended instrumental composition.

Suite—An instrumental composition consisting of multiple, relatively short movements. In the baroque period, these movements would often take the form of stylized dances.

Suling—An Indonesian bamboo flute.

Superparticular—A ratio in the form of $(n+1):n$, such as 3:2, 4:3, or 5:4. Just-intonation intervals are often in this form, which the ancient theorist Claudius Ptolemy considered optimum.

Tack piano—A piano in which thumbtacks have been inserted into the felt hammers to create a bright, brittle timbre on the piano.

Tala—A cyclic rhythmic structure or meter in classical music from India.

Tam-tam—A large, unpitched Chinese gong, often used in Western orchestras.

Taqsim—An unmetered exploration of a mode by an instrumental performer in classical Arabic or Turkish music, similar to the Indian *alap*.

Taryung—A Korean folk-song form.

Tayu—The dramatic storyteller and singer in Japanese Bunraku and Kabuki.

Temperament—A tuning system in which intervals have been compromised from the rational proportions of just intonation to form irrational relationships.

Tertial counterpoint—Harrison's term for counterpoint in which intervals of thirds and sixths, in addition to perfect fifths and octaves, are used as points of rest or resolution. This is the conventional style of counterpoint used in European music.

Tetrachord—A group of four pitches that span a perfect fourth. The ancient Greeks used this structure as the basis for their musical scale system.

Texture—The musical characteristic that describes the relative roles and distributions of melodies.

Threnody—A lament or song of mourning.

Timbre—The characteristic of sound that distinguishes different instrumental tone colors, even though they may be playing the same pitch at the same loudness.

Transposition—Transforming a melody by moving all the pitches up or down by a fixed interval or number of scale steps.

Tremolo—A rapid fluctuation in loudness in a musical tone. On plucked string instruments, it is achieved by rapidly strumming a string.

Triad—A collection of three pitches, in which, when reduced by octaves to lie closest to one another, the second pitch is a third higher than the lowest (or root) pitch, and the third pitch is a fifth higher than the root. Triads have been the basis for European harmony since at least the sixteenth century.

Tungso—A large Korean bamboo flute, similar to the Chinese *xiao* and the Japanese *shakuhachi*.

Tuning system—The method by which musicians decide what precise pitches will be represented on instruments or in a musical system.

Tutti—An Italian term meaning that everyone plays.

Twelve-tone method—Schoenberg's system for composing using a row, or predetermined ordering of all twelve pitches within the octave. In twelve-tone compositions, all pitches must appear in this order or in the order of various transformations of the row, such as transpositions, inversion, or retrograde.

Usul—A cyclic rhythmic pattern that is the basis for metered classical compositions in Turkey.

Viol—A family of European bowed string instruments that, unlike the violin family, have frets and six strings.

Viola da gamba—The larger member of the viol family, played vertically between the legs somewhat like a cello.

Virginal—A small harpsichord in which the strings are positioned laterally, popular in the early seventeenth century.

Wayang kulit—The classic Indonesian shadow-puppet theater.

Xiao—A large Chinese bamboo flute.

Xun—A Chinese ceramic globular flute (ocarina).

Yangqin—A Chinese dulcimer or trapezoidal zither played with small wooden mallets.

Yazheng—A bowed Chinese zither, spelled "yacheng" by Harrison.

Yueqin—A Chinese lute-type instrument with a large round resonator.

Zheng—A large Chinese zither with intermediate bridges under each string. Harrison often spelled it "cheng" or referred to it as a "psaltery."

Zither—A string instrument in which the strings are stretched over a board or box resonator.

APPENDIX B: LIST OF HARRISON'S COMPOSITIONS

The standard catalogue of Harrison's compositions is in Miller and Lieberman, *Lou Harrison: Composing a World*, which we designate ML here. ML includes separate numbering for Harrison's numerous minor compositions in the periods 1934–1936 (numbered 35.1 through 35.43) and 1936–1940 (numbered 90.1 through 90.24). Harrison frequently completed, revised, or created new versions of pieces, sometimes decades after he began them. ML usually lists revised pieces once and orders them according to the completion of the last version. We have sometimes listed works both at the time of original composition (corresponding to this book's narrative) and at the time of revision or completion. A few pieces, references to pieces, or other details have been discovered since ML's publication, and we have included new pieces without corresponding ML numbers. Otherwise this list depends on ML, which should be consulted for further details.

1: 1927 *Elegie* for piano

2: Nov. 11, 1931 *Sonatina in G minor* for piano

3: Jan. 25, 1932 *Sonata no. 1 in C* for piano

4: May 6, 1932 *Sonatina no. IV in A Major* for piano

5: May 1932 *Organ Sonata no. 1* for organ

6: May 14, 1932 *Pianoforte Sonata no. 7* for piano

7: May 23, 1932 *Prelude in C no. 2* for piano

8: May 30, 1932 *Sonata for Piano* for piano

9: 1932 *Psalm Sonata no. IV* for piano

10: 1934 *Blue Glass* for flute and piano—lost

11: 1934 *Detail of Adoration of the Lamb* for fiddles, harmonium, and harp—incomplete

12.1: c. 1933–1934 *Allegro* for violins and cello—incomplete

12.2: c. 1933–1934 *Variations* for violin and piano

13: 1935 *American Pastoral with Byzantine Furnishings* for piano

14: 1935 *The Censor Swingers* for piano

15: 1935 *The Geography of Heaven* for four violins, two violas, two cellos, two basses, and organ ad lib—in quartertones

16: 1935 *Movement* for two horns, strings, and piano

17: 1935 *Music for Handel in Heaven* for violin and viola

18: 1935 *Sonata* for string quartet

19: 1935 *Sonata 4th* for reed organ and piano

20: 1935 *Song* for tenor, violin, and piano

21: 1935 or early 1936 *Waterfront 1934* for percussion

22: Mar. 1936 *Sonata #1* for piano—3 mvts.: "Ostinato," "Discussion," "Jubilation"

23: 1936 *Hill-Rise* for piano

24: Apr. 1936 *Midnoon* for harp and strings

25: Apr. 1936 *Song* for tenor, two pianos, and string quartet

26: May 1936 *Project no. 2* for piano

27: Aug. 7, 1936 *Fugue for String Foursome* for string quartet

28: Sept. 4, 1936 *Double Fugue* for unspecified instruments—rev. and used as mvt. 3 of *Suite for Symphonic Strings* (1960 ML 173)

29: Sept. 5, 1936 *Ground in E minor* for piano—reused in *Summerfield Set* (1987 ML 274)

30: Nov.–Dec. 1936 *Suite* for string quartet

31: Dec. 4, 1936 *Sonata for Unaccompanied Violin* for violin—ed. by Gary Beswick, 1963

32: Dec. 23, 1936 *(untitled)* for orchestra—incomplete; for John Dobson

33: 1936 *Overture for a Tragic, Heroic Drama* for orchestra

34: 1936 *Sonata for Edward MacDowell* for flute and organ or strings—only mvt. 2 extant

35.1: c. 1934–1936 *Adagio* for flute, harmonium, strings, and piano—only mvt. 2 extant

35.2: c. 1934–1936 *Adagio* for flute, two mandolins, guitar, and cello

35.3: c. 1934–1936 *Adagio* for piano

35.4: c. 1934–1936 *Allegro Maestoso* for piano—incomplete

35.5: c. 1934–1936 *Antiphon* for piano

35.6: c. 1934–1936 *Aubade for Gabriel* for chorus, strings, and percussion

35.7: c. 1934–1936 *Autumn* for piano and strings

35.8: c. 1934–1936 *Choral* for organ

35.9: 1934–1936 *Choral preludes* for clavichord

35.10: 1935–1936 *Concerto* for piano and string quartet—incomplete

35.11: c. 1934–1936 *Dance* for two pianos—three mvts.

35.12: c. 1934–1936 *Dance for a Little Girl* for piano

35.13: c. 1934–1936 *Discussion* for strings

35.14: c. 1934–1936 *Feelingly* for piano

35.15: c. 1934–1936 *Fore-Piece to St. George; or, After the Dragon* for orchestra

35.16: c. 1934–1936 *Gothic Piece* for harpsichord

35.17: c. 1934–1936 *Mass* for chorus and two pianos—only two mvts. complete

35.18: c. 1934–1936 *Minuet* for piano

35.19: c. 1934–1936 *Moderato Espressif* for strings and organ

35.20: c. 1934–1936 *Moderato Espressivo* for piano

35.21: c. 1934–1936 *Pastoral and Minuet* for piano

35.22: 1935–1936 *Pavan* for two recorders and bass viol

35.23: c. 1934–1936 *Piece for Cello: Green Trees in a Field*

35.24: c. 1934–1936 *Piece for Two Players at One Piano*

35.25: c. 1934–1936 *Prelude for an Organ Toccata*

35.26: c. 1934–1936 *Rondeau* for piano

35.27: c. 1934–1936 *Rondeau for Pianoforte*

35.28: c. 1934–1936 *Serenade* for flute, violin, and guitar

35.29: c. 1934–1936 *A Small Fugue to Be Crooned* for piano

35.30: c. 1935–1936 *Song: Pastoral Night Piece, or, a Request* for fiddles and male voice

35.31: c. 1935–1937 *Song* for low voice, flute, clarinet, horn, and strings—for John Dobson

35.32: c. 1934–1936 *Song* for string quartet, piano, and other unidentified instr.—two mvts., second incomplete

35.33: c. 1934–1936 *Three Songs from the Geography of the Soul* for voice, piano, string quartet, and harmonium—"Excursion in Other Landscapes," "Unity in Strength," "A Little Girl Walked"

35.34: c. 1935–1937 *Two Pieces for John Dobson* for piano, piccolo, trumpet, harmonium, and cello—"Apples" and "Slowish"

35.35: c. 1934–1936 *Untitled* for flute, clarinet, cornet, trombone, two violins, viola, and cello

35.36: c. 1935–1936 *Untitled* for flute and harmonium—four mvts.

35.37: c. 1934–1936 *Slowish and Serene* for violin and piano

35.38: c. 1934–1936 *Untitled* for piano, trumpet, and drums

35.39: c. 1934–1936 *Untitled* for flute, viola, and cello

35.40: c. 1934–1936 *Untitled* for string quartet and four percussionists

35.41: c. 1934–1936 *Very Fast* for piano

35.42: c. 1934–1936 *We Are Always Winter* for speaking chorus and three percussionists

35.43: c. 1934–1936 *A Whatnot* for harpsichord, violins, flutes, and guitars

36: Dec. 1936–Jan. 1937 *Overture* for flute, clarinet, bassoon. violin, viola, and cello

37: Jan. 8, 1937 *Overture* for piano or orchestra

38: Jan. 15, 1937 *Largo Ostinato* for piano—rev. 1970; rev. and orchestrated as *Third Symphony* mvt. 3 (1982 ML 243); for John Dobson

39: Jan. 23, 1937 *Last Music* for alto or baritone, flute, clarinet, harp, strings, and organ ad lib.

40: Jan. 1937 *Fugue* for orchestra or piano

41: Feb. 10, 1937 *Slow (Symphony for Organ)* for organ

42: Feb. 23, 1937 *Simfony for Organ*

43: Feb. 27, 1937 *A Bit of Rotten Chopin on Order of J. Cleghorn* for piano

44: 1937 *Changing World* for two pianos, percussion, recorder, and voice

45: May 24, 1937 *Saraband* for piano—publ. in *New Music Quarterly* July 1938

46: May 25, 1937 *Saraband* for piano

47: June 11, 1937 *Symphony #1* for orchestra—only one movement complete

48: June 16, 1937 *France 1917—Spain 1937* for string quartet and two percussionists—rev. 1968 with subtitle "About the Spanish War" and referred to as a "Peace Piece"

49: June 17, 1937 *Allegro Moderato* for strings—part used in 1968 revision of *France 1917–Spain 1937*

50: July 1937 *3 Runes for Strings* for string orchestra—only first mvt. "Oracle" survives

51: Sept. 1937 *Winter's Tale* for two violins, viola, cello, flute, trumpet, and percussion

52: Sept. 12, 1937 *Ritual #2: Dance* for harp

53: Sept. 13, 1937 *Ritual #3* for flute, clarinet, and piano

54: Sept. 13, 1937 *Ritual #4* for flute, clarinet, and bassoon

55: Sept. 14, 1937 *Ritual #5* for violin and piano—incomplete

56: Sept. 16, 1937 *Prelude for Grandpiano* for piano—for Henry Cowell

57: Sept. 20, 1937 *Piece for Pianokeys* for piano

58: Sept. 21, 1937 *Ritual #6* for organ or piano or flute and piano

59: Oct. 5, 1937 *Pieces* for harpsichord or piano—only first mvt. survives

60: 1937 *Passacaglia* for piano—also titled *Consort 5* and *Ritual #8*, rev. as *Canticle #2*, mvt. 1 (1942); rev. again for *First Suite for Strings*, mvt. 3 (1948 ML 135)

61: 1937 *Ritual #7* for unspecified instruments

61a: 1937 *Three Dances of Conflict* for piano—for Carol Beals

62: 1937 *Threnody and Chaconne* for violin

63: 1937 *Piano sonata #2 [ms. untitled]* for solo piano—two twelve-tone mvts.: Moderato, Largo

64: Jan. 3, 1938 *Concerto Grosso* for oboe, English horn, bassoon, and strings

c. 1938 *A Clear Midnight* for chorus—unfinished; text by Walt Whitman

c. 1938 *Beforepiece to the Medea* for horn, soprano, and four percussionists—presumably incidental music for Greek drama at Mills College

c. 1938 *Tenth Ritual* for piano, four hands

c. 1938 *Recitative and Chorale*

65: Spring 1938 *Electra* for flute, harp, violins, cello, cornet, and piano

66: Spring 1938 *Tribunal* for piano, four hands

1938 *Dance for Lisa Karon* for piano

67: 1938 *Conquest* for flute or ocarina or recorder, piano, conch shell, and percussion

68: Nov. 1938 *Rondo* for violin

69: 1938 *Third Sonata* for piano

Dec. 1938 *Chorale*—lost, mentioned in a review of the Dec. 1938 Mills dance recital

70: Feb. 22–Mar. 8, 1939 *Fifth Simfony* for four percussionists—for Sherman Slayback; ed. Dec. 3, 1970

71: Mar. 29, 1939 *Counterdance in the Spring* for three percussionists—later formed second movement of *Tributes to Charon* (1982 ML 241)

72: Apr. 12, 1939 *Fourth Violin Concerto* for violin and percussion—for Marian Van Tuyl

73: Apr. 15, 1939 *First Concerto for Flute and Percussion* for flute and two percussionists

74: May 2, 1939 *Uneasy Rapture* for piano and percussion—lost dance for Marian Van Tuyl

75: Apr. 28–May 2, 1939 *Usonian Set* for piano—mvts. are "Reel," "Rangesong," and "Jig"

76: May 11, 1939 *Canon: Langorously Latin* for piano

77: May 15, 1939 *Bomba* for five percussionists

78: May 26, 1939 *The Trojan Women* for flute, clarinet, piano, harp, and strings—three mvts.: "Prelude," "Ground," and "Chaconne." "Prelude" later arranged as *Overture* for orchestra, performed by Pierre Monteaux and the S. F. Symphony and broadcast June 13, 1940

79: 1939 *Reel, Homage to Henry Cowell* for piano

80: 1937 or 1940 *Choephore* for recorder and percussion—lost except for a recording of processional

81: Jan. 15, 1940 *Rune* for six percussionists—incomplete?

82: 1940 (before Apr.) *Goin' to Be a Party in the Sky (Skyparty)* for piano and strings

1940 *Lysistrata*—lost dance score for Lester Horton mentioned in a letter to Cowell

83: June 21, 1940 *Canticle #1* for five percussionists

84: Summer 1940 *Something to Please Everybody* for piano, flute, little organ, and percussion—partial score in Lester Horton archive

85: Summer 1940 *Sixteen to Twenty-Four* for piano and percussion—lost

86: 1940 *Omnipotent Chair* for violin and two percussionists

87: Oct. 28, 1940 *Pied Beauty* for baritone voice, trombone or cello, flute, and percussion

88: 1940 *Sanctus for Contralto* for piano and alto voice

89: 1940 *Labyrinth* for chamber orchestra

1940 *Air* for violin and unspecified percussion ostinato—rev. 1970s for violin, *gendèr*, and *yazheng* drone (ML 226)

c. 1941 *Concerto #5 for Violin* for violin and five percussionists—comp. in 1959 as *Concerto for Violin with Percussion Orchestra* (ML172)

90.1: late 1930s *Antipodes* for unspecified instr.

90.2: c. 1938 *Eumenides* for piano, harp, percussion, bassoon, and violin—incidental music for Greek drama at Mills College

90.3: c. 1936–1940 *Implicity for 5 Strings*

90.4: c. 1936–1940 *Minnesingers* for piano

90.5: c. 1936–1940 *Movement for String Foursome* for string quartet

90.6: c. 1936–1940 *Prelude* for cello and two percussionists

90.7: c. 1939 *Processionals* for piano—two mvts., possibly corresponding to *Two Dances of Commemoration—Parade—Procession*, mentioned in a review of the May 1939 Mills dance recital

90.8: May 1939 *Ecstatic Moment* for piano—for choreographer Ruth Anne Heisey

May 1939 *Little Social Satires*—lost, mentioned in a review of the May 1939 Mills dance recital

May 1939 *Sociable Meeting*—lost, mentioned in a review of the May 1939 Mills dance recital

May 1939 *Opening Dance* for piano—for choreographer Marian Van Tuyl

90.9: c. 1940 *Second Suite* for solo violin with opt. percussion ostinato—for Sherman Slayback

90.10: c. 1939–1940 *Second Usonian Set* for string quartet

90.11: 1936–1937 *Set of Fragments: Lovesong* for solo violin and muted strings

90.12: c. 1938–1940 *Song of Joy: "We Beat Upon Gold Gongs"* for piano and strings

90.13: 1936–1939 *Song Project #2* for voice and percussion

90.14: c. 1939–1940 *Suite* for solo violin with opt. percussion ostinato—for Mervin Leeds

90.15: c. 1938–1939 *Suite of Pieces for Martha Hill* for piano—three mvts.: "Prelude," "Saraband," and "March"

90.16: c. 1939 *Theme and Variations* for piano— possibly corresponds to Van Tuyl's dance *Theme and Variations on This Hectic Life* mentioned in a review from summer 1939

90.17: c. 1936–1940 *Tragic Pantomime* for orchestra

90.18: c. 1936–1940 *Untitled* for orchestra—mvts. 2, 3 extant

90.19: c. 1936–1940 *Andante* for piano and strings

90.20: c. 1936–1940 *Fastish* for two pianos—incomplete

90.21: 1937 or 1938 *Untitled* for piano—three mvts.

90.22: c. 1938 *Untitled* for violin and cello—two mvts.

90.23: c. 1936–1940 *Variations* for violin and piano

90.24: 1936–1938 *Viola Concerto* for viola and percussion

91: 1941 *Labyrinth #3* for eleven percussionists— later incorporated into *Orpheus* (1969 ML 202), mvts. 2, 3, 5, and 8

91a: Jan. 21, 1941 *Suite for Recorder and Lute* for alto recorder and lute

92: Feb. 6, 1941 *Song of Quetzalcoatl* for four percussionists

Feb. 26, 1941 *Jephtha's Daughter* for narrator and percussion—rev. Mar. 1963 (ML 183)

93: 1941 *Simfony #13* for four percussionists

94: Apr. 8–9, 1941 *Suite for Flute*

95: Apr. 1941 *Double Music* for four percussionists—collaboration with John Cage

95a: May 18, 1941 *Exposition of a Cause* for piano— for unknown choreographer

96: Aug. 1941 *Green Mansions* for piano (four hands), recorder, and percussion—choreographed by Letitia Innes, based on story by William Henry Hudson

97: Oct. 8, 1941 *King David's Lament for Jonathan* for tenor and piano—text from John Milton, incorporated into *Three Songs* (1985 ML 261)

98: Oct. 30, 1941 *May Rain* for voice, prepared piano, and tam-tam—text from Elsa Gidlow

99: 1937–1942 *Canticle #2* for string orchestra— two mvts.: "Rich and Singing" (rev. of 1937 *Passacaglia* ML 60) and "Ricercare on Bach's Name"

100: Feb. 1942 *Canticle #3* for five percussionists, incl. ocarina—slightly rev. 1989

101: 1942 *In Praise of Johnny Appleseed* for three percussionists

102: Feb.–June 1942 *Canticle #4* for chorus

103: June 2, 1942 *Suite for Percussion* for five percussionists

104: June 1942 *Canticle #5* for five percussionists— rev. as mvt. 1 of *Canticle and Round for Gerhard Samuel's Birthday* (1993 ML 291)

105: 1942 (before summer) *Fugue for Percussion* for four percussionists

106: Oct. 3, 1942 *Canticle #6* for flute and percussion—not the same piece as ML 109

107: Fall 1942 *The Beautiful People* for trumpet and piano

108: Sept.–Dec. 1942 *Music for the River Merchant's Wife* for piano

109: Sept.–Dec. 1942 *Canticle #6* for orchestra— mvt. 1 revised as mvt. 2 for *Elegiac Symphony*; mvt. 2 revised as mvt. 5 for *Elegiac Symphony* (1975 ML 211)

110: 1943 (before summer) *Gigue and Musette* for piano—incorporated into *Rhymes With Silver* (1996 ML 300)

111: May 1943 *Suite for Piano*

112: 1934–1943 *Six Sonatas for Cembalo*—slightly rev. 1982

113: 1943 *Serenade for Three Recorders* for soprano recorder, alto recorder, and tenor recorder

114: 1943–1944 *[Untitled symphony]* for orchestra—two sketched mvts.; incomplete?

115: Sept. 14, 1944 *Waltz in A* for piano—collected with ML 122 as part of *New York Waltzes* (1951 ML 151)

116: May–Nov. 17, 1944 *Schoenbergiana* for string quartet—original ms. is untitled; arranged in 1962 for wind sextet by Robert Hughes under this title

117: May–Nov. 17, 1944 *Serenade in C* for piano—arranged in 1962 by Robert Hughes for flute, oboe, clarinet, horn, and bassoon

118: c. 1944–1945 *Party Pieces* for piano—joint composition with John Cage, Virgil Thomson, Henry Cowell, Ben Weber, and Merton Brown; arranged by Robert Hughes in 1963 for flute, clarinet, horn, bassoon, and piano

119: c. 1944–1945 *A 12-Tone Morning After to Amuse Henry* for piano

120: Jan. 1945 *Alleluia* for chamber orchestra

121: Feb–May 16, 1945 *Motet for the Day of Ascension* for string septet and harp

122: Sept. 1, 1945 *Waltz in C* for piano—collected with ML 115 as part of *New York Waltzes* (1951 ML 151); for Edward McGowan

123: Dec. 6, 1945 *Triphony* for piano—arranged as *String Trio* (1946 ML 129); heavily rev. as mvt. 5 of *Suite for Symphonic Strings* (1960 ML 173)

124: Dec. 6, 1945 *Polka and Jarabe* for piano—for choreographer Jose Limón but unused

126: 1945–1946 *Sonata in D* for piano

127: Feb. 13, 1946 *Changing Moment* for piano—for choreographer Jean Erdman

128: May 14, 1946 *Ground* for two pianos—revision of ML 99

129: 1946 *String Trio* for vioin, viola, and cello—arrangement of *Triphony* (1945 ML 123)

130: 1946 *Fragment from Calamus* for alto or baritone and piano—orig. with string quartet; text by Walt Whitman, incorporated into *Three Songs* (1985 ML 261)

1943–1946 *Easter Cantata* for solo alto, chorus, two trumpets, two trombones, percussion, harp, and strings—largely composed in New York but completed in 1966 (ML 191) on commission from the Associated Students of Hartnell College

131: Jan. 1946–Jan. 15, 1947 *Praises for Michael the Archangel* for organ—rev. as mvt. 4 of *Elegiac Symphony* (1975 ML 211)

132: 1947 *Western Dance* for piano—arranged as *The Open Road* for piano, flute, bassoon,

trumpet, piano, violin, cello, and bass; choreography by Merce Cunningham

133: 1947 *Air (Air in G minor)* for tenor recorder—rev. for flute and drone in 1970

1947–1948 *Symphony on G* for orchestra—not completed until 1966 (ML 187)

134: Mar. 19, 1948 *Cupid and Psyche* for chamber orchestra—sketches only

135: 1946–1948 *First Suite for Strings* for string orchestra—mvt. 3 is revision of mvt. 1 of ML 99; extensively revised in 1995 as *New First Suite for Strings* (ML 296)

136: Sept. 1948 *Homage to Milhaud* for piano

137: 1948 *Suite #2 for Strings* for string orchestra

138: 1949 (before Jan. 23) *The Perilous Chapel* for flute, cello, percussion, and harp

139: Summer 1949 *The Marriage at the Eiffel Tower* for flute, clarinet, trumpet, violin, cello, double bass, piano, and percussion

139b: 1961 *Suite from "The Marriage at the Eiffel Tower"* for orchestra—arrangement of *The Marriage at the Eiffel Tower* (1949, ML 139)

140: Summer 1949 *The Only Jealousy of Emer* for celesta, piano, flute, cello, and bass; incidental music for play by W. B. Yeats

141: 1949 *Suite for Cello and Harp*

142: Nov. 8, 1949 *Little Suite for Piano*—three mvts.: "Pastorale," "Quadrille," and "Chorale"; for Remy Charlip

143: 1949–Jan. 22, 1950 *Solstice* for flute, oboe, trumpet, celesta, tack piano, two cellos, and bass

144: Summer 1950 *Almanac of the Seasons* for ensemble, singer, and narrator—lost; one mvt. rev. for *Suite for Symphonic Strings*, mvt. 8 (1960 ML 173)

145: Mar. 22, 1951 *Chorales for Spring* for piano—two mvts: "Adjustable Chorale" and "Chorale for Spring"; mvt. 2 later arranged as mvt. 2 of *Suite for Symphonic Strings* (1960 ML 173)

146: 1951 (before July 9) *Io and Prometheus* for piano—originally titled "Prometheus Bound"; arranged for chamber ensemble with vocal parts in 1985

147: July 31, 1951 *Portrait of Abby Shahn on Her Birthday* for piano

148: 1951 *A Glyph* for prepared piano and percussion

1951 *Holly and Ivy at a Quarrel Be* for voice and piano—rev. in 1962 as *Holly and Ivy: A Carol* (ML 180)

149: Aug. 1949–Oct. 1951 *Seven Pastorales* for flute, oboe, bassoon, harp, and strings

150: Oct. 22–23 1951 *Nocturne* for two violins and tack piano—arranged for strings in 1958–1959 under the title *Nokturno*; two mvts.; mvt. 1 arranged as mvt. 9 in *Suite for Symphonic Strings* (1960 ML 173)

151: 1951 *New York Waltzes* for piano—three mvts.: "Waltz in C" (1945 ML 122), "Hesitation Waltz" (c. fall 1951), and "Waltz in A" (1944 ML 115)

1951 (before May 25) *Songs in the Forest* for flute/piccolo, violin, vibraphone/marimba, and piano—for choreographer Donald McKayle; this version may be lost, but rev. in 1992 (ML 286)

152: 1949 comp. 1951 *Alma Redemtoris Mater* for baritone, violin, trombone, and tack piano

153: 1951 *Double Canon (to Carl Ruggles)* for piano—rev. as mvt. 2 for *Concerto for Organ with Percussion Orchestra* (1973 ML 207)

154: 1951 *Festival Dance* for two pianos—rev. 1996

155: 1951 *Group on a Row the Same* for keyboard, trombone, vibraphone, voice, and viola—unfinished; three mvts. each for different instruments; a fourth movement for bassoon was added in the 1960s

1951 *A Thought on the Anniversary of Katherine Litz and Charles Oscar* for piano

156: 1951 *Suite for Violin, Piano, and Small Orchestra* for violin, flute, oboe, tack piano, celesta, percussion, and strings

1951 *Happy Birthday, Garrick* for voice and piano—a brief offering to Julien Beck on the occasion of his son Garrick's second birthday

157: 1947, comp. 1952 *Fugue for David Tudor* for piano—rev. as mvt. seven of *Suite for Symphonic Strings* (1960 ML 173)

158: Feb. 12, 1952 *Serenade for Frank Wigglesworth* for guitar—arranged for harp in 1968; can also be played on harpsichord

159: Mar. 12, 1952 *Mass to St. Anthony* for chorus, trumpet, harp, and strings—choral melodies and some accompaniment originally written Sept. 1939; new version of two mvts. written in 2001 (ML 309)

160: Mar. 23, 1952 *A Little Gamelon for Katherine Litz to Teach By* for piano

161: Apr. 5, 1952 *Praises for the Beauty of Hummingbirds* for two violins, flute, celesta, and percussion

162: 1952 (before Apr. 23) *Praises for the Beauty of Hummingbirds and Hawks* for chamber orchestra

1952 (before May) *A Pleasant Place*—lost work choreographed by Louise Lippold

1952 *Old Times Tune* for string quartet and piano—rev. as *Old Times Tune for Merce Cunningham's 75th Birthday* (1993 ML 290)

c. 1952 *Adagio Grande* for tack piano?—incomplete

163: Aug. 1952–Apr. 1953 *Rapunzel* for three singers and chamber orchestra—slightly rev. 1996; text by William Morris

164: Summer 1953 *The Pool of Sacrifice* for chorus, soloists, and metallophone—lost, incidental music to Noh drama by Seami Motokiyo

165: 1953 *Little Song on the Atom Bomb* for voice, two violins, viola, and harp—rev. in 1968 as *Peace Piece Three*; text by Harrison

166: 1953 *Air from Rapunzel* for soprano, flute, violin, viola, cello, harp, and piano—arrangement of scene from *Rapunzel* (1953 ML163)

167: 1955, mvt. 1 begun 1951 *Four Strict Songs* for eight baritones and orchestra—arranged in 1992 for SATB chorus; text by Harrison

168: July 29, 1955 *Recording Piece* for five percussionists and tape machine

169: Oct. 8, 1955 *Simfony in Free Style* for two recorder players, four viol players, harp, trombone, percussion, and tack piano

170: 1955–1956 *Incidental Music for Corneille's Cinna* for tack piano

171: 1954–1958 *Political Primer* for solo baritone, chorus, and orchestra—unfinished; recitatives performed separately; overtures incorporated into *Elegiac Symphony* (1975 ML 211) and *Third Symphony* (1982 ML 243)

172: 1959 *Concerto for Violin with Percussion Orchestra* for violin and five percussionists—first two mvts. completed c. 1941, last movement completed 1959; also known as *Koncherto por la violono kon perkuta orkestro*

173: 1960 *Suite for Symphonic Strings* for string orchestra—includes new versions of "Chorale for Spring" (1951 ML 145), *Double Fugue* (1936 ML 28), *Triphony* (1945, ML 123), *Fugue for David Tudor* (1952 ML 157), *Almanac of the Seasons* (1950 ML 144), and *Nocturne* (1951 ML 150)

174: 1961 *Concerto in Slendro* for violin, celesta, two tack pianos, and two percussionists

175: 1961 *Moogunkwha Se Tang Ak* for Korean court orchestra

176: 1961 *Quintal Taryung* for *danso*, *tungso*, and optional *janggu*—can also be played on alto and tenor recorders

177: 1961 *Sonata for Psaltery*—also known as *Psalter Sonato*

178: 1962 *Prelude for Piri and Reed Organ*

180: 1962 *Holly and Ivy: A Carol* for tenor, harp, two violins, cello, and bass; or chorus, string orchestra, and harp—rev. of *Holly and Ivy at a Quarrel Be* (1951)

181: 1962 *A Joyous Procession and a Solemn Procession* for chorus, trombones, tambourines, gong, hand bells, and bass drum—for the nuns at the Immaculate Heart College, Los Angeles

1961–1963 *Nova Odo* for chorus and orchestra—first two movements; third movement not completed until 1968 (ML 200)

182: Jan. 20, 1963 *Majestic Fanfare* for three trumpets and percussion

183: Mar. 1963 *Jephtha's Daughter* for narrator, percussion, flutes, and opt. drones—rev. of 1941 version

184: 1963 *Pacifika Rondo* for orchestra of Western and Asian instruments

185: 1963 *At the Tomb of Charles Ives* for alto trombone, two psalteries, two dulcimers, three harps, tam-tam, five violins, viola, cello, and bass

c. 1964 *Mezmelodio* for psaltery or *zheng*—arrangement of mvt. 2 of *Pacifika Rondo* (1963 ML 184)

c. 1964 *Ritmicas: Homago al Rodan* for flute, clarinet, horn, and bassoon—collaboration with Robert Hughes

186: 1964 *Wesak Sonata* for psaltery (*zheng*)

187: 1966 *Symphony on G* for orchestra—completion of work begun 1947–1948; last movement "Chaconne and Fugue" comp. 1964, replaced with Rondo last movement by Feb. 1966

188: Oct. 4, 1964 *Elegy for Harpo Marx* for three harps

189: Dec. 21, 1964 *Garden at One and a Quarter Moons* for psaltery (*zheng*)—for Robert Hughes; rev. 1966

190: Dec. 12, 1964 *Avalokiteshvara* for harp and two percussionists

191: 1966 (before Apr.) *Easter Cantata* for solo alto, chorus, two trumpets, two trombones, percussion, harp, and strings—completion of work mostly written 1943–1946

192: 1966 *Reflections in Motion* for percussion, violin, and plucked strings—partially improvised with subsequent layered tape parts but never realized

193: 1966–1967, 1978 *Music for Bill and Me* for harp

194: Feb. 7–Mar. 14, 1968 *Haiku* for unison chorus, *xiao*, harp, wind chimes, and gong

195: 1967 *Music for Violin with Various Instruments, European, Asian, and African* for violin, reed organ, drums, psaltery, and *mbiras*

196: 1967 *Beverly's Troubadour Piece* for harp and percussion

197: Nov. 1967 *In Memory of Victor Jowers* for clarinet or English horn and piano or harp

198: 1968 *Peace Piece One: From the Metta Sutta* for unison chorus, trombone, two harps, reed organ, string quintet, and three percussionists

199: 1968 *Peace Piece Two* for tenor, two harps, strings, and three percussionists—text by Robert Duncan

200: 1968 *Nova Odo* for chorus and orchestra—last mvt. comp. by summer 1968, first two mvts. written 1961–1963; text by Harrison

201: 1973 *Nuptiae* for reed organ, flutes, bells, rattles, *kulintang*, and two-part chorus; text by Harrison

202: 1969 *Orpheus—for the Singer to the Dance* for tenor, chorus, and percussion orchestra—includes movements of *Labyrinth #3* (1941 ML 91); text by Robert Duncan

203: 1969–1971 *Young Caesar* for narrator, singers, and various non-Western and Western instruments played by five instrumentalists—libretto by Robert Gordon

204: Mar. 28, 1972 *Ductia in the Form of a Jahla for Leopold Stokowski* for harp and percussion

205: 1971 *La Koro Sutro* for chorus with American gamelan, harp, and organ

1971 *The White Snake Lady* for Chinese instruments—mostly improvised

Apr. 2, 1972 *Solo* for tenor bells instrument of American gamelan—for Anthony Cirone

206: June–Oct. 15, 1972 *Festive Movement* for flute, clarinet, violin, cello, and piano

Dec. 12, 1972 *Lyric Phrases* for unspecified instr. with opt. drone and percussion ostinato—kit; mode determined by the performer

207: 1972–1973 *Concerto for Organ with Percussion Orchestra* for organ, piano, celesta, glockenspiel, vibraphone, tube chimes, and gongs

c. 1974 *Three Short Movements for Percussion* for two percussionists

208: Apr. 14, 1974 *Sonata in Ishartum* for harp

209: 1974 *Suite for Violin and American Gamelan*—collaboration with Richard Dee

210: 1974 *Arion's Leap* for two syrinxes, three *yazheng*, metal-strung transfer harp, troubador harp, and percussion—for Charles Shere; very brief

Dec. 22, 1974 *Little Homage to Eratosthenes* for wire-strung harp and bells

211: Nov. 1975 *Elegiac Symphony* for orchestra—includes revisions of Overture from *Political Primer* (1958 ML 171), *Canticle #6* (1942 ML 109), and *Praises for Michael the Archangel* (1947 ML 131)

212.1: 1976 *Gending Samuel* for Javanese gamelan—rev. as *Ladrang Samuel* and *Lancaran Samuel* (Feb. 1981), collected with *Gending Pak Cokro* and *Bubaran Robert* as *Music for Kyai Hudan Mas*; for Samuel Scripps

212.2: 1976 *Gending Pak Cokro* for Javanese gamelan—collected with *Gending Samuel* and *Bubaran Robert* as *Music for Kyai Hudan Mas*; for K. R. T. Wasitodipuro

212.3: 1976 *Bubaran Robert* for Javanese gamelan, later added piccolo trumpet—original version collected with *Gending Samuel* and *Gending Pak Cokro* as *Music for Kyai Hudan Mas*; rev. 1981

213: July 1976 *Lancaran Daniel* for Javanese gamelan

214: July 1976 *Lagu Sociseknum* for Javanese gamelan

215: Jan. 10, 1977 *Binary Variations on "Oh Sinner Man"* for soprano recorder, alto recorder, tenor recorder, soprano crumhorn, alto shawm, treble viol, and viola da gamba

Jan 18, 1977 *Once White and Gold* for piano, alto recorder, and soprano—collaboration with Kerry Lewis, William Colvig, and Richard Dee

216: May–July, 1977 *Gending Paul* for Javanese gamelan—for Paul Dresher

217: July 1977 *Gending Jody* or *Lancaran Jody* for Javanese gamelan—incorporated into *Scenes from Cavafy* (1980 ML 227); for Jody Diamond

218: July–Aug. 1977 *Music for the Turning of a Sculpture by Pamela Boden* for Javanese gamelan

219: 1978 *Waltz for Evelyn Hinrichsen* for solo piano or harp—later arranged for guitar; orchestrated and incorporated into Third Symphony (1982 ML 243)

220: 1978 *Serenade* for guitar; optional percussion added 1988

221: 1978 *Main Bersama-Sama* for gamelan *degung* and horn

222: 1978 *Serenade for Betty Freeman and Franco Asseto* for gamelan *degung* and *suling*

1978 *Plaint and Variations* for guitar—for guitar refretted in Pythagorean tuning; incorporated into *String Quartet Set* (1979 ML 224)

223: 1979 *Threnody for Carlos Chavez* for gamelan *degung* and viola

224: 1978–1979 *String Quartet Set* for string quartet—first movement based on *Plaint and Variations* for guitar (1978)

225: 1979 *Discovering the Art of Korea* for four players playing various Chinese and Korean instruments, harp, and percussion—film used only part of the original recording

226: 1940 *Air* for violin, *yazheng*, and *gendèr*—rev. of work from 1940

226a: 1974 before March *Payatamu and the Corn Maiden*, dance-drama for singers, flute, viola, harp, and percussion

227.2a: 1980 *Gending Bill* for Javanese gamelan—also known as *Gending William Colvig*; incorporated into *Scenes from Cavafy* (1980 ML 227)

227: 1980 *Scenes from Cavafy* for baritone, male chorus, Javanese gamelan, *kecapi*, harp, and *yazheng*—includes "Gending Cavafy," "Gending Bill," "Lancaran Jody," "Gending Ptolemy," and "Gangsaran from the Procession of Bacchus"

227.3: 1985 *Gending Ptolemy* for Javanese gamelan—incorporated into *Scenes from Cavafy* (1980 ML 227)

228: Sept. 23, 1980 *Double Fanfare* for two six-percussionist ensembles

229: 1981 *Gending Alexander* for Javanese gamelan—for Michael Zinn

230: Mar. 3, 1981 *Ladrang Epikuros* for Javanese gamelan—*balungan* used in mvt. 1 of *Double Concerto* (1982 ML 240)

231: Mar. 10, 1981 *Gending Hephaestus* for Javanese gamelan—*balungan* used in mvt. 3 of *Double Concerto* (1982 ML 240)

232: May 7, 1981 *Estampie* for organ—for Susan Summerfield

May 29–30, 1981 *Round for Annabelle and April* for two soprano instruments—arranged and incorporated into *Third Symphony* (1982 ML 243) and *Grand Duo* (1988 ML 276)

233: Jan.–July 1981 *Gending Hermes* for Javanese gamelan—for Vincent McDermott and the gamelan at Lewis & Clark College

234: May–July 1981 *Gending Demeter* for Javanese gamelan—rev. 1983

235: Oct. 16, 1981 *Gending in Honor of the Poet Virgil* for Javanese gamelan—for Trish Nielsen; rev. Feb.–Mar. 1985

236: early 1982 *Gending Claude* for Javanese gamelan—for Claude Lorrain

237: Feb. 21, 1982 *Lancaran Molly* for Javanese gamelan—for Molly Davies

238: 1982 *Gending Dennis* for Javanese gamelan—for Dennis Russell Davies

239: Feb. 25, 1982 *Gending Pindar* for Javanese gamelan

240: 1981–1982 *Double Concerto* for Javanese gamelan, violin, and cello—first mvt. adapted from *Ladrang Epikuros* (1981 ML 230), third mvt. adapted from *Gending Hephaestus* (1981 ML 231)

241: 1982 *Tributes to Charon* for three percussionists—includes a new mvt. "Passage Through Darkness" together with "Counterdance in the Spring" (1939 ML 71)

242: 1983 *Beyond the Far Blue Mountains* for Javanese gamelan—a film score consisting of previously composed gamelan works: *Serenade for Betty Freeman and Franco Asseto, Gending Demeter, Main Bersama-Sama, Gending Dennis, Gending Pindar, Lancaran Molly,* and *Gending Claude*

243: 1982 *Third Symphony* for orchestra—incorporates arrangements of Overture from *Political Primer* (1958 ML 171), *Reel: Homage to Henry Cowell* (1939 ML 79), *A Waltz for Evelyn Hinrichsen* (1978 ML 219), *Estampie for Susan Summerfield* (1981 ML 232), and *Largo Ostinato* (1937 ML 38)

244: 1982 *Elegy to the Memory of Calvin Simmons* for chamber orchestra with oboe solo

245: Oct. 11, 1982 *Gending in Honor of Herakles* for Javanese gamelan

246: 1980–1982 *Richard Whittington* for Javanese gamelan, harp, and singers—for shadow-puppet performance

247: May–June 1983 *Gending in Honor of James and Joel* for Javanese gamelan and two *suling*—for James Broughton and Joel Singer; used in film *Devotions*

248: Aug 9, 1983 *Lagu Lagu Thomasan* for Cirebonese gamelan—three short *balungan*: "To Honor Jennifer," "To Honor Allen," and "For the Children"

249: 1983 *Lagu Cirebon* for Cirebonese gamelan

250: July–Oct. 1983 *Ketawang Wellington* for Javanese gamelan

251: 1983 *Lagu Victoria* for Cirebonese gamelan

252: 1983 latter half *The Foreman's Song Tune* for chorus and Javanese gamelan—incorporated into *Coyote Stories* in 1987

253: Aug.–Nov. 1983 *For the Pleasure of Ovid's Changes* for Javanese gamelan—rev. Dec. 1986

254: 1983 *Gending in Honor of Sinan* for Javanese gamelan

255: Feb.–July 1983 *Gending in Honor of Palladio* for Javanese gamelan—rev. 1983 and 1984

256: Feb. 29, 1984 *Lagu Elang Yusuf* for Cirebonese gamelan—incorporated into *Incidental Music to Goethe's Faust* (1985 ML 260); for Elang Yusuf Dendabrata (Elang Muhammad Yuwana Yusuf)

257: 1984 *Gending in Honor of Max Beckmann* for Javanese gamelan—rev. 1991

258: 1983 *Gending Vincent* for Javanese gamelan—for Vincent McDermott

259: Apr. 6, 1985 *Lagu Pa Undang* for gamelan *degung*—used in *Incidental Music to Goethe's Faust* (1985 ML 260)

260: 1985 *Incidental Music to Goethe's Faust* for soloists, chorus, orchestra, solo harps, and gamelan

261: 1985 *Three Songs* for male chorus, piano, and strings—includes arrangements of *King David's Lament for Jonathan* (1941 ML 97) and *Fragment from Calamus* (1946 ML 130)

262: 1985 *Piano Concerto with Selected Orchestra* for retuned piano, strings, harps, trombones, and percussion

263: June 10, 1986 *Gending in Honor of Aphrodite* for Javanese gamelan, harp, and chorus—original gamelan version from *Richard Whittington* (1982 ML 246); chorus and harp added to make a standalone piece in 1986; rev. further in 1989 and 2002

264: 1986 *New Moon* for flute, clarinet, trumpet, trombone, violin, bass, and percussion—dance work for Erick Hawkins

265: Mar. 21–Aug. 8, 1984 *Ladrang in Honor of Pak Daliyo* for Javanese gamelan—rev. 1986

266: 1986 *Mass for St. Cecilia's Day* for male chorus, harp, and drone

267: Dec. 27, 1986 *A Cornish Lancaran* for Javanese gamelan and soprano saxophone—uses *balungan* of *Lancaran Samuel* (1976 ML212.1); a second section added in 1989

1987 *Varied Quintet* for violin, virginal, harp, and two percussionists incl. American gamelan bells and *jaltarang*—five mvts.: "Gending," "Bowl Bells," "Elegy," "Rondeau in Honor of Fragonard," and "Dance"

268: 1987 *Varied Trio*, arrangement of *Varied Quintet* for violin, piano, and percussion

269: 1987 *Ariadne* for flute and percussion with optional dancer

270: 1986–1987 *Concerto for Piano with Javanese Gamelan* for Javanese gamelan with piano

271: 1985–1987 *Philemon and Baukis* for violin and Javanese gamelan

272: 1987 *The Clays' Quintet* for trumpet, cornet, mandolin, harp, and percussion

1987 *Scattered Remains of James Broughton* for harpsichord, gendèr, drum, and other percussion—film score

273: 1987 *Air for the Poet* for chamber orchestra—arrangement of a section of the score to *The Scattered Remains of James Broughton* (1987)

1987 *Four Coyote Stories* for Javanese gamelan with baritone—part served as basis for last movement of the Fourth Symphony (1990 ML 281)

274: 1987 *A Summerfield Set* for piano or other keyboard; rev. 1988

275: 1988, 2001 *Young Caesar* for singers, chorus, and chamber orchestra—standard opera version of ML 203; rev. first for Portland Gay Men's Chorus and again in 2001 for canceled Lincoln Center performance

276: 1988 *Grand Duo* for violin and piano

277: 1989 *Pedal Sonata for Organ* for solo organ

278: Dec. 1989 *Soedjatmoko Set* for female voice, unison chorus, and Javanese gamelan

279: 1989 *Ibu Trish* for gamelan *degung*

280: 1990 *Piano Trio* for violin, cello, and piano

281: 1990 Fourth Symphony for orchestra with baritone—also known as *Last Symphony*; incorporates arrangement of part of *Four Coyote Stories* (1987)

282: 1990 *Threnody for Oliver Daniel* for solo harp

283: 1991 *Homage to Pacifica* for gamelan, chorus, bassoon, harp, percussion, female voice, and psaltery—includes "In Honor of the Divine Mr. Handel," "In Honor of Mark Twain," "In Honor of Chief Seattle," and other mvts.; vocal part developed by Jody Diamond

284: 1991 *Round for JaFran Jones* for Balinese gamelan

285: Feb.–Mar. 1992 *Now Sleep the Mountains, All* for chorus, six percussionists, piano four hands, and piano two hands—text from Alcmaeon, trans. Andrew Bowman

286: 1992 *Songs in the Forest* for flute/piccolo, violin, vibraphone/marimba, and piano—rev. of work from 1951

287: Mar. 1992 *White Ashes* for piano and chorus

288: 1992 *Tandy's Tango* for solo piano—for choreographer Tandy Beal

289: Oct.–Nov. 1992 *Set for Four Haisho with Percussion* for four *haisho*, two percussionists, and reader

290: Dec. 11, 1993 *An Old Times Tune for Merce Cunningham's Birthday* for piano and string quartet—based on work from 1952; arranged for piano solo by Michael Boriskin

291: Dec. 17, 1993 *Canticle and Round in Honor of Gerhard Samuel's Birthday* for three percussionists—mvt. 1 arranged from *Canticle #5* (1942 ML 104) by Allen Otte

292: Apr. 1994 *Gending Moon* for Javanese gamelan with *suling* and male voice

293: 1994 *Vestiunt Silve* for mezzo-soprano, flute, two violas, and harp

294: May 1994 *Book Music* for Javanese gamelan, *suling*, Ptolemy duple metallophone, and percussion—a set of pieces to surround Harrison's poetry readings

295: 1994 *Lazarus Laughed* for flute, oboe, trombone, harp, percussion, and strings—score for radio drama

296: 1995 *New First Suite for Strings* for string orchestra—extensive rev. of *First Suite for Strings* (1948 ML 135)

297: 1995 *Suite for Cello and Piano*—for Robert Korns

298: 1995 *A Parade for MTT* for large orchestra

1996 *At the Tomb of Messiaen* for ondes martenot or voice or saxophone and organ—rev. of *Prelude for Piri and Reed Organ* (1962 ML 178)

299: Oct. 31, 1996 *Suite for Sangen* for shamisen—for Akiko Nishigata

300: 1996 *Rhymes With Silver* for violin, viola, cello, piano, and percussion

301: 1997–1998 *Concerto for Pipa with String Orchestra* for *pipa* and string orchestra

302: Sept. 15, 1991, comp. 1997 *In Honor of Munakata Shiko* for Javanese gamelan

303: Jan. 26, 1998 *Music for Remy* for oboe and percussionist—for Remy Charlip

1998 *Lancaran Antony* for Javanese gamelan

304: Aug. 1998 *Orchard* for Javanese gamelan

305: Apr. 17, 1999 *Dartington Hall* for Javanese gamelan

1993, compl. 1999 *A Dentdale Ladrang* for Javanese gamelan

306: 2000 *Sonata for Harpsichord* for harpsichord—for Linda Burman-Hall

307: Nov. 1999 *Short Set from Lazarus Laughed* for flute, cello, and celesta—arrangement of three mvts. from *Lazarus Laughed* (1994 ML 295)

308: May 22, 1999 *For the Repose of My Friend James Broughton* for Javanese gamelan

309: Jan. 5, 2001 *Mass to St. Anthony: Kyrie and Gloria* for chorus, piccolo, and five percussionists—new arrangement of two movements of *Mass to St. Anthony* (1939, 1952 ML 159)

310: 2002 *Scenes from Nek Chand* for steel guitar in just intonation

311: 1998–2002 *Ladrang Carter Scholz* for Javanese gamelan

312: 2002 *Another Orchard* for Javanese gamelan

313: 2002 *To Honor Mark Bullwinkle* for Javanese gamelan

Arrangements

125: c. 1945 *Onward Christian Soldiers* for chorus, organ, and trumpet

179: Late 1961 or early 1962 *Nak Yang Chun* for chorus, three flutes, three trombones, celesta, harp, piano, two percussionists, and strings—arrangement of traditional Korean work with restoration of choral parts by Harrison and Lee Hye-Ku

1963 *Suite for Toy Piano* for orchestra—arrangement of work by John Cage

1977 *Christmas Music* for winds, tack piano, marimba, harp or celesta, and chorus—based on three of Charles Ives's songs about Christmas

NOTES

References to "The Lou Harrison Archive" refer to the Lou Harrison collection in Special Collections in the McHenry Library at the University of California Santa Cruz.

Part 1
1. Collins, "San Francisco's American Festival." In addition to this mayoral proclamation, the San Francisco City Council would later pass a resolution declaring May 14, 2002, Lou Harrison Day.
2. Ross, "Mavericks."

Chapter 1
1. Brett Campbell, "Divine Lou Harrison."
2. Notebook #3, Lou Harrison Archive.
3. Harrison interview, March 20, 1995.
4. The first movie version of this play, starring Mary Pickford, had appeared the preceding year. Verna Felton would become famous as the matriarchal voice in several Disney films. Felton and her family were close friends of the Harrisons during the years in Portland. (Harrison interview, March 20, 1995.)
5. Shere, "The Making of Lou Harrison." Miller and Lieberman, in *Lou Harrison: Composing a World* (p. 5), quote from the Feb. 16, 1920 review in the *Oregonian*: "His blasé chirrup, 'I should worry,' when Judy told him not to break a cup, brought down the house."
6. Harrison (interview, March 20, 1995) admitted that the experience of being given away to an actress mother surrogate around the same time his brother was born caused "some troubles" psychologically.
7. Harrison, *The Path at West Holding*, 28.
8. Harrison interview, April 6, 1995.
9. In similar foreshadowing of his adult occupations, he also started but never finished making a violin but did complete a marionette.
10. Leyland, *Gay Sunshine Interviews*, 176.
11. Charlip interview, June 18, 1997.
12. Harrison interview, April 6, 1995
13. Harrison interview, March 20, 1995.
14. Notebook #3, Lou Harrison Archive.
15. Dobson interview, July 11, 2000.
16. Harrison interview, March 20, 1995.
17. Harrison interview, April 6, 1996.
18. Gunden, *The Music of Lou Harrison*, 3.

19. Harrison, "Oleanders," in *Joys & Perplexities*, 92.
20. Harrison interview, July 20, 1997.
21. By the time he graduated from high school, Harrison calculated that he had attended eighteen different schools. (Stone, "Interviews with Pauline Oliveros and Lou Harrison," 44.)
22. Harrison interview, March 20, 1995.
23. Stone, "Interviews with Pauline Oliveros and Lou Harrison," 44.
24. The score is in the juvenilia file of the Lou Harrison Archive. It bears a dedication to "Helen Jhonson" [*sic*], but he later learned that he dedicated it to the wrong person. It was her sister who died. (Harrison interview, March 20, 1995.)
25. Harrison interview, March 20, 1995.
26. Harrison interview, April 6, 1996.
27. Harrison interview, April 6, 1995.
28. Harrison interview, April 6, 1996.
29. That the several other piano pieces that survive in his archives today represent only a small sampling of his output during this time is clear from the fact that one is titled Piano Sonata #7.
30. Celso, "A Study and Catalogue of Lou Harrison's Utilization of Keyboard Instruments," 2.
31. Harrison interview, June 12, 1997.
32. Harrison interview, March 20, 1995.
33. Harrison interview, April 6, 1996.
34. Harrison interview, July 1, 1996.
35. Clipping, dated 1932 but otherwise unidentified, in Lou Harrison Archive.
36. Quoted in Celso, "A Study and Catalogue of Lou Harrison's Utilization of Keyboard Instruments," 2.
37. Harrison interview, March 20, 1995.
38. Harrison interview, April 6, 1996.
39. Ibid.
40. Quoted in Celso, "A Study and Catalogue of Lou Harrison's Utilization of Keyboard Instruments," 16.
41. Introduction to Harrison, *Six Sonatas for Cembalo or Pianoforte*.
42. The song originates in Sharp, *English Folk Songs* v. II, 289–290. Harrison would resurrect and complete this piece as *Variations on "O, Sinner Man"* in 1977. This version would include instructions to hand-pluck the strings of the harpsichord.
43. Harrison interview, April 6, 1996.
44. The program for the graduation ceremony is in the Lou Harrison Archive, but the composition is lost. Presumably, Harrison graduated in December at age seventeen because he had skipped two semesters when he entered the California school system.
45. Harrison interview, April 6, 1996.

Part 2
1. This was one of Harrison's oft-repeated characterizations; for example, in Rockwell, "A West Coast Composer."
2. Kosman, "The Melody Maker."
3. Harrison interview, October 1, 1996.
4. The College had just that year changed its name from San Francisco State Teachers College. Today it is known as San Francisco State University.
5. Harrison interview, August 22, 1999.
6. Harrison interview, July 1, 1996.
7. Harrison interview, July 1, 1997. See also Stryker and Van Buskirk, *Gay by the Bay*, 23–25.
8. Harrison interview, July 1, 1996.
9. Cushing, "San Francisco Scene."

10. Dobson interview, July 11, 2000.

11. The following description comes from Harrison interview, April 10, 1987; American Society of University Composers, *A Conversation between Ben Johnston and Lou Harrison*; and Dobie, *San Francisco's Chinatown*.

Chapter 2

1. Dobie, *San Francisco's Chinatown*, 269.

2. American Society of University Composers, *A Conversation between Ben Johnston and Lou Harrison*.

3. From Harrison's notebook from 1935–1936 now at Mills College Special Collections.

4. Dobson interview, July 11, 2000.

5. Ibid.

6. Ibid.

7. Notebook #50, Lou Harrison Archive.

8. Dobson interview, July 11, 2000.

9. Notebook #50, Lou Harrison Archive.

10. Harrison interview, July 1, 1997.

11. Dobson interview, July 11, 2000

12. Harrison interview, July 1, 1997.

13. Harrison interview, August 22, 1999.

14. Ibid.

15. Harrison interview, October 1, 1996.

16. Harrison interview, August 22, 1999.

17. Harrison interview, July 1, 1996.

18. Judith Malina (quoting Sidney Cowell), undated interview with Eva Soltes.

19. Harrison interview, July 1, 1997.

Chapter 3

1. Harrison, "Tens."

2. Information on *Fanati* comes from a Harrison interview of July 1, 1997, and from Higgins, "Cowell's Lost *Fanati*." Harrison also wrote an extended description from memory in a 1976 draft letter to Sidney Cowell in the Lou Harrison Archive.

3. Sachs, *Henry Cowell*, 57–58. See also Michael Hicks, *Henry Cowell*, 56–57.

4. Mostly written 1916–1921 but not published until 1930.

5. Cowell, *New Musical Resources*, 10–18.

6. Kitaro Tamada, the *shakuhachi* player, was the proprietor of a flower shop in Mountain View, and after Cowell by chance heard him play, Tamada became Cowell's teacher. See Sheppard, "Continuity in Composing." The March 7, 1935 program is reprinted in Mead, *Cowell's New Music*, 317.

7. When the concert started late because of a double-booked clarinetist, Cowell passed the time with an impromptu lecture on Schoenberg, "jollying the audience along," Cowell called it, just as he did in the classroom. The group filled out the concert only by playing his *Chamber Symphony* twice (Harrison interview of June 9, 1997). Harrison remembered other details that we could not confirm, such as riding in the taxi with Schoenberg and going to the post-concert reception at the Cowell house. In Mead, "Henry Cowell's New Music Society" (456–457), critic Alfred Frankenstein remembered driving Schoenberg and his family to and from the concert (but no reception). Harrison also would have been present when Schoenberg conducted the Bay Region Federal Symphony (a WPA orchestra) in September 1937, and he frequently attended other events at the Cowell house.

8. Harrison interview, April 6, 1996. See also Duckworth, *Talking Music*, 101–102.

9. Letter in Lou Harrison Archive, reprinted in Garland, *A Lou Harrison Reader*, 30–31.

10. Letter from Harrison to Cowell in Lou Harrison Archive.

11. Sidney Cowell, "Henry Cowell's View," 29.

12. Harrison, *Charles Ives: Violin Sonatas*.

13. Henry Cowell, *New Musical Resources*, 29–32.

14. Quoted in Celso, "A Study and Catalogue of Lou Harrison's Utilization of Keyboard Instruments," 83. Harrison's pianist friend Douglas Thompson gave the piece its official premiere at a recital at the California School of Fine Arts (now the San Francisco Art Institute) the same month it was completed. The program is in the Lou Harrison Archive.

15. Harrison interview, July 19, 2000.

16. Henry Cowell, *New Musical Resources*, 69–70.

17. He didn't publish his ideas until 1930. (Seeger, "On Dissonant Counterpoint.")

18. Harrison's choice of a baroque dance form reflects his "Mission Period" interest in early music. He composed several sarabands around this time. He was already familiar with Schoenberg's twelve-tone Suite op. 25, which also used baroque dance forms.

19. Yasser, *A Theory of Evolving Tonality*, 62–104. Quintal counterpoint is sometimes called "quartal," since the fourth is the inversion of the fifth and thus functionally identical. Harrison distinguished imitative and non-imitative, and formal versus informal types, contrasting the "formal" European technique of careful attention to each and every harmony resulting from the combination of lines to the more "informal" treatments of combinations he heard in Ives's polyphony as well as in cultures of Asia (Harrison, *Music Primer*, 11–13).

20. Harrison interview, July 19, 2000.

21. Harrison judged these early works successful enough that he incorporated them both into much later works. The *Double Fugue* was orchestrated and included in the *Suite for Symphonic Strings* of 1961, and the *Ground* became the middle movement of 1988's *A Summerfield Set*.

22. Harrison interview, March 11, 1997. See also Harrison, "Learning from Henry." John Cage referred to Cowell as the "open sesame" of American music (Cage, "History of Experimental Music in the United States,", 71).

23. From Cowell's unpublished autobiography, quoted in Nicholls, *American Experimental Music*, 68.

24. Duckworth, *Talking Music*, 102; Stone, "Interviews with Pauline Oliveros and Lou Harrison," 45. Bach famously included his own name as a fugue subject in *The Art of the Fugue*. In German nomenclature, the letters B-A-C-H correspond to the pitches B♭, A, C, B♮. Harrison may have been referring to a piece titled *Ritual #7 on the Name of Bach* dated August 1937 in Notebook #125, Lou Harrison Archive.

25. Henry Cowell, "Towards Primitivism," 153. The issue included scores by Russell, Beyer, Harold G. Davidson, Ray Green, Doris Humphrey, and Gerald Strang (*New Music Orchestra Series* 18 [1936]).

26. Harrison would use a version of the *jaltarang* in his *Labyrinth* of 1941, *Strict Songs* of 1955, and *Varied Trio* of 1988.

27. Henry Cowell, "Drums Along the Pacific," 48–49.

28. Miller, "The Art of Noise," 220.

29. Harrison interview, August 22, 1999.

30. Jane Dudley, "The Mass Dance." Much of this information about revolutionary dance comes from Franko, *Dancing Modernism/Performing Politics*.

31. The first performance of the dance was probably in late 1935 or early 1936. See Miller and Lieberman, *Lou Harrison: Composing a World*, 280.

32. Rathbun, "Lou Harrison and His Music," 7.

33. Dobson interview, July 11, 2000. Lou Harrison Archive programs show that the group repeated the show on May 17, 1936 (two days after Harrison's nineteenth birthday), at the second annual dance festival dedicated to the "Growth and Development of San Francisco" at Veteran's Auditorium. That production also featured another group dancing to three pieces by Cowell, followed by another (lost) Harrison work, "Tomorrow," dedicated to "youth graduating with confidence." Shortly after, Harrison accompanied Beals in a solo piece of his called "March," in a performance at the little theater at the Palace of the Legion of Honor.

Chapter 4

1. See Michael Hicks, "The Imprisonment of Henry Cowell," and Sachs, *Henry Cowell*, 381. In some respects, Sachs's research updates that of Hicks.
2. Sidney Cowell relayed the story of the blackmail attempt from an assistant to the district attorney, whose own sons had played on Cowell's property. See Sachs, *Henry Cowell*, 287, 309, 341, 381. Harrison also had heard the blackmail account, probably from Olive Cowell.
3. Sachs, *Henry Cowell*, 279.
4. Harrison interview, June 9, 1996.
5. Hicks, "The Imprisonment of Henry Cowell."
6. Many of Ives's biographers have written about the rift and eventual reconciliation between Cowell and Ives because of the charges against Cowell, based primarily on the accounts of Ives's wife, Harmony, and the letters she wrote. (Though the letters are in her hand and voice, it is generally accepted that Ives usually dictated them.) Gann, in "Ives the Non-Homophobe," argued that it was Harmony, not Ives himself, who tried to shut out Cowell, on the basis of a supportive letter in Ives's own handwriting sent to Cowell in prison. In any case, there was little contact between them until Cowell was safely married and back in New York in 1941. Gann also argued that Ives probably knew of Harrison's homosexuality when they met in 1947 (see chapter 13).
7. See Hicks, "The Imprisonment of Henry Cowell," and Sachs, *Henry Cowell*, 279, 283. Harrison recalled that Olive Cowell told him that the confession was in response to a promise of leniency. According to Hicks, the district attorney strongly denied that there was ever such a promise.
8. Sachs, *Henry Cowell*, 313–319.
9. Slonimsky, *Perfect Pitch*, 161–167.
10. Letter from Harrison to Olive Cowell, August 21, 1937, in the Henry Cowell Collection of the New York Public Library, quoted in Lechner, *Composers as Ethnographers*, 201–202.
11. Harrison interview, August 8, 2001.
12. In a 1937 article for the journal *Dance Observer*, Cowell proposed such an approach as a solution to the perennial problem that a composer faces in creating a form to closely match a dance that would be frequently evolving in rehearsals. (Henry Cowell, "Relating Music and Concert Dance," 1, 7–9.)
13. Cowell and Harrison share credit for the work on the recital program. (Program in Lou Harrison Archive.)
14. In 1963 Harrison expanded *Jephthah's Daughter* to include drones and flute melodies. Harrison returned to the kit method in his later dance works *Ariadne* (1987) and *Rhymes with Silver* (1996).
15. Copy in Lou Harrison Archive.
16. Harrison quoted in Perlis, *Charles Ives Remembered*, 198.
17. The sixty-two-year-old Ives usually had Chester or his wife write for him during these years because of his failing eyesight and unsteady hand. Letter from Chester Ives to Harrison in Ives Collection, Yale University. Facsimile in Rutman, "The Solo Piano Works of Lou Harrison," 111–113.

18. Harrison interview, April 6, 1996. The quote refers to Harrison's Ives-influenced pieces in general, of which the *Variations* was only one.

19. Ibid.

20. Ibid.

21. Perlis, *Charles Ives Remembered*, 200.

22. Harrison letter to Ives, February 16, 1937, in Ives, *Selected Correspondence*, 251.

23. Harrison, *Music Primer*, 1–4. Harrison quotes nine different methods of motivic transformation as enumerated by Schoenberg's student Adolph Weiss.

24. Harrison, *Charles Ives: Violin Sonatas.*

25. Critic Virgil Thomson heard these same devices in Cage in 1945: "His continuity devices are chiefly those of the Schoenberg school. There are themes and sometimes melodies, even, though these are limited, when they have real pitch, to the range of a fourth, thus avoiding the tonal effect of dominant and tonic. All these appear in augmentation, diminution, inversion, fragmentation, and the various kinds of canon." Thomson, "Expressive Percussion."

26. Harrison, *Music Primer*, 1.

27. A brief analysis is in Leta E. Miller, "Solemn Play," xxii–xxv.

28. Harrison wrote scores to several outdoor productions of the classical Greek dramas that Mills College annually staged to coincide with commencement. However, the *Eumenides* does not appear in surviving lists of productions at Mills, and Harrison did not remember the score. See Mills College, *Mills College, 1852–1937*, 29.

29. Harrison would also use isorhythm in some of his percussion ensemble works, including *Labyrinth* (1941) and *Canticle #3* (1942).

30. Harrison, *Concerto for Violin with Percussion Orchestra*. Harrison dedicated the *First Concerto* to Cowell, who played one of the percussion parts at its first performance, at the Bennington Summer Workshop in 1941. The other players were composers Otto Luening and Frank Wigglesworth, who would later become friends of Harrison in New York.

31. Harrison, program notes in program for premiere of *Schoenbergiana*, 1962 in Lou Harrison Archive.

32. Rathbun, "Lou Harrison and His Music," 88.

33. Harrison interview, June 9, 1996.

34. Harrison, "Schoenberg in Several Ways," 21.

35. Shere, "The Making of Lou Harrison."

36. Even though Cowell didn't meet Schoenberg until 1932, he knew enough about his technique to mention it in 1930 (Henry Cowell, *New Musical Resources*, ix). Schoenberg's student Adolph Weiss was the secretary of the Pan-American Association of Composers in New York in the early 1930s. Harrison had the opportunity to meet Weiss at a New Music Society concert in San Francisco in April 1936. See notes by Nicholls, "Introduction," 146–147; and Feisst, "Henry Cowell und Arnold Schönberg," 57–71.

37. Harrison, *Music Primer*, 14–15. Through his analyses of scores in the public library, Harrison even discovered errors in the published edition of Schoenberg's *Wind Quintet* op. 26.

38. Harrison interview, July 20, 1996.

39. Harrison, "The Violin Concerto in the Modern World," 4–6.

40. Harrison interview, April 6, 1995.

41. Seeger, "On Dissonant Counterpoint," 25–31. Harrison returned to this problem of using a consistent set of intervals both melodically and harmonically at the end of his career, in the third movement of his Fourth Symphony (1993).

42. Although the *Prelude* and *Saraband* appeared together, Harrison did not intend for them to be paired or considered a single piece. In Cowell's absence, managing editor Gerald Strang was running the *New Music Quarterly* from Los Angeles, where he was Schoenberg's assistant.

43. Copland, "Scores and Records," 125.
44. Rutman, "The Solo Piano Works of Lou Harrison" (p. 56), includes an analysis and points of comparison between the *Prelude* and the Bach fantasy. See also Celso, "A Study and Catalogue of Lou Harrison's Utilization of Keyboard Instruments," 87–88.
45. Harrison interview, August 22, 1999.
46. Harrison, *Music Primer*, 15–16. The *Prelude* uses the major third, minor second, and tritone, along with inversions, while the *Saraband* melody uses the major third, minor second, and perfect fourth.
47. Celso, "A Study and Catalogue of Lou Harrison's Utilization of Keyboard Instruments," 86.
48. Ibid., 47.
49. Ibid., 78. The melodic intervals are rigorously limited to the minor second, major third, and minor seventh.
50. Rathbun, "Lou Harrison and His Music," 100. He added, "I tried . . . using the minor second and minor third instead of the major third . . . [but] the minor third and the minor second are just a little too tight . . . [they] just don't go anywhere."
51. Similar interval choices are common in the scores Harrison wrote while he was at Mills College, including his music for Euripides's *Electra* and the dance piece *Ecstatic Moment*.
52. Celso, "A Study and Catalogue of Lou Harrison's Utilization of Keyboard Instruments," 84.
53. The Elgar reference is from a Harrison interview of July 21, 2000. In Alan Baker, "An Interview with Lou Harrison," Harrison remembered listening to the first recording of Ives's *Set for Theater Orchestra*, which included "In the Night." Some forty-five years later, Harrison revised and orchestrated the *Largo Ostinato* to form the third movement of his Third Symphony.
54. Harrison interview, July 20, 1996.

Chapter 5
1. Fisher, "Golden Gate Witnesses a Dance Experiment"; Fried, "Dancers Present Modernist Cycle." *Chronicle* critic and future Harrison supporter Alfred Frankenstein was also positive when reviewing a later performance: "Harrison has a particularly happy gift for writing excellent, interestingly scored, and unobtrusive dance accompaniments." (Frankenstein, "Dance Recital Draws Throngs to Playhouse.")
2. Dobson interview, July 11, 2000.
3. Fisher, "Golden Gate Witnesses a Dance Experiment."
4. Notebook #49, Lou Harrison Archive.
5. Despite other dates given for Harrison's employment at Mills, Miller established this date through several sources. See Leta E. Miller, "The Art of Noise," 256 n. 39; and Miller and Lieberman, *Lou Harrison: Composing a World*, 321 n. 71. Harrison would begin taking the commuter train to Oakland when the Bay Bridge opened in 1938. The Pataky company performed the "Country" section of *Changing World* again that November 1936, and Flade choreographed his *Prelude for Grandpiano* at San Francisco's Community Playhouse.
6. Harrison interview, August 8, 2001.
7. Miller and Lieberman, *Lou Harrison: Composing a World*, 79.
8. Celso, "A Study and Catalogue of Lou Harrison's Utilization of Keyboard Instruments," 28.
9. Though Harrison remembered learning Labanotation from Pataky, Miller ("The Art of Noise," 221), apparently on the authority of an interview with Carol Beals, said that Harrison and Beals took a course in Labanotation together at an earlier time. Miller speculates that it was at the studio of choreographer Ann Mundstock, another student of Laban, who was teaching such a course in 1936. (Cowell was also teaching a course at the same studio.) It is possible that Harrison learned Labanotation from both sources.
10. Miller and Lieberman, *Lou Harrison: Composing a World*, 82.

11. Harrison interview, August 22, 1999.

12. Teck, *Music for the Dance*, 60.

13. Frankenstein, "L.A. Horton Group Dances Novel Version of 'Salome.'" See also Bizot, "Lester Horton's 'Salome.'"

14. Dobson interview, July 11, 2000.

15. Ibid.

16. Harrison interview, August 22, 1999. In the early 1950s, Dobson built a cheap but powerful reflecting telescope out of humble materials—a design that became known as the Dobsonian mount—and started gazing at galaxies and stars from San Francisco street corners, attracting children and adults whom he would teach to make their own telescopes. Expelled from the monastery for these distractions, in 1968 Dobson cofounded the Sidewalk Astronomers organization (Levy, "Walden of the Sky," 84). Both Harrison and Dobson remained active into their ninth decades—white-haired, ponytailed rebels (Harrison rejecting equal temperament in much the way Dobson scorned the Big Bang theory) in their respective fields.

17. Harrison interview, August 8, 2001.

18. Teck, *Movement to Music*, 73.

19. Reynolds and McCormick, *No Fixed Points*, 337.

20. Harrison interview, July 1, 1996.

21. Warren, *Lester Horton*, 61.

22. *Lou Harrison and John Cage, Panel at Cornish School.* See also Duckworth, *Talking Music*, 104.

Chapter 6

1. The course Cage took from Cowell was titled "Primitive and Folk Origins of Music." See Leta E. Miller, "The Art of Noise," 217; David Nicholls, "Cage and the Ultra-Modernists"; Michael Hicks, "John Cage's Studies with Schoenberg," 127. Cage also took a course from Cowell titled "Creative Music Today."

2. Schoenberg taught him mostly standard harmony and counterpoint (and was none too impressed with Cage's work in this area), never the twelve-tone method or any other new techniques. See Revill, *The Roaring Silence*, 47–49; and Michael Hicks, "John Cage's Studies with Schoenberg."

3. Stuart Saunders Smith, "The Early Percussion Music of John Cage."

4. Tomkins, *The Bride and the Bachelors*, 84.

5. The score doesn't specify what instruments should be used, and it displays the notes on a grid rather than using conventional staves and measures. While Cage has acknowledged his debt to Cowell, he said that the inspiration to write for percussion came from his work in 1935 or 1936 as an assistant to abstract animation pioneer Oskar Fischinger, who told him that each kind of material had a "spirit" inherent in it. See Pritchett, *The Music of John Cage*, 12; and Nicholls, *American Experimental Music*, 184.

6. Tomkins, *The Bride and the Bachelors*, 88.

7. Stevenson, "John Cage on his 70th Birthday," 8–9.

8. Harrison, undated interview.

9. Glanville-Hicks, "Musical Explorers," 134.

10. Harrison interview, July 1, 1997.

11. Cage, "Counterpoint."

12. Leta E. Miller, "The Art of Noise," 223.

13. Broughton, *Coming Unbuttoned*, 146.

14. Berger, *Reflections of an American Composer*, 103–104.

15. Harrison interview, July 1, 1996.

16. Mills College workshop production program, Lou Harrison Archive.

17. Harrison letter to Warren, March 14, 1968, reprinted in Warren, *Lester Horton*, 232–235. Among the library materials Harrison would explore was Burlin's *The Indians Book*, which would help to inspire his 1955 *Strict Songs*.

18. According to a 1940 letter to Henry Cowell in the Henry Cowell Collection, New York Public Library, Harrison also scored Horton's dance version of Aristophanes's *Lysistrata* for a performance in Los Angeles.

19. Warren, *Lester Horton*, 232–235.

20. The 1940 census records Harrison and Slayback living at 1461 Kearny Avenue, just by Pioneer Park and the Embarcadero, and shows Metcalf at 1459. It also records that Harrison worked thirty-seven hours a week at his job as a "music teacher" (presumably at Mills) and had an annual income of $800. Harrison later moved a mile away to 1384 Jackson, on the cable car route, according to telephone directories.

21. Harrison and Slayback visited her cooperative house in Marin County, named Madrona, where Harrison met her many friends, who included Ansel Adams and Robinson Jeffers. Gidlow is profiled in many sources. See the descriptions in Stryker and Van Buskirk, *Gay by the Bay* (pp. 21–22), and in Gidlow, *Elsa, I Come with my Songs* (p. 296).

22. Harrison interview, July 1, 1997.

23. Stone, "Interviews with Pauline Oliveros and Lou Harrison," 46.

24. Cage, "Goal: New Music, New Dance," 296.

25. Cage, "The Future of Music: Credo," 4–5. Cage's argument for the legitimacy of environmental and industrial sounds not only reflects the influence of futurist composer Luigi Russolo's *The Art of Noise* and Carlos Chávez's *Toward a New Music*, but also prefigures Cage's later use of silence and magnetic tape to focus the audience's ears on the world around them (Nicholls, *American Experimental Music*, 189–191).

26. Though Harrison clearly remembered introducing Cage to Bird in 1938, Cage's earlier biographers say that Cage began working in Seattle for Bird in 1937, before Harrison and Cage met. This is the basis of the date of Cage's article "The Future of Music: Credo" given in *Silence*. However, more recent research has called the dating of Cage's article into question, and the documentary evidence suggests that Cage went to Seattle in 1938, when he also organized his first percussion concert there. See Miller, "The Art of Noise," 224–225 (and on the subject of the dating of Cage's article, 230, 259 n. 79). Miller dates the article to a lecture Cage gave in 1940. See also Bell-Kanner, *Frontiers*, 106–109.

27. Harrison peripherally knew Beyer in New York, but few people knew her well, it seems. Cowell advocated her works, and she mounted a letter-writing campaign to secure his parole. See Polansky and Kennedy, "Total Eclipse," 719–778.

28. Cage, "For More New Sounds," 243–245.

29. Harrison quoting Cage in *Music Primer*, 94.

30. Alan Baker, "An Interview with Lou Harrison"; and Harrison, *Music Primer*, 95. For example, Cage's *First Construction in Metal* (1939) is made up of sixteen sixteen-measure sections, for a total of 256 measures. Cage divides the sections into subsections of four, three, two, three, and four measures and then groups them by the same proportions; that is, the first four sections form a unit, followed by three sections, two, and so on. Therefore, the large-scale structure reflects the small-scale structure, or, as Harrison put it, "the whole having as many parts as each unit has small parts, and these, large and small, in the same proportion" (Harrison, *Music Primer*, 10).

31. Harrison quoted in Don Russell Baker, "The Percussion Ensemble Music of Lou Harrison," 135. One precedent for such a palindromic form was Arnold Schoenberg's "Mondfleck" from *Pierrot Lunaire* (1912). The *Fifth Simfony* was dedicated to Slayback and dated February 22 to March 8, 1939. The title suggests that this was not Harrison's first percussion ensemble for the concert stage, but the first four "simfonies" do not survive.

32. Harrison, *Music Primer*, 10–11.

33. Siwe, "Lou Harrison at the University of Illinois," 31. See Harrison, *Music Primer*, 1–2.
34. The root rhythmicle is an eighth note followed by two eighth rests and two more eighth notes, for a total duration of five eighth notes. The next diminution removes one of the eighth rests, and then the last two eighth notes become sixteenth notes, and so on. Further analysis is in Leta E. Miller, "Solemn Play" (p. xxviii).
35. Harrison finally completed the full piece in 1982 as *Tributes to Charon*.
36. The title, which reveals Harrison's growing interest in Latin American music, is simply an invented name that Harrison thought sounded somewhat Afro-Cuban. It is what was called in the works of Cuban nationalist poet Nicolás Guillén *jitanjáfora*: a word invented for its onomatopoeic qualities.
37. Harrison later wrote, "Much of the kinetic, & emotional, effect of any piece is determined by the number of attention-points presented in any time unit" (Harrison, *Music Primer*, 17–19).
38. Job, *Looking Back While Surging Forward*, 81. This choreographic version of Euripides premiered at the Golden Gate Exposition on Treasure Island in June 1939. The surviving movements are a "Prelude," "Ground," and "Chaconne." Harrison would later adapt the solemn "Prelude" for orchestra. The score for *Uneasy Rapture*, for piano and percussion, is lost.
39. Teck, *Movement to Music*, 73. Cage biographers have attributed the invention of the water gong to Cage when, like Cowell, he was asked to provide music for a 1938 swimming ballet at UCLA. Experimenting with ways to make the instrument audible to the swimmers, Cage lowered the gong into the water, causing the pitch to rise. See for example Revill, *The Roaring Silence*, 55; and Miller, "The Art of Noise," 219. However, Harrison remembered that Cowell had shown them both the technique, presumably when he was composing for the Stanford water ballet in May 1936 (Carey, "Double Music," 45).
40. Contemporary dance reviews mention several Harrison scores that are otherwise unknown. Sherbon, in "College News" (August–September 1939), mentions Harrison's scores *Alarm and Sequel, Two Dances of Commemoration—Parade—Procession, Little Social Satires*, and *Sociable Meeting*, all from the Mills spring dance recital. The list also includes *Ecstatic Moment*, which corresponds to an extant manuscript in the Lou Harrison Archive labeled "R.A.H." for Ruth Anne Heisey, the choreographer. At the same May 1939 performance, Harrison danced to his own *Usonian Set* and to Cowell's *Exultation*. Goode, in "The Dance at Mills College," mentions Harrison's score to Van Tuyl's *Theme and Variations on This Hectic Life*, and Sherbon, in "College News" (January 1939), mentions Harrison's *Chorale* at the Mills December 1938 recital.
41. Harrison interview, April 7, 1996.
42. Harrison in Marin, *Cherish, Conserve, Consider, Create*.
43. Leta E. Miller, "The Art of Noise," 240.
44. Carey, "Double Music," 45.
45. More than $750 in 2016 dollars.
46. Carey, "Double Music," 39.
47. Harrison's dissatisfaction with later brake drums led him to ship his few remaining old ones around the country for performances of his works (Rathbun, "Lou Harrison and His Music," 127). In an interview in Carey, "Double Music" (p. 43), Harrison said, "The brake drums could be ear-splitting you know! They are four sections of trumpets is what they amount to. And we played them with metal pipes on the interior rim and they just were deafening. Very piercing. I've been to concerts when this is played you know, and I sit there politely and unless they've consulted with me before, and they play the most delicate chamber music. We weren't at all delicate about it."
48. No snare drum rolls appear in those scores because, Harrison explained, none of them could play one (Stone, "Interviews with Pauline Oliveros and Lou Harrison," 46). This limitation was suspected by critic Alfred Frankenstein ("A Varied and Rich Concert," 12).

49. Harrison, "Statement," 32.
50. Frankenstein, "A Program of Percussion."
51. Carey, "*Double Music*," 43.
52. Duckworth, *Talking Music*, 106. See also Carey, "*Double Music*," 38.
53. Siwe, "Lou Harrison at the University of Illinois," 32. The date for this performance is from Leta E. Miller, "The Art of Noise," 225. Harrison would collaborate with Benton in 1971.
54. Duckworth, *Talking Music*, 99.
55. Harrison remembered Cowell showing him an article by McPhee, which probably would have been "The Balinese Wajang Koelit and Its Music." Harrison knew McPhee first as a promising young Canadian composer whom Cowell had published in the *New Music Quarterly* and Wallingford Riegger had written about in Cowell's *American Composers on American Music*. McPhee's later articles on Balinese music would also influence Harrison. Interestingly, Henry Eichheim, a composer from Santa Barbara who had been writing scores influenced by the music of Java and Bali since the 1920s, gave a talk in February 1936 at Mills College and played recordings of gamelan music, but Harrison had not yet started working there.

Chapter 7
1. Harrison, *Music Primer*, 27.
2. Rathbun, "Lou Harrison and His Music," 68.
3. Ibid., 65.
4. Even the rhythm plays an important role in determining the relative importance of the different tones, and hence the character of the mode, a lesson Harrison learned from the seemingly unlikely source *Handbook of Irish Music*; many Irish tunes were modally sophisticated (Harrison, *Music Primer*, 13; Henebry, *Handbook of Irish Music*).
5. Weisgall called attention to these sides of Cowell in "The Music of Henry Cowell."
6. Cowell had frequently written reels of his own, and his performance of a reel at his "debut" recital at San Quentin had received such an ovation that he left the stage, overcome with emotion ("Henry Cowell Wins First Fight in San Quentin—With a Piano," *San Francisco Chronicle*, July 30, 1936, quoted in Hicks, "The Imprisonment of Henry Cowell," 103).
7. Some of the oldest strata of European folk music use the same pentatonic modes as Chinese and other Asian music, as Yasser pointed out in *A Theory of Evolving Tonality*, 40–41.
8. In 1982, Harrison orchestrated the piece and used it as part of the second movement of his Third Symphony.
9. Although he had only seen the score in the library, Harrison later suggested it to John Cage in New York (Harrison interview, April 7, 1996). Through Harrison and Virgil Thomson, Satie would become an important influence on Cage.
10. Rathbun, "Lou Harrison and His Music," 58.
11. The text is from the King James Bible, II Samuel 1:26. He would revise it in 1972 and arrange it for men's chorus in 1985.
12. The opening of Harrison's "Kyrie" is the same as the Kyrie melody of Josquin's *Missa Pange Lingua* and the Phrygian mode hymn on which it is based.
13. Quoted in Richard Brown, *Lou Harrison: Mass to St. Anthony*.
14. Rathbun, "Lou Harrison and His Music," 67.
15. In his pocket music notebook, Harrison sketched out most of the single-line melody for the entire piece but only some of the accompaniment for the "Kyrie" and "Gloria" sections. Although Harrison remembered his original sketches being for only voices and percussion, the "Kyrie" sketch has a polyphonic string accompaniment that would later form the basis for the 1952 version of the *Mass*. Other movements show that he intended to add drones to them as well (Notebook in Lou Harrison Archive).

16. Rathbun, "Lou Harrison and His Music," 60.
17. Harrison quoted in Perlis, *Charles Ives Remembered*, 200.
18. Rathbun, "Lou Harrison and His Music," 60.
19. Harrison found this in Burlin, *The Indians' Book*, 304–307. Kwakiutl is the term Burlin used, but the accepted name for the people of the region is Kwakwaka'wakw.
20. Fried, quoted in Miller and Lieberman, *Lou Harrison: Composing a World*, 15.
21. Frankenstein was reviewing a concert at the San Francisco Museum of Art two months after the premiere, which also featured two other Harrison pieces ("Composers' Forum Presents Second Session"). He also praised the *Sanctus*'s "dignity and individuality" and called it "the most 'advanced' of the many manners represented" at the premiere (Frankenstein, "Radiana Pazmor 'Refreshing'").
22. Lou Harrison, "Jaime de Angulo," 6.
23. Because he couldn't write standard musical notation, de Angulo invented his own, which Cowell later helped him translate. See De Angulo, *Jaime De [o]Angulo*.
24. Carlos Chávez, *Towards a New Music*, 28. The book would also influence Cage. Harrison played some of Chávez's music in a dance concert by Van Tuyl's company in October 1936. The two became friends later in life, and in 1979, Harrison would write a poignant *Threnody* in his memory.
25. The movements suggest chords based on stacking mildly dissonant fourths instead of traditional thirds, as per Cowell's suggestion in *New Musical Resources*, 113–114. Later in New York, Harrison would systematize a style of counterpoint based on stacking fourths. Henry Cowell wrote his own *Amerind Suite* for piano in 1939.
26. In reference to Falla, Harrison called the fifth sonata his own *Nights in the Gardens of Spain* (Celso, "A Study and Catalogue of Lou Harrison's Utilization of Keyboard Instruments," 82).
27. Harrison, *Six Sonatas for Cembalo or Pianoforte*. The *Cembalo Sonatas* were initially published in *New Music Quarterly* in October 1943 and then revised and edited by Susan Summerfield for Peer in 1990. Summerfield suggested new ornamentation in the Peer edition, but Harrison's ambition to include drawings of the California missions was not realized.
28. Van Tuyl repeated this program at the end of the following summer session (August 2, 1940), and the program for this performance is in the Lou Harrison Archive.
29. The program for the April 5, 1940, recital is in the Lou Harrison Archive.
30. Sachs, *Henry Cowell*, 348.
31. Harrison interview, June 9, 1996. For the details on all the work that went into petitioning for Cowell's release, see Sachs, *Henry Cowell*, especially 339–349.
32. Harrison interview, July 20, 1996.
33. Cage, "How the Piano Came to be Prepared."
34. Quoted in Revill, *The Roaring Silence*, 71.
35. Henry Cowell, "Drums Along the Pacific," 46–47. Unfortunately, Cowell had to write his article about the West Coast percussion music scene without being able to attend this concert. Almost immediately after his release, he was required to travel to White Plains, New York, where he would begin his job as the secretary of Percy Grainger.
36. Frankenstein, "A Splendid Performance Opens Red Cross Series." Frankenstein attended a rehearsal but noted that Cage told him that there would be moving lights and projections for the performance. Harrison also described the set in Siwe, "Lou Harrison at the University of Illinois," 32.
37. Another unusual sound source for the concert was sirens, called for by a piece by the Cuban composer José Ardévol. Harrison and Cage had to get special permission to use the instruments because of the war (Upchurch, "Memories of John and Lou"). One of the "sirenists" was Harrison's friend, the architect Irving Morrow.

38. Siwe, "Lou Harrison at the University of Illinois," 59.
39. "Fingersnaps and Footstomps." Cage introduced the reporter to his wife, Xenia, who was performing, "but I didn't start practicing percussion on her until after we were married."
40. Pence, "People Call It Noise—But He Calls It Music," reprinted in Kostelanetz, *John Cage*, 61–62.
41. Quoted in Frankenstein, *Concert Percussion for Orchestra*.
42. Manuscript in Fleisher Music Collection, Free Library of Philadelphia. The instruction was not included when the score was published by Belwin Mills in 1999.
43. Celso, "A Study and Catalogue of Lou Harrison's Utilization of Keyboard Instruments," 108. This score was lost for many years until it appeared in the Lester Horton Collection at the Library of Congress (box 15, folder 20). The surviving score apparently is not complete, as the music for the striptease and some other scenes exist only as excerpts in the medley that concluded the performance.
44. Frankenstein, "At Mills—Strip Tease!" This review is quoted in Miller and Lieberman, *Lou Harrison: Composing a World* (p. 87), from a clipping provided to them by Bella Lewitzsky, because it otherwise does not exist on the microfilm of the paper (not every edition was filmed).
45. Rathbun, "Lou Harrison and His Music," 59.
46. Cage applied for work with the federal projects, but the WPA determined that what Cage did was not "music" and so assigned him to be a "recreational leader" in hospitals and community centers. There he created musical games that anticipated his process works of the 1950s and '60s while using everyday objects as percussion instruments. See Revill, *The Roaring Silence*, 72–73; and Gena and Brent, *A John Cage Reader*, 170.
47. Letter to Cowell c. 1940 in Henry Cowell Collection, New York Public Library.
48. Cage, *Selected Letters*, 34–35.
49. Yates, "A Collage of American Composers, Part 4," 4.
50. Carey, "*Double Music*," 40–41, 46.
51. Ibid., 41. Harrison also noted in this interview that most performances of *Double Music* are too slow and suggested a tempo of half note equals 84. Carey includes a comprehensive analysis of the piece.
52. Frankenstein, "The New Records in Review."
53. "Will consider it open hostility if you go on with this madness," the telegram read, but by then the disc had already been produced and distributed. Cage recounted this story in Revill, *The Roaring Silence*, 74; Dufallo, *Trackings*, 225; and *Lou Harrison and John Cage, Panel at Cornish School*. It may be that Varèse was afraid that Cage's recording might be mistaken for one of his own. The telegram is in the Lou Harrison Archive.
54. This was the same school, descended from the famous Bauhaus school of Germany, whose students had designed the decor for the percussion concert at Mills the previous summer.

Chapter 8
1. Working in Harrison's favor was the fact that, unlike many modern pieces, the slow *Trojan Women* overture would require very little rehearsal time. Monteux let Harrison know that the relative difficulty was the only reason that he did not choose *Canticle #6*. "If this were Paris," he told Harrison, "I would perform it" (Harrison interview, August 8, 2001). While *Canticle #6* itself would remain unfinished, Harrison would adapt its scherzo-like movement as well as an opening modal passacaglia for his *Elegiac Symphony* in 1975.
2. Frankenstein, "San Francisco Rejuvenated."
3. Harrison interview, June 9, 1996.
4. Quoted in Don Russell Baker, "The Percussion Music of Lou Harrison," 76.
5. Harrison would again turn to symbols of connections to nature in works such as his *Strict Songs* of 1955. He would return to the *terza rima* technique in *Pacifika Rondo* of 1963.

6. In 1969 he would borrow its movements to serve as interludes in his large oratorio *Orpheus—For the Singer to the Dance*.
7. Program in Lou Harrison Archive.
8. Harrison interview, July 1, 1996.
9. Harrison interview, April 6, 1995.
10. Ibid.
11. Cowell, *New Musical Resources*, 67–69. Cowell himself had experimented with the idea in such pieces as his 1917 *Quartet Romantic*.
12. Each pair of entries of the subject during the opening exposition is related by a perfect fifth, so that, for example, a four-part fugue in the home key of C would have entries in the keys C, G, C, G, though the octaves of each would vary. The second and third entries of the subject in *Fugue for Percussion* are in time ratios 3:2 ("perfect fifth" slower) and 2:1 ("octave" slower) relative to the first.
13. Ravenscroft, "Working Out the 'Is-Tos and As-Tos'"; and Stuart Saunders Smith, "Lou Harrison's *Fugue for Percussion*."
14. Rathbun, "Lou Harrison and His Music," 125. In 1957, Leopold Stokowski, who had conducted several of Harrison's percussion works, rejected the *Fugue* as unplayable. Today the *Fugue* is performed regularly and has been recorded several times.
15. Frankenstein, *Concert Percussion for Orchestra*.
16. Harrison interview, July 1, 1996.
17. Quoted in Miller and Lieberman, *Lou Harrison: Composing a World*, 89.
18. Harrison, quoted in Facchin and Ferrarese, *A Homage to Lou Harrison*, vol. 3.
19. Program in Lou Harrison Archive.
20. Frankenstein, "A Recital on Percussion Instruments," quoted in Miller and Lieberman, *Lou Harrison: Composing a World*, 21.
21. Harrison letter to Cowell, undated (probably 1942), Henry Cowell Collection, New York Public Library.
22. Harrison interview, March 20, 1995.

Chapter 9

1. Harrison interview, July 3, 1997.
2. Ibid.
3. Ibid.
4. The *Los Angeles Times* lists a performance at UCLA on April 15 and reviews a performance at the Wilshire Ebell Theater on June 4. Advertisements in the *Los Angeles Times* beginning August 5, 1942, show the Lester Horton Dancers performing before the feature films at the Orpheum Theater, where, according to Warren (*Lester Horton*, p. 98), they did four shows a day. However, apart from some benefit performances that September, there is no evidence for a regular concert season in Los Angeles during 1942–1943. Horton choreographed at least four films for Universal during this period.
5. Quoted in Neff, "An Unlikely Synergy," 177.
6. Tusler, "Interview with Peter Yates," 60.
7. Harrison interview, July 3, 1997.
8. He and Harrison would become close enough that Dahl would stay at Harrison's apartment during a trip to New York the following year (Linick, *The Lives of Ingolf Dahl*, 107).
9. Harrison interview, July 3, 1997.
10. Ibid.
11. Yates, "Music: A Trip Up the Coast," 10. In San Francisco, Harrison had written another quintal counterpoint gigue as part of a projected symphony titled *Canticle #6*, later to become part of his *Elegiac Symphony* in 1975.

12. Harrison later arranged the *Gigue and Musette* for his dance suite *Rhymes with Silver* of 1996. Its swift changes of harmony are also reminiscent of Ravel's "Forlane" and "Minuet and Musette" from his own neo-baroque *Tombeau de Couperin*.

13. Harrison interview, July 3, 1997.

14. Ibid; Blum, "The Bell-Like World of Lou Harrison"; *Lou Harrison and John Cage, Panel at Cornish School*. Hanns Eisler described Schoenberg similarly in Bunge and Eisler, "Ask Me More about Brecht," 414. Schoenberg's assistant was Harold Halma, who would later become well known as a portrait photographer.

15. Harrison, "Schoenberg: The Late Works," 138.

16. Harrison interview, April 7, 1996.

17. Thomson, "Schoenberg's Music," reprinted in Thomson, *A Virgil Thomson Reader*, 255. At the time Harrison met him, Schoenberg was at work on his piano concerto, an anguished journey through the hatred and suffering of the war. Harrison would eagerly attend the premiere of this work in New York the following year (Kostelanetz, "A Conversation, in Eleven-Minus-One Parts," 389).

18. He was more often than not disappointed with his American students, who, in addition to Cage, had included the pianist and raconteur Oscar Levant and film composer David Raksin.

19. Cage related several stories of Schoenberg's harshness during Cage's study with him. See Cage, *Silence*, 265–66, 271; and Cage, *A Year from Monday*, 46. See also Michael Hicks, "John Cage's Studies with Schoenberg," 129.

20. Harrison, introduction to *Suite for Piano*. See also Blum, "The Bell-Like World of Lou Harrison."

21. Rutman, "Lou Harrison and His Music," 11.

22. Cizmic, "Composing the Pacific."

23. Cage, "Mosaic" in *A Year from Monday*, 46.

24. For one version of this story, see Rutman, "Lou Harrison and His Music," 11. Harrison identified the quartet in an interview on July 19, 2000.

25. Schoenberg lamented the fact that even those scores that were available were much more expensive in America than in Europe, where government subsidies to publishers allowed students to acquire invaluable personal libraries (Van Leuwen Swarthout and Schoenberg, "First California Broadcast," 300).

26. Harrison interview, July 21, 2000; Pound, *Cathay*, 11–12. The modern transliteration of the Chinese poet's name is Li Bai, but his name appears as Li Po in this volume. Harrison may also have been intrigued by Pound's commentary, in which he argues that this type of poem represents a bridge between East and West. Harrison also vividly remembered settings of Li Po's poetry on a broadcast by the microtonalist Harry Partch while still in the San Francisco Bay Area in 1932 or 1933 (Harrison interview, June 12, 1997). In the 1960s and '70s, Harrison would perform Chinese music to accompany recitations of Chinese poetry, including by poet Kenneth Rexroth.

27. Harrison interview, July 3, 1997.

28. Harrison would later explicitly reference thirteenth-century Notre Dame polyphony in *Seven Pastorales* and *La Koro Sutro*.

29. Stravinsky, *Poetics of Music*, 64–65.

30. Krenek, *Studies in Counterpoint*, 1.

31. Excepting the transpositions of the cantus firmus of the "Conductus" movement, the piece uses only the prime (original) form, the inverted row transposed a perfect fourth up, and the retrograde forms of those two row forms.

32. Harrison, *Suite for Piano*.

33. Rathbun, "Lou Harrison and His Music," 10–11.

34. Harrison, *Suite for Piano*.

35. Cizmic, "Composing the Pacific." That very summer of 1943, Schoenberg would write a tonal, melodic piece of his own: *Theme and Variations*, for amateur wind band.

36. Rutman, "The Solo Piano Works of Lou Harrison," 11.

37. Harrison completed his *Suite* in May 1943, and Mullen premiered it on May 8, 1944. Perhaps coincidentally, Ingolf Dahl was composing a piano suite at the same time, which he performed on the April 5, 1943, Evenings on the Roof concert (Linick, *The Lives of Ingolf Dahl*, 107).

38. Warren, *Lester Horton*, 101; Martin, "The Dance: A New Guild."

39. Harrison interview, June 12, 1997.

40. Rutman, "The Solo Piano Works of Lou Harrison," 11–12.

41. In a letter of May 4, 1945, the composer Roy Harris, then working for the US Office of War Information, asked Schoenberg for his list of ten leading contemporary American composers. Schoenberg replied on May 17 with many disclaimers—that such a list is bound to be incomplete, that he has only had the opportunity to study the scores of a handful of American composers, etc.—but provided a list of names of those "whom I considered characteristic for American music": "Aaron Copeland [*sic*], Roger Sessions, William Schumann [*sic*], David Diamond, Louis Gruenberg, Walter Piston, Anis Fuleihan, Henry Cowell, and among my students, Adolphe Weiss, and Gerald Strang. And among younger and lesser known people I would like to mention: Lou Harrison and Miss Dika Newlin." Cage is conspicuously absent (Schoenberg, *Arnold Schoenberg Letters*, 234).

42. Rathbun, "Lou Harrison and His Music," 68.

Part 3

1. Harrison interview, July 5, 1997.

2. Cocteau, *The Infernal Machine*, 171.

3. Harrison interview, July 5, 1997.

4. Around this time, both Kurt Weill (*Street Scene*, 1946) and Duke Ellington ("Harlem Air Shaft," 1940) wrote music evoking the urban clamor of New York tenement living.

Chapter 10

1. John Steinbeck, a family friend of Xenia's from California, took them out to a $100 lunch when the Cages were literally down to their last nickel (Kostelanetz, *Conversing with Cage*, 12).

2. Ibid., 11.

3. The museum had been founded by Virgil Thomson's Harvard friend Alfred H. Barr Jr. in 1929 (Watson, *Prepare for Saints*, 96).

4. Some of the other headlines: "Percussion Concert Produces Cacophony," *New York World Telegram* (February 8, 1943); "It Comes in a Flowerpot, but They Call It Music," *PM* (February 8, 1943); "Percussion 'Music' Heard at Concert," *New York Times* (February 8, 1943), 14. See the bibliography in van Emmerick, "A John Cage Compendium."

5. In 1988, Campbell would reach millions more thanks to a series of interviews with Bill Moyers broadcast on PBS as *The Power of Myth*.

6. A later film of the dance is included on Erdman, *Dance and Myth: The World of Jean Erdman —Part 1*. See also Teck, *Music for the Dance*, 56.

7. Warren, *Lester Horton*, 103–107. See also John Martin, "The Dance: A New Guild."

8. It would not re-form until 1948, when, back in Los Angeles, Horton created the first established multiracial dance group in America (Dunning, *Alvin Ailey*, 48).

9. Anna Sokolow's piece was called "Songs of a Semite," and Harrison was apparently playing music of Richard Neuman and Alex North. The program is preserved in the Jewish Women's Archive: http://jwa.org/node/8945.

10. Thomson, "A War's End." See also Lederman, *Life and Death of a Small Magazine*.

11. Swed, "Remembering *Modern Music*," 58.
12. Letter from Harrison to his mother, 1943, Lou Harrison Archive.
13. Harrison, "Summer and Early Fall, New York."
14. Harrison, "First-Time Fashions, New York, 1944."
15. Harrison, "On Quotation."
16. Harrison, "Modernism 'Sacred and Profane.'"
17. Harrison, "First-Time Fashions, New York, 1944."
18. Yates, "Lou Harrison." Yates noted that Harrison was planning to move back west and that he considered the West Coast "the future cultural center of the world."
19. Letter from Harrison to Bill and Dorothy Harrison, September 1943, Lou Harrison Archive.
20. Flint, *Wrestling with Moses*, 3–4.
21. Ned Rorem interview, October 2005.
22. Ginsberg, quoted in Miles, *Call Me Burroughs: A Life*, 101.
23. Judith Malina interview, October 2005.
24. Eva Soltes interview with Lou Harrison, undated. This resolution lasted only until 1952's *Praises for the Beauty of Hummingbirds*, which includes parallel thirds throughout.
25. Most of the books were in storage in Paris, trapped by the war (Tommasini, *Virgil Thomson*, 317, 327).
26. John Rockwell, introduction to Thomson, *A Virgil Thomson Reader*, xiv.
27. Watson, *Prepare for Saints*, 317.
28. Thomson, *The State of Music*, 117.
29. Harrison interview, July 3, 1997.
30. Draft letter in correspondence folder, Lou Harrison Archive. Alas, his staff replied, that would not be possible, and Harrison would not have a piano at home until much later.
31. While at home, Thomson always wore pajamas or a bathrobe (Weber, *How I Took 63 Years to Commit Suicide*).
32. Quoted in Duckworth, *Talking Music*, 26.
33. Tommasini, *Virgil Thomson*, 321. See also Zinsser, "Virgil Thomson, Writer," 340.
34. Zinsser, "Flunking Description."
35. Harrison interview, July 5, 1996.
36. Harrison, "Ajemian-Masselos."
37. Bowles, *Paul Bowles on Music*, xii.
38. Harrison, "On the *Chôros* of Villa-Lobos," 85–87. Harrison recalled getting in an argument with Cage, who said it was beneath a composer of Harrison's caliber to be interested in Villa-Lobos (Harrison interview, August 22, 1999).
39. Eva Soltes interview #273.1 with Lou Harrison, undated.
40. Harrison notebook in Mills College Special Collections.
41. Harrison, *Party Pieces*.
42. Harrison, Cage, Cowell, Thomson, and other composer friends participated at various times. Their different handwriting is easy to distinguish in the manuscripts, and in fact they were for this reason keepsakes for Harrison, reminding him of his close circle of New York friends. Cage's *Party Pieces* is Robert Hughes's arrangement of the pieces for woodwinds and piano.
43. Harrison interview, June 12, 1997.
44. Harrison's poet friend Harold Norse described him this way in Norse, *Memoirs of a Bastard Angel* (p. 243).
45. Norse, *Memoirs of a Bastard Angel*, 241. Norse, who later lived with Brown in Rome, used the unconvincing pseudonym "Burton Gray" to refer to him.
46. Cage planned a collaboration with Brown and Harrison, a kind of game similar to the one that had produced *Double Music*, now predictably titled *Triple Music*, but it never materialized (Cage, "A Composer's Confessions," 44).

47. Rorem interview, October 2005. See also Rorem, *Facing the Night*, 175. When he met Harrison, Heliker was teaching painting at the American People's School in the Bronx (run by the dancers Ruth St. Denis and Ted Shawn) and was socially if not always artistically associated with the Village's abstract expressionists (Goodrich and Mandel, *John Heliker*, 14–15).

48. These works include his *Family Suite* for three recorders (1943), "Carol" for two recorders (1943), and *Hymn and Fuguing Tune No. 4* for three recorders (for the Cowells' 1944 anniversary).

49. Boriskin, "An American Original," 34.

50. Weber, *How I Took 63 Years to Commit Suicide*.

51. Minna Lederman recalled that Thomson and Cage seemed to always be together (Lederman, "John Cage," 152). Suzanne Robinson argued that Thomson's relationship with Cage amounted to "homosexual patronage," but there's no evidence of a sexual relationship between them. Thomson was a patron of Harrison, Peggy Glanville-Hicks, and others as well (Robinson, "A Ping, Qualified by a Thud," 83).

52. Rorem, "Virgil (1944)," 74.

53. Leyland, *Gay Sunshine Interviews*, 166.

54. Harrison, "Literature: All About Music," 17.

55. Tommasini, *Virgil Thomson*, 353–361. Later, the *Tribune* was unable to intervene when another of its columnists, Jerome Bohm, was convicted on similar charges and served two years in prison. Like Cowell, Bohm had allowed some teenaged boys the run of his house, and one of them reported sexual contact there (ibid., 424–425).

56. Harrison interview, June 19, 2000.

57. *Lou Harrison and John Cage, Panel at Cornish School*; Harrison interview, June 19, 2000.

58. Weber, *How I Took 63 Years to Commit Suicide*.

59. Sherry, *Gay Artists in Modern American Culture*, 42–43.

60. Thomson's use of the term "little friends" to refer to this group comes from an interview with Harrison on July 5, 1996. References to the term in Tommasini (*Virgil Thomson*, 291–293) refer to a different group and come somewhat earlier. Cage later become Thomson's biographer (O'Donnell and Cage, *Virgil Thomson*), but Thomson essentially controlled the project and hired Cage to provide the musical analyses, resulting in some bad feelings between the two. See Tommasini, *Virgil Thomson*, 440–449.

61. Eva Soltes interview with Judith Malina, undated.

62. Tommasini, *Virgil Thomson*, 240.

63. Robinson, "A Ping, Qualified by a Thud," 88–89.

64. Tommasini, *Virgil Thomson*, 349.

65. Thomson, *Virgil Thomson*, 353.

Chapter 11

1. This poem first appears in the fourth edition of Whitman, *Leaves of Grass*, 144.

2. Celso, "A Study and Catalogue of Lou Harrison's Utilization of Keyboard Instruments," 116–117. Harrison's song resembles Ives's own setting of a fragment of Whitman published in *New Music* in 1933. Harrison's song was his first standalone publication, brought out by Bomart in 1950. Despite its similarities to Ives and Ruggles, Harrison said that he hoped the song would remind listeners of "the Elizabethan songs of John Dowland."

3. Letter from Cage to Thomson in Thomson archives, Yale University. See Robinson, "A Ping, Qualified by a Thud," 110.

4. Rorem interview, October 2005. "If they shake it and look away, they want you," his protégé Ned Rorem recalled Harrison advising him, "but if they shake and look at you, they're not interested."

5. Harrison interview, July 5, 1997.

6. McGowan pushed the YMCA and other organizations to accept black members and helped form the Methodist Federation for Social Service, which advocated "school and neighborhood projects to combat racial and religious prejudice." It also lobbied on behalf of labor and against fascist Spain ("Anti-Bias Work Urged"). This item gives McGowan's church as Epworth Church in the Bronx.

7. McGowan introduced Harrison to Robeson after the performance, and Harrison reminded the great baritone that they had met once before after one of his San Francisco performances. In an interview on July 5, 1996, Harrison remembered that when Robeson won the Stalin Peace Prize in 1952 and was unable to leave the United States because the State Department had revoked his passport, McGowan traveled to Poland to accept it on his behalf. Duberman (*Paul Robeson*) does not mention McGowan's trip, but he does cite a pamphlet McGowan wrote defending Robeson as an African American leader during the height of the McCarthyist hysteria. A copy of the pamphlet is in the Robeson Archives, Howard University.

8. Harrison interview with Eva Soltes, undated (#191 videotape).

9. Hajdu, *Lush Life*, 114–115.

10. John Cage, "A Composer's Confessions," 40. A June 1946 *Junior Harper's Bazaar* article about Cage's previous loft on Sutton Place noted that he "has launched a trend in living: Artists, musicians, and writers are beginning to invade slum & industrial districts bordering on the lower East River" (reprinted in Kostelanetz, *John Cage*, 85).

11. Undated Harrison interview. See also Notebook #61, Lou Harrison Archive.

12. Cage wrote that it evoked "the loneliness and terror that comes to one when love becomes unhappy," foreshadowing the impending breakup of his marriage to Xenia (Cage, "A Composer's Confessions," 40). Despite all the effort Cage poured into *The Perilous Night* (music that would later inspire a series of paintings by Jasper Johns), the reviews, except for Harrison's in *Modern Music*, were unkind (Harrison, "Season's End").

13. In the question-and-answer section of Cage's Norton Lectures of 1988, Cage recalled Harrison showing him the *I Ching* in San Francisco (Cage, *Questions and Answers*). However, Harrison claimed that he had discovered the *I Ching* in Los Angeles and gave a copy to Cage in New York (interview, April 7, 1996).

14. Alan Baker, "An Interview with Lou Harrison."

15. Notebook #45, Lou Harrison Archive.

16. Harrison, "Refreshing the Auditory Perception," 141–143. Though the quartet would languish among Harrison's papers, in 1962 his student Robert Hughes arranged it for wind sextet, in which version Harrison gave it the title *Schoenbergiana*.

17. Harrison, *Music Primer*, 11–13. However, his thoughts on this topic are first found in his notebooks from New York, including Notebook #45, Lou Harrison Archive.

18. Harrison remembered his New York quintal counterpoint compositions being influenced by Kauder's *Counterpoint*. However, he was misremembering, because Kauder's book was not published until 1960. As Kauder was teaching his theories in New York at the time, and his works in this style were commonly on concert programs in New York during the 1940s, it is likely that Harrison was remembering other sources for his familiarity with Kauder's theories during the New York period. Kauder's ideas on counterpoint were well enough known that reviewer Harman Carter ("Records: Folk") referred to his "pet theories."

19. "The possibilities of such polyphony are still far from being completely realized and explored, in spite of the considerable influx of pentatonic melody into modern music" (Kauder, *Counterpoint*, 126). Henry Cowell (*New Musical Resources*, 113–114) proposed such sonorities as an extrapolation from conventional chords, which are built on stacks of thirds. He cites examples in Schoenberg and Rudhyar, but composers as disparate as Debussy, Hindemith, and Berg had also used them.

20. Miller and Lieberman, *Lou Harrison: Composing a World*, 39.

21. He would later call this form of instrumental counterpoint with its idiomatic ornaments "a specialty of Northwest Asia"—that is, Europe (Harrison interview, June 12, 1997).

22. Ibid. His sketches for the *First Suite* list a viol consort as one possibility for the instrumentation and name a movement "Consort à 3," a typical title from these seventeenth-century models. When revising the *First Suite* in 1995, Harrison renamed the first movement (which he otherwise left alone) "Fantasia," another standard title from the period. Harrison's friend Frank Wigglesworth, who shared Harrison's interests in old counterpoint, also wrote a *Fantasia* for strings in 1947.

23. Quoted in Randall, "Alan Hovhaness." See also Kostelanetz, "A Conversation, in Eleven-Minus-One Parts," 389–390.

24. Quoted in Page, *Mysterious Mountain/Elegiac Symphony.*

25. Harrison, "Alan Hovhaness Offers Original Compositions."

26. For example, see Bernstein, "Music That Sings." Randall ("Alan Hovhaness") also quotes an oft-repeated story about Bernstein calling Hovhaness's first symphony "ghetto music" when a recording was played at Tanglewood.

27. Quoted in Randall, "Alan Hovhaness."

28. Harrison, "Summer Music," 21.

29. Celso, "A Study and Catalogue of Lou Harrison's Utilization of Keyboard Instruments," 29.

30. Harrison interview, July 15, 1996.

31. Harrison regularly read the pulp magazine *Astounding Science Fiction*, where "Nerves" appeared in September 1942. In March 1944, the same magazine printed the story "Deadline" by Cleve Cartmill, which had such an accurate description of an atomic bomb that counter-intelligence agents investigated Cartmill and *Astounding.*

32. Harrison interview, July 3, 1997.

33. Harrison interview, July 5, 1996.

34. Ibid.

35. Letter to his mother, 1943, in Lou Harrison Archive.

36. Thomson, *Virgil Thomson*, 354. See also Tommasini, *Virgil Thomson*, 368–369.

37. Harrison interview, July 13, 1996. See also Lou Harrison, "Happy Birthday Virgil," an item from 1977 at the Lou Harrison Archive.

Chapter 12

1. Coomaraswamy, *The Transformation of Nature in Art*, 24. The internal quote is a reference to Thomas Aquinas.

2. Tomkins, *The Bride and the Bachelors*, 99.

3. Thomas Mace, *Musick's Monument*, 118. Harrison also used another quotation from Mace in *About Carl Ruggles.*

4. Mace, *Musick's Monument*, 236.

5. Amirkhanian, "Remy Charlip on John Cage," 21.

6. Patterson, "The Picture That Is Not in the Colors," 183–184.

7. *Lou Harrison and John Cage, Panel at Cornish School.*

8. Harrison, "Music for the Modern Dance," 12.

9. Cage was commenting on the music of Lou Harrison, Alan Hovhaness, and others; see Cage, "The East in the West," 115.

10. John Cage, "A Composer's Confessions," 40. Cage did not use the term "harmony" in the very general sense to refer to any simultaneous pitches, which of course do occur in his works.

11. Harrison, "Ruggles, Ives, Varèse," 11.

12. Harrison to Ives, letter of October 23, 1944, Lou Harrison Archive.

13. Cage, "A Composer's Confessions," 42–43. The composer in question was Roy Harris, though, to be fair, part of Harris's point was that composers should avoid being exploited by those who thought they should work for free. See Sprague, "Composing for Cash." Cage also railed against commercialism in a devastating review of George Antheil's

1945 autobiography *Bad Boy of Music* (Cage, "The Dreams and Dedications of George Antheil").

14. Harrison, "Music for the Modern Dance," 12.
15. Ibid., 11.
16. Cage, "In Defense of Satie," 78.
17. Cage, "Forerunners of Modern Music (1949)," 63.
18. Harrison interview, July 17, 1996.
19. Harrison, "Crackpot Lecture" in Lou Harrison Archive.
20. Notebook #59, Lou Harrison Archive.
21. Coomaraswamy, *The Transformation of Nature in Art*, 10–11; Thomas, *Summa Theologica*, I.117.I. See also Coomaraswamy, *The Transformation of Nature in Art*, 15. Cage's paraphrase of Thomas appears in several places, including "On Robert Rauschenberg" (p. 100).
22. Draft letter from Harrison to Ives dated October 23, 1944, in Lou Harrison Archive.
23. Such pieces as the *Seven Pastorales* (1949–1951), *Alma Redemptoris Mater* (1949–1951), *Holly and Ivy* (1951, revised 1962), and *Vestiunt Silve* (1951, completed 1994) explicitly reference his interest in medievalism, as does his 1952 setting of William Morris's "Rapunzel."
24. Harrison, *About Carl Ruggles*, 5. Harrison's reference to "light and airy music" comes from seventeenth-century composer Christopher Simpson.
25. Ibid., 5–6.
26. Ibid., 18–19.
27. Thomson, *American Music Since 1910*, 33–34.
28. Quoted in Duckworth, *Talking Music*, 106.
29. Thomson, "On Being American."
30. Rorem, *Facing the Night*, 175.
31. Letter from Ruggles to Henry Cowell, January 9, 1945, quoted in Ziffrin, *Carl Ruggles*, 181. Ruggles also wrote the only review of Harrison's *First Concerto* for flute with percussion when it was performed at Bennington College.
32. Harrison, *About Carl Ruggles*, 18.
33. Alan Baker, "An Interview with Lou Harrison."
34. Harrison, *About Carl Ruggles*, 8–9. That description, incidentally, could also apply to the Javanese gamelan music that would later so beguile Harrison.
35. Harrison interview, July 7, 1996. See also an undated paper by Harrison on Ruggles in Lou Harrison Archive; and Miller and Lieberman, *Lou Harrison: Composing a World*, 44. The date for the meeting comes from Ziffrin (*Carl Ruggles*, p. 185), but this account does not mention the racist rants.
36. Seeger, "Carl Ruggles," reprinted in Henry Cowell, *American Composers on American Music*, 14–35. In one perspective, this non-repetition principle loosens the strictures of Schoenberg's twelve-tone method while still avoiding the emphasis of any particular pitch. Other composers who made use of this principle include Merton Brown and Ruth Crawford.
37. Harrison interview, July 7, 1996. The manuscript was originally titled *Trio for Piano*, but in 1995, the rediscovery of this version among his papers led to its being published by Peters as *Triphony*. See Boriskin, "An American Original: Lou Harrison," 34.
38. Harrison interview, August 8, 2001. The harpsichord itself was still a rarity in the United States. Leta E. Miller ("Solemn Play," p. xli) notes that in a 1945 review, Harrison complimented a Bach performance for using a tack piano rather than an unaltered piano when a harpsichord was unavailable (Harrison, "Oratorio Society Gives B Minor Mass of Bach"). In 1946, German composer Paul Dessau used the tack piano, which he called the *Gitarrenklavier*, in his score for Bertolt Brecht's play *Mutter Courage und ihre Kinder*.
39. This work became the *Fugue for David Tudor* when he completed it for the famous avant-garde pianist at Black Mountain College in 1952.

40. Schoenberg's *Klavierstücke* op. 11, a favorite of Harrison's, has a similar motive. Schoenberg used the term "developing variation."

41. Harrison, *About Carl Ruggles*, 19.

42. Ibid., 15. See also Gilbert, "The 'Twelve-Tone System' of Carl Ruggles."

43. Coomaraswamy, *The Transformation of Nature in Art*, 23. The *Natya Sastra* is an ancient and foundational Indian text of theater, dance, and music.

44. Notebook #45, Lou Harrison Archive. Harrison remained an "angelophile" in later life (Weyland, *Gay Sunshine Interviews*, 176).

45. Filmmaker and Harrison's friend James Broughton remembered Virgil Thomson introducing him to the church in 1942 (Broughton, *Coming Unbuttoned*, 55).

46. Campbell would later denounce even some populist Vatican II reforms, like English-language liturgy and priests facing their congregations. See Kennedy, *The Now and Future Church*, 83.

47. Notebook #45, Lou Harrison Archive.

48. Seeger, "On Dissonant Counterpoint," 28–29. Thomson wrote in "Atonality Today," "Present-day efforts by twelve-tone composers to build a rhythmic technique comparable to their tonal system have initiated a second period in atonal research and composition. If the first problem in atonality is to avoid familiar tonal relations, its second is surely to avoid familiar metrical ones."

49. Harrison quite likely helped Merton Brown with his "dissonated" *Cantabile* for strings, published in *New Music* 19, no. 2 (January 1946). In his review of the publication, Harrison called Brown's work "both sensitive and tender in its melodic address" (Harrison, "Mostly Chamber Music," 124–125).

Chapter 13

1. Harrison, "First-Time Fashions."

2. Harrison, "Barone Conducts Concert by N.Y. Little Symphony."

3. Harrison interview, July 11, 1996.

4. Perlis, *Charles Ives Remembered*, 203, 205. See also Ives, *Selected Correspondence*, 292.

5. Perlis, *Charles Ives Remembered*, 205; Alan Baker, "An Interview with Lou Harrison." To Perlis, Harrison said, "I was hesitant, but [Ives's] reaction usually was to do whatever I thought best."

6. Harrison, "Reflections at a Spa." Harrison wrote this review in 1944. Ives's "Second String Quartet" would be premiered in New York two years later. Harrison would also review its performance at the Yaddo Festival in September 1946: "Music of this kind happens only every fifty years or a century, so rich in faith and so full of the sense of completion" (Harrison, "Yaddo Festival," *New York Herald Tribune*, Sept. 22, 1946, reprinted in Burkholder, *Charles Ives and His World*, 345).

7. Harrison letter to Charles Ives, October 23, 1944, in Lou Harrison Archive.

8. Harrison interview, July 11, 1996.

9. Straus, "Symphony by Ives in World Premiere."

10. Thomson, *American Music Since 1910*, 23.

11. Draft of letter from Harrison to Ruggles, April 5, 1946, in Lou Harrison Archive.

12. Fuller, "Airborne Over New York," 120.

13. Straus, "Symphony by Ives in World Premiere."

14. Swafford, *Charles Ives*, 422.

15. Ives letter to Harrison, apparently May 1947 or soon after, Yale Ives Collection, reprinted in Garland, *A Lou Harrison Reader*, 20–28. Of course "Vickey Herbert" refers to the popular operetta composer Victor Herbert.

16. Quoted in Perlis, *Charles Ives Remembered*, 203.

17. Draft of letter to Ruggles, March 1, 1945, in Lou Harrison Archive.

18. Harrison letter to Harmony Ives, July 24, 1946, in Lou Harrison Archive.

19. Kostelanetz, *Conversing with Cage*, 41. See also Cowell and Cowell, *Charles Ives and His Music*, 123–127.
20. Alan Baker, "An Interview with Lou Harrison."
21. Ives letter to Harrison, in Garland, *A Lou Harrison Reader*, 23.
22. Shere, *The Making of Lou Harrison*.
23. Baker, "An Interview with Lou Harrison."
24. Ibid.
25. Ibid.
26. Swafford, *Charles Ives*, 421. Harrison was there when Masselos premiered the "First Sonata" at Manhattan's Town Hall in 1949.
27. Mead, "Henry Cowell's New Music Society," 369.
28. Kostelanetz, "A Conversation, in Eleven-Minus-One Parts," 390.
29. Leta E. Miller, "Method and Madness in Lou Harrison's *Rapunzel*," 88.
30. Cage 1947 letter to Cowell, Henry Cowell Collection, New York Public Library.
31. Harrison interview, July 13, 1996.
32. Harrison, "Renaissance Music."
33. Harrison interview, July 13, 1996.

Chapter 14
1. Cage, *Silence*, 56. This story also formed one of the koan-like narratives of Cage's piece *Indeterminacy*.
2. Don Gillespie interview, October 30, 2005.
3. Harrison interview, July 15, 1996; Ives, *Selected Correspondence*, 334–335.
4. Harrison believed his extensive x-rays were the result of the notorious misdiagnosis of George Gershwin's fatal brain tumor a few years earlier (Kostelanetz, "A Conversation, in Eleven-Minus-One Parts," 390).
5. Kostelanetz, *Conversing with Cage*, 42. The letter, dated May 13, 1947, is reprinted in Ives's *Selected Correspondence* (pp. 334–335). It says that "the charges amount to about ten dollars a day" and that Harrison would be able to pay it back in time. Ives refused to be paid back.
6. Harrison interview, July 15, 1996.
7. Cage letter to Cowell, 1947, Henry Cowell Collection, New York Public Library.
8. Harrison interview, July 15, 1996.
9. Anahid Ajemian interview, October 30, 2009.
10. Harrison interview, June 12, 1997.
11. Harrison interview, July 15, 1996.
12. Harrison interview, July 7, 1996.
13. Harrison interview, August 8, 2001.
14. Harrison interview, August 11, 2001.
15. Salzman, notes to *Lou Harrison and Carl Ruggles*; Rathbun, "Lou Harrison and His Music." 86.
16. Harrison interview, August 8, 2001.
17. Rathbun, "Lou Harrison and His Music," 87.
18. Shere, "The Making of Lou Harrison." In 1969, when CRI recorded *Symphony on G* with the Royal Philharmonic Orchestra, the orchestra inserted a metal plate between the piano hammers and strings as a substitute for a true tack piano. When he heard the tape, Harrison objected so vigorously to this expedient and other decisions that he refused to allow the recording to be released. He instead offered to pay for Gerhard Samuel to travel to London and conduct if CRI would re-record the piece. They did and released the recording on their American Masters Series: *Lou Harrison/Carl Ruggles* (CRI 715). (Harrison interview, June 12, 1997.)

19. Thomson, *The State of Music*, 99. Naturally, Thomson's own scores show a clear preference for the French style.
20. Harrison, undated interview.
21. Later works that would use this form include his *Suite for Violin and American Gamelan*, *Third Symphony*, and *Concerto for Pipa with String Orchestra*.
22. Rathbun, "Lou Harrison and His Music," 87–88; Harrison interview, August 11, 2001.
23. Rathbun, "Lou Harrison and His Music," 88.
24. Harrison interview, August 8, 2001.
25. Ibid. Rathbun, in "Lou Harrison and His Music" (p. 88), writes "'The Swan' sans Swan."
26. Harrison interview, August 1, 2001. See also Rathbun, "Lou Harrison and His Music," 88.
27. Rathbun, "Lou Harrison and His Music," 88.
28. Ibid., 89.
29. Ibid., 86.
30. Anahid Ajemian interview, October 30, 2009.
31. Harrison interview, July 13, 1996.
32. Harrison interview, July 7, 1996.
33. Stevens, who had already designed a yacht that had won the America's Cup in 1937, would go on to become perhaps the most influential figure in twentieth-century sailing. Merton Brown had also dedicated a work to him and may have introduced him to Harrison.
34. Hovhaness's influence would become more apparent when Harrison revised the piece in 1970 for flute and added a drone.
35. Harrison interview, July 15, 1996.
36. Draft letter from Harrison to his mother, May 6, 1947, in Lou Harrison Archive.
37. Harrison interview, July 15, 1996.
38. Harrison interview, June 13, 1997.
39. Cunningham performed *The Open Road* on their tour. After that, thanks to an award from the American Institute of Arts and Letters, they decamped for Europe, where Cage would meet Pierre Boulez, play the *Sonatas and Interludes*, and find some Chinese paper to bring back for the recuperating Harrison.
40. The year after Harrison won the grant, it went to Cage. Peggy Glanville-Hicks, recalling that Thomson had admitted to arranging the grant for Cage, wrote to him asking if he would do the same for her. She was awarded the Arts and Letters prize in 1953. See Robinson, "A Ping, Qualified by a Thud," 120.
41. The myth also formed the basis for a Hindemith ballet score he had reviewed earlier in New York (Harrison, "Mid-Winter in New York 1944," 159).
42. An exception was the third movement, which was adapted from a passacaglia he had written in San Francisco. Harrison still wasn't satisfied with the result, and he would further revise this movement and the suite as a whole until its final incarnation as *New First Suite for Strings* in 1995.
43. Henry Cowell, "Current Chronicle," 451.
44. Serinus, "A Conversation with Lou Harrison."
45. Gabel, "Lou Harrison."

Chapter 15
1. These descriptions of *The Perilous Chapel* are of a later production found in Erdman, *Dance and Myth: The World of Jean Erdman—Part 2*.
2. Revelations 21:1. The program is in the Lou Harrison Archive.
3. Erdman, *Dance and Myth: The World of Jean Erdman—Part 2*.
4. Larsen and Larsen, *A Fire in the Mind*, 256. The tension between Joseph Campbell and those intellectuals concerned with social causes continued throughout his life. During

World War II, he was an apologist for, if not fascism, certainly isolationism, at a time when such viewpoints were decidedly unpopular.

5. Daniélou, *Introduction to the Study of Musical Scales*, 1. This version of the quote comes from the second edition, in which Daniélou's English has been "revised" by the editor (Daniélou, *Music and the Power of Sound*, 1).

6. In Daniélou, *Music and the Power of Sound*, see especially 35–37. Note that musicians conventionally express these ratios with the larger number in the numerator.

7. Ibid., page 7, quoting, presumably in his own translation, De Mengel (*Voile d'Isis*, 494).

8. Kostelanetz, "A Conversation, in Eleven-Minus-One Parts," 391.

9. Harrison, "Season's End, May 1944," 236.

10. Kostelanetz, "A Conversation, in Eleven-Minus-One Parts," 391. Anahid Ajemian also remembered Harrison arriving at her apartment, tuning hammer in hand, to try out the tuning on her grand piano (Anahid Ajemian interview, November 17, 2009).

11. Daniélou, *Music and the Power of Sound*, 204.

12. Henry Cowell, *New Musical Resources*, 3–28.

13. John Cage's 1944 piece inspired by Campbell is called *The Perilous Night*.

14. Teck, *Music for the Dance*, 56.

15. Harrison interview, August 8, 2001. Other pieces that feature chaconne endings include his *Mass to St. Anthony* (1952), *La Koro Sutro* (1972), *Suite for Violin and American Gamelan* (1974), and *New First Suite for Strings* (1995). The evening of dance and music also included works by Debussy, Scarlatti, Satie, and Cage (his prepared piano pieces *Daughters of the Lonesome Isle* and *Phoelian*), along with Harrison's *Changing Moment*. The program from this performance, dated January 23, 1949, is in the Lou Harrison Archive.

16. Henry Cowell, "Current Chronicle," (1949), 296.

17. Remy Charlip interview, June 18, 2004. In later years, Charlip often related how he thought of that moment whenever he shaved and by habit left his upper lip for last.

18. Bob Hicks, "Pen Stroke of Genius."

19. Edward Johnson, *Writing & Illuminating & Lettering*. See Leta E. Miller, "Method and Madness in Lou Harrison's *Rapunzel*," 89.

20. Cocteau, *The Infernal Machine and Other Plays*, 163–164.

21. Perloff, *Art and the Everyday*, 186.

22. Bird had actually produced the ballet earlier at the Cornish School in 1938, where she asked her new accompanist, John Cage, to provide music. He in turn invited a number of composers, including Henry Cowell (then incarcerated), to collaborate, Les Six-style, each composing a different movement: a waltz of the telegrams, a wedding march, a funeral march for the general, and so on.

23. Thomson, "French Music Here."

24. Harrison interview, July 11, 1996.

25. Celso, "A Study and Catalogue of Lou Harrison's Utilization of Keyboard Instruments," 147.

26. In his acknowledgments, Blesh wrote that Harrison "worked enthusiastically and indefatigably with difficult and virtually unscoreable material to produce the most nearly accurate scorings ever, to my knowledge, made of Afro-American music. They reflect his serious approach" (Blesh, *Shining Trumpets*, 106–107).

27. Letter from Bonnie Bird, March 15, 1950, in the Lou Harrison Archive. Bird and Harrison discussed other possible collaborations, but Harrison was too immersed in his own studies and proposed other composers' works instead. Charlip wrote Harrison, saying that *Dance News* called it the best group dance of the season (1951 postcard in Lou Harrison Archive).

28. Harrison interview, July 13, 1996.

Chapter 16

1. Ajemian, "Remembering Seymour Barab."
2. Duncan, *Letters*, 18. Harrison was never quite satisfied with his adaptation of the "Song" to this chamber duo because of the loss of the impressionistic background contributed by the rest of the orchestra.
3. Harrison, liner notes to *Virgil Thomson, Lou Harrison*, Columbia LP ML 4491. The series would also include William Masselos's recording of Ives's "First Piano Sonata," which he and Harrison had worked on together.
4. Ibid.
5. Presumably inspired by Harrison's evocation of static serenity through this old form, John Cage would write two *Pastorales* himself later in the winter of 1951–1952. These pieces, for prepared piano, would be two of his earliest to incorporate chance operations using the *I Ching*.
6. In the same *Musical Quarterly* issue that contained Cowell's review of *The Perilous Chapel*, Colin McPhee published "The Five-Tone Gamelan Music of Bali."
7. This description and the descriptions in italics on pp. 151–152 are based on the later production shown in Erdman, *Dance and Myth: The World of Jean Erdman—Part 2*, although some sections of Harrison's score are deleted or changed in this recording.
8. She had already asked a Juilliard student to score it, but the result "bore no relation to the underlying feeling of my piece." So Erdman discarded that score and approached Harrison to write new music to suit her existing choreography (Teck, *Music for the Dance*, 57).
9. Harrison attributed the Hawaii-born Erdman's perseverance to her inheritance. He called it "pineapple money" (Harrison interview, August 8, 2001).
10. Erdman, *Dance and Myth: The World of Jean Erdman—Part 2*.
11. Teck, *Music for the Dance*, 56.
12. Erdman, *Dance and Myth: The World of Jean Erdman—Part 2*.
13. Carolyn Brown, *Chance and Circumstance*, 4.
14. Erdman, *Dance and Myth: The World of Jean Erdman—Part 2*.
15. Jean Erdman interview in Soltes, *Lou Harrison: A World of Music*.
16. Harrison often mapped out a tonal plan for his large-scale works. He remembered a remark he had heard from classical music critic Alfred Frankenstein, who claimed that complaints about his radio show increased when he failed to arrange the pieces he played according to their keys. He was convinced that starting and ending the multi-hour program in the same key gave a satisfying, if subliminal, sense of closure. Harrison said he found the same sensitivity to tonal cycles in the works of Handel (Harrison interview, July 21, 2000).
17. McKayle interview, August 2011. McKayle studied the techniques at second hand with a dancer with the stage name Hadassah, whose ethnically influenced choreography, including Indonesian dance, was well known in New York. See Danitz, "Hadassah (Spira Epstein)"; and McKayle, *Transcending Boundaries*, 61.
18. Her letter is quoted in Larsen and Larsen, *A Fire in the Mind* (p. 260).
19. McPhee, "The Five-Tone Gamelan Music of Bali." In 1947, McPhee published a breezy autobiographical account of his time in Bali, *A House in Bali*, but this book includes little technical information about the music itself. The results of his research would not come to fruition until 1966, when his monumental *Music in Bali* would be published posthumously. By then, Harrison had turned his attention to other Asian music and Javanese gamelan.
20. McKayle, *Transcending Boundaries*, 61.
21. Henry Cowell, "Current Chronicle" (1950), 452.
22. Glanville-Hicks, "Musical Explorers," 139.
23. Bell-Kanner, *Frontiers: The Life and Times of Bonnie Bird*, 141.

24. Harrison's model was Stravinsky's *Les Cinq Doigts* (1921), another piece for beginning pianists in which the right hand hardly changes position (Celso, "A Study and Catalogue of Lou Harrison's Utilization of Keyboard Instruments," 98).
25. The text comes from the English poet Nicholas Breton's *Fantastickes: Serving for a Perpetuale Prognostication* (1626).
26. Larson, *Where the Heart Beats*, 209.

Chapter 17
 1. Norse, *Memoirs of a Bastard Angel*, 205.
 2. Malina, *The Diaries of Judith Malina*, 152.
 3. Remy Charlip interview, June 18, 2004. See also Tytell, *The Living Theatre*, 35, 46.
 4. Malina interview, October 13, 2005.
 5. Broyard, *Kafka Was the Rage*, vii.
 6. Malina interview, October 13, 2005.
 7. Grimes, "Harold Norse, a Beat Poet, Dies at 92."
 8. Norse, *Memoirs of a Bastard Angel*, 205–206.
 9. Rorem, *Wings of Friendship*, 315.
10. Bacharach, in *Anyone Who Had a Heart* (p. 30), and in an unpublished interview with Brett Campbell recalled a sixteen-minute ballet score that he had heard that Harrison composed for Martha Graham in which thirteen minutes were silent. However, we have not found such a score, and Harrison never claimed to have composed a score for Graham. Graham's list of works does not include any Harrison scores.
11. "I Remember Lou."
12. Malina, *The Diaries of Judith Malina*, 154.
13. Malina interview, October 13, 2005.
14. Malina, *The Diaries of Judith Malina*, 148.
15. Malina interview, October 13, 2005.
16. Malina, *The Diaries of Judith Malina*, 151.
17. Malina interview, October 13, 2005.
18. Harrison interview, August 8, 2001.
19. Malina, *The Diaries of Judith Malina*, 152.
20. Harrison interview, July 16, 1996.
21. Ibid.
22. Malina, *The Diaries of Judith Malina*, 153–154.
23. Ibid., 152.
24. Ibid., 157; Malina interview, October 13, 2005.
25. Malina interview, October 13, 2005.
26. Harrison interview, July 16, 1996.
27. Harrison interview, July 15, 1996.
28. Letters from Callantine to Harrison, dated May 27, 1951, and December 30, 1952, Lou Harrison Archive. After their breakup, Callantine enrolled at the University of Oregon, earning a master's degree in psychology and going on to a career as a school psychologist. She never married or had children. Interestingly, she retired to Boulder Creek, California, just north of Santa Cruz and nearby Harrison's residence. In an interview of July 16, 1996, Harrison admitted that she had "appeared here in the last decade" but otherwise did not discuss her. When Callantine died in 2004, she bequeathed a scholarship in her name to Cabrillo College, the community college where Harrison taught near the end of his life.
29. Malina interview, October 13, 2005.
30. Malina, *The Diaries of Judith Malina*, 152.
31. Ibid., 156.
32. The note and song are in the Lou Harrison Archive.

33. Malina, *The Diaries of Judith Malina*, 160.
34. Malina interview, October 13, 2005.
35. Norse, *Memoirs of a Bastard Angel*, 207.
36. Norse to Harrison in honor of his thirty-fourth birthday. In correspondence files, Lou Harrison Archive.
37. Norse, *Memoirs of a Bastard Angel*, 207–208. The program also included pieces by Thomson, Glanville-Hicks, Bowles, Russell, Ives, José Ardévol, Ernst Toch, Lionel Novak, Ellis Kohs, and Richard Franko Goldman, along with experiments with electronic sound by the Canadian filmmaker Norman McLaren. See also the description of the concert in Malina, *The Diaries of Judith Malina*, 162–163.
38. Norse, *Memoirs of a Bastard Angel*, 207.
39. Berger, "New Music Society"; Berger, "Composers Are Nostalgic for the Turbulent 1920s"; see also Robinson, "A Ping, Qualified by a Thud," 99. Ironically, Harrison had earlier written, "The radio and phonograph are not musical instruments, Sears-Roebuck to the contrary," in "Summer Music."
40. Robinson, "A Ping, Qualified by a Thud," 99.
41. McKayle, *Transcending Boundaries*, 48.
42. Ibid. An announcement of the May 25 performance appears in the *New York Times*, May 20, 1951.
43. It is unclear whether the original dance performance included the poems, the style of which certainly corresponds to those he was writing at Black Mountain College in 1952. Harrison revised *Songs in the Forest* for a Black Mountain reunion concert and publication in 1992.

Chapter 18
1. Harrison, "Songs in the Forest," in *Joys & Perplexities*, 12.
2. Cage, "In Defense of Satie."
3. Silverman, *Begin Again*, 76. According to some reports, students responded by burning Beethoven records, even prompting a food fight in the dining hall.
4. Martin, "The Dance: Graham." The article reproduces a photo of Litz's dance. Litz had previously collaborated with Cage and Cunningham. Writing in January 1950, Martin ("The Dance Agenda") notes that Litz was injured and unable to continue her solo recital performances and that she was to return with a group work that April.
5. Martin, "Litz, Cunningham Give Dance Solos."
6. Interview with Viola Farber in Harris, *The Arts at Black Mountain College*, 168.
7. Remy Charlip interview, June 18, 2005.
8. Harrison, "Music of the Modern Dance."
9. Though he necessarily wrote the piece for piano, he envisioned it for strings from the beginning and only realized this vision when he adapted and expanded the piece as the second movement for his *Suite for Symphonic Strings* in 1960. However, in a compromise with practicality, the 1960 version does not require *scordatura* but uses stopped pitches as if they were open strings (Rathbun, "Lou Harrison and His Music," 93–94). When Cage told Harrison about Franklin's technique, he had recently finished his own very static, nearly monochromatic string quartet and had dedicated it to Harrison.
10. After Morton Feldman had introduced them in New York the previous year, the twenty-four-year-old Tudor and Cage had become close friends and collaborators. Cage was at that time composing his monumental *Music of Changes* for Tudor. Harrison would later retitle *Prometheus Bound* as *Io and Prometheus*, and in 1985 he arranged it as a kit for a chamber ensemble and voices for a new Jean Erdman production in Greece. See Teck, *Music for the Dance*, 60.
11. Beam, "Tales of a Jargonaut." Jonathan Williams also remembered Harrison dressing formally, although Harrison maintained that he stopped regularly wearing neckties in 1947. Harrison is open-collared in photographs of him at Black Mountain.

12. Harrison interview, July 19, 1996.
13. Harrison's resume is in the Black Mountain College papers of the North Carolina State Archives (BMCP.II.14), quoted in Harris, *The Arts at Black Mountain College*, 204.
14. Harding, "My Black Mountain."
15. Plessix Gray, "Black Mountain: The Breaking (Making) of a Writer."
16. Garland, *A Lou Harrison Reader*, 74.
17. Harris, *The Arts at Black Mountain College*, 221.
18. Holzaepfel, "Reminiscences of a Twentieth-Century Pianist"; Olson and Maud, *Selected Letters*, 138–44; Tom Clark, *Charles Olson*, 205.
19. From the North Carolina Museum of Art, *The Arts at Black Mountain College 1933–1956* (research project), BM spool 118: Harrison, transcript p. 19, quoted in Rathbun, "Lou Harrison and His Music," 75–76.
20. Williams, *A Palpable Elysium*, 126.
21. Duckworth, *Talking Music*, 110; Harrison interview, July 17, 1996.
22. Harrison interview, July 19, 1996.
23. Malina, *The Diaries of Judith Malina*, 186.
24. One account of this incident is in Harris, *The Arts at Black Mountain College*, 205.
25. Mary Fitton Fiore, Black Mountain College student, in "The Fra-a-grant Flowers," 267.
26. Harrison interview, July 17, 1996.
27. Harris, *The Arts at Black Mountain College*, 206.
28. Harrison wanted the Black Mountain College Music Press to publish a short work by Merton Brown, another by Cage, and one by himself by that fall. However, the money, which was to support the first two publications, covered only one, Cage's *Haiku*, which appeared in September 1952 (Draft letter to Ives in Lou Harrison Archive).
29. Harrison did not remember the source of his version of the "Holly and Ivy" poem, but there are several published variations that are close to his lyrics, including one published by folk song collector Cecil Sharp in *English Folk Carols* (pp. 17–18). *Holly and Ivy* remained unperformed until Harrison revised it in 1962.
30. As with *The Perilous Chapel/The Perilous Night*, the one-time musical partners—perhaps equally stimulated by their bucolic sojourns at Black Mountain College and Stony Point respectively—both called their 1952 compositions *Pastorales*. But that's where the similarity ends, as Cage's aleatoric *Two Pastorales*, with their long pauses, thin textures, and unconventional sonorities, sound nothing like Harrison's melodic evocations.
31. Harrison interview, September 24, 1997. Writing with such formal restrictions also recalls their earlier percussion music, in particular Cage's square root form.
32. Weil, *Waiting for God*, 77.
33. The spartan refectory menu did not provide many temptations (Harrison interview, July 5, 1996).
34. Harrison, interview #191 with Eva Soltes, undated.
35. Two flutes, oboe, harp, celesta, tack piano, tam-tam (a Chinese gong), two cellos, and bass.
36. Harrison interview, June 10, 1997.
37. Although Harrison spoke in Woodard's article "Composer a Hero in World of New Music" of borrowing this mode from Roy Harris, Harris's string quartet is not really modal. The scale could, however, be derived from Harris's consistent combinations of major thirds and minor seconds that form the basis of his theme. Harris's Second String Quartet was recorded in 1934 and would have been available to Harrison in San Francisco during the period that he worked in Wilson's Record Library.
38. In 1936, Colin McPhee had published the article "The Balinese Wajang Koelit and Its Music," which details the intricate interlocking figurations of this revered chamber gamelan.

39. Harrison's description of *jhala* is repeated several places; for example, in Leta E. Miller's "Solemn Play" (p. l). Alan Hovhaness wrote his *Jhala* op. 103 in 1952. As they shared an interest in Indian music, it is likely that they corresponded with each other about the technique around this time. Hovhaness would use the technique in later works as well, so that Brian Silver ("Henry Cowell and Alan Hovhaness," p. 76) mistakenly called *jhala* "the technique [Hovhaness] has made most distinctly his own."

40. "Ajemian Sisters in Dual Recital." The concert also featured David Tudor and works by Debussy, Mozart, and Schumann.

41. The appearance of the *Suite* on the program would be overshadowed by the historic first performance of electronic tape music in the United States, pieces by Otto Luening and Vladimir Ussachevsky, which, characteristically, Stokowski supported in a brief lecture to the audience despite the conductorless future they implied (Daniel, *Stokowski*, 565–567). See also Taubman, "U.S. Music of Today Played at Concert."

42. In this recording, the conductor famous for conducting his own liberal arrangements of Bach and Wagner added a measure and a half to the end of the piece, enraging Harrison, who by that time had moved back to California. However, Harrison eventually calmed down and accepted Stokowski's wisdom and this revision to the score (Robert Hughes, quoted in Miller and Lieberman, *Lou Harrison: Composing a World*, 231). The recording would be released on CRI with Cowell's *Persian Set* in 1957. In 1972, Harrison would write a piece in honor of Stokowski's ninetieth birthday, and in 1990 a piece in memory of Oliver Daniel.

43. Harrison interview, June 10, 1997.

44. Harrison interview, July 13, 1996. Van Emmerick, in "A John Cage Compendium," lists a performance at the Henry Street Playhouse that May that also included Harrison's *A Pleasant Place*, choreographed by Louise Lippold. This lost work is also mentioned in Harrison's letter to Wigglesworth of February 12, 1952 (Lou Harrison Archive).

45. Draft letter from Harrison to Wigglesworth, February 12, 1952, in Lou Harrison Archive. Harrison recalled that an actor friend of McGowan's had left his guitar with Harrison when he moved to Paris (Harrison interview, July 5, 1996).

46. Guitars with frets in other tuning systems were generally found only as experimental instruments in museums at this time, although Harrison would begin to have access to guitars in other tunings in 1978. The *Serenade* has since been recorded on a guitar in Harrison's preferred tuning. See Schneider, "Lou Harrison's Guitars." Later, he also called this piece *Serenade for Frank Wigglesworth* and *Serenato por Gitaro*. It should not be confused with his 1978 *Serenade for Guitar with Optional Percussion*.

47. Harrison admitted to the misguided notion that revising the instrumentation could lead to a performance at the Church of St. Mary's the Virgin in New York. Ironically, in 1962, when Harrison visited Immaculate Heart College in California, a Sister Theresa asked for the original percussion version, having learned about its existence from Peter Yates. See Rathbun, "Lou Harrison and His Music," 66. Also, in an encounter with a monk in Vermont, it was the trumpet that had to have special sanction for a performance in the sanctuary. Despite Harrison's recollection, this string accompaniment was not entirely new but had been sketched out for the Kyrie movement in his San Francisco notebook, now in the Lou Harrison Archive.

48. In fact he originally wrote out the score on only three staves, changing it only after complaints from conductors.

49. Rathbun, "Lou Harrison and His Music," 68.

50. Ibid. We believe that Rathbun mistranscribed Harrison's interview to read, "The mode writes itself" where we have "The mode rights itself."

Chapter 19

1. Revill, *The Roaring Silence*, 161. Cernovitch would later become a well-known lighting designer.

2. Cage, *Silence*, x; Duberman, *Black Mountain*, 373.

3. Clarkson, "Stefan Wolpe and Abstract Expressionism," 78–79.

4. Quoted in Harris, *The Arts at Black Mountain College*, 228.

5. Harrison, "Music for the Modern Dance," 11.

6. Ibid., 11–12.

7. Undated letter in New York Public Library, New Music Edition Archives, quoted in Miller and Lieberman, *Lou Harrison: Composing a World*, 47. Ussachevsky was the Columbia University composer who had taken over editorship of *New Music*.

8. William Morris, "How I Became a Socialist," 243–244.

9. Harrison's letter (c. 1993) to Peter Oskarson, Lou Harrison Archives.

10. Harrison later found that he accidentally left out one parenthetical word from the original poem.

11. Rathbun, "Lou Harrison and His Music," 72–73.

12. Technically speaking, Harrison's row is not completely invariant (a "trick" row)— only the first five of the six pairs display the sort of symmetry that results in invariance. This means, for example, that the last ten notes of the retrograde inversion transposed up three semitones are the same as the first ten notes of the original row, eventually reducing, in Harrison's view, the number of distinctly different rows to twenty-four instead of the forty-eight he had to work with in the *Symphony on G*. Because his use of it often involved cyclic rotations (as in the symphony) and certain tones were taken out to serve as drones or ostinatos, the compositional result was just the same. Miller and Lieberman (*Lou Harrison: Composing a World*, p. 215) and von Gunden (*The Music of Lou Harrison*, p. 114) stress the near-combinatoriality of the row (the fact that hexachords of different row transformations can combine to create eleven of the twelve possible pitch classes), but that property (even if he had been the sort to have worked something like that out) is of little importance, because Harrison rarely mixed row forms.

13. Williams, *A Palpable Elysium*, 126.

14. Morris, "Rapunzel," in, *The Defence of Guenevere and Other Poems*, 122.

15. Harrison, undated interview with Eva Soltes.

16. The *New York Times* reviewer of *Rapunzel*'s premiere in 1959 noted this parallel, pointing out that the prince utters the same words, "I am not happy here," that Mélisande does in Debussy's opera (Taubman, "Opera: Two Premieres").

17. Harrison's friend Paul Goodman wrote two plays directly in the form of Noh in 1950–1951, and Nick Cernovich published another in the first issue of *Black Mountain Review* in 1951. See Harris, *The Arts at Black Mountain College*, 214; Cernovich, "A Play in the Tradition of Noh."

18. Harrison interview, July 19, 1996.

19. Shere, *The Making of Lou Harrison*. See also Harrison's letter to his parents, March 15, 1953, in the Lou Harrison Archive.

20. See, for example, Harrison's letter to his parents, March 15, 1953, Lou Harrison Archive.

21. Letter to his mother, January 8, 1953, Lou Harrison Archive.

22. Letters to his parents, January 8, 1953, and March 15, 1953, Lou Harrison Archive.

23. January 8, 1953, letter to his parents in Lou Harrison Archive.

24. Letter to Frank Wigglesworth, January 27, 1953, Lou Harrison Archive.

25. Letter from Carl Carmer, president of the MacDowell Association, February 25, 1953, Lou Harrison Archive.

26. Letter to Frank Wigglesworth, January 27, 1953, Lou Harrison Archive.

27. Nicolas Nabokov was the musical director of the American Academy in Rome and was organizing the International Conference of Contemporary Music. See Saunders, *The Cultural Cold War*, 220–223. Ben Weber, in *How I Took 63 Years to Commit Suicide*, confirmed that Virgil Thomson chose the participants.

28. The *New York Times* reported, "Radioactivity from the cloud produced by the ninth blast in the 1953 atomic series was so heavy, that motor and pedestrian traffic was halted in the St. George area of southwestern Utah" ("Nevada Atom Test Affects Utah Area").

29. Harrison interview, June 9, 1996. Harrison remained on friendly terms with Wolpe even after Wolpe delivered a lecture titled "Thoughts on Pitch" during the 1952 summer session criticizing the use of other tuning systems. See Clarkson, *On the Music of Stefan Wolpe,* 118–120. Harrison even wrote a canon in honor of Wolpe's birthday.

30. Duberman, *Black Mountain,* 373.

31. Cage, quoted in Duberman, *Black Mountain,* 347.

32. Remy Charlip interview, June 18, 2005. The quote comes from a letter from Charlip to Harrison remembering the incident written around 1983 (Lou Harrison Archive). The incident, while indefensible, is certainly uncharacteristic. Harrison was shocked at Carl Ruggles's anti-Semitic tirade a few years before and later disdained Ezra Pound for his anti-Semitism. The slur against his recently deceased mentor Schoenberg is especially surprising but may represent a post-*Rapunzel* frustration with the twelve-tone system and the avant-garde it had spawned. Virgil Thomson was sometimes accused of anti-Semitism (Tommasini, *Virgil Thomson,* 330–331; Emerson, "Fascinating Schism").

33. Miller and Lieberman, *Lou Harrison: Composing a World,* 95.

34. Letter from Harrison to his mother, April 14, 1953, Lou Harrison Archive.

35. Letter from Antheil dated June 10, 1953, Lou Harrison Archive. Follow-up letters are dated July 24, 1953, and August 26, 1953.

36. Alan Baker, "An Interview with Lou Harrison."

37. Harrison interview #188 with Eva Soltes, undated.

Chapter 20

1. Notebook #65, Lou Harrison Archive.

2. Harrison interview, June 13, 1997; Bob Hughes interview, March 17, 2004.

3. Letter from Bradbury dated November 1, 1953, Lou Harrison Archive.

4. Teaching-job rejections are in the correspondence file, Lou Harrison Archive.

5. Notebook #29, Lou Harrison Archive.

6. March 23, 1959, letter to Harrison from Bill Jonson, Lou Harrison Archive. Jonson happened to be the conductor of the production of *Porgy and Bess* that Price was in when she was learning Harrison's piece in 1953–1954.

7. Price's performance in the revival of Thomson's opera *Four Saints in Three Acts* had so impressed Thomson that he asked Nabokov to make one of the award categories chamber music with soprano specifically to feature her at the festival. The category worked out well for Harrison.

8. Saunders, *The Cultural Cold War,* 220–225. Nabokov's idea of "advanced music" tended toward atonalism of the Schoenberg school rather than the more radical experiments of Pierre Boulez and John Cage. The polemical Boulez sent Nabokov an especially abusive letter, deriding the festival as "gathering a few puppets in a well staked-out cesspit." See Wellens, *Music on the Frontline,* 124. Nabokov's own music freely alternated between gentle atonality and tonal neoclassicism.

9. In "On Being American," Thomson identified Harrison and Merton Brown as young American "chromatic" composers. Although Thomson did not mention Ben Weber in that article, Thomson was aware that he, Harrison, Brown, and Elliott Carter represented the "Schoenberg fountainhead," as he put it, among younger New York composers. Harrison's recent move to California might have helped Nabokov, because he did not want the American delegation to exclusively comprise New Yorkers (Weber, *How I Took 63 Years to Commit Suicide*).

10. Letters from Brown to Harrison in Lou Harrison Archive correspondence file; see letter of July 27, 1953.

11. Letter from Norse to Harrison, October 8, 1953, Lou Harrison Archive.
12. Serinus, "A Conversation with Lou Harrison."
13. Steinberg, "Leontyne Price Soloist in Rome."
14. De Menasce, "Thoughts After a Festival."
15. Henze, *Bohemian Fifths*, 129–130.
16. Harrison interview, June 12, 1997.
17. Walsh, *Stravinsky: The Second Exile*, 316–317.
18. Thomson, *Virgil Thomson*, 412. Wellens, in *Music on the Frontline* (pp. 121–122), points out that serial composers were in fact in the minority on festival concerts. However, contemporary critics consistently noted the unusual proportion of atonal scores, especially from those younger composers invited to the competition. See, for example, Steinberg, "Contemporary Conference in Rome in April." In "Peragallo Work Wins Rome Prize," Steinberg also pointed out that all the award winners were twelve-tone compositions.
19. Harrison interview, June 13, 1997.
20. Soltes, *Lou Harrison: A World of Music*.
21. Interview with Wigglesworth quoted in Harrison and Miller, "Selected Keyboard and Chamber Music," xl.
22. Weber, *How I Took 63 Years to Commit Suicide*.
23. Ibid.
24. Celso, "A Study and Catalogue of Lou Harrison's Utilization of Keyboard Instruments," 10–11.
25. "Lines of 11 & 8 On Harry Partch." This poem, from October 1973, is reprinted in Peter Garland's *A Lou Harrison Reader* (pp. 63–64), where it is misidentified as "Lines of 11 & 3 on Harry Partch."
26. Harrison interview, June 12, 1997.
27. Brett Campbell, "Natural Sounds," 52.
28. For example, if we were to tune the twelve notes of an octave in just intonation, so that all the pitches were related to C by small integers, what would happen if we started to play a piece in another key, say D major? The A that we had carefully tuned to sound good in an F chord in the key of C (that is, a ratio of 8:5 with respect to C) would sound dissonant in the new key (where we would need an A tuned to 27:16 with respect to C, assuming the G and D in a G chord are also justly tuned to C). Even more remote keys would produce some very dissonant harmonies.
29. As in note 28, we arrive at two different pitches for the piano key representing A if we want it to be in tune for both an F chord and a D chord. The approach of temperament is to find pitches that are not quite in tune in either chord but, we hope, not too objectionable either.
30. Keislar, "Six American Composers on Nonstandard Tunings," 178.
31. In these experiments Harrison was helped by another book, Barbour's *Tuning and Temperament*, which appeared in 1951. Although biased in favor of equal temperament, it included invaluable tabulations of dozens of European tunings and temperaments as well as a selection of Greek tetrachords.
32. Lou Harrison, "Microfest 2001 Keynote Address," 1.
33. Harrison, personal communication. See also Harrison, "Schoenberg in Several Ways," 23.
34. Brunner, "The Choral Music of Lou Harrison," 331.
35. Partch had made the partly practical decision to draw the line at eleven, and, through the 1950s, Harrison followed his lead.
36. Kostelanetz, "A Conversation, in Eleven-Minus-One Parts," 391.
37. Harrison interview, July 19, 2000.
38. Burlin, *The Indians Book*, 355–356.
39. See Owsley Brown, *Music Makes a City*. Although the Rockefeller funding would last only four years, the orchestra commissioned more than 150 new compositions and released dozens of records.

40. Letter from Oliver Daniel, September 23, 1954, Lou Harrison Archive.

41. Quoted in Rathbun, "Lou Harrison and His Music," 61.

42. Burlin, *The Indians' Book*, 349.

43. Quoted in Rathbun, "Lou Harrison and His Music," 61.

44. Harrison, *Music Primer*, 27.

45. Ibid., 28.

46. This evil protagonist's innovations bore an uncomfortable resemblance to those of Harrison's teacher and Mann's fellow Southern California refugee, Arnold Schoenberg. According to Alex Ross, Schoenberg confronted Mann's friend Marta Feuchtwanger in a Brentwood grocery store, shouting, "I never had syphilis!" (Ross, *The Rest Is Noise*, 36).

47. Mann, *Doctor Faustus*, 191. While writing the novel, Mann consulted with the music theorist Theodor Adorno on the technical aspects of the music depicted in the novel, so it is likely that this distinction originated with him.

48. Harrison interview, June 12, 1997.

49. Harrison knew of the *jaltarang* from Cowell's *Ostinato Pianissimo* (1934) and *Fanati* (1935), and Cowell also used it in later works. Harrison would feature it in his later works *Pacifika Rondo* (1963) and *Varied Trio* (1987) and would use it in his ensemble of traditional Chinese music.

50. Fox-Strangways, *The Music of Hindostan*, 15.

51. The local review of the January 18, 1956, premiere of *Strict Songs* commended Harrison on the boldness of his simplicity: "His daring is the gift to be simple.... He succeeds... in building a carpet of sounds that is serenely active.... All the participants combined to establish a mood of quiet rejoicing" (Anderson, "Orchestra's Program of Arresting Quality").

52. Zwiebach interview, June 24, 2015.

Chapter 21

1. Notebook #113, dated 1957, Lou Harrison Archive.

2. Letter from Cage to Harrison, May 20, 1955, Lou Harrison Archive.

3. Notebook #49, Lou Harrison Archive.

4. From "To Music, to Becalm His Fever," by seventeenth-century English poet Robert Herrick. Harrison copied this poem into his notebook. Notebook #78, Lou Harrison Archive. Harrison misquotes this poem in *Music Primer* (p. 5).

5. Harrison, "MicroFest 2001 Keynote Address," 7.

6. Harrison wanted each of the pitches to be precisely pre-tuned, rather than approximated by instruments with a continuous pitch gamut (like a string quartet or the trombones in the *Strict Songs*). Although the *Simfony* does call for trombone, it is only for two drone notes in the entire piece, and they double the harp.

7. In the 1950s, serialist composer and fellow Ives editor Elliott Carter would become well known for his use of this technique, but Harrison later pointed out that, typically, Ives himself anticipated them both (Harrison, *Music Primer*, 19).

8. Schlesinger, *The Greek Aulos*, 545. The appendix, "A New Language of Music: Possibilities of the Ancient Modes for Use in Modern Composition," includes many ideas that inspired both Partch and Harrison. For example, she gives directions on the construction of a monochord, which would be a model for Harrison and Colvig when they built several monochords in the 1960s and later.

9. Notebook #49, Lou Harrison Archive. He even went so far as to track down a manufacturer, and they corresponded about the possibility of his obtaining custom-drilled recorders.

10. On the CD accompanying Miller and Lieberman, *Lou Harrison: Composing a World*. Even with the advent of computer technology, Harrison's pioneering idea of free-style just intonation would spawn few imitators, who included his friends Larry Polansky ("Paratactical Tuning") and Bill Alves ("Digital Harmony of Sound and Light").

11. Harrison interview, June 12, 1997.
12. Harrison, *Charles Ives: Violin Sonatas*.
13. Partch had similarly colored the keys of his reed organ, now appropriately renamed the Chromelodeon.
14. Harrison interview in Soltes, *Lou Harrison: A World of Music*.
15. For example, in Harrison's 1968 KPFA broadcast, "The Music of Lou Harrison."
16. Notebook #49, Lou Harrison Archive.
17. Harrison interview, June 12, 1997.
18. Geoff Smith, "Lou Harrison: An Interview." Letters from Partch in the Lou Harrison Archive include thanks to Harrison for helping to get Partch's *Castor and Pollux* published. A letter from Partch of May 28, 1956, responding to Harrison's LP recordings, calls his *The Only Jealousy of Emer* and *Canticle #3* "constantly fresh, lyrical, dynamic and surprising" and says, "I am proud to know you."
19. Partch would later make use of these possibilities in his film score *Windsong* (1958) and in the opening to *Revelation at the Courthouse Park* (1961), where the tape plays along with the live ensemble. However, the musician who would soon make the technique familiar to millions was Ross Bagdasarian, the creator of Alvin and the Chipmunks (1958).
20. It's unclear from the rather elliptical instructions in the score whether Harrison completely understood how the work would be realized, although the use of the tape machine to play back at double speed is clear.
21. In later years, Harrison would disown *Recording Piece*, following his well-known rejection of electronic music and electronic technology.
22. Harrison, *Pittsburgh 1968 Sound Recording and Discussion*, archive recording of a forum, Lou Harrison Archive. Unknown to Harrison, the RCA synthesizer created its tones by electromagnetically inducing the vibration of tuning forks tuned to equal temperament (see Olson and Belar, "Electronic Music Synthesizer"). The descendent of the 1955 RCA synthesizer would become available to some composers, but under the auspices of Columbia University rather than the ACA.
23. In Notebook #139 in the Lou Harrison Archive, Harrison claimed that Mondrian's paintings are "pentatonic" in nature, possibly referring to Mondrian's use of only five colors (the three primaries plus black and white). He also noted the rhythm implicit in those paintings as well as Mondrian's musical references, such as his *Broadway Boogie Woogie*.
24. Harrison interview, June 13, 1997.
25. Harrison interview, June 12, 1997.
26. In the mid-1960s, Campbell moved to Santa Fe, New Mexico, where she became friends with Georgia O'Keeffe. She and Harrison continued to correspond occasionally (Harrison interview, June 13, 1997).
27. Celso, "A Study and Catalogue of Lou Harrison's Utilization of Keyboard Instruments," 10–11.
28. Sachs, *Henry Cowell*, 448.
29. Notebook #147, Lou Harrison Archive.
30. Notebook #38, Lou Harrison Archive.
31. Harrison interview, June 12, 1997.
32. In a curriculum vitae he wrote up in 1955, now in the Lou Harrison Archive, Harrison wrote that he was at work on an opera titled *Full Circle*. Nothing else is known of this project.
33. Celso, "A Study and Catalogue of Lou Harrison's Utilization of Keyboard Instruments," 33.
34. Another notational oddity in *Cinna* is Harrison's frequent use of alto clef (as many of the moving parts in these movements lie directly between the standard bass and treble clefs), which keyboard composers in the baroque period used, but virtually none since then. "Why write way out of range and lots of ledger lines when you don't have to?" he asked. "There are clefs for that. It makes a much neater score. Of course actually it was for myself.

I didn't even think of the convenience of pianists, because it never occurred to me anyone would play it besides myself, because in the days I wrote it nobody was doing anything like that" (Celso, "A Study and Catalogue of Lou Harrison's Utilization of Keyboard Instruments," 101).

35. July 17, 1957, letter from Robert Duncan, Lou Harrison Archive.

Chapter 22

1. From one of Harrison's 1950s notebooks. Notebook #49, Lou Harrison Archive.
2. Ibid.
3. Harrison interview, March 20, 1995.
4. Under pressure, the composer William Grant Still told the committee that Cowell had been involved with communist music organizations in the 1930s (Sachs, *Henry Cowell*, 410). Riegger was named as a communist during an investigation of the music school of which he was the president (see Committee on Un-American Activities, *Investigation of Communism in the Metropolitan Music School*). Rexroth's investigation is recorded in Committee on Un-American Activities, *Investigation of Communist Activities in the San Francisco Area*.
5. Leyland, *Gay Sunshine Interviews*, 179–180.
6. "Science Tackles Radiation Peril."
7. Given Harrison's antigovernment agitation, it surprised the authors to learn that the FBI reported to them that it had no file on him.
8. Harrison, "Political Primer [Text]," 79.
9. "The History of KPFA." Harrison had known Watts in New York and through Harry Partch (both lived in Sausalito) but mostly through their other mutual friend, the poet Elsa Gidlow.
10. Letter to Cowell, c. 1962, Henry Cowell Collection, New York Public Library.
11. Notebook #107, Lou Harrison Archive.
12. Lou Harrison, "Crackpot Lecture," 1959, Lou Harrison Archive. He references Cousins "Retreat from Decency," 24.
13. Miller and Lieberman, *Lou Harrison: Composing a World*, 179.
14. Letter to Henry and Sidney Cowell, 1959, Lou Harrison Archive.
15. Harrison interview, September 25, 1997.
16. Robert Hughes interview, March 17, 2004.
17. Harrison, "Political Primer [Text]," 80.
18. Ibid., 81. This was the proposal of Harrison's much more rambling article titled "The Separation of War and State" from 1955 in Notebook #18 in the Lou Harrison Archive. It is unlikely that this earlier article was ever submitted anywhere for publication, although it was one precursor to the *Political Primer*. Harrison sent the completed text of his *Political Primer* to at least two of his favorite writers—Norman Cousins of the *Saturday Review* and liberal intellectual Walter Lippman—and both graciously responded. Lippman expressed interest and inquired about Harrison's sources, and Cousins wrote that he was "greatly moved" by Harrison's words (correspondence file, Lou Harrison Archive).
19. This last instrument would be the most problematic to tune, because metal bars are not as easily adjusted as the strings of a harp, for example.
20. Harrison interview, August 10, 2001.
21. Alan Baker, "An Interview with Lou Harrison."
22. The numbering of the overtures is not entirely certain because only one of the three seems to have a designation in the sketches: the first overture ("Monarchy"), which became the last movement of the *Third Symphony* (1982–1983). However, it would be reasonable to suppose that the slower movement would be the second ("Republic"). This movement became the opening to the *Elegiac Symphony* (1975), where it acquired the title "Tears

for the Angel Israfel (1)." The powerful opening of the *Third Symphony* would then correspond to the "Democracy" overture. In these later adaptations, Harrison abandoned his insistence on just intonation, allowing him to accommodate a much more conventional (and practical) orchestra.

23. Harrison, "Crackpot Lecture," Lou Harrison Archive.
24. Harrison, *Music Primer*, 44.
25. Harrison interview, June 19, 2000. It may have been around this time that he made a lengthy list of his earthly treasures, providing a glimpse into Harrison's aesthetic and his wide range of enthusiasms. The musical treasures he lists include Ives, Corelli, Brahms, Schubert, Bruckner, Stravinsky, Honegger's oratorios, Rameau, Vivaldi, Handel, Javanese gamelan music, *gagaku*, Korean *a-ak*, Chinese chamber music, and Javanese *macapat* songs. He lists the artists Lorrain, Dürer, Tiepolo, Rubens, Sonia and Robert Delaunay, Michelangelo, Chagall, and Poussin, the Impressionists, and Chinese landscape painters; he lists architects Palladio, Mansart, Robert Adam, Vanbrugh, Sinan, McKim, Mead, and White. Poets and writers include Racine, Goethe, Horace, Virgil, Sappho, Pindar, Shakespeare, William Morris, Dickinson, Whitman, Cavafy, Wang Wei, Tu Fu, Murasaki, Basho, Chiramatsu, and the Noh dramatists. He also lists philosophers, scientists, musical instruments, places, and "Buddhism and all its works" (Notebook #77, Lou Harrison Archive).
26. Letter from Harrison to Cowell, October 20, 1959.
27. Harrison interview, June 12, 1997.
28. Harrison, quoted in Daniel Burwasser, "A Study of Lou Harrison's *Concerto for Violin with Percussion Orchestra* and *Concerto for Organ and Percussion Orchestra*," 17. In further quotes from this interview (pp. 15–16), Harrison remembered significantly rewriting the earlier concerto, but this recollection is not borne out by comparison of the 1959 score with the original manuscript now in the Lou Harrison Archive.
29. Horowitz, ed., *Uncharted Beauty*, 15.
30. Yates, a critic of the recent European focus on Monday Evening Concerts, fulfilled a longtime ambition to program an all-Harrison concert (Crawford, *Evenings On and Off the Roof*, 185). The review by Walter Arlen, "Harrison Works Heard on Monday Concert," was mostly positive. A draft for a thank-you letter to Peter Yates is in Notebook #80 in the Lou Harrison Archive.
31. Murdoch, *Peggy Glanville-Hicks*, 204.
32. Rathbun, "Lou Harrison and His Music," 74.
33. Taubman, "Opera: Two Premieres."
34. Hughes interview, March 17, 2004.
35. Manuscript copy in the Lou Harrison Archive.
36. Hughes interview, March 17, 2004.
37. Ibid.
38. Harrison, "Political Primer [Text]," 81. The reference is to science and science fiction writer Isaac Asimov, whose article "I Feel It in My Bones" discusses radioactive fallout whose traces were absorbed by human bones.
39. Harlan typescript, Lou Harrison Archive. See also Harlan's essay in Garland, *A Lou Harrison Reader*, 96–97.
40. The following summer, Harrison's *Suite #2 for Strings* appeared on another University at Buffalo concert program.
41. Letter to Siegmund Levarie, dated April 7, 1959, in the collection of Robert Hughes, turning down an offer of a teaching position at Brooklyn College Department of Music as well as a visiting position at the University of Seoul, proposed by the Rockefeller Foundation. Ned Rorem eventually got the Buffalo residency that Harrison had declined.
42. Harrison, "Preface," in *Suite for Symphonic Strings* score, 1.

43. Harrison had the opportunity to experiment with these effects during a rare trip out of California in the summer of 1960. Then he attended the Institute of Orchestral Studies of the American Symphony Orchestra League held in Virginia, where the orchestra read parts of the work in progress.

44. Rathbun, "Lou Harrison and His Music," 93. "I did that because I had written two previous pieces for strings all of which are constantly being done by string-tettes. Nowadays they'll play things with the fewest instruments they can get. So I wrote it intentionally so that it can't be played by a small ensemble." This frustration may have been prompted by the 1954 LP of his *Suite #2* for strings, which Columbia had recorded with the New Music String Quartet under the title *Suite No. 2 for String Quartet*.

45. Harrison, *Suite for Symphonic Strings* score, 6.

46. Ibid., 7.

47. Later, he would use a more colorful version of the name: "stampede," assuming that the name "estampie" comes from its nature as a stamping dance, but later he found that it means "a general brouhaha" (Leta E. Miller, "Solemn Play," liii; and Kostelanetz, "A Conversation, in Eleven-Minus-One Parts," 397. Modern etymologists think that the term came from a verb meaning "to resound" and that "stampede" entered English through a Mexican cowboy term originally meaning "uproar." Either meaning suited Harrison, whose use of the latter term for a dance in fact had a precedent in nineteenth-century Texas.

48. Harrison, *Music Primer*, 23.

49. Harrison, *Suite for Symphonic Strings* score, 6.

50. Rathbun, "Lou Harrison and His Music," 94.

51. Ibid., 94.

52. Ibid., 92. Harrison also credited Erwin Panofsky's essay on the epitaph in *Meaning in the Visual Arts* and said that "more than one friend has agreed that the Chorale seems to be the answer to Mr. Ives' 'Unanswered Question'!" (Harrison, liner notes to *Decoration Day, Suite for Symphonic Strings*).

53. Quoted in Shere, "The Making of Lou Harrison."

54. Rathbun, "Lou Harrison and His Music," 94.

55. Ibid., 94–95. See also Harrison's poem "The Four Patrons of the Palaestra" in *Joys & Perplexities* (p. 8).

56. Harrison, "The Four Patrons of the Palaestra" in *Joys and Perplexities*, 8.

57. Rathbun, "Lou Harrison and His Music," 94–95.

58. Harrison was inspired to take on this challenge after hearing the mode in Roy Harris's Third String Quartet. "It's a very difficult mode to make a piece in because it doesn't have a fifth, you know. Still, it's a very poignant, beautiful mode" (Rathbun, "Lou Harrison and His Music," 96). Harrison was referring to the Prelude of movement 3 in Harris's quartet, although Harris was considerably freer in his use of the mode, allowing at times fifths above the tonic. Harris's piece was recorded in 1940, so it is likely that Harrison would have become familiar with at Wilson's Record Library in San Francisco.

59. Hughes interview, March 17, 2004.

60. Ibid.

61. Ibid.

62. Richard Dee interview, March 16, 2004.

63. The offer letter from Nabokov, dated November 9, 1960, is in the Lou Harrison Archive.

Part 5

1. Harrison, *Music Primer*, 129.

2. Harrison interview, September 24, 1997. "Dodecaphonic" is another term for twelve-tone music.

Chapter 23

1. Harrison interview, Sept. 24, 1997. See also Harrison, *Music Primer*, 26. Actually, the Javanese distinguish between the Chinese scales, which alternate major seconds and minor thirds, and *slendro*, in which all the step sizes are roughly equal—that is, larger than major seconds and smaller than minor thirds. Harrison had already made use of the distinction between the first of his *Strict Songs* (in a "Chinese" pentatonic) and the third *Strict Song* (in a tuning system closer to *slendro*). Harrison at this time used the term *slendro* for both, but later in his life he used *slendro* in this more specific way.
2. Harrison, *Music Primer*, 27.
3. Harrison dedicated the *Concerto in Slendro* to Richard Dee, in the expectation that he would play it. Ironically, Dee never played the piece, and it was first recorded with violinist Daniel Kobialka.
4. As Harrison noted towards the end of his life, metal trash cans and washtubs have become very difficult to find (Rathbun, "Lou Harrison and His Music," 101).
5. Harrison interview, September 24, 1997.
6. Quintal counterpoint is the most appropriate type of counterpoint for anhemitonic pentatonic music, according to Joseph Yasser in *A Theory of Evolving Tonality* (pp. 62–104), the book that had first given Harrison the idea for quintal counterpoint.
7. Harrison interview, September 24, 1997. The movement invites comparisons to Bartók's well-known "night music" style, so named for a movement from the piano suite *Out of Doors*. However, Harrison never mentioned Bartók as an influence here or in other works. The creation of harmonious structures through strict mathematics was hardly new to Harrison but would play a central role in his *Pacifika Rondo* of 1963.
8. Harrison, *Pittsburgh 1968 Sound Recording and Discussion,* archive recording, Lou Harrison Archive.
9. Harrison interview, September 24, 1997. He only later discovered that most of these hosts spoke English, a fact that did not alter their interactions.
10. 1961 letter to Hughes, in Hughes's collection.
11. Early press releases about the conference in "Tour of Japan" (New York Philharmonic Archives) indicated that it would include a "gamelang [*sic*] orchestra from Indonesia." However, we could find no record of such a performance. If one had been there, Harrison's life might have taken a very different turn, as he would have had an opportunity to explore Javanese rather than Korean music at this early date.
12. Notebook #39, Lou Harrison Archive. "Cheng" is the old transliteration.
13. Harrison interview, September 24, 1997.
14. Lou Harrison, "Refreshing the Auditory Perception," 142.
15. "East Meets West," 67. See also Burton, *Leonard Bernstein,* 321. The bulk of this money, of course, was secretly provided by the CIA, a fact that would be made public in 1967.
16. The CCF sent Bernstein a box of scores and tapes of suggested Japanese pieces, but he liked none of them. Then Henry Cowell, independently of the committee, gave him a copy of Toshiro Mayuzumi's *Bacchanale*, which Bernstein liked, although he assigned it to his assistant, the young Japanese conductor Seiji Ozawa. Cowell's friendly act backfired when Bernstein programmed *Bacchanale* in place of Cowell's own Japanese-inspired *Ongaku*. It turned out that Mayuzumi was a well-known enemy of the Japanese left and a supporter of right-wing nationalism, so the programming of his piece only confirmed the suspicions of leftist protesters. However, it would be absurd to suggest that Cowell, whose name had just come under suspicion in the McCarthy era, suggested the piece out of a political agenda. Mayuzumi was "abject" and wrote a letter of apology to Cowell. Harrison was likely aware of the controversy, since the press held up Cowell as a "hero" who gave his spot to a Japanese composer, but by the time of the concert, May 5, Harrison was already in Korea. See the New York Philharmonic Archives folder titled "Tour of Japan, Alaska,

Canada and Southern U.S. 1961: Tokyo, Press, Correspondence, Programming Feb 16 1960–Jun 16 1961"; Sachs, *Henry Cowell*, 473–474; Nuss, "Music from the Right."

17. Daniélou, "Music of India," 8. See also Daniélou, "Problems of Indian Music Tradition Today," 64–66.

18. Wellens, *Music on the Frontline*, 103–113.

19. An April 13, 1961 letter welcoming Harrison into the Socialist Party Social Democratic Federation and a bright red membership card are in the Lou Harrison Archive.

20. Harrison interview, September 25, 1997.

21. Garfias, "Some Effects of Changing Social Values on Japanese Music."

22. Crossley-Holland, "Asian Music Under the Impact of Western Culture," 50.

23. Harrison interview, September 24, 1997.

24. Henry Cowell, "Oriental Influence on Western Music," 74.

25. Harrison, *Music Primer*, 45.

26. Elliott Carter's presentation on "Classical Syntax," Makoto Moroi's on electronic music, and Xenakis's on "Stochastic Music."

27. Quotes here and below from Harrison, "Refreshing the Auditory Perception," 141–143. The copy of this book in the UCSC library incorporates Harrison's handwritten corrections. Saraswati is the Hindu deity associated with music and the arts, and Ganesha is the Hindu deity associated with wisdom and intelligence, among other things.

28. This paper is reprinted in von Gunden, *The Music of Lou Harrison*, 163–165. The more detailed description of the mode room is in the second edition of the *Music Primer* (Harrison, *Rū Harison no wārudo myūjikku nyūmon*, 141).

29. From Harrison's introduction printed in a program for a Korean music concert, Lou Harrison Archive. A version of this description is also in a late May or June 1961 letter to Robert Hughes in the archive.

30. Harrison interview, September 24, 1997.

31. Murdoch, *Peggy Glanville-Hicks*, 123–124.

32. Harrison interview, September 24, 1997.

33. Ibid.

34. Letter to Hughes, Lou Harrison Archive.

35. From a translation to English of an article in the newspaper *Chosun Ilbo* (June 11, 1961) in the Lou Harrison Archive. Possibly the translation was prepared by Hwang or someone at the university during his visit.

36. Postcard included in Soltes, *Lou Harrison: A World of Music*.

37. 1961 letter to Hughes, in Hughes's collection.

38. Harrison interview, September 24, 1997. *Gayageum* is the new transliteration. Harrison spelled it "*kayagum*."

39. From Harrison's introduction printed in a program for a Korean music concert, Lou Harrison Archive.

40. "Spring in Nak Yang." Harrison and Lee, *Korean Music*, 21.

41. Harrison, *Joys & Perplexities*, 99. Harrison's friend Anthony Cirone later set Harrison's text to music for percussion and soprano.

42. Preface to the score of *Nak Yang Chun* in the Lou Harrison Archive.

43. For example, his *Overture to the Trojan Women* of 1939 has parallel chords in the harp very similar to these. See chapter 7.

44. Letter to Cowell, 1962, Henry Cowell Collection, New York Public Library.

45. Carey, "Double Music," 40.

46. Harrison enlisted his Santa Cruz friend, linguist Bruce Kennedy, to help him with the translation to Esperanto. This English version is from Harrison, *Joys & Perplexities*, 115–116.

47. Cowell, *New Musical Resources*, 19–20; Rao, "Henry Cowell and His Chinese Music Heritage."

48. Harrison, "Creative Ideas in Classical Korean Music," 35.

49. Harrison, *Joys & Perplexities*, 116.
50. Harrison and Lee, *Korean Music*, 5.
51. Harrison interview, June 12, 1997. Harrison called the rondo "Henry Cowell-y."
52. A 1963 Harrison letter to Peter Yates in the Lou Harrison Archive mentions a proposed performance at the San Francisco Conservatory of Music falling through; a letter to Hughes in the archive mentions a December 1963 San Francisco Symphony performance of a work with *piri*, psaltery, and orchestra, but it too was canceled. *Nova Odo* was finally performed at the 1968 Cabrillo Festival and in Seoul in 1976.

Chapter 24
1. Harrison, "Creative Ideas in Classical Korean Music," 34.
2. Harrison interview, September 25, 1997. See also the translation to English of the article in the newspaper *Chosun Ilbo* (June 11, 1961) in the Lou Harrison Archive.
3. The old romanization of these instruments' names, used by Harrison, are *tanso, tongso,* and *changgo.*
4. Letter to Cowell, circa December 1961, Henry Cowell Collection, New York Public Library.
5. Harrison mentions this ambition in "Creative Ideas in Classical Korean Music," 35. He also mentions this plan, as well as his experiments with homemade *piri* and *zheng,* in a letter to Boyd Compton at the Rockefeller Foundation in October 1961 (Lou Harrison Archive). In an interview on September 25, 1997, Harrison credited Bill Colvig for the construction of these instruments, but the letter to Compton shows that Harrison was already working on them years before he met Colvig. Harrison noted that the Koreans named their versions of the *piri* after their places of origin, including the *tang* (Chinese) *piri* and the *hyang* (Korean) *piri.* When Harrison brought his plastic version back to Korea, scholars there referred to it as the *miguk piri* or "American *piri,*" a name Harrison continued to use thereafter.
6. Harrison, "Creative Ideas in Classical Korean Music," 34.
7. Harrison interview, September 25, 1997.
8. Harrison received interest in publishing the finished work from Wesleyan University Press (which had recently published Cage's *Silence*) and the Institute of Ethnomusicology at UCLA, directed by Mantle Hood.
9. "For the Hovhanessiad: Lines of 8 & 6 in Honor of Hovhaness." Harrison, *Joys & Perplexities,* 45.
10. See letter from Harrison to Boyd Compton of the Rockefeller Foundation, 1962, and letter from Hovhaness to Harrison April 4, 1962, Lou Harrison Archive.
11. "The Tenth Day," 51.
12. For example, see the letter from Hovhaness to Harrison dated April 4, 1962 (Lou Harrison Archive), where Hovhaness says that these Asian instruments "changed my life." See also Badagnani, "The Alan Hovhaness Website." On a subsequent trip to Japan, Hovhaness produced works for the Chinese *qin* and the Japanese koto as well as his Symphony #15, based on Indian ragas and an Indian novel about a spiritual pilgrimage.
13. It's unknown whether Hovhaness's op. 171 was in fact a response to Harrison's request, but it seems likely. Hovhaness's Sonata, like Harrison's Prelude, can also be played by oboe and organ.
14. Letter to Cowell, 1962, Henry Cowell Collection, New York Public Library. Harrison also notes in the same letter the ancient advice that, as *auletes,* they should avoid eating eels and leeks.
15. April 4, 1962, letter from Hovhaness to Harrison, Lou Harrison Archive
16. See Harrison's 1962 letters to Hughes and to his family in the Lou Harrison Archive.
17. Letter to Bob Hughes, 1962, Lou Harrison Archive. The score of *Nova Odo* indicates that he worked on the second movement while there.

18. Letter to his parents, 1962, Lou Harrison Archive.

19. Typescript in Lou Harrison Archive.

20. In addition to frequent concert tours, Liang studied at Yale University in the 1940s. In 1946, Liang performed in New York City, where Harrison would have had the opportunity to hear him. However, that night the *Herald Tribune* assigned Harrison to review a vocal recital instead. See Miller and Lieberman, *Lou Harrison: Composing a World*, 143.

21. In a few years, Harrison would be obliged to reciprocate when Liang's son David Mingyue Liang moved to California to study ethnomusicology at UC Berkeley, and Harrison became the young man's "American father."

22. See Liang Tsai-Ping, "A Short Note in Honor of Lou Harrison," in Peter Garland, ed., *A Lou Harrison Reader*, 87.

23. On *Pacifika Rondo*. Letter to Hughes dated October 31, 1962, Lou Harrison Archive.

24. Program for East–West Center concert, May 26, 1963, Lou Harrison Archive.

25. In Notebook #5, Lou Harrison Archive.

26. Harrison's score indicates that a harp can optionally replace the *gayageum* zither, as it does on the recording with the Oakland Symphony Youth Orchestra. It is unclear whether the harp was used for the premiere.

27. Frederic Lieberman speech at Lou Harrison memorial, February 22, 2003. See also Miller and Lieberman, *Lou Harrison: Composing a World*, 217–220.

28. Harrison had used palindromes in the percussion works *Fifth Simfony* and *Fugue for Percussion*.

29. Program for East–West Center concert, May 26, 1963, Lou Harrison Archive. In addition to Cousteau, it is likely that Harrison's view of dolphins (which would also surface in his *A Phrase for Arion's Leap* of 1974) was influenced by the recent publication of John Lilly's *Man and Dolphin*.

30. He had used the same structure in *Labyrinth* of 1941.

31. Liner notes to *Pacifika Rondo, Two Pieces for Psaltery, Music for Various Instruments*.

32. Program for East–West Center concert, May 26, 1963, Lou Harrison Archive.

33. The famous medieval song *Sumer is icumen in* has the same sort of canonic ostinato accompaniment.

34. Program in Lou Harrison Archive. Harrison uses the same row-rotation technique that he had in his *Symphony on G*.

35. Bowles, *In Touch*, 476 (entry of April 4, 1977). "*Música escrita por un diós*" translates to "Music written for a god." Bowles didn't actually name the piece that he was referring to in this letter, but he confirms that it was the *Pacifica Rondo* in following correspondence.

Chapter 25

1. Harrison, *The Path at West Holding*, 21–22; draft from c. 1992 in Notebook #3, Lou Harrison Archive.

2. Harrison in Marin, *Lou Harrison: Cherish, Conserve, Consider, Create*.

3. Harrison, *The Path at West Holding*, 21–22 (Lou Harrison Archive; see note 1). The quote from Clarence Harrison is also in a 1964 poem in Notebook #120 in the Lou Harrison Archive.

4. Harrison interview, July 5, 1996; Hughes interview, March 17, 2004.

5. "Hymn for the Bodhisatva Avalokiteshvara." Notebook #120, Lou Harrison Archive.

6. An article in *Time*, "Doctrine of the Dropouts," named Watts (a scholar of Zen Buddhism and lecturer at the newly formed San Francisco Zen Center) as a spiritual leader of the religion of "hippiedom," an "undigested mixture of drug-induced visions, skimmed Orientalism and nature worship."

7. Harrison, "Society, Musician, Dancer, Machine."

8. *Avalokiteshvara* can also be played on harp and has been adapted for guitar, with or without optional percussion.

9. The etching is in the possession of Robert Hughes, who does not recall the name of the artist. Perhaps inspired by the publication of Ray Bradbury's *Martian Chronicles*, Harrison noted that one can see one and a quarter moons in the sky of Mars (Harrison, liner notes to *The Music of Lou Harrison*).

10. Letter to Lieberman, 1963, Lou Harrison Archive.

11. Dee interview, March 16, 2004.

12. Among the works Hughes programmed at the Sticky Wicket series were a full production of Gluck's *Orfeo* and Stravinsky's *L'histoire du Soldat* with Victor Jowers narrating.

13. Frankenstein, "Brilliant Bartok Opens Festival." Harrison was represented on a concert that Samuel did not conduct, a harpsichord recital by Harrison's friend Margaret Fabrizio, who performed his early *Cembalo Sonatas*. However, the *Chronicle* review of that concert does not mention the Harrison piece. Frankenstein did note that Harrison was invited to deliver a lecture but was unable to because of his father's death and his mother's illness. Peter Yates gave the lecture instead, using most of the time to praise Harrison.

14. Fried, "Lou Harrison's Aptos Triumph."

15. Quoted in Celso, "A Study and Catalogue of Lou Harrison's Utilization of Keyboard Instruments," 143. Perhaps the difference was, as Harrison said, that after the constraints of the first movements, this last movement allows itself "a great expanse. . . . It flows and develops and climaxes and finally ends so. That's a different kind of working" (Harrison interview, August 1, 2001).

16. Farley, Sharpe, and Sharpe, *The Old Spaghetti Factory*.

17. One of the few other just-intonation composers at the time, Ben Johnston originally met Harrison in 1952 (before either had composed in just intonation) when Johnston came to New York to work with Cage. In April 1967, Johnston organized a symposium titled "Microtonal Music in America" at the conference of the American Society of University Composers, where Peter Yates gave a presentation mentioning Harrison. It may have been then that Johnston first became aware of Harrison's work in just intonation. La Monte Young was also mentioned, but the group of American just-intonation composers at the time was a small club indeed (American Society of University Composers, *Proceedings of the Second Annual Conference*, 75–123). Johnston and Harrison would become friends, and in 1978, Johnston invited him to the University of Illinois at Urbana-Champaign.

18. Commanday, "Lou Harrison Seeks Privacy in Aptos."

19. Harrison, "Society, Musician, Dancer, Machine," 40.

20. Harrison interview, July 19, 2000. The offer came from the well-known musicologist Wilfrid Mellers, who in 1964 founded the music department of York University.

21. Lorle Kennedy (née Kranzler) interview, June 25, 2013.

22. Harrison, "Society, Musician, Dancer, Machine," 40.

23. Kennedy interview, June 25, 2013.

24. Kranzler interview, June 29, 2015. Richard Dee would sometimes drive up to join in the improvisations.

25. Harrison interview, September 25, 1997. "As I approached fifty, I tended towards alcoholism," Harrison admitted (Leyland, *Gay Sunshine Interviews*, 170).

26. Letter to Cowell, c. 1965, Henry Cowell Collection, New York Public Library.

27. During the period of his great enthusiasm for Chávez's music in San Francisco, the young Harrison had briefly met him backstage, but this was his first opportunity to get to know the Mexican composer and conductor. Harrison hoped to interest him in performing his *Suite for Symphonic Strings*, but their collaboration wouldn't transpire until a few years later, when Chávez became the new director of the Cabrillo Festival.

28. Harrison interview, September 25, 1997.

29. Harrison interview, July 24, 2001; letter to the authors from Dee, December 16, 2014. Harrison titled the collective music for the three dances *Reflections in Motion*, but the version

with the tapes was never realized. Harrison also used sliding tones in *Nova Odo* and *Pacifika Rondo*, perhaps in response to Cowell, who recommended them in *New Musical Resources* (pp. 19–20) (Rao, "Henry Cowell and His Chinese Music Heritage").

30. Festival program, June 23–25, 1966, Jacob's Pillow Dance Archive.
31. Harrison, "Society, Musician, Dancer, Machine," 40.
32. Ziony, "Lou Harrison: Shaping the 60s."
33. Perry, *The Haight-Ashbury*, 47.
34. Chloe Scott interview, June 30, 2014. See also Perry, *The Haight-Ashbury*, 94–95.
35. Harrison interview, September 24, 1997.
36. Harrison, "Schoenberg in Several Ways," 24.
37. Hughes, personal communication. The April 6, 1970, concert was previewed in the SIR periodical *Vector*.
38. Notebook #138, Lou Harrison Archive.
39. Notebook #95, Lou Harrison Archive.
40. Harrison interview, June 24, 2000.
41. "The Rich Culture of Mexico," in Northrop, *The Meeting of East and West*, 65.
42. Draft letter from Harrison to Carlos Chávez, February 5, 1956, in Notebook #65, Lou Harrison Archive; Harlan, "Lou Harrison—My Friend and Favorite Composer," 96.
43. Notebook #138, Lou Harrison Archive.
44. Harrison interview, July 24, 2001.
45. Leyland, *Gay Sunshine Interviews*, 171.
46. Cowell's *The Nature of Melody* remains unpublished. See Sachs, *Henry Cowell*, 333–336; and Gann, "Subversive Prophet," 202–219.
47. Wolf, "Item: Blogging."
48. Rorem, "Books on Music."
49. The *Music Primer* was finally calligraphed not by Harrison but instead back in California by Ron Pendergraft, a student looking for a project as part of his work toward a credential in calligraphy.
50. Harrison would later thank Hinrichsen by dedicating a waltz to her, which became one of the loveliest parts of his *Third Symphony* (Gillespie, "Another View on Lou").
51. Letter to Siegmund Levarie, dated April 7, 1959, in the collection of Robert Hughes.
52. Thomson, *The State of Music*, 109.
53. 1974 draft letter to Don Gillespie, Lou Harrison Archive.
54. Leyland, *Gay Sunshine Interviews*, 175.
55. Letter from Charlip to Harrison, 1966, Lou Harrison Archive.
56. The indefatigable Hughes and Samuel used their positions to bring ever more Harrison music to the area too—the *Strict Songs*; *Suite for Violin, Piano and Small Orchestra*; *Symphony on G*; and *Seven Pastorales* in 1966 alone (1966 letters from Hughes, Lou Harrison Archive).

Chapter 26

1. Hughes interview, March 17, 2004.
2. Leyland, *Gay Sunshine Interviews*, 175.
3. Two biographies of Colvig: Bogdanowitsch, "Bill Colvig"; Collins, "A Sound Life."
4. Linick, *The Lives of Ingolf Dahl*, 297–300.
5. Ned Rorem interview, October 24, 2005.
6. Rorem soon congratulated Lou on his match with Colvig, and they maintained an exceptionally warm correspondence ever after (Rorem letters to Harrison of February 2, 1967, and February 22, 1967, Lou Harrison Archive).
7. Colvig in Marin, *Lou Harrison: Cherish, Conserve, Consider, Create*.
8. Notebook #95, Lou Harrison Archive.
9. Collins, "A Sound Life."

10. Richard Dee interview, March 16, 2004.
11. Leyland, *Gay Sunshine Interviews*, 171.
12. Harrison, *Music Primer*, 42.
13. Colvig's monochord design is in Ditrich and Colvig, *The Mills College Gamelan*, 56–58. One of the innovations Colvig contributed was the use of tweezers instead of a bridge to stop the string. Because closed tweezers, unlike an intermediate bridge, impart no extra tension to the string, the pitch is much more accurate.
14. Harrison described the transfer harp as being "much like the vertical Chinese harp, and a descendent of the Sumerian Lyre." He originally envisioned it to be part of the "Mode Room" he proposed at the 1961 Tokyo conference. See Harrison, "Four Items," 2.
15. Harrison had previously encountered the *marimbula* in their 1940 percussion ensemble performance of Amadeo Roldán's *Ritmicas*. Although performances today frequently substitute a marimba, the photograph of that concert clearly shows a *marimbula* at the far left, perhaps also homemade.
16. The other two were his *Suite for Violin, Piano, and Small Orchestra* (1951) and *Concerto for Violin with Percussion Orchestra* (1940/1959). One could also add the future *Philemon and Baukis* (1987) to the list.
17. Draft letter to Calline Harrison in the Lou Harrison Archive.
18. Poem dated June 5, 1967, in Notebook #95, Lou Harrison Archive.
19. Harrison wrote the article in 1969 in response for a request for an article for a *festschrift* honoring Lee Hye-Ku (Harrison, "Some Notes on the Music of Mouth-Organs").
20. Richard Dee interview, March 16, 2004.
21. Ibid.
22. Harrison, "On Harry Partch," unpublished 1985 paper in the Lou Harrison Archive.
23. Specifically, Harrison decided on Ptolemy's syntonic diatonic scale for these instruments: 1:1, 9:8, 5:4, 4:3, 3:2, 5:3, 15:8. As these instruments would later become the core of his American gamelan, that ensemble shared this tuning. Harrison chose D because it was convenient for string instruments to tune to and because he had built a *piri* whose lowest pitch was A 220: the dominant of D (Harrison interview, August 10, 2001). See also Colvig, "An American Gamelan," reprinted in Rathbun, "Lou Harrison and His Music," 149–150, and Gardner, "*La Koro Sutro* by Lou Harrison," 121–122.
24. Gardner, "*La Koro Sutro* by Lou Harrison," 126. The pentatonic scales of Chinese instruments such as the *qin* are traditionally tuned in perfect fifths; that is, a three-limit tuning (even though today Chinese musicians often use twelve-tone equal temperament). A five-limit scale, with its pure thirds, is more appropriate for a diatonic scale and tertial harmonies, so Harrison's decision implied a framework for East–West hybrids.
25. Bellows often gathered Harrison's short harp pieces into a harp suite in performance. They have since been taken up by guitarists such as John Schneider and David Tanenbaum.
26. "Lines to Ned Rorem" in Harrison, *Joys & Perplexities*, 40. This text has "prod" where we have "proud."
27. Letter from Harrison to Colvig, undated but presumably fall 1967, Lou Harrison Archive.
28. Letter from Harrison to Colvig, November 25, 1967, Lou Harrison Archive.
29. Harrison ms., Lou Harrison Archive.
30. Letter from Harrison to Bill Colvig, November 25, 1967, Lou Harrison Archive. See also "150 Police Break Up Antiwar Riot at San Jose State College."
31. Arnold, "War Music and the American Composer during the Vietnam Era," 319.
32. Somewhat confusingly, Harrison numbered the *Little Song on the Atom Bomb* his *Peace Piece #3*, even though it was the first composed of the three so named. He categorized other pieces with similar themes as "peace pieces" even though he did not make "Peace Piece" part of their titles, including his *France 1917—Spain 1937* (1937) and *Nova Odo* (1961–1968).

33. Duncan, "Up Rising."

34. Bloomfield, "Doves Win Music Festival Decibel Poll"; Hughes interview, March 17, 2004.

35. Kretschmer, Reti, and Jarrell, *Ernest T. Kretschmer*, 24.

36. Clipping of a letter to the editor, *Santa Cruz Sentinel*, March 14, 1970, Lou Harrison Archive.

37. Around this time, Lewis played him a work by Krzysztof Penderecki. "I don't like to listen to that kind of music," Harrison said. "It reminds me of gloomy cathedral basements" (Kerry Lewis interview, December 21, 2013).

38. Shere, "The Making of Lou Harrison."

39. Notebook #13 in the Lou Harrison Archive.

40. Commanday, "Lou Harrison Seeks Privacy in Aptos."

41. Notebook #14 in the Lou Harrison Archive.

42. Notebook #95 in the Lou Harrison Archive.

43. Harrison, "Society, Musician, Dancer, Machine," 41.

44. His syllabus listed the topics by week: "1. Vietnam, 2. Confucian & Buddhist, 3. Buddhist & Japan, 4. Korea, 5, 6. Indonesia, 7. S. E. Asia, 8. India, 9 1/2. India, 1/2 Judea & Coptic, 10. Islam Mostly Iran & Turkey, 11. Africa, 12. Amerindians & Hawaii" (Notebook #71, Lou Harrison Archive).

45. Harrison interview, July 21, 2000; Randall Wong personal communication, July 13, 2013.

46. Harrison, *Music Primer*, 48

47. David Lang interview, October 24, 2010.

48. Siddall, e-mail communication, June 12, 2014.

49. "I Remember Lou."

50. Kerry Lewis, e-mail communication, Dec. 21, 2013.

51. Jarnot, *Robert Duncan, the Ambassador from Venus*, 213; Duncan, *Robert Duncan: The Collected Later Poems and Plays*, 198. Reprinted with the permission of the University of California Press.

52. Ibid., 197. Reprinted with the permission of the University of California Press.

53. Ibid., 198. Reprinted with the permission of the University of California Press.

54. Although Harrison's copyist later typeset the *Orpheus* score on the computer, only the segments adapted from *Labyrinth* were published, now titled *The Drums of Orpheus* for percussion orchestra.

55. Harrison interview, July 19, 2000.

56. Harrison, *Pittsburgh 1968 Sound Recording and Discussion*, archive recording of a forum in the Lou Harrison Archive.

57. Copland, *Aaron Copland: A Reader*, 290.

Chapter 27

1. "From Words for Music Certainly," in Harrison, *Joys & Perplexities*, 11.

2. Harrison interview, August 10, 2001; Leyland, *Gay Sunshine Interviews*, 177–178.

3. Rathbun, "Lou Harrison and His Music," 77.

4. Eva Soltes, personal communication.

5. Harrison outlined these parts of chant in his *Music Primer*, 50.

6. Rathbun, "Lou Harrison and His Music," 130. He was convinced that the technique would work after seeing a Chinese opera in English translation while in Hawaii in 1963.

7. Rathbun, "Lou Harrison and His Music," 77.

8. Ibid., 77.

9. Harrison interview, July 20, 2000. Although the model of Bach shows up in some of Harrison's pieces, he often expressed his annoyance at the canonization of Bach (at the expense of Handel) by the "international industry devoted to a theophany of J. S. Bach" (Notebook #122, Lou Harrison Archive). See Harrison, "Cloverleaf," 2; Miller and Lieberman, *Lou Harrison: Composing a World*, 192; and von Gunden, *The Music of Lou Harrison*, 68.

10. According to Colvig ("An American Gamelan") and the *Young Caesar* score, the scale was pentatonic (from D): 1:1, 9:8, 11:8, 3:2, 7:4. At a later date, Colvig added more pitches in the harmonic series to the scale.

11. Letter to Peter Kehrf, June 18, 1980, Lou Harrison Archive.

12. Program in Lou Harrison Archive.

13. Richard Dee interview, March 16, 2004.

14. Veltman, "Harrison Tried Hard to Settle This Score."

15. Ibid.

16. Rockwell, "Harrison Puppet Opera in Premiere."

17. Hayter-Menzies, *Shadow Woman*, 113.

18. Harrison interview, August 8, 2001.

19. Hayter-Menzies, *Shadow Woman*, 134.

20. Dee interview, March 16, 2004.

21. For example, she didn't like the woodblock interpunctuations Harrison added to one of the White Snake's pensive scenes, which Benton herself would be voicing. "It's too heavy," she declared. "She is a lady" (Hayter-Menzies, *Shadow Woman*, 137).

22. Weinberger, *The New Directions Anthology of Classical Chinese Poetry*, xxiii.

23. Harrison, *Joys & Perplexities*, 46.

24. Harrison interview, July 19, 2000.

25. Broughton, *Coming Unbuttoned*, 60.

26. Hamilton, *A Life of Kenneth Rexroth*, 353. The incident occurred in 1975.

27. Linick, *The Lives of Ingolf Dahl*, 609. Colvig felt guilty because he had been so busy building gamelan that he had lost touch with Dahl (Leyland, *Gay Sunshine Interviews*, 175–176).

28. Harrison interview, July 19, 2000.

29. Leyland, *Gay Sunshine Interviews*, 182–183.

30. In 1970, an engineer from Harrison's favorite radio station, KPFA, came to his house and recorded him reading texts from an Esperanto newspaper, which the composer Charles Amirkhanian, a KPFA producer, arranged into a cut-up text and transformed into an original text-sound composition, *Oratora Konkurso Rezulto (Portrait of Lou Harrison, 1970)* that became "the first-ever four-channel broadcast produced by two stations simultaneously: KPFA (Berkeley) and KSAN (San Francisco)." On November 20, 1970, Harrison played drums in a Berkeley concert of George Antheil's music that Amirkhanian produced for KPFA, sparking a revival of interest in Antheil (radiOM, "George Antheil Hertz Hall Concert"). Amirkhanian became one of Harrison's champions in his position as music director of KPFA and the Other Minds music festival.

31. This is the same syntonic diatonic just-intonation scale from Ptolemy used in *Young Caesar*: 1:1, 9:8, 5:4, 4:3, 3:2, 5:3, 15:8.

32. The tubes and bars are arranged with the "white key" notes along the bottom and the F♯ and C♯ raised and above, resulting in a pentatonic scale along the bottom with two "black keys" above—the configuration for a diatonic keyboard suggested in Yasser's *A Theory of Evolving Tonality* (pp. 42–43), a book that influenced Harrison in his youth.

33. This set of instruments varied over time as Colvig introduced improvements over the years. Most notably, the largest resonators of the current version of the bass *gendèr* now have a ninety-degree turn at the bottom, so that all the bars will fit in a single instrument. Colvig and Harrison also increased the range of the tube instruments.

34. See Colvig, "An American Gamelan."

35. Colvig built an instrument he called "sweet bells" or "sweet jangles" in imitation of a Balinese bell tree called a *gentorak*. In later years, after Harrison owned an actual *gentorak*, he used that instead of the original "sweet bells."

36. Harrison, quoted in Gardner, "*La Koro Sutro* by Lou Harrison," 130.

37. This scale resembles one of those found in the Javanese *pelog* tuning system and also resembles the often-melancholy Japanese *in* mode, traditionally used for solo koto music.

38. The movement avoids the tone E, which in the Ptolemy tuning forms a wolf fifth with the B. It is therefore hexatonic rather than fully diatonic like the *Easter Cantata* chorale.

39. Note that the F tonality is a minor third above the home key of D, mirroring the corresponding first *paragrafo*, whose B tonality is a minor third below D. Similar correspondences help form the large-scale tonal plan of the work.

40. Harrison interview, August 10, 2001.

41. Harrison interview, July 21, 2000.

42. Ibid.

43. Because of these challenges, Aslanian's chorus from Salinas had to be replaced just before the premiere with a professional chorus from Berkeley, conducted by Donald Cobb. After the benefit of more rehearsals, Aslanian's group performed it in Salinas that fall, and the work remains dedicated to Aslanian.

44. Because of the difficulty of shipping the original American gamelan around the country for performances of Harrison's pieces, Harrison in 1994 commissioned instrument builder Richard Cooke of Colorado and his company Freenotes to make a copy of the ensemble. Cooke constructed a total of three copies: one is in Colorado, another is at the Percussion Arts Museum in Indianapolis, and another was made for the Boston Modern Orchestra Project.

45. Dee interview, March 16, 2004.

46. In 1977, Harrison, Hughes, and Charles Shere would collaborate on another *Double Music*-like exercise (ms. in Lou Harrison Archive).

47. Harrison, *Music Primer*, 14. In his sketches for the *Suite for Violin and American Gamelan*, Harrison referred to this type of motive, writing, "Item: The falling 4th in Corelli's and Chinese half cadences, also the descent from 6 to 1 (the Landini cadence inverted so to speak) the penta[tonic] basis of all of this" (Lou Harrison Archive). This type of motive is prominent in both the *overt* (open) and *clos* (closed) cadences of the suite's estampie.

48. This account is based on our own analysis, an interview with Dee (March 16, 2004), and Harrison's memory (in an interview on August 11, 2001) that the reprise of the opening melody was Dee's idea.

49. The plan and sketches of the work are in the Lou Harrison Archive.

50. Harrison, program notes for *Suite for Violin and American Gamelan*, Lou Harrison Archive; Harrison interview, July 21, 2000.

51. Much to Harrison's indignation and Dee's annoyance, performing organizations and even record labels often neglected to acknowledge the *Suite for Violin and American Gamelan* as a true collaboration. Harrison always forbade Dee to reveal which parts of the composition were whose, because he felt that they should share credit for the whole work equally. After Harrison's death, Dee no longer considered the details of their collaboration to be a secret. We are indebted to Dee's description of their collaboration in our interview of March 16, 2004. Much of their collaboration can also be deduced from the sketches in the Lou Harrison Archive. His account is repeated in Miller and Lieberman, *Lou Harrison*, 57.

Chapter 28

1. Alan Baker, "An Interview with Lou Harrison."

2. Harrison's most recent large-scale percussion ensemble compositions, the *Concerto for Violin with Percussion Orchestra* of 1959 and movements of *Orpheus* of 1969, were both based on percussion works he had actually written decades earlier.

3. Rathbun, "Lou Harrison and His Music," 49.

4. Harrison interview, August 10, 2001. Also see Rathbun, "Lou Harrison and His Music," 49–50.

5. Other Harrison works applying this technique include the *Reel, Homage to Henry Cowell* (1939), Overture to *The Trojan Women* (1940), and *King David's Lament for Jonathan* (1941). Pentatonic clusters are used similarly in *Spring in Nak Yang* (1961) and *Pacifika Rondo* (1963).

6. Harrison originally intended to "evoke syncopated sections in César Franck," but he found that the finale is instead "commonly construed by audiences as a sort of jazz festival" (Celso, "A Study and Catalogue of Lou Harrison's Utilization of Keyboard Instruments," 133). For further analysis of this work, see Daniel Burwasser, "A Study of Lou Harrison's *Concerto for Violin and Percussion Orchestra* and *Concerto for Organ and Percussion Orchestra*"; and Chen, "Lou Harrison's *Organ Concerto with Percussion Orchestra*."

7. Soltes, *Lou Harrison: A World of Music.*

8. Serinus, "The Adventure Continues."

9. Leyland, *Gay Sunshine Interviews*, 173.

10. Gidlow, *Elsa*, 364. This autobiography also includes a history and description of Druid Heights. See also Silber, "Inside Druid Heights."

11. Gidlow, *Elsa*, 309. Letters in the Lou Harrison Archive reference his work on it in early 1974 and plans for a performance on the *Vallejo*, a local ferry. A cassette of the work exists in Gidlow's archive at the GLBT Historical Society, San Francisco.

12. Probably the best-known interpretation of these tablets came from the LP and accompanying booklet *Sounds from Silence* (Kilmer, Crocker, and Brown). However, this publication was only released two years after Harrison's *Sonata in Ishartum*, so Harrison must have been following earlier scholarly articles by Kilmer and others. Scholarship now equates the Ishartum mode with modern Ionian (major), but at the time Kilmer and others equated it with Phrygian, the mode Harrison chose for his piece.

13. Chalmers showed Harrison his work collecting the various historical and theoretical kinds of tetrachords; that is, four pitches in the span of a fourth. They tried out many scales constructed from these tetrachords, and Harrison encouraged Chalmers to complete his monumental catalogue and analysis. "You finish it, and I will make sure it's published," he promised. It would take Chalmers another twenty years to complete *Divisions of the Tetrachord*, for which Harrison wrote the foreword.

14. Harrison composed *A Phrase for Arion's Leap* in response to a request from his friend Charles Shere, who wanted to include a score in a new journal he was launching, *Ear*. According to Shere ("The Making of Lou Harrison"), its original title included the descriptor "Precision Piece." Harrison, Colvig, and Dee recorded it for the audiocassette periodical *Tellus*, which included it on its issue #14 (1986), devoted to just intonation.

15. "On Bill's Return from the Mountains, September 1973." Harrison, *Joys & Perplexities*, 71.

16. Notebook #104, Lou Harrison Archive. Harrison's note paraphrases Robert Duncan's poem that he had set in *Orpheus*.

17. Harrison interview, July 19, 2000.

18. Notebook #134, Lou Harrison Archive.

19. Kerry Lewis interview, December 21, 2013. Harrison also employed his student Phil Collins and Bob Hughes's wife, Margaret Fisher, as copyists.

20. Letter to Peter Yates, 1974, Lou Harrison Archive.

21. Quoted in Wilson, "Something Beautiful."

22. Partch did not show such a congenial face to everyone. Elsa Gidlow, remembering Partch, simply "wondered why this gifted, creative man was so bitter" (Gidlow, *Elsa*, 365).

23. Harrison, "Review of Harry Partch."

24. Notebook #74, Lou Harrison Archive.

25. From Pauline Benton's translation of the Chinese myth "The White Snake." Hayter-Menzies, *Shadow Woman*, 203.

26. Harrison interview, July 5, 1996.
27. Robert Hughes interview, March 17, 2004.
28. Notebook #95, Lou Harrison Archive.
29. Harrison, *Joys & Perplexities*, 73.
30. Harrison interview, September 24, 1997.
31. Harrison interview, July 5, 1996.
32. Work on the symphony kept Harrison so busy that he apparently turned down at least a couple of opportunities to write ballet scores, including one for Jean Erdman. Letters from Erdman and an uncashed check for "Wind in the Forest" are in the Lou Harrison Archive.
33. Some critics have discerned Elisabeth Kübler-Ross's well-known five stages of grief in its five movements, but such a literal interpretation is as unlikely as associating a performance of Indian classical music entirely with a single *rasa*, or feeling. Although each Indian raga is well known to be associated with a specific emotion, this association is only a starting point for the complex journey of a successful performance.
34. Harrison, liner notes to *Lou Harrison—Elegiac Symphony*.
35. The teenage bassists of Bob Hughes's Oakland Symphony Youth Orchestra played the solos flawlessly in the premiere. However, when the American Composers Orchestra recorded the piece in 1989, the bassists resisted, and Dennis Russell Davies allowed them to play the melodies as stopped (i.e., fingered) notes. Of course then the tuning and unique timbre disappeared, and Harrison's historic innovation, perhaps the most distinctive moment of the symphony, was ruined.
36. That fall, Harrison traveled to New York to participate in the Ives Centennial conference and lectured at an Ives and Schoenberg Centennial concert in Berkeley.
37. Harrison wrote another passacaglia around the same time in San Francisco that later became a movement in the *First Suite for Strings* (1948). However, Harrison dropped the movement when he revised the suite in 1995.
38. Jacobs, "Lou Harrison's 'Elegiac' Symphony."
39. Tircuit, "An Elegant Premiere."
40. The Oakland Symphony Youth Orchestra recorded the *Elegiac Symphony* shortly after the performance. However, one day Colvig, who often made dubs of Harrison's tape collection in response to various requests, accidentally recorded over the master tape of one of the movements. Harrison was so furious that the couple almost went to a marriage counselor for help. During the following summer, Bob Hughes and the orchestra manager, Ethel London, brought the entire orchestra back together to re-record the movement. Because Denis de Coteau was unavailable, Hughes conducted the movement, though he is not credited on the LP, which came out in 1977 on the Berkeley-based 1750 Arch label.

Part 6
1. Notebook #132, Lou Harrison Archive.
2. Marcos, who would later become a notorious symbol of ostentatious corruption in the impoverished nation, had a special interest in the conference and the performing arts in general, as she had originally come to fame as a singer. After delivering a keynote address of bland homilies, the First Lady was prevailed upon to sing, and Harrison was greatly impressed with her beauty and voice. When they later spoke at dinner, he found her very pleasant, and later he sent a thank-you letter; a copy is in the Lou Harrison Archive (Harrison interview, September 25, 1997).
3. Asian Composers League, *Third Asian Composers League Conference—Festival Final Report*, 86–90. "Surd" is a mathematical term for an irrational root. Harrison preferred the term when referring to tempered intervals because, as he pointed out, it comes from the Latin word for "deaf" and is the root of the English word "absurd."

4. Once at a concert of Glass's music, Harrison erupted, "If I hear one more equal tempered triad, I shall scream!" He later regretted that the outburst had been published. "Of the world of New York, the one I like best, or feel closest to, and it's likely because I know him and like him, and that's Philip Glass. He's a good composer and Dennis [Russell Davies] brought him here," said Harrison. "I didn't like his improvisation on the piano, which was equal temperament triads till I thought I was going to scream, but nonetheless, the orchestral works were stunning. . . . I do admire him and like him, and he's a nice man, too" (Alan Baker, "An Interview with Lou Harrison").
5. Harrison interview, July 21, 2000.
6. E-mail communication from Riley, June 9, 2003.
7. Terry Riley interview, June 28, 2015. Riley and Harrison shared top billing (with Partch) in Michael Blackwood's 1994 documentary *Musical Outsiders: An American Legacy*.
8. Sucharitkul, "Crises in Asian Music," 21.
9. Asian Composers League, *Third Asian Composers League Conference—Festival Final Report*, 10.
10. Harrison interview, July 1, 1996.

Chapter 29
1. Harrison, "Go Planetary!" 1.
2. February 1976 letter to Carola Blubaugh, Lou Harrison Archive.
3. Eva Soltes, personal communication; Bogley, *A History of ASEA and the Center For World Music, 1973–74*. A copy of Harrison's resignation letter is in the Lou Harrison Archive.
4. Although he was no longer on the board, Harrison remained concerned about the Center's finances. A letter from Brown dated November 23, 1976 (Lou Harrison Archive), says that Harrison had twice refused to accept the check for $1,000 that Brown had offered him for his residency.
5. Jeff Abell, e-mail communication, October 4, 2013.
6. Harrison, "Item: Thoughts While Designing a Gamelan," 4. Daniel Schmidt initially proposed a *pelog* tuning using these harmonics, and Harrison maintained that they closely matched the *pelog* tuning of Kyai Udan Mas.
7. The "C" is pronounced as "ch" and was sometimes spelled that way by Harrison. "Pak" is a title given to an elder male. Later in his life, Pak Cokro was awarded the name K. R. T. Wasitodiningrat and then Ki K. P. H. Notoprojo (for Kanjeng Pangeran Harya Notoprojo). Later publications may use one of these names. "Ki" is an honorific. For more on Pak Cokro's music and legacy, see Wenten, "The Creative World of Ki Wasitodipuro."
8. Brett Campbell, "The Divine Lou Harrison."
9. Other pioneers in the "American Gamelan" movement not present that summer included Dennis Murphy, whose Plainfield Village Gamelan preceded the Harrison-Colvig instruments, although they were unaware of each other's work; Philip Corner and Daniel Goode, who cofounded the Gamelan Son of Lion with Benary; Henry Rosenthal, who helped found Other Music with Doty; and Paul Dresher, who would soon collaborate with Harrison, Colvig, and Schmidt.
10. Schmidt, e-mail correspondence, August 6, 2015.
11. Oteri, "Barbara Benary." See also Bogley, ed., *Memories of the Center for World Music 1974–2004*.
12. Schmidt, quoted in Miller and Lieberman, "Lou Harrison and the American Gamelan," 159.
13. Notebook #134, Lou Harrison Archive. Harrison's *Fugue* had proven too difficult for his own ensemble in 1942.

14. Harrison, program notes for *String Quartet Set*, Lou Harrison Archive.
15. San Jose State College had changed its name to San Jose State University in 1972.
16. Harrison had seen Partch's last production, a posthumous performance of *The Bewitched*, when it came to Palo Alto in 1975. However, a new production of *Delusion of the Fury* would have been immensely expensive to mount (Danlee Mitchell e-mail correspondence, March 16, 2014). Plans to mount *Delusion* are mentioned in "San Jose to Honor U.S. Composers," an unidentified 1975 newspaper clipping provided by Kerry Lewis.
17. 1976 draft letter to SJSU president John H. Bunzel, Lou Harrison Archive.
18. Harrison interview, July 24, 2000. Anthony Cirone told him in a lunch conversation that the administration was lying to him when they told him that, as a part-timer, he was ineligible for the benefit. Cirone even confirmed this by looking up the law itself the next time he was in the state capital, Sacramento.
19. Letter to Virginia Rathbun, May 1976, Lou Harrison Archive.
20. See Schonberg, "Concert: In Honor of Composers." The event was hosted by Aaron Copland (one of the founders of the ACA). Dennis Russell Davies would also play *The Marriage at the Eiffel Tower* with Harrison's narration in an all-Harrison concert in St. Paul, Minnesota, the following year.
21. Kostelanetz, "A Conversation, in Eleven-Minus-One Parts," 395. Harrison often repeated this story elsewhere.
22. Alan Baker, "An Interview with Lou Harrison."
23. A returned quiz still in the Lou Harrison Archive has a grade of 85. See also Notebook #73, Lou Harrison Archive.
24. Notebook #129, Lou Harrison Archive.
25. Harrison interview, June 11, 1997.
26. *Gending* also has a more specific meaning as a large Javanese musical structure, but generally Harrison used the term in its more general sense, sometimes to refer to pieces not otherwise in an identifiable Javanese form.
27. Traditional Javanese music would never mix pitches 1 and 7 in the same mode, and pitch 4 is used only as an auxiliary pitch rather than a pitch within the mode. Players of the *gendèr* metallophone, for example, could only play either 1 or 7, but both pitches do not exist on the same instrument. Likewise, pitch 4 would not be represented on the *gendèr* or the *gambang* xylophone.
28. Jody Diamond interview, November 18, 2013.
29. Brett Campbell, "The Divine Lou Harrison."
30. In the Central Javanese tradition, the place where the *kempul* would first sound in the cycle is left silent. Longer forms often leave out the *kempul* and have different densities of *ketuk* strokes.
31. *Kepatihan* or cipher notation originated in a European system of using Arabic numerals to indicate pitches of the seven-tone diatonic scale, and this system worked well for the *pelog* scale, which also has seven tones. However, the Javanese conventionally use the numbers 1, 2, 3, 5, and 6 to indicate the pitches of the pentatonic *slendro* tuning system, bypassing 4 and 7.
32. The *bonang* part shown here is the one Harrison composed and would not necessarily be the same as one realized by a traditional Javanese player, although it would not be objectionable either.
33. For further information, including a further analysis of *Bubaran Robert*, see Alves, "Kembangan in the Music of Lou Harrison."
34. Like the *bubaran*, the *lancaran* form is relatively short (eight beats per gong) and associated with the relatively loud instruments, such as the *bonang*. Harrison would come to favor forms in this loud style, which happened to be a specialty of Jody Diamond (Diamond interview, November 18, 2013).

35. Harrison interview, April 6, 2000.
36. The Center for World Music would move around to several different host institutions until finally settling at San Diego State University in 1979. The Center continues today in San Diego, although it is no longer affiliated with the university.
37. Inspired by their instrument building experiments, Gary Kvistad built a series of wind chimes and went on to found the widely successful Woodstock Chimes company (initially Woodstock Percussion). Rick Kvistad became the principal percussionist with the San Francisco Opera.
38. "A Grand Birthday Celebration, Concert"; Celso, "A Study and Catalogue of Lou Harrison's Utilization of Keyboard Instruments," 1.
39. Daniel Schmidt interview, December 7, 2013.

Chapter 30
1. Harrison interview, July 1, 1996.
2. Kerry Lewis interview, December 21, 2013.
3. Celso, "A Study and Catalogue of Lou Harrison's Utilization of Keyboard Instruments," 2.
4. Robert Hughes interview, March 17, 2004.
5. Schmidt, "Remembering Lou."
6. Harrison still had savings left over from a considerable bump in royalties during Ives's centennial in 1974 (Duffie, "Composer Lou Harrison").
7. Quoted in Celso, "A Study and Catalogue of Lou Harrison's Utilization of Keyboard Instruments," 23.
8. Daniel Wolf, in "I Remember Lou."
9. "Sapphic Syllables in Honor of Sinan at His Tomb," in Harrison, *Joys & Perplexities*, 22.
10. Schneider, "Just Lou Harrison," 21.
11. The full title, as published, is *Serenade for Guitar with Optional Percussion*. Harrison came to regret this title, as it created some confusion with his 1952 *Serenade* for guitar. That earlier piece is also referred to as *Serenato por gitaro* or *Serenade for Frank Wigglesworth*. Instead of alternating equally tempered half and whole steps, the scale employs two different sizes of half steps and two different whole steps. The five-limit scale, beginning on D, is 1:1, 16:15, 6:5, 5:4, 45:32, 3:2, 5:3, and 16:9.
12. Schneider, "Just Lou Harrison," 21.
13. Letter to John Schneider, July 22, 1978, quoted in Schneider, "Just Lou Harrison." The previous year, Harrison had supervised the master's thesis of Robert Orr at San Jose State University, titled "The Application of Quarter Comma Meantone Temperament to the Guitar," for which Orr built a guitar in this temperament; so the idea of refretting was certainly current, although we know of no contact between Orr and Stone.
14. Lou Harrison, insert notes to *Music of Lou Harrison*.
15. This work is the first of several that Harrison called a "set." He noted that the word is linguistically related to the French "suite" and used the two terms interchangeably. He also noted that Ives preferred "set" to "suite."
16. Quoted in Rubin, *John Cage and the Twenty-Six Pianos of Mills College*, 23.
17. Harrison interview, July 19, 2002. Colvig is credited in the film as music recording engineer.
18. In particular, Harrison used the Korean mode known as *ujo* (found on the piano's black keys, beginning on E-flat), which is much more common in traditional Korean music than its equivalent in Chinese traditional music. Harrison also called *ujo* the "minor" pentatonic scale, because it is a subset of the natural minor scale and perhaps can be heard to share minor's supposed melancholy affect. On the other hand, China's most common mode, *gongdiao* (the black-key scale beginning on G♭), Harrison called the "prime" pentatonic or the "major" pentatonic.

19. By comparison, the amount of music in a full-length Hollywood feature is generally less than an hour. Later, Harrison intended to release these tapes, but the album was never realized. The surviving sketches in the Lou Harrison Archive include little of the music that was actually used in the film. The original recordings were in stereo but had to be mixed to mono when added to the film (Harrison interview, August 8, 2001).

20. Richard Dee interview, March 16, 2004.

21. Harrison, *Joys & Perplexities*, 59.

22. Typescript in Lou Harrison Archive.

23. Don Gillespie interview, October 30, 2005.

24. Draft letter to Jean Drahmann, February 7, 1980, Lou Harrison Archive.

25. Draft letter to Peter Garland, July 12, 1980, Lou Harrison Archive.

26. Schneider, "Just Lou Harrison," 23.

27. Harrison said, "I'm very much interested in transferring technologies. Instead of the more prevalent thing of introducing high tech to Third World peoples, for example, oh! there's so many things I would like to get from them. I would love to have a gong builder in this country teaching us the technologies from Java and Bali" (Marin, *Lou Harrison: Cherish, Conserve, Consider, Create*).

28. Cage, *Empty Words*, 6.

29. "Nines to John Cage on his 65th Birthday, 1977," in Harrison, *Joys & Perplexities*, 39.

30. Letter to Peggy Glanville-Hicks, December 10, 1976, Lou Harrison Archive.

31. Harrison, "Cloverleaf," 15.

32. The "Crackpot Lecture" typescript in Lou Harrison Archive.

33. He also noted that in the third century CE, when the Romans were making shields and swords out of bronze, the Javanese were using the same tools (as he saw on sarcophagi from the period) to forge great gongs (Alan Baker, "An Interview with Lou Harrison").

34. The finished scale has pitches (in Central Javanese notation) 2, 3, 5, 6, 7 but at a somewhat higher pitch, roughly a quartertone higher than the Western pitches F♯, G, B, C, and D. The intervals to which it was retuned, relative to pitch 3, were 1:1, 5:4, 4:3, 3:2, 243:128—a five-limit just scale. Thus it was relatively straightforward to combine Western instruments with it, once they had tuned to its slightly high absolute pitch.

35. Harrison concert talk at Santa Clara University, October 19, 1994, recording in Lou Harrison Archive. "Sekar" can mean both "flower" and "song" in high Javanese and Sundanese.

36. Jody Diamond emphasized that the horn and *suling* players were not soloists in the sense of European concertos but simply other members of an egalitarian ensemble. She resisted even calling those players "soloists," although Harrison himself referred to them that way (for example, in Alan Baker, "An Interview with Lou Harrison"). She also rejected the notion that Harrison intended any symbolic marriage of East and West by pairing the horn and *suling*, although critics have often heard it that way (Jody Diamond interview, November 18, 2013). In the liner notes to his CD *Gamelan Music*, Harrison wrote that the title "carries the full sense of transcultural warmth and understanding."

37. Harrison used the form of *kepatihan* or Javanese cipher notation that he was used to from the Central Javanese tradition. The numbers normally used in Sunda to notate gamelan *degung* are actually reversed. In 1985, Jean-Francois Denis transcribed the parts into a score in Western staff notation for publication in Diamond's publication *Balungan* (Harrison and Denis, "Main Bersama-Sama").

38. Powell, "Notation or Not."

39. This fact was noted in Spiller, "Lou Harrison's Music for Western Instruments and Gamelan."

40. Harrison's notebooks show his awareness of the principle of *padang-ulihan* (sometimes known as *ding-dong*). Nevertheless, Sri Hastanto argued in "The Concept of Pathet in Central Javanese Gamelan Music" (pp. 53–54) that the melodies of Harrison's *Lancaran*

Daniel failed to realize a satisfactory *padang-ulihan* structure from the Javanese point of view, thus compromising the realization of the elaborating parts.

41. In modern notation, this would be a compound triple meter, often represented by the time signature 9/8, except that all further divisions and groupings are by threes as well.

42. Harrison made it possible to use quintal counterpoint by retuning the gamelan Sekar Kembar to a five-limit just-intonation scale, in which 3:2 perfect fifths and 4:3 perfect fourths are available. Harrison would later extend the principle of quintal counterpoint to encompass intervals sometimes much farther away from true fifths, intervals known as *kempyung* in gamelan.

Chapter 31

1. Harrison interview, June 11, 1997.
2. Harrison, "Item: Thoughts While Designing a Gamelan," 4.
3. Arranged as ratios in a scale from pitch 1, this sequence of numbers becomes 1:1, 13:12, 7:6, 17:12, 3:2, 19:12, and 7:4 (Alan Baker, "An Interview with Lou Harrison").
4. Brown argued that traditionally tuned Javanese gamelans do not use just intonation at all. Because musicians can differ on the preciseness of a "fit" between a theoretical just interval and an empirical interval, and because the harmonic series is theoretically infinite, it is difficult to state definitively whether some Javanese gamelan tunings can be described as just. It is not a concept that seems to be explicitly articulated by Javanese tuners as it has been among European tuners. Nevertheless, whether by chance or choice, some intervals of some gamelan are close to small integer ratios.
5. Alan Baker, "An Interview with Lou Harrison."
6. Harrison, "Thoughts about 'Slippery Slendro,'" 111. In this article Harrison discussed how the slight deviations between different *slendro* could render a melody completely changed. He said that these pitch deviations and the practice of making transpositions "is a liberating and fascinating doctrine, which, in its turn, brings up terrifying problems for a composer hoping that his own interval expression might be observed" (p. 113).
7. Harrison claimed that this tuning was "comfortably close" to the tuning of the gamelan at the Radio Republik Indonesia studio in Surakarta, in "Item: Thoughts While Designing a Gamelan" (p. 6). However, the measurements of Surjodiningrat et al. (*Tone Measurements*) do not agree with this assessment. In fact, none of the step sizes in the twenty-eight *slendro* gamelan they measured was as small as 9:8. The harmonics of Harrison's *slendro* tuning seem to overlap considerably with the *pelog* scale, but they are offset from it (i.e., they are harmonics relative to a different fundamental pitch).
8. Susan Alexander interview, April 13, 2011.
9. Harrison interview, June 11, 1997. Aluminum's light weight also appealed to them.
10. This technique of adding a central boss to metal bars has a historical precedent in Java, where it was used in the now-archaic instrument known as the *slento*, a precursor of the modern *slentem*. Pak Cokro may have told Harrison of this model, but it is equally likely that Harrison and Colvig discovered this shape independently.
11. Jody Diamond ("In the Beginning Was the Melody," 111) points out that this technique can be found in traditional Javanese compositions as well as in Harrison's works.
12. Harrison concert talk at Santa Clara University, October 19, 1994, recording in Lou Harrison Archive.
13. Susan Alexander interview, April 13, 2011; draft letter from Harrison to Virgil Thomson, December 21, 1978, Lou Harrison Archive.
14. Trish Neilson and Daniel Kelley interview, May 11, 2014.
15. Schwarz, "A Polymath, at 80, Tries to Simplify."
16. Woodard, "Composer a Hero in World of New Music."
17. Schwarz, "A Polymath, at 80, Tries to Simplify."

18. Harrison, 1988 Mills Honorary Doctorate Acceptance Speech, Lou Harrison Archive.

19. David Harrington interview, December 30, 2009.

20. Composers Recordings, Incorporated (CRI), was founded by Oliver Daniel and others. This LP, SD 455, also included Harrison's three pieces for gamelan *degung* and was the first of Harrison's recordings to include his gamelan works when it appeared in 1981.

21. Daniel Schmidt interview, December 7, 2013.

22. However, Mills artist and longtime Harrison friend Mark Bulwinkle apparently beat it beyond beauty at one point, removing so much tension that Harrison said, "It sounded like a thunder sheet. I took it down to a beach and turned it into a gong again" (Alburger, "A Garden Interview with Lou Harrison," 12).

23. Diamond interview, November 18, 2013.

24. Ibid.

25. Harrison interview, April 6, 1996.

26. Harrison wrote *Gending Alexander* for another homemade gamelan, this one built by his friend Michael Zinn at the University of Delaware, where it was performed in April 1981.

27. For example, the two lines of the *gendér barung* metallophone, played with the right and left hands, often use this interval as a stable or final harmony. The *kempyung* in the *slendro* tuning system, on average 720 cents, is nearly always somewhat larger than a 3:2 perfect fifth, which is 702 cents. However, Harrison's *slendro* tuning system had two 3:2 *kempyung*, which he would often favor. In *pelog*, the *kempyung* can vary from approximately a tritone to a sixth, but the *pelog* of Si Betty also includes two 3:2 *kempyung*.

28. The English translation of Cavafy's complete poems had been published by Harcourt in 1961 and, in a second edition, 1976. Harrison, who was accustomed to composing with texts in the public domain or by his friends, would have had to purchase the rights to set the original poems either in English from Harcourt or in Greek (his initial intention) from the original publisher, a difficult and possibly expensive proposition.

29. Cavafy, *Collected Poems*.

30. That piece, along with works by Diamond, Neilsen, and others, was supposed to appear on Harrison's next gamelan recording along with his own. But according to Diamond and Harrison, the label ultimately reneged, releasing only a single, all-Harrison disc. The cancellation of the second release infuriated him. The complete set didn't come out until years later, on Nimbus Records (Diamond interview, November 18, 2013). Nevertheless, flush with enthusiasm for the music, Harrison continued to ask many of his old composer colleagues to write for gamelan, but only a few took him up on it, while Terry Riley, John Luther Adams, and others politely declined. Cage would compose his *Haikai* for gamelan in 1986 on invitation from Toronto's Evergreen Club Gamelan.

31. The *slendro* tuning Harrison chose had the intervals 8:7, 8:7, 7:6, 8:7, 147:128, a scale that had two pure perfect fourths (4:3) but lacked the very un-Javanese 9:8 scale step that he had included in his *slendro* for Si Betty and Si Darius. Harrison's memory that Pak Cokro characterized it as a Solonese-type tuning is difficult to support based on the recordings of tunings from that city recorded in Surjodiningrat et al., *Tone Measurements of Outstanding Javanese Gamelans*, though, according to these measurements, it is very close to the tuning of the famous gamelan Mardiswara of Solo's Mangkunegaran palace.

32. Harrison, personal communication. In Indonesia, the players usually memorize the basic melody and their elaborating parts, obviating the need for scores or stands.

33. McDermott interview, November 24, 2013.

34. Some of the beneficiaries, at around $40 each, included his brother and sister-in-law; old friends Thomson, Pak Cokro, Carlos Chávez, Gillespie, Samuel, Broughton, Diamond, Paul Bowles, Remy Charlip, Sidney Jowers, Richard Dee, Hovhaness, and Davies; various Colvigs, Betty Freeman and Franco Assetto, and Sidney Cowell, among many others (letter to International Star Registry, January 21, 1983, Lou Harrison Archive).

35. Harrison speech at CalArts, 1987, Lou Harrison Archive. This systematic augmentation and diminution in form has precedents in some of Harrison's early percussion music, such as *Canticle #1*.

36. Harrison, insert notes to *Lou Harrison: Double Concerto for Violin and Cello with Javanese Gamelan*.

37. Harrison later attributed performers' sensitivity to the tuning to a national difference. He claimed that Americans could tune by ear on the fly "to an astonishing degree. We tried that in England and it did not work. They see an E♭, and they play an E♭ as they've been taught to play, and that's that. They don't adjust to say, the E♭ that's in the gamelan. But in the United States we have much more freedom of sound, and ways of adjusting" (Alan Baker, "An Interview with Lou Harrison").

38. Harrison, *Joys & Perplexities*, 51.

39. Notebook in folder 15.3, Lou Harrison Archive. Harrison had previously used this scale in *Young Caesar, Concerto for Organ and Percussion Orchestra*, and, in a just-intonation version, his *Serenade for Guitar with Optional Percussion* of 1978.

40. Harrison, insert notes to *Soundscapes*, 2.

41. Diamond interview, November 18, 2013.

42. Harrison, "MicroFest 2001 Keynote Address," 9.

43. Harrison was dissatisfied with his choral melody for *Gending Aphrodite* and would continue to revise it periodically for many years, including during his stay in New Zealand in 1983. He would later add another verse and a harp part. The text also appears in Harrison, *Joys & Perplexities*, 1.

44. After the production, "Bulwinkle presented Lou with a smaller puppet set called Bill and Lou's Excellent Adventure that showed Lou and his partner riding their battered Volkswagen bus, canoeing, and smelling the flowers"—see page 205 (Foley, "Lou Harrison: Sounding the Puppet Art," 9).

45. However, Harrison always rebuffed commissions to compose for Western orchestra and gamelan, because most of the former's instruments wouldn't be able to tune to the gamelan (Cizmic, "Composing the Pacific"; and Schwarz, "A Polymath, at 80, Tries to Simplify").

Chapter 32

1. Harrison, program notes for Third Symphony, in Lou Harrison Archive.

2. Draft letter to Gerhard Samuel, June 18, 1980, Lou Harrison Archive.

3. Jody Diamond interview, November 18, 2013.

4. Hughes interview, March 17, 2004.

5. According to Harrison, Davies was partial to this work and others of Harrison's that he considered "masculine, virile," although Harrison didn't think of it that way (Harrison interview, August 11, 2001).

6. Quoted in Celso, "A Study and Catalogue of Lou Harrison's Utilization of Keyboard Instruments," 85.

7. See Leta E. Miller, "Lou Harrison and the Aesthetics of Revision, Alteration, and Self-Borrowing." Harrison had made many of these changes in a 1970 revision of the piece for piano. Miller argues for influences from *zheng* music, but an equally justifiable comparison may be to the second movement of Bach's *Italian Concerto* or the differences between simple and exfoliated baroque melodies exemplified by Bach's "Arioso" in BWV 156 and BWV 1056.

8. Alan Baker, "An Interview with Lou Harrison." Harrison revised the finale for further performances led by Davies the following year. He continued to revise the symphony through 2002, shortly before his death, in preparation for a performance at Ohio State University. Harrison said the finale "wouldn't stop itching" (Gillespie, "Another View on Lou").

9. Allan Thomas, "Skip, Skip, Skip to My Lou," 12.

10. The falling semitone is also prominent in the first "Tears of the Angel Israfel" movement of the *Elegiac Symphony* and in the *Elegy for Harpo Marx*.

11. Eva Soltes interview, February 17, 2012.

12. Schwartz, "ASUC: Reaching Beyond Academe."

13. At the 1982 Cabrillo Festival, Jarrett and Davies performed the two tack-piano parts in Harrison's *Concerto in Slendro*.

14. This is Harrison's memory of their conversation, related in Kostelanetz, "A Conversation, in Eleven-Minus-One Parts," 391.

15. Soltes interview, January 20, 2014.

16. Jennifer Shannon, e-mail communication.

17. Murdoch, *Peggy Glanville-Hicks*, 126–127.

18. Wija was married to US consular agent Katrina Melcher, another musician whom Harrison knew from the Center for World Music. The American consul general (and ethnomusicologist) Andy Toth also showed them around.

19. Harrison, *Music Primer*, 46. Harrison was surprised when, on a visit to a Balinese cassette shop, he found that the first rack was entirely gamelan *degung* tapes. *Degung* is still often available and played in tourist restaurants in Bali. Balinese we have spoken with have claimed that *degung* tuning, being closer to Western diatonic tuning, is easier on Western ears and its soothing *suling* flute melodies more attractive to Westerners than those of the Balinese gamelan.

20. Perhaps not surprisingly, the melody most resembles the Balinese-influenced "Second Gamelon" movement of the *Suite for Violin, Piano, and Small Orchestra*. The form is ABACA, though he allows for other variations. In a letter to JaFran Jones, he asked her to "forgive me my multiple ignorances," but she successfully adapted this unique work for the Balinese ensemble (Harrison, "Letter to JaFran Jones").

21. Harrison had earlier determined, perhaps from a recording, that the *pelog* tuning of Kyai Udan Arum approximated harmonics 30, 32, 35, 40, 44, 47, and 54 (Harrison, "Item: Thoughts While Designing a Gamelan," 4). However, these ratios do not agree with the measurements of that gamelan by Surjodiningrat et al. (*Tone Measurements*). Of course, these tunings sometimes change over time, and Surjodiningrat's measurements were made in 1969 or earlier. The musician Raymond Weisling, then living in Solo, took Harrison and Colvig to visit the gong foundry.

22. ASKI has since been expanded and renamed STSI (Sekolah Tinggi Seni Indonesia— High College of Indonesian Arts). Raymond Weisling and Andy Toth (the American consul general in Bali) also provided introductions.

23. Vincent McDermott, quoted in Miller and Lieberman, *Lou Harrison: Composing a World*, 170. Harrison's reply is a paraphrase from Samuel Johnson quoted in Boswell's *Life*. His difficulty isn't surprising. "What is *pathet*?" Martopangrawit has written. "This question is always on my mind. I think no definition has yet been satisfactory, due to the act that the word '*pathet*' has so many different uses, and each use fulfills a particular need" (quoted in Sorrell, *A Guide to the Gamelan*, 58). Sorrell notes of *patet* that "whole treatises are written on it . . . and even the most expert of Javanese masters approach it with caution and utmost respect."

24. Unusually for Harrison, he did not specify a tuning, but as is common in Java, he asked Pak Daliyo to choose a tuning represented on a famous Javanese gamelan. When it later arrived in its namesake town, Harrison and Colvig decided to adjust its tuning after all, beginning with a variation on the *slendro* tuning Harrison had used for Portland's Venerable Showers of Beauty gamelan, tuning Si Aptos to intervals 1:1, 8:7, 64:49, 3:2, 7:4. Perhaps dissatisfied with the complex interval between pitches 3 and 5, he later adjusted it to 1:1, 8:7, 4:3, 3:2, 7:4. He also transposed pieces a tone down when playing on the set, so that pitch 6 effectively became pitch 1 (Miller and Lieberman, *Lou Harrison: Composing a World*, 124).

25. Harrison revised this work into its final form in 1986.
26. Harrison interview, June 11, 1997.
27. "Süleymanie: Eights"—Istanbul, April 1984. Harrison, *Joys & Perplexities*, 21.
28. Notebook #29, Lou Harrison Archive.

Chapter 33
1. Letter from Edward McGowan, 1985, Lou Harrison Archive.
2. Notebook #57, Lou Harrison Archive (although Harrison wrote the passage in question in 1995).
3. Letter to Peter Garland, July 5, 1985, Lou Harrison Archive.
4. Letter to Bill Harrison, September 1985, Lou Harrison Archive.
5. Widiyanto interview, November 2012.
6. Harrison, *Joys & Perplexities*, 2.
7. Draft letter to Alan Hovhaness, November 12, 1984, Lou Harrison Archive.
8. Draft letter to Yvar Mikhashoff, November 22, 1984, Lou Harrison Archive.
9. Harrison interview, March 20, 1995.
10. Draft letter to Bill Cassady, January 11, 1983, Lou Harrison Archive.
11. Foley, "Lou Harrison: Sounding the Puppet Art," 9.
12. Ibid.
13. Foley staged another performance with human actors a decade later and finally realized a version with *wayang golek*-like rod puppets in 2013. Harrison's gamelan Si Betty directed by Jody Diamond accompanied this version at Harvard University. However, Harrison's music for Western chamber orchestra was still not part of this production. This music is largely unperformed as of this writing, although Harrison adapted one of the harp dances as part of *Clay's Quintet* (1986), and he used elements from the "Walpurgisnacht Estampie" for the second movement of the *Piano Concerto with Selected Orchestra*.
14. Harrison, note in score to *Piano Concerto with Selected Orchestra*.
15. Vincent McDermott interview, November 2013.
16. Yamashita, *Keith Jarrett: Inner Views*, 191.
17. Doerschuk, "[Interview with] Keith Jarrett," 98.
18. Notebook #122, Lou Harrison Archive.
19. Kandell, "Behind Every Pianist Lurks an Unheralded Hero."
20. Harrison letter to Sidney Cowell, November 1, 1985, Lou Harrison Archive.
21. Zech, "Composer's Datebook."
22. Of all the Romantic composers, Harrison said, Brahms was his favorite. "That man knew what he was doing," he said. "Those melodies—some of them are breathtaking" (Harrison interview, July 7, 1996).
23. The drum pattern and the *overt* and *clos* cadences of this movement are taken from the "Walpurgisnacht Estampie" of Harrison's score for *Faust*, but otherwise the Piano Concerto "Stampede" is original.
24. Iverson, "Keith Jarrett Goes Classical." Harrison did adapt the octave bar from his Organ Concerto to make the clusters easier for Jarrett's wounded wing.
25. Mellers, "A New Everlasting Feeling," 35.
26. Duffie, "Composer Lou Harrison." At the request of pianist Ursula Oppens, who played the concerto later, he also allowed a place for a cadenza toward the end of the first movement.
27. "Süleymanie: Eights"—Istanbul, April 1984; see Carr, *Keith Jarrett*, 177.
28. Swed, "Lou Harrison Just Became a Little Bit Better Known."
29. Horowitz, "An American Original."
30. Notebook #122, Lou Harrison Archive. Jody Diamond also reported Harrison's view of these events. After this incident, though, both Harrison and Jarrett continued to speak well of each other in public.

31. Diamond interview, November 18, 2013.
32. Harrison to composer John Luther Adams; see Adams, "Remembering Lou."
33. Notebook #122, Lou Harrison Archive.
34. Foreman, "About the St. Cecilia Society."
35. Marchand, "The Impact of the Second Vatican Council on the Concert Mass," 182.
36. Harrison's lifelong sampling of religious traditions continued on occasion. In addition to visiting the local Buddhist temple, he sometimes donned a yarmulke and accompanied his friends, musicologist Leta Miller and her husband, to the local synagogue. According to family tradition, he had some Jewish blood from the Silver side of the family. Despite his youthful interest in the *Cathay* poems, Harrison had lost interest in the work of Ezra Pound because of the poet's anti-Semitism (Hughes interview, March 17, 2004). Bob Hughes would become an authority on Pound's poetry and music.
37. Notebook #78, Lou Harrison Archive. He also wrote, "Still, in composing them, I was thinking of kanons, somyo, Gregorian, etc." "Somyo" or *shomyo* is Japanese Buddhist chant, and "kanon" refers to Byzantine chant.
38. Harrison, quoted in Marchand, "The Impact of the Second Vatican Council on the Concert Mass," 184.
39. Foreman said that Harrison "found the dogmatic theology [of the text] not to his liking" (quoted in Marchand, "The Impact of the Second Vatican Council on the Concert Mass," 193). The "proper" sections of the mass are those that change for each Sunday and so are rarely set by composers. The "ordinary" sections of the mass are those that remain the same every Sunday.
40. Harrison said that the mode used in the Kyrie, which was written while he was in New Zealand, is a superset of the *pelog* mode he used in *Ketawang Wellington* and one of his pieces for *Richard Whittington* (Thomas, "Skip, Skip, Skip to My Lou," 10).
41. Marchand, "The Impact of the Second Vatican Council on the Concert Mass," 183.
42. Harrison credited stories from Bruce Walter Barton (*The Tree at the Center of the World*) and Peter Blue Cloud (*Elderberry Flute Song*), the latter a collection of contemporary Coyote stories and poems, but in the end he decided to set the traditional tales in Barton.
43. Soltes recalled that Harrison realized only after choosing the Ariadne story for Soltes's dance that there was a connection to India, but he thought he might have made the connection subliminally.
44. Sketch for *Canticle #6*, Lou Harrison Archive.
45. Harrison revised his 1976 piece *Gending Samuel* as *Lancaran Samuel* and *Ladrang Samuel* in 1981. It was the first half of this piece, the *lancaran*, that Harrison adapted as *A Cornish Lancaran*. He was so pleased with the unusual combination that he extended the piece in 1989, and it was in this form that it was recorded.
46. Harrison's sympathy for minimalist composers continued through the 1980s. Around this time, Harrison drafted a review praising Terry Riley's albums *Salome Dances for Peace*, *The Harp of New Albion*, and *Poppy Nogood and his Phantom Band*. "Finally I've a sense of continuity. The line runs through Harry Partch & me to Terry Riley & on to younger ones. We study and know world music, and study and know our tunings" (Notebook #103, Lou Harrison Archive).
47. In Garland, *A Lou Harrison Reader*, 108.
48. Leta E. Miller, "Solemn Play," xlviii–lii.

Chapter 34
1. Teck, *Music for the Dance*, 62.
2. Dunning, "Blunt Words on Ballet from Erick Hawkins." Hawkins later suffered a stroke, delaying the premiere of *New Moon* until 1989, at which time critics discerned a calculated simplicity in both the music and dance. "*New Moon* . . . could have been made only by two

kinds of artists: either an innocent who knows little about his craft; or a sage who, knowing everything, knows how to plunge his arrow right to the essence of his art" (Goldner, "Erick Hawkins Dance Co. Performs 'New Moon'").

3. Facchin and Ferrarese, insert notes to *A Homage to Lou Harrison Vol. 2*.

4. Bob Hughes remembered it as one of Harrison's less successful efforts, and when Hughes offered to work toward programming it, Harrison himself discouraged his efforts (Hughes interview, March 17, 2004).

5. The intervals in the "Prelude" and "Air" movements (minor second, minor third, minor sixth for the first and minor second, major third, major sixth for the second) are also common in Harrison's treatment of the octatonic "Stampede" melodies, drawing those three movements together and contrasting them with the diatonic "Round." Like the last movement of the *Piano Concerto with Selected Orchestra*, the "Polka" uses a Bartókian scale of mixed Lydian and Phrygian tetrachords. This is also the scale of some South Indian ragas, but they are unlikely to be a source for Harrison's inspiration. Further analysis of the *Grand Duo* is in Leta E. Miller, "Solemn Play," lii–liv.

6. Marin's film, from 1984, includes interviews with Harrison and Colvig, Virgil Thomson, and John Cage, and footage of two concerts at Mills College.

7. Colvig datebook, 1986, Lou Harrison Archive. Harrison's professional activities from 1986 to 1993 are catalogued in Charles Hanson's "The Chronicles of Lou." Harrison was also inducted into the Percussive Arts Society Hall of Fame in 1985.

8. Letter to Keith Jarrett, April 28, 1986, Lou Harrison Archive.

9. In his acceptance speech when the school awarded him an honorary doctorate in 1988, Harrison said, "I used to joke about my lack of academic bona fides by saying that I was working toward an honorary degree, and, good heavens! here it is!" He praised "slightly rambunctious Mills, sometimes turbulent Mills, always creative Mills" for maintaining "a kind of vortex or center of fine musicians," including those who'd played his music, like Abel, Steinberg, Winant, Summerfield, and, of course, the gamelan (Harrison Mills College honorary degree acceptance speech, Lou Harrison Archive).

10. March 26, 1986 letter to Van Tuyl, Lou Harrison Archive.

11. Charlip's colorful career after they parted ways and he left Merce Cunningham's company (replaced as designer by Robert Rauschenberg) included directing the National Theater for the Deaf, cofounding one of the first American children's theaters, a faculty position at Sarah Lawrence College and other teaching positions at Yale and Harvard, and honors from the Library of Congress, the *Village Voice* (two Obie Awards), and the *New York Times* (three Best Illustrated Book of the Year awards).

12. Charlip and Soltes, who was also present, had somewhat different memories of the incident (Charlip interview, June 1997; Soltes e-mail communication, June 2015).

13. Undated letter (apparently 1987) from Charlip, Lou Harrison Archive.

14. Although unable to bear to put his "Palace Music" into equal temperament, he asked it to be played on a justly tuned harp.

15. Gabel, "Lou Harrison."

16. Stabler, "'Young Caesar' Fails." Stabler's remarks provoked controversy among letter writers to the *Oregonian* and in the gay press (Leta E. Miller, "Dark Fairy Tales and Obscure Legends," 24).

17. Foley, "Lou Harrison: Sounding the Puppet Art," 9. Foley's judgment was in response to the 2007 production in San Francisco.

18. Harrison, *The Path at West Holding*, 14–15.

19. Rockwell, "A West Coast Composer Looks to the Far East."

20. Harrison, *The Path at West Holding*, 15; notebook #3, Lou Harrison Archive.

21. Shingleton, "Going Buddhist with Lou Harrison."

22. Harrison, *The Path at West Holding*, 17.

23. Soedjatmoko (who, like many Javanese, used only one name) was an Indonesian representative to the United Nations and an ambassador to the United States. At the time of this commission, he had just retired from the presidency of the United Nations University in Japan. He died in December 1989, just days before the premiere of Harrison's work.

24. Poole reports that he heard from a Hindu scholar that the stories Harrison chose are not found in the canonical text of the *Ramayana* and must be Javanese accretions to this great epic. Many such stories apparently originated in Java and Bali and are now part of the *wayang* tradition.

25. Quoted in Campbell, "Become Ocean."

26. Ibid.

27. Adams, "Remembering Lou"; Eva Soltes interview, January 20, 2014.

28. Kostelanetz, "A Conversation, in Eleven-Minus-One Parts," 396.

29. The first movement uses only major seconds, minor thirds, and minor sixths as melodic intervals. The third movement uses only the minor seconds, minor thirds, and perfect fifths. The stampede (originally the fourth, later the second movement) alternates between two related hexatonic scales: D, F, G, A, B♭, C and D, F♯, G, A, B♭, C. The "Coyote Stories" movement uses a pentatonic mode—E, F♯, A, B, D—which, Harrison claimed, "(were it in Javanese tuning) would be called slendro pathet nem" (Harrison, Fourth Symphony score).

30. Harrison, "About My Fourth Symphony," 131.

31. Harrison interview, August 8, 2001.

32. Harrison, "About My Fourth Symphony," 131.

33. Steward, "Coyote and Tehoma."

34. Kostelanetz, "A Conversation, in Eleven-Minus-One Parts," 399–400. At one point Harrison considered selling his archive to a Swiss collector to raise money, but finally he agreed to bequeath it (for free, except for support for Hanson's work on it) to UC Santa Cruz.

Chapter 35

1. Harrison interview, July 7 1996.

2. Harrison's occasional insertion of declaimed poems in his late works has a precedent in the performance of the dance work *Changing World*, which included a poem at its performance in May 1937.

3. Harrison had contributed a poetic memorial when Duncan died in 1988 ("Papers Relating to Robert Duncan Tribute, 1988 April 4" at UC Berkeley).

4. Harrison, "Item: Syllabic Verse Forms," in *Rū Harison no wārudo myūjikku nyūmon*, 146–151.

5. Seeing the letters reproduced exactly the same way every time created a subtly different look to Harrison's script, however, so Scholz began a process of fine-tuning in collaboration with Harrison (Mirapaul, "For Composer Lou Harrison, Penmanship Counts").

6. After all their work, Harrison was angry to discover that US copyright law did not apply to typefaces. He insisted that the fonts be sold for $100 as a software package.

7. Bottoms and Reti, *Rita Bottoms: Polyartist Librarian*, 187–188. Harrison did not tell his friends where the title *Joys & Perplexities* originated. However, just before the book was published, an article appeared in the *New York Times* about programs to help foreign students bridge intercultural communication: Diane Ketcham, "About Long Island: The Pains, Joys, and Perplexities of Learning American Culture."

8. He had discovered that Boethius (following Ptolemy) had speculated on the division of the tetrachord into three pitches rather than four (thus being more properly a "trichord"). Harrison realized that he had already done the same thing when he came up with his *slendro* tuning for *Si Betty* (in which the 4:3 is divided into 8:7 and 7:6) and the tuning for his gamelan *degung Sekar Kembar* (in which the 4:3 is divided into 5:4 and 16:15).

All of these ratios are of the kind that Ptolemy prioritized, called superparticular (i.e., (n+1):n). Harrison realized that, other than these two gamelan tunings, only one other trichord fits these requirements: the one with intervals 6:5 and 10:9. With John Chalmers and Los Angeles microtonalists Kraig Grady and Ervin Wilson, he formulated a tuning that combined all of these possibilities. Accordingly, Colvig built the Ptolemy Duple in 1980, though it was over a decade before Harrison used it in a composition. See Harrison, "Blessed Be Translators, For They Give Us Words" in *Rū Harison no wārudo myūjikku nyūmon*, 136–140; and Harrison, "MicroFest 2001 Keynote Address," 7–10.

9. In Marin, *Lou Harrison: Cherish, Conserve, Consider, Create.*

10. The score does not indicate a particular text for the first movement, and Harrison asked Jody Diamond, who was the *pesinden* in the performance, to provide her own. Her husband, Larry Polansky, suggested the text, and Harrison agreed (Tang, "Interpreting Lou Harrison," 190).

11. Letter to Alan Didout, February 25, 1985, Lou Harrison Archive.

12. Quoted in Zinn, *A People's History of the United States*, 309.

13. However, their failed attempts to combine the microtonal Ptolemy Duple with Hughes's bassoon forced Harrison to rework the movement to avoid problematic combinations of pitches. Hughes tried to adjust by building an extra-long bocal (the tube that connects a bassoon's mouthpiece to the main instrument), but it threw off other intervals. Even after Harrison reworked the movements, Hughes found the result unsatisfactory (Hughes interview, March 17, 2004).

14. In 1971, American screenwriter Ted Perry wrote these words for the film *Home*, a documentary about ecology and the environment. The film left the impression that the words were a speech by Chief Seattle. Unaware that its inspiring environmental message was not authentically Chief Seattle's, Harrison attributed the text he set to the nineteenth-century Indian leader. In 1992, after the *Homage to Pacifica* had been completed, a front-page article in the *New York Times* exposed the text as inauthentic (Egan, "Chief's Speech of 1854 Given New Meaning").

15. Harrison declined to set them all, but he encouraged Imamura to ask other composer friends to contribute, including his student Larry London and Bob Hughes.

16. After the Buddhist church published and recorded all the hymns, Larry London mentioned it to Lou, and his enthusiastic response was, "We're all over the *planet* now!" (Larry London, e-mail communication).

17. Polansky, "17s for Lou."

18. Harrison's piece, written around the time he had returned to Black Mountain for a reunion, was performed at a gala birthday performance for Cunningham at the New York State Theater with dancing by Mikhail Baryshnikov and Mark Morris's White Oak Dance Project.

19. "Homage to Toshiro Kido." Score to *Set for Four Haisho and Percussion*, also in notebook #57, Lou Harrison.

20. Harrison knew the Chinese version of the instrument, known as the *paixiao*, but the Japanese version had unique features. All of the pipes are the same length, and musical archeologists were able to tell that the pipes were tuned by stuffing paper into them, thus stopping them at different lengths. This intonational flexibility appealed to Harrison, although he ultimately chose what would have been a traditional pentatonic tuning based on 3:2 fifths (known as Pythagorean in the West). In the notes to the score, Harrison allows the players to simply tune the instruments by ear. In doing so, he was confident that good musicians would arrive at just intervals. Significantly, Harrison did not make use of the distinctive Japanese *in* mode (as he had, perhaps, in *La Koro Sutro*), as this scale is associated with musical traditions of a much later time in Japan. Anhemitonic pentatonic modes are associated with more ancient music, such as *gagaku*. For a more detailed consideration of this piece, see Kakinuma, "Composing for an Ancient Instrument That Has Lost Its 'Tradition.'"

21. Harrison originally titled the piece *Homage to Toshiro Kido*, like many of his "homage" pieces of this period, but he changed the title on request from the National Theatre. According to Kakinuma, he used the title *Set for Four Haisho and Percussion* but allowed for the presenters to use "suite" instead of "set." The piece appears as *Suite for Four Haisho* in Leta E. Miller and Fredric Lieberman's *Composing a World* (p. 313).

22. While they were gone, Charles Hanson, UCSC musicologist Leta Miller, and UCSC ethnomusicologist Fredric Lieberman went through Harrison's entire collection of manuscripts, creating the authoritative works catalog published in Miller and Lieberman's *Lou Harrison: Composing a World* (pp. 267–316).

23. Swed, "With a Little Bit of Pluck."

24. Harrison would revise *A Dentdale Ladrang* in 1999 and *Dartington Hall* in 1999 and 2000.

25. He would later donate this set of books to UCSC Special Collections.

26. Alexander, *Eugene O'Neill's Creative Struggle*, 101.

27. The scale of O'Neill's intended production probably kept it from ever being produced to his specifications. In the KPFA production, these chants were recorded separately and then mixed into the tape of the final broadcast.

28. When asked to contribute to a memorial concert for his old friend Ben Weber in 1999, Harrison adapted the "Round Dance," a version of "Miriam," and "Caligula's Dance" (not ultimately used in the production) as a *Short Set from "Lazarus Laughed."* He reorchestrated the movements from the original small orchestra for a trio of flute, cello, and celesta (which also plays clusters and knocking sounds). He also intended to adapt his work as a symphonic suite, but that became another of his never-completed projects. The score was recorded in a San Francisco recording studio and became the last score Harrison conducted himself.

Chapter 36

1. Notebook #102, Lou Harrison Archive.

2. Jackson, in "I Remember Lou."

3. Susan Alexander interview, April 2011.

4. Draft of Gay and Lesbian Music Award Acceptance Speech, Lou Harrison Archive.

5. In *Joys & Perplexities* (p. 61), Harrison wrote, "Video is the ejaculate / of the gleaming corporate cocks; / by video they assert & cum / inside your home / to breed / their money fodder."

6. Their relationship extended to more than that friendship, and Smith ("our third," Harrison called him) was an occasional lover of each and both Harrison and Colvig, though he also had a girlfriend. Colvig and Harrison's relationship, though deep and close, was never sexually exclusive.

7. When composer John Adams saw the license plate, he good-naturedly joked to Harrison, "Do you think you're going to be able to hold onto that?" (Robert Hughes interview, March 17, 2004.)

8. Eva Soltes made an unreleased film of Colvig's "tree-sea" hike.

9. Rockwell, "A West Coast Composer Looks to the Far East." He did buy a motor home.

10. Harrison, personal communication, June 16, 1996. Also in Harrison interview with Charles Amirkhanian at his seventieth birthday concert (RadiOM.org, "Lou Harrison 70th Birthday Concert").

11. Charles Hanson interview, July 5, 2014.

12. Harrison interview, July 19, 2000.

13. Harrison interview, August 10, 2001.

14. Notebook #3, Lou Harrison Archive.

15. Harrison interview, July 19, 2000.

16. Harrison interview, July 1, 1996.

17. Notebook #57, Lou Harrison Archive.
18. Hanson interview, July 5, 2014.
19. Kostelanetz, "A Conversation, in Eleven-Minus-One Parts," 409.
20. Kosman, "The Melody Maker."
21. Harrison, program notes for *Parade for M.T.T.*
22. Ibid.
23. Schwarz, "A Polymath, at 80, Tries to Simplify."
24. Harrison, Miller, and Hanson, insert notes to *Suite from the "Marriage at the Eiffel Tower."*
25. The passacaglia originated in a 1937 piano sketch and had later been incarnated variously as part of *Canticle #2* and *Ground* for two pianos, all of which he rejected in the 1995 revision.
26. He told Richard Kostelanetz that only in 1990 did his income from his music publishing royalties make up for his lost teaching income. He credited Davies for vaulting his music to international attention (Kostelanetz, "Lou Harrison: California Eclectic").
27. Woodard, "Composer a Hero in World of New Music."
28. Kostelanetz, "Lou Harrison: California Eclectic."
29. Alburger, "A Garden Interview with Lou Harrison."
30. Colker, "An Original Composition."
31. Builder John Swearingen, quoted in McNeil, "A Symphony in Straw."
32. Harrison interview, September 24, 1997.
33. Schwarz, "A Polymath, at 80, Tries to Simplify."
34. Colker, "An Original Composition."
35. Swearingen, "A Cave for a Composer."
36. McNeil, "A Symphony in Straw."
37. Collins, "A Medal for Lou."
38. Harrison interview, June 19, 2000.
39. Mark Morris interview, June 8, 2013.
40. Dunning, "In Merged Identities, Chaos Becomes Counterpoint."
41. Acocella, *Mark Morris*, 162–182.
42. Swed, "Lou Harrison, 85."
43. Hunt, "Mark Morris on Lou Harrison."
44. This requirement also meant that he had to compose for equal-tempered instruments, though he actually used his own piano's Kirnberger #2 tuning while composing *Rhymes With Silver* (Keislar, "Six American Composers on Nonstandard Tunings," 181).
45. Swed, "With a Little Bit of Pluck."
46. Finane, "The Choreographer."
47. Acocella, "Mark Morris Delivers the Goods."
48. Harrison wrote *Suite for Cello and Piano* for local physician and Cabrillo Festival board member Robert Korns Jr., adapting old sketches for the outer movements. Harrison dated these sketches to 1947-1948, the third movement originally to have been the second half of his *Air in G minor* (1947). However, stylistically the movements are much more similar to works such as *Festival Dance* (1951), written after he had discovered the Indian *jhala* technique. While Harrison was at work on the piece, he received word that Korns had died and so added a middle movement, "Elegy," using interval controls. The suite was premiered at Korns's memorial service in May 1995.
49. Burwasser, "A Chat with Lou Harrison."
50. Boriskin, insert notes to *The Equal Tempered Lou Harrison*.
51. Griffiths, "Celebrating an Escapee from Tradition."
52. Holland, "Marching to a Different Percussionist." One might be reminded of John Cage's dismissal of neoclassicist composers who appropriated the music of eighteenth-century Europe, which, "putting it bluntly and chronologically, does not belong to them" (Cage "In Defense of Satie").

53. Corbett, "Experimental Oriental," 173.

54. Cizmic, "Composing the Pacific."

55. More criticism and discussion of Harrison's musical hybrids can be found in Chacko, "Beyond the Myth of East–West Hybridity"; Cook, "Living in Northwest Asia"; Kartomi, "Traditional Music Weeps"; Perlman, "American Gamelan in the Garden of Eden"; Tang, "Interpreting Lou Harrison"; and Thomas, "Lou Harrison's Double Concerto for Gamelan, Violin and Cello."

56. Jody Diamond interview, November 2013.

57. Davidson, "Maverick in the Mainstream."

Chapter 37

1. Swed, "With a Little Bit of Pluck."

2. Notebook #137, Lou Harrison Archive; Harrison interview, July 19, 2000.

3. Harrison's introduction to *Suite for Sangen*, Lou Harrison Archive.

4. The *in* mode is pentatonic but sometimes includes alternate tones in ascent or descent, and Harrison likewise created different shades to his modes by adding a sixth tone to a pentatonic basis. For example, the first movement has a scale of E, F, G, B, C, but sometimes Harrison switches the C for a C♯.

5. Harrison interview, September 25, 1997.

6. A more comprehensive analysis of *Suite for Sangen* is in Cook, "Living in Northwest Asia."

7. Swed, "With a Little Bit of Pluck."

8. Wu Man, "Lou Harrison."

9. Sire, "Wu Man."

10. Wu Man interview, November 21, 2009.

11. Harrison interview, June 12, 1997.

12. "A 6-tone mode has the important power of preserving the generic sound of its 5-tone relative," he wrote (Harrison, *Music Primer*, 34–35).

13. This scale, known as the nearly whole-tone scale, includes one pitch that breaks the symmetry of the sequence of whole tones. He also used this scale in the similarly hexatonic *Mass for St. Cecilia's Day*.

14. "Troika" means "set of three" in Russian and can be used to refer either to musical trios or to a sleigh ride (pulled by three horses), as in Prokofiev's *Lieutenant Kijé*. Harrison's piece could fit either definition, but it lacks the breakneck excitement of Prokofiev's work.

15. Before his days as an activist, Locke was Harrison's favorite porn star. After Locke became the outspoken president of the People With AIDS Coalition, Harrison corresponded with him, and they met in Aptos when Locke was very ill with AIDS.

16. Wu Man interview, November 21, 2009. The *Concerto for Pipa with String Orchestra* premiered at New York's Lincoln Center, commemorating Harrison's eightieth birthday.

17. Geoff Smith, "Lou Harrison: An Interview."

18. Like his earlier *Gending Aphrodite*, Harrison was not entirely satisfied with this setting of his own poem with gamelan, and he vowed to revise it, although he never did.

19. Harrison interview, September 25, 1997.

20. Harrison interview, June 13, 1997.

21. Although he did not indicate it in the score, Harrison composed the work with the Kirnberger #2 temperament in mind, and Burman-Hall recorded it in that tuning.

22. Kosman, "The Melody Maker."

23. Harrison, *The Path at West Holding*, 27.

24. Collins, "A Sound Life."

25. Ibid.

26. Harrison, *The Path at West Holding*, 30–31.
27. Adams, "John Luther Adams Remembers William Colvig."
28. "Lou Harrison Receives MacDowell Medal."
29. Collins, "A Medal for Lou."
30. Notebook #57, Lou Harrison Archive.
31. Harrison, 2001 draft letter to Mark Bulwinkle, Lou Harrison Archive.
32. Burlingame interview, July 9, 2014.
33. Ibid.
34. Leyland, *Gay Sunshine Interviews*, 188.
35. Veltman, "Harrison Tried Hard to Settle This Score."
36. Harrison, Miller, and Hanson, insert notes to *Suite from the "Marriage at the Eiffel Tower."*
37. Harrison acceptance speech ms., Lou Harrison Archive. Eva Soltes made the videotape of the speech because Harrison no longer wanted to travel.
38. Leta E. Miller, "Dark Fairy Tales and Obscure Legends," 25, 28.
39. Harrison interview, August 10, 2001.
40. Robert Gordon in Soltes, *Lou Harrison: A World of Music*.
41. Veltman, "Harrison Tried Hard to Settle This Score."
42. Sheridan, "Harrison Recognized as MA Composer of the Year."
43. Ibid.
44. Soltes e-mail communication, 2007.
45. The festival first staged it in 1966. This time, the hourlong opera shared the bill with its dedicatee, Virgil Thomson, via a live performance of his music to *The River* played during a screening of the 1937 documentary.
46. Serinus, "'Young Caesar' Finally Gets Its Due."
47. Kosman, "When Caesar Meets King Nicomedes Things Get Steamy."
48. Harrison, May 2001 letter to Sidney Jowers, Lou Harrison Archive.
49. Hanson e-mail message, July 19, 2014.
50. Although the Gloria resembles the sketch he found in the original notebook, the Kyrie accompaniment is newly composed. The sketches for the other movements from 1939 do not indicate any accompaniment other than drones.
51. Ulrich, "FaceTime: Lou Harrison."
52. Fiore, "Reminiscence, Reflections, and Resonance," 211–213.
53. Schneider and Tanenbaum, "Behind the Scenes from Nek Chand"; Fiore, "Reminiscence, Reflections, and Resonance."
54. Translated to ratios, this results in a scale of 1:1, 7:6, 4:3, 3:2, 5:3, 11:6 relative to the fundamental D, or 1:1, 9:8, 5:4, 11:8, 3:2, 7:4 relative to G. Harrison used a similar scale, with its distinctive 7th and 11th harmonics, in the second half of the original *Young Caesar*.
55. For details, see Fiore, "Reminiscence, Reflections, and Resonance"; and Alves, "The Tuning of *Lou Harrison—Por Gitaro: Suites for Tuned Guitars*." The complete scale of the Harrison National steel is, from G, 1:1, 33:32, 9:8, 7:6, 5:4, 21:16, 11:8, 3:2, 14:9, 27:16, 7:4, 15:8.
56. Magnier, "In India, a Secret Garden That Rocks."
57. Harrison interview with John Schneider, 2002.
58. Hanson interview, July 5, 2014.
59. Colker, "An Original Composition."
60. McNeil, "A Symphony in Straw."
61. Hughes interview, March 17, 2004.
62. Swed, "Where Music and Life Entwined."
63. He had to use an equal-tempered National guitar for that March 7, 2002 performance, as the refretted version of the National steel guitar was not yet available. When the

just-intonation National steel was ready, guitarist John Schneider premiered that version at MicroFest in Southern California (Schneider and Tanenbaum, "Behind the Scenes from Nek Chand").

64. Schneider and Tanenbaum, "Behind the Scenes from Nek Chand." Harrison would not live to fulfill the commission for Paiement.

Chapter 38

1. Harrison, *The Path at West Holding*, 20.
2. Letter to Joel Sachs, January 2003.
3. Harrison, in Soltes, *Lou Harrison: A World of Music*.
4. Harrison, undated interview with Eva Soltes.
5. Hanson interview, July 5, 2014.
6. Harrison, *The Path at West Holding*, 4. The bifurcation of events may refer to the "many worlds" interpretation of quantum mechanics (Harrison loved to read about science), which posits that every possible outcome of a decision spawns a new universe, so that every possibility exists in some parallel world.
7. Hanson interview, July 5, 2014.
8. Burlingame interview, July 9, 2014.
9. Ibid.
10. Adams, "Remembering Lou."
11. Foley, "Saying Goodbye to Lou Harrison."
12. Adams, insert notes to *For Lou Harrison*.
13. Lang interview, August 11, 2011.
14. "I Remember Lou."
15. Harrison memorial service, Mills College, March 16, 2013.
16. Williams, *A Palpable Elysium*, 126.
17. The Rex Foundation and Unbroken Chain were the two non-profits established by members of the Grateful Dead that provided funds for the establishment of the Lou Harrison Archive.
18. Foley, "Saying Goodbye to Lou Harrison."
19. Ross, "Mavericks: Lou Harrison."
20. Jody Diamond interview, November 8, 2013.
21. Most of the gamelan scores have now been published individually by the American Gamelan Institute.
22. Colker, "An Original Composition."
23. Charles Hanson, personal communication.
24. Dresher, "Looking West to the East," 91.
25. Harrison, *The Path at West Holding*, 40.

BIBLIOGRAPHY

"150 Police Break Up Antiwar Riot at San Jose State College." *Los Angeles Times,* Nov. 21, 1967.

"Ajemian Sisters in Dual Recital: Anahid, Violinist, and Maro at the Piano Present Premiere of Lou Harrison's Suite." *New York Times,* January 12, 1952.

"Anti-Bias Work Urged." *New York Times,* June 6, 1946.

"Doctrine of the Dropouts." *Time* 91, no. 1 (January 5, 1968): 72.

"East Meets West." *Newsweek,* May 8, 1961: 67.

"Fingersnaps and Footstomps." *Time* 36, no. 5 (July 29, 1940): 48.

"A Grand Birthday Celebration, Concert." *San Francisco Chronicle,* May 16, 1977.

"The History of KPFA." KPFA (2006), http://www.kpfa.org/history.

Lou Harrison and John Cage, Panel at Cornish School. VHS. Seattle, Washington: Cornish School, January 1992.

"Lou Harrison Receives MacDowell Medal." *NewMusicBox* (September 1, 2000), http://www.newmusicbox.org/articles/Lou-Harrison-receives-Macdowell-medal.

"Nevada Atom Test Affects Utah Area." *New York Times,* May 20, 1953.

"I Remember Lou." *Other Minds* (2003), http://otherminds.org/shtml/Irememberlou.shtml.

"Science Tackles Radiation Peril." *Life* 38, no. 12 (March 21, 1955): 32–39.

"The Tenth Day: 3rd January 1960: Eastern Influence on American Music" (Report on a lecture by Alan Hovhaness) in "The XXXIIIrd Madras Music Conference, 1959, Official Report." *The Journal of the Music Academy, Madras* XXXI (1960): 51.

"Tour of Japan, Alaska, Canada and Southern U.S. 1961: Tokyo, Press, Correspondence, Programming Feb. 16 1960–Jun. 16 1961." New York Philharmonic Leon Levy Digital Archives.

Acocella, Joan. *Mark Morris.* New York: Farrar, Straus and Giroux, 1993.

———. "Mark Morris Delivers the Goods." *Wall Street Journal,* April 24, 1997.

Adams, John Luther. Insert notes to *For Lou Harrison.* CD. New World Records 80669, 2004.

———. "John Luther Adams Remembers William Colvig." *NewMusicBox* (April 1, 2000), http://www.newmusicbox.org/articles/John-Luther-Adams-Remembers-William-Colvig.

———. "Remembering Lou." *NewMusicBox* (May 7, 2003), http://www.newmusicbox.org/articles/john-luther-adams-remembering-lou.

Ajemian, Anahid. "Remembering Seymour Barab (1921–2014): Composer, Cellist, Friend." *NewMusicBox* (July 14, 2014), http://www.newmusicbox.org/articles/remembering-seymour-barab.

Alburger, Mark. "A Garden Interview with Lou Harrison." *Twentieth-Century Music* 2, no. 11 (November 1995), 11–13.

Alexander, Doris. *Eugene O'Neill's Creative Struggle: The Decisive Decade 1924–1933.* University Park: Pennsylvania State University Press, 1992.

Alves, Bill. "Digital Harmony of Sound and Light." *Computer Music Journal* 29, no. 4 (Winter 2005): 49–58.

———. "Kembangan in the Music of Lou Harrison." *Perspectives of New Music* 39, no. 2 (Summer 2001): 29–56.

———. "The Tuning of *Lou Harrison—Por Gitaro: Suites for Tuned Guitars*." Bill Alves website (2011), http://www.billalves.com/porgitaro/porgitarotuning.html.

American Society of University Composers. *A Conversation between Ben Johnston and Lou Harrison.* Evanston, IL: Typescript, 1987.

———. *Proceedings of the Second Annual Conference.* New York: American Society of University Composers, 1967.

Amirkhanian, Charles. "Remy Charlip on John Cage." *Ballet Review* 24, no. 2 (Summer 1996): 21–24.

Anderson, Dwight. "Orchestra's Program of Arresting Quality." *Louisville Courier-Journal,* January 19, 1956.

Arlen, Walter. "Harrison Works Heard on Monday Concert." *Los Angeles Times,* January 20, 1960.

Arnold, Ben. "War Music and the American Composer during the Vietnam Era." *The Musical Quarterly* 75, no. 3 (Autumn 1991): 316–335.

Asian Composers League. *Third Asian Composers League Conference—Festival Final Report.* Manila, Philippines, October 12–18, 1975.

Asimov, Isaac. "I Feel It in My Bones." *Magazine of Fantasy and Science Fiction,* December 1957.

Bacharach, Burt, with Robert Greenfield. *Anyone Who Had a Heart: My Life and Music.* New York: HarperCollins, 2013.

Badagnani, David. "Alan Hovhaness Symphonies Part 3: Overview of Symphonies 15–30." *The Alan Hovhaness Website* (2002), http://www.hovhaness.com/Sym_15_30.html.

Baker, Alan. "An Interview with Lou Harrison." *American Mavericks* (American Public Media radio show) (June 2002), http://musicmavericks.publicradio.org/features/interview_harrison.html.

Baker, Don Russell. "The Percussion Music of Lou Harrison, 1939–1942." DMA thesis, University of Illinois at Urbana-Champaign, 1985.

Barbour, J. Murray. *Tuning and Temperament: A Historical Survey.* East Lansing: Michigan State College Press, 1951.

Barton, Bruce Walter. *The Tree at the Center of the World.* Santa Barbara, CA: Ross-Erikson, 1980.

Beam, Jeffery. "Tales of a Jargonaut: An Interview with Jonathan Williams." *Rain Taxi Review of Books,* Spring 2003.

Bell-Kanner, Karen. *Frontiers: The Life and Times of Bonnie Bird: American Modern Dancer and Dance Educator.* Australia: Harwood Academic Publishers, 1998.

Berger, Arthur. "Composers Are Nostalgic for the Turbulent 1920s." *New York Herald Tribune,* May 20, 1951.

———. "New Music Society: 'Imaginary Landscape no. 4' for 12 Radios Heard." *New York Herald Tribune,* May 12, 1951.

———. *Reflections of an American Composer.* Berkeley: University of California Press, 2002.

Bernstein, Leonard. "Music That Sings: The Records in Review." *Theater Arts* 32, no. 2 (February 1948): 14.

Bizot, Richard. "Lester Horton's 'Salome,' 1934–1953 and After." *Dance Research Journal* 16, no. 1 (Spring 1984): 35–40.

Blackwood, Michael, dir. *Musical Outsiders: An American Legacy.* Video. Michael Blackwood Productions, 1975.

Blesh, Rudi. *Shining Trumpets: A History of Jazz*. London: Cassell, 1949.

Bloomfield, Arthur. "Doves Win Music Festival Decibel Poll." *San Francisco Examiner,* August 20, 1968.

Blue Cloud, Peter. *Elderberry Flute Song: Contemporary Coyote Tales*. Trumansburg, NY: Crossing Press, 1982.

Blum, Walter. "The Bell-Like World of Lou Harrison." *San Francisco Examiner,* March 26, 1981, sec. Sunday Magazine.

Bogdanowitsch, Sasha. "Bill Colvig." *Experimental Musical Instruments* 9, no. 4 (June 1994): 16–19.

Bogley, Ron. "A History of ASEA and the Center for World Music, 1973–74." *American Gamelan Institute* (2004), http://www.gamelan.org/centerforworldmusic/cwmpdf/history73.pdf.

Bogley, Ron, ed. "Memories of the Center for World Music 1974–2004." *American Gamelan Institute* (2004), http://www.gamelan.org/centerforworldmusic/cwmpdf/memories.pdf.

Boriskin, Michael. "An American Original: Lou Harrison—His 'Personal' Piano Music." *Piano & Keyboard* 73, (March–April 1995): 30–34.

———. Insert notes to *The Equal Tempered Lou Harrison: Piano Music*. CD. Newport Classic NPD 85520, 1995.

Bottoms, Rita, and Irene Reti. *Rita Bottoms: Polyartist Librarian*. Santa Cruz: University of California Press, 2005.

Bowles, Paul. *In Touch: The Letters of Paul Bowles*, edited by Jeffrey Miller. New York: Farrar, Straus and Giroux, 1994.

———. *Paul Bowles on Music*, edited by Timothy Mangan and Irene Hermann. Berkeley: University of California Press, 2003.

Broughton, James. *Coming Unbuttoned: A Memoir*. San Francisco: City Lights, 1993.

Brown, Carolyn. *Chance and Circumstance: Twenty Years with Cage and Cunningham*. New York: Alfred A. Knopf, 2007.

Brown, Owsley, dir. *Music Makes a City: A Louisville Orchestra Story*. Video. Louisville, KY: PBS, 2010.

Brown, Richard. Insert notes to *Lou Harrison: Mass to St. Anthony*. Oregon Repertory Singers CD. Koch International Classics, 1993

Broyard, Anatole. *Kafka Was the Rage: A Greenwich Village Memoir*. New York: Random House, 1993.

Brunner, David Lee. "The Choral Music of Lou Harrison." DMA diss., University of Illinois at Urbana-Champaign, 1989.

———. "Cultural Diversity in the Choral Music of Lou Harrison." *Choral Journal* 32, no. 10 (May 1992): 17–28.

Bunge, Hans, and Hanns Eisler. "Ask Me More about Brecht." Pp. 413–440 in David Blake, ed., *Hanns Eisler: A Miscellany*. Luxembourg: Harwood Academic Publishers, 1996.

Burkholder, J. Peter. *Charles Ives and His World*. Princeton, NJ: Princeton University Press, 1996.

Burlin, Natalie Curtis. *The Indians' Book: An Offering by the American Indians of Indian Lore, Musical and Narrative, to Form a Record of the Songs and Legends of Their Race*. New York: Harper and Brothers, 1923.

Burton, Humphrey. *Leonard Bernstein*. New York: Doubleday, 1994.

Burwasser, Daniel. "A Study of Lou Harrison's *Concerto for Violin and Percussion Orchestra* and *Concerto for Organ and Percussion Orchestra*." PhD diss., City University of New York, 1993.

Burwasser, Peter. "A Chat with Lou Harrison." *Fanfare* 23, no. 4 (March/April 2000).

Cabrillo Festival of Contemporary Music. "Searchable Program Database" (November 2016), http://cabrillomusic.org/about-us/festival-history-archives.

Cage, John. "A Composer's Confessions." P. 281 in Richard Kostelanetz, ed., *John Cage, Writer: Previously Uncollected Pieces*. New York: Limelight Editions, 1993.

———. "Counterpoint." *Dune Forum* 1, no. 2 (February 14, 1934).

———. "The Dreams and Dedications of George Antheil." *Modern Music* 23, no. 1 (Winter 1946): 78–79.

———. "The East in the West." *Modern Music* 23 (April 1946): 111–112.

———. *Empty Words: Writings '73–'78.* Middletown, CT: Wesleyan University Press, 1979.

———. "For More New Sounds." *Modern Music* 19, no. 4 (May–June, 1942): 243–245.

———. "Forerunners of Modern Music." Pp. 62–66 in John Cage, *Silence: Lectures and Writings.* Middletown, CT: Wesleyan University Press, 1961.

———. "The Future of Music: Credo." Pp. 4–5 in John Cage, *Silence: Lectures and Writings.* Middletown, CT: Wesleyan University Press, 1961.

———. "Goal: New Music, New Dance." *The Dance Observer* 6, no. 10 (December 1939): 296–297.

———. "History of Experimental Music in the United States." Pp. 67–75 in John Cage, *Silence: Lectures and Writings.* Middletown, CT: Wesleyan University Press, 1961.

———. "How the Piano Came to Be Prepared." Pp. 7–9 in John Cage, *Empty Words: Writings '73–'78.* Middletown, CT: Wesleyan University Press, 1979.

———. "In Defense of Satie (1948)." P. 78 in Richard Kostelanetz, ed., *John Cage.* New York: Praeger, 1970.

———. "Introduction." In John Cage, *Party Pieces.* New York: C. F. Peters, 1982.

———. *John Cage: Questions and Answers.* 1990. Harvard University Press.

———. "On Robert Rauschenberg." P. 100 in John Cage, *Silence: Lectures and Writings.* Middletown, CT: Wesleyan University Press, 1961.

———. *Silence: Lectures and Writings.* Middletown, CT: Wesleyan University Press, 1961.

———. *A Year from Monday: New Lectures and Writings.* Middletown, CT: Wesleyan University Press, 1967.

Campbell, Brett. "Become Ocean: John Luther Adams and the Legacy of Lou Harrison." *MicroFest* (April 19, 2014), http://microfest.org/become-ocean-john-luther-adams-and-the-legacy-of-lou-harrison.

———. "The Divine Lou Harrison." *Andante,* January 2003.

———. "Natural Sounds: Composer Michael Harrison Finds Beauty in Ancient and Modern Musical Tunings." *Oregon Quarterly,* September 2015.

Campbell, Joseph. *The Hero with a Thousand Faces.* New York: Pantheon Books, 1949.

Carey, David. "*Double Music*: A Historico-Analytic Study." MA thesis, San Jose State University, 1978.

Carr, Ian. *Keith Jarrett: The Man and His Music.* New York: Da Capo, 1991.

Cavafy, Constantine. *Collected Poems,* translated by Edmund Keeley, Philip Sherrard, and Geõrgios P. Savvidês. London: Hogarth Press, 1975.

Celso, Lynnette V. "A Study and Catalogue of Lou Harrison's Utilization of Keyboard Instruments in His Solo and Ensemble Works." MA thesis, San Jose State University, 1979.

Cernovich, Nicolas. "A Play in the Tradition of Noh." *Black Mountain Review* 1, no. 1 (June 1951).

Chacko, Rachel E. "Beyond the Myth of East–West Hybridity: An Analysis of Lou Harrison's Works for Gamelan and Western Instruments." PhD diss., University of Colorado, 2010.

Chalmers, John H. *Divisions of the Tetrachord: A Prolegomenon to the Construction of Musical Scales.* Hanover, NH: Frog Peak Music, 1993.

Charlip, Remy. *Arm in Arm: A Collection of Connections, Endless Tales, Reiterations, and Other Echolalia.* New York: Parents' Magazine Press, rpt. Tricycle Press, 1969, 1997.

Chávez, Carlos. *Towards a New Music: Music and Electricity,* translated by Herbert Weinstock. New York: W. W. Norton, 1937.

Chen, Yun-Feng. "Lou Harrison's *Organ Concerto with Percussion Orchestra*: The Fusion of Asian Musical Rhetoric with the Western World's Oldest Musical Instrument." DMA diss., University of Washington, 2005.

Cizmic, Maria. "Composing the Pacific: Interviews with Lou Harrison." *Echo* 1, no. 1 (1999).

Clark, Philip. "Chimes of Freedom (Interview with Composer Lou Harrison)." *Wire: Adventures in Modern Music* 222 (August 2002): 28–33.

Clark, Tom. *Charles Olson: The Allegory of a Poet's Life*. New York: Norton, 1991.

Clarkson, Austin. *On the Music of Stefan Wolpe: Essays and Recollections*. Hillsdale, NY: Pendragon Press, 2003.

———. "Stefan Wolpe and Abstract Expressionism." Pp. 75–112 in Steven Johnson, ed., *The New York Schools of Music and Visual Arts*. New York: Routledge, 2002.

Cocteau, Jean. *The Infernal Machine and Other Plays*. Norfolk, CT: New Directions, 1964.

Colker, David. "An Original Composition." *Los Angeles Times*, February 12, 2004.

Collins, Phil. "A Medal for Lou." *Metro Santa Cruz*, August 30, 2000.

———. "San Francisco's American Festival Proved That Symphony Audiences Will Turn Out for Modern Classical." *Metro Santa Cruz*, June 27, 1996.

———. "A Sound Life." *Metro Santa Cruz*, August 9, 2000.

Colvig, William. "An American Gamelan." *Xenharmonikôn* 3 (Spring 1975).

Commanday, Robert. "Lou Harrison Seeks Privacy in Aptos." *San Francisco Chronicle*, August 3, 1964.

Committee on Un-American Activities, House of Representatives. *Investigation of Communism in the Metropolitan Music School, Inc. and Related Fields: Hearings before the Committee on Un-American Activities, House of Representatives*. Washington DC: US Government Printing Office, 1957.

———. *Investigation of Communist Activities in the San Francisco Area, Part 1*. Washington DC: US Government Printing Office, 1954.

Cook, Lisa M. "Living in Northwest Asia: Transculturation and Postwar Art Music." PhD diss., University of Colorado, 2009.

Coomaraswamy, Ananda K. *The Dance of Śiva: Fourteen Indian Essays*. New York: Sunwise Turn, 1924.

———. *The Transformation of Nature in Art*. Cambridge, MA: Harvard University Press, 1934.

Copland, Aaron. *Aaron Copland: A Reader: Selected Writings 1923–1972*, edited by Richard Kostelanetz and Steven Silverstein. New York: Routledge, 2004.

———. "Scores and Records." *Modern Music* 16, no. 1 (November–December 1938): 125.

Corbett, John. "Experimental Oriental: New Music and Other Others." Pp. 163–186 in Georgina Born and David Hesmondhalgh, eds., *Western Music and Its Others: Difference, Representation, and Appropriation in Music*. Berkeley, CA: University of California Press, 2000.

Cousins, Norman. "Retreat from Decency." *Saturday Review* (September 27, 1958): 24.

Cowell, Henry, ed. *American Composers on American Music: A Symposium*. Palo Alto, CA: Stanford University Press, 1933.

———. "Current Chronicle." *The Musical Quarterly* 46, no. 3 (July 1950): 451.

———. "Current Chronicle." *The Musical Quarterly* 35, no. 2 (April 1949): 296.

———. "Drums Along the Pacific." *Modern Music* 18, no. 1 (November–December 1940): 46–49.

———. *New Musical Resources*, edited by David Nicholls. Rpt. ed. Cambridge, UK: Cambridge University Press, 1930, 1996.

———. "Oriental Influence on Western Music." Pp. 71–76 in *Music East and West: Report on the 1961 Tokyo East–West Music Encounter Conference*. Tokyo: East–West Music Encounter, 1961.

———. "Relating Music and Concert Dance." *Dance Observer* 4, no. 1 (January 1937): 1, 7–9.

———. "Towards Primitivism." *Modern Music* 10, no. 3 (March 1933): 153.

———. *United String Quartet*. New York: Peters, 1966.

Cowell, Henry, and Sidney Cowell. *Charles Ives and His Music*. Oxford: Oxford University Press, 1955.

Cowell, Sidney. "Henry Cowell's View of Teaching Composition." P. 29 in Peter Garland, ed., *A Lou Harrison Reader*. Santa Fe, NM: Soundings Press, 1987.

Crawford, Dorothy. *Evenings On and Off the Roof: Pioneering Concerts in Los Angeles, 1939–1971*. Berkeley, CA: University of California Press, 1995.

Crossley-Holland, Peter. "Asian Music Under the Impact of Western Culture." Pp. 50–53 in *Music East and West: Report on the 1961 Tokyo East–West Music Encounter Conference*. Tokyo: East–West Music Encounter, 1961.

Cushing, Maxine. "San Francisco Scene." *Dance Observer* 4, no. 1 (June–July, 1937): 65.

Daniel, Oliver. *Stokowski: A Counterpoint of View*. New York: Dodd, Mead & Co., 1982.

Daniélou, Alain. *Introduction to the Study of Musical Scales*. London: The India Society, 1943.

———. *Music and the Power of Sound: The Influence of Tuning and Interval on Consciousness*. Rochester, VT: Inner Traditions, 1995.

———. "Music of India." Pp. 5–8 in *Music East and West: Report on the 1961 Tokyo East–West Music Encounter Conference*. Tokyo: East–West Music Encounter, 1961.

———. "Problems of Indian Music Tradition Today." Pp. 64–66 in *Music East and West: Report on the 1961 Tokyo East–West Music Encounter Conference*. Tokyo: East–West Music Encounter, 1961.

Danitz, Marilynn. "Hadassah (Spira Epstein)." Jewish Women's Archive (2009), http://jwa .org/encyclopedia/article/hadassah-spira-epstein.

Davidson, Justin. "Maverick in the Mainstream: At Age 80, Lou Harrison, Ancestor of the Minimalists, Gets to Take a Bow." *Newsday*, April 13, 1997.

de Angulo, Jaime. *Jaime de Angulo: The Music of the Indians of Northern California*, edited by Peter Garland. Santa Fe, NM: Soundings Press, 1988.

de Menasce, Jacques. "Thoughts After a Festival." *The Juilliard Review* 1, no. 3 (Fall 1954): 35–43.

De Mengel, G. *Voile d'Isis*. Paris: 1929.

Diamond, Jody. "In the Beginning Was the Melody: The Gamelan Music of Lou Harrison." Pp. 100–103 in Peter Garland, ed., *A Lou Harrison Reader*. Santa Fe, NM: Soundings Press, 1987.

Ditrich, Will, and William Colvig. *The Mills College Gamelan: Si Darius and Si Madeleine*. Lebanon, NH: American Gamelan Institute, 1983.

Dobie, Charles Caldwell. *San Francisco's Chinatown*. New York: D. Appleton-Century, 1936.

Doerschuk, Bob. "Keith Jarrett." *Keyboard*, September 1986: 80–103.

Doty, David. "Instruere." *Ear New Music Review* 7, no. 3 (July–August 1979).

———. "Interview with Lou Harrison." *1/1: Journal of the Just Intonation Network* 3, no. 2 (Spring 1987): 1–4.

———. *The Just Intonation Primer*. 2nd ed. San Francisco: Just Intonation Network, 1994.

Dresher, Paul. "Looking West to the East." Pp. 90–91 in Peter Garland, ed., *A Lou Harrison Reader*. Santa Fe, NM: Soundings Press, 1987.

Duberman, Martin B. *Black Mountain: An Exploration in Community*. New York: Dutton, 1972.

———. *Paul Robeson*. New York: Knopf, 1988.

Duckworth, William. *Talking Music*. New York: Da Capo, 1999.

Dudley, Jane. "The Mass Dance." *New Theatre* (1934): 17–18.

Dufallo, Richard. *Trackings: Composers Speak with Richard Dufallo*. New York: Oxford University Press, 1989.

Duffie, Bruce. "Composer Lou Harrison: A Conversation With Bruce Duffie." Bruce Duffie website (April 10, 1987), http://www.bruceduffie.com/harrison6.html.

Duncan, Robert. *Letters: Poems Mcmliii–Mcmlvi*. Highlands, NC: J. Williams, 1958.

———. *Robert Duncan: The Collected Later Poems and Plays*, ed. Peter Quartermain. Berkeley, CA: University of California Press, 2014.

———. "Up Rising: Passages 25." In Robert Duncan, *Bending the Bow*, 81. New York: New Directions, 1968.

Dunn, Robert. *John Cage* [catalogue of works]. New York: Henmar Press, 1962.

Dunning, Jennifer. *Alvin Ailey: A Life in Dance*. Reading, MA: Addison-Wesley, 1996.

———. "Blunt Words on Ballet from Erick Hawkins." *New York Times*, February 11, 1992.

———. "In Merged Identities, Chaos Becomes Counterpoint." *New York Times*, April 17, 1997.

Egan, Timothy. "Chief's Speech of 1854 Given New Meaning (and Words)." *New York Times*, April 21, 1992.

Emerson, Ken. "Fascinating Schism: How the Uniquely Gifted George Gershwin Fashioned Masterpieces in Both Popular and Classical Music." *Boston Globe,* December 17, 2006.

Erdman, Jean, and Dan Berkowitz, dir. *Dance and Myth: The World of Jean Erdman—Part 1: The Early Dances*. VHS. New York: Mystic Fire Video, 1990.

Erdman, Jean, and Dan Berkowitz, dir. *Dance and Myth: The World of Jean Erdman—Part 2: The Group Dances*. VHS. New York: Mystic Fire Video, 1991.

Facchin, Guido, and Luisella Ferrarese. *A Homage to Lou Harrison, Vol. 2*. Enrico Balboni, Guido Facchin, and Támmitam Percussion Ensemble CD. Dynamic CDs 263, 1998.

———. *A Homage to Lou Harrison, Vol. 3*. Guido Facchin and Támmitam Percussion Ensemble CD. Dynamic CDs 359, 2001.

Farley, William, Sandra Sharpe, and Mal Sharpe, dir. *The Old Spaghetti Factory: A Documentary*. Video. William Farley Film Group, 2000.

Feisst, Sabine. "Henry Cowell und Arnold Schönberg—Eine Unbekannte Freundschaft." *Archiv Für Musikwissenschaft* 55, no. 1 (1998): 57–71.

Finane, Ben. "The Choreographer: Mark Morris Talks About Putting Music First, the Importance of Boring Music, the Problem with Musicians, the Three Hs, and Why It's More Fun Working with People Who Are Really Good at What They Do." *Listen*, Summer 2012.

Fiore, Giacomo. "Reminiscence, Reflections, and Resonance: The Just Intonation Resophonic Guitar and Lou Harrison's *Scenes from Nek Chand*." *Journal of the Society for American Music* 6, no. 2 (2012): 211–237.

Fiore, Mary Fitton. "The Fra-a-Grant Flowers." P. 267 in Mervin Lane, ed., *Black Mountain College Sprouted Seeds: An Anthology of Personal Accounts*. Knoxville: University of Tennessee Press, 1990.

Fisher, Marjory M. "Golden Gate Witnesses a Dance Experiment." *Musical America*, May 25, 1937: 12.

Flint, Anthony. *Wrestling with Moses: How Jane Jacobs Took on New York's Master Builder and Transformed the American City*. New York: Random House, 2009.

Foley, Jack. "Saying Goodbye to Lou Harrison." *The Alsop Review* (2003), http://www.alsopreview.com/foley/jffharrison.html.

Foley, Kathy. "Lou Harrison: Sounding the Puppet Art." *Puppetry International* 25 (2010): 8–10.

Foreman, Frank. "About the St. Cecilia Society." *Alternating Currents* (2000), http://members.cruzio.com/~yogi/chant.htm.

Fox-Strangways, A. H. *The Music of Hindostan*. Oxford: The Clarendon Press, 1914.

Frankenstein, Alfred. "At Mills—Strip Tease!" *San Francisco Chronicle*, July 8, 1940.

———. "Brilliant Bartok Opens Festival." *San Francisco Chronicle*, August 23, 1963.

———. "Composers' Forum Presents Second Session." *San Francisco Chronicle*, January 15, 1941.

———. "Dance Recital Draws Throngs to Playhouse." *San Francisco Chronicle*, November 17, 1937: 14.

———. "L.A. Horton Group Dances Novel Version of 'Salome'." *San Francisco Chronicle*, April 25, 1938.

———. Liner notes to *Concert Percussion for Orchestra.* Manhattan Percussion Ensemble LP. Time S/8000, 1961.

———. "The New Records in Review." *San Francisco Chronicle,* September 28, 1941.

———. "A Program of Percussion." *San Francisco Chronicle,* July 28, 1939.

———. "Radiana Pazmor 'Refreshing.'" *San Francisco Chronicle,* November 15, 1940.

———. "A Recital on Percussion Instruments." *San Francisco Chronicle,* May 8, 1942.

———. "San Francisco Rejuvenated." *Modern Music* 18, no. 3 (March–April 1941): 186.

———. "A Splendid Performance Opens Red Cross Series." *San Francisco Chronicle,* July 19, 1940.

———. "A Varied and Rich Concert." *San Francisco Chronicle,* May 15, 1941.

Franko, Mark. *Dancing Modernism/Performing Politics.* Bloomington: Indiana University Press, 1995.

Fried, Alexander. "Cushing Works Excel in Composers' Concert: S. F. Museum Hall Jammed for 2nd Forum: Many Standees." *San Francisco Examiner,* January 15, 1941.

———. "Dancers Present Modernist Cycle." *San Francisco Examiner,* May 3, 1937.

———. "Lou Harrison's Aptos Triumph." *San Francisco Examiner,* August 25, 1964.

Fuller, Donald. "Airborne Over New York: Spring 1946." *Modern Music* 23, no. 2 (Spring 1946): 120.

Gabel, Jackie. "Lou Harrison." *Sforzando,* February 1998.

Galardi, Susan. "Premieres: The Composer Speaks: Lou Harrison on His Piano Concerto." *Musical America,* October 1985: 15.

Gann, Kyle. "Ives the Non-Homophobe." ArtsJournal (October 17, 2005), http://www .artsjournal.com/postclassic/2005/10/ives_the_nonhomophobe.html.

———. "Subversive Prophet: Henry Cowell as Theorist and Critic." Pp. 171–221 in David Nicholls, ed., *The Whole World of Music: A Henry Cowell Symposium.* Amsterdam: Harwood Academic Publishers, 1997.

Gardner, Patrick Grant. "*La Koro Sutro* by Lou Harrison: Historical Perspective, Analysis and Performance Considerations." PhD diss., University of Texas, 1981.

Garfias, Robert. "Some Effects of Changing Social Values on Japanese Music." Pp. 18–22 in *Music East and West: Report on the 1961 Tokyo East–West Music Encounter Conference.* Tokyo: East–West Music Encounter, 1961.

Garland, Peter, ed. *A Lou Harrison Reader.* Santa Fe, NM: Soundings Press, 1987.

Gena, Peter, and Jonathan Brent. *A John Cage Reader: In Celebration of His 70th Birthday.* New York: Peters, 1982.

Gidlow, Elsa. *Elsa, I Come with My Songs.* San Francisco: Booklegger Press, 1986.

Gilbert, Steven E. "The 'Twelve-Tone System' of Carl Ruggles: A Study of the Evocations for Piano." *Journal of Music Theory* 14, no. 1 (Spring, 1970): 68–91.

Gillespie, Don. "Another View on Lou: Lou Harrison—A Personal Publishing Memoir." *NewMusicBox* (March 1, 2003), http://www.newmusicbox.org/articles/Another -View-on-Lou-Lou-Harrison-A-Personal-Publishing-Memoir.

Gilmore, Bob. *Harry Partch: A Biography.* New Haven, CT: Yale University Press, 1998.

Glanville-Hicks, Peggy. "Musical Explorers: Six Americans Who Are Changing the Musical Vocabulary." *Vogue* 116 (November 15, 1950): 112–113, 134, 137, 139.

Glinsky, Albert. *Theremin: Ether Music and Espionage: Music in American Life.* Urbana: University of Illinois Press, 2000.

Goldner, Nancy. "Erick Hawkins Dance Co. Performs 'New Moon.'" *Philadelphia Inquirer,* February 15, 1990.

Goode, Elizabeth. "The Dance at Mills College." *The Dance Observer* 6, no. 7 (August– September 1939): 252.

Goodrich, Lloyd, and Patricia FitzGerald Mandel. *John Heliker.* New York: Frederick A. Praeger, 1968.

Graves, Robert. *The White Goddess: A Historical Grammar of Poetic Myth*. New York: Farrar, Straus and Giroux, 1948.

Griffiths, Paul. "Celebrating an Escapee from Tradition." *New York Times,* April 29, 1997.

Grimes, William. "Harold Norse, a Beat Poet, Dies at 92." *The New York Times,* June 13, 2009.

Hajdu, David. *Lush Life: A Biography of Billy Strayhorn*. New York: Farrar, Straus and Giroux, 1996.

Hamilton, Linda. *A Life of Kenneth Rexroth*. New York: Norton, 1991.

Hanson, Charles. "Chronicles of Lou." San Jose State University School of Music and Dance (November 2007), http://www.music.sjsu.edu/links/harrison/harrison_chronicles.html (web page discontinued).

Harding, Mildred Adams. "My Black Mountain." P. 296 in Mervin Lane, ed., *Black Mountain College Sprouted Seeds: An Anthology of Personal Accounts*. Knoxville: University of Tennessee Press, 1990.

Harlan, Calvin. "Lou Harrison—My Friend and Favorite Composer." Pp. 96–97 in Peter Garland, ed., *A Lou Harrison Reader*. Santa Fe, NM: Soundings Press, 1987.

Harman, Carter. "Records: Folk." *New York Times,* August 3, 1947.

Harris, Mary Emma. *The Arts at Black Mountain College*. Cambridge, MA: MIT Press, 1987.

Harrison, Lou. *About Carl Ruggles*. Yonkers, NY: O. Bradinsky, 1946.

———. "About My Fourth Symphony." *Current Musicology* 67 (Fall 1999): 129–132.

———. "Ajemian-Masselos: Two Pianists Play Works of Cage at Carnegie Concert." *New York Herald Tribune,* December 11, 1946.

———. "Alan Hovhaness Offers Original Compositions." *New York Herald Tribune,* June 18, 1945.

———. "Barone Conducts Concert by N.Y. Little Symphony." *New York Herald Tribune,* December 2, 1944.

———. "Carl Ruggles." *The Score and I.M.A. Magazine* 12 (1955): 15–26.

———. Liner notes to *Charles Ives: Violin Sonatas*. Rafael Druian and John Simms LP. Mercury LP 50097, 1956.

———. "Cloverleaf: A Little Narrative with Several 'Off-Ramps.'" *1/1: Journal of the Just Intonation Network* 5, no. 2 (Spring 1989): 1–2, 14–15.

———. Liner notes to *Concerto for Violin and Percussion Orchestra*. LP. Crystal S853, 1972.

———. "Creative Ideas in Classical Korean Music." *Korea Journal* 2, no. 11 (1962): 34–36.

———. Liner notes to *Decoration Day, Suite for Symphonic Strings*. Louisville Orchestra LP, Robert Whitney, cond. First Edition Records LOU 621, 1962

———. "I Do Not Quite Understand You, Socrates." Pp. 133–137 in David Dunn, ed., *Harry Partch: An Anthology of Critical Perspectives*. Amsterdam: Harwood, 2000.

———. "First-Time Fashions, New York, 1944." *Modern Music* 22, no. 1 (November–December 1944): 31–32.

———. "Four Items." *Xenharmonikôn* 1, no. 1 (Spring 1974).

———. "From: Lou Harrison's Bureau for the Consideration of Pathetic Complaints: A Prospectus for Musicians (Department of Utopean Fantasy)." *American Composers' Alliance Bulletin* 6, no. 2 (1957): 14, 22.

———. "Go Planetary!" *Ear New Music Review* 7, no. 5 (September–October 1979): 1.

———. "Item: Thoughts while Designing a Gamelan." *Xenharmonikôn* 7–8, (Spring 1979).

———. "Jaime de Angulo: An Introduction." P. 6 in Peter Garland, ed., *Jaime de Angulo: The Music of the Indians of Northern California*. Santa Fe, NM: Soundings Press, 1988.

———. *Joys & Perplexities: Selected Poems of Lou Harrison*. Winston-Salem, NC: Jargon Society, 1992.

———. Insert notes to *La Koro Sutro; Varied Trio; Suite for Violin and American Gamelan*. CD. New Albion NA 015, 1988.

————. "Learning from Henry." P. 167 in David Nicholls, ed., *The Whole World of Music: A Henry Cowell Symposium*. Amsterdam: Harwood Academic Publishers, 1997.

————. "Letter to JaFran Jones." Jeffrey Ohlmann website (September 2003), http://home.att .net/~jaohlma/music/BGSU/Harrison_Letter.html (web page discontinued).

————. "Literature: All About Music." *View* 6, no. 1 (February 1946): 17.

————. Insert notes to *Lou Harrison: Double Concerto for Violin and Cello with Javanese Gamelan*. CD. Music and Arts Programs of America CD-635, 1990.

————. *Lou Harrison—Elegiac Symphony, Robert Hughes—Cadences*. Oakland Symphony Youth Orchestra LP. 1750 Arch Records S-1772, 1977.

————. "MicroFest 2001 Keynote Address." *1/1: Journal of the Just Intonation Network* 10, no. 4 (Summer 2001): 1, 4–12.

————. "Mid-Winter in New York 1944." *Modern Music* 21, no. 3 (March–April 1944): 159.

————. "Modernism 'Sacred and Profane.'" *Modern Music* 23, no. 3 (Summer 1946): 204.

————. "Mostly Chamber Music." *Modern Music* 23, no. 2 (Spring 1946): 124–125.

————. "Music for the Modern Dance." *American Composers Alliance Bulletin*, October 1952: 11–12.

————. Insert notes to *Music of Lou Harrison*. Composers Recordings Inc. LP. CRI SD 455, 1981; rereleased on CD 613, 1991.

————. "The Music of Lou Harrison." KPFA radio broadcast, August 6, 1968.

————. "Music of the Modern Dance." *ACA Bulletin* 2, no. 3 (October 1952): 11–12.

————. *Music Primer*. New York: C. F. Peters, 1971.

————. "On Quotation." *Modern Music* 23, no. 3 (Summer 1946): 167.

————. "On the *Chôros* of Villa-Lobos." *Modern Music* 22, no. 2 (January–February 1945): 85–87.

————. "Oratorio Society Gives B Minor Mass of Bach." *New York Herald Tribune*, March 28, 1945.

————. Liner Notes to *Pacifika Rondo, Two Pieces for Psaltery, Music for Various Instruments*, LP Desto DC-6478, 1971; re-released as *Music of Lou Harrison.*, CD Phoenix PHCD 118, 1991.

————. Liner notes to *Party Pieces*. Brooklyn Philharmonic LP. Gramavision GR 7006, 1983

————. *The Path at West Holding and Other Poems*. Santa Cruz, CA: Cafe Margo, 2013.

————. "Political Primer [Text]." Pp. 78–83 in Carter Scholz, ed., *Frog Peak Anthology* New Lebanon, NH: Frog Peak, 1992.

————. "Reflections at a Spa." *Modern Music* 23, no. 3 (Fall 1946): 297.

————. "Refreshing the Auditory Perception." Pp. 141–143 in *Music East and West: Report on the 1961 Tokyo East–West Music Encounter Conference*. Tokyo: East–West Music Encounter, 1961.

————. "Renaissance Music: Judith Leigner Is Director at Carnegie Chamber Hall." *New York Herald Tribune*, May 7, 1947.

————. "Review of Harry Partch: 'Genesis of a Music.'" *Bulletin of the International Music Council*, April 1975: 4–5.

————. *Rū Harison no wārudo myūjikku nyūmon* [*Music Primer*], edited by Toshie Kakinuma and Mamoru Fujieda. 2nd ed. Tokyo: Jesuku Ongaku Bunka Shinkōkai, 1993.

————. "Ruggles, Ives, Varèse," *View* 5, no. 4 (November 1945): 11.

————. "Schoenberg in Several Ways." *National Centre for the Performing Arts (Bombay) Quarterly Journal* 4 (1975): 20–31.

————. "Schoenberg: The Late Works." *Modern Music* 21, no. 3 (March–April 1944): 138.

————. "Season's End, May 1944." *Modern Music* 21, no. 4 (May–June, 1944): 236.

————. *Six Sonatas for Cembalo or Pianoforte*, edited by Susan Summerfield. New York: Peer International Corp., 1990.

————. "Society, Musician, Dancer, Machine: A Set of Opinions Entirely Attributable to Lou Harrison in 1966." *Impulse: Annual of Contemporary Dance*, 1966: 40–41.

————. "Some Notes on the Music of Mouth-Organs." Pp. 339–350 in Hye-gu Yi, ed., *Essays in Ethnomusicology: A Birthday Offering for Lee Hye-Ku*. Seoul: Korean Musicological Society, 1969.

————. *Songs in the Forest*. New York: Peer International, 1993.

————. Insert notes to *Soundscapes: Three American Chamber Works Performed by the Mirecourt Trio*. CD. Music & Arts. CD-635, 1990.

————. "Statement." *The Dance Observer* 7, no. 3 (March 1940): 32.

————. *Suite for Piano*. New York: C. F. Peters, 1964.

————. *Suite for Symphonic Strings*. New York: C. F. Peters, 1961.

————. "Summer and Early Fall, New York." *Modern Music* 21, no. 1 (November–December 1943): 35.

————. "Summer Music." *View* 3, no. 3 (October 1945): 21.

————. "Tens on Remembering Henry Cowell." Pp. 37–38 in Peter Garland, ed., *A Lou Harrison Reader* Santa Fe, NM: Soundings Press, 1987.

————. "Thoughts about 'Slippery Slendro.'" *Selected Reports in Ethnomusicology* 6 (1985): 111–117.

————. "The Violin Concerto in the Modern World." *Listen*, March 1947: 4–6.

————. Liner notes to *Virgil Thomson: Stabat Mater; Capital, Capitals; Lou Harrison: Suite for Cello and Harp; Suite no. 2*. LP. Columbia Masterworks ML 4491, 1954

Harrison, Lou, and Jean-Francois Denis. "Main Bersama-Sama." *Balungan* 2, no. 1–2 (Fall 1985): 17–19.

Harrison, Lou, and Hye-Ku Lee. *Korean Music: History*. Ms. copies in Lou Harrison Archive and UCLA Ethnomusicology Archive, 1963.

Harrison, Lou, and Leta E. Miller. *Selected Keyboard and Chamber Music, 1937–1994*. Madison, WI: American Musicological Society, 1998.

Harrison, Lou, Leta Miller, and Charles Hanson. Insert notes to *Suite from the "Marriage at the Eiffel Tower."* Brooklyn Philharmonic CD. Musical Heritage Society 515721X, 2000.

Harrison, Lou, and Trish Neilsen, eds. *Gending-Gending California*. 1981.

Hastanto, Sri. "The Concept of Pathet in Central Javanese Gamelan Music." PhD diss., University of Durham, 1985.

Hayter-Menzies, Grant. *Shadow Woman: The Extraordinary Career of Pauline Benton*. Montreal: McGill-Queen's University Press, 2013.

Henebry, Richard. *Handbook of Irish Music*. Dublin: Cork University Press, 1928.

Henze, Hans Werner, and Stewart Spencer. *Bohemian Fifths: An Autobiography* [*Reiselieder mit böhmischen Quinten*]. Princeton, NJ, Princeton University Press, 1999.

Hicks, Bob. "Pen Stroke of Genius: Recalling Reed's Lloyd Reynolds." *The Oregonian*, May 17, 2008.

Hicks, Michael. *Henry Cowell: Bohemian*. Urbana: University of Illinois Press, 2002.

————. "The Imprisonment of Henry Cowell." *Journal of the American Musicological Society* 44 (1991): 92–119.

————. "John Cage's Studies with Schoenberg." *American Music* 8, no. 2 (Summer 1990).

Higgins, Dick. "Cowell's Lost *Fanati*." *The Musical Quarterly* 82, no. 2 (1998): 232–250.

Holland, Bernard. "Marching to a Different Percussionist." *New York Times*, March 27, 1997.

Holzaepfel, John. "Reminiscences of a Twentieth-Century Pianist: An Interview with David Tudor." *The Musical Quarterly* 78, no. 3 (Autumn 1994): 626–636.

Hoover, Kathleen O'Donnell, and John Cage. *Virgil Thomson: His Life and Music*. New York: T. Yoseloff, 1959.

Horowitz, Joseph, "An American Original" in Joseph Horowitz, ed., *Uncharted Beauty: The Music of Lou Harrison—Pacific Symphony American Composers Festival Program Companion*. Santa Ana, CA: Pacific Symphony, 2006.

Hunt, Mary E. "Mark Morris on Lou Harrison, Léo Delibes and Bob Wills and the Texas Playboys." *CriticalDance* (August 25, 2003), http://www.criticaldance.com/interviews /2003/markmorris2003.html.

Iverson, Ethan. "Keith Jarrett Goes Classical." *Downbeat* 80, no. 9 (September 2013): 24–30.

Ives, Charles, and Thomas Clarke Owens. *Selected Correspondence of Charles Ives.* Berkeley: University of California Press, 2007.

Jacobs, James D. "Lou Harrison's 'Elegiac' Symphony." WGBH (January 30, 2011), http:// www.wgbh.org/articles/Lou-Harrisons-Elegiac-Symphony-1753.

Jarnot, Lisa. *Robert Duncan, the Ambassador from Venus: A Biography.* Berkeley: University of California Press, 2012.

Job, Lenore Peters. *Looking Back while Surging Forward.* San Francisco: Peters Wright Creative Dance, 1984.

Johnson, Steven. *The New York Schools of Music and Visual Arts: John Cage, Morton Feldman, Edgard Varèse, Willem De Kooning, Jasper Johns, Robert Rauschenberg.* New York: Routledge, 2002.

———. "'Worlds of Ideas': The Music of Henry Cowell." In David Nicholls, ed., *The Whole World of Music: A Henry Cowell Symposium.* Amsterdam: Harwood Academic Publishers, 1997.

Johnston, Edward. *Writing & Illuminating & Lettering.* London: J. Hogg, 1906.

Kakinuma, Toshie. "Composing for an Ancient Instrument That Has Lost Its 'Tradition': Lou Harrison's *Set for Four Haisho and Percussion.*" *Perspectives of New Music* 49, no. 2 (Summer 2012): 232–263.

Kandell, Leslie. "Behind Every Pianist Lurks an Unheralded Hero." *New York Times,* December 15, 1985.

Kartomi, Margaret. "'Traditional Music Weeps' and Other Themes in the Discourse on Music, Dance and Theatre of Indonesia, Malaysia and Thailand." *Journal of Southeast Asian Studies* 26, no. 2 (September 1995): 366–400.

Kauder, Hugo. *Counterpoint: An Introduction to Polyphonic Composition.* New York: Macmillan, 1960.

Keislar, Douglas. "Six American Composers on Nonstandard Tunings." *Perspectives of New Music* 29, no. 1 (1991): 176–211.

Kennedy, Eugene C. *The Now and Future Church: The Psychology of Being an American Catholic.* Garden City, NY: Doubleday, 1984.

Ketcham, Diane. "About Long Island: The Pains, Joys, and Perplexities of Learning American Culture." *New York Times* (September 27, 1992).

Kilmer, Anne, Richard Crocker, and Robert Brown. *Sounds from Silence: Recent Discoveries in Ancient Near Eastern Music.* LP. Berkeley, CA: Bit Enki, 1976.

Kosman, Joshua. "The Melody Maker: Composer Lou Harrison Gets Overdue Recognition." *San Francisco Chronicle,* October 8, 1995.

———. "When Caesar Meets King Nicomedes Things Get Steamy—But That's Not Shocking Today." *San Francisco Chronicle,* February 19, 2007.

Kostelanetz, Richard. "A Conversation, in Eleven-Minus-One Parts, with Lou Harrison about Music/Theater." *The Musical Quarterly* 76, no. 383 (Autumn 1992): 409.

———. *Conversing with Cage.* New York: Routledge, 2003.

———. "An Interview on Poetry with Lou Harrison." *Twentieth-Century Music* 5, no. 1 (1998): 7–9.

———. "Lou Harrison: California Eclectic." *The World & I* 7, no. 5 (May 1992): 150–155.

———. *John Cage.* New York: Praeger, 1970.

———. *Writings about John Cage.* Ann Arbor: University of Michigan Press, 1993.

Krenek, Ernst. *Studies in Counterpoint Based on the Twelve-Tone Technique.* New York: G. Schirmer, 1940.

Kretschmer, Ernest T., Irene Reti, and Randall Jarrell. *Ernest T. Kretschmer: Reflections on Santa Cruz Musical Life.* Vol. 1. Santa Cruz, CA: Regional History Project, UC Santa Cruz, 1992.

Kunst, Jaap. *Music in Java: Its History, Its Theory and Its Technique.* The Hague: Nijhoff, 1949.

Larsen, Stephen, and Robin Larsen. *A Fire in the Mind: The Life of Joseph Campbell.* New York: Doubleday, 1991.

Larson, Kay. *Where the Heart Beats: John Cage, Zen Buddhism, and the Inner Life of Artists.* New York: Penguin Press, 2012.

Lechner, Ethan. "Composers as Ethnographers: Difference in the Imaginations of Colin McPhee, Henry Cowell, and Lou Harrison." PhD diss., University of North Carolina at Chapel Hill, 2008.

Lederman, Minna. "John Cage: A View of My Own." P. 152 in Peter Gena and Jonathan Brent, eds., *A John Cage Reader: In Celebration of His 70th Birthday.* New York: Peters, 1982.

———. *Life and Death of a Small Magazine.* New York: Institute for Studies in American Music, 1983.

Levy, David H. "Walden of the Sky." *Sky and Telescope* 90, no. 3 (September 1995): 84.

Leyland, Winston. *Gay Sunshine Interviews.* San Francisco: Gay Sunshine Press, 1978.

Li Ch'ing-Chao. *Complete Poems.* New York: New Directions, 1979.

Liang Tsai-Ping. "A Short Note in Honor of Lou Harrison." P. 87 in Peter Garland, ed., *A Lou Harrison Reader.* Santa Fe, NM: Soundings Press, 1987.

Lilly, John Cunningham. *Man and Dolphin.* Garden City, NY: Doubleday, 1961.

Linick, Anthony. *The Lives of Ingolf Dahl.* Bloomington, IN: AuthorHouse, 2008.

Mace, Thomas. *Musick's Monument* [facsimile]. Paris: Éditions du Centre national de la recherche scientifique, 1966.

Magnier, Mark. "In India, a Secret Garden That Rocks." *Los Angeles Times,* December 6, 2011.

Malina, Judith. *The Diaries of Judith Malina, 1947–1957.* New York: Grove Press, 1984.

Mann, Thomas. *Doctor Faustus: The Life of the German Composer Adrian Leverkühn as Told by a Friend,* translated by H. T. Lowe-Porter. New York: A. A. Knopf, 1948.

Marchand, Rebecca Giacosie. "The Impact of the Second Vatican Council on the Concert Mass in the United States." PhD diss., University of California at Santa Barbara, 2007.

Marin, Eric, dir. *Lou Harrison: Cherish, Conserve, Consider, Create.* Film. Film Arts Foundation, dist. by FVM Media, 1986.

Martin, John. "The Dance Agenda." *New York Times,* January 22, 1950.

———. "The Dance: A New Guild." *New York Times,* July 4, 1943.

———. "The Dance: Graham." *New York Times,* December 23, 1950.

———. "Litz, Cunningham Give Dance Solos." *New York Times,* August 13, 1950.

Maughan, Shannon. "Obituary: Remy Charlip." *Publisher's Weekly,* August 16, 2012.

McKayle, Donald. *Transcending Boundaries: My Dancing Life.* New York: Routledge, 2002.

McNeil, M. E. A. "A Symphony in Straw: The Innovative Straw-Bale House of a Bay Area Composer Is Beautiful, Cool in Summer and Quake-Proof." *San Francisco Chronicle,* February 3, 2002.

McPhee, Colin. "The Balinese Wajang Koelit and Its Music." *Jawa* 16 (1936): 322–366.

———. "The Five-Tone Gamelan Music of Bali." *The Musical Quarterly* 35, no. 2 (April 1949): 250–281.

———. *A House in Bali.* New York: John Day, 1946.

———. *Music in Bali: A Study in Form and Instrumental Organization in Balinese Orchestral Music.* New Haven, CT: Yale University Press, 1966.

Mead, Rita H. "The Amazing Mr. Cowell." *American Music* 1, no. 4 (Winter 1983): 63–89.

———. *Cowell's New Music 1925–1936.* Ann Arbor, MI: UMI Research Press, 1981.

———. "Henry Cowell's New Music Society." *Journal of Musicology* 1, no. 4 (October 1982): 449–463.

Mellers, Wilfrid. "A New Everlasting Feeling: Wilfrid Mellers Pays Tribute to Lou Harrison, 80 This Month." *The Musical Times* 138, no. 1851 (May 1997): 31–35.

Miles, Barry. *Call Me Burroughs: A Life*. New York: Twelve, 2013.

Miller, Christopher. "Orchids (and Other Difficult Flowers) Revisited: A Reflection on Composing for Gamelan in North America." *The World of Music* 47, no. 3 (2005): 81–111.

Miller, Leta E. "The Art of Noise: John Cage, Lou Harrison, and the West Coast Percussion Ensemble." In Michael Saffle, ed., *Perspectives on American Music, 1900–1950*. New York: Garland, 2000.

———. "Dark Fairy Tales and Obscure Legends: Autobiography in the Operas of Lou Harrison." *The Opera Journal* 32 (September 1999): 3–42.

———. "Lou Harrison and the Aesthetics of Revision, Alteration, and Self-Borrowing." *Twentieth-Century Music* 2, no. 1 (March 2005): 79–107.

———. "Method and Madness in Lou Harrison's *Rapunzel*." *Journal of Musicology* 19, no. 1 (Winter 2002): 85–124.

———. *Music and Politics in San Francisco: From the 1906 Quake to the Second World War*. Berkeley: University of California Press, 2012.

———. "Solemn Play: A Life of Cross-Cultural Synthesis." Pp. xv–lv in Lou Harrison and Leta E. Miller, *Selected Keyboard and Chamber Music, 1937–1994*. Madison, WI: A-R Editions, 1998.

Miller, Leta E., and Fredric Lieberman. *Lou Harrison*. Urbana: University of Illinois Press, 2006.

———. "Lou Harrison and the American Gamelan." *American Music* 17, no. 2 (Summer 1999): 146–178.

———. *Lou Harrison: Composing a World*. New York: Oxford University Press, 1998.

Mills College. *Mills College, 1852–1937: A Statement Covering the History, Present Position, Plans, and Needs of the Pioneer College for Women on the Pacific Coast*. Oakland, CA: Mills College, 1937.

Mirapaul, Matthew. "For Composer Lou Harrison, Penmanship Counts." *New York Times*, May 15, 1997.

Montague, Stephen. "John Cage at Seventy: An Interview." *American Music* 3, no. 2 (Summer 1985): 205–216.

Morris, Mark. "The Making of My Dance." *New York Times*, March 23, 2003.

Morris, William. "How I Became a Socialist." Pp. 243–244 in A. L. Morton, ed., *Political Writings of William Morris*. London: Lawrence and Wishart, 1984.

———. *The Defence of Guenevere and Other Poems*. London: Longmans, Green, & Co., 1903.

Mullen, Ruth. "Living in the Past: Memories of a Grandmother's Kitchen Spark the Detail-Perfect Restoration of a 1914 Bungalow." *Oregonian*, April 3, 2008.

Murdoch, James. *Peggy Glanville-Hicks: A Transposed Life*. Hillsdale, NY: Pendragon Press, 2002.

Neff, Severine. "An Unlikely Synergy: Lou Harrison and Arnold Schoenberg." *Journal of the Society of American Music* 3, no. 2 (2009): 155–193.

Nicholls, David. *American Experimental Music, 1890–1940*. Cambridge, UK: Cambridge University Press, 1989.

———. "Cage and the Ultra-Modernists." *American Music* 28, no. 4 (Winter 2012): 492–500.

———. "Getting Rid of the Glue: The Music of the New York School." Pp. 17–56 in Steven Johnson, ed., *The New York Schools of Music and Visual Arts*. New York: Routledge, 2002.

———. "Henry Cowell's *United Quartet*." *American Music* 13, no. 2 (Summer 1995): 195–217.

———. "Introduction." In Henry Cowell, *New Musical Resources*. New York: Cambridge University Press, 1996.

Nicholls, David, ed. *The Whole World of Music: A Henry Cowell Symposium*. Amsterdam: Harwood Academic Publishers, 1997.

Norse, Harold. *Memoirs of a Bastard Angel*. New York: W. Morrow, 1989.

Northrop, F. S. C. *The Meeting of East and West: An Inquiry Concerning World Understanding.* New York: Macmillan, 1946.

Nuss, Steven. "Music from the Right: The Politics of Toshiro Mayuzumi's *Essay for String Orchestra*." Pp. 85–118 in Yayoi Uno Everett and Frederick Lau, eds., *Locating East Asia in Western Art Music*. Middletown, CT: Wesleyan University Press, 2004.

Olson, Charles, and Ralph Maud. *Selected Letters*. Berkeley: University of California Press, 2000.

Olson, H. F., and H. Belar. "Electronic Music Synthesizer." *Journal of the Acoustical Society of America* 27 (May 1955): 595–612.

Oteri, Frank J. "Barbara Benary: Mother of Lion." *NewMusicBox* (February 1, 2011), http://www.newmusicbox.org/articles/barbara-benary-mother-of-lion.

Page, Tim. Insert notes to *Mysterious Mountain/Elegiac Symphony*. CD. MusicMasters MM60204K, 1989.

Palevsky, Stacey. "Drawing Inspiration: Not Even a Stroke Can Halt Prolific S. F. Children's Book Artist." *Jweekly*, July 30, 2009.

Partch, Harry. *Genesis of a Music: An Account of a Creative Work, Its Roots and Its Fulfillments.* 2nd ed. New York: Da Capo Press, 1974.

Patterson, David W. *John Cage: Music, Philosophy, and Intention, 1933–1950*. New York: Routledge, 2002.

———. "The Picture That Is Not in the Colors: Cage, Coomaraswamy, and the Impact of India." Pp. 177–216 in David W. Patterson, ed., *John Cage: Music, Philosophy, and Intention, 1933–1950*. New York: Routledge, 2002.

Pence, James. "People Call It Noise—But He Calls It Music." *Chicago Daily News*, March 19, 1942.

Perlis, Vivian. *Charles Ives Remembered: An Oral History*. New Haven: Yale University Press, 1974.

Perlman, Marc. "American Gamelan in the Garden of Eden: Intonation in a Cross-Cultural Encounter." *The Musical Quarterly* 78, no. 3 (Autumn 1994): 510–555.

Perloff, Nancy Lynn. *Art and the Everyday: Popular Entertainment and the Circle of Erik Satie.* Oxford, UK: Clarendon Press, 1991.

Perry, Charles. *The Haight-Ashbury: A History*. New York: Random House, 1984.

Plessix Gray, Francine du. "Black Mountain: The Breaking (Making) of a Writer." Pp. 301–302 in Mervin Lane, ed., *Black Mountain College Sprouted Seeds: An Anthology of Personal Accounts*. Knoxville: University of Tennessee Press, 1990.

Polansky, Larry. "17s for Lou (on Reading *Joys and Perplexities*)." *Have Pig Want Gun: The Frog Peak Newsletter* 9 (2004).

———. "Paratactical Tuning: An Agenda for the Use of Computers in Experimental Intonation." *Computer Music Journal* 11, no. 1 (1987): 61–68.

Polansky, Larry, and John Kennedy. "Total Eclipse: The Music of Johanna Magdalena Beyer." *The Musical Quarterly* 80, no. 4 (Winter 1996): 719–778.

Pound, Ezra, Li Bai, and Ernest Francisco Fenollosa. *Cathay*. London: E. Mathews, 1915.

Powell, Jarrad. "Notation or Not: Some Musings about Writing It All Down." *Balungan* 2, no. 1–2 (Fall 1985): 6–7.

———. Presentation at Cornish College's "Drums Along the Pacific" Festival. March 29, 2009.

Pritchett, James. *The Music of John Cage*. Cambridge, UK: Cambridge University Press, 1993.

RadiOM.org. "Lou Harrison 70th Birthday Concert." Archive of KPFA radio broadcast (May 14, 1987), http://radiom.org/detail.php?omid=AM.1987.05.14.A.

———. "George Antheil Hertz Hall Concert." Archive of KPFA radio broadcast (November 20, 1970), http://radiom.org/detail.php?omid=AM.1970.11.20.c1.A.

Ramakrishna, Mahendra Nath Gupta, Nikhilananda, and Ramakrishna-Vivekananda Center. *The Gospel of Sri Ramakrishna*. New York: Ramakrishna-Vivekananda Center, 1942.

Randall, Mac. "Alan Hovhaness: A Composer Who Took as Many Knocks as Bows." *New York Times,* May 20, 2001.

Rao, Nancy Yunwha. "Henry Cowell and His Chinese Music Heritage: Theory of Sliding Tone and His Orchestral World of 1953–1965." Pp. 119–145 in Yayoi Uno Everett and Frederick Lau, eds., *Locating East Asia in Western Art Music*. Middletown, CT: Wesleyan University Press, 2004.

Rathbun, Virginia. "Lou Harrison and His Music." MA thesis, San Jose State University, 1976.

Ravenscroft, Brenda. "Working Out the 'Is-Tos and as-Tos': Lou Harrison's *Fugue for Percussion*." *Perspectives of New Music* 38 (Winter 2000): 25–43.

Revill, David. *The Roaring Silence: John Cage, A Life*. New York: Arcade Pub., 1992.

Reynolds, Nancy, and Malcolm McCormick. *No Fixed Points: Dance in the Twentieth Century*. New Haven, CT: Yale University Press, 2003.

Robinson, Suzanne. "'A Ping, Qualified by a Thud': Music Criticism in Manhattan and the Case of Cage (1943–58)." *Journal of the Society for American Music* 1, no. 1 (2007): 79–139.

Rockwell, John. "Harrison Puppet Opera in Premiere." *Los Angeles Times,* November 8, 1971.

———. "A West Coast Composer Looks to the Far East." *New York Times,* November 1, 1990.

Rorem, Ned. "Books on Music." *New Republic,* June 3, 1972: 25.

———. *Facing the Night: A Diary (1999–2005) and Musical Writings*. Emeryville, CA: Shoemaker & Hoard, 2006.

———. "Virgil (1944)." *Antaeus* 71/72 (Autumn 1993): 63–82.

———. *Wings of Friendship: Selected Letters, 1944–2003*. Emeryville, CA: Shoemaker & Hoard, 2005.

Rosenblatt, Esther. "The 1940 Mills College Summer Session in Dance." *Dance Observer* 7, no. 7 (August/September 1940): 100–101.

Ross, Alex. "Mavericks: Lou Harrison Passes On; Berlioz Returns." *New Yorker,* March 3, 2003.

———. *The Rest Is Noise: Listening to the Twentieth Century*. New York: Farrar, Straus and Giroux, 2007.

Rubin, Nathan. *John Cage and the Twenty-Six Pianos of Mills College: Forces in American Music from 1940 to 1990*. Moraga, CA: Sarah's Books, 1994.

Rutman, Neil C. "The Solo Piano Works of Lou Harrison." DMA diss., Peabody Conservatory, 1982.

Sachs, Joel. *Henry Cowell: A Man Made of Music*. London: Oxford University Press, 2012.

Salzman, Eric. Notes to *Lou Harrison and Carl Ruggles: Orchestral Works*. Composers Recordings, Inc. NWCR715, 1996.

Santoro, Gene. "To This Musician/Composer, Music Is a Mystical Experience." *Tower Records' Pulse,* March 1987: 26–31, 45.

Saunders, Frances Stonor. *The Cultural Cold War: The CIA and the World of Arts and Letters*. New York: New Press, 1999.

Schlesinger, Kathleen. *The Greek Aulos: A Study of its Mechanism and of Its Relation to the Modal System of Ancient Greek Music, Followed by a Survey of the Greek Harmoniai in Survival or Rebirth in Folk-Music*. London: Methuen, 1939.

Schmidt, Daniel. "Remembering Lou." Presentation at the University of Oregon Music School, April 13, 2003.

Schneider, John. "Just Guitar." *Guitar International* 6 (April/June 2004): 42–50.

———. "Just Lou Harrison." *Guitar Review* 128, no. 13 (2004): 23.

———. "Lou Harrison's Guitars." *Classical Guitar* 21, no. 10 (June 2003): 20–23.

Schneider, John, and David Tanenbaum. "Behind the Scenes from Nek Chand." Unpub. ms., 2006.

Schoenberg, Arnold. *Arnold Schoenberg Letters* [*Arnold Schoenberg: Ausgewählte Briefe*], translated by Eithne Wilkins and Ernst Kaiser, edited by Erwin Stein. Berkeley, CA: University of California Press, 1987.

Schonberg, Harold C. "Chamber Music Series Is Started by Columbia." *New York Times,* February 15, 1953.

———. "Concert: In Honor of Composers." *New York Times,* February 8, 1977.

Schwartz, Elliot. "ASUC: Reaching Beyond Academe; Lou Harrison Is Honored Composer." *Musical America,* September 1982: 34.

Schwarz, K. Robert. "A Polymath, at 80, Tries to Simplify." *New York Times,* March 23, 1997.

Seeger, Charles. "Carl Ruggles." *The Musical Quarterly* 18 (1932): 578–592.

———. "On Dissonant Counterpoint." *Modern Music* 7, no. 4 (June–July 1930): 25–31.

Serinus, Jason. "'Young Caesar' Finally Gets Its Due." *Bay Area Reporter,* February 15, 2007.

———. "The Adventure Continues." *San Francisco Classical Voice,* July 29, 2008.

———. "A Conversation with Lou Harrison." *Secrets of Home Theater and High Fidelity* 9, no. 1 (February 2002).

Sharp, Cecil. *English Folk Carols.* London: Novello, 1911.

———. *English Folk Songs from the Southern Appalachians*, edited by Maud Karpeles. Vol. II. London: Oxford University Press, 1932.

Sheppard, W. Anthony. "Continuity in Composing the American Cross-Cultural: Eichheim, Cowell, and Japan." *Journal of the American Musicological Society* 61, no. 3 (December 2008): 465–540.

Sherbon, Elizabeth. "College News." *The Dance Observer* 6, no. 1 (January 1939): 165–166.

———. "College News." *The Dance Observer* 6, no. 7 (August–September 1939): 255.

Shere, Charles. "The Making of Lou Harrison: Man and Music." Unpub. ms.

Sheridan, Molly. "Harrison Recognized as MA Composer of the Year." *NewMusicBox* (January 1, 2002), http://www.newmusicbox.org/articles/Harrison-Recognized -as-MA-Composer-of-the-Year.

Sherry, Michael S. *Gay Artists in Modern American Culture: An Imagined Conspiracy.* Chapel Hill: University of North Carolina Press, 2007.

Shingleton, Bob. "Going Buddhist with Lou Harrison." On an Overgrown Path (March 21, 2007), http://www.overgrownpath.com/2007/05/going-buddhist-with-lou-harrison.html.

Silber, Judy. "Inside Druid Heights, a Marin County Counter-Culture Landmark." KALW Crosscurrents (September 19, 2012), http://kalw.org/post/ inside-druid-heights-marin-county-counter-culture-landmark.

Silver, Brian. "Henry Cowell and Alan Hovhaness: Responses to the Music of India." Pp. 54–79 in K. Ishwaran, ed., *Contributions to Asian Studies: Part One, Music of India.* Leiden, The Netherlands: E. Brill, 1978.

Silverman, Kenneth. *Begin Again: A Biography of John Cage.* New York: Alfred A. Knopf, 2010.

Sire, Adeline. "Wu Man: A Master of the Chinese Pipa Mixing Music Genres." PRI's The World, (February 21, 2013), http://www.pri.org/stories/2013-02-21/wu-man-master -chinese-pipa-mixing-music-genres.

Siwe, Thomas. "Lou Harrison at the University of Illinois." *Percussive Notes* 18, no. 2 (Winter 1980): 31.

Slonimsky, Nicolas. *Perfect Pitch: A Life Story.* Oxford: Oxford University Press, 1988.

Smith, Geoff. "Lou Harrison: An Interview." *Sound Circus* (February 2001), http://www .soundcircus.com/releases/sc005/lou_int.htm (web page discontinued).

Smith, Stuart Saunders. "The Early Percussion Music of John Cage." *Percussionist* 16, no. 1 (Fall 1978).

———. "Lou Harrison's *Fugue for Percussion*." *The Percussionist* 16, no. 2 (1979): 47–56.

Soltes, Eva, dir. *Lou Harrison: A World of Music.* Video. Performance & Media Arts, 2012.

Sorrell, Neil. *A Guide to the Gamelan.* Portland, OR: Amadeus Press, 1990.

Spiller, Henry. "Lou Harrison's Music for Western Instruments and Gamelan: Even More Western Than It Sounds." *Asian Music* 40, no. 1 (Winter/Spring 2009): 31–52.

Sprague, Marshall. "Composing for Cash." *New York Times,* February15, 1948.

Stabler, David. "'Young Caesar' Fails Despite Noble Narrator, Dancers." *Oregonian,* April 10, 1988.

Steinberg, Michael. "Conference of Musicians in Rome." *New York Times,* May 2, 1954.

———. "Contemporary Conference in Rome in April." *New York Times,* January 17, 1954.

———. "Leontyne Price Soloist in Rome: Offers Setting of Prayer in Chamber Music Category—3 Fragments Heard." *New York Times,* April 15, 1954.

———. "Peragallo Work Wins Rome Prize: Violin Concerto Gets Award at Music Fete—Laurels in Other Categories Divided." *New York Times,* April 16, 1954.

Stevenson, Robert. "John Cage on His 70th Birthday: West Coast Background." *Inter-American Music Review* 5, no. 1 (Fall 1982).

Steward, Daniel-Harry. "Coyote and Tehoma." Pp. 157–162 in Will Roscoe, ed., *Living the Spirit: A Gay American Indian Anthology.* New York: St. Martin's Press, 1988.

Stone, Carl. "Interviews with Pauline Oliveros and Lou Harrison." Pp. 42–47 in *New Music America '81: A Festival of Contemporary Music.* San Francisco: New Music Alliance and the *San Francisco Examiner,* 1981.

Straus, Noel. "Symphony by Ives in World Premiere," *New York Times,* April 6, 1946.

Stravinsky, Igor, and Arthur Knodel. *Poetics of Music in the Form of Six Lessons.* Cambridge: Harvard University Press, 1947.

Stryker, Susan, and Jim Van Buskirk. *Gay by the Bay: A History of Queer Culture in the San Francisco Bay Area.* San Francisco: Chronicle Books, 1996.

Sucharitkul, Somtow. "Crises in Asian Music: The Manila Conference 1975." *Tempo* 117 (June 1976): 18–22.

Surjodiningrat, Wasisto, P. J. Sudarjana, and Adhi Susanto. *Tone Measurements of Outstanding Javanese Gamelans in Yogyakarta and Surakarta [Penjelidikan dalam pengukuran nada gamelan-gamelan djawa terkemuka di Jogjakarta dan Surakarta].* 2nd ed. Yogyakarta, Indonesia: Gadjah Mada University Press, 1972, 1993.

Swafford, Jan. *Charles Ives: A Life with Music.* New York: W. W. Norton, 1996.

Swearingen, John. "A Cave for a Composer: Lou Harrison's Desert Retreat, Joshua Tree, CA." Skillful Means, http://www.skillful-means.com/projects/vault/lou_harrison.htm (web page discontinued).

Swed, Mark. "Lou Harrison Just Became a Little Bit Better Known." *Los Angeles Times,* May 26, 2006.

———. "Lou Harrison, 85; West Coast Classical Composer, Influential Musical Maverick." *Los Angeles Times,* February 4, 2003.

———. "Remembering *Modern Music.*" *The Musical Quarterly* 80, no. 1 (Spring 1996): 58–60.

———. "Where Music and Life Entwined." *Los Angeles Times,* February 12, 2004.

———. "With a Little Bit of Pluck: After Decades of Working in Obscurity on the West Coast, Composer Lou Harrison Is Enjoying a Revival. Let the Gamelans Ring Out!" *Los Angeles Times,* March 2, 1997.

Tang, Wai Chung Joyce. "Interpreting Lou Harrison: Social Criticism in His Post World War II Works." PhD diss., University of Hong Kong, 2006.

Taubman, Howard. "Opera: Two Premieres." *New York Times,* May 15, 1959.

———. "U.S. Music of Today Played at Concert." *New York Times,* October 29, 1952.

Teck, Katherine. *Movement to Music: Musicians in the Dance Studio.* Westport, CT: Greenwood Press, 1990.

———. *Music for the Dance: Reflections on a Collaborative Art.* Westport, CT: Greenwood Press, 1989.

Thomas, Allan. "Skip, Skip, Skip to My Lou." *Canzona* 5, no. 17 (1984): 4–13.

Thomas, Dwight. "Lou Harrison's Double Concerto for Gamelan, Violin and Cello: Juxtaposition of Individual and Cultural Expectations." *Asian Music* 15, no. 1 (1983): 90–101.

Thomas and Dominicans. *Summa Theologica*. New York: Benziger Bros., 1947; 1948.

Thomson, Virgil. *American Music since 1910*. New York: Holt, Rinehart & Winston, 1971.

———. "Atonality Today." *New York Herald Tribune*, February 5, 1950.

———. "Expressive Percussion." *New York Herald Tribune*, January 22, 1945.

———. "French Music Here." *New York Herald Tribune*, January 5, 1941.

———. "On Being American." *New York Herald Tribune*, January 25, 1948.

———. "Schoenberg's Music." *New York Herald Tribune*, September 10, 1944.

———. *The State of Music*. New York: W. Morrow, 1939.

———. *Virgil Thomson*. New York: A. A. Knopf, 1966.

———. *A Virgil Thomson Reader*. Boston: Houghton Mifflin, 1981.

———. "A War's End." *New York Herald Tribune*, January 12, 1947.

Tircuit, Heuwell. "An Elegant Premiere." *San Francisco Chronicle*, December 9, 1975.

Tomkins, Calvin. *The Bride and the Bachelors: Five Masters of the Avant-Garde*. New York: Viking, 1965.

Tommasini, Anthony. *Virgil Thomson: Composer on the Aisle*. New York: W. W. Norton, 1997.

Tusler, Adelaide G. "Interview with Peter Yates, Evenings on the Roof, 1939–1954." In *Oral History Program*. Los Angeles: University of California Los Angeles, 1972.

Tytell, John. *The Living Theatre: Art, Exile, and Outrage*. New York: Grove Press, 1995.

Ulrich, Allan. "FaceTime: Lou Harrison." *San Francisco Chronicle* (March 3, 2002).

Upchurch, Michael. "Memories of John and Lou." *Seattle Times*, March 27, 2009.

van Emmerick, Paul, ed. "A John Cage Compendium." (2011) http://cagecomp.home.xs4all.nl.

van Gulik, Robert Hans. *The Lore of the Chinese Lute: An Essay in the Ideology of the Ch'in*. Tokyo: Sophia University, 1940.

Van Leuwen Swarthout, Max, and Arnold Schoenberg. "First California Broadcast." P. 300 in Walter Frisch, ed., *Schoenberg and His World*. Princeton, NJ: Princeton University Press, 1999.

Veltman, Chloe. "Harrison Tried Hard to Settle This Score." *Los Angeles Times*, February 11, 2007.

Von Gunden, Heidi. *The Music of Lou Harrison*. Metuchen, NJ: Scarecrow Press, 1995.

Wade, James. *West Meets East: An Encounter with Korea*. Seoul, Korea. Pomso Publishers, 1975.

Walsh, Stephen. *Stravinsky: The Second Exile: France and America, 1934–1971*. New York: Alfred A. Knopf, 2006.

Warren, Larry. *Lester Horton, Modern Dance Pioneer*. Princeton, NJ: Dance Horizons/Princeton Book Co., 1991.

Watson, Steven. *Prepare for Saints: Gertrude Stein, Virgil Thomson, and the Mainstreaming of American Modernism*. New York: Random House, 1998.

Weber, Ben. *How I Took 63 Years to Commit Suicide*, edited by Matthew Paris. Unpub. ms., 2003.

Weil, Simone. *Waiting for God*. New York: Putnam, 1951.

Weinberger, Eliot, ed. *The New Directions Anthology of Classical Chinese Poetry*, translated by William Carlos Williams et al. New York: New Directions, 2003.

Weisgall, Hugo. "The Music of Henry Cowell." *The Musical Quarterly* 45, no. 4 (October 1959): 484–507.

Wellens, Ian. *Music on the Frontline: Nicolas Nabokov's Struggle Against Communism and Middlebrow Culture*. Aldershot, UK: Ashgate, 2002.

Wellesz, Egon, ed. *Ancient and Oriental Music*. New Oxford History of Music, Vol. 1. London: Oxford University Press, 1957.

Wenten, I. Nyoman. "The Creative World of Ki Wasitodipuro: The Life and Work of a Javanese Gamelan Composer." PhD diss., UCLA, 1996.

Whitman, Walt. *Leaves of Grass.* 4th ed. New York: William E. Chapin, 1867.

Williams, Jonathan. *A Palpable Elysium: Portraits of Genius and Solitude.* Boston, MA: David R. Godine, 2002.

Wilson, Frank. "Something Beautiful." Books, Inq. (August 14, 2009), http://booksinq .blogspot.com/2009/08/something-beautiful.html.

Wolf, Daniel. "Item: Blogging." Renewable Music (September 24, 2008), http://renewablemusic .blogspot.com/2008/09/item-blogging.html.

Woodard, Josef. "Composer a Hero in World of New Music: Lou Harrison Bravely Bridges Cultures in His Works, with Both Western and Indonesian Influences." *Los Angeles Times,* March 28, 1996.

Wu Man. "Lou Harrison [Interview with Wu Man]." *Dialogue Talk* (June 21, 2014), http:// dialoguetalk.org/wu-man/lou-harrison.

Yamashita, Kunihiko. *Keith Jarrett: Inner Views [Innā Byūzu: Sono Uchinaru Ongaku Sekai o Kataru].* Rising Inc., 2001.

Yasser, Joseph. *A Theory of Evolving Tonality.* New York: American Library of Musicology, 1932.

Yates, Peter. "A Collage of American Composers, Part 4." *Arts and Architecture,* February 1959: 4.

———. "Lou Harrison." *Arts and Architecture* 61, no. 2 (February 1944): 26, 37.

———. "Music: A Trip Up the Coast." *Arts and Architecture* 74, no. 12 (December 1957): 4, 6–7, 10, 33–34.

———. *Twentieth Century Music: Its Evolution from the End of the Harmonic Era into the Present Era of Sound.* New York: Pantheon Books, 1967.

Zech, John. "Composer's Datebook," October 20, 2001. American Public Media. (Radio broadcast).

Ziffrin, Marilyn J. *Carl Ruggles: Composer, Painter, and Storyteller.* Urbana: University of Illinois Press, 1994.

Zinn, Howard. *A People's History of the United States.* New York: Harper & Row, 1980.

Zinsser, William. "Flunking Description." PowellsBooks.Blog (May 27, 2009), http://www .powells.com/blog/guests/flunking-description-by-william-zinsser.

———. "Virgil Thomson, Writer." *The Sewanee Review* 95, no. 2 (Spring 1987): 340.

Ziony, Ruth Kramer. "Lou Harrison: Shaping the 60s" (letter to the editor). *New York Times,* February 23, 2003.

INDEX

1/1 (journal), 441
1750 Arch, 369, 516n40

a-ak, 256–261, 265, 268, 290, 345–346,
  503n25
Abel, David, 386, 387, 527n9
Abell, Jeff, 329
abstract expressionism, 95, 139, 154, 165,
  166, 484n47
Acocella, Joan, 418
acoustics, 26, 214–215, 371, 415, 448
Adam, Robert, 503n25
Adams, John Coolidge, 387, 418, 440, 530n7
Adams, John Luther, x, 382, 396, 427, 438,
  439, 440, 522n30
Adorno, Theodor, 500n47
Africa, music, 26, 40, 41, 142, 287–288, 324,
  327, 328, 422, 450, 512n44
AIDS epidemic, 375, 424, 532n15
Ajemian, Anahid, xv, 107, 132, 136, 147, 169,
  171, 172, 239, 243, 491n10
Ajemian, Maro, 107, 136, 169, 171, 172
Akademi Seni Karawitan Indonesia (ASKI)
  Surakarta, 371, 524n22
alap, 385, 386, 445, 452
Albers, Josef, 163, 282
Alberti bass, 9, 171, 445
aleatoric music. *See* chance operations
Alpert, Richard (Ram Dass), 279
Alsop, Marin, 430
American Academy in Rome, 210, 212,
  497n27
American Academy of Arts and Letters, 137
American Composers Alliance, 172, 229,
  240–241, 332, 396

American Composers Orchestra, 379, 396,
  516n35
American gamelan. *See* gamelan, American
American Gamelan Institute, 534n21
American Mavericks Festival, 1, 2, 412, 420,
  427
American Music Center, 126–127, 391
American Sign Language, 410, 421
American Society for Eastern Arts, 327, 329.
  See also Center for World Music
American Society of University Composers,
  368, 509n17
American Symphony Orchestra League,
  503n43
Amirkhanian, Charles, xv, 387, 402, 432,
  434, 513n30
Anderson, Laurie, 345, 348
Angulo, Jaime de, 65–66
Antheil, George, 32, 182–183, 209, 297,
  486–487n13, 513n30
anti-semitism, 120, 182, 498n32, 526n36
Aptos, California, x, 198, 223, 242, 246–247,
  262, 281, 287, 391, 408–409
Arabic music, 41, 60, 344, 446
architecture, 12, 163, 176, 206, 213, 216,
  228, 281–282, 341, 343–344, 372–373,
  414–416, 425, 433, 435, 503n25
Archytas, 318
Ardévol, José, 59, 478n37, 494n37
Argo Records, 399
Aristotle, 236
Arizona State University, 394
Arrow Press, 126
Artists' Club (New York), 154, 175
Arts and Crafts movement, 177–179

Ashbery, John, 156
Ashokananda, 11, 22, 50
Asian Art Museum of San Francisco, 345
Asian Composers League, 323
Asimov, Isaac, 241, 503n38
Aslanian, Vahé, 307, 514n43
Assetto, Franco, 354, 522n34
Astoria, Oregon, 6
atomic bomb, 109–110, 181, 219, 234, 235,
    260, 268, 270, 292, 324, 486n31, 498n28
atonality, 2, 27, 38–39, 44, 63, 79, 83–84,
    86, 104–106, 108, 110, 117–118, 126, 129,
    132–136, 138, 143, 146, 168, 171, 173,
    211–212, 216, 240, 244–246, 268, 270,
    314–315, 322, 347, 445, 452, 488n48,
    498n8, 499n18
Auden, W. H., 156
aulos, 226, 246, 259, 265, 445, 507n14
Avakian, George, 147
Aztec culture, 55–56, 66, 70, 73, 76, 270

Babbitt, Milton, 347
Babbs, Ken, 279
Bach, J. S., 12, 21, 30, 32, 87, 119, 123, 148,
    168, 216, 302, 379, 419, 445, 470n24,
    473n44, 487n38, 496n42, 512n9; "Ari-
    oso," 523n7; *Chromatic Fantasy and Fugue*,
    43–44, 473n44; *Italian Concerto*, 523n7;
    Musical Offering, 344
Bacharach, Burt, 156, 493n10
Bagdasarian, Ross, 501n19
Balasaraswati, T., 369
Baldwin, James, 103
Bali, Indonesia, 60, 61, 148, 151–152, 161,
    170, 253, 370–371, 492n19; art, 342;
    dance, 151, 161; drama, 328, 371, 528n24;
    Harrison's visit to, 370–371; musical in-
    struments, 309, 360, 412, 513n35, 520n27;
    music, 60–61, 148, 151–152, 161, 170,
    253, 324, 327, 371, 447, 477n55, 492n19,
    495n38. *See also* gamelan, Balinese
Balinese gamelan. *See* gamelan, Balinese
Ballou, Esther, 48, 120
balungan, 333–337, 350–351, 357–364, 367,
    378, 382, 386, 397, 398, 424, 445
banghyang, 290, 345, 445
Barab, Seymour, 147
Baradinsky, Oscar, 119
Barber, Samuel, 93, 100, 210
barcarolle, 304, 388, 445
Barone, Joseph, 124–125

baroque music, ix, 10, 11, 12, 21, 30, 31, 44,
    63, 69, 80, 82, 83, 106, 109, 135, 170, 215,
    225, 230–232, 242–243, 248, 251–252,
    261, 343–345, 387, 402, 413, 418, 426,
    470n18
Barr Jr., Alfred H., 482n3
Bartók, Béla, 5, 80, 278, 505n7, 527n5
Barton, Bruce Walter, 526n42
Baryshnikov, Mikhail, 529n18
Basho, Matsuo, 503n25
Bauersfeld, Erik, 406
Bauhaus, 68, 163, 165, 189, 479n54
Bay Region Federal Symphony, 469n7
Beal, Tandy, 404
Beals, Carol, 33–35, 37, 45, 46, 48, 73, 74, 76,
    125, 139, 144, 182, 230, 277
beat poetry and aesthetics, 95, 154, 155, 163,
    166, 274
Beattie, Herbert, 241
Beck, Garrick, 160
Beck, Julian, 95, 155, 156, 158, 159, 160, 161
Becker, John, 32
Beckmann, Max, 394, 425, 463
Beethoven, Ludwig van, 25, 39, 84, 148, 164,
    380, 382, 494n3
Beijing opera. *See* Chinese opera
Belafonte, Harry, 103
Bellows, Beverly, 290–291, 317, 511n25
Benary, Barbara, 328, 330–331
Bennington College, 68, 92, 472n30
Benton, Pauline, 61, 231, 305–307, 319–320,
    513n21
Benton, Thomas Hart, 81
Berg, Alban, 42, 44, 94, 133, 241
Berger, Arthur, 55, 161
Berkeley World Music Festival, 328, 330
Bernstein, Leonard, 90, 99, 100, 108, 127,
    253, 320, 396, 427, 486n26, 505n16
Beswick, Gary, 288, 296
Beyer, Johanna, 32, 58, 72, 76
bharatanatyam, 385
Bird, Bonnie, 52, 54, 67, 143–145, 153, 159
Black Mountain College, 137, 148, 157–158,
    162, 163–169, 175–177, 179–182, 190, 191,
    214, 218–220, 222, 223, 227, 229, 242, 243,
    245–246, 282, 294, 296, 297, 400, 401,
    403, 410, 487n39, 494n43, 494n3, 529n18
Blackwood, Michael, 517n7
Blake, Melissa, 79–80, 82, 88, 174, 263
Blake, William, 11, 26, 47, 128, 155
Blesh, Rudi, 145

Debussy, Claude, 26, 63, 179, 448, 485n19, 491n15, 496n40

Decker, David, 148

Decker, Ellie, 148

Dee, Richard xv, 198–199, 248, 251, 262, 275, 277, 278, 283, 287, 289, 295, 298, 304, 306, 307, 311–313, 318, 319, 332, 346, 427, 461, 462, 505n3, 509n24, 514n51, 515n14, 522n34; *Suite for Violin and American Gamelan*, 311–313, 320, 332, 386, 390, 404–405, 427, 461, 490n21, 491n15, 514

degung see gamelan, Sundanese

Del Rey, Lester, 109

Delaunay, Robert, 503n25

Delaunay, Sonia, 503n25

Denby, Edwin, 93

Dendabrata, Elang Yusuf, 372

Denis, Jean-Francois, 520n37

Dennison, Doris, 59, 70, 76, 188, 189

Dessau, Paul, 487n38

Diamond, David, 100, 482n41

Diamond, Jody, x, xv, 333, 335, 337–339, 357, 358, 363–364, 376, 381, 387, 403, 405, 420, 439, 440, 462, 464, 520n36, 522n30, 522n34, 525n13, 529n10

diatonicism, 31, 63–64, 66, 81, 106, 118, 148, 174, 217, 222, 237, 244, 290, 310, 366, 375, 384, 389, 446

Dickinson, Emily, 503n25

dissonant counterpoint (secundal counterpoint), 30–32, 41, 43–44, 63, 90, 105–106, 108, 117, 120–122, 139, 282, 447, 452

ditone tuning, 216, 217, 248, 318, 344, 379, 415, 435, 447, 449

dizi, 285, 289, 303

Dobson, John, xiii, xv, 15, 18–23, 35–36, 38, 45, 46, 50, 56, 73, 113, 285, 441, 456, 474n16

dodecaphony. *See* twelve-tone method

Doors, The, 280

Doty, David, xv, 226, 296, 328, 330, 334, 339, 441, 517n9

Dow Chemical, 292

Dowland, John, 21, 484n2

Dresher, Paul, 339, 360, 387, 442, 462, 517n9

drone, 41; in Cowell, 37; in Harrison, 132, 146, 148, 171, 173, 177, 181, 232, 237, 244–245, 246, 268–269, 288, 293, 310, 313, 321, 375, 422, 447, 449, 457, 459, 461, 463, 471n14, 477n15, 490n34, 497n12, 550n6, 533n50; in Hovhaness, 107–108, 173; in India, 170–171

ductia, 244–245, 269, 317, 447, 461

Dudley, Jane, 34

Dufay, Guillaume, 156

Duffy, John, 156, 157

Duncan, Robert, 100, 148, 166, 232, 282, 287, 293, 296–297, 307, 375, 394, 400, 461, 515n16, 528n3

Dunning, Jennifer, 416

Dürer, Albrecht, 503n25

East-West Center (Hawaii), 264, 266–268, 270–271, 298

East-West Music Encounter (Tokyo), 248–249, 251–256, 260, 419

Eastman School of Music, 332

Egypt, music of, 40, 142; musical instruments, 422; poetry, 359–360

Eisenhower, Dwight, 235

ektara, 303

electronic music, 60, 77, 161, 176, 207, 228–229, 277, 279, 323, 347–348, 447, 494n37, 496n41, 501n21, 501n22, 506n26, 513n30

Elgar, Edward, 45, 473n53

Ellington, Edward Kennedy "Duke," 482n42

Emshwiller, Ed, 239

Encounters music series, 300

Ensemble Intercontemporain, 368

Episcopal Church of St. Mary the Virgin, 121, 488n45, 496n47

equal temperament, 447, 499n31, 517n4, 527n14; alternatives to, 21, 207, 379; comparison to just intonation, 167, 214, 217, 220, 222, 225, 232, 321, 323, 352, 362; Harrison's advocacy against, 244, 255, 256, 474n16; Harrison's use of, 219, 260, 270, 274, 303, 314, 366, 386, 388, 390, 392, 395, 403, 404, 418, 419, 531n44; historical use, 141, 216, 263; on instruments, 174, 218, 280, 349, 501n22, 511n24, 533n63

Eratosthenes, 318

Erdman, Jean, 92, 105, 129, 139, 142, 149, 151, 152, 156, 158, 161, 165, 171–172, 173, 180, 181, 459, 482n6, 490n1, 492nn7–9, 494n10, 516n32

erhu, 196, 197, 243, 266, 447

Erlendson, William, 296

Ernst, Max, 91

Esoteric Records, 146

Esperanto, ix, 213, 220, 229–230, 237, 238, 239, 252, 256, 260, 267, 281–282, 307–308, 311, 313, 394, 401, 410, 506n46, 513n30

George, William, 349
Gerard Samuel, 307
Gershwin, George, 82, 489n4, 498n6
Ghana, 328
Gibbons, Orlando, 21
Gidlow, Elsa, 56, 69, 230, 316–317, 386, 458, 475n21, 502n9, 515
Gillespie, Don, 347, 522n34
Ginsberg, Allen, 95, 274, 316
Giteck, Janice, 360, 387
Glanville-Hicks, Peggy, 95, 153, 190, 230, 240, 257, 338, 370, 396, 484n51, 490n40, 494n37
Glass, Philip, 323–324, 450, 517n4
Gluck, Christoph Willibald, 509n12
Goethe, Johann Wolfgang von, 377–378, 411, 463, 503n25
Golden Gate International Exposition, 61
Golden Gate Park, 234
Goldman, Richard Franko, 494n37
Goldsmith, Kenneth, 362–363
Goode, Daniel, 517n9
Goodman, Paul, 156, 173, 497n17
Gordon, Charles, 383
Gordon, Robert, 301–305, 392, 429–431, 461
Gospel of Sri Ramakrishna, 113
Grady, Kraig, 528–529n8
Graham, Martha, 15, 33, 36, 47, 49, 50, 55, 59, 92, 108, 331, 359, 388, 493n10
Grainger, Percy, 37, 66, 230, 282, 342, 478n35
Grateful Dead, 2, 279, 412, 440, 534n17
Graves, Robert, 140
Greece, 64, 244, 312, 317, 359, 373, 385, 494n10; architecture, 415; drama, 24, 48, 457, 472n28; music, xiii, 140, 142, 214, 216, 226, 236, 243, 245–246, 259, 265, 303, 328–329, 445, 448, 452, 499n31; philoso-phy, 216, 236; poetry, 80, 260, 282, 361, 393
Greenwich House Music School, 148, 153, 282
Greenwich Village, New York, 95–96, 154, 156, 175
Greenwood, Henrietta, 33
Gregorian chant, 11, 34, 62–63, 121, 272, 302, 383–384, 448, 526n37
Griffiths, Paul, 419
Gruenberg, Louis, 482n41
guan, 266
Guggenheim Fellowship, 172, 175–176, 180, 181–182, 219, 226, 229

Guggenheim Museum, 89
Guggenheim, Peggy, 89, 91, 92
guitar, 173–174, 226, 343–344, 348, 352, 379, 496, 511n25, 519n13; slide, 3, 432; steel (resonator), 432–433, 435, 464, 533n54–55, 533–534n63
Gulik, Robert van, 84
Gundlach, Ralph, 145
Guntur Sari (gamelan), 375, 396
guqin. See qin
Gyeongju, Korea, 265

Hagen, Uta, 103
Hall, Elizabeth, 188, 189
Halma, Harold, 481n14
Handel, George F., 11–12, 21, 39, 41, 91, 124, 134–135, 269, 302–303, 321, 359, 402, 417, 445, 464, 492n16, 503n25, 512n9
Hanson, Charles, xii, xv, 369, 394–395, 408, 409, 411, 421, 426, 427, 428, 431, 434–438, 440, 441, 528n34, 530n22
Hanson, Howard, 115
happenings, 175–176, 274, 294
Harlan, Calvin, 241–242
harmonic series, 26, 31, 214–215, 217, 288, 303, 321, 327, 352–353, 433, 435, 448, 513n10, 521n4, 521n7
harmony, 26, 30–31, 40, 42, 43, 57–58, 114–115, 121–123, 169, 350–351, 355, 398, 404, 415, 453, 470, 481n12, 486n10, 522n27
harpsichord, 10, 12, 21, 66, 80, 120, 216, 224, 231, 272, 282, 311, 351, 355, 344, 380, 384, 385, 386, 409, 426, 451, 453, 456, 458, 460, 463, 464, 468n42, 487n38, 509n13
Harrington, David, 356–357
Harris, Donald, 436, 438–439
Harris, Ivan, 10
Harris, Roy, 81, 93, 94, 170, 482n41, 486n13, 495n37, 504n58
Harrison archive, Lou, xii, xv, 440, 528n34
Harrison, Bill, 4, 6, 7, 8, 9, 20, 94, 148, 192, 193, 219, 235, 249
Harrison, Calline Silver, 3–6, 8, 20, 27, 46, 56, 148, 168, 180, 182, 192, 193, 209, 219, 223, 249, 271, 273–274, 276–278, 286–287, 320–321
Harrison, Clarence, 3–4, 6–11, 20, 27, 46, 56, 168, 180, 182, 192, 193, 209, 219, 222, 249, 271–273, 276, 320, 391
Harrison, Dorothy, 284
Harrison, Harry "H. O." 6, 9

Ma, Yo-Yo, x, 1, 417–418

MacDowell Colony, 181

MacDowell Medal, 427

Mace, Thomas, 112–113, 486n3

madrigal, ix, 9, 14, 21, 29

Mahler, Gustav, 247

Malina, Judith, xiii, xv, 95, 154, 155–161, 164, 167, 172–173

Mangkunegaran, 371, 522n31

Manhattan Percussion Ensemble, 391

Manhattan School of Music, 161

Manila, Philippines, 323–325

Mann, Thomas, 220–221, 225, 500n46, 500n47

Mansart, Jules Hardouin, 503n25

Mar, David, 441

Marcos, Imelda, 323, 516n2

Mardiswara (gamelan), 522n31

Mariah, Paul, 304

Marin, Eric, xv, 390, 527n6

Mark Taper Forum, 307

Martinet, Jean-Louis, 212

Martopangrawit, 371, 524n23

Masfield, John, 364

Masselos, William, 128, 136, 168, 489n26, 492n3

Mayuzumi, Toshiro, 505n16

mbira, 282, 287–288, 450, 461

McCall, Eileen, 21, 51, 186

McCarthy, Joseph, 181, 234–235, 485n7, 505n16

McDermott, Vincent, xv, 360–361, 371, 375, 377, 462, 463

McGowan, Edward, 102–107, 109–110, 129–130, 137, 374, 459, 485n6, 485n7, 496n45

McKayle, Donald, 149, 151, 161–162, 460, 492n17

McKim, Mead, and White architectural firm, 503n25

McLaren, Norman, 229, 494n37

McPhee, Colin, 61, 151, 152, 231, 253, 270, 419, 477n55, 492n19, 495n38

meantone temperament, 21, 80, 519n13

medieval Europe, culture, 116, 177, 179, 364, 487n23; literature, 113; music, xiii, 11, 25, 31, 63, 64, 84, 85, 91, 95, 98, 116, 120–121, 148–149, 152, 154, 162, 168, 228–229, 244–245, 263, 269, 273, 310, 344, 351, 379, 383–384, 447, 448, 451, 481,n28, 508n33; philosophy, 84, 116; poetry, 120, 148, 162, 405

Melcher, Katrina, 524n18

Mellers, Wilfrid, 509n20

melodicle, 39–43, 48, 58, 63–64, 76, 84, 85, 120–121, 165, 173, 225, 247, 252, 274, 282, 283, 312, 313, 315, 351, 417, 419

Menotti, Gian Carlo, 100, 210

Mesopotamian culture, 40, 317–318, 327, 344, 379, 511n14

Metcalf, Robert, 11, 12, 15, 24, 56, 230, 475n20

metric modulation, 225, 228, 450

Metropolitan Festival Hall (Tokyo), 253

Mexico, 51, 55–56, 210, 269–270, 281–284, 291, 296

Michelangelo, 212, 503n25

microtonality, 26, 31, 41, 142, 217, 224–225, 232, 363, 433, 441, 448, 450, 455, 509n17; *see also* just intonation

Milhaud, Darius, 29, 153, 356, 357

Milhaud, Madeleine, 357, 368

Millay, Edna St. Vincent, 80

Miller, Leta, xv, 526n36, 530n21

Miller, Richard, 154, 155–158, 160, 161

Mills College, xv, 80, 120, 188–189, 283, 363, 381, 387, 439, 473n51, 477n55, 527n9; ASEA/Center for World Music and, 329; Cage and, 54–55; Center for Contemporary Music, 356; Cowell and, 33, 37, 145; dance department, 45, 48, 50, 66–67, 72, 458, 476n40; gamelan, 357, 359, 362, 372, 382, 386; Harrison's employment at, 48–50, 51–59, 63, 66–70, 278, 356–357, 368, 473n5, 475n20; Kirchner and, 240; Milhaud and, 153, 228, 356; music department, 11, 61, 356–357, 369, 376, 384; Partch and, 214, 228; Red Gate Players and, 231, 300, 305; summer dance session, 50, 51–52, 54–56, 58, 59, 67–69, 79; theater productions, 40, 48, 64, 419, 457, 472n28

minimalism, 323–324, 385–386, 440, 450, 526n46

Mirecourt Trio, 362, 390

Mission Dolores, 11, 12, 383

mobile form, 37, 385

mode (musical), 62–65, 114, 143, 145, 148–152, 173, 254, 256, 268, 283, 297, 303, 308–309, 312–313, 353, 361, 364, 367, 378; Balinese, 151–152; Chinese, 150, 423, 511n24, 519n18; diatonic, 31, 63–66, 142, 168, 174, 217, 244–245, 246, 290, 303, 318, 384, 397, 449, 447n12, 515n12; Greek,

Index   577

Society for Individual Rights, 280, 284, 296, 300, 318, 510n37

Soedjatmoko, 395–396, 528n23

Sokolow, Anna, 93, 482n9

Soltes, Eva, x, xiii, xv, 368, 369, 385, 387, 405, 429, 430, 434, 437, 440, 441, 526n43, 530n8, 533n37

Son of Lion (gamelan), 328, 517n9

sonata form, 134, 366, 380

Sonic Youth, 420

Soundings Press, 319, 390

Soviet Union, 37, 92–93, 211, 236

space exploration, 236, 261

Spain, 12, 47–48, 65, 78–79, 485n6; music of, 12, 44, 66, 426

Spanish Civil War, 47–48

Spiller, Henry, 402, 520n39

Spoleto Festival, 430

Springfield, Don, 421

Sputnik, 236

square root form, 58, 71, 221, 283, 495n31

St. Cecilia, 167, 210, 282, 382–384, 463

St. Cecilia Society, 383

St. Denis, Ruth, 484n47

St. James, Margo, 316–317

St. Mark's Cathedral (Venice), 213

Stabler, David, 393

stampede, 380–381, 389, 397, 399, 419, 447, 504n47, 525n23, 527n5, 528n29; see also estampie

Stanford University, 11, 24, 33, 35, 37, 213, 295, 322, 391, 439, 476n39

Stein, Gertrude, 11, 96, 210, 409

Steinbeck, John, 81, 482n1

Steinberg, Julie, 386, 387, 527n9

Steinway pianos, 379–380

Stevens, Don, 385

Stevens, Olin, 137, 490n33

Stevens, Wallace, 80

Steward, Daniel-Harry, 399

Sticky Wicket cafe, 247–248, 262, 273, 275, 276, 292, 509n12

Still, William Grant, 502n4

Stokowski, Leopold, 36, 172, 180, 239–240, 317, 396, 461, 480n14, 496n41, 496n42, 517n13

Stone, Tom, 343–344, 348, 352, 519n13

Stoppard, Tom, 378

Strang, Gerald, 58, 239, 470n25, 472n42, 482n41

Strange, Allen, 348

Straus, Noel, 125

Stravinsky, Igor, 5, 10, 19, 29, 32, 79, 80, 85, 115, 210, 211, 212, 241, 276, 303, 450, 503n25; *Les Cinq Doigts*, 493n24; *L'histoire du Soldat*, 509n12; *Les Noces*, 65; *Octet*, 10; Piano Concerto, 10; *The Rite of Spring*, 10, 13, 212; *Symphony in Three Movements*, 133

straw bale construction, 206, 414–416, 434, 441

Strayhorn, Billy, 103

strict style just intonation, 220–222, 225, 232, 283

string piano, 22–23, 53, 81, 165, 278

Stryker, Dick, 156, 160

Suetonius, 300–301

suling, 350, 354, 361, 401, 452, 462, 463, 464, 520n36, 524n19

Sumarna, Undang, 340, 350, 463

Sumer is icumen in, 508n33

Sumerian culture, 40, 317–318, 327, 344, 379, 511n14, 515n12

Summerfield, Harry, 385

Summerfield, Susan, 356, 366, 384–385, 462, 464, 478, 527n9

State University of New York at Buffalo. *See* University at Buffalo

Surakarta, 358–359, 361, 371, 375, 521n7, 522n31, 524n21

Susilo, Harja, 370

Swed, Mark, 381, 435, 439

Swedenborg, Emanuel, 155

Syria, poetry, 400

syrinx, 303, 392, 461

tack piano, 120, 134, 135, 152, 168, 170, 177, 226, 231–232, 237, 252, 321, 366, 397, 398, 452, 459, 460, 465, 487n38, 489n18, 495n35

Taiwan, 253, 264, 266

tala, 114, 385, 452

Tamada, Kitaro, 74, 469n6

Tanenbaum, David, 432–434, 435, 511n25

taqsim, 344, 452

tarot cards, 174

taryung, 262, 452, 460

Tchaikovsky, Pyotr, 31, 100, 408

Tecco, Romuald, 389

temperament, 21, 80, 141, 156, 214–217, 230–231, 379, 404, 409, 452, 499n29, 516n3, 519n13, 532n21, *see also* equal temperament

BILL ALVES is a Southern California composer of acoustic and electronic microtonal music, music for gamelan, video, and other works. He is author of *Music of the Peoples of the World*, and his discs are available from MicroFest Records, Spectral Harmonies, and Kinetica Video Library. He teaches at Harvey Mudd College at the Claremont Colleges, where he directs the American gamelan.

BRETT CAMPBELL writes frequently about music and other arts for Oregon ArtsWatch, the *Wall Street Journal*, San Francisco Classical Voice, and many other publications. He teaches journalism at Portland State University and performs in Venerable Showers of Beauty gamelan, based at Lewis & Clark College in Lou Harrison's hometown of Portland, Oregon.

CPSIA information can be obtained
at www.ICGtesting.com
Printed in the USA
BVOW11s1440040417
480266BV00002B/4/P